THE NATIONAL HISTORY OF FRANCE
EDITED BY
FR. FUNCK-BRENTANO

WITH AN INTRODUCTION BY J. E. C. BODLEY

THE MIDDLE AGES

THE NATIONAL HISTORY OF FRANCE
EDITED BY FR. FUNCK-BRENTANO

With an Introduction by J. E. C. BODLEY
Each volume Demy 8vo. Price, 12s. 6d. net.

I. THE EARLIEST TIMES. By Fr. Funck-Brentano
II. THE MIDDLE AGES. By Fr. Funck-Brentano
III. THE CENTURY OF THE RENAISSANCE. By L. Batiffol
IV. THE XVIIth CENTURY. By Jacques Boulenger
V. THE XVIIIth CENTURY. By Casimir Stryienski
VI. THE FRENCH REVOLUTION. By Louis Madelin
VII. THE THIRD REPUBLIC. By Raymond Recouly
VIII. THE RESTORATION AND THE JULY MONARCHY By Lucas-Dubreton
IX. THE CONSULATE AND THE EMPIRE. By Louis Madelin [*To be published*]

LONDON: WILLIAM HEINEMANN LTD

THE NATIONAL HISTORY OF FRANCE

THE MIDDLE AGES

BY

FR. FUNCK-BRENTANO

TRANSLATED FROM THE FRENCH BY
ELIZABETH O'NEILL, M.A.

LONDON
WILLIAM HEINEMANN LTD.

First published, September 1916.
New Impressions, January 1918,
February 1922, *September* 1923,
April 1925, *January, July* 1926,
August 1928, *May* 1930.

Printed in Great Britain
at The Windmill Press, Kingswood, Surrey

AUTHOR'S PREFACE

(TO THE FRENCH EDITION)

THE quotations in the following pages are very numerous: the majority in old French. In some cases they have been shortened and the language and spelling modernized. The bibliographies at the end of the chapters do not pretend to completeness. The studies published on the history of the Middle Ages are infinite in number. Only the documents and works which have been most used are mentioned. We have made great use of the works of our predecessors, and especially those of our masters, Jacques Flach, Achille Luchaire, Siméon Luce, and those of Messieurs Ch. V. Langlois, Emile Mâle, Joseph Bédier, and Alfred Coville. It is a pleasant duty to express to them our gratitude and admiration.

Fr. F.-B.

CONTENTS

CHAPTER		PAGE
I.	CENTURIES OF ANARCHY	1
II.	THE FORMATION OF FEUDAL FRANCE	4
III.	THE EPICS	49
IV.	THE ELEVENTH CENTURY	65
V.	THE CRUSADES	99
VI.	A JUSTICIARY IN ARMOUR: LOUIS LE GROS	126
VII.	THE COMMUNES	142
VIII.	THE TWELFTH CENTURY	159
IX.	THE MINSTRELS	181
X.	THE UNIVERSITY	198
XI.	THE CATHEDRALS	213
XII.	LOUIS VII	241
XIII.	PHILIP AUGUSTUS	250
XIV.	A JUSTICIARY IN ERMINE: SAINT LOUIS	289
XV.	THE MINIATURES	321
XVI.	TOWN ASSOCIATIONS AND TRADE ASSOCIATIONS	336
XVII.	PHILIP THE FAIR	352
XVIII.	THE END OF FEUDAL FRANCE	422
XIX.	THE HUNDRED YEARS WAR	431
XX.	A MODERN KING: LOUIS XI	533
	INDEX	551

CHAPTER I

CENTURIES OF ANARCHY

Ninth and tenth centuries. The Barbarian invasions. Destruction of the towns. Impotence of the sovereign authority. Civil struggles—Anarchy. Destruction of Roman civilization. Absence of governance in society.

THE night of the ninth century . . . What is its course? Dimly the records give a glimpse of a people scattered and without guidance. The Barbarians have broken through the ramparts. The Saracen invasions have spread in successive waves over the South. The Hungarians swarm over the Eastern provinces. "These strangers," writes Richer, "gave themselves over to the most cruel outrages; they sacked town and village, and laid waste the fields. They burned down the churches and then departed with a crowd of captives, and no one said them nay."

> The realm they have burnt, wasted, and spoilt,
> Great numbers they carry off captive bound,
> Little children and women of high birth,
> Noblemen too with blows they drive off on foot.
> *(Ogier the Dane, v. 401.)*

The Normans from the north penetrate by way of the rivers to the very centre of France, "skimming over the ocean like pirates." Chartres, in the heart of the realm, was wont to take pride in its name, "the city of stone," *urbs lapidum*. The Normans appear, and Chartres is sacked.

William le Breton boasts the antiquity and wealth of the town of Autun; but the Barbarians have scattered these riches and its site is overgrown with weeds.

"The country is laid waste as far as the Loire," says the chronicler of Amboise, " so completely that where once were prosperous towns, wild animals now roam. The plain where once the harvests ripened now knows only

'The thistle and the sharp-thorned briar.'"
(Virgil, *Bucolics*, v. 39.)

And Paris? "What shall I say of her?" writes Adrevald. "That town once resplendent in her wealth and glory, famed for her fertile lands, is now but a heap of ashes."

In the course of the ninth and tenth centuries all the towns of France were destroyed. Can one imagine the slaughter and plunder concentrated in such a statement?

In the little country villages the houses crumble to dust, the walls of the churches are full of cracks, their roofs gape wide, the tabernacles are overgrown with weeds while ivy clings to their capitals. The house of God has become a den where foxes burrow and birds of prey have their nests, where one may see the lidless eyes of the owl shine unblinking through spiders' webs.

Powerless to resist the invaders, many men-at-arms join them. They plunder together, and as there is no longer any supreme authority, private quarrels, of man against man, family against family, of district against district, break out, are multiplied, and never-ending. "And three men cannot meet two without putting them to death." "The statutes of the sacred canons and the capitularies of our ancestors have become void," writes Carloman in his palace of Verneuil (March 884). Private wars become common. "In the absence of a central authority," says Hariulf, "the stronger break out into violence." "Men destroy one another like the fishes of the sea" (Council of Trosly).

There was nothing but attacks, rescues, captures, and reprisals, which one can picture from the story, told by Richer, of a leader who was conducting his army over the land from which the enemy drew his supplies. He ravaged it with such fury that "he did not leave even her cabin to a poor old woman in her second childhood."

There is no longer any trade, only unceasing terror. Fearfully men put up buildings of wood only. Architecture is no more.

CENTURIES OF ANARCHY

In the time of Charles the Great, and under his great military power, it would have been possible to discern a society in dissolution. And how much more was the disorder to manifest itself afterwards. At the end of the tenth century was there any remnant, ever so small, of the social, political, and economic conditions established in Gaul by the Romans, or even introduced after their time in rough fashion by the Barbarians?

Everything is changed. The monk Paul, who lived in the eleventh century, speaks of a collection of charters, the most ancient of which dated from the ninth century: " What changes! The rolls preserved in the archives of our abbey show that the peasants of that time lived under customs which those of to-day know no longer; even the words which they used are not those of the present day." And further on: " I have found the names of places, persons, and things changed since that time to such a degree that not only have they disappeared, but it is no longer possible to identify them; far from having preserved them, men do not even know them " (*Cartulary of Saint-Père*).

The peasant has abandoned his ravaged fields to avoid the violence of anarchy. The people have gone to cower in the depths of the forests or in inaccessible regions, or have taken refuge in the high mountains.

The ties which united the inhabitants of the country have been burst asunder; customary and legal usage have broken down. Society has no longer any governance.

SOURCES.—*Chron. de Nithard*, ed. Pertz, *Scriptores*, ii. 642–72; *Chron. de Nantes*, ed. R. Merlet, Paris, 1896; *Chron. des comtes d'Anjou*, ed. Halphen and Poupardin, 1913; *Richeri historiarum libri IV*, ed. Waitz, *Scriptores rerum germanicarum in usum scholarum*, 1877; Adrevald, *Miracles de S. Benoît*, ed. Duchesne, *Historiæ Francorum scriptores*, iii. 1661; *Chron. d'Hariulf*, ed. Lot, 1894; *Garin le Loherain*, translated by P. Paris (1862).

HISTORICAL WORKS.—Benj. Guérard, *Prolégom au polyptique de l'abbé Irminon*, 1845; Fustel de Coulanges, *Histoire des institutions de l'ancienne France*, 1879–97, 6 vols.; Jacq. Flach, *Les Origines de l'ancienne France*, 1886–1917, 4 vols.; L. Reynaud, *Les Origines de l'influence française en Allemagne* (950–1150), 1913; Imbart de la Tour, *Histoire de la nation française*, edited by G. Hanotaux, tome iii., *Histoire politique des origines à 1515* (1921).

CHAPTER II

THE FORMATION OF FEUDAL FRANCE

The Family.—Social life is narrowed to the family. The *motte* of earth and wood. The head of the family. Extension of the family. The "Mesnie" (household). *The Fief.*—The household in extending forms the fief. The baron is the head of a family. Reciprocal duties of lord and vassal. Sentiments of devotion and affection which unite them. The serfs. The stone keeps. The feudal hierarchy. *The Town.*—The feudal castle is a workshop. Beginnings of trade. The castle is peopled by *bourgeois*. Coucy. Construction of Ardres. Castles and towns at the end of the eleventh century. Lords of towns. First communal charters. Meilhan-en-Bazadais. The *Lignages*. The big towns of the Middle Ages were formed by a union of fiefs. The communal assembly. *The King.*—The French throne in the second half of the tenth century. Rivalry between the descendants of Charles the Great and those of Robert the Strong. Election of Hugh Capet. He represents the feudal baron on the throne. The King is the head of a family. The Queen directs the royal *ménage*. Authority of the royal family. The great officers personal servants of the sovereign. The royal household. The resources of the Crown. The King as judge. Royalty the pinnacle of the feudal hierarchy. The monarch has an ecclesiastical character.

The Family. IT is in the midst of this anarchy that the work of social reconstruction is to be accomplished by the only organized force remaining intact, under the only shelter which nothing can overthrow, for it has its foundations in the human heart: the family. In the midst of the storm the family endures, grows stronger, and draws together. Obliged to suffice to its own needs, it creates the instruments necessary to it for agriculture and mechanical labour, and for armed defence. The State no longer exists, the family takes its place. Social life is confined to the fireside;

4

FORMATION OF FEUDAL FRANCE

life in common is limited to the bounds of the house and its surroundings, to its walls and enclosure.

It is a little society, near to but isolated from similar little societies formed on the same model.

The French countryside has taken on again an aspect of primitive wildness. Over the uncultivated lands spread virgin forests—waste stretches where, nevertheless, here and there, preferably on the heights, can be discerned modest groups of habitations, each of which forms the domain of that little State, the family, in which the germs of social life are preserved. The family dwells in its domain, girt round with a stockade and protected by ditches. The palisade is called the "hericon"; it is formed of thin stakes planted obliquely in the soil, with the sharp, aggressive points blackened with fire. In the middle of the enclosure is a mound, formed of the soil taken from the ditches, on which is built a wooden structure, a tower, the future keep. It is the residence of the master. In the enclosure lives the family, including relatives, companions, and servants; there it dwells with its cattle, weapons mingling with the instruments of labour. It has there dwelling-places, stables, sheds, storehouses, and barns.

Some of these wooden towers will still exist in the eleventh century. The monk Aimoin, of Fleury-sur-Loire, was to describe one of them. It stood at the Cour-Marigny, not far from Montargis: "The residence of Séguin was a wooden tower. In the upper story dwelt Séguin with his family; there he spent his time, took his meals, and slept at night. In the lower part was a storehouse where were kept all things needed for daily life. The floor of the upper part, made of long planks shaped with an axe, rested on arches."

At the top of the tower, a "guette," or watchman, scans the horizon. Near the top the tower is surrounded by a path for patrol purposes. There is no opening from the ground up to the first story, where there is an entrance door reached by a wooden staircase, which can be quickly destroyed. The tower on its mound, which dominates the exterior line of enclosure bounded by a ditch, is itself immediately surrounded by a rampart protected by another ditch, over which has been thrown a drawbridge, also easily destructible. Finally, within the large

THE MIDDLE AGES

enclosure a circular spot marked out by rough stones is reserved for meetings held under the direction of the head of the family.

Bordering this group of erections are to be noticed embankments of earth resembling *tumuli*; they are the graves of ancestors, or of dead relatives. They are so arranged as to serve as a first line of defence. All these structures are of wood, except the mound proper, the banks and tumuli formed of heaped-up earth.

Many years later, the historian of William the Marshall was to mention one of these primitive mounds which remained between Anet and Sorel (1180) : An old abandoned mound

> Which was but poorly fashioned
> Close girt by a palisade . . .   (v. 3935.)

It was enclosed by a deep ditch. And even down to our time there have remained in the Gironde, at the place called la Tusque (Sainte-Eulalie d'Ambarès), some vestiges of these erections, the humble beginnings of the castles of the Middle Ages.

The fortified mounds (*mottes*) increased rapidly in number in France during the second half of the tenth century. From the beginning of the eleventh, mention is found of defensive buildings of stone, erected on high ground difficult of approach and protected by ravines or marshes; nevertheless, the wooden keeps, built in the tenth century, are to remain in great numbers in the following century. They are to be repaired and kept up, so that they will be found still in the time of Philip Augustus.

> The marches were well defended,
> From Bonsmolins to Arches
> There was not stone or wooden
> Castle which was not well garrisoned.
>   (*Guillaume le Maréchal*, v. 811.)

There lived the family, under the rule of its natural head.

At the beginning of our history the head of the family recalls the *paterfamilias* of ancient times. He commands the group which surrounds him and bears his name; he organizes the common defence, apportions the labour according to individual abilities and needs. He *reigns*—the word is in the

6

texts—as absolute master. He is called "lord." His wife, the mother of the family, is called "lady," *domina*.

Within each of the fortified residences we have described, are produced all things necessary for the support of those who live there. These people make use on the spot of things which they have made themselves. Exchanges are no longer made; and when these are resumed they will be made first of all between immediate neighbours, from one "motte" to the next. For the rest, life is simple: it is agricultural life without movement. A man suffers, loves, works, and dies in the place where he was born. The head of the family is at the same time soldier and farmer, like the heroes of Homer. The lands which he cultivates are grouped round his dwelling-place. To make use of a term of the Economists, they are "agglomerated" there.

The family, under the direction of its head, is able to build its dwelling and to manufacture scythes and ploughs. In the interior courtyard glow the forge fires, where arms are fashioned on the loud anvil. The women weave and dye stuffs.

The family has become for men a country—the documents of the period call it *patria*. And each one loves it with an emotion the more intense because he has it all round him. He sees it live: he feels immediately its strength and beauty and also its sweetness. It is for him a strong and cherished armour, a necessary protection. Without the family, of which he is one of the elements, he could not live.

Thus are formed the sentiments of solidarity which bind the members of a family one to the other. The prosperity of one will ensure that of his relatives; the honour of the one will be the honour of the other, and consequently the shame of one will fall on all the members of the "line."

These sentiments are to grow strong and develop, and to assume ever more power, in proportion as the family itself develops and the work accomplished through and by the family becomes more notable; when the "house" has been built and the "line" has spread. For the family thus constituted is not to remain limited to father, mother, children, and servants.

THE MIDDLE AGES

Already it has grown. The spirit of solidarity which binds its different members together, strengthened by the necessities of the time, keep the various branches joined to the trunk. The younger sons and their offspring remain grouped round the eldest and continue to receive from him a common guidance. This family in the larger sense, which includes the younger sons and their children, the cousins, the servants, and the workmen attached to the house, takes the name of "mesnie" (*ménage*)—*mesnie* from the Latin *mansionata*, house. This social group, sprung from the family and preserving its characteristics, this "greater" family, is destined to play a very large part in the first period of our national history.

The "mesnie" includes the family, the relatives united round the head of the principal branch, the servants, all those who live round, for, and through the "house." At the head of the house is the lord, invested with the character of a patron, paternal like the authority he wields. An old saying ran: "Like lord, like house"; as we say now: Like father, like son.

The household (*mesnie*) includes the kinsmen and the most faithful relatives by marriage. They are fed, reared, instructed in work and soldiering with the nephews, children, and other relatives. The spirit which prevails in the "mesnie" remains strictly that of a family. In several provinces of France, notably in Burgundy, in the eleventh and twelfth centuries the word "mesnie" still means a house in the concrete sense. Certain rights are given in fief over some "mesnies" in a village.

In course of time, through the growth of the family and the ties of a fictitious relationship which attaches to it many strangers, the "mesnie" comes to include a very important group of men. The private "mesnie" which depends immediately on the lord will have become so numerous by the twelfth century that its forces will suffice for a military expedition when it is not a case of a "great war." In feudal struggles a "mesnie" will be seen defending or taking a town. Lambert d'Ardres, in the twelfth century, will speak of the "infinite multitudes" who compose the great seigniorial "mesnies." The brother of the Provost of Bruges, according to Galbert, ruled over a "mesnie" of 3000 friends and relatives.

FORMATION OF FEUDAL FRANCE

The "mesnie" has its eyes fixed on its head, its lord. It assists him with its counsels, it supports him in time of trouble; the strong men follow him in his expeditions.

United around their lord it is the duty of those who form the "mesnie" to love one another as members of one family, so that indeed this reciprocal affection, deep and devoted, which binds the members of the household (*mesnie*) gives it its essential character. The members of a household ought to have for their lord the affection which is shown to the head of a family, and he on his side has the duty of loving, protecting, and guiding them in all gentleness. In *Raoul de Cambrai* the Count of Artois sees his men lying "in the sand." The enemy have killed them with their heavy spears. "His household is there, dead, bleeding: with his right hand he blesses them; he mourns and weeps over them; his tears run down to his waist."

The family, grown and organized into the "mesnie," has its artisans and its labourers who act at the same time as soldiers under the leadership of their head; it possesses a moral organization, again under the direction of the head of the family. The members of this extended family are united as a sort of corporation; they assist each other mutually; they have their tribunal, the tribunal of the lord, *i.e.* of the head of the family; they have their customs, their manners, their traditions; they have their flag—that is to say, their watchword; they have their banner, "the iron haft of which is gilded over"; they take one name, the name of their lord, of the head of the family; they form "such and such a household."

The family, lasting through the generations, is destined to assert its traditions, the qualities of which it will be proud, heroism and honour. Several generations have gone by since that brutal epoch when the family was the necessary refuge for the individual, and yet all would still work, fight, and die for it.

It is the living cell from which France sprang.

SOURCES.—Aimoin, *Miracula S. Benedicti*, ed. Mabillon; *Acta Sanctorum ord. S. Ben.*, iv. 356–90; *La Chançun de Guillelme*, ed. Herm. Suchier, *Biblioth. normannica*, 1911; *Robert de Blois, Sämmtliche Werke*, Berlin, 1889–95, 3 vols.; *L'histoire de Guillaume le Maréchal*, ed. P. Meyer, 1891–1901, 3 vols.; Montaiglon-Raynaud, *Recueil des fabliaux*, 1872–90, 6 vols.

THE MIDDLE AGES

HISTORICAL WORKS.—Jacq. Flach, *Les Origines de l'anc. France*, 1886–1917, 4 vols.; Karl Bucher, *die Enstehung der Volkswertschaft*, 2nd ed., 1898; Viollet-le-Duc, *Dictionnaire de l'Architecture*, 1854–68, 10 vols. 8vo, and *Dictionnaire du Mobilier*, 1868–75, 6 vols.

The Fief. Messieurs Alfred and Maurice Croiset have given us the following picture of ancient Greece at the beginning of its feudal period: "The populations sought their existence in the hard and obstinate labour of the soil; there was no active industry nor any great trade; it was a rough, poor life, servile and unquiet; a life in which war was frequent, and consequently there were incursions and pillagings; every one bore arms. Instead of open towns there were fortified enclosures built of great stones and situated on the hills; and there were war-leaders who defended the men of the fields and gave them shelter behind their ramparts in times of danger."

And such also is the picture which France offers us at the end of the tenth century: "That was the time," writes Benjamin Guérard, "when each one to secure his own safety fortified and entrenched himself as best he could. The steeps were inhabited; the heights were crowned with towers and forts; the walls of the dwellings were furnished with turrets, bristling with battlements and pierced with loopholes. Ditches were dug and drawbridges poised; the river-ways and defiles were watched and defended; roads were barred and communications intercepted. At the end of the tenth century each person had his definite position; France was covered with fortified places and feudal haunts; everywhere society watched and held itself in ambush."

In these "haunts" lived men, rude and valiant, who engaged in war and the work of the fields. "William of Ponthieu, sprung from the blood royal of France, had four sons. The eldest loved only arms; the second cared only for the chase; the third gave himself to rustic labours, content to store wheat in the barns, and his father gave to him in fief the earldom of Saint-Paul; as to the youngest, he devoted himself to the breeding of cattle: his father allotted to him a territory of uneven ground, bristling with thickets, little woods, and quick-set hedges, possessing pastures and marsh-lands" (Lambert d'Ardres).

FORMATION OF FEUDAL FRANCE

Hariulf describes the country thus arranged, and it is simply Ponthieu: "The country is watered by rivers and springs of fresh water; it is wooded, offers pasturage for sheep, and produces corn. The men there are warlike. No towns are to be seen, only strong castles."

Such was the French countryside at the beginning of the feudal period.

* * * * * * * *

The family has become the household (*mesnie*), and the household develops and becomes the fief.

For a "stranger" (*forain*) could enter into the household of the lord by adoption. To be adopted is, according to the Epitome of Saint-Gall, *ad alium patrem se commendare*, to put oneself under the authority of another father; moreover, contemporaries used the word *familia* to indicate the whole number of persons joined under the authority of a feudal chief.

The baron—which word means "master"—at the head of a fief is the head of a family. By this is understood all his trusty followers, his *subjects*, and it is well to ponder this expression. The baron calls his subjects his kindred:

> With you I will go and my great kindred:
> Full twenty thousand in number shall we be.
> (*Ogier le Danois* (the Dane), v. 4932.)

It is a family whose members are identified one with another, like those of the same family when there is question of joy or sorrow. "Yours will be the fault," a vassal will say to his lord, "to me will fall the loss; and you will have part in it, for the penalty goes to him who holds the lordship; moreover, it is for you to compensate me." The lord owes to his vassals protection, help, the means of support. "In his land of Guines," says Lambert d'Ardres, "Count Arnoul gathered his subjects round him and worked for their good; he received them into his house, into his family; he took an interest in them and married them on his land." When the vassal dies the lord takes charge of his widow; if she is young, he busies himself about marrying her again; he takes care of her children. For the annalist who wrote the *Chronicle of the Counts of Anjou*, Geoffrey of the Grey Tunic is the model baron (tenth and eleventh centuries): "He was skilled in war, where his arm witnessed to his valour; lofty and calm, he gave rein to his benevolence; he loved giving; a true enemy to his enemies, he was a true patron (*patrocinabatur*) to his own people: such is the real baronial character."

Thus the lord is the "patron" of his subject; this word also is of the period. A man standing alone is lost in the storm:

> Men without a lord have fallen badly.
> (*Chanson de Guillaume*, v. 289.)

On the other hand, the vassal is bound to his suzerain by the sentiments and duties of a son to a father; he ought to serve him with love, follow him in war, take his advice in important matters, obtain his consent when he gets married or marries his children; he owes him affection, help, fidelity; and these sentiments—begotten by the fictitious relationship created by the feudal tie, but inspired by the ties and sentiments of the real family—are so strong, that they take precedence over the obligations of kinship itself.

The old Duke Aymon encounters in Ardennes his four sons who are at war with his suzerain. What is the vassal to do? betray his "baron" by showing favour to the rebellion of his children, or wring his paternal heart in taking arms against them?

"Alas!" he cries, "why have my sons not fled away; why do they oblige me to give them battle?"

> And if my sons die, my heart shall be sad!

Count Hermenfroi encourages him in his resolution:

> No man of your age, whose hairs are white
> Should perjure himself, for son or for friend;
> Who to his lord a traitor is, his God denies.
> "By my head," cried the Duke, "I intend you well,
> Never truce shall they have, defeat is theirs."
> (*Les Quatre fils Aymon*, v. 2977.)

And the old man, with torture in his heart, sends heralds to his children to announce himself their enemy.

Thus the fief is the "house" grown larger, and some thousands of fiefs are formed through the broad land. In each of them the baron brings together his own family, his

FORMATION OF FEUDAL FRANCE

near relatives, the children of the younger branches of his family, then those who have come to place themselves and their goods under his protection. The alods (*alleus*), that is to say, the freeholds, disappear. They are lordless, and unresisting they die out.

And as this work of co-ordination and subordination is done without ordered direction or uniform impulse, society is in apparent confusion, but with the life and healthy verdure, the fine disorder of the forest.

The fief includes those who have attached themselves to the lord by subordinating their lands to him, and it includes those whom the lord has attached to himself by a grant of land, or again by a gift of money, by an office at his court, or by some other benefit, some " honour " which the beneficiary receives from him in faith and homage. The new vassal, in exchange for the concession granted by the lord, tenders to him an oath of fidelity, placing his hands in his, after which the baron gives him a handful of soil, a branch of a tree, a ball of turf, as a symbol of the fief granted, field, wood, or meadow, and from this moment the vassal, seized of the benefit which the suzerain has given him, becomes his man and owes him his devotion as the lord owes him his protection.

Such are the sentiments which are to make all the inhabitants of a fief, united under the authority of their suzerain, members of a little country. Moreover, we find the word *patria* used in documents to describe the whole of a fief, inhabitants and land, just as it is also found describing the family and the household (*mesnie*).

Within the fief, subject to the lord and his vassals, live the serfs, the rural labourers attached to the soil, which they **The Serfs.** cultivate painfully. The serf is the manual worker tied to the soil which he cannot leave. He is not a soldier, and except at the call of his lord he has no right to carry arms.

One sees serfs who have other serfs working under their orders. For in servitude there are still degrees. The serfs cannot marry without the consent of their lord. For that matter, it was the same with the vassals and with the lord himself, who could not marry without the consent of the King:

THE MIDDLE AGES

a consequence of the family organization which formed the whole State.

Serfdom replaced slavery proper at the time of the dissolution of the Carolingian Empire. Its origin is found in what historians have called the "appropriation of the soil," which persons of servile condition practised to their profit; as in fact it was practised by persons immediately higher in the social scale. It has not been sufficiently noticed that serfdom constituted the lower stage of vassalship. It might be compared to a forced rent.

The condition of the serfs, then beginning to improve, was still very hard at the end of the tenth century. In 998 a certain Stephen made a donation to the Abbey of Cluny in expiation of his violence in having had the foot of one of his serfs cut off. About the same time the Church declared the penalty of excommunication against any person who should have put a serf to death. But let us not forget that if serfdom tied the hard knot by which a man was bound to the soil, at the same time it offered great advantages in those rude times to him who was subject to it; that if the soil held the serf, the serf held the soil; that if the serf was condemned to toil on the land, at least his livelihood was there assured, and that was for him, in those times of violent anarchy, a blessing. Serfdom was not slavery. Its obligations were fixed. The lord could not give orders at his pleasure. In a document of the eleventh century we see some serfs refusing to cart clay because they had never done it before.

The serf worked, certainly, for his lord; but the lord granted to him, as to all his "subjects," assistance and protection. The watchman, who acts sentinel at the top of the wooden tower, has uttered a cry of fear; on the horizon savage bands or enemy foragers are ravaging the land. The castle opens its doors to the poor labourer with his family, his beasts, his goods.

In years of famine the serf finds help with his lord, while the free man of lowly condition dies of hunger. Between the lord and the serf are repeated, in fact, those same sentiments of unity, devotion, of reciprocal affection which we have noted between baron and vassals.

There is the beautiful story of Amis, in *Amis et Amiles*. A hideous leprosy devours the young knight. His wife spurns him; at the hospital no one dares to approach him, but two of his serfs follow him in his life of wandering; they tend him as a mother does her child; they go so far as to beg for him.

And there are other stories more touching still, which remind one of that of the good vassal Renier, in *Jourdain de Blaye*.

A traitor, Fromont, assassinates his lord, Girard de Blaye, and tries to exterminate even to the last member this family, whose chief he has slain. There remains a child, the only son, whom Girard has confided to the care of one of his men, a certain Renier, and his wife, Erembourc. Fromont hears of it and calls on these brave folk to bring to him the son of Girard, whom he would also kill. Renier and his wife deliver up their own child, making him pass for that of their lord. The poet paints the grief of the mother in making this bitter sacrifice: "The mother sets out to give up her son to those who are going to slaughter him. The child smiles, for he knows no evil. The beautiful days of summer are coming, thought the mother, and I shall climb up there to the walls. Thence I shall see the children, the boys of his age; I shall see them playing with shields, and bars, and tilts, struggling together and tumbling over; and my heart will weep at it."

The documents of the twelfth century show, more than once, the peasants rising bodily in a spontaneous movement, to deliver their lord when they have heard of his captivity.

It can be said of the French serfs of the Middle Ages what the Comte de Ségur wrote of the Russian serfs in the eighteenth century: "Certain of always being fed, lodged, warmed by the fruits of their labour or by their lords, sheltered from every need, they never felt the anguish of poverty or the fear of falling into it." Add to that, security, so precious in those barbarous centuries, for the tiller of the fields.

The serf, it is true, of himself possesses nothing; what he has returns to his lord after his death; but this harsh rule has its corrective in the organization of "village houses" of which the serfs form a part, "mesnies" like those of which we have treated. The goods therein are handed down from generation to generation, arousing the interest of the workers in a common prosperity. It is a collective personality which draws together the members of the family, and is preserved in its successive generations. The serf finds in it a stimulus to work and thrift. He can sell, buy, realize privileges. And there can be seen among the serfs wealthy men, influential men, "rich men," as the expression then went.

The keep procures security for the members of the great family; it gives them independence. From its imposing height the massive tower protects its own.

The Keeps. "Huon de Cambrai, Gautier and Rigaut, having no hope of taking the strong town of Lens, contented themselves with laying waste the surrounding country. . . . This was the limit of their progress, for the lands of Enguerran were too well defended (by the keep which Enguerran de Coucy had built and which the Boches have just criminally destroyed) for them to think of venturing there."

From the middle of the eleventh century the wooden "mottes" become more important; their walls rise higher, their moats grow deeper.

The famous Château du Puiset, described by Suger, was built in the twelfth century. It shows the transition between the "motte" of the tenth century, built of earth and wood, and the feudal castle, all of stone, of the twelfth cenutry.

The Château du Puiset had a double circumvallation like the "mottes" we have already described in outline. A first enclosure is formed by a moat and a palisade; but the second, the interior boundary, is already formed by a stone wall. In the centre is the castle mound on ground raised artificially, with its tower still of wood.

The castle of the feudal lord is composed, then, essentially of the keep, *i.e.* a high tower—square in the eleventh and twelfth centuries, round in the following centuries—surrounded by a vast enclosure, palisade or rampart, bordered by a moat. The keep was generally erected on the highest point of the seigniorial territory, sometimes, however, at a point considered weak from the point of view of defence, in order to strengthen it. In the eleventh century the keep still serves as a residence for the baron and his immediate relatives; in the twelfth century it is to be reserved for purely military purposes; then, quite close, within the same enclosure, the " palace " will be built as a residence for the seigniorial family.

We have just seen that the keep is generally built on an eminence. A vast enclosure follows the declivity of the hill. It is therefore on the lowest level and is called the " inner court." There a well will be sunk and there too a chapel and dwelling-houses will be arranged for the companions and servants of the baron. A second court, adjoining the first—for very soon it will be no longer a concentric court—is also surrounded by a line of enclosure: it contains other dwellings in which the artisans attached to the castle live, and some shelters for the "refugees" (*retrahants*) of the domain, for their cattle and goods, *i.e.* for the inhabitants of the fief who, in case of danger, come to find refuge with their possessions in the shelter of the fortress (*ferté*).

> From Senlis to Orleans one may go,
> Thence back to Paris wend,
> From Laon to Reims through all the cities,
> No man of woman born shall there be found
> Who is not in tower or castle shut.
>
> (*Les Quatre fils Aymon*, v. 3221.)

Up to the twelfth century, only the keep and the interior wall will be of stone—and the keep will not always be so, as we have just seen from the Château du Puiset; the other constructions are still of wood, separate from one another, which gives the whole the appearance of an encampment rather than of a fixed dwelling-place. The exterior wall, surrounded by a moat, is generally composed of palisades; it may happen to be formed of piled-up stones.

Sometimes, beyond the outer wall—but more often within the enclosure and protected by its fence—were a vineyard, orchard, the castle garden, a pleasure garden, or even a little wood; the lord, his lady, and their guests find there green shades, with the song of birds. Finally, outside the walls stretch the arable lands, " *gaignables*," fields, vineyards, woods, willow groves and osier beds, fish ponds where sport the red-brown carp, the elusive tench; the private domain of the seigneur.

There is the very soul of the little country which the feudal spirit has formed round the " baron."

THE MIDDLE AGES

One sees such castles defended by a single man-at-arms who is sufficient for the task, for he has under his orders the "refugees" of the surrounding district, the inhabitants of his "country," his faithful subjects, vassals, and serfs, who take refuge with their families, cattle, and goods within the walls of the castle which the lord has built with their help.

> For fifty leagues wandering you might go,
> Nor would a man be found, townsman or peasant,
> Save those who in the castles are set to watch.
> (*Les Quatre fils Aymon,* v. 3185.)

The peasant feels himself sheltered; he is certain of protection; he can work without fear of seeing a band of robbers suddenly appear who will rend from him cattle and goods, and lead him off captive, him and his, driving him with kicks, a pitchfork at his neck. Thanks to this splendid person the feudal baron, the villein works, sows, looks forward to his harvest. "At that time," says the author of the *Chronique d'Espagne,* "the barons, so as to be always ready, kept their horses in the rooms where they slept with their wives."

Insensibly, between the military chief, iron-clad in his stone keep, and his labourers of the open country, necessity strengthens the mutual contract by making it customary. The "subjects" work for the baron, cultivate his land, carry for him, pay certain dues, so much per house, so much per head of cattle, so much on inheritance or sale, for he must keep himself and his family and feed his soldiers. Le Play has compared the feudal castle thus organized to a military workshop whose work consists in the protection of agriculture, industry, and commerce, which can only be done through it.

The baron is happy in the prosperity of his faithful subjects, and they share in the joys of their lord. Aubri marries Guibourc. On the day of the wedding his castle is filled with his numerous "kindred."

> But when he sees his great palace filled,
> The benches with cavaliers full,
> And they play on the viol high and clear and joyously;
> When his people abound in merriment and joy,
> It seems to him that he is full of well-being.
> (*Auberi.*)

FORMATION OF FEUDAL FRANCE

Garin and his son Girbert arrive in their fief of Gorze lès Saint Mihiel: " Great and small had come to meet them. It was good to see the crowd of young men and maidens laughing and dancing to the sound of the pipes and viols " (*Garin le Loherain*).

And thus one can follow the successive transformations by which family affections developed into usages and customs, and by which through their transportation into the social organism the feudal system was formed.

Sink a well in the desert from which beneficent water shall flow, and you will see all round the land grow green and become covered with palms, aloes, and cactus, the formation of an oasis. So, in the eleventh century, the man enterprising enough to raise a " motte " in a ravaged district, sufficiently powerful to build there a keep with its fortified enclosure and to provide it with soldiers, had not long to wait before he saw an active population growing in the neighbouring countryside, work developing, a group of villages growing up, and monasteries being built. On the other hand, the districts where no powerful lords held sway and extended their protection, soon fell into frightful anarchy.

Most of the fiefs were formed thus in France at the outset of the feudal period, spontaneously, through the grouping of the inhabitants of a district huddling in the midst of the storm under the protection of a man powerful through his courage, his family, his property which he was well able to defend, or through alliances which he knew how to use.

The Feudal Hierarchy.

The hierarchy of protection and mutual devotion established between the lord and his men is to be continued between the lord who rules a fief of some importance and a more powerful baron, who will group under his authority, through similar ties, not only his vassals and immediate serfs, but other seigneurs who, while preserving their authority intact over their " subjects," will themselves become the " men " of this superior suzerain. And this superior baron will attach himself in his turn by identical bonds to a lord more important still. It is a superposition of fiefs,—which reminds one of the system of turrets, spires, niches, and arches of the mediæval

19

churches,—of which each, whatever its degree of importance, its power, its population, is like the others in its composition even up to the supreme fief, the keystone of the whole edifice, which is commanded by the suzerain of all the French suzerains —even to the King in his keep of the Louvre, which Philip Augustus is to build and on which all the keeps of France depend.

SOURCES.—*Capitulaires Carolingiens*, ed. Pertz, LL, tome i.; *Chron. de St. Riquier*, by Hariulf, ed. Lot, 1894; *Chroniques des Comtes d'Anjou et des sgrs d'Amboise*, ed. Halphen and Poupardin, 1913; Suger, *Vita Ludovici regis*,e d. Molinier, 1887; *Lamberti Ardrensis eccl. presb. chron. Ghinense et Ardense*, ed. Godefroy-Menilglaise, 1855; *Le Chanson de Roland*, various editions; *La Chançun de Guillelme*, ed. Suchier, *Biblioth. normannica*, 1911; *Garin le Loherain*, translated by P. Paris, 1862; *Ogier le Danois*, ed. Barrois, 1842; *Raoul de Cambrai*, ed. Meyer and Lognon, 1882; *La Chançun des Quatre fils Aymon*, ed. Castets, Montpellier, 1909; *Li coronomens Looys*, ed. Jonckbloet, *Guillaume d'Orange*, The Hague, 1854, 2 vols.; Vict. Mortet, *Textes relatifs à l'histoire de l'architecture* ($XI^{\acute{e}}$–$XII^{\acute{e}}$ *Siècles*), 1911.

HISTORICAL WORKS.—Alfred and Maur. Croiset, *Hist. de la litt. grecque*, 2nd ed., 1896; Brussel, *Nouvel examen de l'usage des fiefs*, 1750, 2 vols.; Benj. Guérard, *Prolégom. au Polypt. de l'abbé Irminon*, 1845; Fustel de Coulanges, *Les Origines du système féodal*, 1890; Jacq. Flach, *Les origines de l'anc. France*, 1886–1917, 4 vols.; Doniol, *Serfs et Vilains au Moyen Age*, 1900; Seignobos, *Le Régime feodal en Bourgogne*, 1882; C. Lamprecht, *Etudes sur l'état econ. de la France pendant la 1re partie du Moyen Age*, translation Marignan, 1889; Guilhiermoz, *Essai sur l'Origine de la Noblesse en France*, 1902.

The Town : The Castles.
The fortress, composed essentially of an enclosure round a keep, contains an autonomous society, which has its government, its judicial system, its customs, its soldiers, its artisans, who have their dwellings and workshops. Under the shelter of the walls the workmen work for their lord, their " patron," and for his numerous " kindred," *i.e.* for the inhabitants of the fief : the peasants of the surrounding district come to seek refuge there in times of danger.

William le Breton describes the Château-Gaillard, built by Richard Cœur de Lion in a loop of the Seine, whence it dominates the Andelys : " He had the crest of the rock rounded and girt it about with strong walls, he freed it from the stones which encumbered it, and after having levelled the interior of this

FORMATION OF FEUDAL FRANCE

enclosure, he caused to be built there many little dwellings and houses capable of holding many people, keeping the centre only for the erection of the keep. The beauty of the place and the strength of the fortress spread the fame of the Gaillard rock." The castle, reputed impregnable, will be taken by Philip Augustus. "He found there a great street," says le Breton, "filled with many dwellings. . . . The King distributed its houses to new citizens."

Thus the great feudal castles sheltered quite a numerous population, a sedentary population continually increased by " refugees " from the castle-ward.

Around certain keeps there is a vast enclosure which appears to be destined to serve as a camping-ground for an army. This space is furnished with huts hastily put up when disturbances break out. They gave shelter to the " subjects " of the flat country, to their families and their cattle—and these disturbances lasted sometimes for months or years. One can imagine with what activity the work went on then in the workshops within the walls.

But from the eleventh century on, thanks to the " patronal " feudal organization we have just described, a relative degree of order is established, a certain amount of industry is developed; it begins to be possible to move from one district to another, and one sees a commercial movement growing up from the need of exchanges—which were first made from one domain to its neighbour. Then, too, in their turn merchants come to establish themselves within the precincts of the castle : the castle, the burgh (*bourg*)—from the German *burg*, a fortress—becomes peopled with burgesses (*bourgeois*); a population which before long spreads beyond the castle walls and builds up the *faubourgs*, whose inhabitants also are anxious to surround themselves with a wall of defence.

" Girard de Roussillon lived at Orivent, a castle which he held from the King. The burgesses thereof are rich, possessing horses, and gold, and silver " (*Girart de Roussillon*).

What is a town in the Middle Ages ? It is a castle which has prospered. It is an important fact, and one which has not been sufficiently noted, that in the documents of the first centuries of the feudal period the words " town " (*ville*) and

THE MIDDLE AGES

"castle" (*château*) are synonymous. Witness the Fabliau de Courtebarbe:

> Into the *town* (Compiègne) they went;
> They listened and heard
> It cried through the *castle*,
> "Here is good wine, fresh and new."
>
> (*Fabliau des trois aveugles.*)

In the twelfth century Suger and Galbert de Bruges will still call towns like Ypres and Bruges "castles." For William le Breton Dijon is a castle, and so is Rouen for the historian of William the Marshall; while for the author of the *Grandes Chroniques* the Château du Puiset is a town.

We have just described the feudal castle surrounded by a fortified enclosure, where the companions of the lord, the artisans who work for his household, have taken up their abode as well as some of his labourers. Now it happens, as a result of fortunate circumstances, and notably through the growth of the fief, that the work of the castellan, of the burgesses, and of the artisans becomes more active; the population increases. Hariulf speaks of the district of Saint Riquier (Centuel), "where there are no towns but the castles are rich and populous." Here is a geographical position favourable to exchanges, at the crossing of high roads or on a waterway; the products of the land are good for trade, and a town develops inside the fortress, the burgh, and in the faubourgs, whose enclosure it soon breaks through, which in its turn has become too narrow.

Moreover, in the eleventh century there is no opposition between the castle of the seigneur and the town of the burgesses. Town and castle are in unity. Look at Coucy. The high keep, surrounded by thick walls and girt with a deep moat, stands in the wide court where the "palace" is built. This latter contains the residence of the lord of Coucy, of his followers, knights, and squires, his liegemen. The whole is surrounded by vast walls flanked by towers; the walls continuing surround the whole town, the houses of which are built to imitate the keep. If the town is about to be taken the inhabitants take refuge with their provisions in the keep, which can offer so efficient and powerful a resistance that throughout the Middle Ages, the Hundred Years War, and the League it will defy every attack.

FORMATION OF FEUDAL FRANCE

Like the castle, the town is characterized in the eleventh century by the fact that it is surrounded by a line of fortifications, generally composed up to the beginning of the next century of a wooden palisade bordered by a moat like that of the fortresses. Like those of the castles proper, the town enclosures afforded refuge to the people of the surrounding districts in case of invasion by an enemy.

And if we will remember that in the eleventh century all the urban governments are seigniorial governments, we shall not be astonished that the words *town* and *castle* were synonymous : the towns were castles.

As late as the fifteenth century the town of St. Romain-le-Puy, in Forez, will present a striking example of the urban structure : an isolated mountain furnished with a triple system of fortifications ; at the top rises the castle with its keep, protecting a convent of Benedictine monks ; half-way down the hill is the circle of fortifications in stone erected for the defence of the burgh, where dwell the burgesses ; finally, at the bottom, another wall concentric with this surrounds the courtyard (*bassecour*), the refuge of the country people.

The circle of fortifications, however, is not sufficient to constitute a town. Many villages are found protected by a rampart since the tenth century, but they have remained villages. Another condition is necessary ; we have just indicated it : the feudal authority of a suzerain must be established.

The Urban Lordship.

The site of the town of Ardres was in the tenth century but waste land, whence its name : *Ardea.* A brewer came to establish himself there, and his little establishment prospered, for the shepherds came there to drink, and on Sundays they might be seen in front of his door amusing themselves, leaping the bars and turning somersaults. A village grew up. Arnoul, son-in-law of Herred de Furnes, resolved to transfer his residence there. He built there, says Lambert d'Ardres, a " motte," a keep, and surrounded it with a moated rampart. The enclosure soon grew larger, a market was set up, a church was built; Arnoul established a judicial system, a seigniorial authority was established : Ardres was a town.

It is owing to the lord's protection that the town flourishes,

23

an armed defence which means unceasing work for the baron. In it he risks his life and those of his men. " Huon de Cambrai hears in the town (St. Quentin) the cries of the burgesses, the groans of the women and girls ill prepared for such chances (*jeux*) (the perils of war). ' Do not grieve,' he cries to them, ' you have nothing to fear while I am alive ; before they should reach you much blood would be shed, and mine to the last drop.' " (*Garin le Loherain.*)

The feudal baron secures the safety of his burgesses, he secures the safe transit of their merchandise within his territory, and so efficacious is his protection that it follows them into distant lands.

" When the burgesses and merchants of Narbonne hear that their lord, the Count Aimeri, wishes to separate himself from his sons and send them into foreign parts, they are deeply grieved.

" The news spreads that the six brothers are about to set out. The burgesses assemble ; two hundred of them ascend to the hall of the castle :

" ' Aimeri, Sire,' says the best speaker, ' we are merchants who traverse land and sea, carrying rich stuffs, ermine, horses, and wines. When we arrive at distant markets, they demand of us : " To whom do you owe allegiance ? To what lord do you appeal ? " We answer : " The Count Aimeri and his sons." And none would be so bold as to offend against us. Now, behold you wish to scatter your sons abroad. Sire, take rather our vineyards, our lands, our farms ; take what you will of our wealth, and distribute it among your children ; but keep them with you to defend us.' " (*Les Narbonnais.*)

The lord maintained peace within his territory by administering justice.

To encourage the trade of his burgesses, he had bridges built, marshes drained, roads repaired, and inns established.

> And had good bridges made and great hostelry.
> (*Elie de Saint-Gilles.*)

And in the *Roman de Brut*, concerning the Seigneur de Belin :

> Good bridges he had made, high roads,
> Of stone, of sand, of chalk,
> First he made a highway.

The lord built hospitals and lazar-houses.

FORMATION OF FEUDAL FRANCE

"Oilard de Wynville," notes Lambert d'Ardres, "hears that, between Guines and Wissant, a lonely spot, covered with woods, was infested by wicked men. Lying in wait in their dens they pounced upon the passers-by." Through this the place was known as *Soutinguevelt*, i.e. "the field of the wicked." Oilard de Wynville freed Soutinguevelt of the bandits who infested it, and secured safe passage there. Such was the origin, says Lambert d'Ardres, of the toll established in the environs of Guines.

Thus the taxes and dues, the customs and tolls, the wine-presses and manorial bakehouses, whose profits went to the lord, represented the legitimate reward for his trouble, his expenses, and his work. The baron set up a market for barter, establishing it under the walls of his castle, an arrangement which was to remain when the towns developed. He kept order there, and policed it and guaranteed the safety of the merchants:

> A lord who held much land,
> Who so much hated deadly war,
> And all men of evil life
> That well he punished them,
> And when he had imprisoned them
> No ransom would he take,—
> Proclaimed a new market.
> A poor merchant comfortless
> Went to it with his little horse,
> He had neither wallet nor servant,
> Trifling was his merchandise.

The honest man ties up his "little horse" in a field of the seigniorial fief. The beast will browse there, for he has no oats to give it. And the mercer leaves his mount in the keeping of the seigneur and, moreover, in God's hands. Now during the night the "little horse" was devoured by a wolf. The mercer goes to the baron's court. "I had placed my beast under your protection and that of God."—"How much was the animal worth?"—"Sixty sous."—"Well, here are thirty; ask God for the rest" (*Fabliau du pauvre mercier*).

In 1172 Guinard, Count of Roussillon, leaves to Peter Martin, a merchant of Perpignan, one hundred and fifty Melgueil sous for the loss a robber has caused him on his lands.

Like the vassals in the country, the burgesses love their

lord, without whom they could not live. Count Richard de Montivilliers is going to set out on Crusade, and his burgesses, whom he has so well guarded, says Jean Renard, that they are now all rich men, are terribly grieved.

> Alas! they cry fearful and sorrowing,
> What henceforth can we do?
> Alas! gentle count so debonair,
> How distraught are we to-day!
>
> (*L'Escoufle*, v. 188.)

And what joy at his return!

"Droon, son of Girard, entered the castle (Roussillon) on horseback. He found a thousand of the people singing and dancing; and three thousand more on the road. . . ."

"When they heard news of their lord (who, after a long absence, was drawing near to the castle), every heart was full: When shall we see him? Let us who love him go forth to meet him!—and you, canons and clerks of St.-Sauveur, make processions in his honour! you, knights, come with us!" (*Girard de Roussillon*).

Literary works are confirmed by the chronicles. Suger recounts how Count Eude de Corbeil was kidnapped by his brother, Hugh of Crécy, and shut up in the castle of the Ferté-Bernard:

"At this news a great number of the people of Corbeil, a castle (*castellum*) enriched by a company of knights of the old nobility, came to throw themselves at the feet of the King. Weeping they told him of the imprisonment of the Count and begged him to deliver him. The King gave them good hope, and their grief was assuaged."

In speaking of the family we described the "motte"; in speaking of the fief we described the keep. This keep, the **The Inhabitants.** primitive castle, will spread out, so to speak, during the twelfth and thirteenth centuries. Not only will the outer wall grow larger, but within this wall, towers, defensive works, and the other seigniorial buildings will be multiplied; so much so that, as Viollet-le-Duc points out, the most important castles seem to be formed of a group of castles enclosed in a common line of fortification, and which could at need, having each an independent existence, engage in a struggle or defend themselves against one another.

FORMATION OF FEUDAL FRANCE

This great castle, formed of several distinct castles, is inhabited not only by soldiers but by labourers; artisans are established there, smiths, carpenters, armourers, harness-makers, tailors, who work for the lord and his numerous "kindred." One can hear, creaking on their iron staves, the signs indicating mercers, butchers, ironmongers, wine and beer merchants.

Such is a great castle at the end of the eleventh century, and such too a town at the same period.

The burgesses are vassals who render to their lord the same services as the vassals of the fields. They are equally subject to the feudal dues. Their share in the communal life consists in taking their place in the lord's court; they are among his councillors when he administers justice, take part in the meetings he calls; their names appear as witnesses at the end of charters bearing his seal. The chief of them are soldiers, knights. "Seven times twenty knights stayed normally in the town of of St.-Quentin," we read in *Garin le Loherain*, " for at that time knights loved to stay in the good towns and in the seigniorial castles, not, as now, in obscure country places, farms, and woods to live with the sheep." (This heroic poem has come down to us in a twelfth-century version.) The text is confirmed by the Chronicles of Richer and Guibert de Nogent.

These knights have fortified dwellings in the town.

"About this time," writes Gilbert de Mons, "there were in Ghent many men powerful through their connections and strong in their fortifications: enemies of one another, they often had recourse to arms." William le Breton on his side tells us how much the inhabitants of Lille loved their houses with their towers: *turritas domos!* Jean de Marmoutiers speaks in identical terms of the burgesses of Tours; they clothe themselves in purple, in vair and minever; their battle-mented dwellings are guarded by massive keeps.

In a town of the thirteenth century we see, then, several classes of citizen: the lord and his immediate family, a noble class generally called the "knights" (*chevaliers*), burgesses engaged in business—the knights and burgesses form the patrician class; artisans and labourers; lastly, real serfs, called the "beggars" (*questaux*).

THE MIDDLE AGES

These different classes existed everywhere, but they are more clearly distinguished in the little towns of the South, which maintained their primitive conditions up to the time of the drawing up of the Customs. Take, for example, Meilhan-en-Bazadais. At the head of the town is a lord of Meilhan, who has surrounded the castle and the " bourg " with a line of fortifications. The town has three parts: first, the castle; secondly, the " rock "; thirdly, the " bourg." These three quarters are inhabited by knights free from all dues; two of them, the " rock " and the " bourg," are inhabited also by burgesses who are liable to the lord for rents. The knights, who form the noble class, are called the gentlemen (*gentels*); they are grouped in *parages* (this word should be remembered). The burgesses (*borgues*) and the gentlemen are the only ones who play a public part in the town. Below them are the inhabitants (*cazats*) (the charter is drawn up in Provençal). Finally, on the lowest rung, are the men of servile condition, the *questaux*. Moreover, the burgesses could also have serfs as well as the lord and the knights. The lord equips a knight to perform in place of the burgesses the military service claimed by the Count of Poitiers. The burgesses, exempt from military service, are given wholly to their business. The lord, according to the feudal custom, owes protection to the people and the people owe assistance to their lord. Knights and burgesses should help each other against all strangers. The lord receives a Bordeaux farthing for each salmon sold on the butchers' stalls, for at Meilhan the butchers sell fish; he receives a Bordeaux penny for each ox sold, and three farthings per pig. The goods of persons dying intestate and leaving no family revert to him, also a part of what is yielded by fines.

Such is, in its essential features, the type of urban constitutions in the early part of the feudal period.

The towns had their households (*mesnies*) like the country districts, family organizations and, at the same time, feudal.

The "Lignages." The important burgesses, the patricians, had their followers (*mesniers*), whom the documents liken to the vassals of the lords. The poetry of the time shows us the heads of these urban households living in their vast abodes, shut in and fortified. These urban households include

FORMATION OF FEUDAL FRANCE

the family, the servants, the domestic artisans, dependants, some *questaux*, i.e. serfs—in a word, the *familia*, of which we have treated.

The phrase, " in the house of a fèvre-mesnier " (a worker of his household), is found in *Aubri le Bourgoing*.

The " mesnie," as it developed in the towns, produced there groups more extensive than itself, the *lignages* or *parages* of the French towns, the *vinaves* of Liège, the Flemish *geslachten*, the *geschlecter* of the Rhine towns. It is at Metz that these *parages* can be studied most distinctly and at a period comparatively close to our own. The names alone, *parages*, *lignages*, *geschlecter*, would suffice to indicate the family character of these urban groups. The *parages* are subdivided into branches, the branches into households (*mesnies*) or " hostels." The *parage* itself bears a family name; each of these *parages* has an organization at once of the family and military, *i.e.* feudal; each of them forms a distinct and autonomous group in the town. They organize military expeditions, make treaties, each on its own account, sometimes with the stranger against one or other neighbouring *parage* of fellow-citizens (*concitoyen*). It is the feudal system in the town.

And as in the feudal organization proper the movement has come from the lower classes. The households (*mesnies*) or " hostels " have gone to form the branches, the branches have formed the *parages*, and these last, under the authority of the suzerain, rule the city.

The material structure of the town was made in the image of its moral structure.

The Urban Fiefs. The town of Paris did not develop, as one might be tempted to think, from a central kernel, growing, spreading from place to place. There were, on the contrary, a certain number of generating kernels, each of which developed, and grew little by little, drawing nearer together in their growth and finally merging in one another. Contrary to the general opinion, the *Cité* did not play the part of a great splash of oil which gained the banks of the Seine and swamped the land as far as the present line of fortifications: it was an indefinite number of little cities, placed, one under episcopal authority, another under the royal authority,

29

others under the rule of an abbey, others still under the rule of a military order, but the greater number under the suzerainty of a simple lord, which formed and developed singly, living cells, growing by the force of their internal energy, up to the moment at which, having approached one another, they rased their walls within the common fortification.

The town of Paris was thus formed by the juxtaposition of a certain number of fortresses each of which had its own system of defence, each surrounded by its own gardens, woods, meadows, and free spaces, each enclosed by a line of fortification, *i.e.* by high walls without any opening to the outside world, and surrounded by a moat filled with water, and each of which was the dwelling-place of a lord who grouped his household round him, of a patrician who governed his clients, of a *paterfamilias* who lived in the bosom of his *familia*.

Paris afforded, therefore, in the thirteenth century, the aspect which Moscow is still to present in the eighteenth, as described by the Count de Ségur : a vast group of castles, each of which is surrounded by its village, protected by its keep, surrounded by its special fortification.

Within each of these enclosures were seen many houses of merchants and artisans, but they were domestic merchants and artisans, *ministeriales domus*, employed in the service of the seigniorial *familia*, resembling the *fèvres-mesniers* of the feudal castles which we mentioned just now. They ministered to the needs of the relatives of the seigneur; they worked and traded under cover of his patronage. Amidst the general prosperity this population grew and multiplied within these various seignories. The lords are then to be seen building within their enclosures, confining themselves to the centre of their property, dividing into dwellings the parts which border on the public ways. Each of these little family towns enjoyed autonomy with its particular enclosure within the common enclosure. Let us reflect that at the beginning of the reign of Louis XIV in the full seventeenth century more than half Paris depended on individual lords—there were thirty-four of them—each of whom had judicial rights over his territory and that one of these urban lordships was to preserve its independence down to the Revolution.

FORMATION OF FEUDAL FRANCE

It was the same in the town of Tours.

A first town had been confined within the line of the ancient Roman camp, near which was built another town, that of St. Martin's Abbey, *Martinopole*, very soon called *Châteauneuf*, also surrounded by a line of fortifications and placed under the authority of a separate feudal lord, in this case the abbot of the monastery. Another abbey, that of St. Julien, was built between the *castrum* and Châteauneuf; so here is a third little town (*bourg*), for St. Julien surrounds itself with walls. There are three towns in one; and now comes a fourth: the town of the Count, the feudal town. A castle is built with its courts, its towers, its keep; and before long it produces a new population. It makes thus a fourth village which is to develop and maintain an independent existence under the suzerainty of the Count of Tours. They are four towns, separate but juxtaposed, and surrounded by a common line of fortification. And now comes a fifth, then a sixth, then a seventh, and an eighth. In the sixteenth century we find that Tours is still divided into thirty-one different fiefs; in the sixteenth century still thirty-one lords justices share judicial authority in the town of Tours. This means that in the beginning we have had thirty-one feudal groups, thirty-one feudal lords, each of whom had his domain, his fortifications, his subjects, his "justice," and that the union of these formed the town of Tours.

In time the industry of the inhabitants filled with buildings the enclosure surrounding each of these fiefs: houses filled the free spaces round the abbeys and keeps, and the interior walls fell, leaving only to the agglomeration one exterior wall of defence: the town of Tours was formed.

For Amboise, a passage of the old *Chronicles of Anjou* enables us to reconstruct this work of formation with striking precision: "There were then (eleventh century) at Amboise three lords (*optimates*) none of whom regarded himself as inferior to the others, and, in fact, was not; none of whom owed service to another, and each of whom had a fortified dwelling. The first was Sulpice I, lord of Amboise, who had caused to be built there a stone tower so high that from the top one could see as far as Tours. (This stone keep had been built on the site of a wooden tower, one of those primitive

THE MIDDLE AGES

keeps already described.) The second of these lords was Foucois de Thorigné, who had his dwelling on the Motte-Foucois; the third was Ernoul, son of Leon de Meung-sur-Loire, keeper of the Count's palace called the Domicile. On him depended the greater part of the *castrum* of Amboise." The same *Chronicle of the Counts of Anjou* speaks also of a fourth strong castle, the one which Count Geoffrey of the Grey Tunic gave to Landri de Châteaudun, and which was situated in the Southern part of the quarter of Amboise called Châteauneuf. The *Chronicle of the Counts of Anjou* shows then, with a common fortification enclosing the *castrum* (town) of Amboise, four distinct lordships, independent of one another, each of which contains a keep and its feudal territory (*cum omnibus que jure turri appendebant*; ... and further on: *cum omnibus feodis pertinentibus*), each of which includes the head of a fief and its dependencies (*domum munitissimam ... cum multis feodis Ambaziaco donavit*), four feudal lordships whose union, under the suzerainty of the Count of Anjou, forms the town of Amboise. Round each of these keeps artisans have gathered and work at home there to satisfy the needs of their respective barons. These four distinct fiefs, united in the same enclosure, yet remain so much strangers to one another that they are seen frequently at war with one another.

Archembaud de Busançais and his brother Sulpice, says the chronicler, fought with Landri de Châteaudun. From their fortified dwellings and from the Domicile of the Count they often attacked Landri and his people. And further on, *à propos* of the struggles of Sulpice I, lord of Amboise, and his brother Lisois against Foucois de Thorigné, Bouchard de Montrésor, and Foulque le Réchin, the Count of Anjou: "They had fortified their keep at Amboise so that, in the town itself, there were often fights to the death."

Here are the details of one of these struggles in the town of Amboise between enemy fiefs: "Foulque le Réchin, with his army, occupied the Domicile (the castle of the Count of Anjou). Thence his balistas and cross-bows rained arrows on the castle of the Lord of Amboise; but the castle retaliated with arrows, and darts from cross-bows and enormous stones.

FORMATION OF FEUDAL FRANCE

The people of the Domicile crushed their opponents with stones launched by trebuchets. Around the walls sounded horns and trumpets. The neighbouring buildings were set on fire. They only ceased to fire the place when the town was destroyed, including St. Mary's Church. And after this, battering-rams and heavy-wheeled chariots were set against the walls, but in vain. After a siege of five weeks the Count of Anjou drew off. At last an agreement was reached, and, says the chronicler, the people of the town rejoiced at the return of peace."

Arles, likewise, was formed by the union of some ten castles, or lordships, or different towns. We say "castles" (*chateaux*), "lordships" (*seigneuries*), or "towns" (*villes*), because the expressions are here synonymous: first, the city which depended on the Archbishop; secondly, the old town (*Vieux-Bourg*), which was divided into three different fiefs, one of which was held by the Count of Provence, the other by the Archbishop, and the third by the family of Porcellet; thirdly, the *market*, which had as its superior suzerain the Archbishop, but was itself divided into two lordships, one of which belonged to the Viscounts of Marseilles and the other to the Provosts of Arles; finally, the new town (*Bourg-Neuf*), the domain of the Seigneur des Baux.

Metz was formed by the union of six different towns, the famous "paraiges," the first five of which have family names; the sixth, of later formation, being called "the commonalty" (*le commun*).

In Burgundy are found unimportant towns divided among five, six, or seven different lords within one palisade or one wall.

As for urban government, when it made its appearance, it was composed either of the court of the principal lord, of the "good men" who had their seats near him on the dais of the great hall (*salle*), or of an assembly comprised of those whose sphere of activity was common to the various lordships of which the town was composed: at Paris the company of sailors, the boatmen who brought to the inhabitants of the Parisian fiefs the necessities of existence, or who exported the products of their industry. In such and such a town of the South the

Urban Government.

THE MIDDLE AGES

common council might be composed of the workers who kept the exterior fortifications in repair; but generally the communal assembly was composed of the heads of the patrician families, of the *lignages* and *parages*, the grouping of which formed the city.

And if it is true that in course of time one does not always distinguish the evidence of these divisions between which the towns of the eleventh and twelfth century were shared—and which the very closeness of the agglomeration has helped to efface—one notices at least the general principle which has governed the formation of the towns in France: they were formed feudally, like the fiefs themselves, by the development of families; and many of them preserved the living traces of this origin up to a late period in their history.

SOURCES.—Hariulf, *Chron. de l'Abbaye de St. Riquier*, *Chron. des Contes d'Anjou*, ed. Halphen and Poupardin, 1913; Suger, *Vie de Louis le Gros*, ed. Molinier, 1887; Victor Mortet, *Textes relatifs à l'histoire de l'architecture, XIe et XIIe Siècles*, 1911; Wace, *Le Roman de Brut*, ed. Le Roux de Lincy, 1836, 2 vols.; *Le Roman d'Aubri le Bourgoing*, ed. Tarbe, 1849; *Girard de Roussillon*, ed. P. Meyer, 1884; J. Renard, *L'Escouffle*, ed. Michelant and Meyer, 1894; *Recueil des fabliaux*, ed. Montaiglon and Raynaud, 1872–90, 6 vols.; *Archives historiques de la Gironde*, tome xxv.

HISTORICAL WORKS.—Viollet-le-Duc, *Dict. de l'architect.*, 1854–68; Legrand, *Paris in 1380*, Coll. de l'hist. gen. de Paris, 1868; Drouyn, *La Guienne Militaire*, 1865, 2 vols.; H. Klipffel, *Les Paraiges messins*, 1863; Fritz Kleiner, *Verfassungsgesch. der Provence*, Leipzig, 1900; Jacq. Flach, *Les Origines de l'anc. France*, 1886–1917, 4 vols.; F. Keutgen, *Urkunden zür Städtischen Verfassungsgesch.*, Berlin, 1899; P. Dognon, *Les Institut. pol. et administ. du pays de Languedoc*, 1897; H. Pirenne, *L'Origine des constitutions urbaines au Moyen Age*, taken from the *Revue Historique*, 1899; by the same, *Villes, Marchés et Marchands au Moyen Age*, taken from *Rev. Hist.*, 1898; G. Espinas, "Les Guerres familiales dans la commune de Douai," *Nouv. Rev. Hist. de droit franc. et étrang.*, July–Aug., 1899; Imbart de la Tour, *Hist. de la Nation franc.*, ed. by Hanotaux, tome iii. (1921).

We have seen how the family was organized amid the turmoil of the ninth century. It developed and produced the household **The King.** (*mesnie*); from the household came the fief; the grouping together of the little fiefs produced the great fiefs: to the north of the Loire the County of Flanders, the Duchy of Normandy, the County of Brittany, which Philip the Fair raised to a Duchy, the County of Anjou, the County

FORMATION OF FEUDAL FRANCE

of Blois, the County of Champagne, the Duchy of Burgundy; to the south of the Loire the County of Poitiers, the Duchy of Gascony, the County of Toulouse, the County of Barcelona; for, if the kingdom of France was deprived, in the tenth century, on the left banks of the Seine and the Rhone of part of the territory which has since come back to her, if Lyons and Besançon belonged to the Empire, on the other hand the County of Flanders, Ypres, Ghent, and Bruges, and the County of Barcelona were included in it.

We have spoken of the impotence of the royal power in the tenth century. The nation organized itself by its own forces. In the second half of the tenth century this process of reconstruction will reach the summit of the social edifice. While the last Carolingians betray their weakness during the invasions, a new family installs itself on the borders of the Seine, where its strength and activity are made manifest. By its traditions and its special organization it is in harmony with the new conditions of society; it is their living expression.

As a rich landowner on the banks of the Loire, Robert the Strong exercised there the functions of Count of Anjou. Commissioned by Charles the Bald, with the title of Duke of the French, to defend against the invaders the region included between the lower course of the Seine and that of the Loire, he showed the pirates his courage. His son, Eude, increased the fame of his father's name in the defence of Paris in 885. He there exhibited a heroism so brilliant that, when the throne of France fell vacant in 887—on the death of Charles the Fat—Eude was chosen King. The election was made by the assembly of the great men (*Grands*) of the country, *i.e.* by the heads of the most powerful families to the north of the Loire.

Eude died in 898, and from this date the crown is seen passing from the one family to the other, from the descendants of Charlemagne to those of Robert the Strong, at the will of the barons. Charles the Simple, a Carolingian, reigned from 898 to 922. He confirmed Robert, the brother of Eude, in his title of Duke of the French. And Robert was proclaimed King by the assembly of the great nobles, when Charles the Simple was deposed after having been conquered by the German Emperor, Henry the Fowler (922).

THE MIDDLE AGES

Far from taking his disgrace patiently, Charles the Simple attacked his rival and killed him outside Soissons. Vanquished in his turn by Hugh the Great or the Fair, the son of Robert, Charles fled into Germany. Returning to France he was captured and imprisoned in the Tower of Peronne, where he died in 929. Hugh the Fair, who could have assumed the royal crown, had preferred to give it to the Duke of Burgundy, his brother-in-law. This latter reigned up to the year 936, when the crown returned once more to the Carolingians, in the person of Louis IV, the son of Charles the Simple, who was called Louis from Overseas (*d'Outremer*), because he was brought back from England to be made king.

It was again Hugh the Fair who disposed of the crown. Louis d'Outremer was hardly fifteen years old when he was anointed at Reims, on the 19th June 936. He was to show energy; but his power had not the necessary roots in the country. He tried to free himself from the tutelage with which Hugh the Fair overwhelmed him. An armed struggle took place between the King and his powerful vassal. In the course of an expedition in Normandy, Louis was captured and delivered to Hugh the Fair, who imprisoned him at Rouen, in the keeping of Thibaud the Cunning, the Count of Chartres (945–46).

Louis d'Outremer gave up the town of Laon to his terrible protector and so recovered his liberty. Will he recover his power?

" Hugh ! " said he, " how many things you have taken from me! You have taken for yourself the city of Reims; you have seized from me the city of Laon, the only two towns in which I found a welcome, my only defence ! My father (Charles the Simple), captive and thrown into dungeons, was delivered by death from like misfortunes; reduced to the same extremities, I have only the show of my ancestral kingship ! "

In 945, however, Lothaire succeeded without opposition to his father, Louis d'Outremer. In 979 Lothaire associated with himself in the kingship his son Louis V. Hugh Capet, son of Hugh the Great (who had died on the 16th June 950), in his turn entered into conflict with him. " The King and the Duke," writes Richer, " displayed so great an animosity against

FORMATION OF FEUDAL FRANCE

one another that the State suffered for several years from their conflict." But what happened while these storms raged over the protective heights? "Properties were usurped, the unfortunate were oppressed; and the wicked overwhelmed the weak with cruel calamities." Then, adds Richer, "the wisest members of the two parties met together to come to an agreement."

Louis V succeeded Lothaire in 986. He was crowned at Compiègne, at the age of eighteen years. For the sake of peace he was content to give himself up entirely to the direction of Hugh Capet; but hardly had Louis reigned a year when he died from an accident while hunting between Senlis and Compiègne (21st or 22nd May 987). He left an uncle, Charles of Lorraine, the legitimate representative of the Carolingian line. The heads of the great families, called together at Noyon by Adalbéron, the Archbishop of Reims, proclaimed as king Hugh Capet, the son of Hugh the Great (1st June 987). This surname, "Capet," already borne by Hugh the Great, and which was to become the designation of the whole race, came from the cloak in which the Duke of France delighted to robe himself, the hood of which came down on the head (*capet*, a little cape). The election of Hugh Capet was due, without any doubt, to his territorial and family position, which made him among the barons north of the Loire the one who possessed to the highest degree the qualities which characterized each one of them.

As early as the year 985 did not Gerbert, scholar of Reims, *i.e.* director of the Cathedral School at Reims, the future Sylvester II, write to some lords of Lorraine:

"Lothaire governs France in name only; the real King is Hugh." Gerbert appears to have been, in collaboration with his archbishop, Adalbéron, the principal agent in the Capetian election.

Listen to the address by which Adalbéron, Archbishop of Reims, had supported the candidature of the new sovereign in the Assembly of the great nobles, at Senlis, May 987:

"Take for your head the Duke (of the French), glorious by reason of his actions, his family, and his men—the Duke in whom you will find a guardian not only of public matters but of your private affairs. You will have in him a father (*eum pro patre habebitis*). Who has not in seeking refuge with him found in him a defence (*patrocinium*) ? Who, deprived of the help of his own people, has not returned, thanks to him, into the possession of his goods ? "

In these few lines Adalbéron sketches the portrait of the feudal lord as we have already seen him.

On the 1st June 987, then, the Assembly of the great nobles, meeting at Noyon, proclaimed Hugh Capet king.

Through the medium of the feudal baron the royal power was thus developed from the paternal authority. " The King," says Hugh de Fleury, " is the image of the father." And let us be careful not to see here only an abstract connection, a remote origin, which would be shown in exterior forms, mere words or formulas ; we discern a direct origin, established by precise and concrete facts, the consequences of which we see continued through the centuries in the most living manner.

The King, Hugh Capet, directly governs his domain, the royal domain ; he exercises authority as in a family over the heads of the greatest domains, themselves suzerains of other vassals, who have, in their turn, other vassals under their orders. This process of formation has been seen working itself out from the base to the summit : it will only be completed under Philip Augustus, in the second half of the twelfth century, when the King will have succeeded at last in getting his authority recognized by the heads of what have been called the great fiefs. In the tenth century, then, France is formed by the hierarchical grouping of a multitude of little States, an aggregate of principalities, of varying dimensions and importance, which are joined together and superimposed, from the thousands and thousands of families which form the base, each of them strongly constituted under their natural head, up to the summit where the King, himself the head of a family, exercises over these other heads of families, the feudal lords, a paternal authority. This authority, which is above all a moral authority, forms the only tie which joins these thousands and thousands of little States to one another : it forms the national unity.

It has often been remarked by historians that it might seem surprising that the feudal aristocracy did not profit at

FORMATION OF FEUDAL FRANCE

Noyon by the chance which put into their hands the destiny of the State, to render themselves supreme, by freeing themselves from royalty and declaring it abolished. The existence of the patronal King, at the head of the social structure, as we have just seen it formed, was a necessity : the authority of the King formed the keystone of the pile. It was indispensable to it. For the nation, parcelled out into an infinity of different States, this coping was necessary; without it, the nation would have fallen back into the anarchy from which it had freed itself with so much difficulty.

Under the paternal authority of the King, France is governed like a great family. The Queen " keeps house for royalty." The State treasure is under her care. In appearing before the King she is able to say to him :

> Behold your loved one and your treasurer.

The chamberlain, who would nowadays be called the Minister of Finance, is her subordinate. Robert II, the successor of Hugh Capet, took pleasure in praising the skill of Queen Constance in the management of the public money.

Next to the father and the mother comes the eldest son. From infancy his name appears in the royal charters. The agreement of these three wills—that of the King, the Queen, and their eldest son—is often mentioned in acts. These three together represent what we should call " the Crown," enjoying that inviolability, that supreme authority which the men of the time attributed to the Capetian trinity. To the father—the King, in fact—the mother, and the son, is joined, if she is still alive, the Queen-Mother, the widow of the late King—" the White Queen," as she comes to be called. For, up to the time of Catherine de Medicis, the King's widow wears white all her life as mourning for the dead Prince. During the reign of her son she continues to share the exercise of power. Though Robert II had long attained his majority and had been associate King when Hugh Capet, his father, died, his mother reigned with him in the real sense of the word.

Then come the brothers. Their rights in these first centuries of the Capetian monarchy are much more extensive than those they will draw later from the appanages. During the first

THE MIDDLE AGES

part of the Middle Ages it was the royal family which administered the country under the direction of its head.

As to the executive power, it is found naturally in the hands of the household servants attached to the reigning family. These are grouped into six " métiers " (*ministeria*), six ministries: the kitchen, the pantry, the wine-cellars, the fruit-loft, the stable, and the chamber, through which are scattered a company of servants under the direction of the great officers: the seneschal, the master of the pantry, the butler, the constable, and the chamberlain, personal servants of the monarch.

The seneschal rules the kitchen and sees that the fire is kindled; he arranges the prince's table. " Seneschal of the provisions," Bertrand de Bar will call him in the twelfth century. The seneschal has "the water announced" and the horns sounded to warn the lords of the palace that they have to get ready for a meal and wash their hands. The seneschal is the gentleman carver; he cuts up the meat for the prince's table. When the meal is finished, he sees to the washing of the vessels, after which he receives from the cook a piece of meat to which the pantler and butler add two loaves and three pints of wine. The seneschal keeps the household of the King in order, and his importance increases as the *nourris*, the people whom the King brings up and admits into his house, increase in number. He keeps the keys of the doors; he arranges the hospitality of the palace and sees to the lodging of newcomers.

The King confides to him the education of his son.

The *chansons de geste* name the different offices of the royal household through which this eminent position is reached. Girbert de Metz, introduced into the Court by the Queen, fills at first the position of huntsman; then he becomes falconer, and finally seneschal at a wage of three Parisian pounds per week.

The word "seneschal," itself, indicates his functions—an expression of German origin and which meant in the beginning a "family servant." And in numerous French documents of the Middle Ages "seneschal" is exactly synonymous with "domestic."

The seneschal gives the pass-word to the sentinel who watches over the safety of the King; he has sovereign justice over offences or crimes committed within the precincts of the palace. In times of war he sees to the arrangement of the royal tent and follows his master in expeditions in which he bears his standard. " A service," says Bertrand de Bar, " which commands all the others." Under the royal authority the seneschal governs France :

> And ought to have France altogether at his discretion,
> He is the Seneschal, he has the Gonfanon.

After the seneschal comes the constable, *comes stabuli*, the count of the stable. He watches over the King's stable, controls the fodder, buys the horses; he takes in hand the cleaning of the stalls by the grooms; he can also keep four of his horses in his master's stables and take from the kitchen meat for his own use. From the fact that he is concerned with the King's stable the constable becomes, as time goes on, Chief of the cavalry and then Commander-in-chief of the army.

The butler ruled over the cup-bearers as the constable over the stablemen. He offered wine to their majesties and had the care of their stores of wine. He distributed wine to guests in the palace and had charge of the silver. He looked after the vineyards of the Crown and administered their proceeds. He was concerned not only to replenish the cellars of the King, but to dispose of the excess of the harvests. He set up the manorial presses and got in the dues for " tonlieu " (toll paid for standing in a market), pressing (*pressurage*), and drilling (*forage*), which led to his acting as judge in the disputes to which these customs gave rise. In this way it was not long before he took part in the administration of the domain and the management of the treasury; which brought him later to the presidency of the Chamber of Accounts (*Chambre des Comptes*).

The grand chamberlain directs the service of the private apartments; he has the superintendence of the furniture and clothes of the King. He introduces into the presence of the Sovereign the vassals who come to tender him their oath of fidelity and homage, and he takes as perquisite (*butine*) on this occasion the cloaks which they wear and which they must leave behind in token of respect at the moment they appear before the prince. In the " chamber " is found what we

THE MIDDLE AGES

should call the "strong-box." And so, behold, the chamberlain is treasurer of the realm. He commands the valets, the tailors, and the stewards (*chambellans*). The last are in the beginning only humble servants, but they keep the accounts of the house, *i.e.* of the Government. They perform the functions of stewards. In this double capacity as head of the *valets de chambre* and Minister of Finance the chamberlain is placed, as we have already said, under the orders of the Queen.

The grand pantler rules over the pantry; he serves at table while the seneschal carves the meat and the butler dispenses the wine; he sees to the cutting of the bread. He is responsible for the table linen and sees to "the steeping and washing of the cloths." He has "inspection and jurisdiction over the bread made by the bakers of Paris and the suburbs."

Last comes the grand chancellor. His character differs a little from that of his colleagues, because, though domestic, his origin was also religious. The Merovingian Kings preserved among their relics the little cope (*capa*) of Saint Martin, the under-garment which the patron of the Gauls was wearing the day he gave up his cloak to a poor man. Thence the name "chapel" (*chapelle*) given to the place where the relics of the Kings were kept, and that of "chaplain" (*chapelain*) by which the clerics who presided over it were described. To the relics were joined the archives. The aforesaid chaplains registered the oaths taken on the cope, which led them at times to the drawing up of acts and patents furnished with seals. Their head was the chancellor. He had always to carry the great seal hung from his neck for fear it should be lost. He is called "the one who carries the seal." He is over the lawyers who draw up the royal letters and the chafe-wax who seals them.

Such were the six great officers of the Crown; they seconded the King in the exercise of his power; they followed him everywhere; they sanctioned by their presence the publication of the acts of government. Their character, so narrowly domestic, changes in time, but not so rapidly as one might be tempted to think. In the fifteenth century still, on the threshold of the Renaissance, Charles VII will have himself served

FORMATION OF FEUDAL FRANCE

on feast-days by the great officers, each in conformity to his office, and during the repast the high steward will read aloud.

These domestics, great officers, with the Queen and with the King's sons, with his relatives and the great nobles of the realm forming the Council of the King—and with the other officers of diverse conditions who form the establishment of the palace, cooks, chamber attendants, chaplains, marshals—form what documents of the period term the "royal family." Their assemblage—to which comes the Queen, the princes, the guests and the relatives of the King, even to his clerks and his valets—forms the household (*domestique*) of the sovereign, what we should call to-day the Government.

The King makes his military expeditions at the head of his "family."

"Family," "mesnie," are the expressions used in documents to describe the troops of the prince on campaign. It is the *manus privata* of the King, whose importance is shown from the time of the first Capetians. It includes his *nourris*, those who dwell near him for the sake of the "meat" which he distributes to them.

In battle they group themselves round him.

"Charles went to Roussillon with his private 'mesnie,'" we read in *Girart de Roussillon*; "he had not summoned his host and yet he was going to make no mean progress."

This royal household, like that which has been already described, tends naturally, by the development of its internal force, to become the larger household (*mesnie majeure*). From all parts of the kingdom people come to enter it. Below the knights (*equites*) and the squires (*milites*) are the "poursuivants," young men who aspire to chivalry and to be trained in the career of arms; then a compact troop of sergeants, foot soldiers (*pedites*), servants attached to the household of the King. In place of helmets the sergeants wear on their heads hats of iron or leather; they do not use weapons deemed noble—the sword or the lance; they carry in their hands a two-edged hatchet, a scythe, or a spear, or a heavy club with iron spikes; but they form, none the less, a *corps d'élite*, in which are found the best archers, the ablest bowmen expert in handling ribaudequins and trebuchets, swivel-guns and

THE MIDDLE AGES

mangonels. He gives them presents, equipment or gifts of money : to one the use of a shop, or the takings of a toll-house; to another a mill, an oven, some acres of land. Closely attached to the prince, they are his personal followers (*privés*).

As for the resources necessary for them, the first Capetians drew them from the exploitation of their own domains. They subscribed to their needs from their private revenues, without levying taxes, thanks to personal rents, the sum of which was brought to them at the three terms of St. Remy, Candlemas, and the Ascension. They were made up of numerous rural exploitations to the profits of which the monarchs added the feudal dues which they received as suzerains of their fiefs.

So we shall not be astonished, in these circumstances, that the first Capetians did not exercise the power of legislation. A father does not legislate in the bosom of his family. The father's wish is law. The Merovingians legislated, as also did the Carolingians, for their authority was not essentially paternal; the Capetians no longer made laws. As the father among his children so the King is, among his subjects, the living law. He governs his kingdom as a family. "The King's wish is law." The ordinances of the King and of his Council, when they enter into the manners of the people, become customary; but if custom does not admit them, they have only a transitory effect. During the sway of the Capetian dynasty, in the whole of France it is custom which makes the law.

Apart from his personal courage, Hugh Capet had owed his election to the authority which he exercised in his duchy, in the Ile de France; he had owed it to the necessity of uniting the great barons, the Counts of Anjou, of Chartres, of Troyes, the Duke of Normandy; he had owed it to his family connections : was he not the brother of Henry, Duke of Burgundy, the brother-in-law of Richard, Duke of Normandy, as well as of the Duke of Aquitaine, whose sister, "Adelaide," he had married ? Certainly his duchy, of which Paris was the capital, and in which was situated the town of Orleans, had not the extent of territory of the Duchy of Aquitaine, the County of Toulouse, the Duchy of Burgundy, or the Duchy of Normandy ; but its situation was favoured by the convergence of navigable watercourses and by the meeting of the great roads which furrowed the north of Gaul. The Duke of France was Abbot of St. Martin de Tours, of St. Denis, of St. Germain-des-Prés, of St. Maur-des-Fossés, of St. Riquier, of St. Aignan d'Orléans. The Archbishop of Reims, the bishops of Beauvais, of Noyon, of Châlons, of Laon, and of Langres were in favour of his power. He was suzerain of Poitou.

On the 3rd July 987 Hugh Capet was crowned in the Cathedral of Reims by Archbishop Adalbéron. At the moment of his consecration he pronounced the following oath:

"I, Hugh, who in an instant am by the divine favour about to become King of the French, on the day of my anointing, in the presence of God and of His saints, promise to each of you to preserve to you the canonical privilege, the law, the justice which are due to you, and to protect you as far as I can with the help of God as is just that a King should act in his realm towards each bishop and the Church which is committed to him. I promise to concede from our authority to the people confided to us justice according to their rights."

Later, Hugh Capet will say in a patent to the Abbey of Corbie: "We have no right to exist unless we render justice to all and by every means." Moreover, his successors will have him represented on their seal holding the hand of justice, which is to remain the emblem of our Kings until the end of the monarchy. In official representations, the King of France holds the sceptre in one hand, the hand of justice in the other; other Kings have themselves shown holding the sceptre and the sword.

In this tenth century Abbo attempts to define the royal person: "It is," he says, "the incarnation of justice." He declares that the office of King consists "in stirring up the affairs of the kingdom for fear some dispute should remain hidden there." Fulbert de Chartres, in the eleventh century, says also: "The King is the pinnacle of justice: *summum justicie caput.*" It is the essential character marking the prince in all the *chansons de geste*. And what is the nature, the source of this justice? Old Bodin will tell us: "The King treats his subjects and distributes justice to them, as a father to his children."

THE MIDDLE AGES

In the midst of his subjects the King was truly the source of justice; all justice emanated from him. Above the numerous local groups, families, lordships, towns, and communities which divided the kingdom, the monarch was the sole common authority and therefore able to intervene in the differences which arose among them. As each of these groups lived and administered itself independently, the only function which remained to the King was to force them to agree for the common good. " As soon as the King is crowned," notes Abbo (tenth century), " he demands from his subjects the oath of fidelity lest discord should arise in any part of the kingdom." Bodin wrote: " The prince should make his subjects agree with one another and all with him," resuming in two lines the history of the kingly function.

Hugh had owed his throne to election. The representatives of the Carolingian dynasty had still some partisans. He therefore took the precaution, the very year of his accession to the throne, of having his son Robert crowned in the Cathedral of Orleans (the 25th December 987). " He showed a letter sent by Borel, Duke of Hither Spain," writes Richer, " in which the Duke demanded help against the Barbarians (the Saracens). He asked that a second King should be created, so that if one of the two should perish in battle, the army could always count on a leader. He said, too, that if the King were killed and the country ravaged, the nobles might be divided among themselves, the wicked oppress the good, and the nation in consequence fall into servitude."

Lines which give us a glimpse of those Saracens of Spain against whom from that time the Christian knights are destined to struggle desperately: and here is the theme of the *chansons de geste*.

The rule of the early Capetians consisted, besides, in the moral direction they gave to the country. The existence of the King was necessary at the top of feudal society, and it was by this very existence that he governed. Moreover, we ought not to be surprised at the small number of Acts preserved under the name of Hugh Capet: a dozen during a reign of ten years. Contrary to what has been said, this is no proof of impotence. The very great moral authority which the Crown already enjoyed under the first Capetian had no need to manifest itself in documents. Entangled as we are to-day in our administrative bureaucracy, we no longer imagine public action except in the form of paper. The German Emperor, Otto II, a contemporary of Hugh Capet, issued more than 400 Acts; he was still a child; but the reason was that the German Government acted then more by administration. France, say the historians, paid attention to nothing but the dozen counts and dukes who really governed them. This again is not correct. Each of these twelve counts and dukes was at the head of a certain number of vassals over whom he had a power of conciliation and paternal protection similar to that which the King exercised over him and his peers; and these vassals, in their turn, were over other vassals (of an inferior status) and in identical conditions.

No writer has given us a picture of Hugh Capet. From the moral point of view he seems to have been the man of his part, conciliatory, clever in negotiation, persuasive. Of simple manners, with no taste for pomp or show, he helped to give to the French monarchy the popular aspect which is to distinguish it from foreign monarchies. "With the Kings of France," writes Guibert de Nogent, "one finds a natural simplicity; they realize the words of Scripture: 'Princes, be among your subjects as of them.'"

Hugh Capet died on the 26th October 996, of small-pox. He was buried at St. Denis. His death had been as edifying as his life: for Hugh Capet appeared already as a prince of ecclesiastical character, head of his clergy: he busies himself with the care of the monasteries of which he is abbot; he fills the bishoprics of Amiens, Beauvais, Châlons, Laon, Noyon, Reims, Senlis, Soissons, Auxerre, Chartres, Meaux, Langres, Bourges, and Puy, presides at councils, draws up rules for monasteries. He dresses himself in Church vestments (*drap d'Eglise*) and takes part barefooted in processions, carrying the reliquary of St. Valois. The first Capetians blessed their subjects and gave them absolution:

> With his right hand he absolves and blesses them.
> (*Chanson de Roland*, v. 340.)

And indeed, says André Duchesne, "the Kings of France

have never been mere laymen, but have the priesthood and royalty united. To show that they share in the priesthood they are anointed exactly like priests (the anointing with holy oils at their consecration), and they still use the dalmatic under the royal robes to show the rank they hold in the Church."

SOURCES.—*Richeri Historiæ, libri IV*, ed. Waitz, *Scriptores rerum germanicarum in usum scholarum*, 1877; Gerbert, *Lettres, 983–987*, ed. J. Havet, 1889; the *Chansons de geste*, quoted in the preceding and following chapters.

HISTORICAL WORKS.—Montlosier, *De la monarchie française depuis son établissement*, 1814, 3 vols.; Fustel de Coulanges, *Les Transformations de la royauté pendant l'époque carolingienne*, 1892; Jacq. Flach, *Les Origines de l'ancienne France*, 1886–1917, 4 vols.; Achille Luchaire, *Histoire des institutions monarchiques . . . sous les premiers Capétiens*, 1886, 2 vols.; Esmien, *Cours elementaire de l'histoire du droit français*, 3rd ed., 1898; André Lemaire, *Les Lois fondamentales de la monarchie française*, 1907; Aug. Euler, *Das Königthum im alt französichen Karls-Epos*, Marburg, 1886; F. Lot, *Les Derniers Carolingiens*, 1891; by the same author, *Etudes sur le règne de Hugue Capet*, 1903; E. Favre, *Eude, Comte de Paris et roi de France*, 1893; L. Halphen, *Le Comte d'Anjou au XIe Siècle*, 1906.

CHAPTER III

THE EPICS

The origin of the *chansons de geste* is well known. The first troubadours are soldiers who celebrate the high deeds of the family to which they belong. After them, the *chanson de geste* reaches the minstrels. " Geste " means " family." Our oldest epics : *The Chanson de Roland* (Songs of Roland), *The Chanson de Guillaume* (Song of William), *le Pèlerinage de Charlemagne* (The Pilgrimage of Charlemagne), *Garin le Loherain* A great epic poet : Bertrand de Barbe-sur-Aube. Connection between the *chansons de geste* and the Homeric poems.

FEUDAL France is built up from the family.
To the family, which affords safety and shelter, which contains the seeds of future destiny and which has progressively formed public life, men devote themselves unreservedly. The greatest efforts are put forth to develop its power and its prosperity. From the cult of hearth and ancestor, from that of domestic honour, the man of that time draws the courage which is to make of him a stout fellow (*prud'homme*), a valiant knight worthy of the name he bears, of the standard under which he fights, of the watchword (*cri*) which guides him.

In that period of faith and action which begins at the end of the tenth century and includes the whole of the eleventh—in which historians have seen the greatest century in our history, " the most creative age of all "—the sentiments which we have just recalled find sublime expression.

According to a theory which was favoured for a long time, our old epic poems, the *chansons de geste,* had their origin in little sentimental melodies (*cantilènes*), short songs, little poems familiar to the soldiers and the people. Originating in the time of Merovée and Clovis, they were supposed to have increased greatly in number under the Carolingians. In these warlike songs the glory of the great princes, Clovis, Dagobert, Charle-

THE MIDDLE AGES

magne—above all, Charlemagne—were celebrated—and that of the most valiant knights, Roland de Bretagne, Raoul de Cambrai, Guillaume d'Orange, Girard de Roussillon. The various *chansons de geste* were supposed to have been each formed by the stringing together and development of several little songs.

It is a theory which the splendid work of M. Joseph Bédier has definitely condemned.

The French epic poems, the *chansons de geste*, were the spontaneous expression of the heroic sentiments which were handed down in the bosom of the great families in which under the same baron were grouped many households (*mesnies*).

The *chanson de geste* is the song of the family (*lignage*), composed to glorify the ancestors. It is born at the fireside, of old traditions, listened to with an eager attention in the solitude of the barred castles, in the evening round the hearth with the dancing flames lighting up the lofty vaults of stone; gatherings which Suger describes in his chronicle.

The sentiments which animate poet and hearers are exclusively feudal. Whither fly the last thoughts of Roland expiring at Roncevaux on the grey rock? To the lands he has conquered, to his sweet country of France, to the men of his lineage and the seigneur who brought him up: such is the very soul of the *chansons de geste*.

The first epic poets were members or vassals of the family which they sang, taking the word " family " both in its exact sense and the larger significance which the fief and the household lent it in the Middle Ages.

Raoul de Cambrai has a companion, Bertolais de Laon, a valiant warrior, able to make poems on the combats in which he has taken part:

> Bertolais said that a song he would make,
> Such as minstrel never sang.
> Very brave and wise was Bertolais,
> In Laon was he born and cherished,
> Of a fine and splendid line he came:
> He witnesses all the high deeds of the fight
> And makes a song; a better you shall never hear;
> It has been sung since in many a palace. . . .
>
> (*Raoul de Cambrai*, v. 2442.)

THE EPICS

It is just the same in the *Chanson de Guillaume*:

> William my lord has a minstrel,
> In all France none sings so well,
> Nor in battle fights more bravely;
> He can sing to him the *chansons de geste*. . . .
> (v. 1260.)

Such were, in France, the first *trouvères*, the first epic poets; then they gave place to professional poets attached to the seigniorial families, who remunerated them. This was notably the case with one of the most famous of them, Bertrand de Bar, who lived, about the middle of the twelfth century, at Bar-sur-Aube, in the household of a powerful baron, Gui de Hanstone. His seigneur had brought him up and made a "rich man" of him, in return for which Bertrand composed for him a *chanson de geste* in which was celebrated his ancestor Beuve de Hanstone. But these epics were soon to emerge from the sphere of the household, to be sung by the warriors who rode along the dusty roads, as is recounted in *Renaud de Montauban*, singing, helmet on head with flags flying, moved by the march and the wind of the plain. Their verses rang out in the midst of battle. The passage of Wace showing us Taillefer at the opening of the battle of Hastings (1066), singing of Charlemagne and Roland, has remained famous through it:

> Taillefer, who could sing well,
> On a quick-going horse
> Went before the Duke, singing
> Of Charlemagne and Roland,
> Of Oliver and his men
> Who died at Roncevaux.
> When they had so far ridden
> That to the English they drew near:
> "Sire," cries Taillefer, "your mercy,
> Long have I served you,
> You owe me reward for my service;
> To-day, if it please you, pay me.
> By whatever reward I ask,
> And if you will, now I ask:
> Grant me, that I may not miss
> The first stroke in the fight."
> The Duke replied: "I grant it thee."

THE MIDDLE AGES

But the long themes of the epics, in their melodious monotony, were unfolded above all under the sonorous vaults of the keep, in the evening by the glancing light of the torches, or in the garden, in presence of the knights seated on the grass by a clear fountain, in the shade of a pine or almond tree; they were heard on feast-days when the lord held his Court.

For the *chansons de geste* have been collected by professional singers who hawk them from castle to castle, from fair to fair, and from one town to another. And through specialization a division of the profession is effected. A separation comes about between the poets who compose the poem and the minstrels who spread it abroad (*par les amples régnés*).

The *chansons de geste* are poems of the family, and their name alone would be sufficient to emphasize the fact. " Geste " means " family," and especially so in the expression " chanson de geste " by which the epics are described.

Count William with the Crooked Nose—Guillaume d'Orange, thus called because of the shape imparted to his nose by the stroke of a Saracen sword—loves his brave minstrel:

> He is skilled to sing the epic praises of his line. . . .
> (v. 1263.)

singing of Clovis, of Charlemagne, of Roland, of Girard de Vienne, and knightly Oliver.

> His kindred they were and his ancestors.
> (v. 1272.)

If Guillaume d'Orange loves to hear in his hall, paved with marble, the poems which sing of Clovis and Charlemagne, Oliver, Girard, and Roland, it is because their blood flows in his veins.

Moreover, the " heroes " of the *chansons de geste* are—much more than the individuals who figure so brilliantly in them—the families to which these individuals belonged, the " proud lineage " raised higher still.

Garin le Loherain is the bloody history of the long feud which divided two families, and the epic ends only after the slaughter of the last descendant of Hardré.

THE EPICS

The family (*lignage*) for which the troubadour wrote has all the virtues, above all those of the warrior :

> Valiant was my father and my ancestry,
> And of a fine family am I come,
> And therefore valiant should I be.
> (*Gormont et Isembart*, v. 218.)

The enemy house has all the vices :

> The whole company goes with Tiedbalt fleeing,
> And Vivien the valiant remains.
> (*Chanson de Guillaume*, v. 332.)

After having separated it from an infinite variety of detail and a wealth of development, you will find in these words the plot of the greater number of the *chansons de geste*. " Fromont and all his people are felons," says Garin.

> So much they achieved that all loved them
> Except the perfidious stock which always abused them.
> (*Chanson des quatre fils Aymon*, v. 16763.)

Ganelon does not stand alone as a traitor ; his whole " kindred " is wicked ; all his descendants are felons, and it could not be otherwise while a drop of his blood should flow in the veins of one of his descendants, even if he were to belong to the remotest generation. The eleventh century would never have admitted the theme of the *Fille de Roland*, which makes a gallant knight of the son of Ganelon. When Renaud de Montauban learns that his brother-in-law has betrayed him, he wants to kill his own children : what could they become, they who, through their mother, belong to the family of a traitor ?

The *chansons de geste*, which have come down to us to the number of a hundred, can be divided into several cycles, each of which is a family cycle : we have thus the cycle of the Aimerides (from the name of Aimeri de Narbonne), as the Greeks had the cycle of the Atrides ; and in it Narbonne takes the place of Mycenæ.

The cycle of the Aimerides, alone, includes twenty-four of our *chansons de geste*, which are divided as follows : the *geste* of Garin de Montglane, the ancestor, three *chansons* ; the *geste* of Aimeri, the father of Guillaume, in which is found the *chef d'œuvre* of Bertrand de Bar, *Girard de Vienne*, eight

53

chansons; finally, the *geste* of Guillaume,—which begins with the old and admirable *Chanson de Guillaume* and finishes with his profession as monk when William of the Crooked Nose becomes a monk in the Abbey of Gellone,—thirteen *chansons*. And what is this long and magnificent story sung in enthusiastic and confident verse—the history of old Aimeri, of his sons, grandsons, and great-nephews, devoting themselves from generation to generation to the defence of Christianity against the Saracens to sustain their valour and the rights of their King whatever might be his ingratitude and injustices—if not the tale, multiple and complex in its windings, however simple and united its fundamental idea, the tale of the efforts made by a family of heroes to exalt their name.

The elements of the *chansons de geste* are then co-ordinated at this end of the tenth century, which shows us feudal France definitely organizing itself by taking a Capetian as its head. During the eleventh, the heroic, century, the epics will take their most powerful form and spread abroad. The oldest manuscripts preserved of our *chansons de geste*, like that of the *Song of Roland*, were written in the second half of the twelfth century—versions of older *chansons*, for none of these poems have reached us in their original form.

It is written in the ancient geste,

we read in the *Chanson de Roland* (verse 3742).

The three oldest French epics the text of which we possess are the *Chanson de Roland*, the *Chanson de Guillaume*, and that queer, amusing product, disconcerting for the period in which it was composed, the *Pèlerinage de Charlemagne*.

The idea which dominates all these poems is the struggle of Christian Europe, under the hegemony of France, against the Saracens; to which three main facts have contributed. In the first place, there was the memory left of the Saracen invasions of the south-east of France in the ninth century; in the second place, the struggles maintained from the middle of the tenth century and throughout the course of the eleventh, against the Saracens of Spain, in which a great number of French barons took part; in the third place, there were the Crusades.

THE EPICS

The oldest and most beautiful of our epic poems, the *Chanson de Roland*, probably goes back in its first form to the end of the tenth century. The extant version dates from the following century. In its first form entirely lost, it must have been simpler, rougher, more rugged, and certainly more beautiful still.

The poem has its foundation in a historic fact. In 778, on his return from Spain, Charlemagne crossed the Pyrenees with his army. On the 15th August his rearguard was destroyed by Basque mountaineers in the valley of Roncevaux. It was commanded by Roland, the Prefect of the Marches of Brittany. It was an episode of secondary importance, the story of which, woven with heroic legends and resumed by a poet of genius, expressed with incomparable force and nobility the sentiments of the French of the period. This song of the eleventh century is one of the finest works, and without doubt the grandest by reason of the breadth and nobility of its sentiments, in all literature.

The legend makes of Roland a nephew of Charlemagne, and his defeat was attributed to the treason of a certain Count Ganelon, who was to become, for the troubadours of the twelfth century, the type of the traitor, as Roland was to become the model of courage and loyalty.

The energy of the affections and the rugged simplicity of the ideas gives to the narrative a potency which will never be repeated. The descriptions of the heroes is made by a single characteristic, as in Homer: Roland of the fine limbs, Charles with the grey beard; the description of a countryside is contained in two lines:

> High are the mountains and the valleys dark,
> The rocks dark grey, the defiles wonderful.
>
> (v. 814.)

By the sublimity and power of its sentiment, by the robust emotion which dominates the poem, the *Chanson de Roland* takes place above all which has ever been written. Its form even is of the greatest beauty, and if it is true that the art of the writer consists in giving to the words he uses the maximum of their effect by the manner in which he employs them, the

THE MIDDLE AGES

Chanson de Roland is, from the point of view of style also, the *chef d'œuvre* of our literature.

In what district was the *Chanson de Roland* written ? Brittany has been suggested, because Roland was its prefect; then Normandy, because of the devotion which the author of the poem professes for St. Michael of the Perils of the Sea (St. Michel-au-peril-de-la-mer). It seems clear to us that the poem had its origin in the Ile-de-France. It is in the Ile-de-France that the feudal forms, which other districts adopted later, have their origin; the Ile-de-France was the cradle of the power of the Capetians, and, as we shall see, of Gothic architecture; and there the most ancient epics took their rise, and notably the *Chanson de Roland*.

When Charles, to avenge Roland, leads back his army against the Saracens, he forms the first two echelons of Frenchmen, by which is meant knights of the Ile-de-France; the third echelon is composed of the Bavarians, whom Charles loves beyond all others except, of course, the French, *who have conquered for him the other nations*;—the fourth echelon is formed of Germans, the fifth of Normans, the sixth of Bretons, of Poitevins, and men of Auvergne, the eighth of Flemings, the ninth of Lorrainers and Burgundians; finally, the last echelon includes once more barons of France. The French of the Ile-de-France form the van and rear of the army. While the other corps are placed under divers heads, the French are commanded by Charlemagne, and the oriflamme floats in their ranks. Charles loves them above all others, for it is they who have subjected all Europe to him; it was for them that the poet wrote.

And what is the name of this poet to whom we owe the finest work in our language ? The *chanson* ends thus :

> Here ends the geste which Turold relates (*declinet*).
> (v. 4002.)

The sense which should be attributed here to the word " decliner " is uncertain. Is it a question of the poet, that is to say, the author of the poem, or of the minstrel who chanted the *geste*, or the copyist who transcribed it ? And, first of all, one must reject the idea of a copyist who would have had the audacity to bring himself thus under the eyes

THE EPICS

of the reader. On the other hand, in several *chansons de geste*, one sees the poet disclosing himself exactly in this same place. And that seems to be a strong reason for believing that Turold was the author, either of the first version, or more probably of the revision which gave to the *Chanson de Roland* the form in which it has come down to us.

Rather later than the *Chanson de Roland*, the *Chanson de Guillaume* belongs to the end of the eleventh century. It is the history of the defeat inflicted by the Saracens on William of the Crooked Nose in the plain of Larchamp-sur-mer (a place name which has proved impossible to identify), and of the vengeance taken by the noble count with the help of the King of France. Its composition is already different enough from that of the *Chanson de Roland*; it has less breadth, its movement is less simple; it is not so sublime; but the characters shown are depicted with an incomparable relief in their rude energy.

A portrait of a woman, that of Guibourc, the wife of William of the Crooked Nose, takes here the most important place, while in the *Chanson de Roland* the feminine rôle is absent. It is an admirable picture of the feudal châtelaine who cherishes (*nourrit*) her lord's men, rules over the castle when the baron is away, and heartens him when he returns vanquished without a single one of his company. The scenes of the *Chanson de Guillaume* have been many times repeated in the family cycle.

Guillaume appears on the walls of Orange after the disaster of Larchamp. At first Guibourc refuses to recognize her baron in the lamentable state in which he presents himself. At last she orders the gates of the castle to be opened to him.

> Count William at the threshold dismounts.
> The lady Guibourc takes his charger,
> And leads him straight to stall;
> Saddle and bridle she takes away
> And gives him oats to eat.
> Then goes to embrace the Count;
> And courteously demands:
> "Sire," she asks, "what have you done with your men,
> Whom you led off, four thousand and seven hundred?"
> "By my faith, lady, the pagans vanquished them;
> Bloody they lie on the field of Larchamp."

57

"Sire," cries she, "what have you done with Vivien?"
"By my faith, lady, bloody and dead he lies."
When Guibourc hears this, her heart grows very sad.
"Sire," she says, "what have you done with Bertram?
The young Bernard of Brusban town?"
"Sister, sweet friend, much fighting he did
In fifteen attacks. He fell on the field."
(*La Chanson de Guillaume*, v. 2328.)

And Guillaume recounts the death of Bernard; Guibourc continues her tragic questioning: "What have you done with Guiot?—with Gautier?—with Guielin?—with Renier?"—They are dead, all dead, and Guibourc, for all response, with a gesture of poignant simplicity:

Wash your hands, lord, and come and eat!

And the next day, persuaded by his wife, Guillaume sets out for Laon, where he gets reinforcements from the King, and at their head he conquers the Saracens.

The *Pèlerinage de Charlemagne* is the shortest of our *chansons de geste*. It has a special character by reason of the predominance of the comic element; one might call it a fable. Charlemagne, piqued by the idle talk of his wife, who has made in his presence a thoughtless eulogy of Hugo the Strong, the Emperor of Constantinople, has sworn to go and confirm with his own eyes the truth of the story. He goes as far as Jerusalem, whence he brings back the most precious relics, the crown of thorns, the chalice of the Last Supper, a nail of the true cross, some milk of the Virgin. . . . On the return journey, in the palace of Hugo the Strong, at Constantinople, take place the lively scenes to which we have alluded.

Garin le Loherain, in the version we possess, dates from the last third of the twelfth century. This version, later than that of the preceding works, is by two authors. The name of the second, Jean de Flagy, is known. The point which is its greatest interest is that the editors of the twelfth century respected, under a more modern form, the facts, ideas, and sentiments of the earlier period, which takes us back to rough and brutal customs.

It is the story of the great war between the men of Lorraine and those of Bordeaux. It has its origin in a quarrel between Hervis de Metz and Hardré de Bordeaux, who has become

THE EPICS

Count of Artois. It continues between the children of Hervis and those of Hardré, between Garin de Metz (le Loherain) and Begon de Belin. The third, the fourth, the fifth generations pursue the ferocious struggle, down to the extermination of the posterity of Hardré.

Manners and language are equally savage: " With all his remaining strength, Begon strikes Isoré, splits his helmet, cuts through the cap, and reaches the skull and cleaves it to the hauberk. Isoré fell this time never to rise again; he was dead. Then Begon, intoxicated with blood, plunges Froberge into the inanimate body and, like a famished wolf on a dead sheep, he tears the entrails from it, carries them off, and advancing to the room in which lie the hostages, throws them into the face of Guillaume de Montclin:

"' Here, vassal,' says he, ' take the heart of your friend; you can salt and roast it! And remember! Garin has never been perjured! Garin has never betrayed the King!'"

As we have said, a hundred *chansons de geste* have been preserved, and this enormous figure represents only a small part of the epic production from the tenth to the thirteenth century; for the French, "who have not the epic sense," have produced—and it is only a question of the French of the langue d'oïl—eight or ten times as many true epics as all the other peoples of Europe together.

We have mentioned the most ancient of these poems. It would be impossible to continue this enumeration; but we ought to mention the *chefs d'œuvre* of Bertrand de Bar-sur-Aube, *Girard de Vienne*, *Aimeri de Narbonne*, *Les Narbonnais*, and *Beuve de Hanstone*.

Girard de Vienne and *Aimeri de Narbonne* were directly imitated by Victor Hugo in *Aymerillot* and the *Mariage de Roland* for the *Légende des Siècles*. We know a little about Bertrand de Bar, that fine *trouvère* who is to be reckoned as the greatest of the French poets whose names are known with certainty. He lived at the end of the twelfth century, at Bar-sur-Aube, where he composed some of his poems, notably *Beuve de Hanstone*, for Gui de Hanstone, who " nourished " him. He had been previously in the pay of Doon de Mayence, whom he left through a grievance; more-

THE MIDDLE AGES

over, from malice he made one of his ancestors, Doon de Mayence, play an odious part in *Beuve de Hanstone*. Bertrand was a cleric. It was also at Bar-sur-Aube that he composed *Girard de Vienne*.

> At Bar-sur-Aube in a castle seigniorial
> Sits Bertrand, pensive in an orchard,
> A gentle clerk who made this song. . . .
> (v. 1–3.)

Perhaps we owe *Doon de Mayence* also to Bertrand.

However this may be, he was a prolific poet and greatly renowned in his own day, as is shown in the verse of *Doon de Nanteuil*:

> For sure he has learnt more in a single year,
> Than Bertrand de Bar knew in all his life. . . .

Thus Bertrand de Bar wrote his epics for the great noble families; just as in the following generation, when the period of epic poetry was past, the poet who composes—still very often in the epic vein—the life of *Guillaume le Maréchal* writes for the family of the noble lord:

> When the kindred, sisters, and brother,
> Shall hear this, much will they have it at heart.
> (19201.)

It has often been asked, what historic element is to be found in the *chansons de geste*, from the point of view of the actuality of the facts?

If one considers the great figures of Clovis, Dagobert, Charlemagne, Hugh Capet, who pass before us in these stories, the actions which are attributed to them are legendary or even drawn from the imagination; as to the heroes of the great families, the tradition complacently handed down in the families and received by the poets attribute to them fabulous actions; but if the scholar can draw nothing from these poems from the point of view of historic fact, he can, on the other hand, reap an ample harvest in seeking there the beliefs, the manners, the ideas, the sentiments of the French people in the eleventh, twelfth, and thirteenth centuries. The characters in these poems are imaginary, or distorted so much that it is impossible to identify them; but the surroundings in which

THE EPICS

they move, the costumes in which they are dressed, the sentiments they express, are rigorously accurate.

It would require many pages to illustrate in detail the way in which the poets draw on reality. Here is one fact among others. It is borrowed from *Renaud de Montauban*, or poem of the *Four Sons of Aymon*.

For some months Renaud has been besieged with his family by Charlemagne. In his castle, he is suffering from hunger. After the cattle, he has had all the horses within the walls killed; there remains to him only his famous horse Bayard. Him at least he would spare, but since his children are crying for food, Renaud, without killing the noble beast, draws from it some blood on which he and his subsist for some days longer. This incident, in a poem not too sparing of improbabilities, seems one of the most unlikely. Truth is sometimes . . . Boileau will say. The poet had heard the accounts of the episodes of the siege of Antioch by Kerboga:

"Many people," we read in the *Gesta Dei per Francos*, "nourished themselves with the blood of their horses, whose veins they sucked; but they took care not to kill them, for they had not lost all hope of salvation."

These *chansons de geste*, which have nothing historical as far as the heroes and the reality of their facts are concerned, were received by those who listened to them as authentic history.

The auditors of the twelfth and thirteenth centuries who heard them were convinced that "it had actually happened." The "reality" of these tales formed for them their chief interest.

> Seigneur, hear a song of great nobility,
> It is all true history. . . .
>
> (*Les Quatre fils Aymon*, v. 1, 2.)

This reflection is repeated in these old poems under the most diverse forms. One might justly say that the epic is, for the people who produce it, the earliest form of history. On the day it ceases to be regarded as history and becomes literature it ceases to be epic, and this observation, which others have made before us, is much truer than one might think, with regard to the Middle Ages. Pierre Dubois was an advocate, a lawyer who devoted his powers and his knowledge, at the end of the thirteenth century, to drawing up for Philip the Fair grave and learned political treatises : " Charlemagne, who has no equal," he cries, " is the only prince, as far as I can remember, who, during a hundred years and more, marched in person at the head of the most distant armies " (*De recuperatione Terre sancte*). Thus, a Pierre Dubois, at an advanced period of the Middle Ages, accepted still as sober history the epic songs of the troubadours.

The form of the *chansons de geste* is simple and abrupt ; but frequently their expressions are splendidly forceful in their conciseness, and magnificent in their colour.

> There was great carpentry of swords,
> And the earth is robed with pagans. . . .
> (*La bataille d'Aleschans*, v. 490.)

Finally, two words on the connection which exists between the Homeric poems and our *chansons de geste*. They paint an identical social state. The Greek poets call " kings " those whom the troubadours call " barons." The beginnings of the great struggles which serve as theme to the story are in both cases concerned with women (*histoires de femmes*). " The demoiselle was not eight and a half years old. She was already the most beautiful maid possible." " Take her and, with her, the honour of my ' land,' " says King Tierri de Maurienne to Garin de Metz. " Alas ! " the Poet adds, " the maid came into the world in an evil hour ; no one shall ever count the number of gallant men who were to die on her account " (*Garin le Loherain*). The adventures of Girard de Roussillon have their origin in an amorous rivalry. At the beginning of the epic poem devoted to Girard de Vienne, the wife of Charlemagne insults the noble baron. Hence violent anger, open revolt. Charlemagne comes to lay siege to Vienne. Like the siege of Troy, this lasts seven years. Among the besiegers is Roland, who cannot fail to remind us of Achilles ; and among the besieged Oliver, calmer, more delicate and cultivated, is Hector.

> Roland is brave and Oliver is wise.

Do not the epic poets make Roland invulnerable like Achilles ? But the Christian spirit gives a sublime issue to

THE EPICS

the duel between the two rivals which Oliver's sister, the fair-faced Aude, was watching from the battlements:

> It was thus that Roland espoused the fair Aude.

As in Homer, the women of our *chansons de geste* remain always young and beautiful: Penelope up to the end of the *Odyssey*, Berthe up to the end of *Girart de Roussillon*. As in Homer, the warriors of the *chansons de geste* are ever young and vigorous: Charlemagne is more than a hundred years old when he splits from head to waist a knight in full armour. Like the Homeric heroes, the heroes of the *chansons de geste* abuse each other like pedlars before closing in fight. As for the Homeric epithet, if it has less savour and picturesqueness in the *Chanson de Roland* than in the *Iliad*, it has still there a singular nobility.

Like the Homeric poems, the works of our old poets were chanted to throngs of the people whose thoughts they kindled with their sublime accents.

Gilles de Paris tells in his *Carolinus* how in the streets, or at the cross-roads, the *chansons de geste* were sung to the accompaniment of the viol: "The venerable name of Charles, glorious descendant of the illustrious Pépin, is on every tongue. His high deeds are sung throughout the world to the sweet accompaniment of the viol."

We read in a letter in verse written in Italy about the end of the thirteenth century: "I was lounging in the streets when I caught sight of a singer perched on a stage, whence he squalled the renown of the Carolingian armies and of the French: the crowd hung in clusters round him, pricking up their ears under the charm of his Orpheus. I listen in silence. These verses, written in French, are deformed by barbarisms, but the poet unfolds according to his fancy the plot of the story."

PRINCIPAL CHANSONS DE GESTE.—*La Chanson de Roland*, various editions; *La Chançun de Guillelme*, ed. Herm. Suchier, *Bibliotheca normannica*, 1911; *Le Pèlerinage de Charlemagne, Karls des Grossen Reise nach Jerusalem u. Constantinopel*, ed. Koschwitz in the *Altfranzösische Bibliothèk*, 1880; *Raoul de Cambrai*, ed. Meyer and Longon, 1882; *Garin le Loherain*, translated by P. Paris (1862); *Girart de Roussillon*, ed. P. Meyer, 1884; Les trois épopées de Bertrand de Bar; *Girard de Viane*, ed. Tarbe, Reims,

THE MIDDLE AGES

1850, *Aymeri de Narbonne*, ed. Demaison, 1887, 2 vols., *Les Narbonnais*, ed. Suchier, 1898-99, 2 vols. ; *Ogier de Danois*, ed. Barrois, 1842.

Le Cycle de Guillaume d'Orange, ed. Jonckbloet, The Hague, 1854, 2 vols., containing *li Coronemens Looys, li Charrois de Nymes, la Prise d'Orenge, li Covenans Viviens, la bataille d'Aleschans*.

Renaud de Montauban or *Roman des Quatre fils Aymon*, ed. Castets, Montpelier, 1909 ; L. Gautier published a *Bibliographie des Chansons de geste*, 1897.

HISTORICAL WORKS.—Leon Gautier, *Les Epopées françaises*, 2nd ed., 1878-92, 4 vols. ; Gaston Paris, *Histoire poétique de Charlemagne*, 1865 ; Gaston Paris, *La Chanson du Pèlerinage de Charlemagne*, in *Romania*, ix. (1880), p. 1 et seq. ; Paul Meyer, *Recherches sur l'épopée française, Examen critique de l'histoire de Charlemagne*, 1867 ; Pio Ragna, *Orig. dell' epopea francese*, Florence, 1884 ; Jos. Bédier, *Les Legendes epiques*, 1908-13, 4 vols. ; Jacq. Flach, " La Naissance de la chanson de geste," *Journal des Savants*, 1909, pp. 27-38 and 116-26 ; E. Petit, " Croisades bourguignonnes contre les Sarrazains d'Espagne au XIe Siècle," *Rev. Hist.*, 1886.

CHAPTER IV

THE ELEVENTH CENTURY

Robert the Pious and his master Gerbert. The rôle of the clergy at the beginning of the eleventh century. Usefulness of the monasteries. The heresiarchs of Orleans. Robert repudiates his wife Rozala to marry his cousin Berthe. Anathema. His marriage with Constance of Aquitaine. Famine years. The reign of Henry I, his opposition to the clergy, his marriage with Anne, daughter of the Grand Duke of Kief. Accession of Philip I; his tutor Baldwin of Flanders. Struggles between the feudatories of the royal domain. The court of the barons. The sons of Tancrède de Hauteville. The Kingdom of the Two Sicilies. The conquest of England by William, Duke of Normandy. Philip I and Bertrade de Montfort. The Investiture dispute. The papal legates and religious orders maintain the Roman pretensions against the King and the French bishops. Cluny. Exemption and immunity. Royal administration: the Provosts.

THE eleventh century opened in France during the reign of Robert the Pious, the son of Hugh Capet. Robert had ascended the throne in 996. He was a young man of twenty-six, tall, broad-shouldered, and already fat, but not so that his weight rendered him heavy in moving.

A Crowned Monk: Robert the Pious.
He had a short nose; the expression of his eyes was profound, gentle, very affectionate, matching the smile on his lips, which charmed by its kindliness. His father had given him a brilliant education at the school of Reims, under the direction of Gerbert.

Sprung from the centre of France, probably from Auvergne, Gerbert is to be regarded as one of the most powerful minds which have ever existed. There were then connected with every cathedral church—that is to say, in every church which had an archiepiscopal or episcopal see—classes under the direc-

65

THE MIDDLE AGES

tion of a "doctor" (*écolàtre*). In this capacity Adalbéron, Archbishop of Reims, had secured Gerbert d'Aurillac, so called because he had passed his childhood in that town in the monastery of St. Géraud. Gerbert was born about 940–45, of a poor family. He had devoted himself passionately to the cultivation not only of sacred literature but also of profane, which was rare in the case of a Churchman. He wrote to a certain Ramnulfe, whom he had charged with the collection of some manuscripts: "Nothing is more precious than the knowledge of great men put forth in books. Pursue the task you have begun, offer to my thirsting lips the waters of the eloquence of Marcus Tullius (Cicero); his genius will soften the cares with which I am besieged."

The knowledge which Gerbert had of mathematics and astronomy went so far for the period that the men of his time accused him of magic. It is by an error, however, that the introduction of Arabic figures has been attributed to him.

Under the direction of Gerbert, Robert learned logic—that is to say, philosophy, mathematics, and grammar, *i.e.* Latin, and music, regarded at that time as a science.

The chronicler, Richer, who was also a pupil of Gerbert, says of his master: "Gerbert fixed the generation of tones on the monochord; he distinguished their consonances into tones and semitones, also into 'ditons' and 'dièzes,' and by a suitable classification of sounds he spread abroad a perfect knowledge of this science."

The monochord consisted of a single string stretched over two bridges, by which the proportions of musical sounds were measured geometrically; the "diton" corresponded to our major third.

The merit of Gerbert was to teach clearly the musical science of his time: he may not have gone beyond what old Boëtius had said in his books *de Musica*. It was only after the death of Gerbert that a monk of Pomposa, Guido d'Arezzo (eleventh century), directed music into new paths. Even if Gerbert did not invent the scale, he was, at least, the first to have the idea of drawing staves in which musical notation should be fixed—four lines—and which are still in use in plain chant; then too he gave to the notes the short and sonorous

THE ELEVENTH CENTURY

names which they have kept, the first syllables of the first verses of the hymn to St. John:

> Ut queant laxis
> Resonare fibris
> Mira gestorum
> Famuli tuorum,
> Solve polluti
> Labii reatum,
> Sancte Johannes.

(So that thy servants may make the marvels of thy actions resound on the slackened fibres of their affections, take away sin from their polluted lips, oh, St. John!)

In the seventeenth century the Italians replaced *ut* by *do*.

The scale is nominally composed of six notes only. The designation *si* will be introduced only at a later date.

Robert retained a profound impression of the instruction he had received through the pains of the Doctor of Reims. On the throne he is to be an educated prince, a scholar. "Regnante rege theosopho," write the chroniclers. He loves books, has manuscripts copied, and buys many. He takes with him, in moving from place to place, part of his library, and we know that when he is going to Rome, " during this long journey the consolation of reading will not fail him." He chants in stall, vested with a cope like the other clerics. From this came the legend that King Robert composed the words of some hymns and religious chants, notably of the response: " O constantia martyrum. . . ." But of the various Latin poems attributed to Robert, some are due to Notker the Stammerer, who lived in the ninth century, while the others are more ancient still. At most, Robert can only have composed the music of these various hymns and responses: and this would be more easily explained by the fact that the old chroniclers, in indicating the author of a chant, make allusion as a rule only to the composer of the music, not of the words.

Nevertheless, we must not allow the erudition of King Robert, his taste for literature and fine religious ceremonies, his musical talent and the part he took in theological discussions, to delude us as to his real character. Neither must we allow his biography by the monk Helgaud, which is almost a " hagiography," a " saint's life," to mislead us. Robert the Pious was a politician and a soldier; admirable on horseback, his broad shoulders supporting with ease the hooded tunic of leather or the hauberk of brass, he traversed the roads of the Ile-de-France at the head of a company (*mesnie*) clad in armour, to confine within the limits of their fiefs the violent activity of his vassals.

We have seen the formation of feudalism: thousands and thousands of local groups spread over the land and forming so many little States—States with precise limits which each will try to extend at the expense of the little neighbouring States whose inhabitants look upon outsiders as strangers, even as enemies. Favoured by the peace which reigns in each of these communities, agriculture develops. And now, following this early progress, new needs arise. The resources of the feudal domain, which has been organized so as to be self-sufficing, cannot respond to more complex demands. Hence the beginnings of a commercial movement, still embryonic, but which will, none the less, furnish to the lord with his armed men round him the temptation to use his strength and transform himself into a brigand. He continues to maintain peace and concord among his " subjects," but he does not always resist the temptation of making some fruitful foray outside his fief. And the consequences of this are apparent. Dwellings are fortified still further, the fortresses surround themselves with higher walls, with ditches deeper still. There is no feudal group, rough and fierce, which does not fear a surprise, while at the same time seeking to surprise its neighbours.

And the necessity of the royal power at the summit of this feudalism appears more and more clearly. A successor of Robert the Pious, Philip I, will use a happy expression to describe his authority, when he says that it is placed at the head of all the others (Patent in favour of the Abbey of Bec).

In the country included between Normandy and Champagne, Flanders and Anjou, Robert the Pious, then, is constantly on the roads riding with sword in hand to restrain troublesome neighbours. He brings to reason Arnould d'Yèvre, Eude de Deols, Geoffroi de Châteaudun. This struggle against the more violent feudatories will be the task of Robert the Pious and his successors down to Philip Augustus.

THE ELEVENTH CENTURY

The same causes which assured the progress of the royal power formed at this period the force of religious ideas and strengthened the authority of the Sovereign Pontiff, represented in France by his legates and by the religious orders.

In this Society, divided up into various States, the royal power in its right to administer justice represents the sole common authority; in the same way the Church represents the only ideas and beliefs which can draw together these separate groups, the only moral idea which can give them solidarity and unite them in a common work. Luchaire has said very justly that the security of the clergy was then a public necessity, and that it was the guarantee of prosperity and social progress.

The influence of the bishops, so great under the Merovingians and the Carolingians, grows weaker under the first Capetians; it passes into the hands of the abbots, heads of the great monasteries, and of the papal legates. And the reason for this is again to be found in the constitution of feudal society. Each bishop was a lord whose action was limited to his diocese, even to the city where he had his see. The great monasteries, on the contrary, while representing, in the person of their abbots, feudal units, enlarged their circle of influence and extended it over the kingdom in which their order was spread. The monks went from one convent to another. One saw them on the roads spreading from one halting-place to another the ideals which they cherished.

Above all, the Order of Cluny, which was to be represented by a succession of very fine abbots, exercised a powerful influence. And then these convents, by the co-ordination of the efforts which united the numerous monks of a single establishment, became the centres of instruction, taking this word in its widest and most practical sense: architecture, agriculture, mechanical arts, and the arts properly so called.

The work accomplished by the religious orders of the eleventh and twelfth centuries, by the Cluniacs and the Cistercians, has been very justly distinguished from that to be achieved by the orders founded later, the Dominicans and Franciscans. The former achieve practical work; they are agriculturists, masons, artisans; they bring waste land into cultivation, make admirable advances in architecture; under

THE MIDDLE AGES

the inspiration of the Faith they form the most fertile centres of secular culture; their successors are to consecrate their efforts to the defence and propagation of doctrine; they will struggle against heresy; they are to perform essentially the work of proselytization.

During the whole of the eleventh century the delicate brushes which adorn the manuscripts are hardly handled outside the monasteries. "At this time," writes a contemporary, "there was in the Abbey of Saint-Melaine, at Rennes, a brother named Valère, of an ingenious mind, clever in practical arts and in making stained-glass windows. He 'irradiated' the monastery with them."

People pointed the finger, says Ordericus Vitalis, at any lord who did not maintain at least one monastery on his lands. Every baron careful of his duties ought to have, for the good of his vassals, a solid keep with a vast enclosure as a refuge in case of alarm, a town with a market as a centre of exchange, and lastly a monastery as a centre of culture and instruction.

As to the Papacy, it represents at the summit of the human hierarchy the point where ideas concentrate, the tie which unites them. Moreover, in spite of the efforts of the French clergy since the Council of Verzy (991) to dispense with their co-operation at least in temporal matters, the authority of the Sovereign Pontiffs, represented by their legates and supported by the religious orders, was destined to increase.

This makes it easy to understand the bond of union which is formed between the Crown and the secular clergy. We have spoken of the ecclesiastical character of the Capetian monastery. The mediæval clergy in France are more "royal" than "Roman." Their head is the King of St. Denis. Assembled under the presidency of Robert the Pious at the Synod of Chelles, the Archbishops of Reims (Gerbert), Sens, Tours, and Bourges, assisted by their suffragans, declare that the Pope has no authority as against the bishops of a province of France, and that the latter have even the right to annul his decisions.

King Robert, writes Richer, "was conspicuous for his knowledge of divine and canon law; he took part in the synods of the bishops, in which he held forth on ecclesiastical affairs and

THE ELEVENTH CENTURY

joined with them in regulating these. On these occasions he showed his talent for speaking." The gifts of oratory were bestowed on most of the Capetians. They often made use of it to address the people directly, and particularly the people of Paris, when they wished to explain to them, in important matters, their policy, and ask for their co-operation.

In his capacity of head of his clergy, Robert the Pious took part in the discussion and repression of the heresies which arose during his reign. That of the Canons of Orleans made a great stir. According to Raoul the Shaven (le Glabre), a woman had introduced it from Italy. Several Canons of Ste.-Croix constituted themselves the zealous preachers of the new doctrine; but we have no really definite information as to the nature of the " error."

" With their frightful barkings they proclaimed the heresy of Epicurus," writes le Glabre; "they no longer believed in the punishment of sins, or in the eternal reward for pious works." In 1022 King Robert summoned in the Cathedral of Orleans an assembly of bishops and barons before whom were dragged the heretics, laden with chains. The wretches, terrified, at first kept silence; then they recovered themselves and entered into discussion with the King. Robert showed himself an informed theologian, a subtle dialectician, and a fluent speaker. The debate lasted nine hours.

At last, wearied out, the accused cried:

" Let us finish with this chatter, do with us what you will! Already we see our King who reigns on high; He extends His arms to us and calls us to imperishable triumphs; He is summoning us to the joys of heaven."

At the door of the church Queen Constance wanted to put out the eyes of one of the heretics with a golden pin. On the Feast of the Holy Innocents fourteen of these unfortunate people were burned alive at the gates of the town. It was the first stake kindled in France for heresy.

Neither its memory nor his responsibility for it troubled King Robert, who dates one of his charters from " the year in which the arch-heretic Etienne and his accomplices were condemned and burned at Orleans."

After all, one must put the correct significance on this

matter of persecutions. They are not special to any religion, any people, or any time. Persecutions have been carried out in the name of every religious idea, and that, not because they were ideas of religion but because they were ideas affecting Society. The Romans only persecuted the Christians when their doctrines shook the foundations, and more particularly the economic conditions, on which ancient society rested.

The manners, ideas, beliefs, and customs of a people crystallize, if one may say so, under the form of religion. It is under this form that they have the most strength, activity, energy, and intensity; it is under this form alone that they act on a primitive people. And the people cling to them only in the degree in which these beliefs are necessary to their social life. It is a movement common and instinctive, irresistible as always when it is a matter of national evolution. With the triumph of a heresy such as that of the Manicheans at the beginning of the eleventh century France would have melted away, unless indeed this new doctrine in another form had become the soul of a new society, different from that which had preceded it—a new society and religion which, in their turn, under pain of ruin, would have been condemned to intolerance.

However deep was his religious devotion, and however keen his eagerness to favour the churches and monasteries, Robert I resisted none the less the encroachments of the ecclesiastical powers: a policy which, from Hugh Capet to Philip the Fair, was that of all the Capetians, including Saint Louis. In a love story, the struggle of King Robert against the Roman Court was to take a dramatic turn.

In 988, at the age of eighteen, Robert had married an Italian lady older than himself, Rozala, daughter of Berengarius, King of Italy, and widow of Arnoul II, Count of Flanders. Rozala had deep black eyes, with a hard and disconcerting expression; her hair, plaited in bands, looked like crows' wings. She had brought as a dowry to the King of France the castellany of Montreuil en Ponthieu, a precious acquisition for the house of Capet, which through it, for the first time, reached the sea. In France Rozala was called Suzanne. This marriage, dictated by political interest, was

THE ELEVENTH CENTURY

not happy. A big, robust fellow, Robert liked little pink-and-white women. It was not long before he conceived a horror of "his old Italian" with her tanned complexion. He repudiated her. Rozala went back to Flanders, to her son, Baldwin le Barbu (the Bearded), whence she claimed, justly but in vain, the restitution of her marriage portion, the Château of Montreuil. Politics having been successful in the matter of marriage only from the point of view of increasing his domains, Robert gave himself up to the splendid illusion of a marriage for love. While Rozala was still alive he married Berthe de Bourgogne, young, fair, little, and plump, with long flaxen hair. The son of Hugh Capet loved her with all his soul. Imagine his fury when Rome ordered him to break this union on the ground of kinship. The kinship of Berthe and Robert was real: they were related in the third degree counting according to the method in use at the time; in the sixth degree counting as we do now. Robert resisted the most urgent commands. Finally, the Pope, Gregory V, a German, summoned a General Council at Rome in order to pass judgment in it on the King of France (998).

The Council decided that Robert must leave Berthe or suffer anathema, and his fair spouse also. Anathema was the gravest punishment the Church could pronounce, much more serious than excommunication, since the person anathematized was not only put out of the Church, but condemned to hell.

Robert the Pious held out and kept his beloved wife by his side. The papal throne launched its thunders, which, as far as that goes, did not seem to alarm the young couple unduly. We see them, as man and wife, making donations to abbeys. A great number of the French bishops ranged themselves on the side of the King. Thus the legends fall to pieces, as to the effects of the anathema pronounced against Robert the Pious and Berthe of Burgundy. According to these their subjects fled at their approach; they could only keep two servants, who threw into the fire the plates from which they had eaten; when they entered a town the bells would be set going until the moment of their departure. From all this, modern painting has drawn some fine pictures. The truth is less touching. Under the title of Sylvester II, a Frenchman,

THE MIDDLE AGES

Gerbert, the master of Robert, succeeded Gregory V. He moderated the violent measures of his predecessor. However, Robert decided to separate from Berthe. The separation was carried out in September 1001. Berthe was not giving any children to her husband, and Robert had no brother who could succeed him, in default of a son.

Robert's third wife was named Constance. The marriage was celebrated in 1003. Constance was the daughter of a French count of the south called Guillaume. But which Guillaume? Guillaume, Count of Poitiers, or Guillaume, Count of Arles, or William, Count of Toulouse? The most recent writers pronounce in favour of the Count of Arles.

Contemporaries speak of Queen Constance as a very beautiful woman; she was called Blandine because of the fairness of her complexion; but she was capricious, haughty, and imperious. She was avaricious, greedy of power, violent in her malice, hard in her desire to dominate. She had the Count Palatine, Hugh de Beauvais, assassinated under Robert's very eyes. A passage of Raoul le Glabre is often quoted, relative to the influence which Queen Constance, coming from the more polished Courts of the south, exercised over the rude men of the north.

"The lords of her suite," says Raoul, "neglected arms and horsemanship; they had their hair cut half-way up their heads; they were shaven like actors, they wore indecent boots and hose." The good monk does not give us any description of these indecent hose. The clergy of the Ile-de-France always took an attitude of withering indignation against these southern fashions: the first manifestation of the opposition of the France of the north and that of the south, which was to show itself so tragically in the War of the Albigenses.

Berthe, from whom Robert had separated, had kept some partisans at Court, notably her son Eude, who was born of her marriage with the Count of Chartres, and had just succeeded his brother Thibaud in the countships of Chartres, Blois, and Tours. Robert himself regretted Berthe, gracious and tender, with the tranquil brow and soft blue eyes. Constance had black hair like Rozala, coarse, dull hair, a severe beauty, a bitter and uneasy disposition. She exasperated her husband.

THE ELEVENTH CENTURY

None the less, she presented him with four sons. Robert planned to have one of them crowned during his own lifetime, and associate him with himself on the throne, as his father, Hugh Capet, had done for him. The transmission of the crown to the eldest sons of the Capetian line was not yet assured; it depended, according to law at least, on election by the nobles. The King could choose as associate to the Crown whichever of his sons he should judge best capable of these functions. Robert's choice fell on his eldest son Hugh, who was crowned by the Archbishop of Reims in the Church of St. Corneille de Compiègne, on the 19th June 1017. Hugh died on the 17th September 1025. The question arose for the second time of choosing an heir to the throne. Constance supported the candidature of her third son, called Robert after his father. However, the King decided this time again in favour of the eldest, the young prince who was to rule after him under the name of Henry I.

In foreign affairs King Robert tried to prevent the German princes extending their power over our eastern frontier. He was also fortunate enough to get hold of the Duchy of Burgundy. The proposals of alliance put forward by Sancho, King of Aragon, and by Ethelred, King of England, the offer which the transalpine princes made him of the Italian crown, show the consideration and authority in which the young Capetian monarchy was already held in Europe.

A consequence of the social organization which we have just described was the frequent occurrence of the famines which desolated France during the reigns of Hugh Capet and of Robert the Pious. There was famine in 987, 989, 1001, from 1003 to 1008, from 1010 to 1014, from 1027 to 1029, and finally in 1031 to 1032, the year which followed the death of the second Capetian King.

These statistics are frightful. The scourge was produced by the division which multiplied the barriers between the fiefs of which the country was composed. There were some hundreds of little States with closed frontiers; innumerable tolls, payments for market rights imposed on the merchant, unsafe roads infested with men-at-arms who had regard only for the people of their own lord. If bad harvests desolated a part of

THE MIDDLE AGES

the country, food could not be brought from another part where the harvests had been plentiful. In the eleventh century, within seventy-three years, forty-three periods of dearth can be counted. That of 1031 is described in moving terms by Raoul le Glabre: " Rich men and burgesses suffered like the poor, and the violence of the Nobles yielded before the common misery." After having eaten the quadrupeds and the birds, they devoured corpses and things too horrible to mention. " Some sought a remedy against death in the roots of the forests and river plants." Human flesh became a food to be fought over. Travellers were attacked by cannibals who, having killed them, cut them up into steaks which they cooked on the fire. Those who thought that they would escape hunger by leaving their homes for other districts were killed in the night and eaten by their hosts. Unfortunate children were enticed by the bribe of an apple or an egg; then in the solitude of the woods they were killed and eaten. Some went so far as to eat corpses taken from the graves. One wretch is seen offering for sale at the market of Tournus and at that of Mâcon human meat, which he had prepared for cooking like butcher's meat. He was arrested and burned alive. The meat which he had brought was buried; but in the night an unfortunate creature, goaded by hunger, disinterred and devoured it: he was burned in his turn.

The famished people at the end of their forces expired, uttering a feeble cry " like the plaint of a bird at the point of death " (Raoul le Glabre). They were buried in the ditches of the fields, until, the corpses becoming too numerous, they were abandoned in heaps at the corners of the roads.

The reign of Henry I opened under these sad auspices. We have just said that Queen Constance would have preferred **A Warrior King. Henry I.** to see her third son, Robert, crowned. And now comes civil war between the two brothers. The rebels were supported by the powerful Count of Blois and by the Seigneur du Puiset, the most redoubtable of the unruly vassals (*hobereaux*) of the Ile-de-France. The beginnings of the struggle proved unfortunate for Henry, who found a refuge with Robert le Diable (the Devil), Duke of Normandy. From this moment luck

THE ELEVENTH CENTURY

returned to him, especially after the death of the Queen-Mother, Constance (July 1032), had deprived his rival of his chief support. Unhappily, to restore peace Henry thought he ought to give to his brother the Duchy of Burgundy, where the latter founded the first and powerful dynasty of the dukes of that name, who before long made themselves practically independent. It was to come to an end only in 1361, in the person of Philip de Rouvres.

Hardly had the new King concluded peace with his brother Robert, than his other brother Eude revolted in his turn. He also allied himself with the Count of Blois, and with the "hobereaux" of the Ile-de-France. War was resumed and filled the country with ruin and devastation (1034–39). At last Henry I was able to take Eude captive and imprison him at Orleans.

We have seen how, in the course of these struggles, Henry had found a useful supporter in the person of the Duke of Normandy, Robert le Diable, an interested supporter, for the King had to yield to his vassal the French Vexin. In 1035 Robert le Diable having gone on pilgrimage to the Holy Land, Henry took under his protection the young William whom Robert le Diable had had as son by Arlette, the daughter of a tanner of Falaise. The King of France defended the son of Robert the Devil on the field of battle at the peril even of his own body. He saved him at the Val des Dunes from the hands of the rebellious Norman barons. At this moment the union between the Norman Duchy and the French Crown seemed established, but it was not long before it broke down.

Henry I was to have as his chief adversary this same William of Normandy whom he had so bravely defended. The war lasted until 1058, and ended to the disadvantage of the King of France, who however succeeded in maintaining the suzerainty of the French Crown over the Norman Duchy.

Henry I, who was quite as pious as his father, showed himself stiffer still with regard to the clergy and the Papacy. Moreover, the chroniclers of the time, being ecclesiastics, are not very favourable to him. Guibert de Nogent accuses him of avarice and of trafficking in bishoprics.

The Sovereign Pontiff, Leo X, a former Bishop of Toul,

THE MIDDLE AGES

had come to France, and having declared his intention of calling a council at Reims, the King forbade the bishops to go to it.

If we consider finally the eastern frontier, we must admire the efforts made by Henry I to re-establish the authority of the Kings of France, as far as the Rhine. He claimed Aix-la-Chapelle " in virtue of his hereditary right "; as to Lorraine, the rights of the Kings of France over these territories, which he said belonged by no title to the German crown, seemed to him not less evident. The figure of our first King Henry, then, stands out with sufficient brilliance; the figure of a man of iron, worthy to preside over the destinies of a nation beholding the unfolding of the trembling wings of the great epics; a figure interesting, too, by his marriage, in the full eleventh century, with Anne, daughter of the Grand Duke of Kief, Jaroslaw Wladimirowitch. It was Roger II, the Bishop of Châlons, who, sent on a mission to these far-off regions, brought back the princess Anne (1051). From her marriage with Henry, a son was born, who received, under the influence of the Queen, the Byzantine name of Philip. As his father had done for him, Henry I took the precaution of having his son crowned during his lifetime. The ceremony took place at Reims, on the 23rd May 1059. An account of the consecration expressly mentions that the new King was elected by the prelates and a certain number of lords whose names are indicated; after which the knights present and the crowd of common people cried three times: " We approve! We wish it to be so!"

But these are already nothing more than ceremonies, cries, and formulas: the succession to the throne is henceforth assured to the eldest son of the King.

Henry I died on the 4th August 1060. Philip I mounted the throne at the age of eight years. The Regency was given to Baldwin, Count of Flanders, uncle by marriage of the new King, whose aunt, Adèle, the sister of Henry I, he had married. For this confidential position Baldwin had been preferred to Robert, Duke of Burgundy, the brother of Henry I, and uncle by blood of the young King.

The Age of Iron.

THE ELEVENTH CENTURY

It is impossible not to pay a tribute of admiration to the manner in which Count Baldwin of Flanders acquitted himself of the royal guardianship. He divided his time between the banks of the Seine and the County of Flanders—continual journeys which are to last for ten years; and everywhere Baldwin has the young Philip to accompany him teaching him his work as King.

This Baldwin of Flanders was a noble prince, pious and liberal, brave and splendid, large in figure and of a striking beauty. He defended the interests of his royal pupil with as much conscientiousness as courage, and energetically maintained the struggle against the unruly squires of the royal domain whose power and audacity were ever on the increase.

Here is feudalism vigorously entrenched within its stone keeps. The " mesnie " of the barons is extended and fortified; their fortresses, masterpieces of architecture, with their ponds covered with a green carpet of conferva, with their thick *courtaines*, their high towers, defy the armies of the time, which have not yet at their disposal the machinery for effective sieges. And certain of these lords—proud of their strength and their impregnable keeps, proud of their ancestors and by reason of the devotion and fidelity of their numerous vassals—are not afraid of braving the power of the King. A number of them have their keeps bristling on the borders of the royal domain: these are the Counts of Dammartin who commanded the environs of Creil, the Counts of Beaumont-sur-Oise, the Seigneurs de Montmorency, the Seigneurs du Puiset, the Seigneurs de Roucy.

Each of these " barons," sovereign in his territory, exercises there royal rights, holds Court and Council, presides over a tribunal, erects forked gibbets; a veritable army follows his standard; he has his own mint. Numerous men-at-arms and young knights live within the precincts of his vast castle, where they are trained under his direction for the career of arms. The daughters of his vassals form the entou age of the châtelaine. And we must be careful not to see in this man-at-arms a mere unruly squire, a " hobereau " greedy and plundering, even though this very name " hobereau " signifies "bird of prey." Our baron is devoted to his "subjects"; he keeps peace among them; he exposes his own body and possessions for their defence; he assures their existence, their work; he opens the way to them for fruitful enterprises. In return, his subjects owe to him services similar to those which he himself owes to the King—military service, service at Court, in council, and feudal aids. The vassal is bound equally to watch over the castle of his baron, to defend it if it is attacked; this is the duty of "estage." And thanks to this reciprocal aid, when circumstances have been favourable, such a baron as Eble de Roucy can conduct a whole expedition into Spain. "He set out against the Saracens," says Suger, "with an army fit for a King."

The castle of the feudal baron is like the royal Court on a smaller scale. The same officers are found there: a seneschal, a marshal, a pantler, and a butler, a chaplain who is sometimes called a chancellor. And we must not think that it was the feudal lord who copied the Sovereign: it was the royal Court which took its origin from the development of the feudal Court.

Let us penetrate now into the castle of one of these barons of the eleventh century. In the shadow of the high tower—at the summit of which the sentinel, to kill time, sings some songs of the watch, or plays on the flute, the timbrel, or the cornet—has been built the palace, the residence of the seigneur. There are two principal apartments: the chamber, which is reserved for him and his family; and the hall, where meals are taken. A part of this latter room, at the extreme end, is slightly raised like a stage, from which a view can be had of the whole apartment: it is the "dais." In the hall the public life is passed, the common life of the castellany. Guillaume au Nez Courbe has been conquered by the Saracens; he returns home wounded. His wife runs to meet him in the courtyard of the castle.

> Then holds she her loved one by his silken sleeves
> And they mount up all the marble steps;

—the marble steps which lead to the hall of the palace. The castle is empty of defenders; they have been killed in the

THE ELEVENTH CENTURY

battle; it was depleted of the young knights who were wont to throng round their lord:

> No man was there who service should them do.
> The Lady Guiburc runs herself for water,
> And after brings a towel;
> Then sat they down at the lowest table,
> For grief they could not sit on the dais.
> He sees the benches, the couches, and the tables
> Where his many vassals (*barnages*) were wont to be.

(It will be noticed that the words "barnage," "parage," "lignage," "family," are practically synonymous.)

> No one he sees throwing dice in the hall
> Or playing with checks and tablets;
> Then he grieves as a noble man should.
> . . . .
> "Dame Guiburc, you have nothing to weep,
> You have not lost your flesh and blood.
> I must grieve and be sad
> Who have lost my noble kindred.
> Now shall I flee to a foreign land,
> To St. Michael in Peril of the Sea,
> Or to St. Peter, God's good apostle,
> Or in a desert wood where none shall find me.
> There shall I become a hermit of some religious order;
> You, go make yourself a nun, and veil your head."
> "Sire," says she, "this can we soon enough do
> When our earthly task we have fulfilled.
> Sir William, with the will of God,
> To-morrow at dawn mount on thy charger.
> Ride straight to Laon,
> To the Emperor (the King of France) who has always held us dear.
> He will come to our aid,
> And if he does not, render to him his fief."
>
> (*Chanson de Guillaume*, from the *Legendes Epiques*,
> Jos. Bédier, i. 86, 87.)

A simple and living picture of the feudal lordship in the eleventh century, and of the sentiments which inspire its inhabitants.

But it was not long before the feudal lords began to suffer from want of money. The dues which they levied on their vassals were payment in kind. These were consumed like the products of their domains by their family, their servants, and their men-at-arms. As trade and industry developed, money acquired a greater value. It became daily more difficult to do without it, and the feudal lords were short of money. Hence the habits of plunder which are to mark the feudal system: the same lord who forms a model of order and justice within the limits of his fief will be transformed into a brigand outside—that is to say, against those who are strangers to his fief.

"Rigaut, with some of his men, overran the country, burned, destroyed towers and mansions, carried off booty; there was not a cow, a sheep, a robe, a piece of stuff or cloth which he did not have carried off to Plessis. His men were all rich for a long time" (*Garin le Loherain*).

Add to all this the armed struggles which were bound continually to arise, from numerous causes, between the little States into which the country was divided: quarrels of neighbours, disputes about domains, love episodes. . . .

> Two cocks were living in peace, a hen came along. . . .

The cocks are named Godefroi de Namur and Enguerran de Boves; the daughter of the Count de Portian arrives on the scene. "The fires of war," writes Guibert de Nogent, "began to kindle between the two rivals, with so much fury that all the people of Enguerran who fell into the hands of Godefroi were hung on forked gibbets, or had their eyes put out, or their feet cut off."

And so the necessity of being put by the ties of liegeman under the protection of those who were stronger went on increasing.

We read in the chronicle of Lambert d'Ardres: "Adèle de Selnesse heard that numerous lords of the land of Guines—after Walbert, Count of Ponthieu and of Guines, had retired from the world to become a monk, leaving his lands to heirs incapable of protecting them—were putting themselves under the protection of other lords, or indeed of bishops, abbots, or provosts, in order to keep their authority and to live in peace and tranquillity under the protection of others greater than themselves, to whom they enfeoffed their lands. Consequently she herself determined to place her free lands in fief,

THE ELEVENTH CENTURY

notably what she possessed at Poperinghe, under the protection of the bishop."

Thus we see the necessity of the royal authority standing out more clearly in proportion as feudal society becomes more developed and accentuated.

At the end of the eleventh century this authority is far from being able to make itself prevail everywhere without opposition. A charter of Geoffrey, Bishop of Beauvais, dated the 18th January 1106, shows that the feudal robbers were ravaging so cruelly in the country round Compiègne that he dispensed the Canons of St.-Corneille from coming to the diocesan synod, on account of the insecurity of the roads.

The numerous barons, who encumber with their towers the royal domain, have become powerful not only by their impregnable strongholds and their men-at-arms : Suger speaks of those barons to whom alliances with the greatest families gave a redoubtable army. Moreover, while the first two Capetians, Hugh and Robert, seem to have been respected in their domains and to have moved about in them freely, this was not the case with their successors, Henry I and Philip.

Finally this latter, by marrying one of his sons, Philip, to Elizabeth, daughter of Guy Trousseau, lord of Mantes and Montlhéry, managed to bring the famous castle of Montlhéry into the royal family.

" Having received the guard of the castle," writes Suger, " Philip I and his son Louis le Gros (the Fat) were as much rejoiced as if a straw had been removed from their eye or barriers which had held them imprisoned had been broken down." The King, adds the Abbot of St. Denis, declared to his son Louis, in our presence, how cruelly he had been afflicted by the exertions the castle had imposed on him. " Mind," said he to him, " mind, my son Louis ! Watch well this tower ! I have watched it through the trouble it has occasioned me. From it so many tricks and frauds have been perpetrated against me that I had never any rest or peace. Its treasons made my faithful subjects unfaithful, and more unfaithful those who had already betrayed me. From far and near my enemies concentrated there. Hardly an evil was committed within my realm without the consent or assistance of those who occupied it. As the territory of Paris is bounded towards the Seine by Corbeil, half-way to Montlhéry, and to the right by Châteaufort, there was such disorder between the Parisians and the people of Orleans that it was impossible to go from one to the other without the permission of my enemies or under the strongest escort. But now through this marriage the barrier has fallen and joyful communications take place between them."

Of these feudal Frenchmen of the eleventh century some were destined to remarkable fortune. A poor knight of Coutances, Tancrède de Hauteville, had twelve sons and several daughters. Five of these sons, Guillaume Bras de Fer (William Iron-arm), Drew, Omfroi, Robert Guiscard, and Roger, may be regarded as the founders of the French Kingdom of the Two Sicilies. According to the testimony of a Byzantine princess, Anna Comnenus, Robert Guiscard (the Prudent) was a big man, with broad shoulders, fair hair, ruddy complexion, steel blue eyes " which darted lightning glances." He left his Normandy, followed by five horse-soldiers and eight infantrymen, crossed France and Italy, and came to settle in Calabria on the top of a high mountain. Thence, as a brigand, he pounced on travellers, destroyed them, and thus secured for himself, in the simplest manner possible, arms and horses. But he was good to the poor and to Churchmen; moreover, the monks of Monte Cassino celebrated his " exploits " which, too, before long were carried out on a larger scale. It is a case now of castles which are surprised by the bands of Robert Guiscard, in Campania, in Calabria, and which thus become by these proceedings—rudimentary enough—the property of the Norman lord, who is still a feudal seigneur such as we have described.

His family, his household, his men bear him an unlimited devotion. He shows towards all his companions, towards all those who have joined their fortunes to his, an incomparable devotion and justice. The Pope, alarmed by the rapid progress of this disturbing neighbour, began by excommunicating him. Then he marched against him at the head of an army composed of Italians and Germans; but after suffering defeat at Civitate (1053), he hastened to take his conqueror as an ally in his struggle against the Empire.

THE ELEVENTH CENTURY

Gregory VII found no helper against Henry IV more reliable or more useful than Robert Guiscard. Without him, the Germans would doubtless have seized the capital of Christianity. Robert received from the Holy See the title of Duke of Apulia and of Calabria. Gregory VII thought of making him Roman Emperor in order to oppose him to Henry IV (1080). Roger, the brother of Robert, had won the title of Count of Sicily. Between the sons of the two barons there broke out, after the death of their fathers, a struggle of rivalry and for power. Roger II, the brother of Roger I, is to dispossess William, the son of Robert Guiscard, and the Sovereign Pontiff will recognize him as King of Sicily, Calabria, and Apulia; and the Norman Kingdom of the Two Sicilies will be constituted (1130).

It is a feudal suzerainty, in which is exercised the patronage which is its very soul, favourable to the " subjects " whom it encourages and whose efforts it protects. From it rises in Sicily under the shadow of the Norman standards a civilization charming in its variety and picturesqueness. Under the suzerainty of the descendants of Tancrède de Hauteville and of their companions, the French genius, the Arab genius, and the Greek join in a fruitful process. The Mohammedan scholars teach in the schools; the " mires," *i.e.* the Jewish doctors, tend the knights; money is struck in Latin, Greek, and Arabic type. An exquisitely eclectic architecture frames Byzantine and Arab themes in buildings of Roman or Gothic style imported from France, as one will see many years later, the themes of ancient art, revived by the Renaissance, mingle with the capricious fantasies of *flamboyant* Gothic.

Thus the epic realized by the sons of Tancrède de Hauteville in Southern Italy seems like a fairy tale. It is explained by the force and social energy of the feudal institutions described above. The conquerors of the eleventh century carried them in their saddle-bags to make them germinate and develop in far-off lands. What formed the strength of the feudal baron was not the extent of the domains over which he ruled, but the force of the ties of affection and devotion which bound him to his men. In whatever place they might find themselves, lords and vassals formed an organized society which, trans-

THE MIDDLE AGES

planted from Normandy to Sicily, preserved its force of action and expansion.

But the great example of French expansion in the eleventh century was the conquest of England by William of Normandy.

William the Conqueror was the son of the Duke of Normandy, Robert le Diable, and Arlette, a woman of low birth. He was a big, surly fellow, with a large stomach and a bald head; his face was red and puffy, with little round eyes " like gimlets." He had an abrupt, energetic manner and decided movements. He had the gift of commanding men and the power of organization. Of a shy temperament, he loved solitude. He had married Matilda, the daughter of Baldwin, Count of Flanders, and never ceased to maintain with her a united household. He succeeded his father as Duke of Normandy and forced the noblemen of the land to respect his power.

Besides, this Norman nobility was distinguished in the eleventh century from the rest of the French nobility, in that it was not divided into a hierarchy of vassals, composed of rear-vassals, vavasors, more important vassals, vassals of the domain, and superior vassals, superimposed one to another up to the royal throne: the Dukes of Normandy extended a uniform power over a single class of noblemen, equally spread over the Duchy. The lords of Bellême alone formed an exception; they had vassals under their orders, and were thus rendered almost independent. This social constitution was a consequence of the Norman Conquest, which had triumphed and organized itself in the country by imposing on the population the government of a conquering aristocracy; while in the other provinces of France the aristocracy issuing from the family, described above, had been formed slowly, had grown progressively, by a formative process, slow, complicated, and diverse.

In Normandy, following on the triumphant and organized invasion, the lords gave to the country a monotonous organization, for the movement is made from above, by authority; while in the rest of France the movement was made from below with the diversity of all spontaneous action, and seemed

THE ELEVENTH CENTURY

to spring from the soil, adapting itself in different places, to the infinitely varied and complex circumstances of local life. Viollet-le-Duc makes a pregnant observation when he writes: "The Norman castle, at the beginning of the feudal period, is always connected with a system of territorial defence, while the French castle is the dwelling of the chief of a band, isolated, defending his own domain, and taking no count of the general defence of the land."

This observation finds a complement in this assertion of the Council of Lillebonne (1080): "It is forbidden in Normandy to make a ditch so deep that a handful of soil cannot be thrown from the bottom to the bank without standing on anything; it is forbidden to set up a palisade except to mark a boundary, or one furnished with works defending the approach; it is forbidden to construct a fastness on any rock or island; or to build a fortress." We are far from the castles of Coucy and Montlhéry.

This organization of the Norman nobility ensured that the Duke of Normandy had all his subjects well in hand; this rendered easier the conquest of England. The King of England, Edward the Confessor, conquered by the Danes, had taken refuge at Rouen, whence, with the help of the Normans, he had organized an expedition which had enabled him to conquer them in his turn (1042). He died on the 5th January 1066, and one of the chief English nobles, Duke Harold—the brother-in-law of King Edward, who had married his sister—the son of Godwin, ealdorman of Wessex, succeeded him on the throne.

It was then that Duke William declared that King Edward had left him his kingdom by will, and that Harold himself had promised to recognize him as King of Great Britain.

William gathered at Lillebonne an army chiefly composed of his Norman vassals, but in which were also knights from the most diverse parts of France, of the north at least, from Brittany, the Ile-de-France, Flanders, Picardy, Maine, and Anjou, an army of fifty thousand men. The Normans and their auxiliaries set out from the mouth of the Dive on the 28th September 1066. On the 29th, at nine o'clock in the morning, the white sails arrived at Pevensey. The decisive encounter took place at Senlac, near Hastings, on the 16th October 1066 The

THE MIDDLE AGES

Normans, who had entered the fight to the strains of the *Chanson de Roland*, won a complete victory, due to the overwhelming superiority of the feudal cavalry, barded with iron, against the Anglo-Saxon footmen armed with axe and bow, as one sees them on the famous Bayeux tapestry. Harold and his brothers were killed. With a remarkable rapidity of decision William marched straight upon London and had himself crowned by the Archbishop of York at Westminster, under the eyes of the stupefied citizens.

With a like promptitude William established order in the country, so that in the March of the following year he was able to return to Normandy. He had granted lands to his companions whom he attached to himself after the feudal model. He and his auxiliaries introduced into England the use and customs of French feudalism, the French language, the tastes, the amusements, and the literature of that country. The suzerainty of the Anglo-Saxon territories was divided among the members of a French aristocracy, and everywhere within them were seen building fortresses, seigniorial residences, after the fashion prevailing across the Channel. England is to become for several centuries a centre of French culture by the same title as the Ile-de-France. The oldest manuscripts of our *chansons de geste* are of English origin and are in the libraries of London and Oxford. Then one will see the language, the customs, the architecture brought from France, shape itself in Great Britain by an intelligent adaptation to the taste and temperament of the English, so as to form a civilization, impregnated with the French influence, but which in its principal features appears fundamentally original.

And the organization of the nobility of Great Britain becomes the replica of the organization which the Norman nobility had given itself in imitation of that of the Ile-de-France, which we have just described, but without those superpositions and ranking of fiefs before mentioned. The English aristocracy will be, like the Norman aristocracy, a rural nobility, in direct contact with the people, and itself immediately under the hand of the King. This difference between the constitution of the English nobility and that of the French nobility, properly so called, had many consequences; notably

THE ELEVENTH CENTURY

it ensured that, from the first day, the new King of England found himself stronger in his country than the King of France would be in his two centuries later.

In France, the King is brought up against the hierarchy and grouping of the fiefs which come at length to form great States within his kingdom. In England the King commands immediately all the fiefs; and we have to repeat what we have just said of the Norman Conquest: in France the work of social organization is made spontaneously, born of a popular movement; in England it is made administratively by the energy of a conqueror.

One can imagine what follows. The King of England was the Duke of Normandy, and the similarity of language, tastes, and customs was to render more redoubtable still the continual incursions, which the English monarchs—for some centuries yet much more French than English—were to be encouraged to pursue into the very heart of our country. In England the conquerors found themselves in France, and in France they found themselves at home.

It has been made a reproach to Philip I that he allowed the union of Normandy and England to come about; people forget that, in 1066, he was a child of fourteen, under the guardianship of his uncle, Count Baldwin of Flanders, and that the latter, in consequence of the marriage of his daughter Matilda with the Conqueror, a most happy union, would not care to thwart his son-in-law.

At least from the time he had taken in hand the direction of his government, when he had attained his majority, Philip I appreciated the menace which the union of Normandy and Great Britain formed for the French Kingdom, and he supported Robert Short Hose, the son of the Conqueror, in his struggle against his father. He had, however, failed in his efforts when William died in Normandy on the 9th September 1087.

William had divided his domains between his two eldest sons, giving Normandy to the elder, Robert Short Hose, and the kingdom of England to the second, William the Red. A third, Henry, received nothing, and yet it was he who was destined to re-establish in his own hands the redoubtable union of Normandy and Great Britain. After having succeeded his brother William the Red on the English throne, he conquered Robert Short Hose at the battle of Tenchebrai (28th September 1106) and took him prisoner. Thus Henry replaced on his own head the double crown of the Conqueror, and he followed up his work by destroying the castles raised in Normandy since the death of his father.

William the Conqueror had resolutely resisted the injunctions of the Holy See ordering him to dissolve on the ground of relationship his marriage with Matilda, daughter of Baldwin of Flanders; Philip I likewise resisted the commands of the Sovereign Pontiffs enjoining him to repudiate Bertrade.

" In 1092," writes Ordericus Vitalis, " a scandal occurred which disturbed the kingdom. Bertrade de Montfort, the Countess of Anjou, was afraid that her husband Foulque le Réchin—which means restive, headstrong—would do with her as he had done with two other wives and repudiate her in her turn. Confident in her noble blood and in her beauty, she sent a man whom she trusted to Philip, King of the French, to disclose to him the passion of her heart. The King was not insensible to this declaration, and when this lascivious woman had abandoned her husband he gladly received her in France. He repudiated his own wife, the noble and virtuous Queen Berthe, the daughter of Florence, Count of Holland, who had borne him Louis and Constance, and married Bertrade, whom Foulque, the Count of Anjou, had had to wife for nearly four years." Is this adventure related accurately by our chronicler? According to some other authors the Countess of Anjou was carried off by Philip I on the 15th May 1092. However this may be, Philip repudiated Berthe from futile motives, and placed on the throne the wife of the Count of Anjou.

He had been overcome with a passion for her which was not to grow weaker. Queen Berthe was relegated to Montreuil-sur-Mer. If we can believe William of Malmesbury, Philip found Berthe too fat and had developed a feeling of disgust for her, more especially as he was himself bulky, big, heavy, and massive, such as we have seen his grandfather, Robert the Pious, and as we shall see his son, Louis VI. He was a glutton and ate enormously, and towards the end of his

THE ELEVENTH CENTURY

life he was so overwhelmed with fat that he could hardly move.

At first Foulque le Réchin, abandoned by his wife, stormed and thundered. Afterwards he calmed down, through the efforts of Bertrade herself, if we can believe Ordericus Vitalis :

"Between these two powerful rivals broke out a storm of threats, but the woman, clever and subtle, reconciled them and made peace between them so effectively that they met together at a splendid feast prepared by her." In October 1106 Philip and Bertrade will come to Angers, where Foulque will receive them with honour. But the Sovereign Pontiff, the great Urban II, showed himself less amenable than the husband. Supported by his legate in France, Hugh of Die, and by several bishops of the country, notably by Ive de Chartres, he had called on Philip to break his union with Bertrade, and on the refusal of the King, he had excommunicated him (Council of Autun, 16th October 1094, held by the legate, Hugh of Die). The ceremony of the Interdict was renewed by Urban himself at the Council of Clermont (18th November 1095). But Philip did not give in. Bertrade continued to be treated as Queen, and the new Pope, Pascal II, to close his eyes to it. He was engaged in the gravest struggles with Germany; driven out of Italy he seeks a refuge in France. The reconciliation of Philip I and the Holy See is sealed in 1106. The King obtains absolution from the Pope, and we shall see Bertrade seated beside him on the throne until the death of the King (July 1108); "after which," says William of Malmesbury, "Bertrade, still young and beautiful, took the veil in the Abbey of Fontrevault, always charming to men, pleasing to God, and like an angel."

But the episode of his love affairs with Bertrade is only a detail of the struggle which Philip maintained against the Holy See : the first act in the long conflict to which, two centuries later, Philip the Fair was to impose so vigorous a dénouement.

Since the Council of Verzy, held under Hugh Capet (991), the French bishops had shown a certain independence towards **The** the Holy See, and from that time the Sovereign **Investitures.** Pontiffs had never ceased to multiply their efforts to regain complete authority over the French clergy; a policy similar to that which they put into practice with regard to the German clergy. From this is to arise the great Investiture Contest between the papal power on one side and the royal and imperial power on the other. In France, as we have said, the Popes had at their disposal two powerful means of action : the legates and the religious orders ; while the episcopate inclined to favour the royal power. The French bishops regarded the King as their head, at least within the kingdom. The permanent legates of the Sovereign Pontiffs, especially when they were fine men like Hugh of Die, Archbishop of Lyons, tended to deprive the King of his authority over the clergy. (Lyons was not at this time part of the French kingdom.) Philip I claimed that it was only with his permission and in virtue of a royal delegation that the Sovereign Pontiff could judge a matter, even of an ecclesiastical character, from the moment that the interests of the kingdom were involved ; while the Popes claimed independent power in religious matters everywhere.

As to the bishops, if they could be elected by the clergy and the people, or by the clergy alone, then installed and consecrated by the Pope, they could only begin to exercise their functions after having received the royal investiture ; and this seemed the more just as the bishops formed one of the cogs in the feudal system and exercised temporal, political, even military powers, and these of the most important character. It is true that the theory of the French kings, as well as that of the German emperors, presented one grave inconvenience, simony. The sovereigns, careful of the material interests of which they had charge, might prove too readily inclined to give their investiture for financial considerations and to the highest bidder. Ive de Chartres recounts to the legate, Hugh of Die, the adventure of the Abbot of Bourgeuil, who presents himself to Philip I with his hands full of gold to receive from him the bishopric of Orleans which Bertrade has promised him :

" Have patience, the King says to him, until I have had enough profit out of your rival (who had already paid out a large sum); afterwards you shall have him deposed as simoniac, and I will give you satisfaction in your turn."

THE ELEVENTH CENTURY

In 1075, Gregory VII had issued the famous decree which forbade the bishops to receive lay investiture. We know what a stir it made, and still more in Germany than in France. The princes of the Holy Empire said :

" The consent of the Emperor ought to precede the election which will take place afterwards canonically and without simony, after which the newly elected person will go to the Emperor to receive from him the investiture with the ring and the cross."

The conflict is set forth in lively fashion by the Abbot Suger when he describes the interview between Pope Paschal II and the envoys of Henry V, the German Emperor, at Châlons-sur-Marne, in May 1107. These envoys were the Archbishop of Trèves, the Bishop of Halberstadt, the Bishop of Munster, and a certain number of burgraves in armour headed by Guelf II, the Duke of Bavaria, an enormous man of redoubtable appearance, and a great shouter. These envoys came with great pomp, mounted on enormous caparisoned horses. They had a severe and haughty air, and seemed to have come to sow terror rather than arguments. Only the Archbishop of Trèves showed himself courteous and pleasant, fluent and wise, and able to speak French easily. In able style he expounded to the Pope the claims of the Emperor. This, according to him, was the right procedure in the election of bishops or abbots : the election made by the clergy ought to be brought to the knowledge of the Emperor before being made public, in order to ensure that the candidate shall be agreeable to him ; after this the election should be proclaimed in a general assembly as having been made at the request of the people, through the offices of the clergy, and with the consent of the Emperor. Finally, the person elected thus freely and without simony should present himself before the Emperor to swear fidelity to him and to receive from him investiture with the cross and the ring. "And that is just," said the Germans. "No one could be admitted to enjoy, without imperial investiture, cities, castles, lands, and dues within the Empire." But the Pope replied through the Bishop of Plaisance, that the Church, freed by the blood of Jesus Christ, could not go back again into slavery, and that it belonged only to the Altar to grant the investiture with cross and ring, and not to the lay power, whose hands the sword had filled with blood.

At these words the representatives of Henry V protested; they railed " in Teutonic style," says Suger, and made a great uproar. "This is not the place to finish this quarrel," they cried, " but at Rome, where it will be settled at the point of our swords."

The Kings of France likewise claimed that it was their right to grant investiture with the cross, before any consecration.

The eleventh century saw a prodigious increase of the Monastic Orders in France. Of them all, Cluny experienced an unprecedented prosperity. We have spoken of the splendid character of the men who directed it.

Cluny shone by the number of its monks and of the establishments which were founded under its patronage; it shone too by the wealth of its abbeys, by the excellence of its literary and artistic culture, by the development and perfection of its agriculture, and it formed thus in France, in the course of the eleventh century, a real power, a fruitful source of life, progress, and prosperity. It was during the last quarter of the eleventh century, about the year 1088, that the reconstruction of the Abbey of Cluny itself was begun, a whole town of stone, dominated by towers and steeples, in the finest Romanesque style, one of the most imposing monuments that have ever been.

New Orders are founded: the Cistercian Order, the Order of Grandmont, the Order of Fontrevault.

Popes Urban II and Paschal II proclaimed that Cluny was directly dependent on the Holy See; this meant the withdrawal of numerous rich and populous monasteries from the authority of the diocesan bishops, and, therefore, from the royal authority. This fashion of making religious establishments depend directly on the Roman Court was called " exemption "; they were exempt from episcopal authority. Philip I tried to meet exemption by immunity: a privilege that the Kings could accord to such or such an abbey, in order to keep it under his influence, by exempting it from certain royal rights, in particular the rights of justice and staying within their domains, military service, and of certain rents or dues; but the Kings never, or rarely, went as far as total

THE ELEVENTH CENTURY

immunity, wishing to preserve rights over the administration of the abbey while attaching the monks to them by their favours.

One sees at a glance the double current which divides the French Church: the Holy See is trying to draw it entirely to itself, by the efforts of the permanent legates established in France, where they convene councils and appear continually armed with the thunders of excommunication; by its theory of investitures, which would deprive the King of all influence over elections; finally by the development of the religious orders which, by means of exemption, would depend directly on the Roman Court, without passing even by the episcopate; on the other hand, the royal power, which is itself an authority of ecclesiastical character, attempts to keep its episcopate under its influence, and with the more care as its prelates are not only ecclesiastical dignitaries, but feudal lords disposing of a secular and very real material power, in the same way as it tries to maintain its administrative and judicial powers over the abbeys. These political matters are reduplicated by financial problems: the Sovereign Pontiff did not give these exemptions without payments profiting the Roman Court.

And one understands now what will be the sentiments of the French episcopate. For, in the final account, this policy of the Roman Court in France, this action of the papal legates, this exalting of the monastic orders by " exemption," is found to be directed against the episcopate; at least it is the episcopate which in the end pays the expenses of the contest, since the policy followed by the Holy See tended to withdraw a section of the clergy, the richest and most influential, from its authority.

The Roman policy tends to oppose to the bishops more independent rivals, in the person of the abbots of the great monasteries. On his elevation to the Papacy Urban II granted to Abbot Hugh of Cluny the use of the mitre, the dalmatic, gloves and sandals. The French bishops never ceased as a body to show themselves hostile to the papal legates, who were, moreover, generally hostile to the bishops. Thus we understand why in the struggle for power which was maintained, practically without truce, from the time of Hugh Capet to

Francis I, between the Sovereign Pontiff and the King of France, the bishops were generally in favour of the King.

However, towards the end of the reign of Philip I, there was a compromise between the two rival powers in the matter of the Investiture quarrel. It was published at the Council of Troyes (May 1107). The theory of Ive de Chartres, who had never ceased to plead for conciliation, was admitted. Assuredly, a prelate is forbidden to receive investiture from the hands of a layman; but on the other hand an ecclesiastical election cannot dispense with the royal approval. The Sovereign Pontiff, to whom the King's help was necessary in his struggle against the Empire, had yielded on the main point; and Philip I, to whom the love of Bertrade de Montfort seemed not less necessary, had yielded in the matter of form.

The policy of Philip I towards the Papal Court was wanting, then, neither in firmness nor ability; and the King, to whom history generally shows itself so severe, appears to have evinced a strong will and a clear sense of duty.

He realized the importance of strengthening his power, his authority over the royal domain, in what we call the Ile-de-France, and, energetically seconded towards the end of his reign by his son Louis Thibaud—soon known as Louis le Gros—he never ceased to struggle against the rebellious lords who encumbered his territory with their stubborn castles. He takes Corbie and annexes it to the royal domain; in 1107 he grants privileges to the merchants who frequent its markets, which become flourishing. At the death of the Count of Vermandois he takes possession of part of his fief; next it is the Vexin, which he invades after Count Simon de Valois has withdrawn into a monastery; Château-Landon and le Gâtinais are seized in their turn, and finally the town of Bourges and the adjacent territory. And these conquests immediately adjoining his domain are at once organized and put in a state of defence by the construction of fortresses.

If we consider the internal administration of the palace, we notice under Philip I an important change. The administration of justice passes from that mass of men, floating and variable, who formed the Court—and which included generally the *optimates*, the faithful subjects passing by or staying with the

THE ELEVENTH CENTURY

monarch—into the hands of officers residing with the King and composing "the palace" proper. And these members of the Palace, in specializing their functions, come to form, some the Royal Council, some the *Parlement*, and others the *Chambre des Comptes*.

In the local administration the Provosts make their appearance. Their functions consist of administering justice in the absence of the King; they are moreover commissioned to receive the different dues from the domain. They are found at Paris, Sens, Etampes, Poissy, Mantes, Senlis, and Bourges; perhaps also at Pithiviers and Compiègne. Under the orders of the Provosts are placed surveyors (*vicarii*), who serve as their secretaries and support them in their judicial functions.

It has been thought that a weakening was observable in the activity of Philip I from the time of his marriage with Bertrade de Montfort. Her first husband, already, had found in Bertrade a very absorbing wife. "She had made him effeminate," says Suger; "seated on the stool on which her little feet rested, he remained there fascinated by her charms." Another Circe, she appears to have "softened" Philip I in the same way. All for love and absorbed in the eyes of his wife, he no longer concerned himself with public affairs; this is at least what the Abbot of St. Denis affirms. Towards 1099 he had associated with himself on the throne his son Louis (Louis le Gros), who immediately gave himself to the task with youthful ardour.

Philip I made a very edifying end, probably at the Château de Melun on the 29th or 30th July 1108.

SOURCES.—*Lettres de Gerbert, 983–97*, ed. J. Havet, 1889; Vict. Mortet, *Recueil de textes relatifs à l'histoire de l'architecture* (XIe–XIIe *Siècles*), 1911; Adémar de Chabanne, ed. Chavanon, 1897; *Raoul Glabre*, ed. Prou, 1886; *Guibert de Nogent*, ed. Bourgin, 1907; *Chron. de Richer*, ed. Waitz, *SS. rerum germ. in usum scholarum*, 1877; Ordericus Vitalis, *Historia ecclesiastica*, ed. Le Prevost, 1840–55, 5 vols.; *Chron. de Helgaud*, ed. Guizot, 1824.

HISTORICAL WORKS.—Jacq. Flach, *Les Origines de l'anc. Fr.*, 1886–1917, 4 vols.; Pfister, *Etudes sur le règne de Robert le Pieux*, 1885; Augustin Fliche, *Le Règne de Philippe 1er*, 1912; Ach. Luchaire, *Louis VI le Gros*, 1890; by the same author, *Hist. des institutions monarchiques sous les premiers Capétiens*, 1883, 2 vols.; by the same, *Les Premiers Capétiens*,

THE MIDDLE AGES

in the *Histoire de France*, edited by Lavisse, ii. 1901 ; A. Freeman, *The History of the Norman Conquest*, 1871, 4 vols. ; Imbart de la Tour, *Les Elections épiscopales dans l'église de France*, 1891 ; Curschmann, *Hungersnöte im Mittelalter*, 1900 ; L. Halphen, *Le Comté d'Anjou au XIe Siècle*, 1906 ; L. Reynaud, *Les Origines de l'influence franç. en Allemagne*, 1913 ; D. Augustin Gatard, *La Musique grégorienne* (1913) ; J. Combarieu, *Histoire de la musique*, 1918–19, 3 vols.

CHAPTER V

THE CRUSADES

Pilgrimages to the Holy Land in the eleventh century. Saracen invasions in Spain. The military nobility in France. The famine of 1095. Urban II at the Council of Clermont. Peter the Hermit. The Crusade of Poor Folk. The Knights' Crusade. Its leader, the Bishop of Puy. Adhémar of Monteil. The capture of Nicæa (19th June 1097). Victory of Dorylæum (1st July). Siege of Antioch (20th October to 3rd June 1098). The finding of the Holy Lance. Capture of Jerusalem (15th July 1099). Godfrey de Bouillon. Conquest of the Holy Land and its organization by the Crusaders. Consequences of the Crusades in the West.

DURING the reign of Philip I the great movement of the Crusades began. The King of France was under sentence of excommunication, as were his neighbours, William Rufus, King of England, and the German Emperor Henry IV; none of the three princes could therefore take part in it.

Since the tenth century, pilgrims from the West had begun to visit the Holy Places in Asia Minor, the cradle of Christianity. These journeys became more numerous through the conversion of Saint Stephen, King of Hungary (979–1038), which opened to the East the way of the Danube. In 1035 Robert le Diable, Duke of Normandy, set out for Palestine with a great number of his subjects. The "journey" of 1063 numbered some thousands of pilgrims.

At Jerusalem there dwelt a quite numerous Christian population, in a quarter of the city surrounded by walls. There were to be seen there convents of men and of women founded by Saint Stephen. Several witnesses attest the good state of the hospitals and churches then possessed in the town by the Christians. But towards the last quarter of the eleventh century the power over the Holy Places changed hands. The Fatimite Caliphs of Cairo, kindly and humane, were driven away by the Caliphs of Bagdad, the Seljuks. In 1070 Jerusalem was taken by Ansiz-ibn Abik. In 1084 Antioch, become Christian again since Nicephoras Phocas, fell in its turn into the power of the Turks.

A new régime, intolerant and hard, was to weigh on these lands: and the moving tales of the pilgrims were to carry back echoes of it on their return. Many inhabitants of Jerusalem and Antioch, exiled from their dwellings, flocked back to the West. Their sorrowful tales are gathered up and spread abroad by the wandering monks.

Add to this a new invasion of Spain by African Mohammedans, the Almoravides. On the 25th October 1087 the Christian army is beaten at Zolaca. We have mentioned the importance that the repeated wars against the Saracens of Spain had taken in the preoccupations of the French chivalry, the many expeditions which the lords from the banks of the Seine, the Loire, and the Saone had directed against them. The moment had arrived for a greater expedition against the Saracens of the East.

Certainly faith, the faith which built the cathedrals, played a great part in the Crusade; but one finds there other causes which contemporaries perhaps did not avow.

The education of the nobility, in the eleventh century, was entirely military. The knights, ardent, robust, keen on movement, were fit only for war. We have seen the utility of this education in its time, but here is the work of the feudal baron accomplished; the fief is organized. Its lord is reduced to turning his soldierly activity against the neighbouring fiefs.

From being beneficial this activity becomes injurious; but how employ the feudal lords?

<blockquote>They do not accord well together,
Rest and honour.   (<i>Cligès</i>.)</blockquote>

Before them is about to open the vast field of the Crusades.

Accidental circumstances played an important part: the famine of 1095. A contemporary chronicler, Eckhard, says expressly that it was the misery caused by the famine, and

100

more particularly in Gaul, which induced so many men to leave their firesides. Sigebert writes in the year 1095 :

"The famine which had been raging for a long time became very grave. The poor plundered the goods of the rich. In the country districts the peasants lived on roots."

The conquering ardour of the Seljuk Turks directly threatened the Christian Emperor of Constantinople, Alexius. He determined to send to the Sovereign Pontiff ambassadors, who came to Urban II at the Synod of Placencia (March 1095). They drew him a lively picture of the evils which threatened the Christian Empire of the East. From the Synod of Placencia Urban II published a first appeal; soon afterwards he came to France, where he was received with transports of joy. " No man living," writes Guibert de Nogent, " remembers the Supreme Head of the Apostolic See coming to visit these countries."

Urban II was a powerful orator, tall, and of noble bearing; he displayed untiring energy.

He appeared at the Council of Clermont. It would be a mistake to believe that this Council had been called specially on the subject of the Crusade. It had to deal with the excommunication of Philip I and the subject of the French Church. The order of the day—if one may use the phrase—contained the subject of the Crusade only in the third line; but hardly had the question arisen when it produced an immense explosion of enthusiasm. Some Christians, driven from Antioch and Jerusalem, mingled with those assisting at the Council. Urban II had not finished his speech when cries of " God wills it ! " broke out on all sides.

Foucher de Chartres saw the knights having sewn on their shoulders in silk or cloth of gold, or indeed in brown or red woollen stuff, the crosses which indicated the vow to set out for the Holy Land.

" As soon as the Council came to an end," writes Guibert de Nogent, " there arose a great clamour in every province of France, and as soon as any one heard the news of the public commands of the Pope, he went to beg his relatives and neighbours to enlist in the way of God."

And there was seen to arise Peter the Hermit; he was a

hermit by profession (*ermite ordonné*). He was born in the Amiénois. Formerly he had planned a pilgrimage to the Holy Places, but had gone back to his native country without having been able to accomplish it. At Clermont the words of Urban II carried him away, and he consecrated himself to the Crusade. "We saw him," writes Guibert de Nogent, "traversing villages and towns, preaching everywhere; the people swarmed round him, overwhelming him with gifts and praising his holiness."

He distributed generously all that was given to him. He made peace between those who were at variance, brought runaway wives back to their husbands, giving them at the same time pleasant gifts. There seemed to be in him something divine, and the crowd went so far as to pluck the hair from his mule or his ass as relics. He wore a woollen tunic and, above it, a cloak of drugget reaching to his heels; he went bare armed and bare footed. He was little and thin, with black hair, bright eyes, an olive complexion; and wore a long grey beard.

His beard fell to the clasp of his belt. . . .
(*Chanson d'Antioche*.)

The chroniclers enter into the minutest details on this subject. Through them we know that Peter the Hermit liked neither bread nor meat, and lived on wine and fish. Sharp, decided, full of energy, he united to a consuming activity an ardent imagination and an enthusiasm which was infectious. People sold their goods, their fields, the family house, to help towards the expenses of the expedition. The poor equipped themselves in modest fashion. Guibert de Nogent has seen peasants shoeing their oxen and yoking them to their long carts, on which they piled up wife and children and their few belongings.

"And these little children," says Guibert, "as soon as they saw a castle or a town asked eagerly if it was Jerusalem." The enthusiasm became such that there was no longer any need to preach the Holy War in the churches: each one preached it with abundance of emotion, in his house to his friends, to his neighbours checked on the doorstep, on the trapdoor of his cellar, in the street even to all comers. "I have heard it said," writes Guibert de Nogent again, "that there

THE CRUSADES

arrived in one of our seaports some men who spoke a strange language: they put their fingers one over another in the form of a cross, thus showing that they wished to enrol themselves in the cause of faith."

Peter the Hermit and his innumerable companies set out about the end of the month of March 1096. It was the true Crusade, the Crusade of the Poor. However, to this disordered host, to which contemporaries already applied the words of Solomon, "The grasshoppers have no king, and yet they march in companies," there was to succeed another army, carefully organized, the army of the feudal barons, who were preparing thoughtfully and methodically the distant expedition.

And already the words of Urban II are seen to be realized: "And they will become soldiers, those who, until to-day, were mere brigands; they who were fighting with brother and cousin will now fight legitimately against the barbarian; and they who fought as mercenaries for a little money will earn the reward of eternal life."

Throughout the kingdom, as Foucher de Chartres puts it, "Urban II had renewed peace." The quarrels of castle against castle, castle against town, vassal against suzerain, family against family, were appeased. "Before the people put themselves in motion for this great expedition," writes Guibert, "the kingdom of France was given over on all sides to disturbances and the cruellest hostilities. Soon tempers changed completely. . . As the blasts of a tempestuous wind can be calmed by a gentle rain, so these quarrels and conflicts between fellow-citizens were appeased."

It is convenient to record here the precious remark of Joinville when he disapproved of the Crusade of Tunis, mistakenly undertaken, he says, "because at that time the kingdom was at peace."

This was the first effect of the Crusade. And a second result was to put an end to the famine: indeed, the barriers between the domains and the provinces were destroyed for the moment at least. As every one wanted to procure the money necessary for the distant expedition, they sold off all that had been accumulated, reserves of corn, wine, and cattle.

The storehouses of the speculators were opened wide; bushels of wheat, barley, maize, and oats were put upon the market. " The famine in grain," says a contemporary, " is turned into abundance, and I saw seven sheep sold for five pence" (about four francs of our present money).

Peter the Hermit, at the head of a numerous company, arrived at Cologne on Easter Sunday, the 12th April 1096. Other companies were commanded by a knight of noble birth but small fortune, Walter the Penniless (Gautier sans Avoir); they left Cologne with the followers of the Hermit and entered Hungary. A widespread error attributes to the armies of Peter the Hermit and Walter the Penniless some massacres of Jews. On the contrary, they conducted themselves during their journey through Germany with a moderation and wisdom which one must admire in armies of that time and made up as they were. The slaughter of Jews only began at Cologne the 29th May 1096, a date at which Peter and his people were already gone. These massacres were ordered by a German lord, Count Enrich de Leiningen; they were carried out by the men-at-arms, Germans, whom he had gathered together.

Walter and his men arrived safely at Belgrade: but there, when they were refused provisions, they began to plunder. After some unfortunate conflicts with the Bulgars, they arrived at last before Constantinople, where they encamped at the gates of the city (July 1096), and awaited the arrival of Peter and his army.

Peter the Hermit actually crossed Bavaria and Hungary at the head of a disorganized crowd. The chronicler Eckhard paints the astonishment caused by these troops, infinite in number, some on horseback, some on foot, others in two-wheeled carts.

It is certain that Peter the Hermit gave proof of remarkable qualities: authority, intelligence, activity. He was a true popular leader; but the task he had undertaken was beyond human power. In proportion as difficulties increased and the replenishing of food and fodder became harder, and as with the length of the march the enthusiasm of the first days died down, and the instincts of disorder and plundering manifested themselves, his authority proved unequal to the control

THE CRUSADES

of the tumultuous mob which he was trailing behind him. "He could not curb this multitude of diverse peoples who were unwilling to listen to him or obey him." His ascendancy was, however, still sufficiently great for him to be able to win at the head of his companies the victory of Semlin (Zimony). A Hungarian army which had advanced against the Crusaders was routed. It lost more than four thousand men, while Peter left only a hundred of his on the battlefield. Semlin was sacked, after which Peter made his followers cross the Save on a bridge of boats.

In these circumstances and others to follow, we find in Peter the Hermit not only an organizer but a war leader. It is true that a leader in war can succeed only at the head of disciplined troops.

The Crusaders suffered a first check at Nissa (Nish), against the Bulgars. Peter lost there the coach which contained his war treasure. Ten thousand Crusaders were killed. The remainder scattered and took refuge in the forests. Peter and the few men-at-arms still under his orders took refuge on the side of a mountain, where they sounded the rally. He was weeping over the fate of so many of his followers who had perished before reaching the Holy Land. At last 30,000 men were united round him and resumed their forward march (July 1096).

At Sternitz (Sofia) Peter received from the Emperor Alexius a message which pointed out to him the complaints to which the insubordination of the Crusaders were giving rise. The Emperor forbade them to stop more than three days in any town before arriving at Constantinople; but he had sent orders, he added, that in all places they should be furnished with provisions.

At this news Peter the Hermit wept with joy. The Crusaders reached Philippopolis, where, before the inhabitants of the town assembled together, he made a moving speech on his enterprise, on the misfortunes they had suffered, the difficulties they had conquered. The inhabitants, profoundly moved, gave provisions, horses, and money. The Crusaders arrived under the walls of Constantinople on the 30th July 1096, three months and ten days after leaving Cologne. We must remember the

THE MIDDLE AGES

conditions under which this expedition was accomplished, the composition of the army of Peter the Hermit. As it was performed, this march of the Crusaders to the banks of the Bosphorus is one of the magnificent enterprises of which history has preserved the memory. Our pilgrims were forced to encamp outside the walls of the Greek capital, in some plains where they found Walter the Penniless and his companions.

To tell the truth, the Emperor Alexius felt more fear than pleasure at the aspect of these first auxiliaries. In what disorder and wild misery were these armed peasants with their wives and children after their long and harsh Odyssey. The more so as a number of them, in spite of the prohibitions, penetrated into the great city, where they entered the sumptuous dwellings, robbed and plundered, embraced the ladies, sometimes not too gently, and pulled about the chambermaids. They set fire to some houses, and tore the lead from the roofs of the churches and sold it to the Greeks.

The Emperor was in a hurry to get these disturbing allies to pass on into Asia Minor. On the 5th August the transportation of the first detachments to the coasts of Bithynia was begun.

Skirting the Asiatic bank of the Bosphorus, Peter marched with his army on Nicomedia (Ismid). He reached Civitot (now Hersek), on the Gulf of Nicomedia. Here, through want of discipline, a part of the German contingent got separated from him. Others, Frenchmen, to the number of 7000 or 10,000, pushed on in spite of the exhortations of Peter up to the outskirts of Nicæa. They ravaged the country and gave themselves up to the most frightful excesses. Imagine, in those rude mediæval days, men of the people, and exasperated by privation. Separated from their leader they knew no restraint. They seized children; and to cook them they cut them into pieces or roasted them spitted on stakes. They inflicted frightful tortures on the adults. They thrust back into the town the inhabitants of Nicæa who had come out to meet them, and with great booty and numerous cattle they returned in triumph to the camp.

The success of this enterprise excited the jealousy of what remained of the German and Lombard contingents, who split

THE CRUSADES

off from Peter in spite of his remonstrances (20th September 1096). Their enterprise did not turn out so well. Surprised by a lieutenant of Suleiman, in the precincts of the castle of Xerigordos, they managed to take refuge there ; but, besieged, tortured by hunger and thirst, they capitulated and were massacred or kept prisoners (7th October 1096).

The remainder of the troops of Peter the Hermit fell into an ambuscade at Civitot. The Turkish army was fresh, numerous, admirably armed, splendidly commanded. By clever manœuvring they drew the Crusaders on into some narrow gorges in which, with the greatest ease, they slaughtered them (21st October 1096).

Vessels sent by Alexius, the Emperor of Constantinople, gathered up the remnants of the popular expedition ; but the great majority of these poor folk had perished. Those who survived, and among them Peter the Hermit, were taken back under the walls of Constantinople, where some awaited the arrival of the army of the knights, while the others went sadly back to France.

The army of knights, which will arrive in the spring of 1097 on the scene of disaster, on the outskirts of Nicomedia and Civitot will be horrorstruck at the sight of the bleached bones. " Oh, with what severed heads and bones the sea borders were covered ! "

The daughter of the Emperor Alexius, the Princess Anne, relates that afterwards quite a mountain was built up of these bones. And later they served as materials for the construction of a fortress by the French. Mixed with lime these bones formed dry and resistant walls.

The lamentable check of the popular Crusade, in spite of the elements of success which it contained, in spite of the valour of its leaders Peter the Hermit and Walter the Penniless, in spite of the valour and faith of the soldiers, shows that the people only perform great actions and create great works when acting in a perfect social co-ordination : in such a social co-ordination as was to ensure the success of the Knights' Crusade.

Divided into five principal corps, this Crusade only took the road well after the departure of Peter the Hermit and his companions. The first of these army corps, composed of men

of Lorraine, of Frenchmen of the north, and men of the Rhine,
counted in its ranks Godfrey de Bouillon, the Duke of Basse-
Lorraine and his brothers Eustace and Baldwin of Boulogne.
By way of Germany, Hungary, Bulgaria, and Thrace, it arrived
in sight of Constantinople on the 23rd December 1096. The
second army, formed of Flemish and Frisian contingents,
under the direction of Count Robert of Flanders, arrived under
the walls of Constantinople in April 1097. They had gone
by way of Italy, through Campania and Apulia, and reached the
port of Bari on the Adriatic. Among them was the chronicler
Foucher de Chartres. "A great number of poor people," he
writes, "and those who were wanting in energy, frightened at the
thought of the hardships which awaited them, sold their bows,
resumed the pilgrim's staff, and made their way back to their
own country." But the majority embarked for the East.
The third army, at the head of which shone Raimond de St.
Gilles, Count of Toulouse and Marquis of Provence, arrived
under the walls of Constantinople about the same time as the
soldiers of Robert of Flanders, *i.e.* in April 1097. It had come
by way of Lombardy, Dalmatia, and Epirus. The fourth
army of knights included the Italians and the Normans established in Apulia, in Calabria, and in Sicily, with Boémond,
Prince of Tarento, the eldest son of the famous Robert Guiscard,
and the nephew of Guiscard, Tancred. They embarked on the
Adriatic at Brindisi, whence they crossed to Durazzo. By way
of Epirus and Thrace they also reached Constantinople in April.
Finally, in May 1097, the French of the centre and the west,
under the command of Robert Short Hose, Duke of Normandy,
crossed the Bosphorus in their turn.

We have given the names of the most illustrious lords who
were in these five army corps; but it would be a mistake to
think that any of them exercised a military command, a power
like that of a general-in-chief, to use a modern expression. Each
feudal baron went independently of the neighbouring baron,
surrounded by contingents assured to him by the men of his
fief, his vassals; he went with the "barnage" of his household:

> From France, from England, from all Normandy,
> Prince, Duke, and Count, each with his mesnie.
> (*Chanson d'Antioche*, Chant i. v. 796.)

THE CRUSADES

Each of these contingents acted in isolation, under the direction of its feudal head, whose standard it followed.

Thus they arrived at Constantinople in little groups, each of which reproduced the picture of the fief they had left. The baron who commanded it was in his turn united to another more important lord only by the feudal ties which might exist between them. In the plains of Syria, in Palestine, the army of the Crusaders will represent a bit of feudal France transported to the East, with its forms, its constitution, its hierarchy. From this will come its weakness for concerted movements, but also its power of resistance and its indestructible cohesion.

The old knights who had already warred with the Saracens in Spain, beyond the mountains, the authentic heroes of the *chansons de geste*, were already vested with a special esteem among their companions-in-arms :

> They have beards whiter than the flowers of the field,
> Below their helmets appear
> Their grey hairs. . . .
> . . . .
> These are the good knights of old,
> Who conquered Spain by their valour.
> (*Chanson d'Antioche*, Chant viii. v. 311–13, 334–35.)

Among the number were to be seen Thomas de Marle, lord of Coucy, Clarembaud de Vendeuil, Guillaume le Charpentier.

Mounted on their swift chargers these knights of ours have the classical equipment of the feudal baron :

> Armed with hauberks and helmets and quartered shields,
> Lances they have strong and straight, with folded gonfalons ;
> Silver and pure gold shine bright in their shields,
> And in their hauberks and helmets steel and iron shine.
> (*Chanson d'Antioche*, Chant viii. v. 242.)

The army of Crusaders is under the direction of one person whose rôle has not been made sufficiently clear, the Papal Legate, Adhémar de Monteil, Bishop of Puy. Let us not deceive ourselves : Adhémar de Monteil, at the head of this feudal France which has been transported to the East, represents an authority comparable to that of the King at the pinnacle of the feudal France which stays at home ; a moral authority, of a character at the same time religious and military,

THE MIDDLE AGES

and which has as its principal function to maintain union and concord, to perform the work of justice and pacification. For Adhémar de Monteil at the head of the Crusaders is as much " baron " as prelate, just as the King, as we have seen, is as much prelate as baron. Adhémar de Monteil is the Archbishop Turpin of the epic poems :

> The Bishop of Puy was brave and eloquent;
> When the service was over from church he turned,
> As fast as he could to his dwelling he went;
> With wonderful arms was he that day equipped,
> He put on a hauberk of beaten metal
> And laced his helmet studded with gems,
> His spurs to his feet he fixed
> And girt the sword to his left side.
>
> (*Chanson d'Antioche*, Chant viii. v. 1.)

Adhémar de Monteil was the real leader of the first Crusade. The moral authority which placed him at the head of the confederation of French lords was reinforced in him by a vigorous intelligence, an energetic character, and a marvellous gift of organization. Especially in all questions of provisioning, which became so redoubtable, so agonizing, he rendered the greatest service. When he dies at Antioch on the 1st August 1098, the lords, in the necessity in which they stand of filling his place, are to elect the Bishop of Martorano (a city in the Kingdom of Naples).

Such then were the leaders of the first Crusade : the Bishop of Puy, then, after his death (1st August 1098), the Bishop of Martorano, up to the time when, at Jerusalem, Godfrey de Bouillon will be chosen Baron of the Holy Sepulchre.

Foucher de Chartres describes the Crusaders encamped under the walls of the Greek capital : " Our tents were set up within sight of the town, and we rested during fourteen days from our fatigues. We could not go into the town ; the Emperor would not allow it ; he was afraid we should do some damage there. We were obliged to buy the necessities of life each day outside the walls. The inhabitants brought these provisions to us by order of the Emperor."

The French and the Byzantines did not trust one another. The latter were afraid of being plundered and ravaged ; the former feared poison or betrayal. The Western knights seemed

THE CRUSADES

gross brutal creatures to the subjects of the Emperor Alexius, who on their side were regarded by the Westerners as knaves and cowards.

The ends pursued by France on the one side and by Greece on the other were, moreover, not identical. Alexius Comnenus had only appealed to the Crusaders in the hope of destroying the Turks, who were becoming formidable to him, and of extending his Empire; while the French intended only to fight for the Faith and to remain masters of the conquered territories.

Penetrating into Asia Minor, the Crusaders advanced as far as the walls of Nicæa, the siege of which they began (15th May 1097). The different army corps were united there, and it appears that they may have recognized for some time the military authority of Boémond, the Prince of Tarento.

Foucher de Chartres estimates the army of the Crusaders at 100,000 men-at-arms, without counting the servants, the archers, and the swarm of clerics, besides women and children : 600,000 souls come from the West would, according to this, be united in the Knights' Crusade. These figures are, perhaps, exaggerated.

It was a regular siege : machines were constructed ; ballistas and stone-throwers beat upon the walls ; the ramparts were mined. But the Turks were skilful in shooting. With iron hooks attached to ropes they hooked up the bodies of the assailants who had fallen at the foot of the walls, and then, with the help of catapults, flung these corpses on the Christians. Provisions were brought to the besieging army in vessels which the Emperor Alexius sent from Constantinople. On the glaucous sea their sails, with daylight shining through them, were the colour of the setting sun. The town was taken on the 19th June 1097 ; it was occupied by the Greek troops. After this the French could grant themselves a little repose, by which they profited to renew their equipment.

On the 27th June they resumed their march eastward.

The Turkish horsemen, on their agile steeds, appeared suddenly, hovered round them, enveloped them. They deafened them with their cries and the noise of their drums.

> They give forth a noise like chained dogs.
> (*Chanson d'Antioche.*)

111

THE MIDDLE AGES

They launched darts and fought while fleeing, drawing their bows on those who pursued them.

A considerable army, led by the Emir Suleiman to the help of the Turks besieged in Nicæa, met the Crusaders in the Plain of Dorylæum (1st July 1097). The Turks, according to the estimate of Foucher de Chartres, numbered 360,000, all on horseback and armed with bow and arrows. Several of the chief French leaders, Godfrey de Bouillon, Raymond, Count of Toulouse, Hugh the Great, Count of Vermandois, the brother of the King of France, had left the main army with their men. Boémond, who was in command on this journey, displayed there the qualities of a great soldier. The Turks began the attack with furious cries, raining on the Crusaders a shower of arrows. Boémond supported his men with rare energy; but, in spite of his efforts, the Christians, for whom this was a war of a quite new kind, were wavering, when Godfrey de Bouillon and Hugh the Great arrived at the head of their contingents. Prelates and priests, vested in white albs, went about among the ranks of the combatants. They heard the confessions of the wounded. The Mohammedans yielded. The Christians pushed their attack. The Turks fled over mountain and valley, and they still fled terror-stricken long after the French had ceased to pursue them.

The Crusaders continued their march on Antioch, traversing Lesser Armenia, where everything had been devastated by the Turks.

From their first encounters Turks and French learned to appreciate each other. "The French themselves," writes Guibert de Nogent, "recognized that they had not seen any race of men which could be compared to that of the Turks for shrewdness of mind and courage in the fight; and further, when the Turks began to fight against them, the French were nearly reduced to despair by the astonishment which the arms used by their adversaries caused them, weapons of which our people had no knowledge. The French could not have imagined the extreme dexterity of their adversaries in the handling of horses and the promptitude with which they avoided the attacks and the blows of their enemies, having the habit of fighting and discharging their arrows in the act of fleeing.

THE CRUSADES

On their side the Turks regard themselves as having the same origin as the French, and think that military superiority belongs of right to these two people among all nations."

The Crusaders crossed the Taurus and set out for Antioch by way of Cilicia. They had to cross burning plains. They were not clothed for such expeditions. Under an implacable sun, how their thick leather tunics plated with scales of brass weighed them down. They suffered from thirst; their horses perished along the route; at certain stopping-places soldiers died in hundreds.

"Then," writes Foucher, "you would have laughed, or wept perhaps, to see some of our men, for want of horses, put their possessions in packages on the backs of sheep, goats, pigs, and dogs, clothes, food, or other necessities of the journey. The backs of the poor beasts were rasped by the friction of the packages. And knights-at-arms were seen riding on oxen."

"By desert and roadless ways," writes Guibert on his side, "the Christians entered an uninhabited country, impracticable and devoid of water. They had no other resource to alleviate their sufferings than some cloves of garlic with which they rubbed their lips."

"And you would see many cemeteries in the fields and woods along the roads made from the tombs of our Crusaders" (Foucher de Chartres).

But faith and the strong feudal discipline bore up the army. They spoke the most diverse languages, for there were there Frenchmen, Flemings, Frisians, Welsh, Bretons, men of Lorraine, of the Rhine, Normans, Scottish, English, Aquitanians, Italians, Iberians, Dacians, Greeks, and Armenians. "But if we were divided by so many tongues, we were none the less united in the love of God" (Foucher de Chartres).

It was through the leaders that division was to slip in. They grew jealous of each other. The conquests which each hoped to make created rivalries among them. Towards the end of September, Baldwin of Boulogne, the brother of Godfrey de Bouillon, and Tancred, Duke of Pouille, followed by their contingents, separated themselves from the main army, and penetrated beyond the Taurus into the country of the Armenians, where they besieged and took Tarsus.

THE MIDDLE AGES

It had been agreed among the Crusaders that the conquered towns should belong to him among the leaders whose banner should first float over it. Tancred planted his "silken gonfalon" on the walls of Tarsus:

> Baldwin has seen it and his heart is angry;
> That day he did a deed of great reproach:
> He bade a friend take down the banner
> And hoisted his own, bordered with gold.
>
> (*Chanson d'Antioche*, Chant iii. v. 317.)

Tancred, furious, wished to march against Baldwin at the head of his contingents. Richard the Pilgrim takes the part of Tancred; while Foucher de Chartres says he is wrong. Under the influence of Boémond, Prince of Tarento, the two rivals were reconciled.

Similar dissensions will be renewed after the taking of Antioch between Boémond and Raimond de Saint-Gilles. To appease them, the suzerain authority of Adhémar de Monteil, and after him of his successor, the Bishop of Martorano, is brought into play.

The Crusading army reached Antioch on the 20th October 1097. In the town was a considerable garrison of Mohammedans. Antioch was defended by its natural position, by the Orontes, by its situation on the side of the mountain, which its walls, reinforced by 450 towers, enclosed with a girdle of stone. The French pitched their tents at a little distance from the ramparts and attacked the place furiously. They came very soon on both sides to acts of the greatest ferocity. The Christians managed to capture some Turks:

> They cut off their heads, and fix them to poles
> And have them set up in the fields. . . .
>
> (v. 618.)

Mournful ornaments under the eyes of the besieged! The Crusaders took prisoner the nephew of the Emir Jagi-Sian, who was defending the town:

> They have cut off the head of the nephew of Jagi-Sian;
> And thrown it within the city from a mangonel.
>
> (*Chanson d'Antioche*, Chant v. v. 409.)

Distinguished among the Crusaders by their pitiless cruelty were those whom Richard the Pilgrim calls "the people of

THE CRUSADES

King Tafur ": a ribald mob of vagrants, but with an exalted faith and a courage proof against everything. These "ribalds" were placed under the high command of Boémond. "King Tafur," assisted by Peter the Hermit, exercised an immediate authority over them. Richard the Pilgrim paints them in picturesque terms :

> They carried with them neither lance nor sword,
> But two-edged weapons ground and weighted with lead.
> The King (Tafur) carries a scythe, well tempered.
> Well he leads his serried company:
> They have bags tied to their necks by plaited cords,
> Their sides are bare and their stomachs empty,
> Their knees are burnt brown, their shoes broken;
> By whatever country they pass they greatly spoil the land.
>
> (*Chanson d'Antioche*, Chant viii., the part preserved by Richard the Pilgrim, v. 87.)

The siege dragged on. Where were provisions to be got in these wasted or desert countries? Famine, and the arrows of the Saracens were scattering death. The privations were so great that some Crusaders deserted the camp; their energy was exhausted; they wanted to get back to their own country. And, among these fugitives, people saw one day with astonishment Peter the Hermit himself; he was fleeing with one of the most redoubted leaders of the army, William, Viscount of Melun, called le Charpentier (the Carpenter). "He was so called," observes a chronicler, "not because he was skilful in cutting wood, but because, in the fight, he struck out like a carpenter." The soldiers of Tancred caught up with the fugitives.

The chroniclers state that le Charpentier passed the whole night lying on the ground in Boémond's tent. The Prince of Tarento wanted to put him to death; but several of the chief Crusaders begged that he might be spared: "I would willingly consent," replied Boémond, "if he swore from the bottom of his heart not to abandon again the holy pilgrimage." Le Charpentier took the oath, as well as Peter the Hermit—an oath which Peter was to keep; but le Charpentier fled away some months later and could not be retaken.

The famine among the French became more and more terrible. They fed on grass, bark, and roots; they ate their horses, their donkeys, their camels, their dogs, and even rats and mice. They devoured the leather straps and thongs of the harnessings of their horses. As a climax of misery their tents were in rags, rotting and torn; many of them had no shelter but the vault of heaven. Some atrocious scenes are described with a singular vigour by Richard the Pilgrim and by Graindor of Douai:

The lord Peter the Hermit sat before his tent,
To him came Tafur and many of his people.
He had more than a thousand swollen with hunger.
" Sir, counsel me, for holy Charity,
For see, we die of hunger and wretchedness."
And my lord Peter replied: " It is through your cowardice.
Go take these Turks who lie there dead,
Cooked and salted they will be good to eat."
And says King Tafur: " It is truth you say."
From the tent of Peter he turns away and has summoned his ribalds;
They were more than ten thousand when together assembled.
The Turks they flayed and their entrails removed,
By boiling and roasting they cooked the flesh;
Thus they ate but tasted no bread.
By this were the Pagans much affrighted,
For the scent of the flesh reached to the ramparts.
Twenty thousand Pagans watched the ribalds;
There was no single Turk who did not weep.
(Chanson d'Antioche, Chant v. v. 4.)

The "ribalds" said to one another: " Why, it is Shrove Tuesday. This Turk's flesh is better than bacon or ham in oil." And when they no longer found in the fields Saracens' bodies to flay, they went to dig for them in the cemetery.

And went to the cemeteries and dug up the bodies;
All together they piled them in a heap,
The decomposed they threw into the Orentes,
The others flayed and dried in the wind.

The lords of the army come to have a look at this terrible banquet, Robert Short Hose and Boémond, Tancred and Godfrey de Bouillon.

Each stopped before King Tafur,
Laughing they ask him: " How do you feel? "
"By my faith," said the King, "I am much restored;
If only I had wherewith to drink, I have eaten enough."
Said the Duke of Bouillon: " Sir King, you shall have it."
Of his good wine he gave him a bottle.
(Chanson d'Antioche, Chant v. v. 61.)

THE CRUSADES

The worst instincts awoke under the prick of sharp misery. "If it happened," says Guibert, "that some one from the army went a little too far from the camp, and another of the same army happened to meet him alone, the one would put the other to death to rifle him."

At last, on the 3rd June (1098), the Christians took the town, thanks to one of the besieged, an Armenian named Firouz, whom Boémond had managed to seduce. He enabled twenty of the French to mount the ramparts at night by means of ropes; and these soon drew forty more up to them. They opened the gates and, to the cries of " God wills it ! " the Crusaders burst into Antioch, where they set themselves to massacre the infidels with fierce conviction.

The joy of the Christians as masters of Antioch was of short duration. On the 15th June, Kerboga, the Emir of Mossoul, appeared in sight of the town with an immense army —500,000 or 600,000 men, if one can believe the accounts; he would have saved Antioch if he had not stopped three weeks at the siege of Edessa, where Baldwin was shut up. In Antioch the Turks had consumed or destroyed all provisions. Kerboga intercepted the communications of the Crusaders with the sea, so that they could only have their supplies replenished by the vessels of the Emperor Alexius. The French army is besieged in its turn, and very soon the horrors of famine are felt anew, aggravated by the horrors of the plague. Some of the Crusaders found nourishment in the blood of their horses, which they sucked from the veins. And the desertions recommenced. Those who, weary of so much suffering, gave up the Crusade to try and get back to their homes, escaped by night, by means of ropes, with the help of which they slid down to the foot of the ramparts. Hence the name of "funambulists"— from the Latin *funambulus,* rope dancer—which was soon applied to them. Among them was one of the lords of highest birth in the army, Stephen, Count of Blois, who got back to France.

Faith sustained the courage of the besieged, fortified by visions and mystic dreams; and then the finding of the Holy Lance, which had pierced the side of Christ, discovered on the 14th June 1098 through the information of a Provençal priest,

Peter Barthélémy, restored courage to all. This marvellous episode is related by witnesses of the Crusade by the writer of the *Gestes*, by an anonymous account published by Bongars and by Raymond d'Aguilers. According to them Christ and Saint Andrew appeared three times to Peter Barthélémy, to inform him of the place in which, under the altar of the Church of St. Peter at Antioch, the Holy Lance should be found. Search was made according to the indications of the priest, and the precious relic came to light. There was great joy and enthusiasm. The resolution was taken to make an armed sortie from the town and to march against Kerboga. Visibly supported by the intervention of Heaven, could the Crusaders prove other than invincible ? It was now that, for the first time, the Crusaders gave themselves a captain. The choice of the army leaders fell on Boémond, Prince of Tarento. Moreover, the command was only put in his hands for a period of fifteen days.

This Boémond, the son of the able Robert Guiscard, was the very type of a feudal knight : with the figure of a Hercules, his hair worn very short on the forehead, he had square fists and a square head with greyish eyes set wide apart. He seems to have surpassed his companions-in-arms in his knowledge of war ; he was clever at posting the combatants at strategic points and getting them to perform manœuvres at the right moment. He held himself during an action behind the army with a reserve of picked soldiers, following with his eye the movements of the troops and ready to intervene at the proper moment.

Before coming to blows, on the 27th June (1098) Boémond sent five messengers to Kerboga to tell him to retire. At their head was Peter the Hermit, who spoke to the Emir with a passion and authority which could not fail to impress the Saracen ; but Kerboga recovered himself and replied that the French had their choice between conversion to the Crescent or death.

They gave battle on the 28th June. The Crusaders were in a pitiable state of dilapidation ; some of them were almost naked. The majority of the knights were on foot ; others were mounted on donkeys or camels, but they were animated by an ardour which doubled their strength.

THE CRUSADES

The description of the battle of Antioch by Richard the Pilgrim and Graindor of Douai is worthy of being given in its entirety. Richard was an onlooker. His story is animated with an epic inspiration. The Christians issue from Antioch and cross the Orontes to give battle to Kerboga.

The wives of the Crusaders themselves are to take part in the action.

> The ladies who went to serve our Lord
> Ran to the hotels (of Antioch) to seize weapons,
> They tie their veils over their heads to shield them from the wind,
> Many collect stones in their sleeves (to throw at the Saracens),
> Others fill bottles with fresh water.
> (*Chanson d'Antioche*, Chant viii. v. 482.)

The battle opens violently; the Tafurs do wonders. Armed with his staff hooped with iron, Peter the Hermit gives the death-blow to every Saracen he can reach. The knights about to die strike their breasts in confession of sin and swallow tufts of grass to simulate the sacred host. Epic scenes !

The author of the *Gestes*, who took part in the action, writes as follows : " Innumerable masses of warriors were seen coming down from the mountains mounted on white horses and preceded by white banners. Our men could not imagine who these warriors could be; but at last they realized that it was a succouring army sent by Christ and commanded by St. George, St. Mercurius, and St. Demetrius." The good chronicler adds : " This is no lie : many saw it."

The great majority of the Turks were massacred : their camp with abundant supplies fell into the hands of the Christians, who were henceforth masters of the whole of Syria.

There can be no doubt that the finding of the Lance gave to the Crusaders their enthusiasm and ensured their victory It is to be noted that the prelates in the army, and notably Adhémar de Monteil, did not give credence to the revelation From the first they suspected a fraud. The soldiers, on the contrary, particularly Raymond of Toulouse, to whom Peter Barthélémy was chaplain, gave it absolute credence. Eight months went by and the discussions between the partisans of the two opposing views went on with such bitterness that, to make an end of it, they forced Barthélémy to undergo the ordeal by fire. This was at the siege of Irkha, the 8th April 1099. The unfortunate priest had to pass through some burning bushes.

Hardly had the Christians seen him emerge from the fire, than they gave forth loud shouts of enthusiasm. They hurled themselves upon him, snatching from his body his clothes in rags, and pulling out his hair as relics. The Count of Toulouse took the poor priest in his arms and carried him home with him; but he had been frightfully burnt in passing through the flames, and died of his wounds two days later. "Those who, for the honour and love of God, had venerated the lance," says Foucher de Chartres, "ceased, reluctantly, to believe in it. Count Raymond kept it for a long time, until he lost it, I know not how."

The happy effect had been, none the less, produced.

The road to Jerusalem was open. The Holy Land had once more changed masters. The Fatimites of Egypt, driven from Palestine twenty years before by the Turks, had made haste to profit by the embarrassments created by the landing of the Crusaders, in recovering their lost territories, and they had just re-entered Jerusalem (August to September 1098).

The Crusaders were again arrested in their march by the siege of Marra. Here the horrors of famine reappeared. And this was to be the case every time the great Crusading army remained in a fixed place. The provisions which the country could offer were exhausted in a few days and the terrors of famine reappeared.

Peter the Hermit went about among the Crusaders making unceasing efforts to alleviate their suffering. He was invested with functions best suited to him, those of treasurer of the poor.

After having been detained some time still at the siege of Irkha, where, as we have just said, Barthélémy suffered the ordeal by fire, the French arrived in sight of Jerusalem—on the 1st July 1099—three years after their departure!

How describe their transports at the sight of the Holy City? "The pilgrims forgot their fatigues," writes Albert d'Aix, "and hastened their steps. Arriving before the walls, they burst into tears."

THE CRUSADES

A number of Crusaders, however, forgot the vow they had made, not to approach the town except with bare feet.

" It was the custom among us," writes Raymond d'Aguilers, " that whoever should first enter a fortress or village and plant his banner there should become its master, and none of those who came after him should dispute his possession of it." So during the last night a considerable number of Crusaders set out in advance to go and occupy the mountain region and the districts bordering the river Jordan. Small was the number of whose who, preferring to conform to the commands of God, advanced towards Jerusalem barefooted."

The town was surrounded by a formidable rampart. There were no resources for a siege. The bed of the Cedron was dried up; the reservoirs were covered over. Once more the admirable character of the popular part of the army showed of what exploits it was capable.

They gathered together all the wood they could find in the places around, and made from it a great number of ladders. On the seventh day of the siege, at dawn, while the horns were sounding, the ladders were put up against the walls, and with a sublime enthusiasm the French threw themselves into the assault. Vain efforts! From the top of the ramparts sorcerers were casting incantations on the French; but it is not to their sorceries that we attribute the check of this first attack: the walls were too high. The besiegers had to give up the idea of capturing the town by escalade. And they set to work to construct machines and wooden towers the height of the rampart. But with what difficulty! for the wood had to be carried far.

The town was taken on the 15th July. The Saracens, writes Foucher de Chartres, had attached two beams to the top of the walls and used them as rams to repel the assailants. But what they had done for defence turned to their injury. The wooden tower having been brought up to the wall, they managed to cut the ropes from which the beams hung, and these became a bridge leading from the top of the tower to the top of the ramparts. The torches flung by the besiegers set fire to the wooden citadel on the wall, and the fire took such proportions that the defenders could not stay there. On the

THE MIDDLE AGES

Friday, about nine o'clock in the morning, the first to put his foot on the rampart, planting there the standard of the Cross, was one Leuthold. The Saracens fled through the narrow streets. Many took refuge in the Temple of Solomon. The building was full of them and even the roof was covered. The Crusaders made of them a frightful carnage; blood filled the Temple a foot high, and the Mohammedans who had taken refuge on the roof were, for the most part, killed by arrows; the remainder were thrown from this height to the ground, where the heads and bones of these unfortunates were broken.

The extermination was complete; women and children, all were slaughtered. In the streets were seen piles of heads and severed feet and hands. Many of these unhappy wretches, and many women, were killed with horrible refinements of cruelty. And everything was given over to plunder. The Crusaders soon noticed that some Saracens had swallowed " besans "—or, to put it better, Byzantine gold pieces—to save them from their conquerors: they set themselves then to split open their abdomens and search among the entrails to get out the pieces of gold; then as this process proved too slow for them, they piled up the corpses on immense pyres and burned them up. The Crusaders, stooping, searched among the ashes for the golden " besans."

They were enabled by the indications of a Syrian to find a piece of the true Cross. The French enclosed it in a case of gold and silver, and the precious relic was carried in procession to the Temple.

On the 22nd July 1099, eight days after the capture of Jerusalem, Duke Godfrey de Bouillon was proclaimed Baron of the Holy Sepulchre. The pious knight refused the title of King: he was unwilling to wear a crown of gold when the Son of God, the King of Kings, had worn a crown of thorns. And one can truly say of the choice made by the Crusaders that it had fallen on the most worthy. The nobility of his race, writes Foucher de Chartres, his military courage, his gentleness, patience, and modesty, marked him out for the suffrages of the army.

The French were still in the intoxication of triumph when they learnt, at the beginning of August, of the arrival of a

THE CRUSADES

great army commanded by the Fatimite Caliph of Egypt. It was made up of Ethiopians and Bedouin hordes. A new victory under the walls of Ascalon (12th August 1099) assured definitely to the Franks the Empire of Palestine.

This first Crusade had cost the lives of 500,000 or 600,000 men.

The Kingdom of Jerusalem was then placed under the rule of Godfrey de Bouillon, who took the humble title of Advocate of the Holy Sepulchre.

Baldwin, Godfrey's brother, was proclaimed Count of Odessa; Boémond, the Prince of Tarento, received the principality of Antioch; finally Bertrand, the son of Raymond of Toulouse, was before long made Count of Tripoli.

This Frank empire, so suddenly set up on the borders of Asia Minor, was moreover very quickly organized. The army of Crusading knights had not ceased to be organized after the feudal manner with the framework and organization we have described in France. This same organization was established *en bloc* on the slopes of Lebanon. The coast towns developed a prosperous life in consequence of the relations established with the West; pilgrims to the Holy Places became more and more numerous; finally, the Orders, half religious, half military, the Templars and the Hospitallers, were founded to defend the conquest.

Peter the Hermit returned to Europe in 1099 or 1100. He was loaded with relics. He founded a monastery in the suburbs of Huy, near Liège, where he died with the title of Prior on the 8th July 1115. Those of the other Crusaders who returned home also prided themselves on a precious booty. Returning from a later Crusade, Count Arnold of Guînes will be carrying hung from his neck in a little silver reliquary a hair from the beard of Jesus Christ. Before long there will be exposed to the devotion of the Faithful some milk of the Virgin, and in a little phial of opaque glass a little of the "darkness" which formed one of the ten plagues of Egypt.

During a century and a half, Crusades are to succeed one another; but there will not be seen again the splendid popular enthusiasm of the Crusade of Urban II and Peter the Hermit.

Saint Bernard, the eloquent Abbot of Clairvaux, will preach

THE MIDDLE AGES

a new Crusade, no longer to the masses of the people, but to prelates and Kings. From this moment these distant expeditions change character and become a question of individual and royal faith, and at the same time of sovereign authority and administration; which will not be able to replace the invincible enthusiasm of the common faith or give feudal cohesion to the armies which had lost it. From one Crusade to another—there were still seven of them—their decline is manifested. Popes, kings, knights are still interested in them; they are proclaimed in brilliant tournaments in which vows to ladies, with the peacock or golden pheasant, mingle with oaths to God and the Apostles: the mass of the people hold themselves aloof from them.

The first Crusade had the greatest influence on the social transformation which had become a necessity in France at the end of the eleventh century. We have seen how the feudal lord had played out his part. After having been of a utility which cannot be sufficiently emphasized, his activity was becoming injurious. A great part of this bellicose aristocracy passed over to the East; it perished or founded new fiefs there.

To meet the expenses of the Crusade a number of lords had sold their domains and pledged their lands. Their wives, left in the castles, are in great distress.

> We have great need of gain,
> For, by God, there is within neither gold nor silver,
> We are eaten up by usury and tortured by creditors.
> (*Baudoin de Sebourg*, Chant xviii. v. 628.)

Philip I profited greatly from this distress. We see him buying Bourges for 60,000 sous from Eude Arpin, who set out to the conquest of the Holy Land with Gozlin de Courtenay and Milo de Bray. This process was repeated again and again. In the absence of powerful vassals the King insinuated his authority in their domains. More and more the monarchy tends to become national.

Sources.—Bongars, *Gesta Dei per Francos*, 1612, 2 vols.; Michaud, *Bibliothèque des Croisades*, 1829, 4 vols. (the fourth volume includes the Arab chronicles, translated by Reinaud); *Collection de l'histoire des Croisades*, published by the Acad. des Inscriptions, since 1841; *Publications of the Société de l'Orient latin*, Paris and Geneva, since 1876.

THE CRUSADES

The most interesting chroniclers to read on the First Crusade are Guibert de Nogent; the anonymous author of the *Gesta Francorum*, doubtless a Norman of Italy; Foucher de Chartres; Raymond d'Aguilers, Canon of Puy; Albert d'Aix; Baudri de Bourgueil, Archbishop of Dol; the Monk of St. Riem de Reims; Pierre Tudebode, priest of Civray, in Poitou; finally, the account by Anna Comnenus, the daughter of the Emperor Alexius, in the *Alexiade*, the history of her father's reign.

In spite of his great reputation, William of Tyre does not represent an original source.

La Chanson d'Antioche, ed. P. Paris, 1848, 2 vols.; *Les Chansons de Croisades*, with their tunes, ed. Bédier and Aubry; *Assises du royaume de Jerusalem*, published by Beugnol in the *Collection de l'histoire des Croisades*, 1841–43.

HISTORICAL WORKS.—Sybel, *Gesch. des ersten Kreuzzüges*, 2nd ed., 1881; Kugler, *Gesch. der Kreuzzüge*, 2nd ed., 1891; Röricht, *Gesch. der Kreuzzüge im Unriss*, 1898; Prutz, *Kulturgesch. der Kreuzzüge*, 1883; Hagenmeyer, *Le vrai et le faux Pierre l'Ermite*, translated by Furcy-Raynaud, 1883; L. Brehier, *L'Eglise et l'Orient au Moyen Age*, 2nd ed., 1907; Gaston Dodu, *Histoire des Institutions monarchiques dans le royaume latin de Jerusalem, 1099–1291*, 1894; F. Chalandon, *Essai sur le règne d'Alexis 1er Comnène*, 1900.

CHAPTER VI

A JUSTICIARY IN ARMOUR: LOUIS LE GROS

Picture of Louis le Gros. His struggle against the "hobereaux" in their stone keeps. Stephen de Garlande, seneschal and chancellor. His fall in 1127. The government of the Abbot Suger. The Abbey of St. Denis the cradle of Gothic Art. The Oriflamme. Rising of the nation at the summons of Louis VI. The Germans beat a retreat. The murder of Charles the Good, Count of Flanders. Louis le Gros has William Clito appointed his successor. Conflicts with England. Henry Beauclerc marries his daughter to Geoffrey le Bel, heir of the Count of Anjou. Death of Louis le Gros.

THE progress which the Crusades ensured to the royal power was still going on at the accession of Louis VI.

He succeeded his father, Philip I, who had died towards the end of July 1108. In fact he was ruling from the beginning of the twelfth century.

He was born in 1081.

Louis VI, called le Gros, was of powerful stature. He had a slim figure; but with advancing age he became so stout that towards fifty it was only with difficulty that he heaved himself up on horseback, and he was obliged, according to the chroniclers, to keep himself "upright" in bed, which means, no doubt, that he was obliged to keep a sitting position.

His face was livid, with such a striking pallor that it was attributed to an attempt at poisoning made on him in his youth by Bertrade, his stepmother. Ordericus Vitalis, who saw him at the Council of Reims (October 1119), describes him as follows: "He was eloquent, big, pale, and fat." Suger, the Abbot of St. Denis, boasts his merry humour. "So amiable and good," says Suger, "as to appear stupid." Add to these characteristics a devouring activity, "even though the weight of his paunch might have kept him in bed."

A JUSTICIARY IN ARMOUR

This prince, who did so much for the common people, for artisans and peasants, was above all a soldier. Follow him along the steep roads, furrowed with swamps, bordered by thickets and quickset hedges, on his strong charger. He has on his head an egg-shaped helmet of burnished brass; his broad shoulders wear a hooded tunic of leather plaited with iron rings, and he holds in his vigorous hand a large sword whose golden pommel encloses a tooth of St. Denis. Rising with the dawn, he is indefatigable in imposing justice and peace. " You would have seen the noble youth riding through the country with as many knights as he could collect, at one hour in the marches of Berry, at another in the marches of Auvergne, and none the less soon in the Vexin when there was need" (*Grandes Chroniques*).

We have see how the feudal nobles, after having organized their own domains in paternal fashion, spread themselves abroad outside them in repeated violences. They knew no other occupation than the redoubtable game of arms, and continued to practise it ; were they not

> the rich barons of France
> Who desire war more than a youth his love ?
> (*Graindor de Douai*.)

Supported by his peasants and his militia of burgesses, by the knights who were his immediate vassals, and by the soldiery furnished by the Abbey of St. Denis, Louis VI reduced in turn the turbulent lords of Coucy, of Montmorency, of Corbeil, and of Mantes, and tried to destroy their keeps. These keeps, says Suger, planted in the heart of the Ile-de-France, " were disembowelling " the King (*regem eviscerabant*).

In attacking the castles, Louis was seen in the front rank like the bravest of his soldiers. At the siege of the castle occupied by Dreux, Count of Mouchy-le-Châtel, he had succeeded in enticing the redoubtable baron with his men out of the enclosure ; then suddenly facing about, he led on his own men, and striking right and left, jostling the besieged, he penetrates with his followers into the interior courts. The castle is in flames ; but in the midst of the flames he pursues his attack, easily distinguished by his herculean strength and his tall figure. In the heat of the fight he is bathed in perspiration, and in cooling down he develops a hoarseness which it will take a long time to cure. After this, Louis makes his appearance in the district of Bourges, where Aimon II, called Vaire-Vache, has taken possession of the castle of Germigny-sur-Aubois, belonging to his nephew Archambaut de Bourbon. From the fortress Aimon and his men spread over the neighbouring country, ravaging it. The King's troops surrounded the place. Aimon saw no salvation except in the royal mercy. " He had no other resource," says Suger, " than to go and throw himself at the King's feet. Louis kept the castle and took Aimon to the Ile-de-France, to be tried by the lords of his Court." " Thus," says Suger, " the King put an end by dint of fatigue and money to the hardships and oppression which a great number of people had had to endure. He formed after this the habit of making often, and always with the same clemency, such expeditions."

Tragic and splendid was the siege of Meung-sur-Loire (1103). The royal troops had made themselves masters of the fortifications. The keep, in which the defenders had taken refuge, was threatened by the flames; then the besieged, to the number of sixty, threw themselves after their lord, from the top of the tower, to the ground, where those who were not killed by the fall were pierced by the lances or the arrows of the besiegers.

The famous expedition against the Château du Puiset took place in 1111. The Château du Puiset, in Beauce, had been built by Queen Constance for the defence of the country. The castellans who had been installed there had soon begun to act like masters. Hugh du Puiset devastated the country and its inhabitants, conducting himself like a mere bandit " He was handsome," says Ordericus Vitalis, " but wicked."

Suger applies to him the verse of Lucan :

> Et docilis Sullam sceleris vicisse magistrum.
> (Anxious to surpass Sulla, master of crime.)
> (*Pharsale*, liv. i. v. 326.)

He killed with his own hands the seneschal, Ansel de Garlande. Louis summoned an assembly at Melun, in which complaints abounded against the " devouring wolf " : these are Suger's expressions. The King took as the base of his operations the monastery of Toury, in Beauce, near Joinville,

A JUSTICIARY IN ARMOUR

of which Suger was Abbot. And we are about to see the man of religion acting as a soldier.

By order of the King, Suger put into the abbey a large garrison and established there dépôts of arms and ammunition. When all is ready the King arrives with his men. Hugh du Puiset refuses to open the gates of his lair. There follows a siege in due form. Suger gives us a description of it, unfortunately too literary. The besieged showered projectiles on those who were pressing them on all sides. To replace their broken shields, the men covered themselves with planks, boards, blinds, and doors. We had had, writes the Abbot of St. Denis, several carts filled with a great quantity of dry wood, mixed with fat and coagulated blood, so as to furnish ready food for the flames and to burn these unhappy " devotees of the devil." These carts, having been set on fire, were pushed against the castle. But it was formidably defended. Swift horsemen rode up and down the surrounding roads giving the death-blow to those who tried to approach. The hope of carrying the place seemed gone, when a priest was seen, bareheaded, without a helmet to protect his brow, with no weapon but a wretched plank, climbing up the escarpment and arriving at the palisade of the first enclosure. Hiding himself under the shelters which were fitted to the loopholes, he begins to tear away its stakes. Seeing his attempt succeed, he signs to those who remain hesitating below. At his call a handful of assailants throw themselves against the palisade; it is torn away. Hugh and the principal defenders of the place take refuge in the keep, where the proud baron soon capitulates.

The King imprisoned him in the tower of Château-Landon; he put up for sale the furnishings and treasures of Puiset, whose towers and walls were rased to the ground, " which filled with joy," says Ordericus Vitalis, " the peasants of the neighbourhood and travellers."

In 1128 Hugh du Puiset set out for the Holy Land, where he acted like a brave soldier and founded the glorious dynasty of the Counts of Jaffa.

The task of Louis le Gros, for ever recurring, was the more arduous as the English King, Henry I (Beauclerc), supported the rebellious barons.

THE MIDDLE AGES

Of these feudal castles become " places of offence," Louis le Gros took or bought some ; and rendered the owners of others favourable to him. Philip I had made Guy de Montlhéry, called le Rouge (the Red), Count of Rochefort, his seneschal, an office in which the new King retained him in order to assure to himself the quiet possession of the tower of Montlhéry, as well as of the castles of Rochefort and Châteaufort. Louis had gone so far as to consent to marry the daughter of Guy le Rouge, though she was not yet of marriageable age. To Ansel and Guillaume de Garlande there succeeded Stephen de Garlande, who wielded the greatest power which had ever been found in the hands of a single royal official, since he added the functions of chancellor to those of seneschal. " How great is your power ! " the Archbishop of Tours said to him, " and what an accumulation of wealth lies in your hands ! You sit as first among the Palatines and dispose at your pleasure of all the kingdom." Stephen de Garlande has left the reputation of an adroit man, skilful in cultivating his own interests and those of his family, rather than a statesman. He was superseded in 1127 by Suger, Abbot of St. Denis. This is a new orientation of the royal Court, and it is remarkable that it should have been brought about under the rule of the most soldierly of all the kings. The clerics are to take precedence over the soldiers. Following Suger there is to be a brilliant series of Palatines : Goshuin, Bishop of Soissons ; Geoffrey, Bishop of Chartres ; Stephen, Bishop of Paris ; Bartholomew, Bishop of Laon ; Renaud, Archbishop of Reims.

Suger, the Abbot of St. Denis, was one of the greatest ministers France has ever known. He was of low birth and small stature. " Little in body and little in race," as runs the epitaph composed for him by Simon Chèvre d'Or. He was bald. His black and piercing eyes shone in an emaciated face. " What one must admire most in him," writes his biographer, the monk William of St. Denis, " is that nature should have lodged a heart so strong, so fine, so great, in a body so frail and thin."

Suger practised fasting and macerations ; his body, already so spare, was further reduced by the severest possible régime, but he had a lively, even mischievous, temperament, and, like

A JUSTICIARY IN ARMOUR

Francis of Assisi, numbered gaiety among the highest virtues. When with others he refused no kind of food and accepted wine.

"There was one of the gifts of heaven," writes a contemporary, "which was refused him: namely, the grace of becoming fatter as abbot of St. Denis than he had been as a simple monk; while others, no matter how thin they were before, no sooner hold the abbatial cross than their cheeks and stomach and even their hearts begin to put on fat."

His cell was a small room, bare and simple, in the splendid monastery which his diligent activity had enlarged and adorned. He lay there on straw covered with a coarse woollen stuff in place of sheets; but to hide his asceticism a coverlet was thrown over it during the day. And shut up in his silent cell he devoted long hours to the study of authors sacred and profane. He would recite by heart twenty, and even thirty, verses of Horace, says the monk William. He had a profound knowledge of history and could enumerate exactly the families of the princes who had ruled over France.

After these hours of reading and meditation, Suger took pleasure in giving to others, in lively discourse, the fruits of his labour. For he was a charming talker and had the attractive art of witty anecdote. Sometimes he went on with his talks into the middle of the night. He had an engaging eloquence and the gift of persuasion, and expressed himself with equal ease in French and Latin.

"I have sometimes seen," writes William again, "the King of France, surrounded by the members of his Government, standing respectfully before this great man seated on a stool; he dictating to them useful precepts as to inferiors, and they hanging on his lips, listening to his words with the deepest attention."

Suger was the happy complement of Louis VI. The King was a man of action, always ready to heave his enormous body on to the back of a big horse; eager for great blows of the sword and breathless assaults. Suger was the man for agreements, for negotiations, skilful at forming happy and harmonious settlements. "The moment disturbance showed itself in the kingdom," says his biographer, "and wars broke out,

Suger appeared as the contriver of concord, the most courageous mediator of peace."

Under his influence, and with the protection afforded by Louis VI, grateful for the education he had received there, the Abbey of St. Denis shone with an unparalleled brilliance. By its beauty and magnificence it became truly the royal abbey, the radiant centre of the history of art in the twelfth century. Builders and carpenters, workers in glass, and sculptors in stone, were summoned thither from all parts of France. We may say that, rebuilt by the efforts of Suger, St. Denis was the glorious cradle of the Gothic style in all its manifestations —architecture, sculpture, painting, the art of the worker in glass and of the goldsmith; from there it spread all over Europe. The stained-glass windows of St. Denis at once realized perfection, with their circular medallions grouped in a luminous border, with their background of a blue so fine and pure, like the azure of the heavens, in which the figures seemed to breathe. The most precious were destroyed by imbecile hands during the Revolution, but what remains still represents the perfection of this wonderful art.

The Abbot of Cluny came to visit the splendid building. "This man," he cried, speaking of Suger, "condemns us all; he builds not for himself, as we do, but for God alone."

St. Bernard, the austere Abbot of Clairvaux, however, criticised the pomp with which Suger had decorated the buildings which surrounded him, while remaining simple in his life, poor in his cell. "The monastery," he says, "is full of knights; it is open to women; business is transacted there; disputes break out; it is true that there they duly render to Cæsar that which is Cæsar's, but do they render to God that which is God's?"

It is a criticism which forms, to our minds, eloquent praise: the Abbey of St. Denis had become, under Suger, not only the home of the monk, but the living anthill which swarmed round the great statesman.

Still, Suger seems to have responded to the criticism of St. Bernard: he introduced into his abbey reforms which restored it to a simpler and more religious way of life.

"The Emperor Henry," says Suger,—he means the German

A JUSTICIARY IN ARMOUR

Emperor Henry V,—" had had for a long time at the bottom of his heart a strong resentment against the lord Louis because in his kingdom, at Reims, in full council, the lord Calixtus (the Pope) had struck him, Henry, with anathema. Before the death of the lord Pope then, this Emperor got together as big an army as he could, then by the advice of the English King Henry, whose daughter he had married, and who, on his side, was making war on the French King, he pretended to march to another point, but intended to attack unexpectedly the city of Reims."

At this news, Louis VI took from the altar of St. Denis the banner of the Counts of the Vexin. Thus, he thought, St. Denis, the patron of the Gauls, would fight among his soldiers. It was a widespread belief that the glorious martyr would never fail to come directly to the assistance of the French when the soil of their country was invaded. After having thus taken the venerated standard from the altar, Louis VI at the head of his troops hastened to meet the enemy.

The ceremony is reported in identical terms both by Suger and by a charter of Louis VI.

The famous oriflamme, for it is a question of that, was, then, originally the banner of the Counts of the Vexin, and it is by this title that the Kings of France came to take it from the altar to carry it into battle : as Counts of the Vexin the Kings of France were vassals or advocates of St. Denis. The oldest description of the oriflamme dates from the reign of Philip Augustus. It is found in the *Philippide* of William le Breton : a little banner composed of a simple silk tissue of bright red, fringed with green, and attached to a staff of silver gilt—a banner like those carried in religious processions.

Guillebert de Metz, who saw it on the altar of St. Denis, gives an exact description of it :

" Likewise the King of France alone carries the oriflamme in battle ; it is a staff all golden, to which is attached a banner of vermilion, which they have the custom of going to seek in the Church of my lord Saint Denis, with great solemnity and devotion. . . ."

" The oriflamme," says Guillebert again, " is a vermilion banner with five fringes, bordered with green tassels (not golden, as say the *chansons de geste*); it is to be carried above and higher than the royal banners. You can believe me, for I have, in my time, seen two of them on the altar of the glorious martyr, one on each side of the altar; and they had as handles two little staffs of silver gilt, from each of which hung a vermilion banner, one of which was called the banner of Charlemagne."

They had then made a replica of the oriflamme, so as to have pendants for both sides of the altar, and also no doubt so as not to expose the original too often to the perils of battle.

A final detail about the oriflamme is given to us by the monks of St. Denis: "And when he (the King) departs from the Church (of St. Denis, whence he has taken the oriflamme), he ought to go straight to the place in which he is staying, turning neither to right nor left for any other business" (*Grandes Chroniques*).

In answer to the summons of Louis le Gros against the German Emperor, people from all parts flocked round the King (August 1124). Adversaries of the dynasty like Thibaud de Chartres, hastened to get equipment and range themselves and their men under the old oriflamme. The great nobles of the kingdom ranged their troops in order of battle under the eyes of the King. The description which follows is interesting to note. It is like that of the armies on march in the *chansons de geste*, then in all their glory. One would imagine that one was reading the famous description of the "echelons" into which Charlemagne divided his army at Roncevaux. The first echelon was composed of the men of Reims and of Châlons, 60,000 horse and foot; then came those of Laon and Soissons, equal in number; the third echelon was formed by the men of Orleans, by those of Étampes, and by the Parisians, to whom were joined numerous troops of the Abbey of St. Denis. "With them," says the King, "shall I fight; they are of my household and I of theirs." So speaks Charlemagne in *Roland*. Thibaud de Chartres and Hugh de Troyes conducted the fourth division. The *Grandes Chroniques* have here a curious observation: Count Thibaud "maintained war as an ally of the King of England against King Louis; at the same time he had come, for the sake of the kingdom's need against the foreign nations." For the French of the twelfth century the German Emperor

A JUSTICIARY IN ARMOUR

was a stranger, but not the King of England, a French prince The fifth division was under the orders of Hugh the Peaceful, Duke of Burgundy, and William, Count of Nevers. The King decided that this division should form the vanguard. The excellent Count Raoul de Vermandois, cousin to the King, had arrived with his men of St. Quentin and the neighbouring country. He was the son of Hugh the Great, brother of Philip I, of that Hugh who, with Suger, was the principal adviser of Louis VI. He formed a sixth division, which Louis le Gros placed on the right wing. The inhabitants of Ponthieu, the people of Amiens and Beauvais, the seventh division, formed the left wing.

The Count of Flanders, Charles the Good, having been warned too late, had not been able to collect more than 10,000 combatants. He would have brought three times the number had he been told in time. This eighth echelon formed the rearguard.

Finally, the Duke of Aquitaine, William VII, the Count of Brittany, Conan III, and Foulque le Jeune (the Young), the bellicose Count of Anjou, displayed an ardour all the greater because the distance they had to come to join the King had not allowed them, for want of time, to collect important contingents.

And hear how these knights hold forth, like a living echo it would seem, of the epic poems and especially of the *Roland*: " Let us march with courage against the enemy; that they may not go back to their homes unpunished, they who have dared to threaten France, the suzerain of the nations. Let them expiate their arrogance, not in our country, but on their own territory—that territory which should rightfully be subject to the French, who have so often conquered it."

At the sight of such an army, which seemed to have sprung out of the earth, the German Emperor stopped in his march, overcome; then turned on his heel with all his men. " At the news of his retreat," adds Suger, " it took nothing less than the prayers of the archbishops, the bishops, and men acceptable for their piety, to prevent the French going to devastate the States of this prince."

And the great minister rightly adds that this pacific victory was more important still than if they had triumphed on the field of battle. Especially as, at this same moment, Amauri de Montfort, at the head of the contingents of the Vexin, was repulsing the English on the Norman frontier. These events of the year 1124 have made less impression in our history than the victory gained ninety years later by Philip Augustus at Bouvines; they are not less glorious.

Suger ends in a fine patriotic passage:

"Neither in modern nor in ancient times has France done anything more brilliant, or shown more gloriously to what a point the brilliance of her power can reach when her forces are assembled, than in this moment when she triumphed simultaneously over the German Emperor and the King of England."

Two years later, Louis VI was bringing to an end the war in Auvergne. It had begun in 1122. William VI, the Count of Auvergne, was persecuting Aimeri, the Bishop of Clermont, and his people. A first campaign had been marked with brilliant success. Louis VI collected in 1126 more numerous troops.

"The King had already become very fat," says Suger. "He had difficulty in carrying the thick mass of his body. Any one else, however poor they might be, would not have been willing or able, with such a physical drawback, to expose himself to the danger of mounting on horseback; but he, against the advice of his friends, gave ear only to his admirable courage, and braved the overwhelming heats of June and August, which the youngest knights could hardly bear: he made fun of those who could not accommodate themselves to the heat, though he was often forced, among the narrow ways of the marshes, to get his men to support him."

Louis laid siege to Montferrand, where the men of the Count of Auvergne had taken refuge. He conducted the siege vigorously. He had a hand cut off such of the partisans of the Count of Auvergne as he managed to capture, and had them led under the walls of the fortress, "so that they could show their comrades their severed hand reposing in that which was left." Then there appeared on the heights William, Duke of Aquitaine, at the head of numerous troops. He came to bring help to his vassal, the Count of Auvergne. But, like the German

A JUSTICIARY IN ARMOUR

Emperor, he came to a standstill impressed by the imposing aspect afforded by the royal army. And he sent a message to the King, the text of which has been preserved.

"May the grandeur of the royal Majesty not disdain to accept the homage and service of the Duke of Aquitaine or to preserve to him his rights. Justice demands that he should do you service, but he would also that you should be to him a just suzerain. The Count of Auvergne holds Auvergne from me as I hold it from you." Consequently the Duke of Aquitaine proposed to submit the difference between the Count of Auvergne and the Bishop of Clermont to the judgment of the royal Court. As a guarantee of good faith he offered hostages. These propositions were accepted by Louis after deliberation with his faithful advisers.

We have spoken in some detail of several of the points on which Louis le Gros brought his great energy to bear.

These deeds are repeated from north to south and from east to west. It was with lance in hand, on his strong war-horse, in his incessant progresses, that the great prince earned the nickname, recalled by the Minstrel of Reims in the thirteenth century, of "Louis the Justiciary," vigilant in defending the people whom the "hobereaux" destroyed, protecting the merchants who traversed the country, the religious troubled in their useful works.

However, the war against the King of England had just broken out for the third time. There were mingled with it complications in the provinces of the north. The County of Flanders depended on the French Crown. On the 2nd March 1127, the Count of Flanders, Charles of Denmark, called Charles the Good, had been assassinated by some knights of that country, inspired by William of Ypres. Behold King Louis at once on horseback, helmet on head, impatient to punish the murderers. And first of all, at Arras, he has the election of a new count made by the chief men of the country. There were many claimants. Among them were Thierry d'Alsace, William of Ypres, and Baldwin IV, Count of Hainault. Under the influence of Louis le Gros they elected William Clito, the son of the Duke of Normandy, Robert Short Hose, whom Henry Beauclerc had deprived of his Duchy. Clito was devoted to the King, whose sister-in-law, Jeanne de Montferrat, he had married. Then the King enters Flanders, where he seals charters and acts as sovereign. The murderers of Charles the Good are besieged in the tower of the church of Bruges, whence, threatened by the flames, they throw themselves to the ground. The most guilty, Bouchard and Bertold, suffered frightful punishments. Bouchard was bound to a wheel and the crows devoured him; Bertold was eaten alive by a dog, together with which they had tied him to the top of a pole. Louis returned to France. But Clito was not the statesman required by the circumstances.

The Flemish towns had already become strong and powerful. The new Count of Flanders did not recognize their interests and despised their "liberties" (*franchises*). Thierry d'Alsace was called in by the disaffected. The action of Louis le Gros was hampered by his struggle with the King of England. He ordered the burgesses of Flanders to send to him eight representatives, to come to an agreement with him over the quarrel with William Clito. The answer of the burgesses was insolent: "Let the King of France mind his own business." Louis VI got the Bishop of Tournai to lay an interdict on the churches of Flanders, and had Thierry d'Alsace excommunicated by the Archbishop of Reims. He himself advanced at the head of an army as far as Lille, in which Thierry was shut up, and laid siege to it. But William Clito, wounded at the siege of Alost, gave up the struggle and became a monk. Thierry had no longer a rival.

This is but a sketch of which the details will be defined under Philip the Fair.

The King of England, Henry I, Beauclerc, was at the same time a soldier and a proved statesman: a prince of great wisdom, says Suger, whose strength of mind and body were equally worthy of admiration.

We do not know if Suger admired likewise his cunning, his cruelty, and his avarice. He was the youngest of the sons of William the Conqueror. We will not stop to give the details of the struggle which he carried on against Louis le Gros almost without interruption for twenty-five years.

A thing which is characteristic of the fights at an epoch

when chivalry reached its climax, is the small number of deaths which they caused. For example, at the battle of Andelys (20th August 1119), which was very fierce, out of 900 knights who took part, only three were killed. " They were clad in armour. Through the fear of God, or from chivalry, the aim was to take prisoners rather than to slay. Christian soldiers do not thirst to spill blood " (Ordericus Vitalis).

The war arose from a fight for the possession of the castle of Gisors, the strategic importance of which was considerable. Henry Beauclerc added to the immense resources at his disposal the active co-operation of his nephew, Thibaud IV of Blois. On his side Louis le Gros tried to stir up the feudal forces of Normandy against the English prince. When, on the 25th November 1120, the son of the English King had perished in the wreck of the *White Ship*—a pleasure party entrusted to a drunken crew—Louis le Gros took up vigorously again the claims of William Clito, the son of Robert Short Hose, to the Duchy of Normandy. The King of England married at this moment the only child remaining to him, his daughter Matilda, to Geoffrey le Bel (the Fair), heir of the Count of Anjou (1127). The foundation was laid on which the threatening empire of the Plantagenets was soon to be erected. The struggle, broken by short truces, was to end only in 1135 with the death of the English King. As he left no son, there were violent struggles over the succession, and the armed combats which these caused in the heart of the Anglo-Norman realm gave a momentary respite to the Capetian monarchy.

It will cause surprise to read that a prince endowed as was Louis le Gros with all the qualities which make a great King—energy, activity, strength of character, devotion to his people, a clear intelligence of its needs, and who, in the accomplishment of his task had not wavered for an instant—should have thought of abdicating to become a monk in the Abbey of St. Denis. The sense of the duties which he had still to perform on the throne prevented him.

In the last years of his life he suffered greatly from his extreme corpulence, which not only embarrassed his movements, but inflicted gout and other complaints on him. He had gained experience and felt himself at the height of his profession as King. Ah! if only with the knowledge he had won he cou'd have regained the agility and vigour of youth! "Alas!" he said, "how frail and pitiful is our nature, which cannot know and act at the same time!"

"Already for some time," writes Suger, "the lord Louis, enfeebled by his corpulence and the continual fatigues of war, was losing his bodily strength while maintaining his mental power. Although he was sixty years of age he had such knowledge and ability that if the continual inconvenience of the fat which overweighted his body had not prevented it, he would by his superiority have crushed his enemies everywhere. Though overwhelmed by his heavy corpulence he resisted so firmly the King of England, Count Thibaud, and all his enemies, that those who were witnesses of his splendid actions, or heard them recounted, praised loudly his nobility of soul while deploring the weakness of his body. Exhausted by sickness, and hardly able to support himself through a wound in the leg, he marched against Count Thibaud, and burned Bonneval, with the exception of a convent of monks which he spared. . . ."

His last expedition in 1137 was directed against the castle of St. Brisson-sur-Loire, near Gien. The lord of the place was robbing merchants. Louis forced him to capitulate, and set fire to his castle. He was returning from the accomplishment of this act of justice when at Châteauneuf-sur-Loire he was taken with a violent dysentery. He accepted but impatiently the doctor's remedies. Every one was allowed to come freely to his bedside; whoever wished could enter his room; to all he turned a cheerful countenance. He took advantage of a momentary improvement to have himself moved as far as Melun. The news of his illness spread, and from all parts there was an immense concourse of people of every class. "The devoted people whom he had maintained in peace," says Suger, "left castle and town, and abandoned the plough to hasten to meet him on the roads. They prayed to God for his safety."

Louis VI knew that his last hour had come. He ordered that a carpet should be spread on the floor of the room in which he lay, and that ashes should be sprinkled on it in the form

A JUSTICIARY IN ARMOUR

of a cross. He had himself laid upon it with his arms outstretched, lying in the grey dust with his face turned to heaven. Louis the Justiciary gave up his noble soul to God, on the 1st August 1137, at the age of fifty-six years.

SOURCES.—Suger, *Vie de Louis le Gros*, ed. Molinier, 1887 ; Le Moine Guillaume, " Vie de Suger," *Hist. de la France* (D. Bouquet), xii. 102–15 ; Ordericus Vitalis, *Historiæ ecclesiasticæ, libri XII*, ed. Le Prévost, 1838–55, 5 vols. ; Galbert de Bruges, *Vie et meurtre de Charles le Bon* (1127–28), ed. Perenne, 1891.

HISTORICAL WORKS.—Ach. Luchaire, *Louis VI le Gros, Annales de sa vie et son règne*, 1890 ; Thompson, *The Development of the French Monarchy under Louis VI le Gros*, 1895 ; Cartéllieri, *Abt Suger von Saint-Denis*, 1898 ; Ach. Luchaire, " Les Premiers Capétiens," in the *Histoire de France*, edited by Lavisse, ii. 1901 ; L. Halphen, *Le Comté d'Anjou au XIe Siècle*, 1906.

CHAPTER VII

THE COMMUNES

The urban aristocracy. The communal revolution was directed in the towns by the patricians, who claimed full seigniorial rights. The troubles of Le Mans in 1069. The commune of Le Mans; assassination of Bishop Gaudry (1111–14). The communal charters; they make a feudal personality of the community. After the proclamation of the communes, the patrician families are masters of the towns. Their rivalries. The rural communes. The commune of Lorris.

LOUIS LE GROS has been called "the Father of the Communes," no doubt because of what Ordericus Vitalis wrote of him: "Louis, in order to repress the tyranny and the brigandage of the rebellious 'hobereaux,' asked for the help of the bishops throughout France: then was established the commune of the people in order that, led by its priests, it should bring its banners to the help of the King in sieges and fights."

The following passage of the Abbot Suger indicates the rôle of Louis le Gros in the communal revolution, the character of which it shows:

"Louis returned towards Amiens (1115) and laid siege to this town, which was occupied by a certain Adam, a cruel tyrant who desolated the neighbourhood with his depredations."

It was a question of a famous tower which dominated Amiens and was called the Châtillon. Adam lived there as the representative of Enguerran de Boves, lord of Coucy and Count of Amiens.

"Having kept this tower closely besieged for nearly two years (1116–17), the lord Louis at last forced the defenders to surrender at discretion; after taking possession of it he destroyed it from top to bottom and so re-established a welcome peace in the country; finally, he deprived the said tyrant and his people of all power over Amiens."

THE COMMUNES

Let us look in another direction, at the town of Beauvais. A lord, Lancelin II de Bulles, Count of Dammartin, had managed to usurp certain dues which Suger calls " Conductus Belvacensis," market dues, otherwise known as " guidage " or " péage." These dues, moreover, were not in any way justified. Louis VI forced Lancelin to give them up.

These facts reveal the causes of the communal movement, which begins to show itself about the end of the eleventh century and develops in the following century. We have seen how the feudal lords had presided over the formation of the towns. In the beginning they had rendered such services that without them the towns could not have come into existence. In arms from morning to night, they ensured the tranquillity of urban labour, and safety of transit over the land within their suzerainty. In return, they legitimately collected market dues, tolls, dues on wine or commodities sold in the towns; they established there manorial ovens and mills to which the inhabitants were bound to come with open purse to grind their corn and bake their loaves; they exercised there the right of " banvin " which gave them the privilege, when the grape harvest was over, of putting on sale before all others the produce of their harvest; they and their people enjoyed the right of lodging (*gîte*) in the town. One knows the infinite variety and the multiplicity of feudal dues.

In their origin, then, these rights had their justification. Towns of little importance, agricultural groups surrounded by a wall or a palisade, stood in need of the protection of a lord; besides, in the beginning, these dues, in view of the unimportant character of the district, represented but a small payment. But what happens? In virtue of the very progress achieved, largely thanks to the lord, his protection becomes useless: it became useless by reason of the peace and order which were being established throughout the realm, and because of the importance and therefore of the power which the town had acquired. In the second place, these contributions, moderate in the beginning, when they were collected in a modest little district, became enormous and excessive when they were paid out progressively by a rich and populous city.

For example: the Count of Blois takes under his protection

the inhabitants of Seris on consideration of a yearly rent of two measures (*setiers*) of wheat per house. This is all very well while Seris is still a little nursling and cannot do without the powerful support of the Count of Blois; but suppose the town, as happens with many others, is transformed into a rich locality, populous and powerful, and the protection of the noble count loses all *raison d'être*: the tax levied on each house will seem an intolerable abuse.

The dues collected on wine entering the gates of a little town of seven or eight hundred souls are a small thing; but what revenues they represent if it is a question of a town of 70,000 or 80,000 inhabitants.

Moreover, in proportion as trade had developed, these taxes on transport, market dues, and tolls had become more and more vexatious. The owner of a sack of wool—and we quote this as an actual example—after having paid a tax of exit on leaving England and a tax for the right of entry on landing at Dammes, in Flanders, had still, in order to cross the Scheldt and the Scarpe from Rupelmonde to Douai, to pay seventeen tolls. As has been said, these dues were legitimately collected by the feudal lords in the days when they ensured safe transit within the limits of their jurisdiction (*justices*); in the time when the baron, on whose lands a merchant had been robbed, was bound to indemnify him for his loss, his vigilance having been in default; in the days, finally, when it was the duty of the lord to see to the upkeep of the roads and bridges; but one can imagine the irritation of the burgesses at a time when, on the one hand, these services had become useless or were no longer performed, and, on the other, the dues represented altogether a sum which as a result of the development of trade has been multiplied more than tenfold. Add to this that the suzerain lords of the towns continued to exercise in them their judicial powers; and justice was, in the Middle Ages, government. In the preceding century, the lords were alone capable of acting as justiciaries; but now in the rich and prosperous towns, where the highest class is educated, the aristocracy claim this right of justice for themselves; and with the more insistence, as it would form the natural complement of the authority which these patricians exert over their clients.

THE COMMUNES

But the lords, in possession of their privileges, intend to preserve them. The burgesses, for whom these privileges have become onerous and vexatious, and who regard them as no longer justified, desire either to free themselves from them or to appropriate them. Such is the origin of the communal movement.

The communal revolution which is seen breaking out in France towards the end of the eleventh century, was the struggle in the towns of the patricians supported by their clients, against the feudal suzerains supported by their vassals.

At this time the patricians are at the same time merchants and soldiers; as the feudal barons, their contemporaries, are soldiers and farmers. The patricians are constantly at war not only against their own lords but against the " hobereaux " of the neighbourhood. The Counts of Ponthieu give charters of freedom to the inhabitants of Abbeville and Doullens, " to remove them from the losses and vexations which they constantly suffer at the hands of the lords of the district."

We must not see in this a democratic movement. An aristocracy has been formed in the towns; it has been formed feudally, by the power of patronage, and in the same fashion as rural feudalism. But in consequence of the development of industry, the clients are artisans instead of labourers; and yet in some towns, which have kept their agricultural character, the clients of the patricians are still to a great extent labourers who live by the cultivation of the soil, and especially kitchen-gardening and the breeding of cattle. In reading the history of the communal revolution at Laon one meets the good country folk who come on Saturdays to buy their vegetables in the town.

The communal revolution was, then, the work of the patricians. They are for that matter, as we have just said, very like the feudal lords. Their children are united by marriage. The families of both are called " lignages " (lineages); the patricians also have seals, armouries, a standard, a banner; they live in fortified dwellings dominated by a battlemented tower; they are of a warlike temper. The patricians go into battle surrounded by their clients, as the barons escorted by their vassals. It is true that most of them are engaged in

THE MIDDLE AGES

trade; some are "navigators," others drapers, and some bankers; but living on the work of their commissioners or workmen, they do not consider themselves less highly placed in the social scale than their neighbour who lives on the labour of the peasants. In all the towns it is the richest burgesses who are to direct the communal revolution, and historians have remarked that it was the towns in which the aristocracy had most prevailed which secured the greatest degree of independence.

The representatives of these patrician families were grouped in hanses, guilds, brotherhoods, for the needs of their industry or trade. Everywhere where the communal movement is to triumph these hanses or guilds not only take possession of the government of the commune, but form the commune itself. From this point of view the communal charter granted in 1127 by the Count of Flanders to the town of St. Omer is characteristic. Hardly anything but commercial privileges are found in it; it is a constitution designed for merchants and in which it is stated that the franchises are granted exclusively to those who are members of the guild. It is the same with the *Charity* of Arras, and that of Valenciennes, and for the "Amity" of Lille. These are the names by which the communal charter was designated in these localities.

Not less significant are the expressions used in 1213 by the ecclesiastical Synod of Paris, when it denounces those "synagogues" which "usurers" and "extortioners"—the wealthy leaders of the merchant *bourgeoisie*—have erected in France under the name of "communes."

The places in which the first aldermen or communal magistrates meet are the merchants' market-places, *i.e.* the places where the merchants discuss their affairs—what we should call the Exchanges; or again it is the cloth market in the towns where the hanse is formed of the drapers. The majority of the big cities had there their first town hall, notably Beauvais, Ypres, Arras, and Paris.

The French towns in which the patricians succeeded the soonest in freeing themselves from the seigniorial domination by forming themselves into "communes" were Cambrai (then in the territory of the Empire), Le Mans, St. Quentin

THE COMMUNES

(before 1077), Beauvais (before 1099), then **Arras**, Noyon (towards 1108), Mantes in 1110, Valenciennes in 1114, Amiens in 1116–17, Corbie towards 1120; Soissons in 1126, Bruges, Lille, St. Omer towards 1127, and Ghent shortly afterwards. In the towns of the South the movement began later—at Montpelier in 1142, at Béziers in 1167, at Toulouse in 1188, at Nîmes only in 1207.

The disturbances of Le Mans seemed like a prologue. The lord of the town, William the Conqueror, was detained in England—a favourable circumstance. And to free themselves from his authority there was formed an association joined by everybody, the patricians and their clients, the bishop and his clergy, and even the knights who had taken up their abode in the town. And immediately the spirit of the urban association showed itself. They set out, banner, bishop, and clergy at their head, to make war on the feudal barons of the district. The burgesses set fire to several of their strongholds, then they hastened " with furious ardour " to lay siege to the castle of Hugh de Sillé, one of the principal lords of the neighbourhood; but the keep held, and the men of Le Mans turned against the castle of Geoffrey du Maine, which they took and destroyed from top to bottom. To confess the truth, this fine courage died down on the return of the Conqueror, and the men of Le Mans went humbly in procession to meet him for the purpose of handing to him the keys of their city.

The establishment of the commune of Laon took a particularly dramatic character.

The town had been the capital of the Carolingians, who lived there with a part of their nobility, a city built on a hill, the Mont Loon of the *chansons de geste*, rendered inaccessible by defensive works, surrounded on all sides by vines and quickset hedges. Following the long sojourn which the Carolingians had made there, the feudal nobility were still, towards the end of the eleventh century, proportionately more numerous at Laon than in other towns. Relations were frequent between the knights and the peasants, their vassals. The town was under the suzerainty of the bishop, who held at Laon a court of justice, and collected there feudal dues. There were found then at Laon, at the end of the eleventh century, three

THE MIDDLE AGES

classes of people : first, the bishop, an ecclesiastical and feudal lord, with his clerks and his household, his servants and his soldiers ; secondly, the feudal lords, *i.e.* the knights living there, with some of their vassals and their squires ; thirdly, the burgesses and their households. Industry was not much developed, and these citizens were for the most part market gardeners.

At the end of the eleventh century the Bishop of Laon, a certain Gaudry, was a singular character. He was not a priest, but a simple subdeacon, grossly ignorant except in matters of war and the chase. He had won the favour of Henry I, King of England, at the battle of Tenchebrai (28th Sept. 1106), where he had taken prisoner Robert Short Hose, the brother of Henry I, and had delivered him into the hands of the King. After this, Henry made him his revising officer, then Bishop of Laon. He was seen clothed in cope and mitre ; but more often with helmet and hauberk. He had to attend him a negro who acted as his executioner. He had had the castellan, Gerard de Querzy, killed in church. Guibert de Nogent and Ordericus Vitalis have drawn the same picture of Bishop Gaudry.

In the episcopal palace were ranged vases full of gold which he had extracted from the English King, and in larger quantities from his subjects of Laon.

For the rest, these subjects themselves were not of a very peaceable temperament. We have seen how, when its work of organization was finished, a part of the feudal nobility had become mere brigands. These habits were found again among the knights living in Laon, and were communicated to their fellow-citizens, the burgesses. Thus the town was changed into a sort of cut-throat place. The nobles pounced at night on the burgesses, threatening them with death, and held them to ransom. On the other hand, the burgesses seized the peasants of whom the nobles were the suzerains, and despoiled them with an equal brutality.

The King himself was not safe from the enterprises of our citizens. He happened to be staying at Laon with his household. His horses could be seen being led to drink, through the streets of the town, in the full daylight or in the dusk of

THE COMMUNES

the evening; and our burgesses watching them on the way and capturing them, after having thrashed their drivers.

One can imagine the excitement produced in such a place by the announcement of the communal charters which had been obtained by the inhabitants of St. Quentin and Noyon. Bishop Gaudry having gone to England, the burgesses of Laon obtained from the clergy and nobles of the town authority to form themselves into a commune in their turn.

We must reprint here once again the celebrated passage from Guibert de Nogent: "The clergy, the archdeacon, and the knights, seeing how things were going, and for the sake of gaining money, made an offer to the people to give them for a financial consideration the power to form a commune. Now let us see what was meant by this execrable and new name. 'All the inhabitants who were due to pay a certain tax were to pay at one single time in the year the ordinary obligations of serfdom, and to make amends by a fine fixed legally if they committed any offence contrary to the laws.' On these conditions they were entirely freed from all the other payments and dues which it was customary to impose on the serfs. The men of the people, seizing this opportunity to free themselves from a host of vexations, gave large sums of money to these misers, whose hands seemed like gulfs which must be filled. The latter, rendered more tractable by this shower of gold, promised the people, under oath, to keep to the letter the agreements made with them."

One asks oneself if the word "execrable," which is found at the head of this famous page, is not an interpolation; for its sense is contrary to the context, opposed above all to the spirit which inspires the work of Guibert de Nogent.

But here is Gaudry returning from England. One can imagine his fury. He breaks out angrily, then calms down when the burgesses have paid out money to him also. And Louis VI equally, for a financial consideration, recognizes the new commune (1111); but in the following year, under the pressure exerted by the bishop, the King revokes his decision, and the commune of Laon is suppressed (1112). This was the beginning of the revolution. The streets of Laon rang with the cry: "Commune! Commune!" And when Guibert de

THE MIDDLE AGES

Nogent warns Gaudry of the danger he is running in resisting the burgesses any longer:

"Good," says the bishop, "what can they do? If John, my negro, were to pull the nose of the most redoubtable among them, would he dare so much as to utter a groan?"

"The violation of the treaties by which the commune of Laon had been formed," writes Guibert de Nogent, "filled the hearts of the burgesses with rage and stupefaction. They ceased to do any work. The butchers and the shoemakers closed their shops; the innkeepers and the wine merchants displayed no merchandise." A general strike!

Far from allowing themselves to be intimidated, the bishop and the knights demanded from the inhabitants a new contribution, destined to destroy the commune, and which equalled the sum they had paid to establish it.

On Good Friday, companies armed with swords and spears, with axes and hatchets, with bows and iron weapons, run through the streets converging on the episcopal palace, and slay its defenders. At the noise, Bishop Gaudry runs to take refuge in the cellar, where he hides at the bottom of a barrel. He is pulled out by the hair. Amidst the jeers of the exasperated burgesses, a serf splits his head with a hatchet. On the slippery floor of the cellar, his blood mingles its unctuous purple with the wine from the barrels which have been staved in. Massacres are multiplied. The dwellings of the clerics and the nobles are plundered and given to the flames. The cathedral is burnt; its immense roof falls with a crash on the reliquaries and silver candlesticks. The adversaries of the burgesses take flight in various disguises. They could be seen, men and women, descending the side of the mountain and slipping through the vineyards by which the town was surrounded. The corpse of the bishop, deprived of its clothing, was dragged through the market-place, where it remained till the next day, naked, soiled, pitiable, a butt for the worst outrages. Only then the burgesses allowed it to be buried.

The movement spread. The burgesses of Laon obtained the support of Thomas de Marle, castellan of Crecy-sur-Serre and of Nouvion l'Abbesse, one of the most redoubtable feudal bandits of the time. He was the son of Enguerran de Boves.

THE COMMUNES

His youth had been passed in robbing pilgrims, by which he had laid the foundation of his enormous fortune. Then, after some years of orgies and debauchery, he had installed himself in his castle, as an open brigand. He made terror reign in the surrounding country, continuing to rob in order to enrich himself further, continuing to kill and torture to amuse himself. " He hung his captives in the air," writes Guibert, " hanging on to them with his own hand, by the most delicate organs, which yielding to the weight of the body were torn away, and through the gaping hole the intestines flowed out. He hung them by their thumbs and laid great stones on their shoulders to increase their weight. He beat them to death with clubs and broke their bones."

It was impossible to count the number of victims whom he had left to rot in the depths of his dungeons. He slowly burned his captives' feet, and when they could no longer walk, because he had tortured them so much, he cut off their feet; since, said he, for that matter, they could no longer use them.

" One day he thrust his lance so deeply through the mouth of one poor wretch that the steel pierced his intestines." The burgesses of Laon had in him a useful auxiliary. But the King intervened and sent his troops against the rebels. The burgesses fled, while the nobles and the clerics returned within the walls of Laon. " Now the knights having escaped massacre," says Guibert, " stole from the houses of the fugitives all their provisions, furniture, and even hinges and bolts." The peasants of the surrounding districts, following the example of their lords—that is to say, of the nobles established in Laon—invaded the captured town and, for several days, plundered and destroyed. The commune disappeared then (1114); one might have thought for ever; but in the year 1128, under the name of the " institution of peace," the inhabitants of Laon obtained their communal charter.

What is in reality the proclamation of a commune at the beginning of the twelfth century ? We have nowadays acts by which the civil personality is recognized in a society ; by a communal charter the feudal personality was recognized as belonging to an urban community.

The commune becomes a feudal person, a collective lordship; an association of non-nobles united to form a collective noble. Like a baron in his keep, it enters into the feudal hierarchy. It becomes the vassal of a suzerain who governs it according to the customs of the nobles, and to whom it will render the service of the nobles, the service of the army and progress, the service of war; and it in its turn becomes suzerain to other vassals. The prerogatives which it has won are exactly those which were attached to the possession of a barony. It has a seal like the feudal lord and, like him, it has its keep, which is called the watch-tower. Should it happen that a King destroys a commune he will have its watch-tower rased to the ground, as he would have the seigniorial keep, if he had captured a fief.

What would the clauses of a communal charter be? We can judge by that of Beauvais:

"The inhabitants of the town shall take an oath to the commune; they will lend each other mutual assistance;—the peers of the commune, otherwise known as sheriffs or councillors (*jurés*), will give justice to all;—if some one after doing an injury to one of the members of the commune should find refuge in a feudal domain, the peers shall demand of the lord reparation for the loss occasioned, and, if the lord refuse this, they will take vengeance on him or his men; the peers shall protect the merchants who come to the market of the town and shall punish those who molest them;—if the commune shall be at open war against declared enemies, none of its members shall lend money to them; should the commune set out to fight an enemy, none of its members shall hold communications with any of these latter;—if the debtor of a member of the commune finds refuge in a feudal domain, the lord of the domain shall pay the debt or expel the debtor, and if he does not do this, the commune shall levy a fine on such of the lord's men as they can manage to capture."

It is an organization at once military and commercial. It was the rich merchants who directed the communal revolution; it was made for their profit. At St. Omer the guild draws from their coffers the funds destined for the fortifications.

It is, nevertheless, an error to say that the movement was not made in favour of the common people, and that they were too humble still to exercise an influence on the course of events. At this time in the towns the interests of the people are bound up with those of the patricians. The people form their clientele. Between the people and their leaders there exist those same paternal ties which we saw a century earlier between the inhabitants of the town and its lords. At the beginning of the twelfth century the patricians render to the companies of traders the same services of protection that the lords rendered to the rural inhabitants at the beginning of the eleventh century. And the same sentiments of unity and reciprocal affection exist between them, the same co-ordination of efforts. It is thanks to the efforts of the merchant-patricians that industry advances and the trades prosper. It is thanks to their efforts that the crafts reach perfection. So that the triumph of the patricians over the lords in the twelfth century was likewise the triumph of the crafts. These relations are to be profoundly modified a century later. It is a mistake to judge the sentiments and conditions in the towns at the beginning of the twelfth century by what they shall have become in the thirteenth.

The communal charter having the effect of making the commune a feudal personality, its chief result was to give to its representatives a judicial authority. In the Middle Ages it was said " the fief and justice are all one." The right of administering justice was the principal attribute of the feudal lord, and it was by it that he governed his vassals; just as it was the principal attribute of the King himself who governed his kingdom by it. And this communal justice exercised by the magistracy, for this is the name by which in the towns in the north they designated what we should call the municipal council, was as extensive as that of the lords. It went as far as the right of punishing by fine, imprisonment, and even death. The municipal bodies had their pillory where they had the condemned exposed and beaten with rods. They had gibbets on which they had people hung and left the corpses suspended. One asks how the communes had been able to snatch from the feudal power the most important of its attributes; why, because they had themselves become, as we have just said, a feudal power. And, to go more deeply into the matter,

THE MIDDLE AGES

the feudal lords had drawn their power from the authority of the family; the heads of the communes drew theirs from the same source. We have seen that the towns had been formed as fiefs under the action of the family. " Lignages " had constituted themselves there which had grouped themselves into " parages." The union of these formed the town. Like the city of antiquity, the French town is in the twelfth century the union of a certain number of families, to each of which are attached a certain number of clients. It is not a democracy but an aristocracy formed by a grouping of patrons and clients. The heads of these " parages," followed by their clientele, brought about the communal revolution, and when the town was free they quite naturally found themselves at its head. Thus is also explained that for the formation of the first sheriffdoms or magistracies no election was made.

It is to be noted also that in a number of towns some " ilots " (helots) are to be found even later than the communal charter, withdrawn from the jurisdiction of the magistracies. Here a slave was under the jurisdiction of the King, further on of a bishop, there of an abbey, elsewhere of some particular lord. What we have said about the formation of the towns will be remembered. A quarter, a street, sometimes a single house will be found withdrawn from the common jurisdiction, answerable to some particular jurisdiction.

A feature which strikes one in studying these communal constitutions is the close solidarity in which they try to unite the members of the urban groups. " All the men of the commune shall help each other with all their might," says the charter of Senlis. " Each man of the commune shall be faithful to his sworn comrade, shall go to his help, shall give him help and council," says the charter of Abbeville. The charters are called " brotherhoods," " charities," " institutions of peace," or more simply " peaces "—the " peace of Amiens," the " peace of Arras." The members of the commune are the members of the peace (*paiseurs*); the town hall will be the " house of the peace "; the communal territory the " enclosure of the peace," the oath of the members the " oath of the peace." For the seigniorial authority, whose principal rôle was to assure peace to the burgesses and to maintain it, outside

THE COMMUNES

by force of arms, within by the exercise of a vigilant and active power, has become weak and remote. And how important it is to replace it by a profound sentiment of reciprocal devotion, concord, and unity.

Moreover, in spite of having given up a great part of their power and their privileges by the communal charter, the lords have not entirely renounced their suzerainty over the town, in which they have still to exercise rights and duties which Beaumanoir will define in the thirteenth century with the precision of his fine genius :

"Each lord who has good towns under him in which there are communes ought to take account each year of the state of the town, and how it is maintained and governed by the mayors, and by those who are set up to watch over and govern it, so that the rich may fear that if they offend they will be severely punished, and that the poor in the said towns may gain their bread in peace."

In these last lines Beaumanoir alludes to the divisions which will break out in the towns in the course of the thirteenth century, and of which we shall have to speak further on.

For it would be an error to believe that the action of the communal charters procured for the towns in France the peaceful delectations of the golden age. We have said that the communes became feudal persons. They acquired their aggressive and warlike spirit. Jacques de Vitry at the beginning of the thirteenth century hardly exaggerates in his sermon to the burgesses :

"The burgesses, relying on their numbers, oppress their neighbours and subject them by violence. Brutal communes which are not content with overwhelming the nobles of their neighbourhood . . . they aim at the ruin of their neighbours, destroy the cities and the other communes by their persecutions. The majority of the communes make rabid war against one another. The members of communes are not only seen attacking their neighbours, but also strangers and pilgrims, defenceless people, whom they overwhelm with illegal exactions and impose upon in every way. . . . Outside war, inside terror."

The burgesses had created the communal movement from

a desire for union. But here are now for the first time rivalries between the principal families which the scigniorial justice had until then kept in peace. The great patricians have in their train each his clientele. There are few French towns which from the end of the thirteenth century are not troubled by these dissensions, which often give rise to bloody conflicts. Beaumanoir expresses himself here again clearly and points out to the lord of the town the line of conduct he should hold :

"When a disagreement arises between the citizens of a good town through misunderstanding or through hatred, the lord should not allow it, and even if one of the parties will not deign to plead, rather he ought to take the parties and keep them in prison until a stable peace is made between them, or stable guarantees if peace cannot be made ; for otherwise the good towns would suffer by the struggles between the families."

In several towns of the South which had managed to free themselves from the seigniorial suzerainty more completely than those of the North, this recourse to the authority of the suzerain to settle quarrels among the families being no longer possible, they were obliged to appeal to those peculiar personages whom they called " podestas." One sees such cities as Marseilles, Arles, or Avignon calling in foreigners, generally Italians, and asking them to govern for a certain time with dictatorial power. Even the constitution of the town was put into their hands, provided that they governed without hate, without favour, without personal profit—the only means of avoiding the conflicts between the patrician families which were quarrelling over the administration. These " tyrants," or podestas, strangers to the civil struggles which were destroying the town, were alone capable of re-establishing order there by the exercise of an absolute power.

After this there will arise dissensions between the patricians and their clientele on the one side, and the popular class, " the commons," on the other. They will fill the end of the thirteenth and the fourteenth century, and will cause rivers of blood to flow. Far from reducing the distance which separated the common people from the patricians, the establishment of the communes only accentuated it, for to their wealth the patricians

THE COMMUNES

now added the government of the city, which was until then in the hands of the lord. And having no longer need of the people in their struggle against the feudal suzerain they will come to speak only with scorn of those " whose nails were blackened by work."

We must say yet a few words about the rural communes. A number of them obtained communal charters from their lords either through their generosity, for money, or as the result of an armed insurrection. From that day the inhabitants chose magistrates, organized a militia, and surrounded themselves with fortifications. The village became a town. Sometimes several villages were seen to unite and form a single community which obtained a communal charter. A number of examples could be cited, of which the most important would be the seventeen villages of the people of Laon, who adopted as their political centre Anizy-le-Château, and received in 1128 the charter of Laon of which we have spoken.

Among these charters granted to the villagers a special mention should be made of the famous privilege granted by Louis VI to the town of Lorris-en-Gâtinais. The King took measures there in favour of his subjects against his own agents. He improved the condition of the people by freeing them from the bond which bound them to the soil. For the future each burgess of Lorris could leave the district and sell what goods he possessed. Forced labours were suppressed, and the service of work due to the King was limited to one day. At least this service due to the King could not take the inhabitants more than a day's journey from their home. Direct contributions were reduced and fixed. The majority of the indirect contributions were suppressed, especially those which involved contributions of food. The fairs and markets of the country were made safe by a special protection, extending to the merchants who went there and to their merchandise. Finally, in judicial matters the royal Provost had the fines which could be inflicted reduced, and procedure simplified. It is one of the most active efforts which have ever been made by a prince to improve the condition of his subjects, and one of the most fruitful. For the example given by the King was followed by his barons, and the number of rural communes which soon received " the Lorris charter " either in the royal domain or in the lands of the barons increased with the happiest rapidity. And each found in it his profit : the tenants who saw their lot improved ; the lords who saw the population of their domains increase, the towns and villages prosper, and, hence, their own power growing and even the dues which they collected from their subjects becoming more important. For if it is true that for each of the said subjects they were lighter, the sum of the amounts collected showed a sensible increase in consequence of the development of the population and the general prosperity.

SOURCES.—*Guibert de Nogent*, ed. Bourgin, 1907 ; Beaumanoir, *Coutumes de Beauvaisis*, ed. Salmon, 1899–1900, 2 vols. ; Aug. Thierry, *Monuments inédits de l'histoire du Tiers-Etat*, 1850–56, 2 vols. ; A. Giry, *Documents sur les relations de la royauté avec les villes en France de 1180 à 1314*, 1885 ; Charters and documents published in the following works :

HISTORICAL WORKS.—A. Luchaire, *Les Communes françaises à l'époque des Capétiens directs*, a new edition published by Halphen, 1911 ; Paul Viollet, *Histoire des institutions politiques et administratives de la France*, tome iii. 1903 ; A. Giry and A. Reville, *Emancipation des villes, les communes, la bourgeoisie*, in the *Histoire Générale* of Lavisse and Rambaud, ii. 1893 ; A. Giry, *Histoire de la ville de St. Omer, et de ses institutions, jusqu'au XIV*^e *Siècle*, 1887 ; A. Giry, *Etudes sur les origines de la commune de St. Quentin*, 1887 ; J. Flammermont, *Histoire des institutions municipales de Senlis*, 1881 ; Maurice Prou, *Les coutumes de Lorris*, 1884 ; Abel Lefranc, *Histoire de la ville de Noyon*, 1887 ; L. H. Labaude, *Histoire de Beauvais*, 1892 ; And. Ducom, *Essai sur . . . la commune d'Agen*, 1892 ; R. Villepelet, *Hist. de la ville de Perigueux*, 1908 ; F. Lennel, *Hist. de Calais*, tome i. 1908 ; G. Bourgin, *La commune de Soissons*, 1908 ; Imbart de la Tour, *Histoire de la nation française*, edited by G. Hanotaux, tome iii., *Histoire politique des origines à 1515* (1921).

CHAPTER VIII

THE TWELFTH CENTURY

In the thirteenth century feudal institutions reached their maturity in France. The peace and the truce of God. The " forty days " of the King. The associations of peace. Chivalry. The initiation of knights. The virtue of love. The life of the castle. The barons as poets and singers. The lady of the castle. The tournaments.

AT the beginning of the twelfth century the feudal organization is completed. Beliefs and traditions have become absolutely fixed. No one has any doubt of the truth of the religion which he practises fervently; and these beliefs have the more power as they are precise and concrete. In the thought of the time the world is limited to the starry vault of the heavens stretched above our heads. Prayers are addressed to God and the saints as to very near neighbours constantly intervening in human affairs, living familiarly on earth as much as beyond the clouds. All this gives to opinions an energy we know no longer.

No one contests the value of the morality which is taught to him, the legitimate character of the bonds between men which no one dreams of changing. No one imagines a social organization preferable to that which surrounds him, or even different from it. Thus as Gaston Paris observes, no one dreams of protesting against the society in which he finds himself or imagines one better constituted, " but all wish that it should be more completely what it is and ought to be."

At the beginning of the twelfth century all the provinces are definitely adapted to the same social forms: those of feudalism—it would be better to say, of protection.

THE MIDDLE AGES

What the father is to his children the baron is to his faithful followers, the patrician to his artisans, the great feudal lord to his vassals, and the King to his feudatories. "Eum pro patre habebitis" (You shall have him for a father), the Archbishop of Reims said in 987. His prophecy came true.

To this maturity of institutions is to correspond an economic movement of a power and intensity which have astonished historians. It has been compared to the economic development of the nineteenth century, but while our time has owed this formidable forward movement to the discovery of the forces of steam and electricity, and the progress of mechanics, the twelfth century owed it to moral causes. The population grew so rapidly that it reached then in France a figure equal to that of our own time.

Succeeding to the eleventh century, the epoch of heroic youth, the twelfth century will give to France the full fruition of its genius. Our literature, our art, our manners will be resplendent throughout Europe. But before reaching so far there will still be many grievous checks, disorders to appease, and many violences to be calmed.

One can easily picture French society at the beginning of the twelfth century such as we have just described it: a multitude of little States each of which is placed under the suzerainty of its patronal head, the baron in armour. The towns themselves had become feudal persons. But these little States are in incessant conflict, against one another. Every one is fighting either for self-defence or attack. It is no longer the anarchy of the ninth and tenth centuries. It is organized war, but it is none the less war, and the country is destroyed by it. For these armed conflicts consist above all in merciless devastations. The poets and the chroniclers of the times have left descriptions of it. Read *Garin le Loherain, Raoul de Cambrai, Girart de Roussillon,* Guibert de Nogent, Ordericus Vitalis.

The Associations of Peace.

The companies of troops were preceded by incendiaries and foragers. "The incendiaries set fire to the villages, the foragers plunder them, carrying off sheep and killing the shepherds. The distracted inhabitants are burnt, or led off

THE TWELFTH CENTURY

with their hands bound, a pitchfork at their neck. The alarm sounds, on all sides there is general dismay." "No longer one saw the mills turning; the chimneys smoked no longer; the cocks had ceased to crow and the great dogs to bark. The grass grew in the houses, even between the paving-stones of the churches; for the priests had abandoned the broken crucifixes" (*Garin le Loherain*). "To devastate the country (Maine) they used various means. The vines were torn up, fruit trees cut down, houses and fortifications destroyed. This rich region was desolated by fire and sword, after which the King of England entered the town of Le Mans in triumph" (Ordericus Vitalis).

The Church endeavoured from the eleventh century onwards to curb these furious passions. Does not Raoul le Glabre already show it to us by the crowds arriving at the councils? They press around their bishops armed with their golden crosses, and raise their hands despairingly to heaven, crying: "Peace! Peace!" The efforts of the prelates result in the proclamation of peace and of the truce of God, to which a number of feudal lords are to give their adhesion. It is forbidden to do violence to priests, churches, women, children, peasants, or to seize their goods. Such is the peace of God. It is forbidden to wage private war from the first Sunday of Advent up to the Octave of the Epiphany, from the first day of Lent up to the Octave of the Ascension, and during the rest of the year from Wednesday evening to Monday morning—that is, during the days of the week which correspond to the days of the Passion. This is the truce of God.

To the truce of God there will come to be added under Philip Augustus the "Quarantine" of the King—that is to say, the obligation to allow forty days to pass between the offence and the declaration of vengeance which is to be taken for it, on one side, and on the other the opening of hostilities. It is obvious that a right of civil war, parcelled out, cut up, delayed, confined into little spaces of time, would find peculiar hindrances to its progress. And to ensure that these prescriptions should be observed, there were formed on all sides the famous associations of peace which came to be veritable armies joined by nobles, burgesses, artisans, and peasants.

THE MIDDLE AGES

Moreover, the work of pacification was facilitated by the tendencies which showed themselves among the feudal nobles themselves; from them was born chivalry. The institution of chivalry is also of French origin; it shone with the greatest brilliance in France. Listen to the Englishman Gerald of Barri celebrating "the French chivalry, whose glory dominates (*exsuperat*) the whole world."

Chivalry.

Chivalry must be distinguished from the feudal nobility, although it issued from it and though all the feudal barons were knights. Chivalry constituted an order to which noblemen were generally admitted after a religious ceremony called investiture and after being dubbed knight by another knight, often the suzerain of the fief to which the recipient belonged. But nobility of birth was not a condition rigorously required. One sees commoners, even serfs, who were armed knights; and sometimes nobles remained candidates (*damoiseaux*) all their lives because of the great expense occasioned by being dubbed knight.

The ceremony of initiation took place in a church, or in the hall of a castle, or even in open country. The essential part of it consisted in the handing of the sword to the lord by the young knight, and in the "striking" (*colée*) three blows with the flat of the sword on the shoulder, or a strong blow of the fist on the nape of the neck by the knight who is receiving the novice. This latter had passed the previous night in prayer at the foot of an altar. In the morning he had bathed and clothed himself in white; then he had received the sacraments of confession and communion, for the Church had come to consider chivalry as an eighth sacrament.

Here are the principal details of the ceremony.

The lord demanded of the novice if he was resolved to live conformably to the good of the Church, to honour, and to the laws of chivalry. The novice swore to do so, after which he was invested, piece by piece, by knights or sometimes by ladies or maidens, with the different parts of the armour which was worn by a knight. He was given his spurs, the hauberk or coat of mail, the cuirass, the armlets, the gauntlets; finally the lord girded on his sword. This was the initiation. After which the lord who was conferring the order rose from his seat and gave the stroke (*colée*) to the recipient who was kneeling before him.

The lord said : " In the name of God, St. Michael, and St. George, I dub thee knight "; and he added : " Be valiant." Finally the new knight was presented with his helmet, shield, and lance, and a horse was led up to him. Before a numerous company he had to leap on it, if possible without using the stirrup, perform a gallop, run a quintaine—that is to say, to run through or to overthrow, with his lance couched, a mannikin clothed in iron armour which was supported by a lance fixed in the ground. The day was finished in feasting and rejoicing, and if the new knight belonged to a rich family in jousts and tournaments.

The moral obligations imposed on the knight formed the importance of the institution ; to remain subject to his suzerain, to fight for the faith, to be faithful to his word, to protect the weak, unfortunate and helpless men, women and children, to fight against injustice.

The mediæval poets have left a description of the ideal knight. He should be " free of heart and handsome in body, gallant, gentle, and modest, not given to talking." Add to this the two great qualities demanded from the " rich men " of the time, valour, and generosity in giving alms.

Under all circumstances the knight must defend his faith. " And in making this solemn promise of maintaining the faith of Jesus Christ, it was the custom in France that the knights hearing Mass should hold their drawn swords upright during the recital of the Gospel " (*Lacurne de Sainte-Palaye*).

If a knight broke the laws of chivalry, failed in honour or broke his oath, he was degraded. The essential part of this last ceremony was that a felon knight had his golden spur cut off level with the heel.

These institutions found their complement in the essential virtue we have already indicated. The lord should love his vassals ; the vassals should love their lord. The author of *Renart le Nouvel* expresses this with striking precision in two lines of verse in which he compares society to a ship :

> And the ship with concord
> Is fortified by the nobility.

THE MIDDLE AGES

Thus is seen to develop the great virtue of the Middle Ages: *love*. Never has the divine and human precept, "Love one another," penetrated hearts more profoundly.

> Love, Charity, and God
> Are all one.
> *(Renart le Nouvel.)*

And the chief result of this love is generosity in giving. The lord, the wealthy, must give. This was a necessary virtue in the Middle Ages, when the means of livelihood or of making a fortune were scanty, and not easily come at; and in the absence of organized credit.

"You will be pleased to ride abroad, to distribute fiefs to knights, vair and minever to those who have nothing. A true knight exalts himself in giving largesse, and, if he is greedy, each day of his life causes loss to others" (*Garin le Loherain*).

"What is knowledge," says Robert of Blois, "if greed goes with it? What is valour in a calculating man?" "Whence comes the authority of princes and valiant knights? From largesse—Generosity is the queen of virtues. The great lords have wherewith to give, and do give. That is the secret of their power."

But man is man after all, and virtues most enjoined by tradition, by custom, even by the very constitution of the society in which he lives, by priests and poets, can fail to be impressed on him. And again there is a limit to the means of doing good. Moreover, the poor and humble must know how to bear suffering:

"There will never be a poor man who does not suffer," says Robert of Blois again.

Such was, in its rude crust of stone and iron, the social mind of the twelfth century: "Be generous, know how to bear suffering, love one another to the best of your ability."

Life in the Castle. The lord lived with his household in his castle. In the twelfth century the nobles have almost entirely given up living in the towns, where they had enjoyed living in the previous century, to dwell in country domains.

The thirteenth-century castle is the centre of a vast system of agricultural works. The artisans' workshops which were attached to it have not disappeared; but they have not been developed, for the towns have given a great impulse to trade, and the castle can obtain manufactured goods from the travelling merchants.

At the centre is the dominating tower, the keep, at the foot of which is built the "palace," the residence of the lord and his immediate family. At the top of the tower the watch scans the horizon. He gives warning of the approach of an enemy, or signals the arrival of visitors for whom the drawbridge must be let down. To kill time he plays the flute, timbrel, or pipe, or sings one of those love songs which have been called "watchmen's songs" (*chansons de guettes*).

The approaches to the keep are guarded by men-at-arms. As at the threshold of the churches, beggars stand at the entrance of the palace:

> At the gate were folk
> Awaiting alms.
> (*Châtelain de Coucy*, v. 2991.)

They stand generally on the lower steps of the great staircase which leads to the lord's dwelling, a staircase which plays an important rôle in feudal life, for the guests of the castle enjoy taking the air and talking on the steps of grey marble. On the platform at the top of the high staircase the baron holds his Court and administers justice to the men of his fief. At the foot of the staircase single combats, jousts, and tiltings take place. On the steps are the spectators; and the combatants go there to rest.

The stone staircase is supported by vaults under which the poor and beggars can take shelter. We read in the *Life of Saint Alexius* that he lived for several years under the steps of the paternal castle before he was recognized.

There were two principal apartments in the feudal castle: the hall and the chamber. In the hall the public life was passed. The lord held his assizes there, received messengers, gave banquets. In the chamber, which he shared with his wife, he received his intimates. In the chamber, round the fire, long gossipings took place on winter nights.

The hall, of vast dimensions, opened off the top of the staircase. At one end was a deep stage running right across the room and raised a few feet from the floor, called the *dais*.

There the lord and his lady received their guests, both seated in arm-chairs (*sièges pliants*). There were the high tables, so called because they overlooked the low tables standing on the floor of the hall. At these high tables sat the lord, his lady, and guests of distinction. The dais was directly lighted by a large window jutting outwards. In the space furnished by this bay in the interior of the room the servants placed a table useful for serving purposes and dessert.

In the hall, great wooden chests, containing the goods of the lord and lady, served as seats. For the furniture of these rooms was of the simplest. They were almost empty. The seats in the hall were stone benches hewn out along the walls or in the bays of the windows. They were supplemented by folding seats which were brought in on occasion; in the same way the table, formed of planks resting on trestles, was put up at meal-times. The credence tables, holding gold and silver dishes, did not make their appearance before the fifteenth century.

The great flags of the floor were strewn with rushes—whence the word *joncher* (to strew)—with sweet-smelling herbs, or sometimes with flowers.

> Fresh rushes and mint they have had brought,
> And soon the dwelling they fill with sweet perfume (*empimenter*).
> (*Les Narbonnais*, v. 2405.)

The word *empimenter* means to perfume by burning juniper wood or Eastern perfumes.

One day Duke Begon was in the Castle of Belin, with the beautiful Béatrice, the daughter of Duke Milo of Blaives (his wife). He kissed her mouth and her face. The lady smiled sweetly. In the hall their children played before them. The eldest was named Garin and was twelve years old. The second, Hernaudin, was only six. Six noble youths shared their sport, running, jumping, laughing, and playing at catch-who-catch-can.

The Duke looked at them and began to sigh. The fair Béatrice noticed it. "What have you to worry about, my lord Begon?" said she; "you so lofty, so noble, so bold a knight. Are you not a rich man? Your coffers are full of gold and silver; your wardrobes of vair and minever. You

THE TWELFTH CENTURY

have hawks and falcons. In your stables are many draught horses and palfreys, mules and valuable horses. You have overcome all your enemies. For six days' journey round Belin there is not a knight who would hesitate to come at your call. Why are you anxious?" (*Garin le Loherain*).

Every feudal lord had a Court, similar to the royal Court, which had, for that matter, sprung directly from the Court of the baron. Since the time of the wooden keeps he had lodged and supported there a large household of vassals, servants, artisans, and domestics. How much larger it had become in the great dwellings of the twelfth century!

The squires, called also the *poursuivants* because they aspired to the order of chivalry, were divided into several classes, according to the services to which they were set. There was the body squire, attached either to the lord or his lady; the squire of the chamber, or the chamberlain; the squire of the table, or the seneschal; the squire of the stable, or the constable; the squire of the wine cellar, or the butler; the squire of the pantry, or the pantler, etc.

Under their orders, servants set up and laid the tables, brought water for the washing of the hands before meals, served the dishes, poured out the wine. They were concerned with the pantry, the wine cellars, the kitchen, the service of the chambers; they saw to the arrangement of the songs and amusements which followed the meals; and before the assembly broke up they presented the sweet wines, sweetmeats, the hot and spiced wines which the guests took before retiring to bed.

The squires accompanied guests to the rooms prepared for them. More important still was their military service. They kept in order the lord's weapons, equipped him with them, took care of his horses, looked after their harness, followed the lord in war and to the Court of his suzerain. They accompanied him to the tournament.

These squires, knights' sons, were destined for the order of chivalry. They were the sons of the vassals or relatives of the lord.

The principal officer at the Court of the baron, as at the Court of the King, was the seneschal. He had among his functions the superintendence of the household. His relations with his lord were very close. A saying ran:

> By the seneschal of the house
> You shall know its lord.

The squires and the young poursuivants-at-arms, who lived in the baron's castle and served him, received from him the education which was to enable them to maintain their rank in feudal society. They were also called the "supported" (*nourris*), and, under this title, regarded themselves as belonging to the lord's family.

> For he is my kinsman who will give me to eat.
> (*Baudoin de Sebourc*, Chant xix. v. 550.)

They received from the seneschal distributions of meat—by this word is understood "food" in general—and from the butler some measures of wine; unless the lady of the castle took this task on herself.

William of the Crooked Nose returns from the disaster of Larchamp. He enters the hall of his castle:

> "Oh! good hall, how long and wide you are,
> On all sides you are adorned:
> Blessed be the lady who has adorned thee.
> Oh! high tables, how lofty you are;
> Linen cloths cover you;
> These vessels filled to the brim. . . ."

But the knights bachelors, the *nourris* of Count William, who are generally at these tables, sit there no longer: they have been killed in battle.

> No sons of French mothers eat there—
> At Larchamp they have had their heads cut off.
> William weeps and Guiburc (his wife) faints;
> He lifts her up and comforts her. . . .

The scene is sublime.

The least important lord would maintain several squires in his castle. There is mention in *Guillaume de Dôle* of a poor lord: "He is not rich: scarcely could he support six squires from his lands."

Auberi addresses his companions:

> "Twenty knights must be living here,
> And I see only two at this supper. . . ."
>
> (*Auberi*.)

THE TWELFTH CENTURY

The vassals are obliged to show themselves at regular intervals, every month or every fortnight, and on great feast-days, at the Court of their lord, where in full assembly they give judgment, under the presidency of their lord, on any quarrels which have arisen among the dwellers in the domain.

These assizes were generally held in the hall of the castle, which received hence the name of the "mandate" (*mandement*):

> And the barons go up to the mandate
> Where the Duke sits between him and his men.
> (*Les Quatre fils Aymon*, v. 447.)

Let us look at the lord in the hall surrounded by his vassals. "He wears a cloak of blood-red cloth, trimmed with minever, with a collar of ermine. His girdle is a wide band of fine gold fastened with a sparkling clasp of precious stones. With the rod of pine which he holds in his hand he strikes the table sharply for silence" (*Garin le Loherain*).

The vassals assembled before him are clothed either in coats and surcoats, or in leather tunics or hauberks, and converse pleasantly with one another. Over the hauberk, with its trellis-work of grey mail, is thrown a cloak of a brilliant red colour:

> The colour of the coat of arms
> Shows us by reason proved
> The martyrdom which God suffered,
> When for us His blood He spent.
> (*Robert de Blois*, v. 1111.)

The helmets are enamelled in bright colours and with flowered designs, and sometimes inlaid with precious stones. The lord takes his place in an arm-chair on the dais, from which he dominates the assembly, and his wife is seated beside him.

These armour-clad men, whose principal occupation was warfare, were not wanting in culture. It would be a mistake to imagine them mere dullards. Certainly they enjoyed above all things the life of war. But how many of them were educated, friends of literature, and collected in their "palaces" manuscripts containing the works of their favourite authors!

Between two battles, during their distant expeditions, one might surprise our feudal dignitaries gathered together to read poetical works: *chansons de geste,* or romances, or works of history.

THE MIDDLE AGES

When they rode in company, they liked to sing to make the road seem shorter :

> Aallard and Guichard began a song :
> Of Gascony were the words and of Limousin the tune,
> And Richard sang well the bass.
>
> (*Les Quatre fils Aymon*, v. 6599.)

The feudal lords are to take a high place among the poets of the twelfth and thirteenth centuries, and several of them will shine in the first rank. They write lays and songs, rondeaus, songs of spring-time, *sirventes* and *tensons*, or, if they keep to prose, it will be, as with Villehardouin and Joinville, to range themselves among our most picturesque historians. William VII, Count of Poitiers and Duke of Aquitaine, is the earliest of our troubadours (he flourished from 1087 to 1127). After him comes Raimbaud d'Orange, the Viscount Bertrand de Born, and Jaufre Rudel, Lord of Blaye. In the family of the lords of Uisel, in Limousin, there is quite a blossoming of musicians and poets. " Guy d'Uisel," his biographer tells us, " was a noble lord of a castle. One of his four brothers was called Elie, and all four were troubadours. Guy made good songs, Elie good tensons (a kind of *jeux partis*), Eble *mauvaises*, and as to Pierre, he sang what the others composed." For the rest, the list of known troubadours, which contains about four hundred names for the twelfth and thirteenth centuries, includes five kings, six counts, five marquises, five viscounts, and a great number of rich barons and valiant knights.

> A song sweet to hear
> And pleasant to listen to
> As a knight I shall make . . .

says the noble Count Raoul of Soissons.

In the lofty keeps of France the language of *oïl* found, as a matter of fact, no fewer poets than the language of *oc* to the south of the Loire. We may mention Amauri de Craon, Roger d'Andely, Thibaud de Blaison, Bouchart de Montmorency, Charles of Anjou, King of Sicily, Peter Mauclerc, Duke of Brittany, the Castellan of Coucy, the Count of La Marche, Guillebert de Berneville, Geoffrey de Châtillon, Raoul de Boves, Perrin d'Angicourt, and Richard Cœur de Lion, Duke of Normandy and King of England. It was among the high feudal

THE TWELFTH CENTURY

nobility that lyric poetry took its rise and from them it spread to the middle class. The powerful Duke Henry III. of Brabant, one of the most magnificent princes of his century, a good poet and the author of some charming songs—of which he composed, like most of the poets of the time, both words and music—gives us a picture of himself, seeking for rhymes while riding in war gear :

> In the morning I mounted
> On my ambling palfrey,
> And the desire had seized me
> To make a new poem.

Luke de la Barre-sur-Ouche, while fighting against the King of England, wrote of him in some poetry which was much applauded. " He raised a laugh at my expense," says Henry I, who although he was called " Beauclerc " was not fond of jokes. In the fight of Bourg-Théroulde, Luke de la Barre fell into the hands of the English King, who, in spite of the protests of the Count of Flanders, ordered that his eyes should be put out. The good monk, Ordericus Vitalis, judges that this was just. On hearing the sentence of his conqueror, Luke de la Barre dashed out his brains against a wall. Jean de Brienne, who is to die in 1237 on the throne of Constantinople, composes pastorals. Count Thibaud of Champagne, the King of Navarre, will be the best poet of his time, the one whose work will be the most delicately finished. A poet, said Thibaud, ought only to have recourse to nightingales, flowers, and stars in the last extremity !

> Leaves and flowers are worthless in poetry.

As for the rôle of the lady of the castle, it seems to have been as important as that of the baron.

The poets of the eleventh and twelfth centuries have sketched her ideal in the *Chançun de Guillaume* and in *Aliscans*, in the person of Guibourc, the wife of Count William of the Crooked Nose. She has her husband's valour. She restores his courage when he is about to waver, and she is the first to send him forth to battle. And the author of *Aliscans* traces for us here scenes of an epic beauty and grandeur.

During the baron's absence she presides over the castle and rules the fief. At all times she governs the seigniorial

THE MIDDLE AGES

household as a good and active housekeeper. It is she who, with maternal solicitude, "nourishes" the youths, the sons of her husband's vassals, who are, according to custom, brought up in the castle. The young Guy recalls her care, on the field of battle, at the moment when, mortally wounded by the Saracens, he is about to die:

> Clear was the day and fair was the morn.
> The sun is shining, the arms sparkle.
> The rays strike on the shield of Lord Guy.
> Softly his eyes are weeping.
> William sees him, and asks,
> "What can it be, fair nephew, Sir Guy?"
> The youth replies: "To my sorrow I see
> Guibourc who nourished me so tenderly,
> Who gave me to eat so early.
> Now is the hour at which she used to offer it.
> Now I am so hungry, already I die,
> I cannot move or lift my weapons,
> Wield my lance or mount Balzan [his horse],
> Nor help myself, nor another injure,
> But to-day I die; this is sorrow and loss;
> God! what sorrow shall my friends have!
> For I am so hungry I am going mad.
> Would that I had my lady to serve me."
>
> (*Chançun de Guillelme*, v. 1733.)

The young maidens, whom the châtelaine has also "nourished" in the castle, she will marry to her husband's vassals, among whom he will distribute lands. Count William has departed to the war against the Saracens. To those of the knights who have remained in the fief and whom she is sending to join her husband, Guibourc speaks thus:

> "And who would not take lands without a wife,
> I have still a hundred and sixty maidens,
> Daughters of kings, there are none fairer under heaven,
> I have nourished them by the grace of William,
> They embroider for me golden tissues and stuffs in wheeled designs,
> Let him come with me and choose the fairest:
> I will give the wife; my lord shall give the land,
> It will be as good as payment could be."
>   One hastened to choose the fairest
>   —On Thursday evening—[the refrain of the song]
>   Who afterwards at Larchamp lost his head.
>
> (*Chançun de Guillelme*, v. 1392.)

THE TWELFTH CENTURY

For the châtelaine is also the mother of a family who sees to the education of the young girls gathered together in the castle, as the lord does for the youths. The distaff and the needle are held in honour among them. They busy themselves, under the direction of the châtelaine, with embroideries in gold and silken thread, and in dyeing materials.

These young girls took hardly any part in the gatherings of the men. When guests entered, they left the room. Only on feast-days they joined the assembly, where their grace and youthful array won admiration. They passed their days in the " Maidens' Chamber " (*la Chambre des Pucelles*) : great households seething with life, in which all is action, colour, and movement, and over which the châtelaine reigns supreme.

Just as the knight-bachelor was taught to ride and tilt, so the young maiden learned in the pale light of the deep windows to do " beautiful needlework."

A knight equipped for battle will not hesitate to offer his beloved a needlecase, knowing beforehand that the gift will please her. There is found still to-day, sculptured on the rough grey stone which covers the grave of a feudal châtelaine, in homage to her memory, a pair of scissors.

So the ladies of the castle in the twelfth century are clever at handling the spindle and the use of the needle. Their graceful industry produced beautiful alms-purses, helmet lacings, capes woven of silk and gold, the altar-cloths of the monasteries, while they sang to amuse themselves :

> All tunes Saracen,
> Songs of Gascony and France,
> Lays of Lorraine and Brittany. . . .
> (*Le roman de Galerent*, v. 1170.)

Here is an example of these songs, which became celebrated under the name of " sewing-songs " (*chansons de toile*), because ladies and maidens sang them while sewing, and because nearly always one finds in them a woman or young girl occupied with her needle :

> THE SONG OF FAIR YOLANDE
> (*Chanson de toile*)
> Fair Yolande in a chamber still,
> On her knee some stuffs unfolds,

THE MIDDLE AGES

Sews with a thread of gold and one of silk.
Her stern mother chides her;
"I chide you for it,
Fair Yolande."

"Fair Yolande, I chide you,
You are my daughter, do your duty."
"My lady mother, what is it for?"
"I will tell you, by my faith;
I chide you for it,
Fair Yolande."

"Mother, for what do you chide me?
Is it for sewing or cutting,
Or spinning or brushing,
Or is it for sleeping too much?"
"I chide you for it,
Fair Yolande."

"It is not for sewing nor for cutting,
Nor for spinning nor for brushing,
Nor is it for too much sleeping,
But for speaking too much to the knight!
I chide you for it,
Fair Yolande."

They learn also to tend the wounds received by the knights in war or tournament; to unlace their helmets, to remove their hauberks. They wash away the blood, and the dust which covers them. They dress the wound with bandages of white linen.

The day, says a lady, passes in the castle:

... in reading my psalter,
And working in gold and silk,
Cyrus of Thebes or of Troy (romances),
And playing songs on my harp,
And playing at chess with some one,
Or feeding my falcon from my hand.
(*Le roman de Galerent*, v. 3881.)

The chroniclers have left us portraits of these feudal châtelaines which differ so much that it would be impossible to derive from them any common features. One, like Blanche of Navarre, the guardian of her young son, Thibaud IV, puts herself at the head of a military expedition, in which she displays the qualities, but also the roughness, of a man. Aubarède,

THE TWELFTH CENTURY

the châtelaine of Pithiviers, has the head of the architect who has built her castle cut off, so that he may not reveal the secrets of the place or be able to build any similar keeps in the neighbourhood. Then she expels her own husband from the castle; but he returns before long in force and kills her with a poignard. Mabel, the wife of Count Roger of Montgomery, reduced the noblemen of her own fief to beggary until they avenged themselves by cutting her head off. The Countess Adelaide of Soissons had her brother poisoned so as to have the full enjoyment of his fief; she had the eyes of her victims put out and their tongues cut off. More dreadful still is the châtelaine of Cahuzac, who takes part in the tortures which her husband inflicts on poor wretches: cutting off hands and feet, putting out their eyes; she took a horrible pleasure in having the breasts of defenceless women cut off or in having their nails torn off so that they could not earn their bread.

A sufficiently large number of these examples might be cited, but if the writers of the time have preserved them for us it is because they were exceptional, and on the other hand, do not the same chroniclers give us to balance against them, the names of women whose lives have been all kindness, gentleness, beneficence, and piety? Of more than one châtelaine of the twelfth century, it may be said, with the author of *Girart de Roussillon* :

> To give, this is her towers and battlements.

To begin with, there is Guibert de Nogent's own mother, a saintly creature, whose whole life was filled with beneficence.

We read in the chronicle of Lambert d'Ardres: " The wife of Arnold the Red was a young lady pleasing to God; she was gentle and simple, diligent, pious, and God-fearing. She was to be seen amusing herself with her young maidens in children's games, singing choruses, dancing in rings, even joining them in playing with dolls. During the great heat of summer, in the innocence of her free heart, she would go and bathe in the lake clothed only in her chemise, not so much for the purpose of washing as for refreshment and exercise. She would swim rapidly in graceful curves, in the smooth water, now lying on her back to disappear, a moment later under the rippling water, appearing again on the surface whiter than snow, whiter than her silky chemise which was dazzlingly white; and this in the presence not only of the maidens of her suite but of the young men and knights. In this and in a thousand other ways she showed the limpid goodness of her character, the undisturbed purity of her habits, which made her beloved by her husband and the knights of the castellany and by all the people."

And no doubt she is an exception among the châtelaines of the twelfth century, just as the cruel viragos we mentioned above were exceptional figures.

The education which the feudal lords gave their sons was exceedingly severe.

The Tournaments. "The serfs," we read in a sermon of the time, "spoil their children when they are small; they give them fine clothes to wear, and when they are grown up they send them to the plough. The nobles, on the contrary, begin by trampling on their sons; they make them eat in the kitchen with the serving-men, and then when they are grown up they 'honour' them." Boys take pleasure in horse-riding, hunting, and fencing bouts. While employed in the service of the suzerain who "nourishes" them, the young men bear their shields; they learn to arm themselves for the battle or the tournament.

The tournament was the repetition, often cruel and bloody, of the methods of battle. "A knight must," says Roger de Hoveden, in speaking of these violent exercises, "have seen his blood flow, had his teeth broken by blows of the fist, been thrown to earth with the full weight of his antagonist on top of him, been twenty times unhorsed and twenty times recovered from his falls, and yet must prove more implacable than ever in battle."

A very false idea prevails of these tournaments, at least in the heroic period. We picture knights in shining armour, with burnished and brightly coloured shields, with fancifully crested helmets on their heads, mounted on horses caparisoned in gold, jousting courteously within the white lists, in the presence of beautiful ladies seated on a dais with armorial bearings.

In the twelfth century tournaments were real wars which developed not only in the precise place appointed for the meet-

THE TWELFTH CENTURY

ing, but encroached on the neighbouring country. There is no document known which at this period forbids the use of sharps swords or pointed lances in the tournament. However, the object of the combatants, protected by their iron carapaces, was not to kill. But they mishandled each other severely, greedy to get possession of each other's horses and harness, trying to take prisoners for the sake of ransom, as in real battles.

" The Normans and English," we read in the biography of William the Marshall, " were grouped for a tournament against the French. . . . Beforehand, in their houses, the French had apportioned the harness and gold of the English; but they had not got them yet."

The lords appeared there with their serving-men and sergeants who helped them in the course of the fight, without however being of very much use, for they ran away at the first sign of danger, knowing that the knights on the other side would not hesitate to massacre them.

Tournaments appear to have been distinguished in the thirteenth century from real wars only by the following points:

1. Tournaments had the *lists*, a part of the ground barricaded off, where the knights could rest, have their wounds dressed, get their weapons mended or change them, or indeed take refuge when they felt themselves too hardly pressed. It was neutral ground.

2. The place of the encounter had been fixed beforehand.

3. During the intervals of fighting the knights of both sides paid reciprocal visits of courtesy.

4. Finally, at the end of the tournament the chief personages engaged in the struggle met together to award prizes to those who had distinguished themselves most.

Real armies were sometimes seen contesting in these jousts. There were three thousand men at the tournament of Lagny described by the biographer of the Marshall. The contestants were seen on horseback advancing with difficulty through the vineyards.

The biographer of the Marshall speaks of a great tournament which took place somewhere between 1176 and 1180 in the district round Dreux. On one side were the knights of France,

Flanders, Brie, and Champagne. On the other were the Normans, Bretons, English, the men of Mantes, the Anjevins and Poitevins. The French and their adherents charged in great disorder. They broke in the attack, and when Henry the Young, the son of the Plantagenet Henry II, and William the Marshall arrived with their contingents they were already routed.

The pursuit was so lively that the King (Henry the Young) remained behind alone with the Marshall. They found in a street Simon de Neauphle, who barred their passage with three hundred foot sergeants armed with bows, picks, and hatchets.

" We cannot pass here," said the King, " and we cannot think of turning back."

" We must just run over them," replied the Marshall.

The sergeants, seeing them coming, opened ranks, not daring to await them, and the Marshall took my lord Simon by the bridle. He led him along, the King following a little way behind. The Marshall did not look behind. A waterspout jutted out across their road, and the Lord of Neauphle got caught on it and was left hanging. The King saw, but said nothing. The Marshall arrived at the dépôt, still holding in leash the French lord's horse. " Take this knight," he said to a squire.—" Which knight ? " said the King.—" Which knight ? Why, the one I am leading."—" But you haven't one."—" Where is he then ? "—" He is hanging on a waterspout."

Such is an episode of the tournament.

Following on this affair, in which the Marshall had distinguished himself, the Count of Flanders sent him, as a mark of homage, a magnificent pike.

" Two knights were told off to present it to him. They set out, a squire going in front of them with the pike. They found William at the forge with his head on the anvil, while the smith, with the help of his pincers and hammers, was forcing away his helmet, warped and battered down on his neck."

William the Marshall was connected with another knight, Roger de Gaugi. " He was an enterprising and resourceful person, but a little too keen on profit." His prowess had obtained him admittance into the household of the King of

THE TWELFTH CENTURY

England. Gaugi knew of the magnificent gains which the Marshall earned in the tournaments.

> Greed seizes and kindles
> His heart; he speaks and tells
> The Marshall he will bear him company.
>
> (v. 3394.)

For two years the Marshall and Gaugi frequented the tournaments, sweeping up horses, harness, money. "I am not talking in the air," says our biographer; "I base my statements on the accounts of the clerks. The accounts of Wigain, the clerk of the kitchen, and others absolutely establish that between Pentecost and Lent (1180) they took a hundred and three knights, without mentioning the horses and equipments which the accountants did not enter."

Another tournament took place later at the same spot. At the beginning of the action the French had the advantage but on the arrival of the English prince, Henry the Young, and his troops, they were routed. Some of them took refuge on a fortified hill defended by a "hericon," *i.e.* a palisade, itself surrounded by a moat. They had tied their horses to the palisade. "William the Marshall performed a great feat. He dismounted and gave his horse into safe keeping, climbed up to the fort, took two horses and drove them down into the moat at the foot of the rampart, then up the opposite bank." But two French knights came up and, seeing him worn out, took the two horses from him.

"The Marshall, again in the saddle, rode towards a barn in which several knights (French) were besieged by a superior number of their enemies." Seeing him coming, the besieged, who knew him, cried out : 'There are fifteen of us, knights; take us as your prisoners. We prefer, as we are reduced to this point, to belong to you rather than to those who are besieging us.'"

Tournaments had their origin in France, and it was there that they had all their brilliance. In spite of his partiality for everything from beyond the Channel, the biographer of the Marshall acknowledges this.

We have just seen William the Marshall in partnership with a sort of ruffian for the sake of the profits to be won from these warlike jousts. In this way there came to be formed a class of professional fighters in tournaments, just as we see formed to-day in many sports. They went from tournament to tournament, realizing a fine profit in horses, plate, and often in good, hard cash. Such a one was the good knight, who had neither vine nor land, described with such picturesque effect in one of our old fables; he had no means of livelihood except what he won by frequenting tournaments, and found himself reduced to a lamentable state of distress, when, at the instigation of the Church, this violent form of sport was momentarily suspended.

SOURCES.—*La chançun de Guillelme*, ed. Herm. Suchier, *Bibliotheca Normannica*, 1911; *Garin le Loherain*, translated by P. Paris, 1862; *Lamberti Ardensi Chronicon Ghisnense et Ardense*, ed. Godefroy Menilglaise, 1855; Guibert de Nogent, *De vita sua*, ed. Bourgin, 1907; Montaiglon-Raynaud, *Recueil des fabliaux*, 1879–90, 6 vols.; *L'histoire de Guillaume le Maréchal*, ed. P. Meyer, 1891–1901, 3 vols.

HISTORICAL WORKS.—Viollet-le-Duc, *Dictionnaire de l'architecture* and *Dictionnaire du mobilier*, ed. cit.; Leopold Delisle, "De l'instruction littéraire de la noblesse française au Moyen Age," in the *Journal de l'instruction publique*, June, 1855; B. Hauréau, *Notices et extraits de quelques MSS latins de la Bibliothèque Nationale*, 1890–92, 6 vols.; Huberti, *Studien zur Rechtsgesch. des Gottes frieden und Landfrieden*, 1892; Sémichon, *Paix et trêve de Dieu*; La Corne Ste.-Palaye, *Mémoires sur l'ancienne chevalerie*, 1781; R. Rosières, *Hist. de la Société française au Moyen Age*, 1884, 2 vols.; Ch. V. Langlois, *La Société française au XIIIe Siècle*, 2nd ed., 1904; Ch. V. Langlois, *La Vie en France au Moyen Age*, according to some moralists, 1908; E. Rust, *Die Erziehung des Ritters in der Altfranzösischen Epik*, 1888; Alvin Schultz, *Das Höfische Leben zur Zeit der Minnesinger*, 2nd ed., 1889, 2 vols.; Thomas Wright, *A History of Domestic Manners and Sentiments during the Middle Ages*, 1862; L. Gautier, *La Chevalerie*, 3rd ed., 1895.

CHAPTER IX

THE MINSTRELS

Trouvères and minstrels. The French language comes from Latin. The talents of the minstrels. Their manuscripts. How the minstrels were paid. Their poverty. Colin Muset and Rutebeuf. The minstrels as authors of fame. Fine words and splendid stories. The troubadours.

IN the life of the castle much pleasure was derived from minstrels. Their name (*Jongleurs*) comes from the Latin *joculares* or *joculatores*. We must not confuse them with the poets (trouvères): the " trouveurs," as they were called in the twelfth century. The minstrel gives to the public the work composed by the poets. The troubadours were the trouvères of the South, those who wrote in the language of *oc* (*oc* = oui), and their name has the same origin: it comes from *trobar*, to find. The trouvères used the language of *oïl* (*oïl* = oui), *i.e.* French proper. The line of demarcation starts on the right bank of the Garonne at its junction with the Dordogne, from which it turns northwards. Angoulême is still in " langue d'oïl "; Limoges, Guéret, Montluçon are in " langue d'oc "; thence the dividing line bends towards Lyons through Roanne and St. Etienne.

Provençal was divided into dialects just as Northern French was. There was Provençal proper, the dialect of Languedoc, of Auvergne, of Limoges, and to the east in Savoy and Dauphiny, an idiom finely flavoured with its suggestion of Latinity peculiarly well preserved. It has been called Franco-Provençal. Of these dialects that of Limoges became the language of literature, just as did, in the *langue d'oïl*, the speech of the Ile-de-France. The *langue d'oïl* and the *langue d'oc* are equally derived from Latin. French is, like Provençal, Latin

181

which has insensibly changed. In the eleventh century Adhémar de Chabannes still speaks of French as " Latin."

" Rollo of Normandy being dead, his son William succeeded him. He had been baptized. The Normans adopted the faith of Christ and, forgetting their barbarous tongue, they took the habit of speaking *Latin*." Moreover, if we take the oldest example of our language, the famous oath taken at Strasburg in 841 by Louis, the son of Louis the Debonnair, to his brother Charles the Bald, it is impossible to say whether this language is still Latin or if it has already become French : " Pro Deo amur et pro Christian poblo et nostro commun salvament d'ist di en avant, in quant Deus savir et podir, me dunat, si salvarai eo cist meon fradre Karlo et in adiudha et in cadhuna cosa si cum om per dreit son fradre salvar dist." (" For the love of God and before all Christian people and for our common salvation, from this day forward, in so far as God may grant me knowledge and power, I will aid my brother Charles by assistance and in all things as by right a brother should.")

No mention of minstrels is found before the eleventh century, but from the reign of Robert the Pious (the beginning of the eleventh century) one finds them mingling with various classes of society.

The French minstrels soon took the lead of the literary movement in Europe.

They come fully into view at the time when the epic is ceasing to be merely local and to belong strictly to the family, at the period which sees it uprooted to be carried from place to place. The minstrels made them heard to the strains of the Irish harp, from castle to castle, from one market to another, from town to town.

The minstrels have been defined as : " Those who make a profession of amusing the people " ; for their talents were varied. A poet says to a young man who intends to become a minstrel : " You must know how to ' trouver ' (compose poems), to jump high, to speak easily, and propose competitions. You must know how to play the tambourine, the castanets, and the symphony (a musical instrument) . . .; how to throw and catch apples with two knives, the songs of birds and

THE MINSTRELS

marionettes. You must know how to play the guitar and the mandoline, and to jump through hoops. You will have a red beard, and make a dog jump over a stick and stand on two paws." In the picturesque adornments of the margins of thirteenth-century manuscripts one may still see the minstrels with their red beards and wigs.

> I will tell you what I can do,

says the minstrel in a fable to one of his companions:

> I am a minstrel of the viol,
> I know the musette and the flute,
> And the harpe and chifonie,
> The gigue and armonie,
> And the salteire and the rote;
> I know well how to sing a tune;

(The harpe, chifonie, gigue, salteire, and rote were musical instruments.)

> Well I know how to use the juggler's cup,
> And make the snail appear
> Alive and leaping on the table;

(Compare the song of the children to make the snail come "alive and leaping on the table": "Mas! Mas! Mas! Show me thy horns!")

> And I know many fine table tricks,
> And from prestidigitations and magic
> Well I know how to make an enchantment.
> . . . .
> And the knowledge and chants of the clergy,
> And the speech of chivalry,
> And to warn good knights
> And decipher their arms.

And this same minstrel will know the heroic *gestes* of *Roland* and *Guillaume*, of *Rainoart, Garin, Vivien,* and *Ogier*. He will be the poetic echo of the most touching idylls, *Perceval, Tristan et Iseut, Flore et Blancheflor*:

> I know well how to serve a knight,
> And of fine tales the whole sum;
> I know stories, I know fables,
> I can tell fine new tales.

THE MIDDLE AGES

> Songs with refrains, old and new,
> Poems satirical and pastorals.
>
> . . . .
>
> I can sing at your desire
> Of King Pepin and Saint Denis,
> Of the men of Lorraine the whole history,
> I know their meaning and have them by heart—
> Of Charlemagne and Roland
> And the fight of Oliver.
> I know of Ogier, I know of Aymon,
> And of Girard of Roxilion,
> And I know of King Louis
> And of Buevon de Conmarchis.
>
> . . . .
>
> I can give counsels of love
> And make crowns of flowerets,
> And love gifts,
> And speak well of gracious service
> To those who are in love. . . .
> (*Fabliau des deux bordeors*, v. 283.)

Others know how to imitate the song of the nightingale, the cry of the peacock, the humming of the bee, the roaring of a bull. Aubry de Trois Fontaines speaks of the prowess of a minstrel whom he saw at Compiègne, where the betrothal of Robert of Artois with the daughter of the Duke of Brabant was being celebrated. He mounted a horse which was walking on a rope.

The author of the *Moral Story* writes that the door was opened willingly to

> Those who can twist their limbs strangely,
> Who all night can sing songs with refrains,
> Who can make the whole household leap and dance;

to those who know how to "make the forked tree" (stand head downwards, legs in the air) on the high table and can make curious grimaces.

Joinville in his turn writes: "There came three minstrels, brothers, on pilgrimage to Jerusalem; they had three trumpets with the horns turned towards their faces. When they began to play their trumpets you would have thought it was the voice of swans coming from the water, and they produced the sweetest and most gracious melodies, a marvel to hear."

THE MINSTRELS

And these same minstrels—they were Armenians—did three wonderful acrobatic feats. A towel was put under their feet and, holding themselves rigid, they turned a complete somersault, their feet returning to the towel. Two of them turned their heads to face behind them, and the eldest also, and when he turned it round again he crossed himself, for he was afraid of breaking his neck in the act of turning."

And these minstrels with their instruments accompanied the armies on march and came into the churches to sing variations on the *Kyrie*, the *Sanctus*, and the *Agnus Dei*.

Some minstrels were themselves poets. It is a minstrel who writes the *History of the Holy War*, and another the *Life of St. Alexius*. The most charming and the greatest of thirteenth-century poets, Colin Muset and Rutebeuf, will both be minstrels.

Our merry fellows carefully preserve the manuscript containing the text of their gay science; they would guard the privilege of their fine poems, or if they part with a copy to a colleague, or a rival, it is for a financial consideration.

> I will tell you of a song held in great honour,
> In the realm of France none is so much praised,
> Huon de Villeneuve kept it close guarded:
> He would not for it take horse or harnessed mule,
> Cloak with vair or minever, or cape of fur,
> Nor of Parisian monies a measureful:
> Now greatly he grieves that it is stolen from him.
> (*Les Quatre fils Aymon*, ed. Castets, p. 10.)

Huon de Villeneuve has made every effort to keep the text of his song for himself; he has refused money and horses for it, a cloak trimmed with fur and a fur cape; but, behold, it has been stolen from him.

In treating above of the *chansons de geste* we saw that the first minstrels had been soldiers. Suger still, in his life of Louis VI, speaks of a brave knight who was also a minstrel, and who leaves the army of the feudal barons of Enguerran de Boves and Eble de Roucy, to range himself under the banners of the King. But from the middle of the twelfth century there is hardly any longer found any but professionals who go from district to district on horseback, their luggage in their saddle-bags, their fiddle and bow strapped to their shoulders, seeking a livelihood by making heard everywhere the themes of their epic poems, the lively refrains of their songs, their songs with the refrain of *vadu,* and their *triboudaines.*

"Like flies on a sweet liquid," writes a thirteenth-century orator, "one sees the minstrels flying to the Courts of princes." The author of the Provençal romance *Flamenca* has described a wedding feast at which 1500 minstrels display the most varied talent :

"Then you could have heard the sound of instruments through the whole gamut of tones. . . . One fiddles the song of the honey-suckle, another that of Tintagruel; one sings the faithful lovers, another the song made by Ivan ; one plays the harp, another the viol ; one the flute, another the fife ; one the gigue, the other the rote ; one says the words while another accompanies him ; one works marionettes, another juggles with knives ; another dances a cabriole : the buzz of many voices fills the room."

Our artists received for their trouble food and lodging, clothes and money.

The author of *Huon de Bordeaux* shows us a minstrel at the royal Court. He begins to play the viol. The lords press round him. In their enthusiasm, one after another they take off their cloaks, which fall in a heap round the minstrel. "We have seen princes," says Rigord, "who after having spent twenty or thirty marks on splendid garments wonderfully embroidered, have given them a week later to minstrels."

After all, devoted as they may be to art and poetry, our minstrels have still to live and support their families. And they do not hesitate to say so :

> Now draw near, lord, I pray you,
> And he who has no money need not sit down,
> For those who have it not are not of my company.
> (*Baudoin de Sebourc,* Chant v. v. 19–21.)

And what discontent when the amount of the payment does not tally with the expectation, when the minstrel has not received from the baron at whose castle he has displayed his talent, the desired recompense. The reception is not the same

THE MINSTRELS

everywhere. There are wealthy men who, in return for the amusement afforded them by the minstrels,

> Make them depart often unshod:
> . . . . .
> Giving them only old clothes,
> And a little of their broken food,
> Throwing it as to dogs.
>
> (*Fabliau des lecheors*, v. 82.)

Colin Muset expresses himself on this subject in peculiarly vivid terms. He is addressing a lord at whose castle he sang, recited poems, and played the violin, and who has given him a meagre pittance.

> Lord Count, I have fiddled
> Before you in your house,
> Yet nothing have you given me
> Nor paid my fee,
> It is shameful—
> By the faith I owe to Our Lady
> No longer will I serve you.
> My alms-purse is ill furnished,
> My pouch ill filled.
> Sir Count, pray tell me
> What you will do for me.
> Sire, if it please you,
> Grant me a good gift
>   From courtesy.
> I have great desire, do not doubt,
> To return to my family.
> When I go there with empty purse
> My wife is not merry.
>
> Why, she says, "Sir Needy,
> In what land have you been
> That you have earned nothing?
> Have you disported yourself too much
> About the town?
> See how your box moves!
> It is well stuffed with air!
> Shame be to him
> Who would be of your company!"
>
> But when I come to my house
> And my wife has seen
> The bag well filled behind me,
> And myself well garbed
> In a furred robe;

THE MIDDLE AGES

> Know that she throws down at once
> Her needle, truthfully,
> She smiles at me for kindness,
> Throws two arms round my neck.
>
> My wife goes to rifle
> My bag without delay:
> My serving-man to water
> And care for my horse;
> My servant-maid to kill
> Two capons to cook
> In garlic sauce;
> My daughter brings me a comb
> In her hand from courtesy:
> Then am I king in my house,
> Very joyful and without care
> Beyond what I could tell you.

And the great Rutebeuf harps on this same theme but in poignant terms:

> Do not blame me if I hesitate
> To go back,
> For I shall have no welcome;
> My coming will not be agreeable
> If nothing I bring.
> This is what most disheartens me,
> That I dare to knock at my door
> With empty hands.

At his house, poor Rutebeuf finds his wife dissatisfied, crabbed, whining. The landlord comes for the rent, his furniture is pledged, and now comes along the hired nurse demanding money " to feed the baby," failing which she will send it back to fill the house with its yelling.

Hear the heart-rending cry which the poet sends out to the foot of the royal throne:

> I cough with cold and with hunger gape,
> Through them I die and am finished with.
> I am without coverlet or bed;
> Lord, I know not where to go.
> My sides feel the straw,—
> A bed of straw is no bed,
> And in my bed there is nothing but straw. . . .
> Lord, I would have you know
> I have not wherewith to buy bread. . . .

THE MINSTRELS

Poverty has deprived him of his friends:

> I think the wind has carried them off.
> Love is dead!
> They are friends whom a breeze carries off.
> It blew before my door,
> And they are gone.

And he ends with these admirable lines:

> The hope of to-morrow,
> This is my banquet!

Thus, as writes Guillaume le Vinier:

> Sometimes the minstrel is singing,
> And he is saddest of all,
> He sings according to his subject
> As the most sorrowful man in the world;
> It is not for pleasure,
> But for need of help
> As a minstrel courteous and free;
> When he has finished his song,
> Gently he asks and prays
> Help to live for a while.

Saint Louis gave money "to poor minstrels without number who, through old age or sickness, could not work or follow their profession" (*Joinville*).

The ministrels frequented fairs and places of pilgrimage. They stopped at the entrance to the shrines, where they recited their poems, often in the open air, to the crowd, sometimes noisy and sometimes attentive. In Paris they made themselves heard preferably on the Petit-Pont (little bridge), which in the Middle Ages seems to have played the rôle of the Pont-Neuf (new bridge) in the seventeenth century. We have seen how Gilles de Paris heard them singing to the people the *gestes* of Charlemagne, with the accompaniment of the viol. In the great square, the jugglers erected their stages from which they recited their verses to the gaping clowns. In certain places taxes were demanded from them; they were expected to pay in money or small-wares. This was the case at Mimizan in Aquitaine (near Mont-de-Marsan). A certain W.-R. de Monos controlled the juggling there, and collected the fourth of the dues paid by the performers. He held this right in fief from the King of England, who was Duke of Aquitaine, for the consideration of a hawk which he owed him annually, or, in default, ten pounds of wax.

And here, with this audience of passers-by gathered in the public square, what a modest harvest it must have been! One of the minstrels who appears in *Huon de Bordeaux* breaks off in an epic poem to exhort his auditors to come next day each with a farthing tied up in his shirt (failing a purse) ; and above all, that it should not be a Poitevin coin but one of Paris, for the Paris farthing was worth four times that of Poitou :

> Come back to-morrow after dinner
> And I beg of you, each bring me
> A farthing tied up in your shirts ;
> For in these Poitevin coins is little value :
> Greedy and parsimonious were they who had them struck,—
> Never give them to a gentle minstrel.
> (*Huon de Bordeaux*, v. 4957.)

For the rest, if the minstrels are too often wretched, it is largely the result of their careless temperament and love of pleasure. One of them says mildly :

> Do not repine if I have your money,
> For as soon as I have it to the tavern it will go.
> (*Baudoin de Sebourc*, Chant xii. v. 921–22.)

Our minstrel, if he has earned a garment or some money, and happens to pass a tavern, cannot resist the invitation of the serving-man of the inn, who hails him from the threshold. He enters :

> When he has got together sous three, four, five,
> Into the tavern he soon goes
> And feasts with it while it lasts.
> And when he has tasted the good wine,
> And the landlord sees he has spent all :
> " Brother," says he, " seek another inn,
> Give me pledge of what you owe."
> And he leaves with him his hose and shoes.
> (*Le Moniage Guillaume*.)

And there he is, like the poor minstrel of Sens, who often had not a whole coat to his back :

> But quite often in his shirt
> Was exposed to wind and blast. . . .
> (*De Saint Pierre et du jongleor*.)

THE MINSTRELS

The wind is cold, the blast is sharp:

>I do not see come April or May;
>Look at the ice!

Tolls for crossing bridges and roads they pay in "monkey money" (*monnaie de singe*), *i.e.* by a trick performed by themselves, or the little animal or monkey which often accompanies them—or even sometimes by some verses of their poems, a couplet of their songs.

Greater comfort was assured to the minstrels attached as domestics (*ministeriales*) to some great house.

Watriquet has sung before some passer-by, "ballads and short rondeaus." His auditors ask him:

>Are you not Raniques?
>—No indeed, by Our Lady, but Watriques,
>Minstrel to the Count of Blois,
>And also to my lord Gauchier
>De Chastillon (the constable . . .).
>(*Fabliau des trois chanoinesses de Cologne*, v. 108.)

Joinville speaks of the "ministrels of the rich men," *i.e.* of the minstrels attached to the household of the great lords, who come to the court of the King with their viols. After the meal, Saint Louis "waited to hear grace said until the minstrels had recited their poems, then rose, and the priests who were before him said grace."

We have seen that some great lords were trouvères or troubadours. They kept minstrels who lived in their castles among their servants. The minstrels accompanied them in their travels. They performed publicly the work of their masters. A certain miniature in the Bibliothèque Nationale represents the poet in silken tunic, sitting proudly in an arm-chair of gold. He holds in his hand the baton of a conductor of an orchestra, with which he marks time for the minstrel, who, standing before him, is reciting in song one of his poems.

Moreover, the great lords did not extend their protection to the minstrels solely for the amusement they afforded them. These poets were the dispensers of fame at a time when they were the only recorders of men's actions. Lambert d'Ardres tells that the author of the *Chanson d'Antioche*, Richard the

THE MIDDLE AGES

Pilgrim (le Pèlerin), refused to mention in his epic story the high deeds of Arnold the Ancient, lord of Ardres, because the latter had refused him a pair of scarlet shoes. "The lord of Ardres," says Lambert, "shunning human glory, preferred to refuse a paltry gift to a buffoon to being sung and praised in his songs to the accompaniment of musical instruments." We have preserved some verses of the *Chanson d'Antioche* by Richard le Pèlerin, but for the most part we only possess his work in the revised version of Graindor of Douai. It has been very justly remarked that Richard Cœur de Lion would never have had the brilliant reputation which he enjoyed in his time, if he had not patronized so many poets and minstrels. Even in his absence William de Longchamp, who remained in England as regent, brought minstrels from France to sing his praises at the cross-roads of the towns before the assembled people.

In time there came a division among the minstrels. Some became poets who composed their own works and only recited them in good company. Others sang or recited to the accompaniment of musical instruments the works of the poets. Finally, a third class included mountebanks, pirouette dancers, and showmen.

This is a humbler class, scorned by the minstrel who is assuming a more refined character:

> A minstrel should conduct himself
> More simply than a maid! . . .
> A minstrel who wishes to act rightly
> Should not imitate the mountebank,
> But on his lips should ever have
> Gentle words and fine language.

Ah! "fine phrases," "seemly words," "splendid stories"; what importance our minstrels attach to them, whether they call themselves "Short-Beard," "Proud Arms," "Break-pot," or "Simple in Love."

Contrary to general opinion, no poets have had in a higher degree a regard for form than the trouvères, troubadours, and minstrels of the twelfth century. Hundreds of years before Malherbe, they know the "force" "of a word in the right

THE MINSTRELS

place." Poor Boileau was lamentably ignorant of his most glorious predecessors.

Courte-Barbe sums up all the aspirations of his craft, and indeed all those of the modern poet, in the following lines, which end with a timid and touching appeal to Immortality:

> A matter here I will tell you
> Of a fable I will relate to you.
> The minstrel is thought wise
> Who gives his time to writing poems,
> To making fine phrases and good tales
> As they are recited before Dukes and Counts.
> Fables are good to hear:
> To many ills and sorrows they bring forgetfulness,
> And many wearinesses and misdeeds:
> *Cortebarbe* made this fable;
> I believe, indeed, that it will not be forgotten.
> (*Le Fabliau des trois aveugles de Compiègne*, v. 1.)

Certainly they love rhyme and "assonance"; but they do not sacrifice to it the sense of their lines. They prefer reason to rhyme. "A plague upon a fine rhyme if it detracts from the sense!"

> I will endeavour and I intend
> To tell a fable in rhyme,
> Without purple patches and ambitious rhymes.
> But if it has assonance
> I care not who speaks ill of it.
> For it cannot be pleasing to all,
> Consonance, without good words.
> (*Fabliau des Trois dames*, v. 1 . . .)

It is true that at times the rhyme is difficult to find. One gets out of it as best one can, by some cunning turn or a little juggling:

> The priest says immediately,
> First loud and then low,
> "Dominus Domino meo,"
> But I cannot in *o*
> Find here assonance.
> (*Fabliau du prestre qui dit la Passion*, v. 50.)

On their wax tablets, on which they imprint with a nimble pencil their gracious or droll fancies, they efface many times

THE MIDDLE AGES

lines they have written, to improve and polish their texts. Cursed wax tablets! In their soft and fickle paste, how many have been lost of these charming works stamped with the Gallic genius of the minstrels! Parchment was dear and was only used for important work, serious productions but not always the best.

The minstrels' art began to decay during the thirteenth century.

The era of the minstrels ends about the beginning of the Hundred Years War. Ministrelsy and Feudal France rose together: they disappear together. "Readers" replace "auditors." Chantecler, as he is called in the *Roman de Renard*, the bold and adventurous minstrel, dressed in a hooded robe, half yellow, half green, or a robe of red silk,—Chantecler, whom one sees with "a green chaplet on his head," in castles, at fairs, on pilgrimages, his fiddle in hand, his memory crammed with epic tales, with courtly romances, lays, ballads, and fables,—gives place to the "man of letters."

. . . .

Some of the troubadours—the poets of the South—were, like the trouvères—the poets of the North—at once poets and minstrels. Some of them were, like the minstrels, at once poets and musicians—inventing not only the words but the tunes of their poems. They had, perhaps more still than the trouvères, a regard for form to such a degree that they came, especially in the first period, to cultivate this for its own sake, to love poetry only for its form, which led them through over-refinement to the recondite word, the *trobar claus*, i.e. to obscure expressions, closed to the profane.

The poetry of the troubadours flourishes, like that of the trouvères from the middle of the eleventh up to the thirteenth century. The period of its greatest brilliance is the twelfth century; while the greatest poets of the North, the authors of the finest poems, flourished at the end of the eleventh century.

The poetry of the troubadours is essentially, and almost exclusively, a lyric poetry, but in this class it is unequalled. Love is its theme, and it puts love in the frame which best becomes it, the beautiful scenes of Nature. "When the green grass and leaves appear and the flowers open in the orchards,

THE MINSTRELS

when the nightingale begins to sing, it gladdens me to hear him and to see the flowers; I am pleased with myself, but more still with my wife," writes Bernard de Ventadour. This taste for Nature at her gayest is pushed to such a degree that Raimbaud d'Orange protests against this orgy of nightingales singing themselves hoarse in flower-decked meadows :

" I sing not for bird, or flower, or dawn. . . . I sing for the lady to whom my thoughts fly. . . ."

We have said that the troubadours wrote in the dialect of Limoges, though a great many of them did not belong to that province. Bernard de Ventadour, Marcabrun, Jaufre Rudel, Arnaud de Mareuil, Giraud de Bornelh, Arnaud Daniel, Bertrand de Born, who flourished in the second half of the twelfth century, are the best representatives of the poets of Langue d'oc.

" Bertrand de Born," says Dante, " sang of arms, Arnaud Daniel of love; Giraud de Bornelh of integrity, honesty, and virtue."

The one whom Dante ranked first was Arnaud Daniel. " He was," he says in his *Purgatorio*, " the greatest artist in his native tongue. He surpassed all others in romances and love poems; say what they may those fools who think that Giraud de Bornelh is his superior." Arnaud Daniel is the poet of opulent rhymes, " dear " rhymes as he called them. Is it this which won him the favour of Dante ? For the verdict of the great Italian poet has not been ratified by posterity. The necessity of adapting the sense to the opulent rhymes, " lugubriously opulent " as Joseph Bédier so well terms them, has caused him more than once to sacrifice lucidity and even poetry itself. Giraud de Bornelh said just the opposite : " If I had the talent for it I should write a little poem which my grandson could understand, and in which all the world could take pleasure." Giraud de Bornelh, says an ancient biographer, was a mason from the district of Excideuil. . . . He was of low birth. . . . He was termed the master of the troubadours and is still estimated as such by connoisseurs, those who appreciate the subtle words expressing well the sentiment of love. In the winter he pursued his studies. In the summer he frequented castles, taking with him two singers to sing his poems. He would never take a wife; and all he earned he gave to his poor relatives and to the church of the town in which he was born.

Bertrand de Born is the soldier poet:

"I am well pleased with the good season of Easter, which brings the leaves and flowers; I love to hear the joy of the birds, which fill the woods with song; but also I love to see, in battle array, horses and armed knights."

"I love to see the scouts and behind them the main body of the soldiers. I love to see strong castles besieged, the fortifications battered down and demolished, and the army on the slope surrounded by moats and palisades of strong and serried staves. . . ."

Peyre Cardinal holds a unique position among the troubadours; he alone, of these poets of love, jests about love:

"Never did I gain so much as on the day I lost my love, for in losing her I found myself, whom I had lost. . . ."

"At last I can sing the praises of love, for it no longer deprives me of appetite and sleep; it no longer exposes me to heat and cold; it no longer makes me sigh or wander aimlessly at night; I no longer declare myself overcome and vanquished; love saddens or tortures me no longer; I am no longer betrayed; heigho! I have departed with my dice.

"I fear no longer jealousy; I no longer commit heroic follies. I am no longer beaten, I am robbed no more; nor do I now dance attendance. I no longer declare myself vanquished by love. I have departed with my dice.

"I no longer declare that I am dying for the fairest, nor that she makes me languish. I no longer beseech her, nor adore her, foolish at her feet. I no longer claim or desire her. I do homage to her no more. I put myself no longer in her power, nor am I subject to her. She has no longer my heart in fee. I am no longer her prisoner; heigho! I have departed with my dice."

But we have here a unique exception, for all the work of the troubadours forms a hymn, repeated and varied thousands of times, to love in fair Nature.

We have seen that it reached its apogee in the second half of the twelfth century. In the thirteenth the poetic vein loses

THE MINSTRELS

its richness. By dint of harping continuously on the same theme, the troubadours arrive in the end at a conception of love, refined and subtilized to such a degree that it has no longer in it anything of this world. Through the religious reaction which follows the Albigensian Crusade, the improvisation is transformed gradually into a hymn of purified love which becomes a hymn to the Virgin, who is the purest, fairest, gentlest of all women.

So much so that there was no longer any other admissible form of poetry than those hymns to Mary, the last blossoms of the old poetry of Langue d'oc, which produced in course of time that interminable series of poems to the Virgin winning the prizes at the floral games.

SOURCES.—E. Koswitz, *Les plus anciens monuments de la langue françaises*, 3rd ed., Heilbronn, 1897; *Œuvres de Rutebœuf*, ed. Jubinal, 1874–75, 3 vols.; *Les Chansons de Colin Muset*, ed. Bédier, 1912; Montaiglon-Raynaud, *Recueil des fabliaux* . . ., 1872–80, 6 vols.; P. Paris, *La Romancere français*, 1833; K. Bartsch, *Alt französiche Romanzen u. Pastourellen*, Leipzig, 1870; K. Bartsch, *Deutsche Liederdichter* from the Thirteenth to the Fourteenth Century, 3rd ed., Stuttgart, 1893; *Les Chansons de Guillaume IX d'Aquitaine*, ed. Jeanroy, 1913; *Les Poesies de Peire Vidal*, edited and translated by Langlade, 1913.

HISTORICAL WORKS.—P. Paris, "Chansonniers du XII⁰ Siècle," in the *Histoire littéraire de la France*, xxiii. 512–838; E. Freymond, *Jongleurs und Menestrels*, Halle, 1883; Jos. Bédier, *Les Fabliaux*, 1893; Edm. Faral, *Les jongleurs en France*, 1911; Jos. Anglade, *Les Troubadours*, 1809. This book of M. Anglade is of a rare value. A. Schultz, *Dar Hofische Leben zur Zeit der Minnesinger*, 2nd ed., Leipzig, 1889; Ch. V. Langlois, *La Société française au XIIIe Siècle*, 2nd ed., 1904.

CHAPTER X

THE UNIVERSITY

The first schools were set up by abbots and bishops. The trivium and quadrivium. Paris the capital of letters. The University. The students. Organization of the University of Paris. The Colleges. The Sorbonne.

IN the sphere of learning the eleventh and twelfth centuries saw an intense movement, as powerful perhaps as in the social and economic sphere, as powerful as in art and literature. Nowadays we should certainly never dream of comparing the brilliance of the science and philosophy of the Middle Ages with that of their art and literature. The reason for this is that sciences make continuous progress. Each of the newcomers who, while profiting by the work of his predecessors, increases them by his personal discoveries, in doing so casts some spadefuls of oblivion on the results achieved by them. Consequently, the progress made in an age gone by will seem of little importance to modern times, by the very fact of the progress made during the following centuries; while a poet or an artist endowed with an inventive genius and a vivid originality produces works to which nothing is added later. Time passes over them like the tide over rocks. Detached and brilliant, they will never cease to bear free comparison with the creations of succeeding generations.

Beginning from the second half of the eleventh century, there is manifested in the nation a great desire for learning.

" On all sides," writes Guibert de Nogent, " people devote themselves ardently to study." When Abelard (1075–1143), condemned by a council, takes refuge in a lonely district on the banks of the Arduson, he sees a flood of disciples coming to him; the desert is peopled around him.

The first schools were set up by the abbots of the mon-

THE UNIVERSITY

asteries and by the bishops in their cities : cloistral or episcopal schools attached to the cloisters of the monasteries or the cathedrals. Every great church had a library. The most famous of these schools in the tenth century was the diocesan school of Reims, in which Gerbert taught. Then followed that of Chartres, in which Fulbert shone. We must mention too the schools of Laon and Orleans.

The monastic schools were not less flourishing. That of Fleury-sur-Loire, with Abbo, enjoyed a great reputation from the end of the tenth century. In the eleventh century it is by his teaching at St. Martin de Tours that Bérenger distinguishes himself. The Parisians group themselves round masters who teach at St. Germain-des-Prés or at St. Maur. The Cluniac establishments deserve special mention.

In these monasteries instruction was given freely. Their resources dispensed them from the need of demanding payment. The schools of the bishops and the chapters made children of rich people pay ; they gave free education to the children of the common people. Some of these establishments were not content with giving free instruction : they provided for all the needs of many pupils.

In the diocesan schools it was generally the bishop's chancellor who performed the functions of schoolmaster ; or at least the schoolmaster was placed under his orders. Both of them had masters to assist them, and when the cloister and the cathedral proved too small to contain the flow of pupils, we see clerics, who had finished their studies, organizing classes in the town by which they spread the knowledge they had acquired. They taught with the permission of the Chancellor who gave them the licence to do so : *licentia docendi*.

The divisions into which the curriculum was distributed in the Middle Ages are well known. They are the *trivium*, including the liberal arts, *i.e.* grammar, rhetoric, and logic ; followed by the *quadrivium*, in which were ranged the sciences, *i.e.* arithmetic, geometry, astronomy, and music. Above the *trivium* and *quadrivium* were the three faculties : theology, law, and medicine.

In the twelfth century the writers of antiquity come into favour again. Among the Greeks hardly any but Aristotle and

THE MIDDLE AGES

Plato are studied; among the Latins the favourite authors are Vergil, Horace, and Lucan. Latin verse is read; and it is also composed, in the lightest vein, even in the monasteries.

Paris becomes the capital of letters and the "arts." Towards the middle of the twelfth century, the schools sprung from the cloister of Notre Dame become numerous. The City, the Petit-Pont, are full to overflowing with them. They overflow on to the left bank and creep up the side of the hill of St. Geneviève.

"Philosophy and all clerkly knowledge flourished in Paris; the study of the seven arts was so great there and in such authority that it was not so full or so fervent in Athens, Egypt, or Rome, or in any part of the world. And it was not only for the delectability of the place, nor for the great quantity of things in which the city abounded, but for the peace and liberty which the good King Louis (Louis VII) had given and which King Philip, his son (Philip Augustus), gave to the masters and scholars. Moreover, they did not only read in this noble city the seven liberal sciences, but decrees, and laws, and physic, and there was read above all the holy page of theology." (*Chron. de St. Denis*). And these "lecteurs" (masters) bore the most illustrious names: from foreign lands there came to take rank among them such men as Saint Thomas and Albert the Great.

The sum of the teaching remained subject to ecclesiastical authority. The first universities, those of Paris, Toulouse, Montpelier, and Orleans, were for a long time only associations of priests and clerks. The students wear the tonsure. For the word "University" does not apply at this time to the sum of the sciences taught; it means "association." There were then the association of the masters and that of the pupils. The first is found constituted during the pontificate of Innocent III (end of the twelfth century). It has statutes, pleads in the Roman Court, for it has lost no time in entering on a struggle with the Episcopal Chancellor who claims to hold it in tutelage. The seal of the University of Paris—which, by the way, does not appear before the first third of the thirteenth century—bears the figure of the Virgin its patron, and that of the Bishop of Paris. These University associations are placed under the

THE UNIVERSITY

superior authority of the Sovereign Pontiff, who watches over them with the more attention as the University of Paris is destined to produce more particularly theologians, as that of Orleans lawyers, and Montpelier doctors.

In matters of religious doctrine the University of Paris will form an authority; on her Councils and Sovereign Pontiffs will depend. At the beginning of the sixteenth century still, Erasmus will say that the French boast themselves to be the first theologians in the world.

A conflict which broke out at the end of the twelfth century between the association of teaching masters on the one side, and the Chancellor of the Bishop of Paris on the other, did much to give precision to the organization of the universities. The Chancellor claimed to demand from the candidates for a licence (to teach) an oath of obedience. The Masters also complained that the Chancellor granted or refused the licence at his pleasure, without taking account of their opinion. There was an agitation in the University: the Masters held meetings. The dispute was put before Innocent III. After an interminable process, the Sovereign Pontiff sanctioned the greater number of the claims formulated by the Paris Masters.

The masters and the pupils, huddled in the little streets of the City, had on their side, in order to ensure the triumph of their cause, emigrated in great numbers to the left bank, where the Chancellor of the Abbey of St. Geneviève also gave them "licences."

For that matter it had become difficult to confine the teaching to a dogmatic rigidity, in face of a youthful generation greedy for knowledge and independence. "Babblers in flesh and bone," writes Stephen of Tournai, "discuss irreverently the immaterial, the essence of God, the incarnation of the Word. One hears at the cross-roads subtle reasoners chopping up the indivisible Trinity." The Abbot of St. Victor, for his part, writes: "Our scholars are pleased when, by dint of subtleties, they have arrived at some discovery! They do not want to know about the conformation of the earth, the virtues of the elements, the position of the stars, the nature of animals, the velocity of the wind, about trees or roots. They think they can solve the riddle of the universe; but they look with bleared, not to say blind, eyes on the supreme Cause, the end and principle of all things."

Our masters come to the point of discussing the acts and decrees of the Holy See itself. The Papal Legate, Benedict Gaetani, the prelate who is to take the name of Boniface VIII when he ascends the pontifical throne, will exclaim passionately (30th November 1290) : " You, Paris Masters, in your desks, think the world should be ruled by your reasonings. But, no ! It is to us that the world has been entrusted. You waste your time in foolishness. And even were your reasonings good there would be a way to answer them, and this is it : ' Under pain of deprivation of offices and benefices it is forbidden to all masters to preach, discuss, or confer on the (papal) privileges, either publicly or privately. I truthfully declare to you, that rather than go back on its word, the Court of Rome would destroy the University.' "

Masters and pupils formed an association independent of the royal power, at once a society of mutual help and a religious confraternity, placed under the patronage of the Holy See.

The masters of the University of Paris in the beginning occupied the streets of the City, near the approaches of the cathedral under whose auspices the first schools had been opened. In the twelfth century, as we have seen, they had crossed the Petit-Pont to group themselves on the slope of the hill of St. Geneviève. There was formed the University town, including masters and pupils, with its privileges, its laws, and its police. The official foundation of the University by the Pope and the King (Philip Augustus) dates from the year 1200. In 1215, in an act of Cardinal Robert de Courçon, there appeared for the first time the words *Universitas magistrorum et scolarium*. It was a real little State within Paris, with its own tribunals, concerned in frequent disputes with the neighbouring State, the town of the Abbey of St. Germain-des-Prés. And what conflicts with the labourers of the Abbey, the cultivators of the Priests' Meadow ; bloody, sometimes murderous conflicts. "They are bolder than knights," says Philip Augustus, in speaking of the students of Paris, "for knights clothed in their armour hesitate to engage in battle ; while these clerks, with neither helmet nor hauberk, and with their

THE UNIVERSITY

tonsured heads, throw themselves into the fight armed only with knives." "The members of Paris and Orleans," says a contemporary, "are turbulent, fighters: they would disturb the whole earth."

It was already the vivid, picturesque, animated life which has gone on ever since. Robert de Courçon might demand that the University student should wear a "round cloak of a subdued colour reaching to the feet," as is becoming to clerics; the habit does not make the monk, or the scholar. "For eating and drinking they have no equals," writes Pierre le Mangeur. "They are gourmands at table, but not devotees at Mass. They yawn at their work; at feasts they respect no one. They detest meditation on the sacred Scriptures; but they love to see wine sparkling in their glass, and they drink it off gallantly."

To the strains of tambourine and guitar, they sing to the beautiful eyes of Marion or Lisette.

> Time flies,
> I have nothing done.
> Time comes again,
> I have done nothing.

Here is a vivid sketch:

> Four Normans scholars and clerks,
> Their bags carry round their necks,
> Within them their books and clothes.
> Very handsome they were and plump,
> Pleasant and merrily singing.
> (*Fabliau de la bourgeoisie d'Orléans.*)

Moreover, there was among them more than one "goliard," a free-lance, without domicile or means of support. Some, in the intervals of study, plied the trade of minstrels, rhyming in French and Latin, tales, fables, ballads, and *jeux partis*; living on resources the most diverse, sometimes most ingenious if not always very honest. "Some of them," says Robert of Sorbon, "are better acquainted with the rules of dice than those of logic." But there were also good scholars studious and well conducted. In the evening they might be seen strolling along the banks of the Seine, beside the Priests' Meadow, repeating the day's lesson or reflecting on the Master's teaching.

Others, among those most worthy of interest, are of poor families. How can they buy the necessary books and pay the professors of theology? They have only St. Nicholas, the patron of scholars, to help them. They make copies for their comrades or hire themselves out as carriers of water. And in the end they manage, all the same, to outstrip those of their companions, who being very rich possess numerous books which they have never opened.

The following letter, written in the twelfth century, is typical of any period:

"To our dear and respected parents, salutation and filial obedience," write some gentle students. "Know that, by the grace of God, we remain in good health in the city of Orleans and that we give ourselves entirely to study, knowing that, as Cato said: 'It is glorious to know something.' We live in a good and handsome house separated from the schools and the market-place by a single building, so that we can go every day to the lectures without soiling our feet. We have also good comrades already well advanced and very desirable. We are glad of it, for the Psalmist said: '*Cum sancto sanctus eris.*' But in order that the end we have in view shall not be hindered by the want of implements we think we ought to appeal to your paternal affection and ask you to send us enough money to buy parchment, ink, an inkstand, and other things which we need. You will not leave us in a state of embarrassment and you are anxious that we should finish our studies properly, so as to be able to return home with honour. The bearer would carry also any shoes and hose you might send. You could also send us your news by him."

These demands for money are repeated in every form:

"See, it is two months since," writes a son to his father, "that I spent the last penny of the money you gave me. Life is expensive; so many things are wanted; one must have a lodging, and what numbers of things there are to buy! You, my father, know well that, without Ceres and Bacchus, Apollo cuts a sorry figure." And what numbers of reasons for asking for the dispatch of precious money (*livres tournois*—Tours coins)! In the town everything is dear—is this not always the case in University towns?—and the exceptionally large

THE UNIVERSITY

number of students makes everything still dearer; the harvests have been bad; the rooms with their lofty ceilings are difficult to heat, and the winter is so exceptionally hard.

But the paternal reply does not fail to be written in the same key:

"Certainly, my dear son, I would send you money, and gladly, but the rains have spoilt my harvests and the birds have pecked the grapes in the vineyards. I should have to go to the money-lenders, and that would be madness." Or, with a frown, the father replies more severely that his son ought to be ashamed to be getting money out of the author of his being, whom he really ought to be assisting.

Then he turns to a heart which he knows is softer, that of his little sister: "A sensible and tactful sister ought to be able to stir up her husband and relatives to help a brother in need. Sweet little sister, I ought to let you, in your love for me, know that I study gladly and, thank God, learn well. But what misery I have to bear! I lie on straw, without sheets; I go without hose, badly dressed, shirtless. I won't mention the bread I get to eat. So I beg of you, sweet little sister, subtly to persuade your husband to come to my help and with as much as he can spare."

And the sweet little sister allows herself to be touched, perhaps a little too much. She sends her brother a hundred sous of Tours (which would be worth now about a thousand francs), two pairs of sheets, and six ells of good cloth. She tells him, however, to take care that her husband shall not know of this, "for if he hears of it, I am a dead woman." "Besides, I firmly believe," she adds, "that on his part he will shortly send you, at my suggestion, some money."

For their studies at the University, the students received money, not only from their relatives, but by a system which one might have thought quite modern, from the churches, which allocated bursaries to them.

The students, who wrote the letter we have just quoted were still at Orleans, but it is at Paris that all have the ambition to go for their studies:

For it is like Paris gold.

THE MIDDLE AGES

(The gold of the Parisian goldsmiths had the reputation of being the best gold in the world.)

> A clerk is not much worth
> Who has not been to Paris
> To study, and stayed there,
> And studied so much
> And so much learned that he has become a master,
> Who there and elsewhere
> Are renowned with the best.
>
> (Robert of Blois, *L'Enseignement des Princes*, v. 1503.)

" Fortunate city," says Philip of Harvengt, speaking of Paris—" fortunate city, in which the students are so many, that their great numbers almost exceed those of the inhabitants." Students came to Paris from all parts of Europe —from England, from Germany, from Scandinavia. " O Paris ! " cries Pierre de la Celle in 1164, " you catch souls with lime." And Lanfranc, the celebrated surgeon of Milan : " Paris, you beget clerks ! Unfortunate me, who have lost so much time far from your most honourable and most holy studies ! "

" At that time " (1210), writes William le Breton, " at Paris letters were brilliant. At no epoch and in no part of the world had such a flow of students ever been seen. This is not only accounted for by the admirable beauty of the town, but by the privileges which the King (Philip Augustus) and his father had conferred on the scholars. . . ."

About the same period (a little before 1190) a clerk of Champagne, Gui de Basoches, gives us a picturesque sketch of the University town. " The Grand-Pont," he writes, " is the centre of things. It is cumbered with merchandise, merchants, and boats. The Petit-Pont is appropriated by the dialecticians, who cross it, walking and discussing things. In the Ile (the City), adjoining the palace of the King, one sees the palace of philosophy where learning reigns supreme, the citadel of light and immortality : the eternal dwelling of the Seven Sisters, the liberal arts whence springs the source of religious science."

It is a fine and joyous life, and one which our students love to prolong. More than one turns a deaf ear when his family summons him home and holds before his eyes the most tempting bribes. To one they propose a fiancée clever and gentle, and, moreover, a brunette : she is elegant, beautiful, wise, and of the highest birth ; she will bring him a big dowry and splendid connections through her relatives. But the student replies that it will always be easy to find a wife, whereas it would be folly to give up the pursuit of knowledge just at the moment when he is on the point of mastering it.

The studies finished by the licence which gave the scholar the power of teaching in his turn : an examination which was accompanied by a banquet given by the new member to his masters and comrades. A Paris student begs a friend to explain all this to his father, whose bourgeois soul will not grasp it alone. He needs the money for this banquet, and this is the only obstacle between him and the final goal.

All the tests have, at length, been undergone, and behold the triumphant letter written to the parents who, far away from their son, must have read it with a feeling of pride :

" Sing new canticles to the glory of God ! Play the viol and the organ ; sound the loud cymbals ! Your son has just maintained a learned thesis in the presence of a numerous assembly of masters and students. I replied to all the questions without hesitation ; no one could stump me. I have given a magnificent banquet at which rich and poor have been regaled as never before. Already I have solemnly opened a school. And how full it has been since the first day ! The neighbouring schools are denuded to furnish me with a great number of auditors."

We have seen that the University included three higher Faculties : theology, medicine, and canon law. Below these we have distinguished the Masters of Arts, who taught the students the branches of the *trivium* and *quadrivium*. They and their pupils were known as the " artists." Each of the three Faculties formed a special corporation. As to the " artists," they were divided into four " nations " according to the native country of the students—the French, the Picards, the Normans, and the English. The four nations appear for the first time in a document of 1222.

In 1245 the four " nations " gave themselves a common head, a Rector. This latter soon became the head of the whole university, the three great Faculties themselves, whose members had all passed through the University of the Arts, agreeing that he should concern himself with their interests.

We must not picture the University of Paris in buildings specially arranged like those in which it is established at the present time. The majority of the masters taught in their own homes. The pupils gathered in a compact body in obscure habitations, sitting on the ground. In the winter the ground was strewn with straw, whence the name given to the street in which many of these schools were found, *rue du Fouarre* (*feurre* = straw). The Master spoke from in front of a desk, on a raised platform. He was dressed in a black robe with long folds and a hood of minever. The lessons consisted of explanations of the texts used for examinations. The fault of this teaching was that it continued to rely wholly on books. According to Fra Bartolommeo of Bologna, logic is Aristotle, medicine means Gallienus, Cicero is rhetoric, and Priscian is grammar. If the pupils became too numerous the teaching was given in the open air, at the cross-roads, in the squares. The meetings of the Faculties were held in a monastery, at Paris at the Maturins, or in the chapter-house of the Cistercians. The " artists " met every Saturday in the Church of St. Julien le Pauvre.

The majority of the students who followed the University courses in the Middle Ages, like the majority of those who follow them to-day, had some practical end in view. They were learning a profession there, intending, when their studies were finished, to enter the Church, or to engage in the practice of medicine or in that of the law.

The corporate organization which the masters and students of the University of Paris had come to form for themselves, while it had some precious advantages—and the most precious of all, independence—had some grave drawbacks. A great part of the energy expended in these centres of learning was wasted in disputes between groups and coteries, in struggles of rival influences. A picture of it is given by the Chancellor, Philip de Grève, at the beginning of the thirteenth century: " Formerly when each taught on his own account and the name ' University ' was not yet known, lessons and disputa-

THE UNIVERSITY

tions were more frequent; there was more ardour for study. But to-day, when you are united in a single body, now that you have formed yourselves into a University, teaching and discussion are rare. Every one hurries as much as possible, teaches little, and takes time from lessons and disputations to go and debate at meetings on the affairs of the community. . . . And while the elders are meeting to deliberate, legislate, and draw up regulations, the younger generation is having the run of the gaming-houses."

Then again, the rivalries between the masters: quarrels between schools, theories, influences. " The crowing of the cock heralds the day," again says Philip de Grève, " but our cocks, instead of announcing the dawn, have become fighting cocks. For what indeed are these quarrels between masters if not cock-fights ? . . . We have become the laughing-stock of the laity. The cocks bridle up and bristle against one another ; they devour each other's red combs and cover themselves with blood. . . ."

What is the cause of these quarrels ? Ambition, pride. As Ovid says :

Immensum gloria calcar habet.
(Ambition has an immense spur.)

To get together a great number of pupils—this is the pride of the masters. They use persuasion and entreaty ; some go so far as to pay their pupils. Strange, sensational doctrines are taught to attract them and pique their interest. The master's favourite pupils are not those who attend most assiduously to his teaching, but those who are clever at bringing him others. A master would never forgive a pupil for following other courses on the same subject concurrently with his, however authoritative their delivery. On their side the pupils were not always swayed by the most scientific motives. Those of Paris, for the most part theologians, sought by preference the masters whom they believed influential with the higher clergy, with regard to the positions they hoped to attain by their mediation.

The mediæval Universities were not richly endowed. They had no possessions : a poverty which formed their strength in their struggles against the Church and the royal power. It

THE MIDDLE AGES

was easy for them to disperse and go and pitch the tents of learning in some other district. In face of these threats of " secession," how often did not their adversaries come to an agreement! Moreover, the expenses which the University organization had to face were of the smallest. The payments collected on the conferring of degrees sufficed for them.

There were some rich students, especially among those who studied canon law. They were seen in the streets preceded by serving-men carrying great volumes. But the great majority were poor fellows.

For the sake of the needy students there were set up from the end of the twelfth century special houses in which they found food and shelter. These houses grew in importance. They are to be endowed with revenues which will go on increasing. They are to become the famous " colleges " which play so large a part in the life of the mediæval University, while they come to modify its aspect and even to constitute the University.

The earliest of these foundations was set up by a burgess of London named Joce, who, returning from the Holy Land, founded at the Hôtel-Dieu (the principal hospital) in Paris a certain number of beds in a special room, destined to accommodate in perpetuity eighteen scholars, but out of gratitude for the livelihood thus assured to them they watched in return the hospital dead and carried the cross and holy water at funerals. Before long they were installed in a house of their own, the " College of the Eighteen," near the Church of St. Christopher. It set an example. In 1209 there is the foundation by the widow of Stephen Bérot, of the College St. Honoré, which takes thirteen students.

On the other hand, one sees masters and students installing themselves in common in big houses which they rent, living together and sharing expenses. Through this, study became more assiduous. Each of these hostels was governed by a " principal." The colleges of which we have spoken were founded with a charitable intention. Under Saint Louis, Robert de Sorbon is to found the Sorbonne College, for poor Masters of Arts who wished to pursue their studies up to the doctorate of Theology. We know what it has become. In

THE UNIVERSITY

the thirteenth and fourteenth centuries appeared the Colleges of Harcourt and Navarre. Students found in these not only food and lodging but fine libraries and masters who acted as tutors. These were houses receiving paying members. The " collegiates " enjoyed such advantages that they came to be considered better than the free students who, in the fifteenth century, are almost regarded as suspicious characters under the name of " martinets " (from the word *martin*, a bâton, with which they were said to be too often armed). The transformation is then complete. The old University, free, independent, without fixed abode or resources, with no other tie than the oath which united its numerous members, has disappeared. Even the instruction given by the regents of the Faculty of Arts is given up in favour of these tutors who provide private instruction in " colleges " and " hostels "—colleges and hostels the union of which, on the site of the old Latin quarter, the rue du Fouarre, the rue de Garlande, the rue de la Harpe, come to constitute the University itself. The great Faculty of Theology is not ashamed to borrow for its ceremonies the buildings of the Sorbonne College.

Such was the character and development of the University of Paris. In the year 1169, Henry II, King of England, in his struggle with Thomas Becket, invoked its arbitration. And this prestige will go on increasing until the day when it will decay—into a disrepute from which it will require several centuries to recover—a punishment for the wretched attitude which the University of Paris takes up in the trial of Joan of Arc.

SOURCES.—Denifle and Chatelain, *Cartularium Universitatis Parisiensis*, 1889–96, 3 vols. in 4 ; *Epistolarium de Ponce le Provençal*, 13th century, Bibliothèque de l'Arsenal, MS. 3807, ff. 56–83.

HISTORICAL WORKS.—Ch. Turot, *De l'organisation de l'enseignement dans l'Université de Paris au Moyen Age*, 1850 ; Al. Budinsky, *Die Universität Paris und die Fremden au derselben im Mittelalter*, 1876 ; Denifle, *Die Universitaten des Mittelalters*, 1885 ; J. A. Clerval, *Les Ecoles de Chartres au Moyen Age*, Chartres, 1895 ; by the same, *L'Enseignement des arts liberaux à Chartres et à Paris dans la 1re moitié du XIIIe Siècle*, 1889 ; Leop. Delisle, " Les Ecoles d'Orleans au XIIe et XIIIe Siècles," *Ann. bull. Soc. hist. de Fr.*, vii. 139–54 ; B. Hauréau in the *Journal des Savants*, 1894 ; Hastings Rashdall, *The Universities of Europe in the Middle Ages*,

Oxford, 1895, 2 vols. ; Ch. V. Langlois, " Les Universités au Moyen Age," *Revue de Paris*, 15th February 1896, pp. 788–820—a study remarkable in its brevity, and on which the author of the preceding pages has especially drawn ; A. Luchaire, " L'Université de Paris sous Philippe Auguste," *Bulletin intern. de l'enseignement superieure*, 1899 ; by the same, *La Société française au temps de Philippe Auguste*, 1899 ; Ch. Haskins, " The Life of the Mediæval Students," *American Hist. Review*, iii. (1898), 203–20 ; by the same, " The University of Paris in the Sermons of the Thirteenth Century," *ibid*. x. (1904), 1–27.

CHAPTER XI

THE CATHEDRALS

The Romanesque style, tenth and eleventh centuries. The Gothic style takes its rise in the Ile-de-France in the twelfth century. The greater number of the cathedrals were built by the efforts of the bishops. Popular enthusiasm. Æsthetic elements in the Gothic style; the pointed arch, the arch in tierce-point, the buttress. The decoration of the Gothic churches is a means of instruction for the people. The sculptures. The stained-glass windows. Artistic and literary influence of France on the Europe of the twelfth century.

AT the beginning of the eleventh century the chroniclers note the zeal of the faithful to rebuild the churches in a new style. "About the year 1002 or 1003," writes Raoul le Glabre, "people began everywhere to restore the churches, and though many of them were still in good condition, they vied with each other in erecting new buildings, one more beautiful than the other. It seemed as though the world were throwing off its decrepitude to clothe itself anew in an array of white sanctuaries"—white sanctuaries on whose pinnacles already shone, with its golden plumage, the Gallic cock.

Nearly all the episcopal churches were rebuilt at this time, a great number of the conventual churches, and even the rural chapels. It is true that some of them were remarkably small. We know through the letter of an Archbishop of Aix (eleventh century) that the oratory on the site of which he had his cathedral built, could hold only ten worshippers: which reminds one of the most frequented Russian churches of to-day.

From this general need of restoration in the eleventh century the Romanesque style took its rise. Attempts had been made right and left to produce structures which should transform the art of building. The comparative peace induced by the Feudal System gave it its impulse. The characteristic mark of the Romanesque style was the substitution of vaults of stone for the dressing left by the Romans, *i.e.* for flat ceilings of timber work and roofs supported on stringcourses. The lintel of the basilicas is replaced by the arch resting on columns. It was a change which soon produced churches with several stages of windows in place of the Roman basilica lighted only on one story.

The Romanesque churches have still a squat effect. They stand heavily enough at the farther end of the squares ornamented with quincunxes; but one is aware in them of a tremulous desire to ascend. The arches which support the vaults relieve the walls, which soon take advantage to raise themselves towards heaven in a transport of faith.

The Romanesque style had its cradle in the centre of France and in Aquitaine, in Auvergne, and in the valleys of the Saône and the Rhone, where it reached its perfection in the second half of the eleventh century.

It was divided into two schools.

The flat-roofed basilicas of the Romans, similarly modified, had produced in Byzantium since the sixth century the churches with cupolas of which St. Sofia is the finest example. Their influence had been felt by the architects of Perigord, where it produced the famous church of St. Front de Perigueux and other churches with cupolas in the surrounding country; while in our other provinces the Romanesque tendency remained purely French.

At the same period in which, through the rise of the vaults, the Romanesque style was forming, stone was replacing wood in the chief buildings, churches and castles, episcopal palaces and hospitals.

In spite of this transformation there remained churches and fortresses built of wood as late as the beginning of the twelfth century.

In nearly all the episcopal cities the cathedrals were rebuilt, as Raoul le Glabre has just told us; but it was above all the monastic buildings, the churches of the abbeys and monasteries, which, during the eleventh century, were to give a magnificent impulse to the Romanesque style. And particularly important

THE CATHEDRALS

was the stimulus which the new architecture received from the Cluniac Order, whose development at that time was prodigious.

The basilica of Cluny, vast and lofty, with its five naves and its five towers, was one of the finest structures ever built. The building went back to 1089; it went on for thirty years. By an act of criminal vandalism for which the governments of the Directory, the Consulate, and the Empire are responsible, this magnificent masterpiece and testimony to the genius of our ancestors was destroyed at the beginning of the nineteenth century.

The abbots staked their self-respect on the beauty of these buildings. They liked their names to be associated with the *opus ædificale*, the work of construction. Without calling in question their sincere desire to raise to God a dwelling befitting His glory, we may say that they loved the edifice which was destined to exalt their memory in the eyes of their successors.

The bishops of the eleventh, and then of the twelfth century, give themselves up enthusiastically to the same tendency. They are seen blindly devoting their energy and their resources to the building of cathedrals. It becomes a fever; Pierre le Chantre calls it *morbus ædificandi*, the building fever. We may quote Bishop Fulbert at Chartres, Geoffrey de Montbray at Coutances, Hildebert de Lavardin at Le Mans, Gerard I de Florines and Gerard II at Cambrai, and then Hugh de Noyers at Auxerre and Maurice de Sully at Paris. These churches are constructed by the bishops from their personal resources, with the help of the lords who make a point of helping them in their pious work, and with the co-operation of the faithful for whose assistance they appeal. They are great edifices in which they establish the see of their fief. For the prelates do not only celebrate there the divine office. They hold their courts of justice and pronounce sentence there.

Robert I, Bishop of Coutances (1025–48) begins the construction of the cathedral with the assistance of Gonnar, the second wife of Richard I, Duke of Normandy, and with that of his canons. Hubert de Vendôme, Bishop of Angers, rebuilds, in the first half of the eleventh century, the cathedral of St. Maurice, with the assistance of his parents. Bishops Walter Mortagne and Maurice de Sully built, the one the cathedral of

THE MIDDLE AGES

Laon, the other Notre Dame at Paris, at the expense of their private fortunes. " Maurice de Sully," says a contemporary, " built Notre Dame much more at his own expense than through the generosity of others." William de Seignelay at Auxerre, Stephen Béquart at Sens, Philip de Nemours at Châlons-sur-Marne, and Raymond de Calmont at Rodez do the same. The church of Mende is due to the initiative of Pope Urban II, a native of that diocese. At Chartres bishops and canons devote their revenues for several years to the building of the cathedral. At Beauvais too, Bishop Milo de Châtillon-Nanteuil and his canons contribute largely to the work of building. Geoffrey I of Montbray goes to Calabria to Robert Guiscard to get money for the church of Coutances. He brings back gold, silver, precious stones, and rich stuffs as presents from the famous Norman leader and his comrades. He was not content to build the church with the three towers, but he furnished it with ecclesiastical ornaments, with tapestries for the walls, with carpets and precious manuscripts. He attached to it choristers and a school, as well as goldsmiths, stained-glass workers, an iron worker, carpenters, a master-mason, and sculptors for the permanent works. The building was begun in 1056.

A great church thus became, like the castle, the centre of a manufacturing activity, vivified by the flocking of the faithful and of the pilgrims who came to venerate the relics. Besides the schools attached to it, the families of the workmen settled there. The labour necessitated by the cathedral life was great and continual. It formed the " people of the work " (*gens de l'œuvre*). A valuable light is thrown on the life of the artisans encrusted at the foot of the cathedrals, by Leger, Archbishop of Vienne. He relates, in 1050, that one of his flock, a doctor named Ato, had improved and adorned, in the cloisters of his church, the little dwellings (*domunculæ*), in which lived the women employed for the weaving of cloth of gold for the divine services. The canons, under the bishop's direction, were concerned with the building, the administration of which was very complicated; and sometimes the best artisans are recruited from their ranks, as at Auxerre, where during the reign of Henry I, Bishop Geoffrey of Champallement institutes

THE CATHEDRALS

prebends for some ecclesiastics, one of whom is an "admirable goldsmith," another a "clever painter," and the third an intelligent worker in stained glass. At Avignon, the Chapter includes masters qualified to teach the art of design.

We must then abandon the theory of Viollet-le-Duc that the great churches were the manifestation of a lay art created by the impulse of the communal movement, the symbol of popular liberty, against the seigniorial stronghold.

Doubtless from the thirteenth century onwards, the monuments of religion served as meeting-places for the burgesses. The vaults resounded with their declarations of their rights. They had markets there; we should say now that they served as exchanges. Feasts were held there which were far from being religious celebrations. Even councils of war were held there, in which military expeditions, in which the burgesses would be called to take part, were discussed. Treaties were signed there. Doubtless too, from the middle of the eleventh century the architects, monks, and clerks are frequently replaced by laymen. The master-masons, the corporations of artisans who work on the buildings, are laymen. But the bishops and his canons are none the less the promoters of the work; from them comes the inspiration and it is under their direction. Without them the work would not be done. It must be said too that the prelates were helped in every way, if only by the confraternities of peace which contributed to the building, the repairs, and the decoration of the church.

At the time when the Abbey Church of St. Remy at Reims was built, through the efforts of Abbots Aicard and Thierry (1003–49), members of the *familia ecclesiastica*, i.e. the vassals of the abbey, gave their voluntary help. We see them on the steep roads perched on long wagons drawn by strings of red oxen, carting building materials. Donations flow in from all sides. They come from the royal coffers: Louis VII makes a present of two hundred pounds to the church of Notre Dame in Paris. Offerings come from the humblest sources. They made use of the results of collections during church services, as in our own day. The granting of indulgences, which was to become later a source of abuse, secured a good deal of money. Finally, appreciable sums were furnished by the exposition of relics which the canons took in musical processions through the countryside. Around the reliquaries minstrels sang moving poems; after which the collection was made.

For the building of the church of Soissons, Countess Adelaide allowed the wood necessary for the carpentry to be taken from her forests; still more, she provided wood already cut and prepared. Elsewhere the owners of quarries allowed them to be drawn upon for the stone needed. For the most part these immense stones were carved in the quarry itself, into square blocks, or into shafts or the bases of columns, or capitals according to designs furnished by the architects, and afterwards taken away on heavy wagons drawn by many yokes of oxen: thirteen pairs, twenty-six oxen says the author of the *Miracles of Ste. Foi* in speaking of the building of a church in Rouergue (middle of the eleventh century).

How shall we describe the enthusiasm of the multitude when they saw,

Kneeling afar off in their robes of stone,

the dwellings destined for God?

" A spectacle wonderful to behold, incredible to relate," we read in the chronicles of the Abbots of St. Trond, " these multitudes who, so zealously and joyfully, brought the stones, lime, sand, and wood necessary for the work; night and day in carts at their own expense. As large stones were not found in the district they brought them from distant parts. The shafts of columns came from Worms in boats which came down the Rhine as far as Cologne, whence they were carted from village to village, without the help of oxen or mules, dragged by men's arms. They took them across the Meuse without any bridge, by means of ropes tied to them; and so materials come to us to the sound of canticles."

The letter addressed, in 1115, by Abbot Haimon to the religious of Tutbury, in England, has remained famous. It is speaking of the church of St. Pierre-sur-Dives:

" Who has ever seen or heard the like? Princes, powerful and wealthy men, men of noble birth, proud and beautiful women, bent their necks to the yoke of the carts which carried the stones, wood, wine, corn, oil, lime, everything necessary for the building of the church and the support of those working at it. One saw as many as a thousand people, men and women, attached to the reins drawing a wagon so heavy was its burden, and a profound silence reigned among the crowd pressing forward with difficulty, in the emotion which filled their hearts."

"At the head of the long procession, minstrels of the highest sounded their brazen trumpets, and the sacred banners in their brilliant colours swayed in the wind. Nothing proved an obstacle. The ruggedness of the mountains, the depth of the streams, the waves of the sea at Sainte Marie du Pont (the mouth of the Orne) could not delay the march. To the carts there were yoked even old men, bent under the weight of their years; and children tied to the reins had no need to stoop: they could march upright under the traces.

"When they had arrived near the foundations of the church the carts were drawn up round it as on the borders of a camp. From dusk to dawn the sound of hymns arose. The carts were emptied by the ruddy light of the torches and during that night many miracles took place: the blind recovered their sight; the paralytic began to walk."

The impulse of faith here described is that of the twelfth century, from which are to spring the Gothic churches, a movement of a still greater amplitude and strength than that of the eleventh century, which had produced the Romanesque churches. It began round about 1130. It was at work most especially in Northern France, and became more marked in the course of the twelfth century. It developed a peculiar intensity during the reigns of Louis VII and Philip Augustus, when it became prodigious. There were very few cities, to the north of the Loire at least, which did not then undertake, on the most magnificent scale, the rebuilding of the dwelling of the Lord.

It is doubtless from this period that a proverb dates, which we have picked up on the banks of the Rhine. They say there of a man who is very happy: "Es geht ihm so gut wie dem lieben Gott in Frankreich" (His affairs succeed as well as those of the good God in France).

The cathedral of Noyon, rebuilt through the efforts of

THE MIDDLE AGES

Bishop Baldwin of Flanders, is completed in 1167. At Chartres, after the burning of the Romanesque church, Bishop Renaud de Monçon begins the splendid edifice which is our admiration to-day. In 1220 its vaults were almost completely finished; the principal rose window was in its place. The roof of the church reminds William le Breton of the shell of a great tortoise: "Behold it," he says, "rising from the ground, new, gleaming with sculpture, an unrivalled masterpiece." The royal cathedral—Reims—with its lofty crown of stones, is begun in 1211 by Archbishop Aubri de Humbert. The foundations of the Cathedral of Auxerre are laid in 1215 by William de Seignelay. And these same bishops who regarded themselves, in accordance with an ancient tradition, as the heads of the city, had sometimes, as at Cambrai, work done on the fortifications of the town.

The Abbot of Mont St. Michel, the famous Robert of Torigni, himself a marvellous builder, said in speaking of Notre Dame in Paris, the choir of which was consecrated in 1181: "When this building is finished there will be no work to compare with it."

We have said that its building, contemporaneous with the reign of Philip Augustus, was due to Bishop Maurice of Sully, who devoted his fortune to it. The cathedral of Laon, begun in 1170 by Bishop Walter of Mortagne, preserves the rough and savage character of the soldier burgesses we tried to portray in speaking of the communal movement. Its outline reminds one of a fortress rather than of the joyous churches of the epoch in which it was built. It stands on the top of the hill, whence it gives the impression of a feudal edifice. One would have thought—in the days before the hideous Boches had overrun the district—that the same hands had built the cathedral of Laon and the neighbouring castle of Coucy. "Nowhere did ancient France appear in such majesty: it is that fine Gothic of the end of the twelfth century with which nothing can compare unless it be Greek Art" (Emile Mâle).

The apse of Soissons Cathedral was completed in 1212.

The new style in which these churches were built has been termed the "Gothic" style; an expression which Raphael seems to have been the first to apply to it. It was used again by

THE CATHEDRALS

Vasari in his famous history of Italian Art. Through him it became general. "Gothic" in the mouth of Raphael signified "barbarous," as it does still under the pen of Molière when he treats of the "Gothic ornaments":

> Those hateful monsters of the centuries of ignorance
> Which the tides of barbarism have produced.

The term has been kept since, although used in a different sense; it has seemed convenient. The correct expression to characterize this style would be "French Architecture." For it is the French style *par excellence*. Just as the Romanesque took its rise in the eleventh century in the centre of France and in Aquitaine from the development of the architectural style of the Romans, so the Gothic style rose in the north of France, in the twelfth century, from the development of the Romanesque style. It is the style of the Ile-de-France, whence it spread later, with the development of the royal power, over the rest of the country, and from France over Europe. Richard of Dietenheim in the thirteenth century brings an architect from France to rebuild the Church of St. Peter, at Wimpfen, in the new style—the new style which is described by those who drew up the charter as *opus francigenum,* the French style: ". . . accito peritissimo in architectoria arte latomo, qui tunc noviter de villa Parisiensi e partibus venerat Franciæ, opere *francigeno,* basilicam ex sedis lapidibus construi jubet." In Italy the Romanesque still prevails in the buildings of John of Pisa at a period when Gothic flourished everywhere in our own land.

The Gothic style is characterized by its aspiration towards clearness, light, joy. Huysmans called it "the unfolding of the soul." Walls are seen rising higher and higher and perforated more and more with window spaces. And thus are achieved those perfect and exquisite works of French Art, the Sainte Chapelle and the Cathedral of Metz, which seem to be altogether made up of stained glass.

Hugh de Noyers, we read in the chronicles of the bishops of Auxerre, had the windows and stained glass of his church enlarged so that the building which, after the manner of the old churches, was dark, shone with a great transparency.

THE MIDDLE AGES

Girard II, Bishop of Cambrai, likewise "lengthened" the windows, which were "too short," says his biographer, to give more light to the house of God.

Higher vaults and larger walls were then necessary, but these, pierced with larger and more numerous bays, offered less resistance to the weight of the roof. From this came the Gothic style. And first of all the ogive, an expression which indicates not the broken arch, the arch in tierce-point which succeeded the semicircular arch, but the arches intersecting in crosses thrown on to each bay and increasing (Latin, *augere*) the power of resistance in the vault. The word *ogive* or *augive* signified "support": "it is easy to build, it is light, for all its weight falls, not on the walls, but on the intersections of the ogives; it is solid, and if, by chance, it is distorted, it does not give way altogether, as the four compartments are independent."

These four arches which sustain the vault throw their weight on four points of support, the resistance of which is increased by buttresses. Such is the principle of Gothic. The broken arch (*arc brisé*) itself, miscalled the ogival arch, is inspired by the same idea: to increase its power of resistance against the horizontal thrust of the vaults. Far from being an essential mark of the Gothic style, the arch in tierce-point, the ogival arch, is, as one sees, only an accessory. It might be called an accident of construction.

And its beauty lies precisely in the fact that it was introduced not through an æsthetic motive, not because, as has been said, the eye had become used to the ogival form in the intersection of semicircular arches, but by very necessity, the technical needs of the construction, whence its harmony with the general effect of the building.

Finally, the buttresses—the third of the essential marks of the Gothic style—also rose from the same cause: the need of supporting and reinforcing the walls against the thrust of the vaults, walls rising higher and higher and pierced more and more with rose windows and brilliant stained-glass, which they aspired to make high and higher still, resplendent with light and colour. Such is the skeleton of the Gothic building: the vault constructed on four projecting ribs—the ogives—which

THE CATHEDRALS

carry the thrusts to the four corners on to supports reinforced and sustained by the buttresses.

And thus is seen at a glance the progress made in building since the time of the Greek temples. These latter can not only have but one story, but they cannot support any weight. The Romans make some progress. Thanks to the arcade the upper part of their buildings can have more weight, but the power they have introduced into building is still imprisoned in the lintel which they have from the imitation of Greek Art. The Romanesque architects emancipate themselves from the lintel: they impose the arcade on columns. They create the vault which gives to their edifice a power of resistance unknown before their time; but they are still subject, in imitation of the Romans, to the superposition of orders. On the abacus of the columns which surround the nave, other columns rise up to the springing of the vaults which they support. The Gothic architects at last invent clusters of columns springing from a single shaft from the ground to the roof.

Add to this the force they have found in the ogives, in the arch in tierce-point, and in the buttresses; and we shall have assembled the principles of their art.

From the middle of the twelfth century, the date of the rise of Gothic architecture, the arches of religious edifices are becoming more and more pointed; but this transition from the Romanesque to the Gothic is not abrupt. In the Ile-de-France and the neighbouring regions one style succeeds insensibly to the other. Between the Abbey of the men of Caen, pure Romanesque on one side and on the other Gothic in its fullest development—the Cathedral of Reims, for instance—there is a whole series of monuments which merge into one another, without it being possible to mark by a precise border-line the division between the two styles. One cannot then, at least in the region of its origin, the Ile-de-France, the heart of the royal domain (including Valois, the province of Beauvais, the Vexin, the region of Paris, a part of the country round Soissons), isolate the art of the ogive from that of the semicircular arch, for it developed insensibly from it. And it will be seen that it was with the monarchy as with the French

THE MIDDLE AGES

language itself—the language of the Ile-de-France—and with the epics that the Gothic style, the French style, was to progress. You will not find Gothic, in its beginnings, in Flemish Flanders, nor in Lorraine or Alsace or Brittany, nor in Languedoc; nor *à fortiori* in Germany, Italy, or Spain. To these countries the Gothic comes fully formed. Between the Church of St. Géréon at Cologne, full Romanesque, and the famous cathedral of that city, which is of a pointed Gothic, you would not find in the district any transition. Moreover, France had already more than a century before produced some masterpieces of Gothic, the Abbey Church of Morienval, St. Etienne at Beauvais, Notre Dame at Senlis, and the Abbey Church of St. Denis (this last begun in 1143), when the foundations of the Cathedral of Cologne were laid on the plan of Amiens.

So completely were contemporaries won over by the new style of building that bishops and lords were seen destroying the old churches in the Romanesque style, and often splendidly built, to raise churches corresponding to the aspirations of their own time.

At Paris Maurice de Sully had a Romanesque church which was dedicated to Our Lady and only went back to the reign of Louis le Gros, what we should have called a new church, rased to the ground. At Laon the church demolished in 1170 by order of Bishop Gautier de Mortagne for the construction of the new cathedral was only fifty-six years old.

Contrary to general opinion, these buildings were achieved with great rapidity. The work was immense, and it seemed as though one saw the stones, already cut and chiselled, come and place themselves on one another and up to unknown heights to the sound of hymns, " as were built the walls of Thebes to the strains of Amphion's lyre."

Notre Dame, the Cathedral of Paris, founded in 1168, sees its choir finished in 1196; in 1220 it was completed. Imagine the vastness of the work: the infinite detail of the sculptures. The Sainte Chapelle was entirely built in eight years. And one must remember the means of construction then in vogue. Our mechanical processes were unknown, as also was the rapid use of reinforced concrete. It is true that some churches begun in the twelfth and thirteenth centuries were completed

THE CATHEDRALS

only in the fourteenth or fifteenth century. This was because the work was interrupted by political events, local troubles, or for the want of money.

As to the artists who raised these great monuments, the most beautiful in which human genius may glory, in spite of the lowliness of their condition through which they were described as "master-masons," or, at the most, as "masters of the work," the name of some of them have been preserved. Pierre de Montreuil produced from his genius the basilica of St. Denis; William of Sens drew the plans of the cathedral of that town and presided over its construction (twelfth century). He was afterwards summoned to England, where he rebuilt, according to a new plan, Canterbury Cathedral. To Jean Langlois we owe that miracle, St. Urbain of Troyes. Jean d'Orbais and, after him, Robert de Coucy, conceived the magnificent cathedral of Reims (Robert de Coucy is the architect of the towers). Robert de Luzarches drew the plans of Amiens Cathedral. To Jean de Chelles we owe the transept of Notre Dame of Paris, and the architect, Villard de Honnecourt (district of Cambrai), after having built the choir of the Cathedral of Cambrai, went to introduce his art into Hungary.

The master of the work generally lived at the foot of the cathedral, where, under heavy awnings of grey canvas, he had established his workshop, his " lodge " (*loge*), to use the expression of the time. It was a little city of workmen governed by the architect, paid and supported according to accounts kept by the clerks of the church. There lived under a common authority the various artisans of the work, from the masons and carpenters, to plumbers, painters, and workers in stained glass. They laboured in closed workshops heated in winter.

The most important room in the " lodge " was the " design room " (*chambre aux traits*), in which the master of the work drew his plans, and made light wooden models of the various parts of the building. These plans or models were known as the " molles."

How were these great artists paid? A contract made in 1261 with Martin de Lonay by the Abbot of St. Gilles in Languedoc for the completion of the abbey church gives us some information on the subject. Martin is to receive yearly

THE MIDDLE AGES

100 pounds of Tours (about 20,000 francs now) for himself and, doubtless, for his assistants. He is to have besides 2 sous (20 francs now) each working day; and the right to take his meals at the Abbot's table except on days of abstinence, when he will eat in the kitchen, where the cook will serve him with a portion one and a half times that of a monk. His horse will be stabled at the abbey. On the other hand, we find that the architects of the Dukes of Burgundy and the Counts of Poitiers formed part of their households by the same right as their painters and miniaturists. In this capacity they received a robe each year, as also did their wives, and wages amounting to 10 pounds (2000 francs) annually at the Burgundian Court and 6 pounds (1200 francs) at that of the Count of Poitiers.

The monuments which these artists conceived, and so magnificently executed, were adapted to the soil on which they stood, to the climate, to the scenes of Nature which surrounded them, to the habits and needs of the men for whom they were made. The incongruity in modern towns has often been pointed out of monuments constructed in imitation of antiquity. Look at the Madeleine in Paris. Can one imagine that this edifice has been built by the same men who live in the neighbouring houses, when the stages of these houses are about as high as one of its capitals? The proportions of the monuments of antiquity were admissible in Greece, where they were of small dimensions. Modern architects who have sought inspiration in them have multiplied them three, four, five times in every part, and this has made them disproportionate to the men who are to use them, and to the surrounding dwellings.

The Gothic architects, on the contrary, according to the luminous observation of Viollet-le-Duc and of Lassus, far from seeking, like the imitators of the antique, relative proportion, have sought human proportion: they mean that the proportions of the monuments which they built are always calculated in relation to man. Bases, capitals, colonnettes, mullions, ribs, and mouldings are of the same dimensions in the case of a big church or a little, of a cathedral or an oratory, because in both cases man is taken as the point of comparison. But in big churches the number of these things is increased; the number of curves and mouldings is greater in a big church in proportion to the greater weight of the vaults which they have to bear, and likewise the number of mullions in proportion to the larger windows. Columns are lengthened or shortened, their diameter increased or decreased, but the capitals and the bases maintain the same height. Ornaments will enter in greater or less number into the decoration of the balustrades which run along the spring of the roofs, but the height of these balustrades will not vary, any more than the dimensions of the ornaments themselves.

Thus the Gothic church, whatever its dimensions, will remain always living, in harmony with the surroundings for which it has been made, in harmony with the men who are to come to pray in it. It will adapt itself always, and in the most charming way, to the buildings which surround it and among which it seems to have sprung spontaneously as the tree in the forest has sprung from the same soil as the green plants which flourish in its shade. On the contrary, the building imitated from the antique suffers from surroundings with which it is incongruous, which it overpowers, and by which it is itself made hideous.

To the justice of these principles one must add a marvellous knowledge of technique. The carpenterings of the Gothic architects are masterpieces. And see the way in which they arrange the draining away of water. The watercourses, openly exposed, are easy to clean. The pipes lead methodically one into another up to the buttresses, the line of which they follow, terminated by those picturesque gargoyles which spit the rain far from the walls into the street gutters.

And the most beautiful feature of a Gothic church is perhaps its ornamentation. The Ancients, Greeks or Romans, had adopted the principle of unity in uniformity; the Gothicists discovered the formula infinitely more fruitful, of variety in unity. On the walls of a Greek or Roman temple, from base to summit everything is continuous; one line is followed With Gothic buildings, on the contrary, it is the *ensemble* which gives the impression of a perfect harmony, while their details are as varied, spontaneous, and free as possible. Hence that impression of life produced by mediæval buildings.

THE MIDDLE AGES

Let us add that the ornamentation of a Greek or Roman building is on plates fixed on various parts of the monument which do not seem to demand them naturally, while in Gothic buildings the ornamentation is suggested by the very elements of the construction. It responds to the ideals, the beliefs of the time. It is at the same time a symbol and a method of instruction. Everything in it is fixed by traditional rules, of the meaning of which no one is at this time ignorant, of which every one has knowledge—a knowledge of which the artists constitute themselves the interpreters.

The churches are orientated from east to west. On the western façade is sculptured the representation of the Last Judgment, which will be lighted up in the evening hours, as in a luminous symbol, by the flaming orange of the setting sun. It has been remarked that a number of the churches of the time, and some of the best built, like Notre Dame in Paris, possessed a choir which swerved more or less markedly from the axis. In some the deviation is very much accentuated, to mark, it is said, the bending of the Head of Christ dying on the Cross. And some eminent archæologists have gone so far as to ask whether the little door opened in the side of Notre Dame in Paris—the " red door "—was not there to represent the wound made by the lance in the Side of the Divine Martyr.

The multitude knew that the lion represents the Resurrection, because lion cubs, issuing without life from the mother, become animate only on the third day through a breath of their father. They knew that the little figures of naked infants on the folds of Abraham's cloak represented the future life, and that a hand issuing from the clouds with a gesture of blessing is the image of Providence. If a head is surrounded by a cruciform nimbus they see in it one of the Persons of the Trinity. The aureole, or "glory," surrounding the whole body marks eternal happiness. Among sacred figures only God, the angels, and the Apostles have bare feet. The artist has an exact knowledge of these rules. Moreover, the people connected with the church, who have commissioned and watch over the work, take care to remind them of them. And the people are not to be deceived on the subject. Thus the Middle Ages saw in art a means of instruction incomparably vivid, powerful, and broad. At the beginning of the eleventh century do not the Acts of the Synod of Arras say : " Simple and unlettered souls find in the Church what they cannot know through books ; they see it in the lines of the plan " ? At the beginning of the following century (twelfth century) Honorius d'Autun was to say in his turn : " Painting is the literature of laymen."

Here is the wonderful prayer to the Virgin Mary which François Villon puts into the mouth of his old mother :

> I am a woman poor and old,
> I know nothing, and no letters have read ;
> In my parish church I see
> Paradise painted, where are harps and lutes,
> And a hell where the damned are cooked.
> The one makes me afraid, the other glad and blithe.
> Give me happiness, noble saint,
> To whom all sinners should have recourse,
> Filled with faith true and untiring ;
> In this faith I will live and die.

Thus the cathedral has been called " the Bible of the poor." The stained-glass windows, the statues, the mural paintings, the figures on the tapestries, do not only relate the sacred Scriptures, the Old and New Testaments, but the principles of morality. One sees there the series of virtues and vices and even the history of the world, the moral and material worlds, the courses of the seasons, agricultural labours, and those of the workshop ; and the reproduction of Nature as God has shown it to us. It is a " mirror " of the world, to use a phrase of that time. It is at Chartres perhaps that this great book of pictures has the most numerous pages, with its 10,000 personages in painting and sculpture. The poem opens with the Creation of the world ; then here come our first parents driven from Paradise. They come on the earth where work redeems their fault, ennobles their life, reconciles them with their Creator.

The fruitful efforts of man working for his livelihood, the sculptors have put in relief in the series of the twelve months, each of which is represented by the rustic labour of the corresponding season of the year. There follow the representation of the virtues and vices, the configuration of the world, animals, trees, plants, flowers, mountains, and waterways. And everything holds together and is harmoniously connected in this immense history, from the signs of the Zodiac, the path of the sun through the constellations, to the grass discreetly growing in the fields; from God in His dazzling glory, to the humble peasant bent over the brown furrows. See the vine winding round the capitals. The wild rose clings to the archivolts; ivy, ferns, spearwort enlace the colonnettes. Here are the flowers, herbs, and fruits dear to the hearts of gardeners—roses, gladiolas, heliotropes, violets, geraniums; even cabbage leaves and herbs used for soup; there are the plantain, cress, parsley, and the little sorrel; apples and pears growing on lattice-work, the raspberry bush with its burden of amaranthine berries, vermilion strawberries among their great green leaves. Here are too the quiet denizens of the woods: the robust branches of oak and elm, the slender branches of the beech, the thin boughs of the birch, the maple, the wild plum tree, lords-and-ladies, and wood anemone. And there is the enamel work of the landscape, broom, umbelliferæ, the blades of ripe corn, and the arum; and the animals of the poultry yard, the chicken and the rabbit; the faithful helpers of man, the ox, the ass, the horse; and exotic animals too—the elephant, the camel, the lion, which crowd together multifarious and joyous. Here is, in its magnificence, the entire work of the Creator on which man also, in the sweat of his brow, has made his valiant mark.

And the vast edifice is animated by it all; life palpitates within it. It crackles from the bases of the slender columns up to the sculptured capitals beneath the vaults, it runs on the crest of the buttresses out on the gargoyles grimacing in sinister fashion at the good folk passing by, with their noses in the air, beneath the walls.

The studies from which the artist worked were made by him with minute care from Nature. The album has been preserved in which Villard de Honnecourt made from Nature the sketches which he thought useful for his art. After he had built the cathedral of Cambrai he traversed France and Switzerland, sketching in his album, now the towers of Laon and the windows of Reims, now a swallow, a parroquet, a fly, a crayfish. He brought a patient care to the study of the least little beast. Abandoning the sterile imitation of the acanthus and old laurel, it is with all the fauna and flora of their country, with the fresh and joyous vegetation of the banks of the Seine and the Oise, that the Gothic artists decorate with an ardent sanity the house of the good God.

It has been remarked already that the Gothic style in the period of its youth, the twelfth century, reproduces spring flowers : its vegetation is still in the bud. The fern has hardly emerged from its downy sheath ; the buds appear at the ends of the boughs still bent back like a spring. In the thirteenth century, Gothic art in its full expansion gathers for its array a vegetation in full maturity : the flowers are fully opened, the stems are long, the leaves are completely unfolded. Finally, the fourteenth and fifteenth centuries will reproduce an autumnal flora, a leafage shrivelled, wrinkled, jagged. The artists seek great ferns which apply the lace of their palms to the humid walls, or else dry plants like thistles and thorns— a vegetation which, like the style itself of which it forms the ornament, will give the impression of a life which, after a supreme and flamboyant brilliance, is on the point of extinction.

Thus, in the course of their existence the cathedrals had, like that Nature of which they were the splendid expression, their vivacious spring-time, their luxuriant summer, and their autumn in which the corollas fall apart and the foliage turns to gold as though impregnated with the flames of the setting sun.

Lastly, we have all the gaiety of the time, the amiable frolics which do not disturb the serenity of a religion for ever young. In a corner of the sacred building the monkey of the minstrels capers in bizarre fashion. Elsewhere it is a monk who has slept peacefully during the singing of the Office and awakens suddenly with a great yawn. Along this balustrade we see a gossip astraddle on an ass, riding the wrong way round ; and a thousand other mischievous tricks of the artist which, in this time of implicit faith, do not detract from the sanctity of the place.

As to the sculptors, those admirable artists who made themselves the interpreters of the multitude in creating these thousand masterpieces, they were hardly conscious of their art. They were hewers of stones. In the contracts they

THE MIDDLE AGES

were treated as simple masons, obliged to work at their task from morning "till supper-time." Henry of Brussels, one of the masters of the work of the cathedral of Troyes, gets married. On the day of his wedding he did not go to work, but the day is counted off his wages.

In fact, the sculptors of the cathedrals were great, more because they made themselves, like the epic poets, the unconscious interpreters of the living beliefs and powerful aspirations of the people among whom they lived, than by their professional skill.

We may say, in conclusion, that the greater number of these statues were painted, as also were the vaults of the churches, vaults of a royal blue dotted over with golden stars.

At Notre Dame the statues in bright colours stood out in the tympans of the porches against a background of bright gold.

It was a polychrome at once bold and harmonious, the finest part of which was formed by the stained-glass windows.

And this is an art which is, above all things, French, according to the testimony of foreigners such as the monk Theophilus who establishes it in his Treatise on Various Arts (*Diversarum artium schedula*). The first Romanesque churches had large flat walls which the painters covered with frescoes treated as mosaics under a Byzantine inspiration. Light penetrated under the vaults only through narrow bays closed by pierced slabs of stone, or through large wooden frames without glass. An example of these primitive devices has been preserved in the church of Lichères (Charente).

The use of ogives and buttresses having made possible the construction of higher and larger walls, the architects dared to pierce them with larger bays which they filled with glass, the more so as the use of triple naves made it necessary that the light should penetrate farther into the church to light the central portion. And with what joy the youthful and vivid minds of the men of the time were to receive the invention of coloured glass, which was to give to the mural surfaces of the churches a brilliance and beauty which no fresco or mosaic could have attained.

The churches now, thanks to the perfection of their con-

THE CATHEDRALS

struction, tend more and more to become luminous shrines, made of translucent mosaics, for as such indeed do the windows appear, filling the edifice with a warm radiance, in which the rays of the sun take on the various colours of the rainbow.

It was in France, then, that the art of stained glass took its rise. The oldest text in which mention is made of stained-glass windows representing stories is furnished by Richer, when he tells us that Adalbéron, Archbishop of Reims, one of the founders of the Capetian Monarchy, in rebuilding his cathedral (969–988) ornamented it with windows containing figures from stories (*fenestris diversas continentibus historias*).

At the beginning of the eleventh century, still in France, this art of storied windows was to make great progress, through the substitution of rings of soft lead for the wooden frames. The supple character of the lead made it possible to follow sinuous outlines. Its use was necessary in the stained-glass window as it was produced in the Middle Ages, not only to support the design but also to enclose the separate colours and so prevent their diffusion. Without it the clearest and most vivid colours, in juxtaposition with others more sombre, would encroach on these, and from a distance would confuse the design. These networks of lead are to play a great rôle even in the design itself. Look at the fine Christ of the Passion at Poitiers: the anatomy of the body is traced by means of the leaden curves themselves.

The monk Theophilus, who lived at the beginning of the twelfth century, in Italy perhaps, but more probably in Germany, gives in his *Treatise on the Practice of the Arts* the technique of stained glass.

" Should you wish to design windows of glass, begin by procuring a smooth wooden board, sufficiently long and wide for you to be able to work on it at two panels of each window. Then take some chalk, and having scraped it with a knife so as to cover the whole board with it, sprinkle it with water, then spread over it a cloth so as to cover the whole board. When your glaze is dry, take the measure of the length and breadth of the panels of the window and trace it on the board with lead or tin. If you want a border to it, trace it giving it the required size and ornamentations. This done, trace the images in as

THE MIDDLE AGES

great a number as you will, first with lead or tin, and afterwards with red or black colours, marking carefully all the lines ; for it will be necessary in painting the glass to make the lights and shadows according to this design on the board. Arranging the different draperies, mark the colour of each of them in its place as well as of all other objects which you wish to represent. Mark in the colour by a letter. After this take a little cup of lead, in which you will put some powdered chalk in water. Make two or three fine brushes of martin's tail or minever, or squirrel's or cat's hair or donkey's mane ; and take a piece of glass of the kind you want, bigger in every direction than the space on which it is to be placed, and, applying it on the surface of the board, you will follow the design, by the lines on the board seen through the glass, repeating them with your brush on the glass itself. And if the glass is so thick that you cannot see through it the lines drawn on the board, take a piece of white glass and placing it on the table trace on it in transfer the lines in question ; after which, when your line is dry, place the thick coloured glass against the white glass, and, lifting it up against the light so as to light it with its rays, sketch in the lines as you see them. You will design in the same way all kinds of glass, whether it be a matter of figures, draperies, hands, feet, borders, or any other object you wish to reproduce in colour."

The cutting of the coloured glass according to the lines of the design was a difficult and delicate operation, for the use of the diamond point (which will not appear until the sixteenth century) was not yet known. They used red-hot iron, the contact of which involved the risk of making the glass fly into splinters.

The workers in stained glass in the eleventh and twelfth centuries used only simple colours—red, blue, yellow, and their composites, green and violet. In places they put white ; dull white, clear white, or greenish white. The shades are rendered by the inequalities of the glass, by its thickness, which is greater or less in places. Certainly from the point of view of an ideally perfect manufacture the sheets of glass used in the windows of the twelfth century would furnish material nowadays to more than one critic. What blisters, and opacities ; what swellings, what inequalities ! But the art of the worker in stained glass was able to draw even from these imperfections the happiest results. To the eyes which regard these windows from a distance what a wealth of colour and warmth they afford! They spread over the wall a translucent tapestry, made up of precious stones glistening and tremulous, instead of the dull cold surfaces afforded by modern windows.

The stained-glass windows of the eleventh and twelfth centuries are composed of pieces of glass coloured in the mass. It is by the juxtaposition of the pieces of coloured glass that the design is obtained. The oldest windows with figures now known are those of Dijon and Reims; but it was in the Ile-de-France in the thirteenth century that were produced, with the full blossoming of the Gothic style, the richest and most beautiful windows. It was at St. Denis, under the direction of Abbot Suger, that the art of the worker in stained glass reached its perfection. The finest of the windows which he commissioned, that incomparable history of the First Crusade, were unhappily destroyed by the Revolution. What remain enable us to form a judgment of these masterpieces.

From St. Denis the glass workers of Abbot Suger migrated to Chartres, then to Angers in the middle of the twelfth century. They afterwards crossed the Straits and went to York, to decorate the cathedral there with their dazzling mosaics.

The finest windows known to-day are all of the end of the eleventh and of the twelfth century. They are the windows of the church of St. Remy at Reims—sacked by the Boches—of the church of St. Denis, of the cathedrals of Chartres, Angers, and Bourges. The design of the figures may appear too archaic and stiff; but what character they have, and what shall we say of the ornamentation, of those borders of flowers and foliage which form them into admirable miniatures, brilliant and luminous? The windows of the thirteenth century, such as some in the Sainte Chapelle, are already harsher and the colours drier. The windows of the twelfth century are recognised by their blue backgrounds, a blue as deep and transparent as the azure of the sky on fine summer days, an atmosphere which palpitates round the figures which it seems to enwrap.

In the thirteenth century this blue ground, at once intense

THE MIDDLE AGES

and very soft, is replaced by a background of blue and red tones which produces at a distance a violet colour, with a shade of peaceful melancholy, which is far from being without charm, but which does not give to the whole work the powerful and profound harmony of an earlier period.

And from the point of view of technique these windows were of an admirable workmanship. Their grooves were filled with putty, which protected the work against the rain. Thus these wonders of art, which have never been surpassed in any branch whatever of the arts, arrived intact at the threshold of modern times. It required the cultivated ignorance of the seventeenth and eighteenth centuries, the grossness of the Revolution, and the infamous savagery of the Germans in 1914 to 1918 to destroy them criminally.

By the time of the death of Philip Augustus nearly all the cathedrals of the royal domain were completed : Paris, Chartres, Bourges, Noyon, Laon, Soissons, Meaux, Auxerre, Arras, Cambrai, Rouen, Evreux, Séez, Bayeux, Coutances, Le Mans, Angers, Poitiers, and Tours. The English Guienne, on the contrary, preserved its old monuments.

By the time of the death of Philip the Fair the royal domain will have expanded. It will have annexed Champagne and French-speaking Flanders ; it will have conquered Lyons. Its influence will have penetrated Auvergne and Burgundy, and these provinces will then be seen adopting in their turn the Gothic style received by them in its completed form. But the provinces under the English domination still stand out, and when they enter at last into the general movement they will find a style which, after its long and glorious career, will no longer have the force necessary for a vigorous renewal.

Thus our great churches are nearly all complete when the Valois ascend the throne. The churches tardily begun in the fourteenth century—always excepting St. Ouen at Rouen—will not be able to be finished. They are, as it were, atrophied during their growth—and this is indeed the suitable expression, so much did it seem that a vivifying sap was rising in their stone arteries.

For the rest, not a single one of our great churches was finished according to the plan on which it was conceived. The

THE CATHEDRALS

prodigious impulse which caused them to spring from the ground is included almost entirely in the reign of Philip Augustus—forty years—which one might extend perhaps up to the year 1240—sixty years in all. And the effort produced in this short space of time might seem superhuman. Nothing even remotely comparable to it has since been seen, just as nothing has appeared since comparable to the wonderful flowering of the epic poems, contemporary with the cathedrals, which furnish for them so magnificent an echo.

It was in the Ile-de-France, that little land smaller than Greece, as great as Greece by reason of its genius, that the Gothic churches and the epic poems were together elaborated to spread subsequently throughout the civilized world. It formed a literary and artistic influence which created from the twelfth century onwards a " French Europe," to use the expression by which will be characterized later the radiation of French culture after the reign of Louis XIV.

The English chroniclers themselves, such as Herbert of Bosham, speak in the twelfth century of "sweet France." Bruneto Latini will in the thirteenth century write his *Trésor* in French, because " the speech of France is more general to all people, and more delectable to hear than any other." And Francis of Assisi will find no greater happiness than in chanting the praises of the Lord in French.

Already Paris exercised her fascination on the whole of Europe. A German poet, Hugo of Trimberg, writes:
" How many people have been to Paris! They learned little there and spent much, but they have seen Paris ! "

The manners of the French châtelaines became for the whole of Europe :

> . . . the touchstone and the example
> Of what should be permissible and done.
> (*Cléomàdes.*)

In the same way in all Germany nothing else was read but the French epic poems translated into German. The best poets, Heinrich von Veldeke, Johannsdorf, Friedrich von Hansen, Rudolf von Neuenberg, and how many others imitated the trouvères or troubadours, Folquet de Marseille and Pierre Vidal. The French language was spoken by all educated

237

people. French expressions and phrases were already entering into the German language to designate things relating to culture and civilization. The French style was substituted for the ancient manner of building. Clothes were cut after French fashions. Domestics served in the French manner. The life of Court and castle was organized à la française. In the castles of the Rhine, French minstrels were welcomed effusively.

We have seen William of Sens building Canterbury Cathedral (1175–81) on the model of that of Sens. The cathedral of Lincoln is built by another Frenchman, reproducing a church the construction of which had been begun at Blois in 1138. We have seen the French architects going to Germany to raise there their *opus francigenum*, while young German architects come to study in France the principles and rules of their art. We have followed the architect Villard de Honnecourt beyond the German frontier into Hungary, where, no doubt, he built the cathedral of Cassovia. Mathieu d'Arras and Pierre de Boulogne directed the building of Prague Cathedral, to which comes later Henry Arler, master of works at Boulogne-sur-Mer. To the son of this latter, Pierre Arler, the cathedral of Ulm is probably due. Stephen de Bonneuil with ten " young men " (*bacheliers*), went to Sweden to build the cathedral of Upsala. The company left Paris in September 1287. Martin Ravège built the cathedral of Colocza, where the stone marking his grave is preserved.

French architects passed from England into Norway, where their influence is especially felt in the plans and decoration of the beautiful blue church of Trondjem.

In Spain also, churches of the twelfth and thirteenth centuries due to architects of our country are very numerous. And these are, dating from the end of the eleventh century, the church of Compostella, then that of Leon, Burgos, and Gerona. The plans of the cathedral of Toledo, the foundations of which were laid in 1226, were designed by Pierre de Corbie. Finally, even in the isle of Cyprus and the Holy Land, some of the most important religious and military buildings were due to our architects of Paris or Champagne.

In Italy it was some French artists, Philippe Bonaventure, Pierre Loisart, Jean Mignot, who built the cathedral of Milan.

THE CATHEDRALS

In Southern Italy Frederick II and Charles of Anjou employed French architects Philippe Clunart, Jean de Toul, and Pierre d'Angicourt.

In Italy as in Germany the influence of the French poets was even greater, in the twelfth and thirteenth centuries, than that of the artists. The majority of our national poems were imported there, and so energetically did our minstrels circulate there the works of the French poets of the South that they came, as we have seen, to form a kind of jargon, a mixture of Italian and French, which the people beyond the Alps came to understand, and which our artists, perched on a stage, gave forth in the public squares or at the street corners. And the avidity with which the peoples of the Peninsula listened to them was so great that the Governor of Bologna thought right to pass a law forbidding the flocking round the French minstrels.

The troubadours obtained an equal success with the trouvères in Italy, Spain, and Portugal.

"I want to compose a love song in the Provençal style," says a poet of the Iberian Peninsula. And which poet? Denis the Liberal, King of Portugal. Spanish troubadours like the Italian troubadours, wrote in Provençal up to the fourteenth century, and it is known that Dante himself composed much verse in that tongue. The Courts of Aragon, Castile, Leon, Navarre, and Portugal resounded with poems and songs composed in our language of *oc*.

France then has known two great centuries of creative organization—the eleventh century, the century of feudalism, and the seventeenth century, the century of royal power, followed by those two great centuries of literary and artistic expansion, the twelfth and the eighteenth centuries.

SOURCES.—Theophilus, *Essai sur divers arts*, ed. L'Escalopier, 1843; Vict. Mortet, *Textes relatifs à l'histoire de l'architecture* (XIe–XIIe *Siècles*), 1911.

HISTORICAL WORKS.—Viollet-le-Duc, *Dictionnaire d'Architecture*, ed. cit.; J. B. A. Lassus, *Album de Villard de Honnecourt*, 1858; Anthyme Saint-Paul, *Histoire monumentale de la France*, new ed., 1911; L. Gonge, *L'Art Gothique* (1890); Emile Màle, *L'Art religieux du XIIIe Siècle en France*, 1902—a splendid work of rare value from every point of view. H. Stein, *Les Architectes des Cathedràles Gothiques* (1909)—a precious little volume of which we have made great use; Cam. Enlart, *Manuel d'archéologie française*, 1902–16, 3 vols.; Ol. Merson, *Les Vitraux*, 1898; Luc. Magne, *L'art appliqué aux metiers : Decor sur verre*, 1913; L. Reynaud, *Histoire générale de l'influence française en Allemagne*, 1914; Alwin Schultz, *Das Höfische Leben zur Zeit der Minnesinger*, 2nd ed., 1899, 2 vols.; Emile Màle, *L'Art allemand et l'art française au Moyen Age*, 1917.

CHAPTER XII

LOUIS VII

The direction of the Government remains in the hands of Suger. Eleanor of Aquitaine. Conflict with the English Crown. St. Bernard's Crusade. The King's divorce. Louis VII married again to Adèle de Champagne. Birth of Philip Augustus. The progress of the royal power. Character of Louis VII's government.

LOUIS VII, known as Louis the Young (*Le Jeune*), was fifteen or sixteen years old when he succeeded his father Louis le Gros (1st August 1137). He had been " associated " to the throne and consecrated at Reims on the 25th October 1131. At the moment of assuming the Crown he had just married Eleanor, daughter of William X, Duke of Aquitaine, who had died in Spain on pilgrimage to the shrine of St. James. In his last moments William had begged the nobles of his Duchy, standing round him, to marry his daughter the heiress to his States, to the son of the King of France. The sentiment of national unity was coming into existence. The marriage doubled the extent of the royal domain in the hands of the Capetians.

Louis VII was careful to maintain Abbot Suger in power. If any influence could have opposed the work of the great minister it would have been that of the young Queen Eleanor, a vivacious and gay Southerner, pretty, graceful, sprightly, wayward, and fanciful. She was ardent and passionate. The young King, who was acquainted up to the day of his marriage only with the graver manners of the North, was charmed by her. He was won by her graces, her mischievous, kittenish cajoleries, the pretty ways she had learned in a Court where her grandfather, William IX of Aquitaine, had been a delightful troubadour.

Eleanor had brought from the South frivolous notions, not so much subject to the discipline of the Church, and she tried to withdraw her young husband from the authority of the prelates, which was too strict for her liking. Thus the influence of Suger was not absolutely paramount. The King resists the Sovereign Pontiff in the matter of the nomination of the new Bishop of Bourges. He attacks Thibaud of Champagne, who is protected by St. Bernard; so that in the end the Pope lays him under an interdict.

The struggle against the feudatories goes on, at least against the great feudal lords; for the "hobereaux" of the royal domain are no longer to be feared. In the chief of these the Montmorencys, the Dammartins, the Clermonts, the Beaumonts, the monarchy has found servants. The great feudal lords had pursued this same struggle against their own unruly squires, and they also had triumphed over them within the limits of their respective fiefs. Thus they can in their resistance to the Crown adopt a more ambitious policy. Louis VII takes possession of Champagne; Reims and Châlons are occupied. At Vitry thirteen hundred people are burnt alive in a church, a fact which strikes the imagination of the King and helps to impel him, by way of expiation, towards the Holy Land. Thibaud allies himself with the Counts of Flanders and Soissons in proclaiming the betrothal of his son and daughter with their daughter and son. By this he broke openly with his suzerain; for a feudatory had no right to arrange the marriage of his children without the consent of the King. The situation was most threatening when Innocent II died (24th September 1143). His successor, Celestine II, will show himself more conciliatory. Peace is re-established (1144). Louis VII yielded on the matter of the bishopric of Bourges. However, an event occurred which was to involve the gravest consequences. Geoffrey the Fair, Count of Anjou, taking advantage of the troubles to which the succession of his father-in-law, Henry I, was giving rise in England, seized Normandy. Louis VII was skilful enough to have handed over to him in return for his acquiescence in this conquest several keeps in the Vexin and the famous castle of Gisors-sur-Epte, which was of capital importance from its position on the frontier between Normandy and the royal

LOUIS VII

domain. The foundations of the redoubtable empire of the Plantagenets were none the less established. The first years of the reign, in spite of the youth of the sovereign, did not fail to augur well for the future. The young King was evincing intelligence, decision, and energy when he had the unfortunate idea of taking part in a new Crusade (the second), of which he even appears to have been the promoter, in memory of the tragedy of Vitry. Edessa had just fallen into the hands of the Mohammedans. The French barons were evincing repugnance towards the remote expedition, and the new Pope, Eugenius III, was not entering enthusiastically into the views of the King, when at the Council of Vézelay the burning eloquence of St. Bernard stirred up new enthusiasms (1146). The town could not hold the crowd which had flocked to it. The Abbot of Citeaux preached in the country from the top of a wooden tower which had been put up for him. The King of France stood beside him. The scenes of Clermont were repeated. Thousands of crosses prepared beforehand were scattered among the crowd like seeds in a field. The preacher's clothes were torn from him and made into crosses. "The Abbot Bernard," writes Eude de Deuil, "hid a robust soul under a frail and seemingly dying body. He went about like the wind, preaching everywhere, and the crosses were multiplied." " I opened my mouth," writes the Saint himself; " I spoke : the villages and towns have become deserts. One sees everywhere only widows whose husbands are alive," *i.e.* on Crusade. But it was no longer the great popular impulse of 1099. With his powerful mind St. Bernard organized a vast movement by which the Mohammedans were to be attacked simultaneously, both in the Holy Land and in Portugal—for the African Mohammedans still ruled in Lisbon—as well as the pagan Slavs beyond the Elbe.

At the same time as the King of France, the German Emperor Conrad took the cross. The rivalries between the French and Germans, who made a reproach to each other of their different habits, customs, and fashions, and in the East the hostility between Latins and Greeks, led to a frightful disaster. The Germans were massacred near Dorylæum, the French at the siege of Damascus (1148).

THE MIDDLE AGES

Louis VII was too much in love with his wife to bring himself to part with her. In Syria Eleanor's temperament gave itself free rein. An enervating heat fell from the heavens, and the manners of the country were easy. The women clothed themselves in transparent silk. Eleanor found once more the pleasant ways of the South. Ah! these men of the North, harsh, unpolished, jealous! For the King was jealous. At Antioch (March 1148) there was a violent scene, followed by a real scandal. In her thin imperious voice Eleanor declared that her husband could depart if it seemed good to him: she intended to stay in the town. Louis VII had her taken to Jerusalem as a captive. A family quarrel before the eyes of the Crusaders! Finally, from Jerusalem, where Louis VII had the misfortune to be belated, the remnants of the French army returned to Europe without having been able to strike an appreciable blow at the Mohammedan Empire.

A fact which could, in a measure at least, counterbalance this grave check was that, during the absence of the King, Suger had administered his States with incomparable wisdom. The reign of Louis VII seemed to be developing in the happiest possible manner when the conjugal scenes of Antioch produced their consequences. "Some of the relatives and kinsmen of the King," a chronicler relates, "came to him and told him that there were between him and Queen Eleanor ties of consanguinity."

On the 18th March the union of the King and Queen was dissolved. Eleanor went back to her beautiful Aquitaine, where she wasted no time in mourning over her broken union. On the 18th May she married quite gaily Henry, the son of Geoffrey Martel, Count of Anjou—he was surnamed Plantagenet because it was his custom to stick a jennet (*genet*) in his scarlet bonnet embroidered with a leopard. To Henry Plantagenet Eleanor brought, not only her voluptuous graces, but—what perhaps the noble lord prized still more—her magnificent domains in the South.

Suger had died on the 13th January 1151. We may safely affirm that, in his lifetime, he would not have allowed these precious ties of consanguinity to be produced.

Henry Plantagenet, the son of Geoffrey Martel, Count of

LOUIS VII

Anjou, grandson through Matilda his mother of Henry Beauclerc, King of England, and great-grandson of the Conqueror, possessed Touraine and Anjou, Normandy and Maine. Behold him too, through his wife, master of Poitou, Guienne, and Gascony, with suzerainty over Aunis, Saintonge, Angoumois, Quercy, la Marche, Auvergne, and Perigord. In the following year he finds himself heir to the crown of England, which he assumes in 1154, and when his son shall have married the heiress of the Duchy of Brittany, which he is to govern as regent, he, the King of England, will be the ruler of three-quarters of the French realm.

This would have meant the ruin of the throne of the fleur-de-lis, if popular traditions had not preserved to the King his rôle of protector and suzerain, Grand Justiciary of the land. But they preserved it to him with such great energy that, solely through the power of this office of protector, the King of St. Denis will win back the whole kingdom.

To tell the truth, Louis VII tried to make a struggle, but the forces were unequal, the more so as Henry II of the Plantagenet house was a man of great courage. On the 31st August 1158 the two sovereigns meet outside Gisors. A treaty of peace is concluded. It is even stipulated that Henry, the eldest son of the English King—he was three years old—shall marry Marguerite the third daughter (aged six months) of Louis VII. Henry went back to England with the little bride-to-be in his custody. But shortly afterwards the war recommenced. Henry II, as Duke of Aquitaine, claimed the County of Toulouse. Louis VII hastened to the assistance of Count Raymond V, and as his forces were weaker than those of the Plantagenet, he shut himself up with Raymond in the town. Here an unexpected sight was seen.

So deeply was implanted in the minds of the men of that time the respect due to the royal suzerainty that the powerful King of England, Duke of Aquitaine and Normandy, Count of Anjou and Governor of Brittany, declared that it was impossible for him to besiege a place in which was the King of France, his suzerain. So he decamped with his formidable army, scruples which even the Chancellor of England, the famous Thomas Becket, treated as mere quibbles.

THE MIDDLE AGES

On the 4th October 1160, Constance, the second wife of Louis VII, died. Hardly a few weeks had passed before Louis married again, Adèle de Champagne; to which Henry II, King of England, retorted by concluding the marriage of his eldest son with the little Marguerite of France whom he had in his keeping. The new husband and wife could count nine years between them. Louis VII had no son by his marriage with Constance. His neighbour across the Channel had hoped that he would never have one. War broke out again, followed by another treaty of peace.

The King of England, Duke of Normandy, recovered Gisors; the Count of Toulouse was abandoned.

At this moment the destinies of the Capetian dynasty appeared to be compromised. Events relatively of minor importance, when they are compared to the consequences, suffice to show that the moral foundations on which the French King's power rested, represented a force which it would not be easy to shake.

Thomas Becket, the Chancellor, was elected, on the 3rd June 1162, Archbishop of Canterbury and Primate of England. From that day forth, he, who had never ceased to show himself the most ardent protagonist of the rights of the English Monarchy, the boldest of the councillors of Henry II, displayed an equal zeal in defence of the privileges of his Church. Henry II had attempted to submit the clerics of his kingdom to his judicial authority and to make them pay taxes like the laity. To this Becket opposed an unexpected resistance. Henry tried to bend him. The Archbishop would not yield. The struggle became so violent that Becket had to flee to France, where Louis VII received him with great honour.

Louis VII was a very good man; too good. Instead of profiting by the circumstances to increase the embarrassments of his redoubtable neighbour, he set himself to arrange several interviews between the prelate and the English monarch in the artless desire of effecting a reconciliation. The third of these interviews, at the Ferté-Bernard (20th to 22nd July 1170), ended in an agreement. Becket went back to his see. But the dispute soon broke out again. At the castle of Bures-lès-Bayeux, in December 1170, Henry II allowed these words to

LOUIS VII

escape him: "A man who has eaten my bread, who came to my Court poor and naked, and whom I have placed above all others, dares to raise his foot and kick me in the teeth. And there is no one to avenge me on this cleric!" The words fell on the ears of four English barons. On the 29th December they assassinated Thomas Becket on the altar steps in his cathedral of Canterbury.

The stir made by this event cannot be imagined. The victim was resplendent with the palms of martyrdom. On his tomb miracles were worked. In that time of ardent faith Henry II felt that his power was being thus undermined.

Then on the 21st August 1165, Adèle de Champagne gave to Louis VII the son he had waited for so long. The description of the joy of the people reveals the intensity which monarchical sentiment had already assumed. In the middle of the night the news runs through Paris. The town wakes up and bursts into illumination. At the cross-roads bonfires blaze. Thousands of torches are borne through the streets. Cries of triumph re-echo noisily. The people pull the beadles out of bed and make them open the churches, into which the crowds fling themselves to sing their thanksgivings. From the highest lord to the humblest peasant all unite their joy in a general clamour.

Awakened by the tumult, Gerald de Barri, an English student, rushes to his window. Two poor old women were running along with all the strength of their stiffened limbs, waving lighted candles. Gerald asked them in his French with an English accent what was the meaning of all this nocturnal uproar.

"We have a King given us by God, a proud heir to the throne, who will put your King to shame and sorrow!"

The good old women did not know how truly they spoke. The little fellow just born was to be called Philip Augustus.

From one end of France to another, even to the humblest townships, messengers ran to carry spontaneously the truimphal tidings. Henry II saw the hope vanish which he had formed when he had had the marriage of his son with Louis VII's daughter concluded, the hope of seeing his son one day unite in his hands the sceptres of France and England. The moral

THE MIDDLE AGES

reproach imputed to Henry II by the assassination of Thomas Becket was rendered graver still by the disagreements in which the English King was involved with the delicious Eleanor, destined decidedly to import as many difficulties as charms into the lives of her successive husbands. She won over her sons. In open revolt against their father they took refuge at the French Court. Louis VII hastened to recognize Henry, the eldest, as King of England, and to have a seal made for him ; and the young King to publish acts in which he took the style of reigning monarch under the name of Henry III. He was supported by the Pope, with whom he had turned to account the fact that the murder of Thomas Becket had not yet been avenged. War breaks out again. The feudatories are involved in it. In England a number of great lords rise against their suzerain. The King of Scotland enters into the struggle. But Louis VII had not the military qualities, the energy, or the activity of his vassal. He suffered nothing but reverses. The King of Scotland was defeated. On the 30th September 1174 peace was signed at Montlouis (near Tours). Henry II in his triumph limited his demands to the restitution of the castles which had been taken from him in Normandy. But he kept his wife Eleanor a prisoner for several years.

In the last year of his life, Louis VII, then nearly sixty years old, was struck with paralysis of the right side. He then abandoned the cares of the government to his son Philip Augustus—whom he had had consecrated in Reims Cathedral on the 1st November 1179 by Archbishop William " with the white hands."

Numerous barons took part in the ceremony, even some foreign princes owing allegiance to the German Crown. The Count of Flanders—acting as Constable of France—carried the royal sword.

We can form a fairly clear impression of the character of Louis VII. He was very gentle and very good : some said to the degree of stupidity. He talked familiarly with the first comer. His palace, open to all, had the simplicity of a bourgeois residence. Conversing with the Englishman, Walter Map, Louis VII said pleasantly : " As for your prince, he wants for nothing : valuable horses, gold and silver, silken fabrics,

LOUIS VII

precious stones, he has them all in abundance. At the Court of France, we have only bread, wine, and gaiety." The German students in Paris thought good to laugh about it. They ridicule the fact, writes another Englishman, John of Salisbury, that the King of France converses civilly with his subjects and does not live separated from them by a barrier of sergeants and guards. A third Englishman, Henry of Hereford, says that Louis VII governed peaceably and always as an honourable man.

However amiable might be the character of the King, his government was not lacking in firmness. He displayed it, above all, in the exercise of justice. Moreover, during his reign of forty-three years the kingdom prospered. Peaceful years predominated. New towns were multiplied; old towns grew. Everywhere progress was made in agriculture, and vast forests were cleared.

SOURCES.—The same as for Chapters XI and XIII.

CHAPTER XIII

PHILIP AUGUSTUS

Coalition of the Nobles of the realm. Tragic death of Henry II, King of England. Richard Cœur de Lion. The Crusade of the two Princes. Deliverance of St. Jean d'Acre (13th July 1191). Captivity of Richard Cœur de Lion. Brigands in the pay of the Princes. Cadoc and Mercadier. Ingeburg of Denmark. Assassination of Arthur of Brittany. Conquest of Normandy. The Fourth Crusade: Villehardouin. The Latin Empire of Constantinople. The Albigensian Crusade. Bouvines (27th July 1214). Creation of Bailiffs (*Baillis*). Louis VIII in England. The works ordered by Philip Augustus in Paris. Death of Philip Augustus. Reign of Louis VIII.

PHILIP AUGUSTUS was barely fifteen years old when he mounted the throne on the 18th September 1180 —a young man who was destined to preside over one of the most fruitful reigns in our history. With a strong, acute, and active mind, a tenacious will, and a far-seeing energy, he had the qualities of a great prince of that day. He will know how to divert the turbulent Nobility towards useful enterprises, contribute to the consolidation of the communes, and for the benefit of his policy to assert the royal authority in distant provinces. " I desire that at the end of my reign the monarchy shall be as powerful as in the time of Charlemagne," and there wanted little to the fulfilment of his wish.

The surname " Augustus " he got from the fact that he was born in August. When he is getting old, the Chronicle of Tours will sketch this picture of him :

" Philip was a handsome, strapping man, with a pleasant face, bald, of a ruddy complexion and with a temperament inclined to good cheer. He was a skilful engineer, a good Catholic, farseeing and with strong opinions. With him there mounted on the judge's seat right and justice. Beloved of Fortune, fearful for his life, easy to rouse and appease, he

PHILIP AUGUSTUS

was very severe towards the Nobles who resisted him, and took pleasure in fermenting discords between them. He never, however, made an enemy die in prison. He loved to be served by insignificant folk." It is easy to picture this man with the tall figure, broad shoulders, thin and bald, and with the piercing eyes.

At his accession he found the powerful Plantagenet, Henry II, King of England, master of half France and preparing to lay hands on Auvergne and Languedoc. Philip of Alsace, Count of Flanders, had seen his power growing, not only by his marriage with Isabelle de Vermandois, who had brought him Vermandois and Valois, but also through the formidable economic development of his domains.

To the wealth of the County of Flanders was comparable that of the County of Champagne. The markets of Troyes had become the most important in Europe. Through this and through his magnificent family connections the power of Henry I, the Liberal, Count of Champagne, had increased. His sister was the wife of Louis VII. One of his brothers, William of the White Hands, was Archbishop of Reims and Papal Legate. Another of his brothers, Thibaud V, Count of Blois and of Chartres, was Seneschal of France, the title of the chief officer of the Crown. Lastly, the youngest, Stephen, Count of Sancerre, was the best soldier of his time. Together they formed the faction of the " Champenois," just as in the sixteenth century there would be that of the " Lorrains " (the Princes of Guise).

Is it not a miracle that in face of such rivals, Philip Augustus should in his small domain watered by the Seine and the Oise, have been during the course of his reign able to undermine the English power and to double the extent of the royal territory ?

And first of all there was his marriage with Isabella of Hainault—or Elizabeth, for it is the same name, Isabella being the Spanish form—daughter of Count Baldwin V. As a dowry she brought Artois : Arras, St. Omer, Aire, and Hesdin. The " Champenois " felt their power weakening. They formed a league under the inspiration of Philip Augustus' own mother, allying themselves with the Count of Flanders, the Count of

Namur, the Count of Hainault, and the Duke of Burgundy. The conspirators tried to secure the adherence of the German Emperor Frederick Barbarossa. Victory was certain, they assured him, and thus he would be able to extend the limits of the Empire up to the seas round Britain: here is already the horrible dream of William II.

War broke out in 1181. It was to last five years.

From Crêpy-en-Valois the Count of Flanders sent troops to attack Senlis, the old town of the Capets; but Isabella of Vermandois, the wife of the Count of Flanders, dies. Philip Augustus claims her heritage and begins by taking possession of it. It is Vermandois and Valois. He sows division among the allies. He brings pressure to bear on his wife to persuade her father, the Count of Hainault, to abandon the coalition. He threatens to repudiate her. "In 1185," recounts Gilbert de Mons, "Queen Isabella became odious to the French, because her father was lending assistance to the Count of Flanders as he was bound to do (as his vassal). The Nobles of the Court urged the King to divorce her. A day had been fixed on which the repudiation was to be pronounced at Senlis, when Queen Isabella, having put off her fine raiment and put on the humblest clothing, walked barefoot through the streets of the town calling aloud on God to remove from her royal spouse his pernicious councillors. The people were touched. They loved their good Queen: and here they come before the palace, a great crowd in which were seen beggars, cripples, lepers. They cried on the King with loud and lamentable groans begging him to retain his wife; to which Philip Augustus consented. But he adopted towards her a cold, reserved manner. Even in her own country he treated her as a stranger, so much so that, when in the following year Baldwin of Hainault had come to see his daughter at Pontoise, Isabella threw herself in tears at his feet, imploring him to lend his aid to her husband, the King, against the Count of Flanders; and Count Baldwin promised to do all he could, saving his allegiance to the Count of Flanders, his suzerain."

The coalition was hard hit by this defection. The Count of Flanders demanded peace. The King of France obtained (July 1183), besides the confirmation of the cession of Artois, his wife's dowry, sixty-five castles in Vermandois, and Amiens, the capital of Picardy.

The Duke of Burgundy was reduced in a rapid campaign.

It will cause surprise that Henry II, the King of England, did not at this point think of supporting the members of the coalition against the French prince; but at this time he was at the height of his struggle with his three sons. It is Philip who attacks the English King; but the war, begun in May 1187, came to an end in June. By the Treaty of Châteauroux (23rd June) Henry II ceded to Philip Augustus Issoudun and the lordship of Fréteval-en-Vendômois. Philip's activity is relentless. He receives at his Court Richard—the future Cœur de Lion—who has become, by the death of his elder brother, heir to the crown of England. He makes an alliance with the German Emperor Barbarossa, and passing through Tournai takes advantage of it to give to the inhabitants a communal charter and to obtain from them a contingent of three hundred men. And it is well known how great is to be the devotion of the people of Tournai to the French Crown during some centuries.

The struggle with England was about to be resumed when there was spread abroad this news : " Saladin, the tyrant of Egypt, has taken Jerusalem, and has carried off the Holy Cross." It is the epoch when heroic passions break out to the strains of the epic poems.

At Gisors, on the 21st January 1188, Philip and Henry II meet and give each other the kiss of peace. Both of them take the cross. What a farce! In May, Philip invades the domains of the English monarch, seizes Châteauroux and Argentan. War spreads over the various lands which the Plantaganet owns in France.

Through the voice of her legates, Rome utters heart-rending cries. And what about the Holy War?

The interview of Bonmoulins (18th November 1188), on the borders of Perche, only emphasized the rivalry of the two princes. Richard, the son of Henry II, the heir to the English Crown, appeared there at the side of Philip Augustus. When the sovereigns separated, Richard followed the King to Paris. Richard attracted to his suite a great number of the barons inhabiting the provinces in France which belonged to the English allegiance. Maine was invaded by the troops of the King of France. Henry II hastened to shut himself up in Le Mans. He was ill, tired, disheartened. On the 12th June 1189, Philip Augustus, accompanied by Richard, appeared beneath the walls. The English King fled from the burning town as far as the castle of Fresnai-sur-Sarthe, twenty miles away. After Maine, Philip Augustus conquered Touraine. A great number of the barons, who had still adhered to the side of the English monarch, now abandoned him. Henry II resigned himself to an interview with his youthful adversary at Colombiers, in the environs of Tours, on the 4th July 1189. " The two Kings met," we read in the *Life of William the Marshall*; " all the great barons who were there saw plainly from King Henry's face that he had suffered greatly. The King of France himself saw it, and said to him : ' Sire, we know that you cannot stand,' offering him a seat. But Henry refused to be seated, saying that he only wished to know what was demanded of him and why he was despoiled of his territories."

The two Kings agreed on peace ; after which they set out together to the Crusade. They agreed each to communicate to the other the names of their secret adherents and allies.

At Chinon Henry II had to take to bed. " He wished to know the names of those who had been against him," we read in the Life of the Marshall. " He therefore sent Master Roger, the Keeper of the Seal, to the King of France to demand the promised list. Master Roger went to Tours, where he copied the list of those who had promised to help the French. On his return Henry asked him the names : ' Sire,' replied he with a sigh, ' the first name on the roll is that of your son Count John.' "

John Lackland was the only son of Henry II who had seemed to remain faithful to him. The great King had concentrated on him all the tenderness of his wounded heart.

When King Henry, pursues the chronicler, heard that the being he loved best in the world was faithless to him, he could only say : " You have said enough." He turned over in his bed. He was seized with trembling ; the blood grew torpid in his veins. His skin grew dark. He was ill for three days, uttering unintelligible words.

PHILIP AUGUSTUS

"At last death broke his heart, and a jet of congealed blood spurted from his nose and mouth. And there happened to him at his death a thing which had never before happened to so great a baron. They had nothing wherewith to cover him. He remained so poor, so forlorn—quite naked—that he had neither linen nor wool to cover him." The poet adds: "It is truly said that *the dead have no friends.*"

Richard Cœur de Lion hastened to take advantage of his cordial relations with the King of France. An agreement was made. Philip Augustus restored to him the greater part of his new conquests; he kept only the territory of Issodun and Graçay-en-Berry. The two Kings renewed their vow to set out for the Holy Land at the same time. And the departure was made from Vézelay on the 4th July 1190. The first days seemed like a scene of enchantment. The two princes at the head of their troops descended the Rhone valley in brilliant procession. Young girls in white came singing to present baskets of flowers. But after Marseilles the good understanding was disturbed. Richard was pompous, haughty, and arrogant; Philip was reserved, suspicious, and egotistical. He reproached Richard for breaking his promise in not having married his sister Alice; to which Richard replied with rudeness. The quarrel became so bitter that, in March 1191, to save the expedition, the two princes concluded an agreement, a veritable treaty of peace, as if they had been at open war. Its terms are published by Rigord. They arrived before St. Jean d'Acre. The town, heroically defended, had been beseiged for two years by the Christians. The Christian barons in the East were divided by differences which the rivalry between Philip and Richard was to increase further. Guy de Lusignan, King of Jerusalem, conquered at Tiberias, found a redoubtable rival in the person of Conrad, Marquis of Montferrat. Philip took the side of Montferrat, and Richard that of Lusignan. One wonders how the affair would have terminated if the place had not capitulated on the 13th July 1191. It was plainly a first success; but the Crusade was only beginning. Saladin was not conquered; he was still master of Jerusalem. Then Philip Augustus declared that he was going back to France. He declared that he was

THE MIDDLE AGES

very ill. The air of Palestine did not agree with him. This illness consisted chiefly in the question of the succession to the Count of Flanders, who had died suddenly before St. Jean d'Acre. Philip made fine promises to Cœur de Lion : far from injuring his interests in the West, he would watch over them like a brother. He left him 10,000 men of his army commanded by the Duke of Burgundy. On the 25th December 1191 the King of France had returned to Fontainebleau.

Philip Augustus at once prepared his attack on the English Crown. An unheard-of circumstance proved favourable to him beyond his dreams. On his way back from the Holy Land, Richard Cœur de Lion fell into the hands of his personal enemy, Leopold, Duke of Austria, who had him thrown into prison. The two princes had had some violent quarrels before St. Jean d'Acre. Philip invaded Normandy and seized the Vexin, but he failed before Rouen. Richard Cœur de Lion had just been delivered by Duke Leopold to the German Emperor. Philip insisted with this latter that he should indefinitely keep the English King in prison. Frightful negotiations were begun. The details thereof were to be read publicly at the Diet of Mainz. Philip Augustus and John Lackland, Richard's brother, offered the Emperor 80,000 marks if Richard were detained until the feast of St. Michael (29th September), and 150,000 if Richard were delivered up to them. Then the King of England made up his mind to yield. He consented to all the demands of Henry VI, owned himself his vassal, and was set at liberty. On the 23rd March 1194, Richard Cœur de Lion entered London, whence he hastened to cross the Channel to recover his Duchy of Normandy.

The war lasted from the month of May 1194 to April 1199. It is a new war ; in many ways no longer a feudal war, by **The Brigands.** reason of the important part which money plays in it—a fight between the pound of Tours and the pound sterling. And there are then seen to appear on the same plane as the noblest knights, those men-at-arms half brigands, half soldiers, skilful at ambushes and ambuscades, at bold rescues, the Mercadiers and the Cadocs.

A soldier of fortune, at the head of his bandits the " Coter-

256

eaux" (mercenaries), Mercadier became the brother-in-arms of Cœur de Lion. Through the whole of France, from Normandy to Aquitaine, the King and the adventurer are seen riding together cheek by jowl. The bulletins in which Richard informed his prelates and barons of his victories rarely failed to sing the praises of the valiant Mercadier. Before starting out for the Holy Land he had given into his keeping seventeen castles in Quercy.

Since the year 1183 Mercadier had been seen, traversing Limousin with his companions, plundering, burning, sacking, sparing neither woman nor child, holding to ransom towns and monasteries.

Mercadier was particularly clever at surprising places in the half-light of the morning. He took also an important part in the affair of Gisors, when Philip Augustus was defeated on the 29th September 1196. But the stroke for which the English King was most grateful to him was the capture of Milly (19th May 1197), when he took possession of Philippe de Dreux, the Bishop of Beauvais and first cousin of Philip Augustus, one of the most redoubtable warriors of his time.

As a curious type of the soldier bishop, this Bishop of Beauvais might well have served as model to the contemporary poets who trace in the *chansons de geste* the picturesque silhouette of Archbishop Turpin. He divides his time between the battlefield and the sanctuaries of piety. After having massacred the adherents of the King of England and delivered towns and villages to the flames, he set out with equal ardour on pilgrimage, barefooted, to the shrine of St. James of Compostella. His lieutenant, an archdeacon, was not less pious, nor less of a fighter; the two companions terrorized the whole of Normandy.

But to come back to Mercadier. In the course of the Flemish campaign of 1198 he managed to make a large fortune. The country was rich, the markets thronged. What seizures and surprises were furnished him by the merchants returning from gatherings at Ypres or Bruges, with their purses weighted with golden florins! On the other hand, King Richard made him a gift of large domains in Perigord. Mercadier rises to the height of some fine rôles. He makes pious benefactions

THE MIDDLE AGES

to monasteries to assure himself of heaven, and is anxious to be proclaimed protector of monks. He was a freebooter placed by the King of England at the head of his armies.

We will not follow the two adversaries, Philip Augustus and Richard Cœur de Lion, through this five years' struggle, a jumble of turns and reversions of fortune. It was marked, on the side of Richard, by the building of the Château-Gaillard (Saucy Castle), a formidable stronghold, regarded as the masterpiece of the defensive fortresses of the period. The war assumed a character of atrocious cruelty. On both sides prisoners were blinded and maimed. " The King of England," says William le Breton, " had three knights whom he had taken prisoner flung down from the rock of Château-Gaillard and their necks and bones were broken. After this again he had the eyes of fifteen men put out and gave them as guide one who had had one eye left to him, so that he could conduct them to the King of France. Then the latter inflicted the same injury on a like number of Englishmen and sent them to their prince led by the wife of one of them, and he had three others cast down from the summit of a rock so that he might not appear inferior to Richard."

Cœur de Lion had great qualities as a soldier. He was daring but clear-sighted, skilful in striking great blows in the right place. After the defeat of Courcelles-les-Gisors (27th September 1198) the position of Philip Augustus seemed critical.

The Truce of Vernon, concluded through the pressing intervention of Innocent III, imposed hard sacrifices on him. Out of all his conquests he kept only Gisors. Seeing his fortunes suddenly restored, Richard Cœur de Lion, with Mercadier, besieged the Viscount of Limoges, a rebellious vassal, in his castle of Châlus-en-Limousin. On the 26th March 1199 an arrow, sped from the great tower, wounded the English King in the shoulder. The castle was taken a few days later and the companions of Cœur de Lion hanged all the defenders, with the exception of the archer who had wounded the King. However, gangrene had set in in the wound, and Richard was informed that there was no hope for him. The English King asked to see his murderer.

"What evil had I done to thee that thou shouldst kill me?"

"Thou hast slain with thine own hand my father and my two brothers, and wouldst have killed me also. Take what vengeance thou wouldst; I am ready to suffer all the cruelties thou canst invent, provided that thou thyself art to die, thou who hast done so many and so great evils in the world."

Richard replied to the archer that he would pardon him.

"I want not thy pardon. I am happy to die."

This young hero was named Pierre Basile.

"Thou shalt live in spite of thyself," replied the King, "a living witness of my humaneness."

And after seeing that he was given a hundred sous in English money, the King had him set at liberty.

Richard died. Hardly was he dead when Mercadier had Basile, who was entirely unsuspecting, sought out, and burnt alive before his eyes.

Richard Cœur de Lion was of an enthusiastic, chivalrous, most attractive character. Himself a poet, he showed himself generous to the trouvères and troubadours, and they have celebrated in magnificent words his brilliant qualities.

John Lackland, the youngest brother of Richard, succeeded him. He was as knavish and cunning as his brother had shown himself open and chivalrous; cruel, greedy, sensual and wicked, but he had the qualities of his race. He had the intellect of a politician and the shrewdness of a diplomat. He was more refined than the majority of the men of his day, but his vices made him odious.

John had had a rival to the throne, the young Arthur of Brittany, son of the deceased Geoffrey, eldest brother of John Lackland, and Constance, Duchess of Brittany. Had Geoffrey survived Richard, all the latter's domains would have come to him. In virtue of the right of succession, Arthur of Brittany claimed the crown which his father would have worn, and the support of Philip Augustus. In his quality of suzerain the King of France proclaimed young Arthur heir to Normandy and Brittany, which were held from him. War began. It was proceeding with varying fortunes when suddenly the King of France seemed to be paralysed. He was struggling with the

THE MIDDLE AGES

difficulties which his conflict with Ingeburg of Denmark was raising for him.

It is a strange story. Isabella of Hainault, the first wife of Philip Augustus, had died at the age of nineteen (1190) after having given birth to a son. Philip Augustus asked Knut II, the King of Denmark, for the hand of his sister Ingeburg, asking him at the same time to yield to him the claims on the crown of England which he had from Sweyn II and to help him in substantiating them. It was the constant desire of Philip Augustus to repeat the expedition of William the Conqueror. The young princess, aged eighteen years, arrived in France on the 14th August 1193, and Philip married her at Amiens. He himself was twenty-eight years of age. Ingeburg was fair and slender. There was a disconcerting charm in her blue green eyes, that smooth blue of the Northern seas when the sky is very clear. Contemporaries speak of her grace and beauty. Philip Augustus had received her with evident gladness, but behold, on the day after the wedding, when the coronation was to take place, Philip draws away from her, waving his hands as though repelling a phantom and giving the strangest signs of horror and repulsion. He grew pale and trembled. What had passed between husband and wife during the night? This will never be known. Sorcerers, so the doctor and chaplain of the King will say, had prevented the consummation of the marriage, and this is the reason which Philip Augustus will put forward before the Roman Court. The King wanted to return the young woman immediately to the Danish mission which had conducted her, but they replied that their part in the matter was finished. The King had Ingeburg shut up in the Convent of St. Maur. He came there to pay her a visit, crossed the threshold of the room, and immediately came out again. "It is impossible for me," he said. "to live with this woman." A complacent assembly of nobles and prelates meeting at Compiègne pronounced a divorce (5th November 1193) under the eternal pretext of ties of relationship. The great-grandmothers of Isabella, the first wife of Philip Augustus, and Ingeburg were supposed to have been sisters, daughters of Charles the Good, Count of Flanders. Now Charles the Good had never had any children. Innocent III treated the proceedings at Compiègne as mere buffoonery.

Poor Ingeburg, strictly cloistered, did not know what was going on. She neither spoke nor understood French. Those who had accompanied her from Denmark were kept away from her. Even in the convent she was treated wretchedly. When the Archbishop of Reims presented himself before her to notify her, through an interpreter, of the decision which had been made, the young wife burst into tears, and then recovering herself, she exclaimed in Latin, "Mala Francia!" (Wicked France!), and added " Roma ! " to indicate that she appealed to the Pope.

By order of the King, Ingeburg was transferred to a dependency of the Abbey of Cisoing, in the diocese of Tournai, where she continued to be disgracefully treated. She, who had brought to her husband, besides her shadowy claims to the English Crown, a fine dowry in very real gold, was obliged to sell some of her furniture and clothes for her living expenses. Philip Augustus obstinately refused to see her again. Knut II, on his part, made a formal protest before the Sovereign Pontiff. Philip Augustus took every step to impede the course of the law, had the Danish envoys driven from Rome, and then arrested outside Dijon, deprived of their correspondence, and thrown into prison. In his anger against the young wife who defied him, Philip made her confinement still more rigorous. From the convent where she was, he had her transferred to a fortress. One can imagine what followed. The King of France, not allowing himself to be checked by the papal decision which declared the sentence of divorce passed at Compiègne null and void, set himself to seek another wife. The search was not easy. The parents, dazzled by so magnificent an alliance, eagerly followed up the first parleys, but the young ladies proved recalcitrant. " I know how the King of France behaved to the King of Denmark's sister," says the daughter of the Count Palatine, " and this example scares me." And she married Henry of Saxony. A similar refusal was made by Jane of England, who was to become the Countess of Toulouse. Another maiden from Germany was dispatched on her journey by her parents with a fine retinue apparelled for the wedding.

THE MIDDLE AGES

But she arranged to pass through the territory of a lord who was in love with her. The gallant formed an ambush, carried off the beauty, who made a laughing struggle and married him. In the end Philip Augustus married Agnes de Méranie, the daughter of a Bavarian lord. Rome issues an interdict, and with the greater justice as, if there were no ties of kindred within the prohibited degrees between Philip and Ingeburg, these did exist between him and Agnes.

Here, then, is the King of France entangled once again in the complications of a sentence of interdict. The bells are silent in all the churches, the churches shut their doors to hymns and prayers; the mournful graveyards refuse the dead. The corpses abandoned by the sides of the roads filled the land with stench and terror. Then, too, Philip Augustus decided to sign a treaty with John Lackland on the 22nd May 1200 at Le Goulet. Moreover, the treaty was not too unfavourable to him. He received the County of Evreux and a sum of 20,000 pounds sterling. On the other hand, the King of France consented to the marriage of his son Louis— later Louis VIII—to Blanche of Castile, the niece of John Lackland. Saint Louis was the son of this marriage. John Lackland came to Paris, where a sumptuous reception was arranged for him; but at the end of the year the war was resumed.

In Aquitaine, John Lackland had by the sordidness and egotism of his policy very soon brought the chief barons to rise against him. He had taken from Hugh the Brown (le Brun), the son of the Comte de la Marche, his fiancée, Isabelle Taillefer, to marry her himself (30th August 1200). The lords of Aquitaine appealed from their immediate suzerain to their superior suzerain, *i.e.* the King of France. John was summoned to appear in Paris before the Court of Peers. It was the first great example of those appeals made by Aquitaine which are to play an important rôle during the following century and are to prove a source of inextricable difficulties for the English Crown. The sentence of the Court of Paris was delivered in 1202, probably on the 28th April. John Lackland was found to be at fault. Information as to the details of the judgment is, unfortunately, not forthcoming, and even its exact text is

PHILIP AUGUSTUS

not known. "The Court of France," says Raoul, Abbot of the Cistercian monastery of Coggeshall, "declared that the King of England should be deprived of all the fiefs which he held from the King of France, for not having fulfilled the conditions on which the said fiefs were held, and for having disobeyed his suzerain in almost every way."

This is an important date. From this day the thoughts of the Kings of France will constantly revert to this solemn act by which the English Kings were despoiled of their French possessions.

Philip invaded Normandy, but the young Arthur was defeated at Mirebeau and fell into the hands of the English monarch (31st July 1202). Here again a frightful tragedy is enacted. In the tower of Rouen John Lackland assassinated his nephew with his own hands (April 1203). The news spread, emphasized with horrible details. And there was seen growing more marked a movement of reprobation similar to that which had almost overthrown Henry II after the assassination of Thomas Becket. It is the time at which Philip Augustus seizes Château-Gaillard (6th March 1204), the formidable fortress which formed the key of Normandy. The Capetian found himself master of the whole province in two months. The ability of the French King had been seconded by the indifference of John Lackland, who did not think it necessary to interrupt a chess party to receive the Norman envoys.

Philip Augustus acted with equal decision in Poitou and Aquitaine. One must admire the efficacious policy of the young prince who destroyed in three years the work so laboriously built up by William the Conqueror, Henry Beauclerc, and Henry II. Rarely have such important events been brought about by such simple means, operating with such clear-sightedness and precision.

In order to gain the necessary respite the King had made a show of yielding to the Pope on the subject of his divorce from Ingeburg. In March 1201 he had appeared, together with the Queen, at Soissons, before an assembly of judges presided over by the papal delegate. The envoys of Knut II spoke with vehemence, reminding Philip Augustus of his promises and oaths. The King's advocates replied in subtle

THE MIDDLE AGES

and eloquent speeches. The poor Queen was much embarrassed in her effort to answer their dialectics confused with Latin phraseology, when from the midst of the assembly there rose an unknown clerk. He pleaded the cause of innocence with so much force and emotion that the assembly was overcome. Sessions succeeded each other. The cardinals could find no motive for divorce, when, to the general surprise, Philip Augustus suddenly declared that the Queen was completely restored to favour. He went towards her, gave her his hand, led her to the bottom of the steps, took her up behind him on his horse, and departed in the style of a youthful lover. The interdict was removed. Agnes de Méranie, discarded in her turn, died at the Castle of Poissy; but now John Lackland is conquered and Philip wants to repudiate Ingeburg again. He has her shut up in the tower of Etampes and closely guarded. He wants to get her herself to demand a divorce to enter religion. The material privations and the moral tortures to which the unhappy Queen was exposed gave rise to fears for her health. She is insulted by those who serve her. She is deprived of the consolation of the practice of her religion. "Father," she writes to the Pope, "I look to you that I may not perish. It is not because of my body, but my soul that I am troubled. I am dying every day." She asks the Sovereign Pontiff to annul beforehand all statements or oaths which may be forced from her by violence. In her calm resistance the young and captive queen acted admirably. " Young in years," writes Stephen of Tournai, " she had the prudence of a head whitened by age." The Papacy was magnificently represented by Innocent III, who displayed in this painful drama his lofty wisdom, his resolute energy, and his great goodness. The King of France had already broached negotiations for a fourth marriage with the daughter of the Landgrave of Thuringia, when as a submissive son of the Church he yielded and took back his wife (April 1213). There was general rejoicing. Ingeburg regained her position as Queen of France and was never again deprived of it.

For twenty years, the time to which his first meeting with Ingeburg went back, Philip Augustus had desired on several occasions, and seemingly quite sincerely, to be reconciled with her, and each time he had felt himself repelled by an unconquerable aversion. Now we see him in the fifties. Age softens the whims of love and puts political considerations in the forefront. After having driven the English from France, Philip Augustus resumed the same plans which had prompted him to demand the hand of Ingeburg, so that his wife and the King of Denmark and the Sovereign Pontiff had become necessary to him once more.

As for Ingeburg during the many years she still lived—for she only died in 1237—she occupied herself with noble works of beneficence in which shone forth the beauty of her soul, "more beautiful still," says Stephen of Tournai, "than her radiant countenance."

To return to the contemporary events of the Fourth Crusade. It was decided on at a tournament at Ecri-sur-Aisne at which the barons of Champagne had jousted against the Flemings and Picardese. After a plentiful exchange of buffets and blows, they had fraternized and decided to attack the Saracens. Fulk, the Vicar of Neuilly-sur-Marne, was its preacher, recalling by his passionate eloquence both Peter the Hermit and Saint Bernard. He came to preach at Champeaux, where a market was held in a cemetery. "There," writes Jacques de Vitry, "usurers, light women, the greatest sinners, after having despoiled themselves of their garments, threw themselves at the preacher's feet confessing their sins. Sick people had themselves carried to him. The crowd rushed after him, destroying his robe to share its shreds among them. Vainly he drove away the more impatient with a stick. He could not protect his garments from the piety of the spectators. Every day he required a new cassock." He must have given the cross to more than 200,000 pilgrims.

The Crusade of Villehardouin.

Once more, crowds of the people are seen departing without any experienced leader and perishing on the way in the most lamentable manner. The real Crusade was formed of feudal barons. Thibaud of Champagne being dead, Philip Augustus advised that Boniface de Montferrat, the brother of the old rival of Guy de Lusignan, should be taken as leader.

However courageous they might be, the knights who joined

THE MIDDLE AGES

in this new expedition to the East were not the rude soldiers of the First Crusade. We find among them trouvères and troubadours who compose pretty love songs, both verse and music, as a farewell to their lady, while she sews on the shoulders of their cloaks the white cross of the Crusaders. Hearken to Robert de Blois :

> Departure from the sweet country
> Where the fair one is, has made me very sad,
> I have had to leave her whom I have most loved,
> To serve the Lord God, the Creator ;
> And none the less I remain in her love,
> For all to her remain of my heart and my thought ;
> If my body is going to serve Our Lord,
> I have not for this my good love forgotten.

Another, among the most valiant captains of the Crusade, Villehardouin, Marshall of Champagne, has given a vivid description of the expedition.

Like the previous expeditions, the Crusade had Jerusalem as its first objective. Six ambassadors, among whom was Villehardouin, were sent to Venice to settle the conditions on which the flourishing Republic of Merchants would transport the Crusaders by sea. The messengers were received by the Doge Dandolo. The Venetian Government agreed to put vessels at the disposal of the French armies at a price of four marks per horse and two marks per man.

Venice was to receive besides half of the conquests. Always business men ! It was also decided that the disembarkation should take place in Egypt and that the Crusaders should march directly on Babylon (Cairo), " because the Turks could be destroyed better by way of Babylon than any other land." As a matter of fact, Cairo, was the centre of the Mohammedan power, a decision which will explain the Crusade of Saint Louis. And given the end that the French knights had in view, this plan was well conceived ; but they afterwards allowed themselves to be circumvented by the cunning Venetians, who were interested in the re-establishment on the Byzantine throne of Isaac the Angel, driven from it by his subjects. And the French knights could at the same time gratify an old feeling of resentment against the Byzantines, for it was

PHILIP AUGUSTUS

a widespread opinion in France that the Greeks of Constantinople had caused the check of the previous expeditions by their perfidious policy.

The feudal army arrived at San Stefano on the 23rd June 1203.

"And when they got a full view of Constantinople," says Villehardouin, "which they had never before seen, they thought that there could not be so rich a city in the world. When they saw those high walls and the rich towers which enclosed her, and those rich palaces and lofty churches of which there were so many that they could not believe their eyes; and they saw the length and breadth of the city, which was queen of all others; you must know that there was none so bold but that he trembled; and it was no wonder that they were moved, for never had so great a feat been attempted by any people since the history of the world began."

The usurper, Alexius III, fled. Hardly were the Crusaders masters of the town than the multitude of soldiers demanded a march on Jerusalem. But the leaders already discovered a new field for their activities. Isaac the Angel and his son Alexius IV not having kept their promises, the agreement between them and the Crusaders was considered to be broken. Quarrels between Greeks and Latins led to fights. Part of Constantinople was given to the flames. After having left the town the French returned to it as victors (11th April 1204). Some rebels had seized Isaac and his son and killed them. Baldwin IX, Count of Flanders, was proclaimed Emperor. Dressed in the imperial robes, *i.e.* in the chlamys lacquered with gold eagles, silk hose, and purple sandals enriched with precious stones, he was crowned at St. Sofia (9th May 1204). The Byzantine Empire was divided among the French knights. Boniface of Montferrat was nominated King of Thessalonica and Macedonia.

The institutions of French feudalism were seen planted and taking root on the shores of the Bosphorus as they had done two centuries earlier on the parched plains of Syria. Within the limits of the old Empire of the " Basileus " there is formed a new France (*nova Francia*); the expression is due to Honorius II (letter to the Queen of France, 20th May 1224). At the

THE MIDDLE AGES

French Court of Constantinople the pleasant songs of the trouvère, Quene de Béthune, and the melodious verses of the troubadour, Rambaud de Vaqueras, are heard:

> A song easy to understand
> Will I make, for it is my trade,
> So that each may learn it
> And sing it at his will. . . .
>
> (*Quene de Béthune.*)

Villehardouin received the fief of Mosynopolis. About 1210 he dictated his History of the Conquest of Constantinople for the information of those belonging to him, a picturesque precursor of the good lord of Joinville, like him a native of Champagne. The French conquest extended over Morea, Achaia, and Greece. One finds Dukes of Athens and of the Archipelago. These good knights from France drew up codes, founded towns, struck coins with their effigy or arms, and with a liberalism astonishing for that period maintained a reciprocal tolerance among the enemy cults.

The Latin Empire of Constantinople disappeared in 1261, but the feudal lords had taken root in the country. The excellent Catalan chronicler, Ramon Muntaner, will write still about the end of the thirteenth century: "The princes of Morea choose their wives from the best French houses. Their vassals, barons, and knights do the same, only marrying wives descended from French knights. It was said, too, that the noblest knighthood in the world was the French chivalry of Morea. As good French was spoken there as in Paris."

Philip Augustus had remained a stranger to these brilliant events; but in France itself he worked successfully for the greatness of his country. So great already was his power that his activity extended to Germany, where he intervened in the struggle between the Guelfs (the House of Saxony) and the Ghibellines (the House of Hohenstaufen).

By his cruelties and exactions John Lackland had stirred up the English clergy. Innocent III placed him under the ban of Europe (January 1213). Philip Augustus was charged by the Pope with the task of driving John from a throne which he was no longer deemed worthy to fill and of placing on it his own son, the future Louis VIII. Philip Augustus prepared for a descent on England, but John was reconciled with the papal throne, acknowledging himself as its vassal. At the moment of embarking, Philip Augustus was stopped by the legate of Innocent III. He submitted, as he said, willingly, but in his own mind he only postponed his plans.

His attention was for the moment required for one of the most important events in our history, the Albigensian War.

For many years the south of France had been inclined towards religious ideas alien from Roman orthodoxy. It is a question of the doctrine of the Albigenses and that of the Vaudois. The Albigensian doctrine was also known as the heresy of the Cathari, from the Greek καθαροι, the pure.

The Albigensian War.

The Visigoths who had settled in the south of France were Arians, and did not admit the divinity of Christ. Their kingdom was invaded by Catholic dukes, counts, and bishops. But the time of humble and poor missionaries was already past, the time when the leaders of souls influenced the people because they were themselves of "the people." Moreover, the Arian ideas continued to spread at the centre of the mass of the people, and to take there a form more and more concrete, in the direction of the pagan beliefs in good and bad spirits. They were applied to the Gospels, whence came the conception of a principle of Good, namely, God, and of a principle of Evil, Satan, the organizers of the World. It was the old Manichæan dualism.

Such seems to have been the foundation of the heresy of the Cathari. As to precise details, it is difficult to find them, contemporaries having made every effort to remove all trace of them. We can, nevertheless, conclude from certain formulas of solemn renunciation that the Cathari recognized a class of elect among men, *the Perfect*, whom God had distinguished from the mass of believers. In this respect they seem to have been precursors of the Jansenists. The Cathari, like the Vaudois, preached scorn of ecclesiastical dignities and protested against the tithes demanded by Churchmen from the labourer. With progress in material affairs and the departure of the Catholic leaders for the Crusades, the sects spread.

THE MIDDLE AGES

From the land of the Albigenses they prevailed in Languedoc from Toulouse to Beaucaire.

As to the doctrine of the Vaudois it had its origin in Lyons, where it had been taught during the last quarter of the twelfth century by a rich merchant, Pierre Valdo, a sort of saint and apostle. After having distributed his goods to the poor, Valdo had set to work to preach in the streets, in the public squares, and at the cross-roads. His disciples, of whom there were soon a great number, were known as the " Poor Men of Lyons." They spread as far as Montpelier in the South and Strasburg in the North. Their doctrine was a reversion to the primitive teaching of the Church. They did not admit the real presence of Christ in the host, or the cult of the saints, or purgatory, or the powers attached to ecclesiastical ordination. Valdo and his disciples—the Vaudois—taught, in short, at the end of the twelfth century the principles which were afterwards to be the basis of the Protestant religion. Let us add that in the eyes of the clerics the Vaudois appeared less " perverse " than the Cathari or Albigenses proper. We are not speaking of the Crusading knights, who will make no distinction in the South between the Vaudois and the Cathari, or indeed between Vaudois, Cathari, and Catholics.

In the year 1145 St. Bernard had undertaken to fight against heresy. In 1163 the Council of Tours denounced the dangers which the Faith suffered from the Albigensian doctrine which was gnawing " like a cancer " into a part of France. It was putting division among citizens, bringing discord into the bosom of families. In 1178 the progress of the new religion was so great that Louis VII and Henry II had projected a crusade against it, but this expedition reduced itself to a missionary progress. It had but mediocre results. The Count of Foix, the Viscount of Béarn, the Viscount of Béziers, the Count of Comminges declared in favour of the heretics. Finally, Raymond VI, who in 1196 had succeeded his father Raymond V, Count of Toulouse, declared himself an Albigensian. The greater part of the South was won to heresy.

Before taking severe measures Pope Innocent III wished to have recourse to the arms furnished by the arsenal of reason. The Bishop of Osma, accompanied by the admirable monk who was one day to become Saint Dominic, went into the contaminated lands. They frankly recognized that the disorders among the clergy, the luxury, the dissipated lives of numerous prelates, abbots, and vicars were at the root of the evil. They came to the conclusion that it would indeed be useful to bring the Church back to her original purity as the Vaudois desired, but without injury to the integrity of the Faith. They set the example, going barefooted along the roads begging the necessities of life, and conversing with the heretics, whom they strove to lead back to the right path by the gentle force of argument. Unfortunately, other highly placed Churchmen took a different tone. They demanded the extermination of the heretics; mortified limbs which must be cut off from the body by steel and fire, lest the whole body . . . but we know the frightful sophism.

Among these prelates, Folquet de Marseilles expressed himself the more vehemently because he thought he ought to make good haste along the road to Paradise, having previously trodden quite other paths. In February 1206 he was promoted to the Episcopal See of Toulouse.

At his instigation the Papal Legate, Pierre de Castelnau, excommunicates Raymond VI, Count of Toulouse (1207). By way of response, one of the Count's squires assassinates Pierre de Castelnau in an inn (12th January 1208).

"When the Pope heard that his legate had been killed," we read in the *Chanson de la Croisade des Albigeois*, "the news wrung his heart. He buried his face in his hands and called on St. James of Compostella and St. Peter of Rome. And his prayer finished, he extinguished the candle which was burning. There were present the Abbot of Citeaux and Master Milo who speaks Latin, and twelve cardinals, whose seats formed a circle in which was taken the resolution through which so many men have perished violently and so many ladies have lost clothes and covering."

In June 1209 an army of Crusaders met at Lyons. "I will not trouble to recount how they were armed," says the author of the *Chanson de la Croisade*, "or what was the price of the crosses, made of strips of material woven of silk and gold, which they wore on their breasts."

This alludes to the way in which the money necessary for the expedition had been got together. Rich merchants, bankers, usurers, Cahorsins, had advanced funds as though it were a commercial enterprise. Afterwards they were to receive as compensation stuffs, wine, corn, even estates and castles taken from the Albigenses. They considered it a very good investment.

On the 21st the Crusading army arrived before Béziers. The Viscount Raymond Roger protests in vain his constancy in the Faith. The town is taken and sacked, given to the flames and bloodshed. In the Church of the Madeleine alone, where some women, old people, and children had taken refuge, seven thousand poor wretches were slaughtered. The town was destroyed. After this the war takes its course, mingled with savage executions. The defenders of the fortresses are hung on the seigniorial gibbet. Knights captured in combat are strangled and hung " to the flowering olives "; or again they are dragged, gasping, through the streets tied to their horses' tails. The burgesses of the towns are burnt alive, in crowds, in the middle of fields, where their calcined bones are piled in smouldering heaps. Poor old women, flung to the bottom of pits, are crushed there by great stones. " The grass of the fields was red as the rose, for no prisoners were taken " (*Chanson de la Croisade*). And amidst the immense enthusiasm, miracles flourished along the bloody path of the Crusaders like lilies in a pure heart. In the fiercest fights, amidst the tumult of attack, clerks sang the *Sancte Spiritus* and the *Veni Creator*, under the banners of the army on the march, " in procession and in voices so loud that the sound could be heard half a league away " (*Chanson de la Croisade*).

A squire from the Northern provinces, Simon de Montfort l'Amaury, had lost no time in distinguishing himself by the ardour of his faith, as well as by his courage, his energy, and his military talents. The faith of Simon de Montfort filled Saint Louis with admiration, and the good King used to take pleasure in relating the following anecdote about him. " Some Albigenses came up to the Comte de Montfort saying they had come to see the host which, they had been told, had been changed into flesh and blood in the hands of a priest at the altar ; but he said to them : ' Go and see it, you who do not believe; I am not anxious to do so, since I firmly believe it.' "

Robust in his faith, Simon was severe in every way, though at the same time an adroit politician ready to follow good counsels. He was elected by the Crusaders Viscount of Béziers and Carcassonne, the lordships of which Raymond Roger was deprived. The Crusade had found its leader. Simon de Montfort pursued the campaign with an overpowering swiftness. Places fall one after another into his hands, and each encounter with the Southern troops, badly organized and led, undecided whether to submit or fight, is marked by a victory. In 1212 Raymond VI no longer commanded anything except Toulouse and Montauban. The conquest, moreover, was still characterized by the most atrocious cruelties. The official historian of the Crusade, the monk Pierre de Vaux-Cernay, gives us its note. " With great joyfulness our pilgrims burned a great number of heretics."

These Frenchmen of the North seemed, to the more refined population of the South, men of repulsive rudeness and brutality. Above all, they inspired repugnance by their drunkenness. Thus amidst the clashing of steel and under a tide of blood was swamped the " gay science," the magnificent language of the troubadours, the courtly poetry which flourished in the noble Courts of Comminges and Languedoc.

Peter II, King of Aragon, resolved to march to the aid of his neighbour, the Count of Toulouse, to whom he had married one of his sisters, and another sister to his son. Relations of every kind were at that time frequent between the south of France and the north of Spain. The two slopes of the Pyrenees were bound by ties of active sympathy.

At the moment of buckling on his hauberk Peter II wrote to a noble lady of Toulouse that he was setting out to the war for the love of her, a stroke of gallant chivalry worthy of a brave and courteous prince and a friend of the troubadours. The letter was to fall into the hands of Simon de Montfort. He took a harsher view of it : " How could I respect a King who, for the sake of a woman, marches against God ? " This anecdote gives us a picture of both adversaries.

The King of Aragon, accompanied by the Counts of

THE MIDDLE AGES

Toulouse and Foix, arrived before the walls of Muret where Simon de Montfort was shut up. The allied princes had considerable forces at their disposal: 2000 horsemen and 40,000 footmen, the latter furnished by the communal militias, and including sergeants-at-arms, youths, and servants.

Simon de Montfort had with him only a thousand knights and two or three thousand footmen, but he did not hesitate to issue from the town and offer battle to an army ten times bigger than his own. His fanaticism carried him away. He knelt before the Bishop of Uzès, saying, "My God, I give you my soul and my body." In the first rank of the Crusaders marched the Bishop of Toulouse in all the splendour of the pontifical vestments, holding above his head a piece of the true cross. The battle began on the 12th September (1213). The Northerners made a furious attack.

Simon de Montfort had grouped his knights in a mass which fell solidly on the enemy. The latter were divided into two bodies, one under the orders of the King of Aragon, the other under the Count of Toulouse. According to the custom of chivalry, the fighting took place in independent groups, by households, each feudal lord being surrounded by his vassals. After having crushed one of the two bodies of knights opposed to him, Simon de Montfort overwhelmed the other through the swiftness and density of his attack.

Two knights, Alain de Roucy and Florent de Ville, who had sworn to kill the King of Aragon, managed to get up to him and cut his throat. To the Southerners this was the signal for a stampede. The Counts of Toulouse, Foix, and Comminges were the first to flee. A Catalonian knight came to announce the defeat to the thousands of the men of Toulouse assembled in the fields of the Garonne, who had not yet taken part in the action. Terror-stricken, they sought refuge in the boats moored in the middle of the river which had been used to bring ammunition and provisions from Toulouse. They jostled each other, overcrowded the boats, and were drowned by the hundred in the flowing stream. A frightful carnage was made of the survivors. The number of victims among the men of Aragon and Toulouse ran into thousands: twenty thousand according to Pierre de Vaux-Cernay. The Crusaders lost hardly a hundred men. The corpse of the King of Aragon was despoiled by plunderers of its rich armour and clothing. His white body, covered with blood, was found lying quite naked on the green grass.

It was a decisive victory. Simon de Montfort was master of Languedoc.

These wars between Christians and vassals of the same king did not fail to give rise to protests. Guillaume le Clerc writes:

> When Frenchmen go against men of Toulouse
> Whom they hold as heretics,
> And the Roman legate there
> Conducts and leads them,
> It is not well. . . .

The Holy Places have fallen once more under the rule of the Crescent. Is this the moment for Christians to be killing one another?

And what a singular rôle is that of the Churchmen, who march with soldiers and excite them to carnage!

> But the clerk should go to his scripture
> And to his psalms, to sing,
> And let the knight go
> To his great battles in the field:
> While he is in front of the altar.

It must be confessed that, once master of Languedoc, Simon de Montfort proved himself a clever organizer. At Pamiers in 1212 four ecclesiastics and four French barons, together with two knights and two burgesses of the South, were chosen to draw up statutes destined for the new conquest. These were the famous Statutes of Pamiers, in which Languedoc found a constitution better adapted to the transformations effected in the past century. A check was put on the excesses of the unruly squires, and the inhabitants of the district hailed the changes which were made, almost with gratitude. But the troubadours regretted the times of the Courts of Love, where their noble poetry brought forth, in quiet nests of loveliness, shining eggs of gold.

"This is what I saw before my exile," writes Aimeric de Péguilhan. "Before my exile (in Italy) if, for love, a ribbon was bestowed on us, immediately joyous meetings and invītations arose. It seems to me that a month now is twice as long as a year in the days of chivalry. What sorrow to see the difference between the society of to-day and that of yesterday."

Under these wars of religion deeper causes are to be found. A society different in its manners from that of the North had been formed south of the Loire. The Crusaders behaved like brutes, destroying everything. "They made," we read in the Chronicle of the Churches of Anjou, "a frightful carnage of heretics and Catholics, between whom they did not stop to discriminate." It would be impossible to condemn their excesses too indignantly; but in the violence of the conflicts they bound Northern France to the France of the South by ties which were destined never more to be broken. With their rude and bloody hands they made a clear space for the influence of the Ile-de-France which, at the heels of the monarchy, was to conquer politically, intellectually, and artistically the whole country.

In fact, from the beginning Philip Augustus treated Simon de Montfort as a royal officer. He regards him as a judge. Simon de Montfort administers justice in his name. The Council of Lateran, meeting in November 1215, had left Toulouse to Count Raymond on the insistence of the Sovereign Pontiff. Simon, who wanted the whole domain, came to lay siege to the town. The defence of the place was heroic and gay. "Everybody," we read in the *Chanson de la Croisade*, "set to work with a will: the common people, young knights and maidens, ladies, married women, boys, girls, and little children. Singing ballads and gay songs, they worked at fences, ditches, and earthworks. . . ." At last, the aim of a stone-thrower manœuvred by some women of Toulouse struck Simon de Montfort on the brow and scattered his brains within his burnished helmet. "There was in the town a machine for casting stones, made by a carpenter," says the author of the *Chanson*; "the stone was thrown from the top of St. Sernin by the ladies and girls who were working the engine. And the stone went straight to its mark, and struck the Count of Montfort on his brass helmet, so accurately that it smashed his eyes, brain, teeth, forehead, and jaw. See the Count stretched on the ground dead, bloody, and black." Two knights ran and covered the body with a blue scarf, to hide the

PHILIP AUGUSTUS

fact of his death. But the news spread, sowing terror. The besiegers burned their constructions, their wooden fortresses, and decamped towards Carcassonne. "Straight to Carcassonne they carry him for burial, and to celebrate his obsequies at the monastery of St. Nazaire. And we read in his epitaph that the Lord of Montfort is a saint and martyr, and that he will rise again and rejoice in the beatitude of God. If by killing men and spilling blood, by damning souls, by consenting to murders, by giving ear to perverse counsels, by kindling great fires, by destroying barons to take their lands by violence, by slaughtering women and massacring children, one can in this world win Jesus Christ—the Lord of Montfort should indeed be crowned and resplendent in heaven, And may the Virgin's Son, Who makes right shine forth, Who gave His Flesh and Blood, watch over right and justice and show forth the right between the two sides." It is difficult not to subscribe to these lines, attributed to the troubadour Peire Cardinal.

Thus Count Raymond VII of Toulouse got the upper hand again, and the son of Simon de Montfort will be seen leaving his domains to the King of France.

Could not then the unity of a great country be achieved without such cruel crises?

Hardly was the Albigensian War over when the spectacle of the clashing of arms was to be seen at the other extremity of France.

Bouvines. The King of France had given the throne of Flanders to Ferrand of Portugal, making him marry Jeanne, the eldest daughter of Count Baldwin, who had become Emperor of Constantinople. At first Ferrand showed a certain amount of gratitude, but soon, led on, it is true, by his subjects who were bound by their commercial interests to England, he had consented to become the liege man of John Lackland, on consideration of a money payment. We have mentioned the material prosperity of the great Flemish towns; their cloth merchants and weavers had need of English wool. Even before the marriage of Ferrand of Portugal to the daughter of Count Baldwin they had allied themselves with John Lackland against Philip Augustus.

Renaud de Dammartin was not as great a prince as the

THE MIDDLE AGES

Count of Flanders, but he was bold and enterprising, and he had had his domains augmented through the protection of Philip Augustus. He married Countess Ida of Boulogne, and to the important lordship which his wife brought him Philip Augustus added three Norman Counties: Aumale, Mortain, and Varennes. Renaud de Dammartin had thus become an important feudatory. Discontented at not receiving from Philip Augustus the support which he had asked for in a struggle against Philippe de Dreux, the warlike Bishop of Beauvais, Dammartin entered, in the presence of the Count of Flanders, the service of the King of England. This latter succeeded also in taking into his pay the Count of Holland; and the German Emperor, Otto VI of Brunswick, was drawn into the Coalition. John Lackland thought the moment had come for him to attempt to recover the French provinces of which Philip Augustus had deprived him. The beginnings of hostilities were marked by a great success for the members of the Coalition. Philip Augustus was besieging Ghent. A little French garrison was established at Damme, the port of Bruges, where was stationed the fleet of four hundred ships which Philip Augustus had equipped for a descent on England. The English came up and burned nearly all the vessels which the garrison of Damme found it impossible to defend. The German Emperor began a campaign while Ferrand plundered Artois. Renaud de Dammartin laid siege to Calais. The Coalition had conceived a plan on a grand scale. While the Flemish, Germans, and Dutch were to invade Northern France through Artois, and advance on Paris, John Lackland was to land in Poitou and with all his forces, augmented by the contingents which he could levy in these districts, as well as in Aquitaine and Anjou, was to march on Paris and attack it from the South. The Capetian power would be crushed in a gigantic vice. To the lords of Aquitaine, energetic, restless, and warlike nobles without nobility, needy Gascon younger sons, John Lackland sent money But Philip Augustus also exerted himself to keep faithful allies in these lands, notably the famous Guillaume des Roches, a rich landed proprietor and a brave captain, and his son-in-law, Amauri de Craon.

John Lackland landed on the 12th February at La Rochelle.

PHILIP AUGUSTUS

He made incursions into Saintonge, Poitou, Angoumois, and Limousin. Philip Augustus sends his son against the invaders, threatening him from the South, while he himself is to march against the Imperial troops, the Flemish and Dutch, who threaten the North. The brilliant victory of Prince Louis over John Lackland at La Roche au Moine in Anjou (2nd July 1214) is of happy omen. Leaving tents and baggage, stone-throwers and trebuchets, John Lackland flees for all he is worth. On the 15th July he is at La Rochelle. Philip Augustus heard the news at Peronne, whence he was watching the troops of the Coalition grouped on the frontier of Hainault.

The plateau of Bouvines dominated, at a height of about ten yards, the marshy plains stretching between Lille and Tournai, one of the few spots in the district in which one did not slip about in mud and which was fully exposed. Otto's army was entrenched at Valenciennes, 80,000 men, of whom 1500 were knights. Philip Augustus, following up his plan of cutting the Imperial troops off from their communications with Flanders and England, left Peronne on the 23rd July. On the 26th he was at Tournai. Otto and his troops turned round and went to install themselves in a strong position, defended by marshes on the Roman road which leads from Bavai to Tournai. The enemy armies were separated by fifteen kilometres. The Imperial troops were already counting on victory. The King of France was to be killed and his kingdom divided among the conquerors. In this fine allotment of spoil, Paris was to fall to the Count of Flanders.

However, on Sunday, the 27th July, in the morning, Philip made an attempt to bend back on Lille. The Coalition troops attempted to follow him without any fixed order of marching. Their one fear was that the King of France should escape them. Philip Augustus continued his march as far as Bouvines, situated on the highest part of the plateau, where he arrived about midday. His troops had begun to cross over to the left bank of the Marcq by a bridge which the French King had had made wider—the bridge of Bouvines, which was at that time thrown ninety-eight metres up the river from the present bridge. The King had removed his armour and was resting in the shade of an ash tree watching the operation of the crossing of the river, which was just finishing. "He was steeping a slice of bread in a cup of pure gold and the weather was very hot," writes Philippe Mousket, when there ran up the famous Hospitaller, Brother Guérin, the chief adviser of Philip Augustus, the grey Eminency of the reign. Brother Guérin had just been elected Bishop of Senlis. He announced the enemy's attack. The King springs to the saddle. He gives the order to the contingents of his communes to cross the river again. To gain time for the operation to be completed the French rearguard, commanded by the Viscount of Melun, resisted with obstinate courage the attack of the Imperial troops. Otto, who expected to find an enemy army in retreat and divided by the stream which one part would have crossed, was surprised at running up against a complete army drawn up in order of battle.

The French King was stationed in the centre of his troops. Beside him, Galon de Montigny carried the royal standard sown with golden lilies on an azure field. It was a radiant July day and the Imperial troops would have the sun in their eyes. Opposite Philip Augustus was the Emperor Otto, resplendent in golden armour and flanked by the Imperial standard, a dragon surmounted by a golden eagle. William le Breton gives us a description of it. "A stake stood up from a chariot and round this was curled a dragon. He could be seen from afar. He held up his tail and swelled out his wings. He seemed to suck in the wind, showing his horrible teeth in his enormous jaws. Above him soared an eagle. These animals were of gleaming gold and shone like the sun." Speaking of the German eagle, the Chronicler of St. Denis shows him with " face turned towards the French with gaping jaws as though he would swallow all."

Brother Guérin commanded the right wing of the royal army. Over his coat of arms of grey mail was thrown the tunic of the Hospitallers, red with a black cross. He faced the left wing of the Coalition army commanded by the Count of Flanders. The left wing of the French was under the orders of the famous fighting prelate, Philippe de Dreux, Bishop of Beauvais. It would have to measure itself against the right wing of the Allies under Renaud de Dammartin.

PHILIP AUGUSTUS

The enemy hosts confronted each other along two parallel lines.

Brother Guérin fulfilled the functions of General-in-Chief of the French army. He had arranged the troops, no longer leaving the different households grouped round their respective barons, but mixing them together according to strategical requirements.

The combatants realized the gravity of the moment. The tumult and clatter of arms which mark the beginnings of battle were not heard in their ranks; an impressive silence reigned. Philip Augustus addressed his men:

" Our hope and trust is in God. King Otto and his army have been excommunicated. They are the enemies of religion. The money which supports them has been extorted from the tears of the wretched." And stretching out his hands—like the Kings of the *chansons de geste*—Philip Augustus blesses his subjects.

The trumpets sounded, the clerics chanted the psalms, and the battle began.

Contrary to the statement generally made, the soldiers of the communes—the militias of Beauvais, Valois, Senlis, Vermandois, and Picardy—played only a secondary part. The legend of the communal militias of 1214 is on a par with that of the volunteers of 1792-93. The victory of Bouvines was decided by the impetuous courage of the French knights. They are seen at several points, in massive squadrons, travelling like an immense projectile from one part to another of the enemy ranks. In the midst of the fray Philip Augustus, who fought as a knight, became entangled among the German infantry. A ruffian seized him under the throat at the opening of the cuirass, with one of those javelins of which the point is furnished with a double hook. He pulled it with his two hands like a woodcutter does a rope tied to the fork of an oak tree. The King fell from his horse and disappeared under a heap of German ruffians: a lump of sugar under a swarm of ants. Guillaume des Barres, " the flower of knighthood," and Pierre Tristan released the King with great sword-strokes and he got back to saddle. A handful of knights, however, reached the Emperor, and Gerard La Truie put out an eye of his horse under its brass frontal. Mad with pain, the animal gallops off with Otto. Des Barre pursues him and comes up with him at the moment that the animal falls exhausted. He seizes the Emperor by the throat and with so tight a hold that he might have choked him had not some German knights forced him to loose his hold. But Otto, seized with terror, ran away shrieking. "We shall see his face no more," said Philip Augustus. The Emperor with the Golden Eagle ran all the way to Valenciennes.

On the left wing of the French the action still remained indecisive when at the centre and on the right wing victory was assured. In this left wing the Bishop of Beauvais, with prodigious strength, struck without respite, with his heavy iron weapon crushing the knights under their iron carapaces. As he was invested with the episcopal dignity, the Pope had forbidden him to spill blood by using an edged weapon. The folk whom he bore down were none the less duly killed. Salisbury, the English leader, underwent the experience. Renaud de Dammartin, traitor to his King, fought desperately. He was taken towards evening, having rolled under his horse. Count Ferrand gave himself up to the brothers of Mareuil. The number of dead was not so large as might have been expected. "Each of the knights," says William le Breton, "covered his limbs with several plates of iron; he covered his breast under tunics of leather, stuffed doublets, and various plastrons. The moderns are more careful about protecting themselves than the ancients were. As dangers become more threatening precautions are multiplied and new methods of defence are invented against new methods of attack." Nevertheless, they had not yet arrived at tanks and aircraft, 420's and torpedoes. The number of prisoners too was considerable. There was not enough rope to bind them. "The people to be bound were more numerous than their conquerors," says Le Breton.

The enthusiasm with which the battle of Bouvines filled the whole of France was, perhaps, more remarkable than the victory itself. It is an explosion of joy in which vibrates with a sublime emotion the ideal of one's country. The poets of the time, celebrating gentle France in song, expressed the sentiments of all.

PHILIP AUGUSTUS

"Who could describe in writing," says William le Breton, "the hymns of victory, the innumerable dances, the songs of the clerics, the chimes of the bells under the golden cocks, the adornment of the sanctuaries, the white hangings of the houses draped in cendal and silk, the strewing of roads and streets in which brightly coloured flowers and green branches were spread."

It was harvest-time. Reapers and binders, sheavers and spreaders, abandoning their work, crossed the fields in great haste, rakes and scythes over their shoulders, and went in great haste to range themselves along the route. Wiping with their forearms the sweat from their dusty brows, they gazed upon "Ferrand enferré" (Ferrand "pierced") in his chains.

Peasants, old men, women, and children made a mockery of his name, which could also be that of a horse. And it happened that the two draught horses which drew him a prisoner in his litter were exactly the sort the colour of whose coats led to the giving of this name.

"What shall we say of the welcome given to the conquerors by the Parisians?" it is an Englishman speaking. "The houses were hung with brightly coloured cendal (a thick silk), the streets shone with a thousand torches and lanterns; they resounded with plaudits and song. During the whole day and the night which followed, the echoes took up the notes of the trumpets and the hymns of joy." The students drank and sang for a week.

The vanquished met a terrible fate: Renaud de Dammartin, cast into the depths of a dungeon, was chained to a tree trunk which two men could not have lifted. The Count of Flanders was imprisoned in the tower of the Louvre, where he was to remain for thirteen years. The Emperor Otto, dethroned in favour of his rival Frederick II of Hohenstaufen, fled to Cologne with his wife, disguised as a pilgrim. He died in obscurity at Brunswick (19th May 1218).

With the news of the victory of Bouvines the few Aquitainian barons who supported John Lackland deserted him also; but the Pope intervened.

On the 18th September 1214 peace was concluded between

the French and English Crowns at Chinon. John Lackland paid £60,000 to his rival, and gave up to him Anjou, Brittany, and the greater part of Poitou. The two victories won by the French armies at La Roche au Moine and Bouvines had another consequence. They emboldened the English feudatories who forced from John Lackland the ratification of the Great Charter, by which limits were set to the royal power. " Why do they not ask for my crown also ? " cried John Lackland.

The year 1214 marks the highest point of the government of Philip Augustus. On every side men claim the King's protection. Towns and villages, abbeys and corporations, wish to be placed directly under his patronage and to be withdrawn from the claims of local authorities.

Philip Augustus was a statesman, a politician, and a soldier. Historians have pointed out that he deserves even more than Louis VI to be called the protector of the communes.

But the most important act of Philip Augustus in the history of the internal administration of France was the creation of the first " bailiffs " (*baillis*). The administration of the provosts, almost exclusively appertaining to the demesne, had become inadequate. It was at the moment of his departure for the Crusade that Philip Augustus instituted the *baillis*, superimposed on the provosts and extending their functions over a larger district. These first *baillis* had ill-defined functions, at the same time judges, administrators, and collectors of taxes. They were, above all, judges, itinerant judges commissioned to verify the judgments of the provosts. Philip Augustus established *baillis* at Orleans, Sens, Senlis, Bourges, Gisors, in Vermandois, then in the Northern towns, Amiens, Aire, Arras, and St. Omer, as well as in Normandy, in the district of Caux and in the Cotentin. But in the beginning at least the authority of each of these *baillis* was not limited to the territory whose principal town they occupied. The Seneschals of the South corresponded, as we know, to the *baillis* of the North, but with a very different character, at least in the beginning. They are great and powerful lords like Guillaume des Roches or Aimeri de Thouars, to whom the King has recourse in their respective provinces to entrust to them a superior administrative authority similar to that which the Seneschal of the

PHILIP AUGUSTUS

Crown has from his functions at the Court of France : whence, moreover, their name is derived.

Philip Augustus had a very active financial policy which doubled, and more than doubled, the revenues of the Crown, not only by developing with more care the demesnes of the King and in extracting from the feudal dues all they could be made to yield, but in creating new sources of revenue.

While Louis VII had protected the Jews, Philip Augustus exploited them. He threatens to expel them and obliges them to ransom themselves. He lays on them a fixed tax, which yields £1200 in 1202 and £7550 in 1217.

He substitutes payment in kind for labour dues and makes the towns pay money in lieu of service with the army. His financial adviser was a Templar, Brother Aimard, who appears to have been, together with Brother Guérin the Hospitaller, the guide whom he most regarded. Louis VII had already kept in pay horse troops, which had formed a sort of contingent. Philip Augustus gave to this institution a fixed character which it had not known before.

Moreover, he is seen habitually in military expeditions surrounded not by feudal vassals but by a troop of horse soldiers, the King's knights, followed by sergeants and bowmen : mercenary troops—in whose ranks are already roughly outlined the silhouette of a regular army.

After Bouvines, Philip Augustus never knew an enemy who dared to measure himself against him. He remained in his castles in the Ile-de-France, whence he directed the government. His son Louis was commissioned to pursue in the provinces, and very soon in England, his ever-active policy.

Profiting by the disputes of John Lackland with his vassals, the King of France dreams of winning for his son Louis the crown of the English King. Had not Louis married Blanche of Castile, the niece of King John ? Innocent III had just quashed the Great Charter at the request of the English King. The barons across the Channel entered into relations with the King of France. The latter put forward that John Lackland had been condemned by the peers for the murder of Arthur, which was not, in fact, true. Consequently the son of John

THE MIDDLE AGES

Lackland could not inherit from a father deprived of his possessions.

But the Sovereign Pontiff protected John, who had declared his intention of taking the Cross for the deliverance of the Holy Land. He was, above all, unwilling that the power of the King of France should increase without a counter-balance.

Philip Augustus pretended to disapprove of his son Louis, while at the same time he provided him with soldiers and subsidies.

Innocent III excommunicated Louis, who embarked for Great Britain. Here everything succeeded with the son of Philip Augustus. And the French prince might well already have believed himself master of the Crown of the Plantagenets when John Lackland died on the 19th October 1216.

The Papal Legate immediately had the young Henry III, aged nine years, crowned at Westminster. The aspect of affairs was about to change. If the English barons preferred Prince Louis to King John, perfidious, cunning, sensual, and greedy, they liked better the government of a nine-year-old child than the authority of an active and energetic knight. The arms of Louis of France suffered a grave check beneath the walls of Lincoln Castle. The English were commanded by William the Marshall and by a brigand, Fauquet de Breauté. Then the French fleet was destroyed within sight of Calais. It was commanded by a famous pirate, Eustache Le Moine (24th August 1217). The historian of William the Marshall has given us the description of the naval action. The vessels attacked by boarding each other. The English conquerors plundered the French vessels, " but one man, armed with a hook, intending to draw towards him on a bridge a fine scarlet coverlet, found that it was only a patch of blood." On the 11th September following, Louis signed a treaty by which he renounced his claim to the English Crown for an indemnity of 10,000 marks.

The last years of the reign were occupied with important works. Philip Augustus had been a great builder. Paris owes a great deal to him. It is estimated that the town counted 120,000 inhabitants in his reign. The streets were muddy, black, and beaten tracks in which splashed liquid mud. Philip Augustus had them paved.

In the field cemetery, on the site of the present market, there was held among the tombs a market of edibles, in which the smell of herrings, cabbages, and cheese mingled with that of the corpses which pigs came to root up, while fine ladies took the air at the proper hours in aggressive elegance. Philip Augustus, deeming that the cemetery no longer presented an aspect suitable " to a place where a great number of saints were buried " (William le Breton), had it surrounded (1186) by a wall of square stones outside which the market, the pigs, and the fine ladies could establish themselves. He built the great tower of the Louvre and deposited his treasure there. Finally, it was he who surrounded the northern part of the town from Seine to Seine with a continuous wall (1190) broken at the ends of the streets by " bastilles," *i.e.* fortified gates, an enclosure of which fragments still remain.

In the midst of an activity rude, industrious, sometimes unscrupulous, but always useful, death came to surprise the admirable King. He was fifty-seven years old. He was consumed by a fever which dragged on for a year, and he died at Mantes on the 14th July 1223.

Louis VIII gave his confidence to his father's officers and pursued his work in the same spirit. Brother Guérin took the title of Chancellor. The new King was a little thin man, nervous, decided, with an aquiline nose and bright eyes. From the first day he adopted a very resolute attitude towards the English, who claimed the conquests made from John Lackland. He marched with a considerable army into Aquitaine, where some barrels of Parisian pounds helped to secure victory. Louis VIII conquered Poitou, Limousin, and Perigord, but Bordeaux remained to the English. After this the King turned against Languedoc and Provence. There was still the question of the Albigenses. At the head of considerable forces, Louis laid siege to Avignon. The town resisted with admirable energy. It was necessary to dig an immense ditch, a regular moat, and to take famine as an auxiliary. After Avignon the chief towns of the South, Nîmes, Narbonne, Carcassonne, Beaucaire, Castres, and Montpelier, opened their gates to the King, and the castles followed their example.

It remained to make a study of the organization given to the country by Simon de Montfort. The statutes of Pamiers were rendered more exact and complete. The country remained divided into seneschals' jurisdictions, and subdivided into provostships, but the franchises of several towns were reduced. Amauri, the son of Simon de Montfort, through lack of money had yielded his rights over the conquered districts to the French King. Louis VIII decided that all the goods, the castles, and lands confiscated on account of heresy should fall to the Crown. Unhappily, he added to these decrees a decision which condemned heretics to the stake.

Louis VIII was returning towards the Seine when he succumbed at Montpensier, on the 8th November 1226, to the illness supervening on dysentery contracted at the siege of Avignon.

SOURCES.—Leop. Delisle, *Catalogue des actes de Philippe Auguste*, 1886 ; works of Rigord and of William le Breton, ed. H. F. Delaborde, 1883–85, 2 vols. ; *Gisliberli Chron. Hanoniense*, ed. W. Arndt, *SS. rer. germ. in usum Scholarum*, 1869 ; *Chronique de Hainaut par Gilbert*, translated (into French) by Godefroy-Menilglaise, Tournai, 1874, 2 vols. ; *Histoire de Guillaume de Maréchal*, ed. P. Meyer, 1891–1901, 3 vols. ; Geoff. de Villehardouin, *Conquête de Constantinople*, ed. Nat. de Wailly, 3rd ed., 1882 ; *Chanson de la Croisade contre les Albigeois*, ed. P. Meyer, 1875, 2 vols. ; P. de Vaux-Cernay, ap. *Histoire de la France* (D. Bouquet), xix. 1–113.

HISTORICAL WORKS.—A. Cartellieri, *Philippe Auguste*, 1899–1910, 3 vols. ; by the same author, *Abt Suger von S. Denis*, 1898 ; Ach. Luchaire, " Louis VII," " Philippe Auguste," " Louis VIII," in the *Histoire de France*, ed. Lavisse, iii. 1901 ; by the same author, *La Société française au temps de Philippe Auguste*, 1909 ; H. Geraud, " Ingeburge de Danemark," *Bibl. Ec. des Chartes*, 1844, pp. 1–27, 93–118 ; Borelli de Serres, *La Réunion des provinces septentrionales à la Couronne par Philippe Auguste*, 1899 ; H. Malo, *Renaud de Dammartin*, 1898 ; Ch. Bémont, " La Condamnation de Jean sans Terre," *Revue Historique*, xxxii. (1886) 33–72, 290, 311 ; H. Delpech, *La Tactique au XIIIe Siècle*, xxxvi. 95–135 ; Jos. Auglade, *La Bataille de Muret*, 1913 ; J. Longnon, " Bouvines," *Revue Critique des idées et des livres*, 25th June 1914, p. 641 seq. ; Ch. Petit-Dutaillis, *La Vie et le règne de Louis VIII*, 1894.

CHAPTER XIV

A JUSTICIARY IN ERMINE: SAINT LOUIS

BLANCHE OF CASTILE

A CHILD of twelve ascended the throne on the 8th November 1226.

Louis IX was born at Poissy on the 25th April 1214. His mother, the widow of Louis VIII, held the regency during his minority.

Blanche of Castile. White by her title, as the widow of a deceased King was called " the white Queen," white in heart and countenance, writes William le Breton, the Queen with the fair name says Thibaud of Champagne, was the daughter of Alfonzo VIII, King of Castile. She had been brought to France at the age of twelve, and since then had not left the country of her adoption, but had continued to live there surrounded by familiar friends from her native land. She was to keep always her Spanish accent, which did not fail to call forth the raillery of the writers of the time. She had a haughty character, ardent, active, imperious. She was thin, dry, and sharp. She had exercised great sway over her husband, an authority which she was to maintain over her son. Profoundly imbued with the beliefs of her time, she had rigidly brought her child up in them.

Blanche retained the ministers of Louis VIII—that is to say, of Philip Augustus—with Brother Guérin in the first rank. Unfortunately this great man died in 1227. Next to him was Barthélemy Roye, who had been Chamberlain of France for twenty years. Age had already undermined his intellect. The great feudal nobles, so forcibly kept in hand by Philip Augustus, thought the moment had arrived to regain their lost influence. Pierre Mauclerc, the Count of Brittany, Hugh of Lusignan, Count of La Marche, who had married the widow of John Lackland, and Thibaud le Chansonnier (the Singer), Count of Champagne, formed a coalition with the Count of Bar and some others. "After the King was crowned," says Joinville, "there were some barons who demanded of the Queen that she should give them much land; and because she would do no such thing, they called together all the barons at Corbeil. And the sainted King (Louis IX) related to me that neither he nor his mother, who were at Montlhéry, dared to return to Paris until the Parisians came with arms to conduct them. And he told me that the road from Montlhéry was full of people, armed and unarmed, as far as Paris, and that all cried on Our Lord to give to him (the young King) a good and long life, and to defend and keep him from his enemies."

The allied lords did not find themselves in sufficient force to resist the power of the people concentrated round the royal ideal. The Count of Bar was the first to make honourable amends. As to the poet Thibaud, he fell in love with Blanche of Castile.

In the month of January (1227) Ferrand, the Count of Flanders, was set at liberty, with the necessary guarantees. At length, by the Treaty of Paris (April 1229), the able regent put an end to the bloody conflicts of which the Albigensian War had sown the seeds. Raymond VII, the son and successor of Raymond VI, Count of Toulouse, abjured heresy. Blanche, his only daughter, was affianced to Alfonse de Poitiers, the brother of Saint Louis, who thus extended the Capetian suzerainty to Beaucaire, Nîmes, Carcassonne, and Béziers. It was a pacific conquest which was completed at Sens, on the 27th May 1234, by the marriage of Saint Louis himself with Marguerite, the daughter of Raimon Berenger IV, the Count of Provence. Moreover, Thibaud de Champagne yielded to the King, for 40,000 pounds, the suzerainty of the counties of Blois, Chartres, Sancerre, and the Viscounty of Châteaudun.

Nevertheless, the regent must suffer the reproach of listening too readily to priests and Spaniards; of letting the government fall into the hands of clerics ; and of putting mere nobodies at the head of the State. She was mocked for the devotion with which she had so suddenly inspired Count Thibaud, that fat man, pot-bellied and slow, a droll figure for a lover. Lastly, there was the reproach which always arises so easily against queens of foreign origin of sending the nation's money across the frontiers. The verses of Hue de la Ferté have given lively expression to these grievances. The poet addresses the King :

> Sire, why do you not summon
> Your barons to make peace ;
> And bid come forth the peers,
> Who are wont to govern France,
> And with their followers
> They will give you aid ;
> And make the clerks go
> Sing in their churches ?

As for Thibaud de Champagne, is he the man to wear helmet and hauberk ? The barber's towel and basin would suit him better.

The passion of King Thibaud for Blanche of Castile has its place, not only in our political history, but also in the history of our literature. She inspired him with songs of which he composed both words and music, and which are among the most beautiful of all time. " He would often dwell on the remembrance of the sweet look of the Queen and of her beautiful face, declare the monks of St. Denis, and then a sweet and amorous sentiment would fill his heart. But when he remembered that she was so great a lady, and of such good and pure life that he might not take pleasure in her, his sweet and amorous feeling changed to great sadness. And because deep thought begets melancholy he was advised by certain wise men to study the fine notes of the viol and sweet and delectable songs. And so were composed by him and Gasse Bruslé, most beautiful poems, the most delectable and melodious which have ever been heard in song and on the viol. And they were inscribed in the great halls of Provence and Troyes. They are called the songs of the King of Navarre. For the kingdom of Navarre fell to him when his brother died without heir of his body."

THE MIDDLE AGES

Queen Blanche replied to the love poems which Thibaud addressed to her, like an honest woman and in a piquant manner which kept the gallant at arm's length.

Thibaud de Champagne was extremely fat. What will become, he asks the Queen, of the god of love when we are no more, for if you were to die I should not survive you for a moment? The following reply is put into the mouth of Blanche:

> By Jove, Thibaud, as far as I can see,
> Love is not nigh to death;
> I know not if you are mocking me,
> For you are not yet very thin. . . .

Thibaud claims that if he has put on flesh it is because he feeds on hope; to which comes the reply:

> Silence, Thibaud! You should not begin
> A discourse wanting in all sincerity,
> You say it to conciliate me—
> You who have so mocked me. . . .

King Thibaud dreams none the less of embracing her whom he loves:

> I know full well that my lady is loved by a hundred
> And more still . . . it provokes me to anger,
> But I love her more than any living man:
> Would to God I might clasp her lovely body. . . .

To which Raoul de Soissons replies: " I should like to see you embracing your beloved! The width of your stomach is greater than the length of your arms! . . . Embrace a woman! . . . Be content to look at her! . . ."

> Sir, you have done well
> To gaze on your beloved;
> Your fat and puffy belly
> Would prevent you reaching her.

Louis IX was not declared of age until he was twenty-one. Joinville gives a sketch of him at a banquet given by the young King at Saumur. He was dressed in a coat of violet satin with an upper coat and mantle of vermilion satin edged with ermine. This was the garb of royalty. Joinville adds: " He had a cotton hat

King and Saint.

on his head ill becoming so young a man." His clothing was very simple in comparison with that of the lords seated round the King, notably that of Thibaud de Champagne, who also wore a coat and mantle of satin, but with bands and clasp of gold and a golden crown on his head. Thus Louis IX was to exhibit himself all his life in the humblest garb, even before the time when, after his return from the Egyptian Crusade, he adopted costumes of an excessive simplicity. He wore robes of cendal—a coarse silk—of a dark blue shade " embellished with his arms," *i.e.* with the fleurs-de-lis ; and sometimes he wore camelin, a common material, of a mixture of wool and cotton of a brown shade. It was remarked that not only the nobles of the Court but clerics like Robert de Sorbon were dressed in richer stuff than the King. He liked to declare that one ought to dress in such a way that elderly people could not say " one dressed too much," and young people that " one did not dress enough."

Marguerite of Provence, who loved fine clothes, complained to the King that he dressed too simply.

" Madame, to please you, then I will dress in splendid clothes ; but you, on your side, must suit yourself to my taste and give up your beautiful garments."

The King heard no more on this subject from his wife.

Saint Louis was very tall. He stood a head higher than those around him. " Never was there so fine a man under arms," says Joinville, " for he stood above all his people from the shoulders upwards." This high stature is found again in his grandson, Philip the Fair, and his great-grandson, Philip the Long. He was slight, thin, lightly built, pleasing and gentle in his movements. Such he was when in 1248 he was seen by Fra Salimbene, when Saint Louis was preparing to depart on his first Crusade. He was clothed as a pilgrim with cape and staff. " Truly," adds the Italian monk, " he seemed more like a monk vowed to religion than a soldier trained to the profession of arms."

Saint Louis was fair, but he became bald very early. Contemporaries are agreed as to the gentleness of his look. They speak of his " dove's eyes." The smooth beauty of his face impressed the Arabs who saw him in Egypt.

THE MIDDLE AGES

Two features dominate the character, life, and government of Saint Louis : his piety and his love of justice.

Ancient France has been defined as an aristocratic republic governed by judicial institutions under the direction of a supreme magistrate, the King. After the glorious evolution of the twelfth century these institutions reached their maturity. Here is definitely constituted that paternal France whose germs we have seen unfolding in the tenth century. Under the King who assures justice to his vassals, and the vassals who assure justice to the lesser vassals, the nation lives with a life intense and independent. In occupying himself with justice alone, the King secures peace and concord in his kingdom, and through concord and peace he gives it glory and prosperity. "He shunned discords," writes Guillaume de Saint-Pathus, "he avoided scandals and hated disagreements. For which reason the waves of assault were held back on all sides and disturbances driven away."

"Dear son," Saint Louis will say to him who was afterwards to become Philip the Bold—"dear son, if it should be that you come to reign, see that you have the mark of a King—that is to say, that you are so just that you will never refuse justice on any consideration. If it happen that a dispute between rich and poor comes before you, support the poor rather than the rich, and when you have heard the truth, do justice to them. And if it happen that you have a dispute with another, support the claim of the other before your council, and do not show your great interest in the dispute until the truth be shown, lest those of your council should fear to speak against you ; for this you should not desire."

"The King," says Joinville, "governed his land well and loyally, as you will see from what follows." And here is this government :

"He had his business arranged in such a way that my lord of Neele (Simon de Nesles) and the good Count of Soissons (Jean II le Bégue), and we others, who were around him, when we had heard Mass went to hear the pleadings at the gate, which are now called the Requests. And when he came back from the church he would send for us, and seating himself at the foot of his bed he would make us sit round him and asked us if there were any one to settle with who could not be satisfied without him. And we mentioned them, and he sent for them and asked : ' Why do you not take what our people offer you ? ' And they said : ' Lord, they offer us but a little.' And he said to them : ' You ought to accept what they are willing to do.' And thus the holy man exerted all his powers to bring them to a right and reasonable course."

Such are the famous scenes which are to produce the Requests of the " Hôtel " when the King can no longer deal in person with matters brought to the palace, absorbed as he will be in the more and more numerous occupations to which the aggrandizement of the royal demesne and the development of his authority will give rise.

After which Joinville presents us with this familiar picture, of the Wood of Vincennes :

" Many times it happened in the summer that he (the King) went to sit in the Wood of Vincennes, after hearing Mass, and leaned against an oak and made us sit round him, and all those who had affairs to attend to came to speak to him without disturbance of an usher or any one else. And then he asked : ' Is there no one who has a plea ? ' And those who had rose, and then he said : ' Keep quiet, all of you, and judgment will be dealt to you in turn.' And then he summoned my lord Perron de Fontenines (the famous lawyer) and my lord Geoffroy de Villette (*bailli* of Tours in 1261–62), and said to one of them : ' Judge this case for me.' And when he saw anything to correct in the words of those who spoke for him or those speaking for any one else, he himself made the amendment with his own lips."

In Paris the good King acted in the same way. For this purpose he went to the Garden of Paris, *i.e.* to the garden of the King's residence (the Palais de Justice) at the summit of the City, a spot now occupied by the Place Dauphine.

" I saw him several times in the summer," says Joinville, " going to judge cases for his people in the Paris Garden, dressed in a coat of coarse stuff, with an outer coat of tyretaine (a stuff half wool, half cotton) without sleeves, a mantle of thick black silk fastened round his neck, his hair well combed out and without a hat, but with a coronet of white peacock's feathers on his head. And he had a carpet spread for us to sit round him; and all the people who had matters to bring before him stood round him, and he gave judgment in the way I have described before in the Wood of Vincennes."

Such was essentially the government of Saint Louis, an incessant labour which included great and small, from the common people, whose affairs he quickly settled (*expediait*) at the palace gate or under green boughs in wood or garden, to the feudal lords whose quarrels he appeased, and the good towns where he strove to put an end to disputes between Patricians and artisans. " Blessed," said he, " blessed are the peacemakers."

And as he could not be everywhere at the same time, in the innumerable nooks and corners of his kingdom, he instituted his famous inquirers (*enquêteurs*), who journeyed through the provinces charged with the inquiry into the manner in which *baillis*, seneschals, and provosts administered justice. Saint Louis generally chose religious for these missions, Dominican or Franciscan Friars.

The reputation as an administrator of justice which the pious monarch thus acquired spread beyond the frontiers. The princes of the Marches of the Empire came to submit their disputes to him. Wishing to end their quarrels, they addressed themselves, not to the German Emperor, but to the King of St. Denis. Still more foreigners came as simple individuals to the royal Court in spite of distance, to Reims, Paris, Melun, or Orleans, to beg the ivory hand, whose pacific action was felt throughout Europe, to put an end to their differences. And now we come to the famous " *dit d'Amiens*." The English barons were struggling against King Henry III, who had not taken care to respect the Provisions of Oxford, an act by which the English Nobility had surrounded the exercise of the royal power with new barriers. In December 1263 the two sides, weary of their quarrels, referred them to the decision of the King of France. He pronounced his judgment at Amiens on the 24th January 1264. It was completely in favour of Henry III.

Some years before, the good King had given a striking proof of his desire for justice by the way he had tried to put a

A JUSTICIARY IN ERMINE

definite end to the long conflict between the French and English Crowns, a fact which had doubtless won for him the confidence of King and barons across the Channel.

Profiting by the dissensions which had arisen between the French Court on one side and some lords of the South and West on the other, Henry III had broken with Louis IX (16th June 1242), judging the occasion to be favourable for winning back the provinces of which Philip Augustus had deprived John Lackland. The English landed at La Rochelle, they proposed to join forces with the Count of Toulouse and the Count of La Marche; but the victory won by Louis IX under the walls of Saintes—known as the battle of Taillebourg—broke the Coalition (22nd July 1242). Treaties were concluded at Bordeaux. Although he had conquered his rival, Saint Louis restored to the English Crown part of the conquests of Philip Augustus—Limousin, Quercy, and Perigord. His brother, Alfonse, Count of Poitiers, had no children. If he should die without heirs, the English monarch was to receive also Agenais and the greater part of Saintonge, that part situated south of the Charente. In return, Henry III definitely renounced for himself and his successors Normandy, Anjou, Touraine, Maine, and Poitou. Moreover, he formally acknowledged himself as a vassal of the French King for the domains which the English Crown still preserved in our country.

Joinville tells us that the King's Council made the liveliest opposition to these astounding concessions. " Sire," said the barons to Saint Louis, "we are greatly surprised that you are willing to give to the English King so large a part of the land, which you and your predecessor (Philip Augustus) won from him through his misdeeds. It seems to us that if you think you have no right to them you are not making satisfactory restitution to the English King unless you give him all the conquests made by yourself and your predecessor; and if you think you have a right to them it seems to us that you are throwing away what you give back to him."

To this the holy King replied :

" Lord, I am certain that the predecessors of the King of England rightly lost the conquest which I hold. The land I am giving him, I do not give because I am bound to him or his heirs, but for the sake of the great love existing between my children and his, who are first cousins. And it seems to me that what I give I employ well, for he was not my man and now has done me homage."

It is none the less certain that Saint Louis made a very grave mistake in this case, and one for which the country might justly have called him severely to account. He broke in an alarming way from the policy of his grandfather, which he should always have had before his eyes. At one stroke he destroyed so many efforts made by the Frenchmen of France for the unity of their country, so many troubles and sufferings borne by them; and prepared enduring calamities.

But at least Joinville has revealed the motives which actuated the holy King, and primarily that need of unity, peace, and concord so deeply rooted in him. By a natural impulse of the man, he attributed to others a character like his own, with the same kindness and an equal sense of justice. He believed that his generosity would secure a durable peace between the two countries. He judged things out of his charity. His grandfather, as a clear-sighted politician, had, on the contrary, discerned the germs of future discords in the very settlement which was now concluded.

Saint Louis could not appreciate that those feudal institutions which he saw so well established round him were soon to crumble. He had consolidated, he said, the ties of fidelity and homage by which the English Kings were subject to the Kings of France, and does not a vassal owe aid and devotion to his suzerain? But in a few years these feudal ties were to count no longer. To understand fully the actions of Saint Louis as King it is necessary to take full account of his religious faith. This sentiment had in him assumed a strength which we can only imagine with difficulty. For Louis IX, Catholic dogma was the truth. The lightest doubt could not cross his mind. He was convinced that, quite close by, God watched over men, assisted the faithful, helped him himself to rule. Thus God, religion, and its holy cult formed the principal end towards which his efforts were directed. His mother, Blanche of Castile, had brought him up to practices which Churchmen themselves considered excessive. Is it not Guillaume de

A JUSTICIARY IN ERMINE

Saint-Pathus, the Queen's confessor, who shows us the King remaining so long on his knees with his elbows supported on a bench and lost in prayer that the members of his suite, among whom were many clerics, yawned with weariness? At other times, in his room, he would remain for hours prostrate with his face against the ground, absorbed in ardent prayer, so long that on rising he was dazed and rubbed his eyes, asking his stewards : " Where am I ? "

By abstinences, fasts and privations, the hair shirt, and the discipline, he contrived to ruin his health, to the great detriment of the matters over which he had charge. Under the influence of an extreme piety he published against blasphemers those terrible edicts by which their tongues were to be pierced with a red-hot iron. Some historians have professed to see in these edicts only a menace, a formula of malediction, a sort of anathema; but these edicts were put into force in a horrible way, and more than once; to such a degree that even Churchmen came to regard them as excessive. Finally, we must regretfully confess that Saint Louis authorized the establishment in the South of France of the tribunals of the Inquisition.

We have said that Louis IX was guided in his government by the advice of his mother, " the white Queen." His chamberlain, Pierre de Laon, a man of great intelligence and profound virtue, had equally a great influence on his decisions; and then there were the Churchmen.

Saint-Pathus reports that, on a certain day, at the breaking up of the Parliament, a good woman named Sarrette waited for the King in his palace at the foot of the grand staircase, and when he passed near her, " Fi ! Fi ! " she cried out to him. " Are you King of France ? It were better that another should be King; for you are King only under Friars Minor and Preaching Friars and priests and clerks. It is a great pity that you should be King, and it is a great wonder that you are not driven out of the kingdom ! "

The sergeants of the Guard would have thrown the good woman out at the door, but the King prevented them, and going up to her said, with his sweet smile :

" You certainly speak the truth : I am not worthy to be King. And if it had pleased Our Lord it would have been better that another than I should have been King, and one who would have understood better how to rule the kingdom."

And he gave orders that money should be given to the good woman.

The candid poet Rûtebeuf for his part declared that he hated the "hypocrites," "pharisees," and all the religious pretenders habited in black and grey who replaced in the Councils of the King the "Naymes de Bavaria," the wise counsellors trained to war and affairs, the glorious assistants of Charlemagne.

Certainly Saint Louis was hardly a "hypocrite." His piety was gay and attractive. If it is true that he forbade the knights to sing in his palace "frivolous songs"—"sing hymns rather"—we have seen his liking for minstrels, more frivolous in this than his grandfather, Philip Augustus, who had banished them from Court. After a meal he would put off the pious readings proposed by the monks, choosing instead some lively subject of conversation: "There is no book so good after eating as a few jokes."

He asked Joinville in the presence of Robert of Sorbon: "Seneschal, which is the better, an honest man (*prud'homme*) or a *béguin*?"

Louis XIV would say: "An honest man or a devotee" ("*Honnête homme ou dévot*"). Robert of Sorbon pronounced in favour of the devout, while the Seneschal of Champagne exalted the honest man. And Saint Louis agreed with the latter.

"Master Robert, I would much rather have the name of an honest man; let me be this, and you may keep the rest; for *prud'homme* is so great and good a thing, that the very name is a mouthful."

Since we are speaking of Saint Louis at table, let us give the menu of a dinner which the good King gave in the refectory of a convent of monks at Sens in 1248 to some noble guests: his three brothers, to the Cardinal Legate, and the Archbishop of Rouen. Fra Salimbene was present at it. "At dinner," he writes, "we had first cherries and then very white bread. We were served at the same time with wine in great abundance, as became the magnificence of royalty. And after the manner

A JUSTICIARY IN ERMINE

of the French some were anxious to invite and persuade those who were unwilling to drink. Afterwards they gave us new beans cooked in milk, fish and lobsters, eel pies, rice with milk flavoured with almond and sprinkled with cinnamon, roast eel with fine sauce, turtles and curds, and finally a quantity of fruit."

For the rest, Saint Louis' piety did not prevent him standing firm against the demands of the clergy. On occasion the Sovereign Pontiff found in him an adversary. It happened that the King was asked to attend an assembly of prelates held in Paris. Hardly had he entered than the Bishop of Auxerre harangued him in the name of his colleagues:

" Sire, the lords here present, archbishops and bishops, have bidden me say to you that Christianity, which ought to be protected by you, is perishing in your hands."

Saint Louis, alarmed, crossed himself. Excommunications were giving rise to the greatest abuses. There was no part of France in which there were not a great number of interdicts, and most often for some motive of temporal interest. Now the prelates wished that the King should force the excommunicated by the confiscation of their possessions to give satisfaction to those who had pronounced sentence on them. Saint Louis replied that he would willingly do so, but only when it had been proved to him in each individual case that the interdict had been justly pronounced. In other words, he was asking that the cases should be submitted to him. But the prelates protested against this claim, and as Saint Louis quoted as an example the case of the Count of Brittany who had been unjustly excommunicated, and that by the judgment of the Court of Rome itself, as shown by the fact that it had afterwards absolved him, the French prelates did not insist and took care not to refer again to their request.

Saint Louis, governed by his sentiments of piety and charity, multiplied foundations of monasteries, churches, infirmaries, hospitals, almshouses, the most famous of which has survived, that of the *Quinze-Vingts* for the blind. He acquired in 1239 from the Latin Emperor of Constantinople the Crown of Thorns, and, in 1249, a piece of the true Cross. It was as a shrine for the Crown that he had the Sainte Chapelle begun in 1242 on the plans of Pierre de Montreuil, a pure gem of Gothic architecture. The sublime edifice was completed in 1248. The building had cost £40,000, which would represent eight million in our time.

To his piety he united a humility, which he imposed on himself, for it was not natural to him. He washed the feet of the poor and even of lepers. He made them eat at his table. In the refectories of monasteries he loved to serve the simple monks. On a certain day in the Abbey of Royaumont there were many religious at table and few servers to carry the dishes. The King went to the kitchen window, where he took the vessels full of food. And because the dishes were too hot he wrapped his hands round several times in his cloak because of the heat of the food and the vessels, and several times the food was spilt on his cloak. The abbot remarked that he was spoiling his cloak, and the King replied: "It does not matter; I have others."

But in a second monastery, in which he expressed the wish to serve the monks in the refectory, the abbot advised him to refrain: "It is not for a King to do; it would be talked about for good or evil, to which it is better not to give an opening."

Marguerite de Provence made him a similar and equally sensible reply, on the day when he suggested that they should both enter religion, he as a monk and she as a nun. His wife rejoined that they had better things to do even in the interests of religion than to go into monasteries to mumble prayers.

For the rest, the canonization of the holy King and the cult which has been vowed to him are amply justified by his exquisite goodness. In his "Instructions" to his daughter, the Queen of Navarre, he says: "My dear daughter, keep a kindly heart towards those whom you hear of being unhappy in mind or body, and help them willingly with consolation or alms according to your power." Advice which all his life he put into practice, and with a charming graciousness, a disarming courtesy, gaily, even humorously.

The legislative work of Louis IX has been greatly exaggerated. The title of a compilation of laws known as the "Institutions of Saint Louis" has caused the illusion. It is only a collection of local customs of Anjou and Orleans, to

A JUSTICIARY IN ERMINE

which were added two ordinances, one relating to the provostship of Paris, the other to the prohibition of judicial duels. They were questions of procedure; the second, it is true, very important and representing substantial progress in the administration of justice. The part of the " Instructions " which Saint Louis drew up for his son, Philip the Bold, and which treated of internal wars, was animated by the same spirit. We have seen that the private wars, recurring incessantly, chiefly consisted for the feudal lords in ravaging each others' territories. It was a terrible scourge to the inhabitants of a country without fortresses. " If it happen that it is necessary to make war," says Saint Louis to his son, " give careful orders that the poor people, who have nothing to do with the matter, be protected from injury, through the burning of their goods, or in any other way. For it is more becoming for you to put constraint on the wrong-doer in taking his goods or his towns or castles by siege, than to ruin the possessions of poor folk."

Saint Louis suffered from a chronic malady about which Saint-Pathus gives us the following details : " Suddenly the King would become deaf, losing his appetite and power of sleep. He moaned with pain. Each of these crises lasted three or four days, during which the invalid never left his bed. When he was on the point of getting better, his right leg would swell and become as red as blood ; then slowly he returned to his normal condition ; the King was now well again."

Was this the illness from which he was suffering when, in 1244, he resolved to take the cross ? Joinville describes the scene. Louis IX was in such a bad state (*méschief*) that one of his nurses " wanted to pull the sheet over his face, and said that he was dead " ; but another, " who was at the other side of the bed," contradicted this, and a dispute began in the course of which the King gave again signs of life. " And as soon as he could speak he asked that the cross should be given to him, which was done." The Queen-Mother was overcome with joy when she learned that her son had recovered consciousness, but only to give place to a deep despair when she was told that he had vowed himself to the Crusade. In vain Blanche of Castile united her efforts with those of Queen Margaret and of the King's Confessor, as well as of the Bishops of Paris and

Meaux, to persuade him at least to put off the execution of his plan until he was quite recovered. Saint Louis belonged to the class of gently obstinate people. "Lord Bishop," he said to the Bishop of Paris, "I beg of you to put on my shoulder the Cross of the pilgrimage beyond the seas."

The situation of the Christians in Palestine had become critical after the battle of Gaza (9th October 1244), in which **The Egyptian Crusade.** the French, united with Malik-Mansur, the Soudan of Emessa, had been defeated. Gautier de Brienne, Count of Jaffa, had been made prisoner as well as the Grand Masters of the Temple and the Hospital. Speaking of this alliance of Gautier de Brienne with Malik-Mansur, the Arab historian Makrizi observes that this was the first time that the banners of Christ had been seen waving in the same ranks as the Mohammedan standards.

The Crusade was preached by Innocent IV at the Council of Lyons (1245). But at the same time he proclaimed the Crusade against the Emperor Frederick II, whom he had just excommunicated; with the result that Frederick hastened to warn the Sultan Nedjin-Eddin by a messenger disguised as a merchant. The Crusaders made their preparations under the direction of Saint Louis, while the Mohammedans organized their resistance.

The French King appealed to his vassals, barons, and burgesses. Salimbene saw him traversing the bishopric of Auxerre in the company of a Franciscan friar who was preaching the Crusade and giving the cross to those who pledged themselves to it. The people sympathized with the King.

> Behold the time! God seeks you out,
> With outstretched arms blood-stained! . . .

cries Rutebeuf in his magnificent style.

The barons showed less enthusiasm. They should all have been like the lord of Joinville. He had summoned his vassals for Easter Eve (18th April 1248). By a happy coincidence a son was born to him the same day, to whom they gave the name of John. The first days of the week were full of feasting, drinking, and the singing of songs and carols. But on the Friday, Joinville assembled his men, telling them

A JUSTICIARY IN ERMINE

he was going overseas, and that he wanted, before setting out, to make reparation for any wrongs he might have done to one or other of them. He left this to their judgment.

They embarked at Aigues-Mortes on the 28th August 1248. The King took his wife and his three brothers. The fleet was to put in at the isle of Cyprus where large supplies had been prepared. From Cyprus the King proposed to set out to attack Egypt. It was a well-conceived plan. Cairo was the key of the Holy Land. In the King's absence the French regency was entrusted to Blanche of Castile.

Joinville describes the imposing aspect of the supplies prepared in the isle of Cyprus : " The King's stores were such that his people had made in the fields on the seashore great piles of barrels of wine bought two years before. They had piled them up on one another so that seen from the front they looked like storehouses. Wheat and barley had been heaped up in the fields, and they looked like mountains ; for the rain which had fallen during a long period on the grain had caused it to sprout on the top so that it looked like green grass. Now it happened thus that when they wanted to carry it into Egypt they cut off the dirt on the green surface and found the wheat and barley as fresh as though newly threshed." The majority of the barons vowed to the Crusade had not arrived at Aigues-Mortes, so that the King had to await them in the isle of Cyprus until the month of May in the following year, whilst the Arabs, having been warned, were multiplying their means of defence. Finally, on Friday the 21st May 1249, the fleet weighed anchor.

It was a magnificent sight : eighteen vessels whose white sails covered the sea with a multitude of " cloths " (*touailles*), thousands and thousands of sheets dazzlingly white in the rays of the sun against the great blue sea. Arab fishermen who had put off from the African coast in their boats shaped like slices of melon, mistook the Christian fleet at a distance for an innumerable flight of gulls poised on the crest of the waves.

The French arrived in sight of Damietta, at the mouth of one of the branches of the Nile, on the 27th May 1249. Under the orders of the Emir Fakhr-Eddin, the Arabs in order of battle occupied the upper parts of the beach. The Moham-

THE MIDDLE AGES

medan army appeared brilliantly equipped. "The noise," writes Joinville, "which they made with their timbals and their Saracen horns was horrible to hear."

The French threw themselves into boats and hastened towards the shore. When Saint Louis saw that the oriflamme had reached the shore, seized with impatience he leaped into the sea. With the water up to his armpits he marched with a golden helmet on his head, his shield at his neck, his sword in hand. On the shore he towered above his men with his great height. A strong squadron of Turkish knights flung themselves on the French. "When we saw them coming," says Joinville, "we fixed the points of our shields in the sand, and the wood of our lances with the points towards them. When they saw them thus ready to pierce their bellies, they turned right round and fled."

In a short engagement two lieutenants of Fakhr-Eddin, Emirs renowned for their courage, were killed. The Arabs were thrown into confusion. Fakhr-Eddin made his army cross the bridge of boats leading to the eastern bank of the Nile. The French found themselves masters of the western bank. The Emir led his army southwards up to Achmoun-Tanah. The Mohammedan inhabitants of Damietta, seized with terror, fled after him, abandoning their fortifications. The French entered the town in the morning of the 6th June 1249. They found in it a considerable quantity of weapons, machines of war, and munitions. But the Arabs had set fire to the bazaars where provisions were accumulated.

"At the news of the capture of Damietta," writes an Arab historian, "there was general consternation in Cairo. They reflected gloomily how much this success would increase their (the French) strength and courage. They had seen the Mohammedan army flee before them. They found themselves masters of a considerable quantity of arms and ammunition." The Sultan of Cairo, Nedjin-Eddin, had fallen ill and was growing worse. Would it be possible for him to take the needful measures? "No one doubted," concluded the Arab, "that the kingdom would become the spoil of the Christians."

Saint Louis' first care was to send a message to the Sultan

A JUSTICIARY IN ERMINE

inviting him to make peace and adore the true Cross. Nedjin-Eddin replied :

"In the name of the all-powerful and merciful God, salvation to our prophet and his friends ! I have received your letter : it is full of threats and you glory in the great number of your soldiers. Are you ignorant of the fact that we know how to wield arms and that we have inherited the courage of our ancestors ? No one has ever had the audacity to attack us without our proving our superiority. Let me remind you of our triumphs. We drove the Christians from their countries ; the strongest towns fell into our power. And remember the words of the Koran : 'Those who fight unjustly shall perish.'"

Ill as he was, the Sultan took the most energetic measures. He had fifty of his officers, guilty of having abandoned Damietta, strangled. He had himself carried on board a warship, in which he sailed down the Nile to meet the Crusaders, as far as Mansourah. He had all available vessels rigged out and equipped with soldiers and munitions. He had the fortifications of the town strengthened. Arabs and Bedouins flocked to his call. At Damietta, Saint Louis called a council. The Count of Brittany and the chief barons thought it would be best to capture Alexandria, a port well defended and sheltered, and in which the vessels which brought supplies to the army would find good anchorage. But the Count of Artois, the brother of Saint Louis, thought it best to march straight on Cairo. "And he said also, that he who wished to kill a serpent should crush its head." Saint Louis adopted this opinion, which his brother had been practically alone in maintaining.

And this might not have been the worst advice if the King had decided to march at once on Cairo, thus taking advantage of the confusion into which their defeat had thrown the Saracens. But they dragged on at Damietta, where was seen a repetition of the laxity, which, in similar circumstances, had enervated the earlier Crusades : feasts, orgies ; after superhuman efforts an irruption of luxury and pleasure. The barons gave themselves over to much eating and strange foods. The soldiery fell into similar excesses and worse. Joinville adds that, through cupidity, the Crusading lords let shops and

THE MIDDLE AGES

the right of having a stall in the town at exorbitant prices, so that the traders from the Mediterranean lands gave up coming to provision the army. Already the Turks, on their swift horses, were skirmishing on the plain of Damietta, where they surprised some of the French in isolated groups. Some Christian prisoners were taken off to Cairo.

Nedjin-Eddin, who directed the defence, died in November 1249, in his fortieth year, after having named as his successor his son Touran-Chah, who lived at Damascus.

Saint Louis heard of the death of the Sultan in spite of the precautions of the Saracens to hide it. He immediately assembled his troops and ordered them to march on Cairo. He came to camp at Fariskour on the eastern bank of the Nile, thirteen miles from Damietta. On the 13th December the French were at Bermoun, twelve miles from Mansourah. The Emir Fakhr-Eddin had taken command of the Mohammedans under the regency of the favourite Sultana of Nedjin-Eddin, while awaiting the arrival of the new Sultan. He sent letters to the inhabitants of Cairo to warn them of the approach of the French. The town was in disorder, the inhabitants preparing to depart. The French might well trust in the success of their expedition. They appeared before Mansourah. They were separated from the Saracens by one of the branches of the Nile, that which Makrizi calls the "Achmoun Arm." The Crusaders set up their camp, which they fortified and surrounded with ditches. They constructed machines of war, mangonels and trebuchets, and movable towers from which they hurled projectiles on the Saracens. To replenish their stores, boats plied up and down the river as far as Damietta. The water of the Nile, delicious for drinking, was a great help to them. The Crusaders, imitating the Arabs, put it in vessels of porous earthenware called alcarazzas, which they hung outside their tents. The water, through evaporation, became fresh in the vessels, which the good Joinville, not knowing anything of the laws of physics, attributes to the wonderful qualities of the Nile water.

Impatient to come to blows, Saint Louis decided to throw a causeway across the arm of the river—an immense labour and one which the Mohammedans rendered useless by hollow-

A JUSTICIARY IN ERMINE

ing out the soil on the eastern bank as fast as the French pushed on their endeavour. From one camp to the other, across the Nile waters, Crusaders and Saracens overwhelmed one another with their murderous engines. The Saracens used carrier pigeons. They were acquainted with the use of Greek fire and even gunpowder, as this much-disputed passage of Joinville would seem to indicate :

" Our extinguishers were equipped for the extinguishing of fire ; and because the Saracens could not aim directly at them, through the two wings of the pavilions which the King had had made, they aimed straight towards the clouds, so that the arrows fell directly towards them. The manner of the Greek fire was this : it came well forward as big as a barrel of verjuice, and the tail of fire which issued from it was as big as a large sword. It made such a noise in coming that it was like thunder ; it seemed like a dragon flying through the air. It threw so great a light that one could see the army as though it was day by reason of the great size of the fire which produced the great light. Three times that evening they hurled at us Greek fire, dispatching it from the towered arbelist."

What indeed could have been this Greek fire which passed through the air with a noise like that of thunder ?

The Crusaders were impatient for a hand-to-hand fight, the only form of combat in which they could hope to triumph. They were grieving to realize the futility of their efforts to throw a dyke across the Achmoun arm when a Bedouin, for a large sum of money, revealed to them a ford not far from Mansourah. The French crossed there on the 8th February 1250. Fourteen hundred horsemen crossed the arm of the river, and after putting to flight several bands of Saracens who had come to meet them, they attacked Mansourah with such fury that they swept into the town.

Fakhr-Eddin was being shaved in his bath. He dresses hastily, leaps to horse, tries to rally his soldiers, but falls pierced with strokes in the midst of a band of Crusaders. The Saracens flee on all sides. The French pursue them beyond Mansourah on the Cairo road. Carrier pigeons announced the disaster to the inhabitants of Cairo, and soon the first refugees arrived to confirm it. All night the gates of Cairo remained open for the townspeople, who fled wildly. Joinville shows Saint Louis, at the head of his knights, advancing " with a great sounding of trumpets and timbals." High above all the crests shines his helmet, surmounted by two golden lilies crossing each other at right angles ; in his hand is a gleaming sword.

He had penetrated into Mansourah, where the Sultan Touran-Chah had arrived the day before, from Damascus. The King of France had already crossed the threshold of the palace. Saint Louis thought that victory was his : the Sultan a prisoner, the road to Cairo cleared, the capital of the Mohammedan Empire defenceless in his hands.

The Arab historians recognize that if the French knights had been able to hold until their infantry had crossed the Nile, the Mohammedans would have been lost. Then a tragic reverse occurred. Under the leadership of Bibars-Eboudakdari, who was very soon to be King of Egypt, the horsemen of Baharia, the famous Mameluks, resumed the offensive. Some of the French were pursuing the fugitives along the Cairo road. An attack was made on those who remained in the town. The inhabitants joined their efforts to those of the soldiers. From the top of their flat roofs they threw down on the French, constricted in the narrow streets, beams, stones, earthenware vessels, which knocked them over and crushed them under their heavy armour. Joinville gives us again the picture of these tall knights, sheeted in iron on their heavy chargers, attacked by the fleet Saracens, who showered on them from a distance a multitude of sharp arrows. Six Turks had seized the King's horse, trying to drag him along, but Saint Louis freed himself with great strokes of his sword. When the knights, who had pursued the fugitives along the Cairo road, returned to Mansourah intoxicated with their victory, their comrades had no longer any thought but to save their lives. The Count of Artois, the lord of Coucy, the Earl of Salisbury, William Longsword, were dead. The French beat a retreat; the flower of chivalry had fallen. " A second carrier pigeon," say the Arab historians, " bearing the news of the victory won over the French, restored calm to the town (Cairo). Joy succeeded despair. Every one congratulated one another. Public rejoicing organized itself spontaneously."

A JUSTICIARY IN ERMINE

Having recrossed the Nile the French shut themselves up anew in their camp, where they soon suffered cruelly from famine. In vain they awaited the boats which, ascending the river from Damietta, ought to have brought them provisions. This is what had happened.

Touran-Chah had had several boats made which could be taken to pieces. He had them transported down the riverside, across the sandy plain on the backs of camels, put together, and launched. These vessels, full of armed men, intercepted the boats full of food which were coming up from Damietta to the Crusading army. Communications between the French camp and Damietta were interrupted, and very soon the most terrible famine made itself felt in the army.

The Crusaders could not understand why boats came no longer from Damietta. " We had no news of these things," writes Joinville, " until a small boat belonging the Count of Flanders which escaped them by the water told us, and that the vessels of the Soudan had taken eighty of our ships which had come to Damietta and killed the men in them." The famine, which enforced a wretched diet, developed under the heat of the African sky that terrible malady of camps, dysentery. A large convoy of thirty-two boats laden with provisions was again intercepted by the Mohammedans on the 16th March (1250). At this news an immense discouragement fell upon the Crusaders. Saint Louis proposed a truce to Touran-Chah : the exchange of Damietta for Jerusalem. The Sultan, convinced that the Christians were ruined, rejected these proposals.

The bodies of the men killed in the battle of the 8th February infected the army. " The corpses," writes Joinville, " came to the surface of the water, floating up to the bridge between our two armies (the army of the Saracens and that of the French), and could not pass because the bridge touched the water. There were so many that the whole river was full of dead from one bank to the other and for a length of a small stonethrow."

On the evening of Tuesday the 5th April the King gave the signal for the retreat to Damietta. The sick were to go down the river in boats, but the Mohammedans organized a pursuit. They massacred the sick by night on the banks of the Nile by the light of fires which they had kindled. A new combat began on the height of Fariskour. This is the second battle of Mansourah (5th–6th April 1250). Driven back on every side, the French withdrew into a village called Minieh, which occupied the top of a hillock of sand. Saint Louis, very ill, rode a little draught horse with a silk coverlet. He had on a scarlet cap edged with minever. "Behind him," says Joinville, "there remained of all the knights and sergeants only my lord Geffroy de Sergines, who conducted the King to the village of Minieh, in such a manner that the King told me that my lord Geffroy de Sergines defended him from the Saracens as a servant guards his lord's goblet from the flies. For each time the Saracens approached he took his sword which he had put in his saddle bow and put it under his arm and ran upon them, driving them away from the King. And in this way he led the King to the village and put him down in a house. . . ."

Elsewhere Joinville shows us Gaucher de Châtillon struggling alone in a small street of the village against the Turks who attacked him:

"This street ran straight through the village so that one could see the fields at each end. In this street was my lord Gaucher de Châtillon, naked sword in hand. When he saw the Turks coming into this street he ran upon them with his sword and 'threw' them out of the village; and in their flight before him, the Turks, who aimed behind as well as before, covered him with darts. When he had chased them out of the village he pulled out the arrows, and put on his coat of arms and rose up on his charger, stretching out his arms with his sword, and cried: 'Châtillon! Knights! Where are my good men?'"

Alas! his good men were killed or taken prisoners.

"When he turned round and saw that the Turks had entered at the other end he ran on them again, sword in hand, and drove them off; and thus he did three times in the manner described above."

Surrounded by some faithful followers, the French King had taken refuge in the house of Abi-Abdaellah, lord of Minieh. Weakened by dysentery, he fainted several times. They

A JUSTICIARY IN ERMINE

laid him "on the lap of a woman from Paris like one quite dead."

The Arab historian Saad-Eddin as well as Joinville and Saint-Pathus relate that when the King of France was restored to consciousness he could have fled either on horseback or by boat as did the Papal Legate; but he was unwilling to abandon his men, staying among them till the last moment. At last the good King gave himself up as a prisoner into the hands of the eunuch Djemad-Eddin-Muhsun-El-Sahil. Saint Louis and his brother, Alfonse of Poitiers, were loaded with chains. They were shut up together at Mansourah in the house of Ibrahim-ben-Lokmar, the Sultan's secretary, under the guard of the eunuch Sahil. Ten thousand Frenchman had perished in this day's fight, while hardly a hundred Mohammedans had met their death.

"The King of France," writes an Arab, "was made to embark on the Nile in a warship. He was escorted by an infinite number of Egyptian boats which led him in triumph to the sound of timbals and tambours. On the bank the Egyptian army advanced beside the fleet. The prisoners followed the army with their hands bound." Under the walls of Damietta the Mohammedans found themselves embarrassed by too great a number of prisoners. In the night they were led in bands of three or four hundred to the banks of the Nile and, after having their heads cut off, were thrown into the river.

The Sultan only allowed Saint Louis to keep near him his one cook, Ysembart. This latter prepared his meals, chiefly made up of cakes, bread, and meat. The King's teeth were loose in the gums. He was so thin that "the bones of his spine seemed all points." He was so weak that Ysembart had to carry him from one seat to another, but his strength of character never failed.

At length the question of ransom was considered. Damietta would be given up in exchange for the King's person. As to the other prisoners taken by the Saracens, their ransom was fixed at the round sum of 500,000 pounds, about a hundred millions in the money of to-day.

Hardly was the treaty concluded than there broke out among the Saracens a revolution at Court. The favourite

THE MIDDLE AGES

Sultana, Chageret-Eddin, the widow of Nedjin-Eddin, had exercised the regency up to the arrival of Touran-Chah. A dispute broke out on the subject of a rendering of accounts. The Sultana formed a party with Bibars, the head of the Mameluks. On the 2nd May 1250, Saint Louis was in his tent with his brother when there broke out a great noise outside. The conspirators were attacking the Sultan. He took refuge at the top of a wooden tower on the banks of the Nile. The Mameluks set fire to it. Touran-Chah flung himself from the top of the tower into the river, where he was dispatched with arrows. The Sultana Chageret-Eddin was declared Queen of Egypt. She was the first slave who had ever ruled the country. After having bought her, Nedjin-Eddin had become attached to her. Bibars, the chief of the Mameluks, succeeded her on the throne. He founded a new power, that of that military guard which had surrounded the Sultans up to the day on which it had seized the power. The Mameluks dominated Egypt up to the nineteenth century.

They proceeded to the execution of the treaty. The days of the 7th and 8th May were spent in paying out to the Saracens part of the ransom. It was necessary to pay later three hundred thousand pounds. If we can believe the instructions given, some hundred years later (1360), to the commissaries charged with the raising of the money for the ransom of King John, the expenses occasioned by the Egyptian expedition and the ransom of the prisoners produced such an impoverishment of the kingdom in France, that they were obliged to make leather money. "And there is still some of this in the tower of the Louvre," adds the writer of the circular.

Saint Louis set sail for Palestine, which he still hoped to deliver, while his departure inspired the Arab poet Essahib-Giemal-Edden-ben-Mahoub with verses which have been translated as follows :

" Carry to the French King when you see him these words written by an advocate of the truth.

" You landed in Egypt sure of capturing it : you thought it was peopled only with cowards, you who are but a drum filled with wind !

" You thought that the time for ruining the Mohammedans

had arrived, and through this false notion closed your eyes to the difficulties.

" You have left your soldiers on the plains of Egypt where their tombs are open along your path.

" What remains to you of the seventy thousand who accompanied you ? Dead, wounded, captive.

" May God inspire you often with like designs ; they will cause the ruin of the Christians, and Egypt will have nothing to fear from their fury.

" No doubt your priests promised you victories.

" Give ear to a more enlightened oracle.

" If the desire of vengeance impels you to return to Egypt, he assures you that the house of Lockmar (in which Saint Louis was imprisoned) is still there, that the chain is ready, and that the eunuch (who guarded Saint Louis) is on the alert."

Saint Louis remained four years in Palestine repairing or building fortresses, Acre, Jaffa, Cæsarea, Sidonia. He was seen mingling with the masons, carrying stones and basketsful of quicklime. The good King often took part in the combats which became frequent round St. Jean d'Acre. " He carried in person the decomposed and smelling bodies to bury them in the ditches." He offered the King of England, through messengers, to give him Normandy and Poitou if he would join him with his men-at-arms in Asia Minor. This would have destroyed the work of Philip Augustus. Happily for France the proposal was rejected.

About the end of November 1252, Blanche of Castile, regent of the kingdom during the King's absence, died in Paris. When the news reached Saint Louis, he realized that his duty at length recalled him to be among his subjects. It was, however, only on the 24th April 1254 that he re-embarked for France with his wife and children.

It is difficult, at so great a distance of time, to appraise the work of Saint Louis in Egypt and Syria. If his success did not correspond to his efforts, at least these efforts were not barren. Saint Louis left great memories in Egypt which produced consequences glorious for the French name, and still effective in our own day. In Syria he strengthened for half a century the tottering power of the Christian princes,

THE MIDDLE AGES

contributing there also to the maintenance of French influence.

After his return to France, Saint Louis visited several parts of his kingdom, to inquire into the character of judicial administration. He was able to verify the sacrifices which the country had had to impose on itself to cope with the Egyptian expedition.

The Return to France.

The piety of the King increases, and his humility and charity too. He only dresses now in dark colours, deep blue, brown or black. The materials of his garments are of wool or common camelin. The furred parts are of moderate price, being of deer, hare, or lamb. He was equally restrained at table, having the poor to eat in his room and serving them himself.

In pursuance of his rôle of peacemaker, he made with the King of Aragon a treaty similar to the one he had made with the King of England. In it was found the same desire for harmony, the same thirst for justice (Treaty of Corbeil, 11th May 1258). In exchange for the claims which the King of Aragon put forward to various French provinces, Saint Louis renounced the claims of the French Crown to Roussillon and the province of Barcelona. The King of Aragon kept in France only the suzerainty of Montpelier. Isabella, daughter of James I of Aragon, married Philip, the son of Saint Louis, who was one day to become Philip III, and the Spanish prince gave up to his cousin Marguerite, wife of the French King, his rights over Provence, and to the King of France himself his pretended rights over Languedoc.

At length in 1262 there occurred an event whose consequences contemporaries could not yet foresee. A French pope, Urban IV, offered to Saint Louis, through Albert de Parma, one of his notaries, the kingdom of Sicily as a fief of the Holy See. Louis IX declined the offer of the Sovereign Pontiff for himself and his children; but his brother, Charles of Anjou, accepted it. Such was the origin of those Italian expeditions which were to appeal to the French for two centuries, and cost them so much exertion, blood, and money.

The deliverance of the Holy Places remained the constant preoccupation of the King. On the 25th March 1267, the

A JUSTICIARY IN ERMINE

feast of the Annunciation, before a numerous gathering of the great nobles and in presence of the Papal Legate, Saint Louis, according to the custom of the French Kings, himself spoke and set forth to his nobles the reasons working in favour of a new Crusade.

The Crusade of Tunis.

From this day forth he was always thinking of it. The King took three years to prepare for this new expedition; but he was very ill, and it was with a feeling of despair that his most devoted helpers saw him persisting in his resolution. Joinville expresses it strongly: "Those who recommended the Crusade to him were guilty of mortal sin; for the whole kingdom was at peace and he with all his neighbours . . . a great sin did those commit who advised the Crusade in view of his great bodily weakness. He could not bear to be carried in a vehicle or to ride on horseback. His weakness was so great that it gave him pain when I carried him in my arms from the house of the Count of Auxerre to the Franciscan monastery, where I took leave of him. And even though he was so feeble, if he had remained in France he could still have lived and done much good and many good works."

But when, in his gentle obstinacy, Saint Louis had come to a decision it became difficult to divert him from it. He pressed Joinville to take ship with him. The good seneschal refused, and the reasons he gives are interesting to note. " While I had been in the service of God and the King across the seas (Egyptian Crusade) the sergeants of the King of France and of the King of Navarre (Count of Champagne) had destroyed and impoverished my people. . . . And I said to them (Saint Louis and the Count of Champagne, who were pressing him to join the Crusade) that if I wished to act according to the will of God, I should remain here to aid and defend my people; for if I should risk my body . . . there where I saw quite clearly it would be to the disadvantage and injury of my people, I should offend God Who gave His Body to save His people."

These are valuable lines. They show how, during the Crusade, the King's men, profiting by the absence of the nobles, continued to extend the sovereign authority over their domains. They also show all the services the lords could still render to

THE MIDDLE AGES

their tenants, when, remaining amongst them, they occupied themselves zealously with their interests as did the good Lord of Joinville.

The royal fleet set sail for the African coast on the 1st July 1270. The King had been persuaded by his brother, Charles of Anjou, titular King of Sicily, to direct his arms on Tunis, in order to destroy in their dens the Barbary pirates who infested the Mediterranean. Circumstances, moreover, seemed to him to favour an attack, for the country was weakened by a terrible famine. On the 21st July, Saint Louis landed in sight of Tunis and laid siege to the town.

The French fortified their camp. The lack of water involved them in great suffering. From the neighbouring heights the Arabs, with enormous machines, raised clouds of burning sand which covered the encampments of the Crusaders. It is impossible not to be reminded of the asphyxiating gas of the Boches. And then the plague made its appearance. Nevertheless, the French won a brilliant victory under the walls of the town, and already the Tunisians were despairing of their fate when, on the 25th August 1270, the holy King died in his tent, succumbing to extreme weakness aggravated by dysentery. He breathed his last on a bed of ashes, his hands joined, his eyes turned towards Heaven.

His reign has remained one of the most popular in our history. It coincided with the period in which the feudal institutions of which the monarchy formed the keystone, reached their maturity. Now no one has better or more completely personified these institutions than Saint Louis. We have tried to show that they were essentially founded on the exercise of justice, on love, and reciprocal devotion. And this circumstance, more than any other cause, has perhaps formed the greatness and beauty of this reign.

The Son of Saint Louis. Philip III, surnamed the Bold, who succeeded his father, Saint Louis, on the throne, was like him pious and good. Of a generous nature, he gave to the poor and surrounded himself with Churchmen. More even than his father he had the air of a monk wearing the Crown, in spite of the passion with which his second wife, Mary of Brabant, inspired him. At the beginning of his reign

A JUSTICIARY IN ERMINE

he was dominated by his favourite the Chamberlain, Pierre de la Broce, who succumbed to Court intrigues and was hanged in the June of 1278. After this Mathieu, Abbot of St. Denis, had the direction of the government. This abbot continued the traditions of Saint Louis, of whom he had been a councillor.

On the death of Alfonse de Poitiers, the brother of Louis IX, his immense heritage reverted, by default of heirs, to the French Crown. But Henry III, the King of England, put forward some claims founded on the Treaty of Paris (1259). After his death (1272), they were taken up by his son, Edward I, one of the most remarkable of the princes who have occupied the English throne. In conformity with the promises made by his father, Philip III gave up Agenais to the English monarch (Treaty of Amiens, 23rd May 1273). Another part of the heritage of Alfonse, the Comtat-Venaissin, was given up to the Sovereign Pontiff.

The end of the reign was marked by the Aragon expedition, the origin of which is found in the rivalry which broke out in Sicily between Peter III of Aragon and Charles of Anjou. The insurrection of the Sicilian vespers, in which the French were massacred, was caused by the instigation of the Spanish emissaries. Soon afterwards the Catalonian fleet won a victory over that of Charles of Anjou, and Peter of Aragon had himself proclaimed King of Sicily. Pope Martin IV was French by birth. He declared Peter of Aragon deprived of his crown and freed his subjects from the obligation of fidelity. Philip III accepted the kingdom of Aragon from the hands of the Pope. He had still to win it. The expedition against the excommunicated Peter III took the form of a crusade. It has been truly remarked that the campaign of 1285, in Spain, was the first war of conquest entered upon by the Kings of France beyond their natural frontiers. Philip III led an imposing army across the Pyrenees. On the 28th June he laid siege to Gironne. A serious reverse for the French King was the destruction by Roger de Loria, of his fleet with stores to replenish the supplies (4th September). Philip III was attacked by the disease of the army. Gironne was taken, but the army had to beat a retreat with the state of the King

THE MIDDLE AGES

growing daily worse. The son of Saint Louis died on the road from Paris to Perpignan, on the 5th October 1285.

SOURCES.—Joinville, *Vie de Saint Louis*, ed. N. de Wailly, 1881; G. de Saint-Pathus, *Vie de Saint Louis*, ed. Delaborde, 1889; Makrizi, *Histoire de l'Egypte*, translated by Blochet; *Les Etablissements de Saint Louis*, ed. Viollet, 1881–86, 4 vols.

HISTORICAL WORKS.—Edg. Boutaric, *Saint Louis et Alfonse de Poitiers*, 1870; H. Wallon, *Saint Louis et son temps*, 1875, 2 vols.; Elie Berger, *Histoire de Blanche de Castille*, 1895; Ch. V. Langlois, in the *Histoire de France*, edited by Lavisse, iii. 1901; L. Brehier, *L'Eglise et l'Orient au Moyen Age, les Croisades,* 2nd ed., 1907; Ch. V. Langlois, *Le Règne de Philippe le Hardi*, 1887.

CHAPTER XV

THE MINIATURES

The first books with miniatures are executed in the monasteries. Imitation of the Byzantines. The decorative art of the eleventh century. The art of miniature begins to be laicized under Philip Augustus. The Psalter of Ingeburg. A workshop of the miniaturists. The manufacture of colours. The taste for Nature. The circumstances of the miniaturists. Painting with oils. The miniaturists Honoré and Jean Pucelle. The French painters of the Renaissance.

"AND as the writer who has finished his book illuminates it with gold and blue, so the said King illuminated his kingdom . . ." says Joinville, speaking of the good works of Saint Louis. The comparison is charming and appropriate with regard to a reign in which the art of miniature shed such an attractive lustre.

What was a miniaturist? This name was originally applied to the *miniator*, the person who drew in red, in *minium*, the tall initials of the manuscripts.

Under the Merovingians and the Carolingians the majority of the books with miniatures were produced in the monasteries. There was no abbey without its *scriptorium*, a workshop in which writers and illuminators worked. They copied Byzantine works, giving them a heavier rendering. They put their originality into the complexity and exaggeration of forms and designed grotesque monsters which they surrounded with tortured ornament.

We should not find earlier than the eleventh century a miniaturist drawing his inspiration from Nature and life. It is true that, after having abandoned their first guides, the Byzantines, the artist of the eleventh century no longer ventures on full-page compositions. His brush was reduced

321

to the ornamentation of the initials, but with fancy, ingenuity and often with the most agreeable delicacy.

One of the reasons which kept the illuminators so long in these narrow ways was that they were, nearly all, up to the middle of the twelfth century, religious. Hence this lack of fire. Not that religion would have been incapable of producing great artists; but the composition and details of their work were imposed on them by tradition. It was a hieratic art.

Towards the end of the twelfth century, under Philip Augustus, there begins to glow, on the white sheets of vellum, a new art. The miniaturist has left the monastery and become a layman. In Paris, under Philip Augustus, is founded that famous school of miniaturists which Dante, a century later, will declare to be the best in the world:

> ... and the honour of this art
> Which is called illumination in Paris.
> *(Purgatorio,* XI. v. 80.)

The Psalter of Ingeburg of Denmark, preserved at Chantilly, forms a remarkable example of the art of the Parisian miniaturists under Philip Augustus. We may quote equally one of the gems of the Bibliothèque de l'Arsenal: the Psalter described as " of Saint Louis," which seems to have belonged to Louis IX after having passed through the hands of Blanche of Castile.

The use of colours also becomes more varied. Up to the last third of the twelfth century, the miniaturists hardly employed any but the simplest colours—blue, red, black, sometimes pale yellow, not to speak of their backgrounds of gold. Now appears a new colour, a composite colour—green. Thus the use of green affords us a valuable means of dating the miniatures of this period.

What we should call the primitive period of the miniature goes as far as the reign of Philip Augustus. The thirteenth century corresponds to the period of stained glass. The brush traces pages which might seem to be designs for stained-glass windows. It seems certain, too, that our artists drew their inspiration at this period from the sublime stained glass, the

THE MINIATURES

glory of the cathedrals. In this imitation, they go so far as to keep, in their little pictures, the black lines which represent the lead settings, in which in church windows the pieces of coloured glass are inserted.

At the same time the illuminator seeks to free himself from the narrow rules which the hieratical traditions imposed on the composition of pictures. In a descent from the Cross the body of Christ was to be held in a certain way, the Virgin's cloak should be of a fixed shade, the Magdalen kneeling in a place precisely fixed. From the beginning of the thirteenth century the artists make efforts to vary the poses of their personages, and to give variety to the groups. At times the blue, red, and brown of the robes present shades different from those which were up to then held sacred. The first artist whose brush dared to clothe the Virgin in a robe which was not blue appears as a bold innovator. They were bids for freedom as yet hesitating. Towards the middle of the thirteenth century there comes the artist who, in a picture of the Nativity, represents the Divine Child resting in the arms of His mother, instead of showing Him, according to rule, lying in the crib under the muzzles of the ox and ass:

> Between the ox and the grey ass
> Sleeps the little Son. . . .

It was a new movement whose revolutionary audacity we can hardly imagine now.

Finally, from the reign of Saint Louis, one comes across, more and more frequently as the years flow on, miniatures on parchment, no longer of religious subjects.

It has often been remarked, à propos of the miniatures of the twelfth and thirteenth centuries, that they are nearly all of very fine quality, while from the second half of the fourteenth century, beside works of great merit there appear a great number of mediocre productions. It is because, in the twelfth and thirteenth centuries, only sovereign princes and very exalted personages could put manuscripts ornamented with miniatures in their libraries. Later parchment will be manufactured more cheaply, and colours also, at the same time losing their quality, and Books of Hours will become commoner, within reach of more modest purses. By a natural consequence their quality will diminish.

Let us penetrate now into those old workshops, the humble cradles of modern painting. We find there, gathered round a master or patron, four or five poor folk, men and women. They are bent over their work. The volume to be illustrated has been sent in loose leaves to the head of the workshop. The calligrapher has finished his work, being careful to leave blank the pages, margins, or squares destined for pictures and initials, where the miniaturist is to apply his brush. The head of the workshop examines these blank spaces carefully and then divides the work among the collaborators. Often the scribe has noted, with regard to the blank space, the scene which the miniaturist is to represent; or even on the blank space itself. This direction, if it is written in the margin, must be effaced; if it is drawn in the blank space, it will be covered by the painting.

The head of the workshop, having mastered these notes, divides the leaves among the collaborators. He adds some verbal instructions or writes them on the manuscript, or he may make some rapid sketches, either in the margin or in the very place which the miniature is to fill.

Through a fortunate negligence these sketches which ought to have been effaced were sometimes left. The leaves of more than one manuscript lay them before our eyes to-day. And these sketches, jotted down in the margin of the miniature which they inspired, are nearly always superior to it. Thus the work of the master is distinguished from that of his assistants. An expression which has come down to us, " made by a master hand" (*fait de main de maître*), is thus explained. William the Marshall in his Book of Truth (*Livre du Voir dit*) describes a chapel decorated artistically:

> And a very beautiful chapel
> Painted with gold by a master hand. . . .

We come now to the preparation of the colours. They are diluted in water with pine or fir gum added to it, except minium (red lead) and ceruse (white lead), for which white of egg is preferred. We have several books of recipes drawn

THE MINIATURES

up by artists or amateurs of the time. The first is the celebrated treatise of the monk Theophilus, *Schedula diversarum artium*. Its compilation is not so old as has been thought. It seems difficult to date it farther back than the twelfth century. Scholars have even thought they could identify the monk Theophilus with a certain Rogkerus, a celebrated goldsmith, who lived about the beginning of the twelfth century in the Benedictine monastery of Helmerhausen, near Paderborn.

A second collection, two centuries later, since it dates from the fourteenth century, is that in which Jean le Besgue gives the rules and recipes of the miniaturists for the composition of their little pictures and of their colours.

The striking point in the old miniatures is the brightness of the gold portions. They shine even now like plates of glowing metal. They are sheets of beaten gold resting on parchment. Theophilus speaks of them as follows:

" To apply gold or silver, take some of the light part of beaten white of egg, without water. With this coat by means of a brush the place where the gold or silver is to go. Moistening in your mouth the end of the same brush, you will touch with it the corner of the leaf ready cut. Then lifting it very quickly place it on the prepared place and spread it out with a dry brush. At this moment it behoves you to take precautions against the air: hold your breath, for if you breathe you will lose the leaf and only find it again with difficulty. When this is in position and dry, place another, if you wish, on top of it in the same way, and a third if necessary, so that you may give a more brilliant polish with a tooth (of a bear, beaver, or wild boar) or with a stone (agate or amethyst)."

" Begin by rubbing the gold quite gently," says Le Besgue, " then harder, then so vigorously that the perspiration stands out on your forehead."

The brilliance given to the gold leaf by the burnisher kept all its sparkling character after several centuries.

In giving their orders, the patrons demanded that the material used should be of proper quality: the painter shall use, we read in a contract, " fine gold," and " good and sufficient " colours.

THE MIDDLE AGES

Moreover, our artists used chiefly vegetable colours. If we may believe Jean le Besgue, the blue was extracted straight from the corn-flower.

"To make paint of an azure blue, take the pure juice of corn-flowers, and make on wood or parchment a field of white of lead, then put the juice over the said field, in three, four, or five layers or more, if need be, and you will have the colour of azure."

To gather the flowers necessary for their pretty compositions the miniaturists went with the first light of dawn into the fields, their feet wet with the dew. "Go in the morning, at sunrise, to the fields and gather various corn-flowers and other plants," says Jean le Besgue.

They extracted carmine from the sap of ivy.

Our illuminators realized fully the captivating charm of the beauty of Nature, which they reproduced in their delicate works, as did their colleagues the sculptors of the cathedrals. All the flora of our country, its fauna, birds, butterflies, delicate plants, are reproduced with graceful fancy in their picturesque framings. Not only do they take from the fields the flowers necessary for the manufacture of their colours; they gather there also models which they carry back in shining armsful to their workshop, where they copy their forms and shades with loving faithfulness:

> . . . It was the sweet month of April
> When the weather is suave and soft
> Towards all folk and lovers;
> The nightingale, in the morning,
> Sings so clearly in the trees
> That all creatures languish with love;
> The lady has risen,
> Having long lain awake:
> She has gone into her garden,
> With bare feet wet with dew. . . .

Thus the Middle Ages had, in the most charming way, the feeling for Nature, and expressed it with a frank sincerity, in the tympans of its churches, in the verses of its poets, in the fine illuminations of its painters. The Books of Hours generally open with a calendar in which are noted the principal feasts

THE MINIATURES

of the year; and our artists, to give the character of each month, celebrate here rustic labours and the satisfactions they can give.

Nature sleeps in January; and one stays at home, in the house fast shut, the back to the fire and the front to the table. This is the intimate and picturesque image with which the illuminators represent the first month of the year. Jean Corbichon says that " February is represented in painting as an old man who sits at the fire warming his feet, because then the cold is at its height, the sun being too far away from us." Round the house, luminous, there stretches the country. The sky hangs low, the plain sleeps under the snow on which the crows throw the dark stains of their folded wings. In March the fields awake. This month is represented by the vine-dressers who prune the vine shoots, or a wood-cutter who shuffles with his lagging steps the brown leaves of the forest. In April the miniaturist takes pleasure in showing the thickets which are taking on colour, the fields of a tender green where the enamel work of the flowers sows a speckled field of bright colour. It is the time of the renewal of love in its first stirrings. The betrothed exchange pledges with a tenderness they believe eternal, a bunch of flowers, a green crown, a gold ring, a silver necklace. Round them little boys and girls weave chaplets of flowers. The month of May is symbolized by a cavalcade under the verdant arches of the forest. The ladies have put on the livery of May, " gay green "; their heads are laden with flowers. It is the feast of the Queen of May. On the 1st May every one was expected to wear a green sprig under pain of being mobbed, whence the saying, " I take you without green " (*Je vous prends sans vert*). Or, again, the young folk dance in the fields singing their roundelays:

> In May when the fields are flowering
> And the rose is new,
> I rode through a cornfield
> All the length of the path.
> There I saw a shepherdess
> Who was very joyful,
>   And sang:
> " Margueron, shame be to her
> Who refuses well to love."

THE MIDDLE AGES

> Margueron has heard
> This one who calls to her;
> This song is much to her taste,
> She leaps with joy at it.
> Then I saw another damozel
> Who wore a wreath of flowers,
>   And said:
> "Margueron, shame be to her
> Who refuses well to love."

Sometimes, too, the month of May is represented by hunting with the falcon: "It is represented in painting as a young man on horseback who carries a bird on his hand" (Corbichon).

June is characterized by haymaking. "It is represented in painting as a reaper who reaps the field, for at that time the grass is ripe and ready to gather in." Some artists put the harvest at this time: witness the reaper who cuts down the corn with a scythe, the corn which bends its heavy ears; a little way off girls tie up the sheaves, and the peasants shear their sheep. Other miniaturists of a more precocious temper show us already harrowing in June. Generally the harvest is reserved for July. In August, says Corbichon, "the corn is gathered into the barns, and therefore the painters represent it as a thresher who threshes the corn with a flail." At other times it is hunting with the falcon. September is represented "in painting as a grape-gatherer who cuts the grapes and puts them in a basket." Among the sticks supporting the vines, bruised and coloured by autumn, vine-dressers, men and women, are seen bending over the luscious bunches with which they fill their hampers; or again in the sheds, with their wood burnt by the weather, the grapes are pressed in the vats. At another time the grape-gatherers are replaced by a woman gathering apples. Or, indeed, the artist has already depicted sowing in this month. This is, however, oftener put in October. "October is represented in pictures," says Corbichon, "as a man throwing seeds in the soil." They are peasants, serious and mournful, who with an ample movement scatter the seeds of new harvests. Beside them is the harrow, drawn by oxen or horses, which will throw the soil back on the seeds. And already, under the very eyes of the labourer, flocks of sparrows have come to swoop down on the field to pick at them. Some

THE MINIATURES

of these little pictures, in which one sees the rustic life of former days, remind one of the worn peasants, the robust and peaceful landscapes, the grave poetry of François Millet.

Sometimes the acorn crop is put in October, though ordinarily it belongs to November. Under the vaults of the groves of oak, golden in this late autumn, a peasant knocks off the fruit of the lofty trees with a long pole. He has strewn the ground with them, and his flock greedily feeds on them. " In painting," says Corbichon, " this month is represented as a peasant who knocks the acorns from the oaks to feed his pigs." Less often the illuminator represents in November " the death of the pig " : a feast-day at the farm, when the black puddings are taken all hot from the shrivelled fat, and moistened by a great quantity of cider or claret; but this picture, dear to our forefathers, was oftener reserved for December. " In painting, December is represented as a butcher who kills his pig with a blow." Sometimes the beast is roasting on the spit in front of the happy hearth. December may also be represented by the putting of the bread into the oven, or by the noisy trumpeting in the forest with the dogs rushing upon the quarry, under the eyes of the kennel men, who blow out their cheeks while sounding the horn.

From the religious pictures, so carefully illuminated by our miniaturists, will spring the great painting of the Renaissance. Often the composition of such-and-such a famous picture of the sixteenth century is admired, the " Last Supper " of Leonardo da Vinci, for example, or the " Laying in the Tomb " by Titian; in it the genius of the artist is honoured, when it is really only the reproduction of the arrangement adopted since the thirteenth century and perfected from age to age by the humble miniaturists of olden times.

As for the historical scenes, they are distinguished by an anachronism the more daring in proportion as it is unconscious. Whatever may be the epoch represented, the Egypt of the Pharaohs, or the Rome of the Cæsars, furniture and costume are invariably those of the times in which our illuminators lived. Sometimes, with an ingenuous scrupulosity, the artist puts on the personages of antiquity costumes a generation or two old; as though to represent the contemporaries of Themistocles or Romulus Augustulus, we were to give them the fashions of the reign of Louis Philippe or of the Second Empire. In our old miniatures Pompey appears surrounded by cardinals dressed in long scarlet robes; Julius Cæsar makes his entry into the Eternal City at the head of a train of artillery, and Nero holds forth in the foreground of a screen on which is represented the Crucifixion. These *naïvetés* are comparable to those of the old Christmas carols which the soul of the people created about the same period, in which the Virgin and Saint Joseph wander in Bethlehem, from one inn to another, from the " Golden Lion " to the " Shield of France " and to the " White Horse," repulsed from door to door because of their wretched appearance, before finding refuge in the stable where the Divine Child is to be born.

But let us go back to the workshop where our illuminators, men and women, bent over the white sheets of parchment, work with their delicate brushes at the minute work.

Though they are grouped in the workshop under the same head, they are not all equally skilful; whence the differences of execution observable among the miniatures of a single manuscript. They have all been carried out in the same workshop, under the same direction, but by hands not equally expert.

We can imagine only with difficulty to-day the incredible patience of these precise workers. In many places they needed six or seven layers of the same colour to obtain the desired effect.

In wet weather an interval of eight or ten days, sometimes more, was necessary between one layer and the next. The use of driers was not known. Two months or longer were necessary for the purple of a cloak or the green of a wood; but from this there came also that intensity and depth, that precision of colour, that unchangeable purity and clarity which are our admiration. As to the circumstances of these delightful artists, they were generally of the humblest. They were labourers in the true sense of the word, just as the sculptors were stone-cutters. They traded with their pretty pictures in the same way as their neighbours sold candles or combs, cups or hauberks. In our days we often see carpenters who

THE MINIATURES

are at the same time sellers of wine. In the Middle Ages it was the miniaturists who joined their profession to that of innkeepers, and doubtless the sale of claret and beer profited them more than that of the little masterpieces created by their brushes.

Moreover, our painters were organized in corporations, and their statutes resemble those of other trade guilds.

"Article I.—No one shall be admitted to the said trade as master, nor can he work in Paris, nor have an apprentice, until he has made a masterpiece or a trial, and is testified as efficient by the jury of the said trade."

Article V. advises the painter who works on wooden panels to choose only sheets of very dry wood : moreover, he is not authorized to begin his picture until the sheet of wood has been inspected by the masters of the trade.

By these statutes of the thirteenth and fourteenth centuries it is seen that oil painting, on wood as well as on canvas, was practised in the Parisian workshop two centuries before its discovery by the brothers van Eyck.

"Article XV.—Likewise no painter, who is making a painting in oil or distemper, shall work on canvas which is not sufficient and strong enough to stand the painting; and he shall do nothing on tin, which is no good either for oil or distemper."

In the time of Saint Louis, our artists were grouped in the same quarter as the other corporations. The illuminators nearly all chose to live in the rue Eremboux-de-Brie, corrupted now into rue Boutebrie, in the neighbourhood of the Church of St. Severin. There were found, side by side, illuminators, parchment makers, and booksellers.

As to the names of these charming painters, they have, for the most part, remained unknown. We have said that they considered themselves merely artisans, and artisans do not sign their work. Among these comrades the earliest who has left traces of his name was he who illustrated, in 1285, the manuscript now preserved in the Bibliothèque Nationale under the heading Manuscrit français 412. He at least thought of tracing on the last leaf of the volume, if not the name he bore—that would have been, it seems, to ask too much—

THE MIDDLE AGES

at least his Christian name and the date at which he did his work:

> The illuminator has Henri for name,
> God keep him from shame.
> This was made in the year M.CC.IIII.XX et v (1285).

In a tax roll for the year 1292 we find two more Christian names of miniaturists: the family name is always wanting. They are Nicolas and Honoré, both qualified " heads of workshops." We meet this Honoré in 1288 in his workshop in Paris, where he has just finished a *Decretals of Gratian* now preserved in the Bibliothèque de Tours. His workshop is naturally situated in the rue Boutebrie; Honoré works there with his daughter and his son-in-law, Richard of Verdun, who design and paint under his direction.

Honoré appears to have been a person of importance among his colleagues. He is the one who pays the highest tax of all. He was employed by King Philip the Fair; and made for him, in 1296, the beautiful Psalter which is preserved in the Bibliothèque Nationale under the quotation MS. latin 1023.

Perhaps Honoré should be considered the master of Jean Pucelle, the artist who is placed in the first rank of the miniaturists previous to the brilliant school of the fifteenth century, with men like Pol de Limbourg and Jean Foucquet. Pucelle and his pupils can claim the honour of having inaugurated in the decoration of manuscripts the direct and faithful copy of Nature. See in the margins of their beautiful books, or in the boughs with which they decorate their great capital letters, those various birds, familiar denizens of our farms and woods, roguish blackbirds or pheasants with their red-brown plumage, plump bullfinches, and goldfinches with their red hoods. See, at the bottom of the page, this swift hare which jumps across the ferns to the barking of the dog which chases it. Above flutter butterflies and dragonflies. Nature is reproduced here from life, with the exception of the trees, still always presented in masses of " anonymous " foliage, if one may use the expression. We must wait for the painters of the Flemish generation, those of the fifteenth century, to get the variety of trees represented in their individuality.

THE MINIATURES

Honoré and Jean Pucelle were Parisians, as were also those other painters of a delicious grace, Jean Chevrier, Anciau de Cens, Jaquet Maci; these are they whom Dante declared the masters of their art.

Several works of Jean Pucelle are preserved. A hundred years after the death of this clever artist his name was not forgotten; which is surprising at a period when, as we have pointed out, the idea of the qualities which make an artist was not yet formed. A hundred years after the death of the painter, people still spoke in praise of "A little Hours of Our Lady, called the *Heures de Pucelle*, illuminated in black and white, for the use of preachers." This delightful volume, commissioned by Charles the Fair for his third wife, Jeanne d'Evreux, enriched by the master with exquisite cameos and completed in 1327, is now the property of the Baroness Adolphe de Rothschild. To Pucelle we owe also the Breviary of Belleville (Bibliothèque Nationale MS. latin 10483) and the Bible written by Robert of Billyng (Bibliothèque Nationale MS. latin 11935).

These are doubtless the most characteristic works produced by the miniaturists; for the wonderful pictures on parchment of the fifteenth century, those of Foucquet, of the brothers Male-wel (Pol, Hermann, and Jannequin of Limbourg), those of Bourdichon, no longer know the art of ornamenting the margins, the letters, the pages of a book; they are little pictures which are not of the body of the volume and can be detached from it: a thing which has in fact happened to a great number of Foucquet's miniatures.

Moreover, Pucelle and his companions dominated the art of decorating books from the end of the thirteenth century to the end of the fourteenth. We have said that the reign of Philip Augustus had corresponded in the history of the miniature with the period of stained glass; the reign of Philip the Fair saw the beginnings of the decorative period which is to flourish up to the end of the fourteenth century. But the painters who will work for Charles V, those even who are to illustrate the manuscripts commissioned by his brother Duke Jean de Berry, not excepting Jacquemart de Hesdin himself, will descend from John Pucelle, the continuator, if not the pupil, of the miniaturist Honoré. For a century or more, it will seem impossible, we do not say only to do better, but even to do differently.

From the beginning of the fourteenth century, a number of painters from the North and East, Flemings, Limbourgians, Burgundians, come to settle in Paris. There are the workshops of repute; there live or sojourn the princes, the "rich men," those who give useful commissions. In the fourteenth century there are thus seen coming to Paris Peter of Brussels and John of Ghent. They learn there the principles of their art in the workshops of the rue Boutebrie; up to the time when, having become artists by their feeling so rich and full of savour for real life, they give the impulse to the great Flemish art of the fifteenth century.

While the Parisian miniaturists carried their art to perfection the Italians developed mural paintings, frescoes. We have seen how in France the tendencies of the Gothic style avoided, more and more, walls in order to obtain buildings more and more open to the day, screens pierced with immense bays in which the coloured light of the stained-glass windows was like a song. Painting no longer found space on the walls of the churches; while in Italy it assumed magnificent proportions under the brushes of the Giottos and the Cimabues. Moreover, the French of the Renaissance, drawing their art from the painting of the manuscripts, will do "small painting," at least as regards their delicate and minute character and their processes. They will be men like Foucquet, Jean Perréal, François Clouet, Corneille de Lyon, up to the invasion by the Italians, under Francis I, with the Primitives and the School of Fontainebleau; while, from the fourteenth century, and up to the blossoming of the Renaissance, the Italians will give themselves to that which one may agree to call—if it is a question of dimensions—great painting.

SOURCES.—Theophilus, *Schedula diversarum artium*, ed. L'Escalopier, 1843; Jean le Besgue, Bibl. Nat. MS. lat. 6741; Bartholomew de Glanville, *De proprietatibus rerum*, translated by Jehan Corbichon, *Le proprietaire des choses*, Lyons, undated; *Les métiers et corporations de la ville de Paris*, ed. R. de Lespinasse, 1896–97, 3 vols.

HISTORICAL WORKS.—Emeric David, *Histoire de la peinture au Moyen*

THE MINIATURES

Age, new ed., 1863 ; Paul Mantz, *La Peinture française du IXe à la fin du XVIe Siècle*, 1897 ; Lecoy de la Marche, *Les Manuscrits et la Miniature*, undated ; **J. H.** Middleton, *Illuminated Manuscripts in Classical and Mediæval Times*, Cambridge, 1892 ; Henry Martin, *Les miniaturistes français*, 1906 ; Henry Martin, *Les Peintres de mss et la miniature en France*, undated. We have drawn especially on these last two volumes.

CHAPTER XVI

TOWN ASSOCIATIONS AND TRADE ASSOCIATIONS

Trade corporations have their origin in the family. Hanses and Guilds. The Brotherhood of Valenciennes. The Eschevinages. The Patricians and the Commune. The Corporations. Etienne Boileau's Book of Trades. Strikes.

WE have just seen that the miniaturists were organized in trade associations.

Origin of the Trade Associations. These trade societies, which played so great a part in the history of feudal France, and whose statutes were put into writing during the reign of Saint Louis, do not go back to a very remote date. The oldest dated only from the second half of the twelfth century.

The corporations of artisans in the Middle Ages had their origin in the feudal lordship. Like all the institutions of the period, they sprang from the organization of the family.

We have seen the lord maintaining in his castle domestic artisans. Some castles prospered and became towns, in which the artisans became numerous in course of time. They were grouped into associations: such as the confraternity of St. Euchère, founded at St. Trond between 1034 and 1055. It is not yet a trade society; it is the artisans of a household who are grouped together regardless of their trade. They are associations of mutual help with subscriptions, called "fraternities." They have corporate property, an administration, and a dean (*decanus*). We have seen the towns formed by the agglomeration of a certain number of lordships. Each of these lordships had its domestic artisans. The towns grew and prospered, and one saw the artisans of different households joining together to make their work easy and render it perfect.

These artisans, grouped into associations of peace, of mutual

TOWN AND TRADE ASSOCIATIONS

help, of technical perfection, soon worked no longer for their master only, but for the customer who approached them. To their master, who remains their lord, they continue to render payments in kind or in manual work, dues, and services, but their workshop, which becomes at the same time their shop, is open to all comers. From the court of the castle or monastery, the artisans spread beyond into the town and suburbs, where they group themselves no longer as the artisans of the same lordship but as of the same trade. The corporation is formed.

On the other hand, the urban lords have become traders. The very rôle of protector or patron which the urban lord has to fill with regard to the working part of his household, leads him to occupy himself with the distribution of the articles which it manufactures, with the provision of materials required for its work; and he will do it the more energetically as he makes a profit by it. Thus is formed the urban patrician class, feudal in character like the rural patricians or feudal nobles properly so called. It is formed by a parallel movement with the working class: it has grown and prospered with and through it. A fact which scholars have remarked in the early part of the Middle Ages is thus explained, that the artisan first appears as a mere workman, using the materials furnished by his client. The weavers manufacture cloth with the wool which the wool drapers send them. In their respective trades, tailors, carpenters, and shoemakers do the same. And this is not astonishing when one remembers that in the beginning these artisans were " domestics."

But here are the Patricians also forming associations like the artisans. The hanses and guilds grouped the trading patricians, the heads of the city, while the corporations united the artisans. They were associations resembling each other in many ways, and in the beginning called by the same name, brotherhoods (*frairies*), fraternities.

Hanses and Guilds.

The seigniorial associations—by which we mean the patrician groups—are earlier in date than the associations of workmen. That is self-evident. These lords, growing rich on the work of their households, had the idea of forming associations to extend their enterprises, long before it was possible for the

337

THE MIDDLE AGES

artisans to group themselves in their turn. We have just seen that the oldest known groups of artisans go back to the second half of the twelfth century. Patrician associations, such as the Fraternity of Valenciennes, are known from the beginning of the twelfth century. This word alone, *frairie* (brotherhood), indicates the spirit of this association of merchants.

Take their charter, of which the following is the preamble:

"Brothers, we are images of God, for it says in *Genesis*: 'Let us make man to our image and likeness.' We are united in this idea, and we shall, with the help of God, be able to accomplish our work if brotherly love is spread among us; for through the love of our neighbour we attain to the love of God. Then, brothers, let not any discord be among us, according to the words of the Gospel: 'I give you a new commandment. Love one another, as I have loved you, and I shall know that you are my disciples because you love one another.'"

Several of the articles of the ordinance reveal the state of disorder into which the country was yet plunged. "If one of the brothers, *i.e.* one of the members of the corporation, go to the market without arms"—we must understand this to mean without his coat of mail and his bow—he is condemned, to the profit of the society, to a fine of twelve pennies. This military character of our merchants, the result of their feudal origin, will persist through long years. In the twelfth century, Jehan le Galois d'Aubepierre, in his fable of the *Pursefull of Sense*, will still speak of a merchant, the lord Reniers, who returns from the market at Troy, after accidents which have reduced him to a wretched condition. Behold him

> As badly dressed as a highwayman
> On foot, without shield or lance. . . .

M. Jourdain, in the thirteenth century, was clad in iron, like a knight.

But let us return to the Fraternity of Valenciennes.

The Brothers are not allowed to leave the town except several together, so that they may assist one another, under any circumstance, with advice, purse, and sword. A Brother is, for instance, obliged to contribute, in case of need, to the ransom of his comrade or his merchandise, if they have been captured. If the carriage of a Brother is broken through coming across an obstacle, or if his horses fall from accident or fatigue, his comrade is obliged to assist him according to his ability. If one of the comrades has finished his business in a place, he ought, none the less, prolong his sojourn for twenty-four hours, in company with a Brother who shall ask him to do so. If it happened that a member of the society so far forgot himself as to strike or injure another member, he was condemned to a fine or even dismissed from the Fraternity. No one was admitted into the " Charity "—another designation used to describe the Society—if he had a feeling of hatred against one of the members. The fines were paid, sometimes in money, sometimes in hogsheads of wine, for the Brothers of Valenciennes were liberal drinkers. The most curious articles of the charter are even devoted to the gatherings in which the Brothers of the Exchange—the Exchange of commerce —met together for the purpose of drinking. Let us picture to ourselves these merchants of the eleventh century seated round great tables of rough wood in the premises of the Fraternity. Each has before him a large pot of wine. " On the day when the Brothers drink together," says Article IV, " they will give wine to the poor, in quantity equal to one-tenth of what they themselves shall have drunk." No one shall have arms, or bring young men or children, " so that the Brothers may be together in peace and holy religion without disturbance." We must not be shocked by the word " religion " applied to the libations of these merchants : the meeting was opened with prayers, and a very serious deportment was *de rigueur*. " When the Brothers drink together no one must go in or out singing ; each Brother should speak only to the one sitting next him, and if he speak to another he must pay a fine of four pennies."

If a Brother comes to die, his comrades watch the body during the night, and if he has wished to be buried outside the town they accompany the bier during three days and three nights.

Some articles, added to the charter, enable us to judge of the prosperity which the Fraternity will have reached a century later.

THE MIDDLE AGES

The charters of Valenciennes are not the only ones of this time which have come down to us. Several others have been preserved, notably those of St. Omer and those of Tournai.

For many years these patricians remained closely united with the artisans who composed their households and whose work they directed, protected, and encouraged. **Eschevinages.** It was with their support that they carried through the communal revolution of which we have spoken, and after having crushed or diminished the authority of the principal suzerain of the town, duke or count, bishop or abbot, they formed the eschevinages or municipal governments. They were governments which kept, in the beginning, their feudal character: the *échevins* (sheriffs) are above all judges and soldiers.

These *échevins*, who do not appear before the end of the eleventh century, are at this period the representatives of the patrician families; they are the heads of these families. By forming a group they become the government of the city. The communal revolution freed the patrician families from the immediate authority exercised by the principal lord. They deprived him especially of his right of administering justice. But from this day, too, these various families entered into a struggle against one another. Intestine quarrels became the scourge of the mediæval towns in the period following the communal revolution. There is no patrician family which, relying on its household of artisans and labourers, does not aim at predominance in the city and is not jealous of rival families. Previously the lord had put a vigorous curb on these struggles. He is no longer there, or at least he has lost the greater part of his power. Hence the necessity to guard, by means of an organization of entire peace and fraternity, against conflicts which threatened to recur constantly. Such was the origin of those first urban organizations of which we have just spoken, of the fraternity guilds and hanses, which are to become the municipal organization itself. Moreover, like the hanses and the merchant organizations the urban organizations are called "associations of peace." They replace the action of the feudal lord of which they have been deprived. These guilds of merchants occupy themselves with the repair and improve-

TOWN AND TRADE ASSOCIATIONS

ment of the fortifications of the town, with putting a guard in the watch tower and supporting a watchman.

Hoc est carta pacis et concordie et consulatus—This is the charter of the peace of concord and the consulate (Eschevinage)—we read in the municipal charter of Avignon.

Moreover, the eschevinage is sometimes identical with the guild itself. In some towns only the members of the guild or the hanse can belong to it.

At first, in the twelfth century, the authority of the *Magistrat* (the municipal corporation), like that of the feudal lord, is exclusively judicial and military. Later the *échevins* unite with these financial activities. We must, too, distinguish carefully between the eschevinages founded before the middle of the twelfth century and those created later. The first are essentially feudal organs. After 1150, with the development of the commercial movement, appear economic preoccupations.

From the *Magistrat*—as the eschevinal college is called—the people of the artisan class, those who work with their hands, the men " with blue nails," are excluded. The people are equally excluded who hawk through the town edible commodities or articles of clothing, small dealers with baskets, those who pursue small trade within a small space.

The *échevins*, called in many towns " the peers " (*pairs*), are recruited by the method of co-optation. There is no question of popular election. At Rouen the name of " peers " was given to the members of a college of a hundred patricians who chose the *échevins*. The consuls of Narbonne themselves nominated their successors. At Poitiers, the town corporation is formed by the Confraternity of St. Hilary, an association of a hundred members, the Patriciate.

At first, and up to the middle of the twelfth century, the eschevinages had no place specially devoted to their meetings. Their gatherings generally took place in the hall of the merchants, or in the room in which the merchant guild discusses its affairs. To administer justice our *échevins* sit in the open air. Saint Louis, in the shade of the oaks of Vincennes, or on the lawns of the Jardin de Paris, was not making any innovation. To administer justice the *échevins* establish themselves in the middle of cross-roads or in the square before the church. But their deliberations on matters of communal interest, which were the same, in their estimation, as the commercial interests of their guild, are carried on behind closed doors. At the end of the twelfth century, the peers of Senlis condemn to a fine a burgess who had boasted that he knew what passed at their meetings.

This anecdote indicates the division which had been produced between the Patricians and the People. After having made use of the artisans and the agricultural workers of their households, to deliver themselves from the seigniorial authority, the patricians organized in communes, gave a great impulse to their industrial or commercial enterprises, and set themselves to exploit their subordinates, by extracting from them the greater part of the profits which might result from them. The towns became divided into two classes—the patricians on one side, composed of those whom the Latin texts describe under the name *majores*, and on the other the popular class, composed of those described in the Latin texts as *minores*, the working class, as we should say now.

The terms of the charters which exclude the workers from the magistracy (*Magistrat*) indicate the scorn professed for them by the patricians. Look at the charter of Damme (1241) which rejects from the eschevinage, in terms far from flattering to the artisans, "robbers, coiners, and those who have not refrained from all manual work for a year and have not acquired the hanse of London," *i.e.* have not become members, by paying a large sum, of the patrician guild.

In the towns in which admission to the *Magistrat* was not forbidden by a formal text, it was actually made impossible for them. Beaumanoir explains this with his usual precision: " We see several good towns in which neither the poor nor the middle class have any part in the administration of the town, as have all the rich because they are feared by the commune on account of their wealth or their lineage. So it comes about that some are dean, mayor, or sworn members or *recheveurs*, and the next year they create them from their brothers, their nephews, or their near relatives, so that in ten or twelve years all the rich people have their part in the administration of the good towns. . . ."

TOWN AND TRADE ASSOCIATIONS

The customs, which the patricians, at the head of the eschevinage, had imposed on the large towns, were even injurious to the honour of the working people. There were circumstances in which a patrician could, with impunity, strike an artisan. An insult was punished by a fine heavier in proportion as it was addressed to a man in a high position. In certain towns the abduction of a maiden of the patrician class was punished by a very heavy fine; while a girl of the people could be kidnapped with impunity.

Thus, not finding in their patrons the protectors under whom their industry had taken its rise, the artisans came to organize themselves in trade societies. We have **The Trade Societies.** said that the first corporations of workmen included all the artisans of the same household, without distinction of trade; they were, at first, only associations of protection and mutual assistance. But soon the organization became specialized, and the different corporations each included the artisans of a particular trade. There were formed corporations of weavers, of fullers, of butchers, of carpenters, of stone-cutters . . . and for some time yet they were only associations for mutual protection; but which transformed themselves insensibly into technical associations for the perfectioning of the craft and the maintenance of the manufacturing traditions which had been developed. They became professional corporations.

We have a great deal of information about the trade societies of the twelfth and thirteenth centuries, and these have given rise to numerous studies. The corporations of Paris are familiar to us through an admirable work, the Book of Trades by Etienne Boileau, drawn up in the reign of Saint Louis through the industry of the famous Provost of Paris who bore this name.

Etienne Boileau collected the statutes of the corporations of Paris in order to fix the customs of the workers for fear they should come to be changed. It is unnecessary to add that the Provost introduced nothing into them on his personal initiative. He has simply left us a compilation of the uses and customs which the various trades of Paris had spontaneously imposed on themselves since the twelfth century. Etienne

THE MIDDLE AGES

Boileau wrote from the dictation of members of the crafts.

In the middle of the twelfth century Jean de Garlande occupied himself with the subject of industry in Paris. We owe to him a list of the merchants and manufacturers, as well as of the principal articles exposed in their "shops"; but the trade associations were not yet formed. On the contrary, here they are constituted during the reign of Saint Louis, and how perfectly! How one realizes, in listening to the depositions before Etienne Boileau of these dyers and weavers, these fullers and makers of saddles, these brewers of beer and hucksters, the great part which this population of workmen played in history, and the perfection in which it kept, for so many centuries, the products of its labour.

The dominant preoccupation, common to the statutes of the most diverse corporations, is to assure the fairness of the manufacture and the excellence of the merchandise sold. In the introduction placed at the head of the collection the Provost declares that he had gathered together this body of customs because it happened that there had been sold to foreigners (*as estranges*) "some things which were not as good and honest as they should have been."

In the first, to be admitted master the apprentice should give proof before the committee of the corporation of the knowledge and skill required. The workers in silk express themselves as follows: "Whoever wishes to pursue the said trade as a master, it will be necessary for him to know how to do all the processes himself, without advice or help from any one else, and he shall for this purpose be examined by the guardians of the craft." There is no question yet at this period of the masterpiece unless it is in the statutes of the makers of saddles.

Then the committee exercised the strictest watch to ensure the use of primary materials which were beyond reproach. A number of crafts prescribed working on the street front, *i.e.* in a workshop giving on the road, in sight of the passers-by. The statutes of the saddlers only authorize the entire completion of a saddle when it is to be sold so that the client may see the solidity of the work, before the ornamentation is pro-

TOWN AND TRADE ASSOCIATIONS

ceeded with, the painting and varnishing which could hide defects. The same rule occurs in other trades; with the makers of images, for instance, who are bound to show their statue in a single block before it is covered with colours. A second piece would be authorized for the crown of the Virgin or saints.

We read in the statutes of the cooks :

"No one should cook geese, beef, or mutton if these meats are not of good quality and with good marrow. No one should keep for longer than three days cooked meats which are not salted. Sausages must not be made except from good pork." As to puddings made with blood, their sale is prohibited, as they are " dangerous food."

Edible commodities found to be bad in the shops are condemned to be burnt, *i.e.* to be thrown into the fire, and a fine is inflicted on the seller. The makers of tallow candles declare in this connection in touching terms : " For the false manufacture of tallow candles is too harmful to poor and rich and too shameful." The goldsmiths demand that the gold used shall be of the standard of Paris, adding proudly that, " Paris gold surpasses all the golds of the world."

Next to the quality of the manufacture, that which the statutes of the corporations seek to safeguard most carefully is the place in the sun of every industrious and honest workman. It did not seem just to our forefathers that a manufacturer, because he was more skilful or more fortunate or more farseeing than his neighbour, should have the right to expand unduly in stifling and destroying him. Here is the energetic defence of the interests of small and moderate businesses, the protection of the humble against being crushed by the great workshops. A master was not authorized to direct several workshops, or, in his own, to employ more than a fixed number of apprentices. The rules provided that an article should be made and sold by the same master, and further, he was forbidden to have a stall and a hawker at the same time. If he kept a hawker he could have one only, and some trades went so far as to require that this hawker should be no other than the master himself, or his wife.

It was forbidden to corrupt the " valets," that is to say, the workers; forbidden even to entice by tricks of advertisement the clients of one's neighbour; forbidden to the weavers, dyers, and fullers to plot together to influence the price of raw materials, or to monopolize supplies and prevent every one having work according to their means.

In some towns the rules go even further. "If some one," says one of them, "has made a purchase at Montpelier, and an inhabitant of Montpelier was present at the sale, he has the right to take a part of the purchase, and the seller is bound to deliver a part of it to him. Only in cases when the purchaser has made a purchase for his own personal use or for that of his family shall he not be bound to give up a part of it."

It was forbidden for several merchants to join together to ruin a competitor, or to come to an understanding together so as to sell articles at a lower price. These manœuvres, which lead nowadays to "trusts," were stigmatized under the name of "alliances."

Salesmen, say the rules, should not buy of any merchants freights or cargoes of eggs or cheeses to be delivered in a future journey or at any deferred period. It was the destruction of sale on account, beginning with speculation in merchandise. And these rules of the thirteenth century justify their prescription with the same amazing clear-sightedness. "For the rich merchants would monopolize all the edibles and the poorer could not reserve anything for themselves, and the rich could sell all again as dearly as they pleased."

And the trades were not only careful to raise a barrier against the subjection of the workshops by the big manufactories, but above all to put an obstacle in the way of the harm which speculation works on productive labour. The solidity and stability of industrial labour being thus guaranteed, the artisans were anxious to secure its transmission in the bosom of each family. Some trade associations have strict rules to attain this end. "No one ought to have the trade of a weaver," say the weavers, "unless he is the son of a master. It is true that in Paris, as in Flanders, the weavers formed a fraternity proud of its power, a kind of aristocratic trade among the others. In all the corporations the sons and relatives of masters were favoured, if only by the free gift of apprenticeship and right to become a master. Moreover, a master could not have in his workshop more than one " strange " apprentice ; the others, children or relatives, were the private apprentices.

Our artisans of the twelfth and thirteenth centuries had fully realized the importance of apprenticeship. The book of Etienne Boileau treats of it with the greatest care. It has been truly said that the apprentices were the spoilt children of the community. The rules enjoin on the masters to watch carefully over the education of the apprentice. Some, in forbidding more than one apprentice to the master, point out that the instruction of a single pupil suffices to absorb his attention. The time of the apprenticeship should be completed. It is a long time : four, six, or eight years. The master who provokes the departure of an apprentice is liable to a fine ; but if it happen that an apprentice deserts his workshop, the master must await his return for a year and a month before replacing him. These good artisans, so severe in all that pertains to morality, are full of indulgence for the youthful pranks of the apprentices, for their " folly," say the texts, and their " jollity."

These were rules which were observed with the more rigorous care, inasmuch as they were the work, not of a legislative power, but of the artisans themselves.

The masters or patrons are the industrial leaders of the period ; the apprentices are their pupils and successors : they form the permanent and productive element in the middle classes. Beneath them, and under their direction, lives that which we call to-day the working class, those whom the statutes describe as the *valets*, or the *sergents*, or the *alloués*. Workmen, apprentices, and masters live in common, work together, and break bread at the same table. It is the intimate union of the factory and the fireside, this latter spreading its beneficent warmth over the workshop. The master exerts over his workman not only a technical but also a moral patronage. The workers espouse the cause of their patron ; they group themselves round him for his defence. Moreover, we shall see the working class as a whole standing close round the heads of the workshops in the struggle in which they are to engage with the Patricians. When the communal militias march out of the town, the worker marches armed beside his master. It

THE MIDDLE AGES

is the paternal workshop, always animated, let us be clear on the subject, by the very spirit which produced feudalism.

The thrifty workman earns enough to establish himself in his turn. He can also attain to a mastership by marrying the widow or daughter of a master, a thing which frequently happened in the intimacy of a common life. The workmen, besides, form part of the corporation; they exercise a great influence in it owing to their numbers.

The number of hours of work is limited. We required nearly a century after the great Revolution to bring us back to that. The Parisian trades put into practice the " English week," which was, in the twelfth to the thirteenth century, the French week. From the French it passed to the English, who, in their spirit of tradition, preserved it. From England it has come back to France: as a stranger. Night work is forbidden. And we find always the same spirit of kindness. The work of upholsterers of highly polished surfaces was forbidden to women as too fatiguing.

Respect for women is one of the chief features of these customs; it is joined to the practice of a worthy and moral manner of life. Should the behaviour of a workman cause scandal he is dismissed from the trade; or even exiled from the town until he has improved. The master fuller who keeps a workman of bad life is condemned to a fine. The beer-makers —or, as we should say, the brewers—impose a fine of twenty sous for bad manufacture or—and this is an admirable feature— on the master who permits the sale of his beer in bad places.

The corporations have chests for assistance replenished by the fines. They are destined for the help of old members of the trade who have fallen into destitution. There is a similar care for orphans. " The masters of the corporation shall have them taught a trade and provide them with all things."

When a working tailor spoils a piece of stuff, the committee imposes on him as a penalty a day's work at mending the garments of the poor. The trades connected with food make frequent distributions to the necessitous. Article X of the goldsmiths' statutes says that the corporation shall cause to be opened, on each Sunday and Feast day, the shop of one goldsmith (the others remaining shut); and the profits of the

TOWN AND TRADE ASSOCIATIONS

sales in this shop on this day were used to prepare a fine repast on Easter Sunday for the poor of the Hôtel-Dieu (hospital), in order that on this great Feast even the poor should have feasting and merriment.

The observation of these regulations was rendered easier by the fact that the various corporations remained grouped each in one of the quarters of the town. Mortar was made in the rue de la Mortellerie; the leather dressers (*mégissiers*) were established on the quay of the Mégisserie, and the goldsmiths on the Goldsmiths' (*Orfèvres*) Quay. The saddlers and the stirrup makers occupied a part of the rue St. Denis, called the rue de la Sellerie. We have already shown the painters in miniature near by in the rue Erembourc-de-Brie, which was often called the "Street of the Illuminators." To buy haberdashery the good wives betook themselves to the rue Trousse-Vache; and the squires and sergeants, to get bows, arrows, and weapons, stopped at the stalls which surrounded the porte St. Ladre. The counters of the money-changers ran along the paths of the Grand-Pont (great bridge), later known as the Pont-au-Change, while the important corporation of weavers predominated in the Quarter of the Temple, rue Vieille-du-Tempe, rue Bourg-Thibout, rue de la Courtille-Barbette, rue des Rosiers, rue des Escouffes, rue des Blancs-Manteaux. The dealers in old clothes and furniture gave its picturesque aspect to the parish of St. Merry. During the weeks of Lent, when the church bells rang for Compline, the shops were closed.

To expose the perfection of the customs which the artificers of the Middle Ages had succeeded in giving themselves, there is for that matter no need to shake off the dust of parchments. Do not those incomparable edifices, the pride of our public squares, which no contemporary nation could rival, preserve the glorious testimony of this prosperity?

The craftsman loved his labour because the work produced was indeed his own work. Division of labour was not known. Let us take a candlestick or a pair of andirons in copper. To-day they pass from the hands of the founder into those of the moulder, then into those of the chaser, afterwards to the burnisher, and finally into the hands of the gilder. In the thirteenth century the manufactured article never left the one workshop.

THE MIDDLE AGES

The net cost was indeed higher; but the finish, the solidity, the artistic character of the manufactured article, have disappeared with the satisfaction which the artisan felt in producing a work all his own, to which he applied, cordially, all his skill.

It is not that there were not then as in every epoch some lazy folk. Many a comrade preferred the tavern to the workshop:

> At terce (9 a.m.) he says that it is Nones (3 p.m.),
> And at Nones that it is night,
> And as soon as he can off he goes.
> He does not care so long as he is paid
> And can eat and drink
> In the tavern. . . .
>
> (*Le Besart de Dieu*, v. 1134.)

Rutebeuf said:

> He wishes to be well paid
> And to do little. . . .

Strikes. It is not either that strikes did not take place, with restraint of blacklegs and peaceful picketing. Beaumanoir devotes these oft-quoted lines to these:

"It is an alliance against the common good, when any sort of people agree or pledge themselves not to work at so low a wage as before, and thus cause their wages to be increased by their power, and agree among themselves that they will not work for less, and bring injuries and threats to bear on the comrades who will not join their alliance (the *chasse aux jaunes*).

Beaumanoir indicates the inconveniences of strikes from his point of view: "And thus if one allowed them it would be against the general good, and there would never be profitable sale of goods, for those of each trade would take bigger salaries than would be reasonable, and the community cannot allow work to stop." The legist who was the bailiff of Philip the Fair recommended repressive measures. "And for this reason, as soon as such alliances come to the knowledge of the sovereign or other lords, they ought to lay hands on them and keep them close prisoners for a lengthy period. And when they have had a long term of punishment in prison, a fine of 60 sous (1200 francs now) should be levied on each of them."

TOWN AND TRADE ASSOCIATIONS

These lines are inspired by events which must certainly have occurred more than once; but the artisans, as a rule, remained attached to their patrons in the struggle in which these latter were about to engage with the urban patricians: the principal cause of the great conflicts which are to mark the reign of Philip the Fair.

SOURCES.—G. Fagniez, *Documents relatifs à l'histoire du commerce et de l'industrie en France*, 1898–1900, 2 vols.; *Le livre des métiers d'Etienne Boileau*, Coll. de l'hist. gen. de Paris, 1879; *Les métiers et corporations de la Ville de Paris*, ed. R. de Lespinasse, same collection, 1886–97, 3 vols.; *Les Métiers de Blois*, ed. Alf. Bourgeois, 1892–97, 2 vols.; Beaumanoir, *Coutumes du Beauvaisis*, ed. Salmon, 1899–1900, 2 vols.

HISTORICAL WORKS.—Jacques Flach, *Les Origines de l'ancienne France*, 1886–1917, 4 vols.; Levasseur, *Histoire des classes ouvrières en France*, 1857; G. Fagniez, *Etude sur l'industrie au XIIIe Siècle*, 1877; Et. Martin-Saint-Léon, *Histoire des corporations de métiers*, 1899; Ch. V. Langlois, *La Vie en France au moyen age*, 1908.

CHAPTER XVII

PHILIP THE FAIR

Portrait of Philip the Fair. Life at the French Court. Feudal robbery. Popular revolts. The Royal administration, bailiffs, and beadles. The first States-General. The Legists. The Appeals of Aquitaine. Sources of the difficulties with England. The depredations at sea between English and French. War between Philip IV and Edward I. Alliance between the King of England and the Count of Flanders. Defeat of the English at Beauregard and of the Flemish at Furnes (1297). Boniface VIII, his conflict with Philip the Fair. Guillaume de Nogaret. The rising of the Flemish communes, Peter Coninc and Guillaume de Juliers. The "Matins of Bruges" and the battle of Courtrai (1302). The Treaty of Paris (20th May 1303). The outrage of Anagni (7th September 1303). Death of Boniface VIII. Victory of Mons-en-Pevele (18th August 1304). Election of Clement V. Financial administration: Enguerrand de Marigny. Trial and condemnation of the Templars. Scandals at the French Court. Death of Philip the Fair. Philip the Catholic.

THE Crusade of Aragon ended in a check. After the death of Philip the Bold, on 5th October 1285 at Perpignan, the command of the army was assumed by his eldest son, then seventeen years of age. From the first moment he was opposed to this distant and fanciful expedition beyond the Pyrenees. After he had carried out the obsequies of his father in the cathedral of Narbonne, Philip the Fair returned to Paris.

The Reign of the Devil.

King Philip IV, called already by his contemporaries Philip the Fair, was a fine young man with broad shoulders and robust limbs. When the Court met he stood a head above the assembly, in this recalling his grandfather; but while Saint Louis was slender and thin, the vigour of his grandson corresponded to his great stature. If he pressed with his clenched fists on the shoulders of two men-at-arms he made them bend to the ground. " His thighs and legs were so long," wrote the Templar of Tyre, " that his feet were only a palm's distance from the ground when he rode." He carried himself very erect and with a native majesty. " No one seeing him among others," notes a contemporary, " would have required to ask which was the King." Blond ringlets framed a face of striking whiteness. He had large blue eyes, blue like steel. Their expression was hard and haughty. The majesty of his look overawed those who came before him. The Bishop of Pamiers, Bernard Saisset, lost his tongue and avenged himself by a boutade :

" Our King," said he, " resembles the horn-owl, the finest of birds and yet the most useless. He is the finest man in the world ; but he only knows how to look at people fixedly without speaking."

All that one learned about the young monarch was in keeping with his grave and dignified exterior. An Italian speaks of his " venerable youth." His morals were beyond reproach though perhaps a little ruthless : one of his first acts was to expel women from the Court.

Philip the Fair had an austere piety. Every morning he assisted at Mass ; twice a week he kept rigorous fast ; he wore a hair shirt next his skin ; he made his confessor give him the discipline. Even his adversaries did not represent him otherwise. They would have said with Guillaume de Nogaret :

" He is chaste, humble, modest in bearing and speech. He is never angry. He hates no one ; he is jealous of none ; full of grace and charity ; pious, merciful ; pursuing at all times truth and justice. Detraction finds no place in his mouth. He is fervent in his faith, religious in his life. He builds basilicas and practises works of piety. . . . God works miracles through his hands."

He raised some sumptuous piles, such as the Palais de Justice, whose towers are reflected in the waters of the Seine. When it was a matter of doing honour to the House of France, he displayed a dazzling splendour ; but his daily life was of an extreme simplicity. At his table only three dishes were served. On fast days four dishes were allowed. Philip the

THE MIDDLE AGES

Fair permitted only wines gathered in his vineyards, and these were not situated in Champagne, Burgundy, or Bordeaux. At the King's table, however, only water coloured with wine was drunk. Dessert was of fruits grown in the royal orchards; in Lent, of nuts, figs, and dried raisins.

His dress was as simple as his table. With his family his ministers and his officers he led a familiar existence, and he was equally familiar with his subjects. The Florentine Barbarino expressed his surprise to see this terrible Philip the Fair, who "cast his shadow over the whole of Christendom" (Dante), return the greeting of three roysterers of the lowest class, and allowing himself to be detained by them at the corner of a street in order to hear their complaints. The King stood upright with his feet in the mud; he wore a white head-dress; the three soldiers spoke to him with their caps in their hands. And Barbarino does not omit to note the difference between these royal customs and the haughtiness of the Florentine lords.

His one distraction was the chase. He had at Fontainebleu a pack of forty-two harriers. Knowing from this how to make themselves agreeable to him, his subjects brought him vultures and falcons.

Unlike his father, who was no scholar, Philip the Fair had received through the care of his tutor the chaplain, Guillaume d'Ercuis, a good education. He understood Latin and retained his taste for study.

Such was the prince of whom the famous historians Michelet and Renan have written: "One would readily say that his reign is the reign of a devil."

Under Saint Louis feudal society had reached its highest development—the "golden age," the feudal lords will call it fifty years later; but already there were premonitions of decay.

Thanks to the protection which the lords had assured to labour in the country and the organization that the patricians had given to the towns, agriculture had prospered, industry was born, commerce had developed; a relative peace reigned in the land. By very reason of this progress, of which the lords and patricians had been the chief agents, their rôle became useless, though they continued to receive the rights and enjoy the privileges which it had assured them when it had been necessary.

PHILIP THE FAIR

One saw the feudal barons continuing to levy their dues on the countryside and even in the towns, rights of justice, rent and tithe, toll and market dues, rights of relief and exchange, *meilleur catel, champart, corvée,* and *banalités.* Champart involved the paying to the feudal lord of a share in the harvest; corvée meant the furnishing of a number of days' labour. The crenellated walls of the castle keep, which, in the formative period of feudalism, had offered their protection to the countryman who had assisted in their construction, no longer defended anything but an unjustifiable exploitation, and the peasant dreamed only of demolishing them.

The trader who transported his merchandise from one part of the country to another came into collision with similar obstacles. At road-crossings, in the passage of bridges, at fords, at the raising of locks, in entering canals, on the fringe of the woods, at each corner, turning, or cross-roads, he saw appear the agents of some local fisc, flanked by men-at-arms who cast themselves upon his baggage like birds of prey and only loosed their hold when they had extorted ransom.

The writers of the thirteenth century, in particular Jean de Meun, the author of the *Roman de la Rose,* which Philip the Fair read frequently, interpreted the popular passions.

Of the first ages, Jean de Meun writes :

> Rich were all equally,
> And they loved each other loyally,
> The simple folk of good life :
> Then was love without seigniory.

He makes the villeins, speaking of the nobles, say :

> We are men as they,
> Members have we as they,
> We have as great heart as they.

Moreover, continues the poet, what is the virtue of this nobility which exploits the commonalty ?

> It is too bereft of morals,
> And weaned from its ancestors
> Who bore themselves nobly.
> They are the offspring cast-off,
> Counterfeit and badly sprung,
> And in them is no lineage.

THE MIDDLE AGES

Let us open the doctrinal of Jean de Weert : " At the end of the thirteenth century, entire provinces were destroyed by the rivalries of noble families, the lords of the country taking one side or another, and fighting on the back of Jacques Bonhomme. A man of the people has no longer any security for his possessions. From his keep poised on the neighbouring ' motte,' like a bird of prey of which he bears the name, the ' hobereau ' pounces upon his neighbours ; those who possess rich houses are carried off to the battlemented castles and thrown into some dungeon ; they are there put to torture until they have given up some part of their goods. The merchants are robbed ; or else the nobles go into partnership with the brigands, to whom they give shelter in their keeps in order to share with them the spoil of their victories. Other of the lords hire themselves out as mercenaries. They take no interest in the cause they espouse : their interest is engaged in slaughter and pillage as a means of improving their future. Such are the nobles," concludes Jean de Weert. " What hast thou left me, dear husband ? " cries the widow of the lord of La Roche-Guyon. " Poverty reigns in thy dwelling ; thou hast abstained from all brigandage on thy neighbours and on the poor."

In the towns the situation is similar. The patriciate is itself *déclassé*. The absorption of the municipal liberties by the royal power is the theme of the lamentations of modern historians. But what had these municipal liberties become ? The population of the towns was divided into two classes : the patricians and the commonalty. The patricians have all the privileges—privileges which in their origin had been justified by the part played by them in the formation, development, and defence of the city, but which for some years now had no longer any justification. Beaumanoir thus describes the situation : " The poor and the middle class had none of the offices of the town ; the rich held them all. These were skilful in evading all control, and it was in vain that any one brought an accusation of fraud or imposition against them, however well founded. And the poor could not endure them ; but they knew not the proper way to secure their rights except to attack them."

As the patricians feared riots, they forbade the artisans to gather together more than seven at a time, to make collections among themselves, or, as the documents say, to club together (*boursiller*). Those who broke these regulations were punished with the utmost severity, were driven from the town, and had their eyes put out.

These precautions did not prevent revolts. At Puy, in 1296, the people pursued their enemies into the church, where the latter succeeded in barricading themselves. The people pulled off the roof, penetrated the edifice, and after piercing the eyes of the tax collectors whom they found there, the artisans threw them from the top of the building on to the pavement. In 1279, in order to suppress a popular rising at Provins, so many of the common people were hung that there were no more left in the town. The following year, at Arras, the trades corporations walked the streets, bearing their banners. The workmen cried, " Death to the *échevins* and rich men." Some of the mutineers had their heads cut off, and the excitement died down. Then a number of the rioters were dragged through the street naked and panting, their heads bumped on the paving-stones, and the poor wretches at the point of death. Others were hung.

A short time afterwards the popular party took its revenge. They seized the government of the town. The patricians had to flee. The great poet Adam de la Halle, who took their part, followed them into exile. It was on this occasion that he wrote his famous *congé* which perhaps inspired the " testament " of Villon :

> Arras, Arras, town of pleasure;
> And of hatred and of calumny,
> Which used to be so noble. . . .

A charming motet of the same Adam de la Halle shows the " good company " of the town :

> Leaving friends, houses, and armour,
> Fleeing by twos and threes,
> Living in a foreign land. . . .

At Douai the same year, the working class rose against the traders. Twelve aldermen were killed. On 15th November the riot was suppressed with bloodshed.

These popular movements were repeated at Châlons, Rouen, Ypres, Bruges, Lille, Alby, Cahors, Bordeaux, and Tournai.

THE MIDDLE AGES

The clergy went through a similar crisis. It was marked by the Council of Rouen in 1299.

France is in a state of disintegration. One after another the institutions which from the foundation to the full establishment hold up the edifice, crack and break down. But has the royal power in this crisis the means to hand for the accomplishment of its task? The feudal lords cry to him, " The King has no right to know or to see our lands."

Among the great feudal lords, some like the King of England, Duke of Aquitaine, are as powerful as the King of France; others like the Duke of Brittany and the Count of Flanders rule over provinces which live a foreign life. The people of Languedoc detest the French. From one frontier of the country to another there exist a multitude of usages, customs, traditions, jurisdictions, and privileges, contradictory and different, but tenacious, which the King cannot touch; the great mass of the nation is in rebellion against the ruling class, who do not the less continue to enjoy the resort to public action; everywhere disorganization, anarchy, the danger of seeing several provinces become independent or fall into foreign hands. Behold the reign of the devil of which Michelet and Renan speak.

In this vast country, bristling with local independencies, the King was represented by thirty-six officers, called in the North " baillis," and in the South " seneschals ":

The Legists. great personages who received from the royal treasury very high pay. From time to time the King sent them instructions. To carry out these instructions the *baillis* and seneschals had under their orders certain officers called " provosts " in the North, " beyles " in the South. These provosts were not chosen by the King; they leased a commission given to the highest bidder. They became proprietors of a commission thus acquired. Their functions consisted chiefly in receiving the produce of the royal domains and the judicial fines.

The provosts had under their orders sergeants, also called beadles (*bedeaux*). Sergeants and beadles were also proprietors of their commissions by right of purchase. In the exercise of their functions they carried a short round wand, decorated with fleurs-de-lis. These functions were at the same time those

PHILIP THE FAIR

of our *huissiers* and of our *gendarmes*. The people detested them. A popular preacher, Friar Nicholas de Biard, wrote: " As the wolf intrudes in order to carry off the sheep, so the beadles watch the occasion to steal that which does not belong to them."

These persons who, in number and function, were the firmest and in reality the sole support of the royal authority in the country, were not in favour with the King. In the eyes of the Court they appeared to be " an infinite multitude who devoured the substance of the people." In 1303 Philip the Fair ordered the number to be reduced by four-fifths.

Baillis, provosts, and beadles, these were all the King had at his disposal for the government of the country. A singular government ! The *baillis* held the travelling assizes ; but they had not the right to sit in the domains of the lords nor in those of abbeys, nor where the jurisdiction of the *échevins* ran. Where, then, could they sit ?

Baillis and provosts took the oath to be good and faithful servants of the King and . . . to respect local immunities, which were in essence an obstacle to the authority of the King. In 1303 they were equally enjoined to receive the orders of the King with respect . . . at least when the said orders were not contrary to the interests of the prince. As each of them held himself to be judge of this interest, they did as they would.

Moreover, let us consider the territory a *bailli* had to administer. Brittany belonged to the jurisdiction of the bailiwick of Tours. One can imagine what would be the action of a *bailli*, installed at Tours, in the neighbourhood of Rennes or of Quimper, given the state of communications the suzerainty of the Dukes of Brittany, the local immunities, the thousand and one independent jurisdictions, the occupations with which our *bailli* was overwhelmed, his ignorance with regard to what concerned the people who were under his administration.

And yet, in this realm, organized as we have seen, although the prince had not in his hands the necessary jurisdictions to make his authority valid, this authority was the only force that could sustain the crumbling society, preserve the union of the provinces, reconcile the warring classes.

It is one of the arresting moments of French history. The

THE MIDDLE AGES

King is without power and he is all-powerful; it would not be possible for him to impose his will in any place, and in every place this will is imposed. He has more than the complicated machinery of an administrative bureaucracy at his disposal: he has the belief in a King.

In the situation in which the country finds itself, the French feel instinctively that the person of the King alone can preserve the integrity of the country in face of the crisis which threatens it; they see that it alone can check the social strife, give progressively to the nation the community of law and custom that it needs; and they put into this sentiment an energy that will make it triumph over all obstacles.

One ought to add that Philip the Fair possessed in a remarkable degree the qualities useful to a French King at this time.

He feels that his power lies in the sentiment which binds him to his people, and he makes his government the government of the appeal to the people. Philip the Fair never took an important step, never went through any formidable crisis, never engaged in any enterprise involving grave consequences, without approaching the nation, without taking its advice, without laying before it his line of conduct, without striving to justify himself in its eyes. There were popular assemblies, travelling missions, meetings in the garden of the palace, letters patent spread abroad everywhere. There is mutual confidence and devotion; the people are attached to the King and vow him a blind fidelity.

In critical circumstances Philip the Fair calls together assemblies in which scholars have discerned the first attempts at States-General. His subjects sent there representatives. Is it to give their opinion there, to expound their interests, to give advice or counsel? Consult the powers given by the electors to their deputies. Some are deputed "to hear what the King shall say"; others "to approve what the King wishes"; and others "to carry out the King's pleasure." Nothing is more characteristic.

This faith in the monarchy had not only innumerable faithful adherents in all classes of the Nation: it had its fanatics.

The French were then seen becoming wild partisans of the

royal authority and of its extension. Five centuries later a similar movement will break out, produced by similar causes and leading to similar results. The "Jacobins" will be fanatics of "liberty," which meant for them "administrative concentration," as their precursors the "Royalists"—the word comes from the thirteenth century—will be fanatics of the throne. These Royalists are to produce the famous "legists" and the class, which so rapidly extended, "the knights of the King."

Side by side with the feudal nobility produced by the progressive development of the family, there was created, after three centuries, an administrative nobility. This latter drew its title from the royal authority which was to reorganize the nation. One of the most illustrious of these "knights of the King," Guillaume de Nogaret, thus defines them :

"They are not nobles, but knights, knights of the King, since the King has accepted them for his men, and from this comes their honour and dignity, and they are called 'knights of the King.' There are an infinite number of them in the realm of France."

They are men of a new class. They possess a knowledge of the law ; they have the passion for the royal power ; they have studied Roman history and dream of a universal monarchy like that held by the Cæsars. In them is the sentiment of their country, which they wish to see mighty and respected ; they have the vision of the old frontiers of Gaul, which their efforts will help to reconquer. It is no longer the power of their family which makes their force, nor the might of their sword ; it is their personal intelligence, their devotion to the royal power. They are the true creators of the modern State. And since the State is then concentrated in the Court of the King, they are directed by a dominant idea, which—like the idea in the brain of the Jacobins of 1793 of an administrative centralized France—becomes in them a fixed idea : the extension of the rights of the King.

To understand the work of the legists is to justify it. The extension of the rights of the King was, at this epoch, the one means of organizing—that is to say, of pacifying and saving the country. And with what passion were they transported against everything which could form an obstacle to the realization of their dream of the grandeur and unity of their country. Do not let us lose sight of the Jacobins of 1793. These are the same men, the same characters, following the same end by the same means: the destruction of local authorities and immunities—what the men of 1793 called "federalism"—and foreign conquests. "The legists," writes Renan, "set up this *noblesse de robe* whose first act was to establish the omnipotence of the King to weaken the power of the Church, and whose final act was the Revolution."

Philip chose these legists, following the counsel of Gilles de Rome, from the middle class. He confined the seigniorial nobility to the service of the Court and the army. Some members of this nobility he made high personages bearing on their dress picturesque armorial bearings; but beside them "the little people of the Council of the King" had in their hands the direction of the State.

From the first day there was established between the King and his legists an inviolable compact. They mutually understood each other and supported each other resolutely.

Among his legists Philip the Fair found men of the rarest gifts, and these he promoted to the highest offices of the State.

The most eminent was without doubt the Auvergnian Pierre Flote, who from a simple sergeant became Chancellor of France, the first layman in France to be invested with this dignity. He filled the most diverse missions—administrative, judicial, and diplomatic. His eloquence brought him a European reputation. It was he who pronounced in the name of the King, on 10th April 1302, in the assembly of the States, meeting in Notre Dame, the discourse against Boniface VIII which made so great a stir. We have unhappily only preserved a phrase of it; but we have the address delivered in London, 15th June 1298, before Edward I, when he speaks with such force and pride of what filled his soul, of the greatness of the King of France.

Boniface VIII held him in execration and pursued with sarcasms "this one-eyed man who was blind in spirit." He called him shortly "the little one-eyed advocate"; and it is this impression that posterity has preserved of him. Pierre

PHILIP THE FAIR

Flote had become a very high and powerful lord by rank, character, and fortune. He was followed by a princely train. His daughter was married to the Constable of France, Gaucher de Châtillon. He was himself a tried soldier. He saved Lille at the beginning of the campaign of 1302 by throwing himself, at the opportune moment, with a body of troops into the fortress, and fell under the walls of Courtrai, arms in hand, in the battle of the Golden Spurs. Moreover, if the commander of the French Army, the Count of Artois, had given heed to the counsels which Flote gave him before the action, the battle would not have been lost.

Round Pierre Flote were other legists to whom the King confided the most varied functions, above all those of " inquisitor-reformers."

These inquisitor-reformers of Philip the Fair, chosen from among the knights and clerks of the King, were numbered in hundreds and the missions with which they were charged in thousands. They are the successors of the famous inquisitors of Saint Louis; but while the mission of these was confined to rendering justice of appeal, the inquisitor-reformers of Philip the Fair not only hear the appeals which the inhabitants made from the sentence given by the local judges, but occupy themselves with the general organization of the realm, restore corrupt customs to the state in which they existed " in the time of the good King Louis," care for the maintenance of bridges and roads, and, above all, guard with a vigilant eye the rights of the King. Moreover, their rôle included the stopping of the usurpations of the clergy, seeing that the abbeys pay the mortmain taxes, enforcing the collection of impositions, and preventing the nobles trampling on the people. The knight, Hugh de la Celle, was sent to Poitou, where he remained four years. His mission was to put an end promptly " without any formal process," writes the King, " to armed attacks, and to murders which desolate the country and to the usurpations of royal officials." And this last trait ought not to surprise us when we think of the character of these officials, proprietors of a commission which they have bought and for which they naturally seek to secure the greatest possible return. " In order to dissuade the subjects from denouncing their crimes,"

THE MIDDLE AGES

writes the King himself, " our officials state that, if they are suspended from their offices, they will quickly be replaced; they say that the numerous inquests of which they have been formerly made the subject came to nothing, and that those which are made in the future will not be any more formidable. Some threaten the complainants, others are clever enough to obtain from our relatives and friends letters to cover up their offences; others again purchase the silence of their victims." Thus is the tableau complete.

The King turned his attention more particularly to the provinces of the south-west—Gascony, Limousin, Quercy, Perigord, Agenais, comprised under the general name of the "Duchy of Aquitaine." Their immediate sovereign was the King of England, who was the more to be feared as, at the moment, the English crown was worn by a man of the courage of Edward I.

The Appeals of Aquitaine.

One can do this justice to him, that he carried out faithfully the obligations which bound him to the new King of France. The Wednesday of Whit week, 1297, he repaired to Paris, equipped as a vassal, and in the great hall of the palace took the oath of fidelity and homage between the hands of Philip the Fair for the lands which he held from his crown.

For his part, Philip the Fair, following the line of policy traced by Saint Louis, made in 1289 a new treaty with the Crown of England by which he ceded to it the towns of Limoges, Cahors, and Perigueux, which in strict right he had the power to retain. He ceded the part of Saintonge situated to the south of Charente. With regard to the parts of Quercy to which the English monarch made claim, Philip the Fair refused to deprive his crown of them; but by way of indemnity he assigned to the English King £3000 of the Tours currency. In return, modelling himself here also upon Saint Louis, he took care to exact recognition once more for the sovereignty of the Crown of France over the whole of Aquitaine.

Like the other provinces of France, Aquitaine was divided into two hostile factions. On the one hand were the high feudal nobility and the city patricians, on the other hand were the lesser nobles of the country and the popular party in the towns.

PHILIP THE FAIR

The latter faction, the lesser nobility and small bourgeoisie, assisted by the working class, sympathized with the English government, whose representatives in Aquitaine supported it in the struggle against the great nobles and the patricians who sought the favour of the King of France.

The party of the King of France fortified itself by the system of the " avoueries "—that is to say, it drew to itself the men who, to escape from the suzerainty of the immediate lord, declared themselves the men of the superior and distant sovereign, and therefore less troublesome—in fact, of the King of France.

These *avoués* of the King were grouped in the new towns, the famous new towns of the thirteenth century—they were called "bastides" in the South. They were places fortified and protected by royal charters, which governed themselves independently of local sovereigns with the claim to take orders only from the King of France. It was particularly on the northern frontiers of Aquitaine, abutting on the royal domain, that the bastides were multiplied, though reaching to the Spanish frontier.

Already one can appreciate the sources of conflict between the King of France and his vassal the King of England, the Duke of Aquitaine. Then there were the " royal cases."

By this term were described offences which touched " the general security of the kingdom "—an elastic definition which the legists took care not to state more precisely. Royal cases, said they, are those which "touch the King." But in the whole realm, including Aquitaine, the cases which touched the King, *i.e.* the King of France—were under the King's jurisdiction. And as soon as an offence of the royal case quality had been committed in Aquitaine there appeared officers, armed with shields bearing the fleur-de-lis and supported by a considerable escort who set themselves to arrest, imprison, sequestrate, confiscate, question, draw up statements, and to act judicially as though they were in Paris.

This was, in fine, the business of appeals.

In feudal law every one condemned by the tribunal of his immediate sovereign enjoyed the privilege of appeal to his

THE MIDDLE AGES

superior sovereign. What happened? A given person lost his case before the officers of the Duke of Aquitaine—that is to say, the King of England. He appealed on it to the Court of France. From that moment, in so far as it concerned him, all action of the local powers was suspended. He found himself, his relations, his goods, his possessions under litigation, placed under the authority of the King of France. One must remember the leisureliness of communications and the long processes of the period.

It is no longer possible to execute malefactors in Aquitaine. An assassin is condemned to death. He appeals. From this moment the executioner is held at a distance and one sees appear the representatives of the Court of Paris, who take our man from the prison where he has been in custody in order to remove him elsewhere. Thus, as the English officers held, " murders and thefts remain without any punishment." The same occurred in civil matters. The party which lost appealed to the Court of France. From that moment the goods under litigation were sequestrated, and there were at times entire fiefs with serfs and tenants, the administration of which was thus suspended for months or years.

The officers of the King of England tried to prevent the appeals. They strove to accommodate the parties and come to a direct understanding with them. When it came to persuade a condemned person that the better part for him was to let himself hang, the matter was not easy. If the attempt miscarried, the English officers set themselves to condemn the appellant systematically in any other suits he might have begun. It was an exemplary warning. Seeing this, the French King declared that appellants were wholly withdrawn from the jurisdiction of the Duke of Aquitaine, to be solely amenable to the Court of France, and this in all the matters in which they were engaged. Another habitual practice with the representatives of the English monarch was to seize the goods of the party who was going to lose before judgment was pronounced, so that they could argue afterwards that the seizure was anterior to the appeal. The appellant thus found himself deprived of the use of his property over the whole duration of the procedure of the Court of France, which was often very long. But then

PHILIP THE FAIR

there arrived French sergeants who compelled the English officers to release what they had taken.

Sometimes the English King's emissaries threw into prison without any judicial formality those who appealed to the Court of France; there they constrained them by threats, blows, or by the most cruel tortures to withdraw their appeal. They threatened with death the clerics or notaries who dared to draw up the appeal. At other times, seizing the appellants, they forced apart their jaws to the extreme limit by introducing wooden wedges into their mouths, to such purpose that the miserable wretches were unable to utter the least sound, and, after having bound them in the public road, they cried to them mockingly, " Appeal about it to the King of France ! "

The appellants were equally exposed to the violences of the opposite side whom the English officers supported. The King of France because of it came to authorize them to carry arms. As a consequence, their adversaries also armed themselves; relatives and friends took part on one side or the other, and while waiting for the dispute to be decided at Paris, they murdered each other in the streets of Bayonne or the rugged roads of Limousin.

The seneschal of Saintonge who, on the frontier, was charged with the duty of making the French King's authority respected in Aquitaine, gave to the appellants sergeants and guards. These came armed with the baton, marked with a fleur-de-lis which made them inviolable. At the house of the appellant, they hung up a shield bearing a fleur-de-lis above the main door. On the limits of his properties they drove in stakes on which they hung other royal shields. This did not prevent the appellants fortifying themselves on their lands and surrounding themselves with paid troops for greater safety. Thus in the English provinces of France centres of resistance to the English King multiplied themselves under the ægis of the King of France. The adversaries of the government of London defied it publicly, escorted by French sergeants ; but at other times the French sergeants were attacked, chased from their guard-room, and beaten unmercifully—a source of fresh conflicts between France and England.

The environs of Dax and Riom were cut up by veritable

little armies of appellants who levied contributions on their adversaries and declared themselves, from the fact of their appeal, withdrawn from the authority of the local magistrates. Under cover of these disorders, bands of brigands roamed through the country, doing open violence to the people, sacking houses and churches, killing, stealing, plundering, and saying to the officials of the English seneschal of Aquitaine who came to bring them to reason, " We are appellants to the Court of France, and we have nothing to do with you." They had even procured, no one knows how, some French sergeants-at-arms to cover their crimes with the august patronage which these represented.

From the fact of the appeals, the administration of the County of Aquitaine had become impossible. Unless one of the two parties, the King of France or the King of England, renounced his rights—that which neither the one nor the other was disposed to do—the situation was inextricable. Whatever goodwill Philip the Fair and Edward I felt towards each other, the French suzerainty over the provinces of the South-west, possessed by the Crown of England, made a conflict inevitable.

Nevertheless, if we find in the situation of Aquitaine the true cause of the war which will break out between France and England, that will not be the pretext.

Between the seamen, subjects of the King of France, *i.e.* the Normans and Flemings, on the one side, and those subject to the King of England, *i.e.* the English and Gascon seamen, on the other, there had been for some years a perpetual struggle. The cause of these conflicts, incessantly renewed, was the custom of letters of marque given by one country or the other. Let us take one example out of a thousand. An Englishman named Brown, the owner of cloth to the value of £200 in the ship of a citizen of Bayonne, named Duverges, complains to the King of England that the said cloth had been taken with the said ship by the French, in view of Dover. As compensation he demands the power to seize £200 worth of wine which is in a French ship anchored in the port of Winchelsea. The latter vessel belonged to some people of Calais, and when they saw themselves deprived of their wine, they demanded,

PHILIP THE FAIR

in their turn in the Court of France, a letter of marque—such was the name of these authorizations—to act on the sea against the people of England or Bayonne, and take from them merchandise up to the value of 200 pounds sterling. The letters were granted; some merchants of Bayonne were robbed; but they hastened to petition the King of England to authorize them to recover 200 pounds worth of goods from the people of the King of France. There was no reason why this game—a game of bloody robberies—should ever cease. There were even reasons why it should not finish and should lead to more and more complications. These letters of marque were given by hundreds. One can imagine the sort of encounters between French and English seamen from the coasts of Spain to those of Zeeland.

These struggles assumed an extreme ferocity. Normans and Flemings, like the English and Bayonnais, were proud of hanging at their mast-heads the seamen of the other side whom they had contrived to capture. They found pleasure in regarding these corpses tossed about by the wind. On one occasion the Normans seize some merchandise carried on an English vessel in the open sea, after having drowned its whole crew. The English retort by cropping the ears of the seamen whom they find on a French ship. On another occasion, the French or English set the boats adrift after having previously cut off the hands and feet of the whole crew. In the sun on the open sea, lying on the bridge, the miserable wretches expired in terrible agony. It would take too long to pass in review the infinite series of massacres and pillages.

The officials of the King of France and those of the King of England united their efforts in the attempt to re-establish peace between the rival nations. The seamen of both parties who could be gathered together were assembled in a given port, and they were made to take an oath to keep the peace; but, far from calming down, the conflict assumed greater and greater proportions. The ships of both nations only went out now in fleets in order to give mutual assistance, and when two opposed fleets encountered each other, true naval battles occurred.

On 24th April 1293, a great number of English seamen

left Portsmouth on more than two hundred ships. Some days later the Normans, on 225 well-equipped vessels, put out from the harbour of Charente. The encounter took place on 15th May 1293, near the coast of Brittany, off Cape St. Mathew. The vessels were all provided with "fortified towers" which turned them into warships. At the top of the masts floated long banners of red cendal two yards broad and thirty yards long. These banners, say the English sailors in the narrative they have left of these events, called in French "Boucan," mean "death beyond repair and mortal combat in every place where sailors are." The battle was terrible. The English were victorious. The French ships were taken or sunk. Some Normans on light skiffs contrived to regain the coast of Brittany. It was reported to the King of France that, in the English fleet, were sixty strong warships which had been fitted out with a view to an expedition in Palestine. The English government, then, had encouraged the enterprise. Some days after the victory, some English and men of Bayonne surprised la Rochelle. They penetrated into the town, killed, pillaged, burned, and then returned laden with booty.

Philip the Fair sent an ambassador to London to demand justice. He demanded the restitution of the captured vessels, the liberty of the French sailors who had been taken prisoner, and considerable indemnities. Edward I took a high line. The English Court, he replied, has tribunals which hear charges and give equitable decisions. This brought on him a citation from Philip the Fair, in his quality of suzerain, dated 27th October, summoning him to appear as Duke of Aquitaine before the Parliament of Paris, to justify the crimes committed by his subjects, or in default know himself condemned. While waiting for the appearance of the English King, Philip the Fair pronounced reversion of the lands held by Edward I under the suzerainty of the Crown of France.

Passions were greatly excited. At Bordeaux there was a massacre of the French. At Fronsac some officers of Philip the Fair were murdered. Two of his sergeants, who had been sent as guards of the Château of Cuiller, were hung. Jean de St. Jean, who commanded in Aquitaine as lieutenant of Edward I, had the head cut off of a knight belonging to the suite of Raoul de Nesle, Marshal of France.

Edward I, who had been cited before the Parliament of Paris for 14th January, did not appear. He was declared contumacious, and the Court of France declared confiscated all that the English Crown held under the suzerainty of the fleur-de-lis.

We must make no mistake : we are on the threshold of the Hundred Years War. The complex and disorderly struggle which was to endure a century and a half, and to carry us from the Middle Ages to the Renaissance, began with this rupture between Philip the Fair and Edward I—a social war rather than a national war ; a long fermentation of conflicting elements from which will emerge a new social state : the Renaissance.

The policy of Edward I, at the beginning of the conflict, has not been understood. He sent to France his brother, Edmund of Lancaster, to order his lieutenant in Aquitaine, Jean de St. Jean, to restore to Philip the Fair the duchy which he reclaimed. There was even a ceremony of remission at Valence d'Agen, 5th March 1294, when the Marshall of France, Raoul de Clermont-Nesle, received in the name of his master, from the hands of the seneschal of Gascony, Jean de Havering, the reversion of the lands which Edward I held under French suzerainty. At the same time the keys of Bordeaux, Bayonne, and Agen were sent to the King of France.

What was the purpose of Edward I ? He wished to delay the action of the King of France, since already Raoul de Nesle was on the frontier of Agenais with a powerful army. The English troops were still in England, and fighting the Welsh. In other words, Edward hoped to reconquer by force of arms the lands of which the Crown of France had just retaken possession, and to find himself, after this conquest, delivered from the suzerainty which made the government of these provinces impossible for him.

Whilst, at Valence in Agenais, Jean de Havering handed over to the representative of the French King the possession of Aquitaine, from north to south of this province the English officers and their adherents were organizing resistance. And when the French officers presented themselves in order to take over the towns, Jean de St. Jean made them shut the gates in their face.

Philip the Fair saw the plan of his rival. He had not a moment to lose. While Edward still struggled against the Welsh, the Marshall of France, Raoul de Nesle, invaded Agenais and Gascony, and sent troops into Agen, Bordeaux, and Bayonne.

On his side Edward acted with all possible care. He equipped a fleet and an army. In Aquitaine he could count on the popular party—that is to say, on the trade corporations and on the lesser nobility. An able diplomacy, well provided with money, wasted no time in securing him a powerful bundle of alliances with which he enclosed France. First he arms his two sons-in-law, the Duke of Brabant and the Count of Bar, against Philip the Fair; then the King of Germany, Adolph of Nassau, to whom he gives much money, in consideration of which Adolph declares war against France, 31st August 1294; then the Count of Holland, the Count of Gueldre, the Bishop of Cologne, the Count of Juliers, the Count of Savoy, an important league of Free-County lords. The corrosive action of the English gold attacks even the interior of the French realm. Edward I fails in the case of the Duke of Brittany—whose fidelity Philip the Fair recompenses by erecting his duchy *en paierie*—but he succeeds in the case of the Count of Flanders.

The situation was the same in Flanders as in Aquitaine. The King of France exercised there the rights of suzerainty, which made the government of his State extremely difficult for the lord of the land. Moreover, the Count of Flanders, at this time Guy de Dampierre, was in need of money. He was a French lord, a native of Champagne. He had accompanied Saint Louis on the Crusade, and was the godfather of Philip the Fair. He was seventy years of age, with a long white beard, and he limped because his heel had been cut in an expedition against the Dutch. In his two marriages he had had a great number of children, of whom sixteen had survived. He was a good father. During his long life he could be observed occupied incessantly in procuring good establishments for his numerous progeny; and he threw into this the more ardour from the fact that he had

PHILIP THE FAIR

little money to give them. He was in a lamentable state of poverty. It is painful to see this feudal knight struggling without intermission in the crooked fingers of Jewish usurers, of Cahorsins or Lombards. He owes money to every one, to his tailor, to his wine merchant; he borrows from all comers, even from his servants; then, on the day of reckoning, his coffers are empty.

But behold, one fine morning the King of England offers him much money and a marriage beyond his hopes for the little Philippine, the goddaughter of Philip the Fair. Philippine would espouse the eldest son and heir of Edward. One day she would be Queen of England. The old Count was dazzled. He knew he had no right, as a French peer, to conclude such an alliance without the consent of his suzerain. He also knew that at Paris this consent would be refused : England was in a state of open war with France. Edward I reassured him. Was not he, King of England and Duke of Aquitaine, there to defend him against all attacks ? Moreover, the temptation was too strong. On 31st August 1294, Guy de Dampierre concluded the treaty of Lierre in Brabant, by which Philippine of Flanders was affianced to the heir of the English Crown.

But Philip the Fair fought his neighbour beyond the Channel with his own weapons. To the King of Germany, Adolph of Nassau, he sent by an Italian financier, called in France "Monseigneur Mouche," more money than Edward I had sent him, to such purpose that Adolph, after having declared war against France, did not move. And the Duke of Brabant, seeing this, did not move either. The two confederates none the less kept the English money. To the Count of Savoy, Philip the Fair opposes his hereditary enemy, the Dauphin of Viennois; he allies himself with the Count Palatine of Burgundy, Otto IV. In the Italian ports he recruits entire fleets—vessels, soldiers, and captains. The Genoese and Venetians were the finest seamen of the time. He sends subsidies to the Scots, and with their King, John Balliol, concluded an alliance, the exact counterpart of the alliance signed between Edward I and Guy of Dampierre. He assured himself of the active support of Duke Thibaud of Lorraine, of the valiant Count Henry of Luxemburg, of the Bishop of Cambrai, of the Count of Hainault; and profiting by

THE MIDDLE AGES

the antagonism between the Dutch and Flemish, detached from the English alliance Count Florent of Holland in order to secure him as an adherent to his cause. Finally, we should note the treaty concluded between Eric, King of Norway, and Philip the Fair. Eric promised to put at the disposal of France a fleet of 200 galleys, " long vessels, driven by sail as well as by oars " ; and lastly the alliance of Philip the Fair with the King of Majorca.

The King of France heard of the pact concluded between the King of England and the Count of Flanders. He ordered the latter to come to speak with him. His letters were dated 28th September 1294. In the following month Guy de Dampierre was at Paris. Philip treated his vassal very harshly. He told him that by the fact of his alliance with a declared enemy he had proved himself " disloyal," and he ordered him to have his daughter Philippine brought to Paris ; and commanded that until this was done he and his two sons who had accompanied him should be imprisoned. Shortly afterwards, the little princess, aged seven years, was at the Louvre, where from this day she was brought up under the eye of Philip's wife, Jeanne de Navarre, with the royal children of France. Followed by his two sons, Guy de Dampierre returned home.

The war between France and England had taken its full course. On 26th October 1294 the English fleet which bore the army raised for the reconquest of Aquitaine made its entry into the Gironde. At Bayonne the popular party regained control, put to flight the French officers, and delivered the town to the English. On his side Philip the Fair had fitted out a fleet with Admiral Mathieu de Montmorency in command. It appeared before Dover and landed there 15,000 men. Edward I announced to the people that the plan of the King of France was to stamp out every trace of the English language. The attempt miscarried and the French re-embarked after having burned a few buildings and pillaged several convents.

A second English fleet left Portsmouth on 15th January 1296. It ravaged the Ile de Rhé, landed in Guienne, took Blaye, Bourg-sur-Mer, did not dare to attack Bordeaux, where Raoul de Nesle was in command, and went as far as La Réole, where also the popular party threw open the gates to the English.

PHILIP THE FAIR

On 27th April 1296, Edward I achieved a great success. At Dunbar he crushed the Scottish army, and on 10th July John Balliol, the King of Scotland, was forced to come to him and make his submission. But by this time the King of France had raised a second army, which was commanded by his brother Charles de Valois. This army marched through Aquitaine. La Réole was retaken and the heads of the English party were hanged. Edmund of Lancaster, the brother of Edward I, was beaten and took refuge in Bayonne, where he died from his wounds.

Henry de Lacy, Earl of Lincoln, succeeded Edmund of Lancaster. Philip the Fair sent against him the prince, who had the reputation of being the first soldier of his time, Robert II, Count d'Artois. The adversaries met at Bonnegarde, in Landes, and in a decisive engagement the English were routed. Jean de St. Jean, the energetic and able lieutenant of Edward I in Aquitaine, was among the prisoners. The falling night and the neighbouring forests covered the flight of the beaten army, of whom not one would have escaped.

Some months later, the same Robert d'Artois, at the other end of France, fought a battle that was not less important. The troops of the Count of Flanders and of the German princes, equipped by Edward's gold, were placed under the command of a German knight, renowned for his feats of arms—William of Juliers, the elder. This army was the sole hope of Guy de Dampierre. The battle was fought on 20th August 1297 in the plain of Furnes. The chroniclers show Robert d'Artois, on his heavy horse, " armed with a fine steel jazeran (coat of mail) and a high gorgiere, and, over these, a mantle of blue satin, covered with golden fleurs-de-lis. In front of him, knights sounded the cornets and trumpets, which filled the air with the sound of their fanfares."

The victory of Robert d'Artois was complete. Guillaume of Juliers, the elder, was among the prisoners, mortally wounded.

The situation of the old Count Guy de Dampierre was desperate. Betrayed by fortune, feebly assisted by the King of England, on the point of being abandoned by his relatives, he took counsel with his two elder sons, Robert de Béthune and Guillaume de Crèvecœur. "Then," writes a contemporary, "they were disconcerted because money, friends, their towns, and every help began to fail them." The Count had no longer any refuge except the mercy of the King.

Followed by his two eldest sons and some faithful knights he set out for Paris.

But when from afar he saw the city the old Count Guy became so pensive and melancholy "that when one spoke to him he did not know what to reply."

"When they had reached the perron, in the great court of the Palace (now the Palais de Justice), where he found the King, Guy and his two sons dismounted, and they climbed the steps to the top with the Count of Savoy, who led them before the King." . . . "Then they threw themselves all three on their knees before the King as a great sign of humility and handed themselves over to him, recommending themselves to his good graces, giving themselves entirely to his noble will. The King looked at them well, but said not a word; and so sent them away. Then were they wholly abased that the King had not spoken."

Philip the Fair assigned as a residence for Guy de Dampierre the Château of Compiègne, to Robert de Béthune that of Chinon, and to Guillaume de Crèvecœur that of Issoudun in Berry. The tower of Compiègne, in which Guy de Dampierre was enclosed, was of timber-work, so contrived that every one from outside could see the Count. And people came from afar to regard the captivity of the rebellious vassal "from which he often suffered so much shame that he wished he was dead, and he was already old and hoary."

In the monastery of Vyve-Saint-Bavon, in Flanders, on 9th October 1297, a truce was concluded. The treaty was founded upon the principle "ki tient se tiegne"—that is to say, that each of the belligerents should continue to occupy, until the definite peace, the territories of which he was master at the moment of the armistice. As the arms of Robert d'Artois had just put Flanders and Aquitaine into the hands of Philip the Fair, the agreement was all to the advantage of the King of France, who at once set about the energetic organization of the conquered lands.

PHILIP THE FAIR

The truce of Vyve-Saint-Bavon had been negotiated through the mediation of Pope Boniface VIII. Benedetto Gaetani, who took on the pontifical throne the name of Boniface VIII, had been elected by the College of Cardinals on 24th December 1294. His family was of Catalonian origin, but it had settled in the Volscian district and had taken rank among the Italian nobility.

The Two Swords.

He himself was born at Anagni about 1217. He had pursued his studies at the University of Paris, where he had distinguished himself in the study of law. Through his mother he was a nephew of Pope Alexander IV. His family connections and a great capacity for affairs, a very brilliant mind, gracious and prepossessing manners, rapidly assured him a preponderating place at the Roman Court. He was charged with the management of the pontifical finances. While administering them in the most advantageous manner for the Holy See, he at the same time acquired a great personal fortune and trebled the extent of his inherited territory by adding to it the magnificent fiefs of Selvamolle. To increase, fortify, make prosperous and flourishing the lands which constituted his seigniorial grandeur and that of his family, came to be his chief preoccupation. He was distinctly a man of his time. Arable lands came to be added to arable lands, woods to vineyards, pasturages to *gaignables*, fiefs to castles; his vassals, clients, tenants, increased in number; his keeps were full of armed men.

Boniface VIII ascended the throne of St. Peter at the age of seventy-seven years.

The study of antiquity had given him an insight into other civilization than that in which he was born. He had realized the beauty of the religion of antiquity, and, from this admiration for a cult other than that to which he belonged, he had come to ponder the truth of dogma. Dante stigmatized the numerous atheists who existed in the Italy of his day. Between these fine and cultivated sceptics and the crude believers represented in France by the grandchildren of Saint Louis, the contrast can be imagined.

A French contemporary of Boniface VIII said of him: "He was learned, wise, and subtle." He was worldly and elegant. He took pleasure in the company of artists and

THE MIDDLE AGES

among the ladies who, after the fashion of the time, held their courts of love. He liked the company, too, of the Italian knights and the men-at-arms who garrisoned his castles and passed their watches in reciting Horace and Virgil. His air, wrote Ernest Renan, was more that of a knight than that of a priest. At this date bishops still led armies. The charming figure of William of Juliers, Archbishop of Cologne, who led the Flemish soldiers to victory helps us to understand Boniface.

They both had the fault of not weighing their words. Boniface forgot that a Sovereign Pontiff could no longer maintain the attitude with which, as an agreeable monsignor, he had amused the Florentines. He despised the scandal that his free and worldly airs naturally provoked. An elevated character certainly, but in it was mingled a certain irresponsibility. He furnished his palace with works of art of the most profane character. He had his image carved in stone, from which the French concluded that he wished to have himself adored. He delighted in rendering courteous songs which he had made in honour of the ladies. What a magnificent prince of the Church he would have made in the sixteenth century! Moreover, he excited in the mind of Ernest Renan the liveliest admiration. Among his Italian contemporaries he found some cultivated minds who understood him; but in what stupefaction was he not to plunge Philip the Fair, simple, rugged, of the same grain as Saint Louis.

A Cardinal de la Pouille reports a conversation at the time of Celestine V in which Gaetani took part. Many priests were discussing which was the best religion. Gaetani interposed:

"What are religions? Human creations. Is there any other life than the present? The universe had no beginning and it will have no end."

Of Heaven and Hell he said: "Is there any one living who ever came back from them?"

It is obviously necessary to allow for paradox, the desire to shine. The faith of Gaetani was certainly pure and profound, but he believed it necessary to bow to the taste of the Italian nobility, in which one loved to play the ready wit.

When he became Pope, Gaetani checked the Inquisition;

he took away from it some of its victims and made it release some heretics. We see in this his best title to honour. The writings of Arnaud de Villeneuve alarmed some strictly pious souls : Boniface VIII protected him. He loved neither mystics, hermits, nor mendicant orders. They were dangerous visionaries in his view, and useless parasites. He loved energy, action, life broad and liberal. Moreover, he found monks and hermits dirty and evil smelling.

We must add that Cardinal Gaetani had been elected Pope under strange circumstances. On 5th July 1294 the choice of the Sacred College had fallen upon a hermit of Mount Majella, a reputed Saint, Celestine V. A rustic and mystical nature, the brilliant rôle assigned him overwhelmed him. Hardly was he proclaimed Sovereign Pontiff than he thought of returning to a better life—that is to say, to his cell of Sulmona. Gaetani persuaded him to abdicate, which he did on 13th December. On the 24th of the same month, Benedetto Gaetani was elevated to the Pontificate. Boniface VIII gave to his consecration, 2nd January 1295, an extraordinary brilliance. The King of Sicily and the King of Hungary marched on foot before him bare-headed holding the bridle of his horse.

But the devout ex-Pope was on the road returning to his hermitage. Boniface VIII reflected that it was not prudent to leave this feeble spirit in the hands of his adversaries. He had the old hermit pursued. Celestine, warned, wished to fly, to take refuge in Greece ; but Boniface's men arrested him at the moment when he was going to embark, and he was led back to Rome, with marks of profound respect, so as not to revolt the people who followed him in crowds, snipping off pieces of his habit and pulling out the hair of the ass on which he was mounted. At Rome, Boniface VIII received his predecessor with the greatest respect ; and with the greatest respect he caused him to be imprisoned in his Castle of Fumone, where Celestine V soon died.

Boniface VIII is consumed with the passion to dominate. Certainly he wishes to do good ; but he only understands by this his own greatness. The magnificent dreams of Gregory VII and of Innocent III were revived in him, exalted by his pride. In the Roman Campagna he made the might of his

THE MIDDLE AGES

house prevail. He wished to dominate the Kings throughout Christendom.

One must read his Bulls, written in so nervous and so living a style, adorned with fine Latin expressions and sonorous periods : " The Roman Pontiff sits on the throne of justice : a peaceable judge, he dissipates evil by the movement of his thought."

The man who wrote these lines was to come into collision with the greatest moral power of his time, with the French monarchy in the person of Philip the Fair.

From the first years of his reign, among the difficulties of government, the young sovereign had felt keenly the embarrassment which the privileges of the clergy caused him. They claimed to be answerable only to the ecclesiastical tribunals, and to be exempt from taxation and municipal charges. The Archbishop of Bordeaux, who was one day to be Pope under the name of Clement V, refused to acknowledge the King of France as suzerain. A number of monasteries claimed to depend only on the Roman Court.

Conflicts of jurisdiction between the officers of the King and the clergy were incessant. From the beginning of his reign, Nicholas IV held himself to have power to rebuke, on this subject, the young King. But he had replied in a style in which one could already perceive the Prince who is determined to maintain the independence of his crown :

" Our most Holy Father without doubt took pity on our youth when he exposed to us the manner in which, as has been told him, the Church of Chartres would be injured by us. . . .

" The poor vagrant proved a good prophet in saying ' The exactions of the clergy will cease only when they have wearied the goodwill of France.' "

In 1294 broke out the struggle with England. Considerable resources were necessary. Several religious orders refused to contribute to the expenses of the war. The Order of Citeaux appealed on the matter to the Roman Court. In vain the clergy of the diocese of Reims pointed out to the Sovereign Pontiff that in lending assistance to those who resisted the royal authority he was causing profound trouble in the realm.

PHILIP THE FAIR

Boniface VIII judged the occasion favourable for the consolidation of the spiritual power.

In order to make the situation of the kingdom perfectly clear, Philip the Fair sent to Rome the Prior of la Chaise, Pierre de Paroi. Paroi spoke at length with Boniface VIII, endeavouring to make him realize the inconveniences of his meddling in the temporal affairs of the realm of France. Boniface VIII did not intend to give way. At length, the Prior said brusquely:

" His Holiness ought to guard himself against failing in the respect which is due a monarch so august as the King of France, since His Holiness is accused of professing heretical doctrines and of not using fitting decency in his conduct."

One can imagine the fury of Boniface VIII. These were diplomatic fashions which he had not expected. Pierre de Paroi has described the scene. In reading it we hear the roaring of the old lion:

" ' Who said that to you ? ' cried the Pope.

" I named to him Philip, the son of the Count of Artois," tranquilly goes on the Prior of la Chaise, " and Monseigneur Jacques de St. Pol, because he could do nothing against them."

Boniface VIII could command himself no longer. He shouted:

" These knights are donkeys. Behold the pride of the French! Get away, thou ribald! Evil monk! God confound me if I do not destroy the pride of the French! I shall dethrone the King of France! All the other Christian kings will join me against him!"

The decree *Clericis laicos* was dated 24th February 1296. With unusual harshness, Boniface VIII forbade secular princes to levy contributions on the clergy without the authorization of the Holy See. Philip the Fair replied on 17th August by the ordinance which forbade the exportation of gold and silver beyond the realm. This was to dry up, by checking the contributions of the French clergy, an important source of the papal revenues. Philip the Fair knew the old Pope's passion for gold, that thirst for gold which Dante stigmatizes in his Inferno, where he places the victim of Anagni:

" Are you already there, Boniface, are you already there ?

THE MIDDLE AGES

Are you yet satisfied with those riches for which you prostituted the Church?"

The Bull *Ineffabilis amor*, of 20th September 1296, in which the Sovereign Pontiff replies to the ordinance of 17th August, is a masterpiece of irony. It distils gall; it rends in its caresses. In reading it over, the old Pope, a writer by birth and a good Latinist, must have been proud of his pen. The ordinance of the King of France, said he, is foolish and tyrannical. Has he dreamed of laying rash hands on the interests of the Pope and cardinals? And that at a moment when his realm is disturbed, when his own subjects fall away from him, when the Kings of Germany, England, and Spain are preparing to attack. "Unhappy one," cried he, addressing Philip the Fair, "do you forget that without the help of the Church you could not resist them? What is to happen to you if, after gravely offending the Holy See, you make of it the ally of your enemies and your chief adversary?"

These were not vain threats. But Philip the Fair stood fast, and replied by the pen of Pierre Flote.

It was in reply to the Bull *Ineffabilis amor* that Flote produced the admirable protest which affirmed the independence of the crown of France, and is designated in history by its opening words, *Antequam essent clerici* ...

"Before there were any clergy, the King of France had the care of his realm, and he framed for it certain rules in order to protect it against its enemies. . . . The very privileges of the clergy only exist by the permission of the secular princes. And these privileges, whatever they may be, cannot prejudice the task, which is incumbent on kings, of ruling and defending their realms. . . .

"The Lord said: 'Render to Cæsar the things that are Cæsar's. . . .' The enemy has invaded the land and the clergy have not paid any contribution to those whose duty it is to protect them and their goods. . . . The Pope goes even further: he forbids the clergy to pay subsidies to the King. . . . So that although it would be lawful to the clergy to give money to actors and to women, to keep off the poor, to squander money on ornaments, on cavalcades and in feasts, these clerics, enriched, grown fat, and stuffed by the devotion of princes, would be forbidden to lend help to the same princes against unjust aggressors!"

To threats Philip the Fair replies by threats:

"Beware! Beware! To speak like this is to lend assistance to the enemies of the Crown; it is to commit the crime of *lèse-majesté*."

The controversy began on such a plane that already one expects to see the conflict break out violently; but, behold, Boniface suddenly gives way. A Bull of 31st July 1297 permits the clergy to pay subsidies to the Crown.

The Pope was in the throes of a grave difficulty. He had on his hands two "crusades," one against the Aragonese of Sicily, the other against the Colonna family. The latter were one of the great feudal houses, which in thirteenth-century Italy had come to form veritable small States. Two of the Colonna, James and his nephew Peter, were members of the Sacred College. They had voted for Benedetto Gaetani, for the Gaetani family had for some years been a dependant of the Colonna family. Once he had ascended the pontifical throne, Boniface intended to modify the respective positions of the two "Houses." The Gaetani were overwhelmed with gifts, with dignities, with favours. The conflict broke out sharply when Peter Gaetani, promoted Count of Caserta, bought the lands of the Annibaldi, in the Maritime Province—lands which for many years the Colonna had coveted. And hence between the Colonna and Gaetani one of those family strifes—like that of the Montagues and Capulets—which the Middle Ages, and particularly the Middle Ages in Italy, knew so well. The Colonna Cardinals go about repeating that Boniface was not elected Pope in a regular manner. He cites them to appear before the Sacred College. The two Cardinals judge it more prudent to take refuge in their castle of Longuezza. They are declared heretics, schismatics, blasphemers; they are excommunicated. The places where they shall go to live are placed under an interdict. They are declared incapable of exercising any office, of making a will, of performing any public act, themselves, their relatives, and their descendants to the fourth generation.

Peter had five brothers—John, Eude, Agapet, Stephen, and

THE MIDDLE AGES

James known as Sciarra, all soldiers. Stephen made an ambush on the Appian Way and carried off the pontifical treasure which was being transported from Anagni, where the paternal house of Boniface VIII was, to Rome. Most of the noble families of the Roman Campagna were jealous of the rapid growth of the Gaetani. The Colonna gathered partisans round them. But they were defeated by the Pope's adherents. Sciarra Colonna heroically defended Palestrina, the last foothold of his family. The town was taken. With a fine gesture, inspired by the ancient world, Boniface VIII had it rased to the ground, and the ruins sown with salt—" as the Romans," he said himself, " had done to Carthage."

Sciarra Colonna escaped, disguised as a drover. Pirates seized him and put him in chains. For four years he was a galley slave ; he rowed at the bottom of the keel ; the bandits struck him with leather thongs. He would not disclose his identity for fear he should be handed over to Boniface. At last, when the galley had cast anchor in view of Marseilles, he made himself known. His cousin, Egidio Colonna, Archbishop of Bourges, the councillor of Philip the Fair, had him ransomed by the King of France. One can imagine the mountain of hatred that had grown up in his heart

Egidio Colonna, better known under the name of Gilles de Rome, a disciple of St. Thomas, himself called the most profound doctor, a commentator on Aristotle, put at the disposition of his family, who were athirst for vengeance, his high situation at the Court of France, his intellectual gifts, and his authority.

Papal policy never ceased, during the Middle Ages, to foster the division between the Courts of France and Germany. The German Emperor, King of the Romans, was supported in Italy by a powerful party, the Ghibellines. On the other hand, the King of France represented the greatest power of the epoch. His religious character increased his authority. The union of the two crowns destroyed the temporal influence of the Roman Pontiff. The Popes who were the most devoted to the Capetians, those who, like Clement V, appeared to be only the agents of the King of France, did not cease to pursue in Germany an anti-French policy. This is no reproach to

384

PHILIP THE FAIR

them. The policy was then a necessity for the Popes, above all for those who, like Boniface VIII, wished to secure to the Roman Crown a temporal dominion.

On 2nd July 1298, the King of Germany, Adolph de Nassau, who was the ally of the King of England against Philip the Fair, was killed at the battle of Gœlheim by his competitor, Albert of Austria, an adherent of French policy, who was soon to marry a sister of Philip the Fair. Boniface refuses to ratify the election of Albert. He treats him as a murderer and a usurper, and excommunicates him. On 9th December 1299 there takes place at Vaucoulers, near Toul, the famous interview between the Kings of France and Germany, when the two sovereigns make their alliance. The Flemish ambassadors at the Roman Court have described the fury of Boniface VIII when he heard of the event. He cried out before the cardinals, "These princes wish to disturb everything."

He repeated : " Yes, the King of France takes bad advice." At one moment he still hopes to bring round Philip the Fair, and he presses him to break with the new King of Germany ; but the King of France means to keep his powerful ally.

The year 1300 closes the thirteenth century. On this occasion a solemn Jubilee was decreed at Rome. Boniface VIII, an old man of eighty-three years, was beside himself. He had himself carried in the streets under a canopy of golden silk, blessing the crowd who bowed down before him. In front of him marched a herald with two swords : representing the one the temporal and the other the spiritual power. Another herald-at-arms cried, " O Peter, look here upon thy successor ! O Christ, behold Thy Vicar ! " To the ambassadors of Albert of Austria, who demanded that he should recognize their master as Emperor of Germany, he replies, " I am Cæsar ! It is I who am the Emperor." He forbids the Hungarians to choose a King ; he threatens the King of Naples with anathema. He writes to the Florentines : " All the faithful, whoever they may be, should bow the neck to the orders of the Sovereign Pontiff."

He is no longer master of his characteristic fits of passion. The Archbishop of Genoa, having presented himself for the ceremony of the ashes on the first day of Lent, Boniface threw the vase full of ashes in his face. " Remember that you are a Ghibelline " (a partisan of the Imperial dominance in Italy), he cried, " and that with all the Ghibellines you will return to dust." On another occasion, when one of the ambassadors of the King of Germany, the sub-prior of the Strasbourg Dominicans, bowed before him in order to kiss his toe, the Pope gave him so vigorous a kick in the face that he made it bleed.

It was at this moment that Philip the Fair, still anxious for conciliation, sent to Rome as ambassador one of his favourite legists, Guillaume de Nogaret, in order to make the character and necessities of his policy understood there. Nogaret appeared with a brilliant equipage before the Sovereign Pontiff. He endeavoured to show in detail that the alliance concluded between the Kings of France and Germany had no other object than peace, the good of the Church, and finally the crusade beyond the seas, the constant aim of the Roman Pontiffs. Boniface VIII would hear nothing. Albert of Austria was a usurper, and excommunicated ; as to the King of France, the Pope uttered insults and threats.

Then Nogaret considered " the wickedness of the Roman Pontiff and the affliction of the Church of France which he devoured." These are his expressions. He took him privately, he says, and counselled him to amend his ways. He reminded him that he was heretical, simoniacal, a thief and an assassin, and that he had horrible vices ; and that all this was notorious. Nogaret—we are following his own account—says all this to the Sovereign Pontiff " very humbly, entreating him deferentially, to look to his reputation and to spare the Church and the realm of France."

Boniface demanded if, in France, the ambassadors were not chosen from fools. He defied Nogaret to repeat his discourse in public. But when numerous witnesses were introduced, Nogaret repeated his accusations.

"Do you speak in your own name or in that of your master?"

" I replied," writes Nogaret, " that I had said all this on my own authority, inspired by my zeal for the faith in view of the miserable condition to which the Church of France had been reduced, which had been placed under the patronage of the King."

PHILIP THE FAIR

"At these words," says our ambassador, "Boniface behaved like a madman. He uttered frightful threats, insults, blasphemies which, for the love of Christ, I listened to patiently. Yet I wept for the Church of Rome, I wept for the Church of the Gauls. I continued for some days to argue with him, but in vain. On my return to my master, I gave him an account of what had passed, asking him to defend the Church; but he, as a pious son, averted his eyes from these scandals."

This Guillaume de Nogaret, though not possessed of the capacity of a Pierre Flote, was nevertheless one of the most useful assistants of Philip the Fair. In the hands of the King he proved a marvellous instrument. He was born at St. Felix de Carmaing in Haute-Garonne. In 1291 he was professor of Law at Montpellier; in 1294 he was Chief Justice in the Seneschal's jurisdiction of Beaucaire. In 1296 he entered the council of the King. The registers of the *Olim* make him a clerk, but oftener he is called "Knight" and "venerable professor of laws." The King had made him Lord of Cauvisson and of Massillargues. He married his daughter Guillemette to Guillaume de Clermont-Lodève. The Marshall of France, Mile de Noyers, wrote to him familiarly as "my dear friend, Monseigneur de Nogaret." His activity ranges over the most various spheres: he organizes the Crown archives, has a hand in making the Seine navigable, and settles the financial questions raised by the Flemish campaigns.

He was an ardent patriot. He said, "I think that had I killed my own father if he attacked my country, all the ancient authors are agreed on this point that it could not be urged against me as a crime. I should deserve, on the contrary, to be praised for it as an act of virtue." Danton could not have said more.

The celebrated Bull *Ausculta fili* (Hear, O my son!), addressed by Boniface VIII to Philip the Fair, was dated on 5th December 1301. Written in a nervous, incisive style, with a strong vein of restrained irony, it was bound to wound Philip profoundly:

"Hear, O dearest son, the warnings of a father, and open thy heart to the exhortation of the master who holds on earth the place of Him who alone is Master and Lord. . . . Oh, well-beloved son, do not allow thyself to be persuaded by any one that thou hast no superior and that thou art not subordinate to him who is placed at the summit of the ecclesiastical hierarchy." The King of France, Boniface went on to say, grinds the churches, oppresses the nobles and commons, scandalizes the people. The counsel which the Sovereign Pontiff has not ceased to give him has remained without effect. The King of France falls from sin to sin, and sin has become a habit with him. He makes himself the judge of Churchmen, takes possession of their property, levies taxes upon the clergy, oppresses the Church of Lyons although it is situated outside his realm (Philip the Fair was attempting at this date to compel Lyons to re-enter the dominion of the Crown). Boniface reproaches the King even on his financial administration and for changing the currency. The Bull ended by announcing the approaching convocation of a General Council at which the King will be judged.

One anecdote, among many others, indicates the irritation into which this Bull threw the King of France. On 23rd February 1302, in an assembly of the great personages of the kingdom, Philip the Fair declared to his three sons that if it should ever happen to them to be so weak as to admit that the King of France held his crown of any other than God, they should consider themselves as under his curse.

The thesis of Philip the Fair was brilliantly taken up, on 10th April 1302, by the Chancellor Pierre Flote speaking to the delegates of the three orders of the kingdom, assembled in the Church of Notre Dame. We know from Geoffroi de Paris that the Chancellor's address produced profound emotion. And when the speaker, in the name of the King, appealed to the devotion of all Frenchmen to defend the independence of the Crown, prolonged acclamations filled the high naves of the Church. The nobility replied by the voice of Robert d'Artois, that for this cause they were ready to shed their blood. The lawyer Pierre Dubois, deputy of the bailiwick of Coutances, spoke in the same sense in the name of the Commonalty. The adhesion of the clergy was given under a less forcible form, but it was none the less formal. Only the Bishop of Autun and the Abbot of Citeaux refused to put their seals to the foot of the protest against Boniface VIII. The movement was so strong

PHILIP THE FAIR

that the act of protest of the King was signed not only by all the French princes present, but also by some vassals of the Holy Empire, by Ferry, Duke of Lorraine, by Jean, Count of Hainault and of Holland, by Count Henri of Luxemburg, by Jean of Châlon Arlay, and even by Louis de Nevers, grandson of the Count of Flanders.

And without delay, the Commissioners of the King spread through the provinces. They went two by two, carrying the copies of the documents relative to the difference between the Pope and the King.

On the arrival of the Commissioners the people were assembled by the sound of bells, or by the blast of trumpets, sometimes in a church, sometimes in a cemetery, or in a cloister garth, or on the market-place, or under the market house. At times they were content to call together the principal townsmen in the consulate. The royal Commissioners addressed the most diverse publics, the canons of cathedrals, monks in their monasteries, municipal bodies, and tumultuous gatherings of the people in public. A platform was erected in the open air. The Commissioners mounted it, read their documents, and delivered a short speech. They were interrupted by cries, " Yes. Yes. I agree. I agree. Long live the King ! "

At length special envoys set out for Italy with letters for the Pope, drawn up, some in the name of the clergy, others in the name of the noblesse and the last from the commons of France. In a different tone all affirmed the independence of the French Crown.

The Sovereign Pontiff received the delegates on 24th June 1302 at Anagni, his birthplace. Boniface VIII took the high line. He called Flote Belial and Achitophel, and declared that he was a heretic. Flote was blind in one eye, as we know, which made the Pope say of the kingdom of France, " In the kingdom of the blind the one-eyed are Kings." The Count d'Artois was also called Achitophel. Coming to Philip the Fair, Boniface declared that he loved him much, but that the King had driven him to extremities. " We know the secrets of his kingdom," he added. " No detail is concealed from us ; we have weighed all its activities. We know what the Germans, Burgundians; and Languedocians think about France." He followed with sustained attention the efforts of the English Court; which still maintained its allies in arms during the treaties concluded with France. The English party in Aquitaine grew stronger. " Our predecessors have deposed three Kings of France," concluded Boniface; " and, although we are unworthy to unlatch the shoes of our predecessors, since the King has done that which his ancestors who were deposed have done—and even worse—we shall depose him as a rascal (*sicut unum garcionem*)."

In Flanders, Boniface found some unexpected allies. Philip the Fair had given the Flemings as Governor a brave knight, the uncle of the Queen, Jacques de Châtillon, Count of St. Pol. Connected with the nobles of the country and imbued with feudal ideas, he governed through the nobility in the country and in the towns in favour of the Patricians.

In the hope that the King of France would deliver them from the Patrician tyranny; the popular party had at the outset received him and his people with favour. The disappointment they experienced in the policy of Jacques de Châtillon was only the stronger. The younger sons of Gui de Dampierre, of whom the youngest; Gui de Namur; above all was filled with ardour and intelligence, re-entered the country. The workmen found an admirable tribune, a powerful voice with the crowd, in the person of a weaver of Bruges, Pierre Coninc. The author of the *Chronique Artésienne* sketches him in a few lines : " There was at this time at Bruges, a man called Pierron le Roy (Coninc in Flemish means *roi*). He was of small stature and of poor lineage and a weaver. And he had till then gained his livelihood by weaving and had never had so much as ten pounds, nor had any of his line ; but he did not lack words, and they came so easily and so finely that it was a great marvel. Moreover, the weavers, fullers, and cloth-workers had such confidence in him and such affection that he neither said nor commanded anything that was not done on the moment." Coninc was sixty years of age.

Having found in Coninc a great tribune, the Flemish discovered in the person of Guillaume de Juliers the younger an admirable captain. He was the younger brother of Count Guillaume de Juliers who had been beaten and killed at Furnes by Robert d'Artois. He had to avenge the death of his brother, and he was the grandson of the old Gui de Dampierre. Guillaume de Juliers the younger was also called Guillaume le Clerc, because he was a priest, archdeacon of the Church of Liège. He was still little more than a child and of a very delicate constitution. Naturally lively and ardent, his glance was full of fire and it seemed as though an inward flame consumed him. With a devouring activity he was impetuous, rash, stimulated by obstacles which he loved to find in his way. And he triumphed over them by the audacity of his spirit. On his arrival in Bruges, Guillaume de Juliers declared himself the lieutenant of his grandfather, the Count of Flanders, and placed himself at the head of the rebels. To the rash and impulsive character which pleases the people, to the youth which they love, to the illustrious nobility which flatters them when it bows before them, he added an elegant bearing and a seductive beauty. "God had lavished natural gifts upon him," wrote a Chronicler of Ghent. "He was young and handsome and full of spirit, eloquent, and of powerful understanding." "He was only a child," says the Dutch Chronicler, Louis van Velthem, "but, O wonder! The people took confidence in seeing this child come from the East. The countries blessed God." Splendidly clothed, and bearing on his shield the lion of the house of Flanders, he traversed the streets of Bruges on his fiery horse. For him, the coffers which held the town's treasures were ever open. The finest costumes, rare arms, bright-coloured stuffs, were thrown at his feet by the people, mad about their hero, proud of his brilliance as if it were their own. He advanced surrounded by a cortege of soldiers and priests, musicians and girls in gay clothing. He kept about him magicians whose rôle was to forecast the future. Then came the escort of horsemen in armour, of Flemish heralds at arms; and then, always pushing and rough, the crowd which acclaimed him.

"He alone was obeyed," writes the Chronicler, Guillaume Guiart, "and he became master over all." One saw him during many years draw after him the populace of the great towns, proud of its outcries, and fall on the field of battle, weary of carnage, drunk with blood. Then he was made Archbishop of Cologne.

On 18th May 1302 the Governor, Jacques de Châtillon, his

THE MIDDLE AGES

Councillors, Pierre Flote and the Bishop of Auxerre, who lodged in the town of Bruges with a sufficiently great number of French knights, were wakened by cries in the middle of the night. The Chronicle of Flanders says agreeably : " Soon the majority saw that there would be great plunder and that these hired Frenchmen, who were full of gold and silver, of plates and dishes, of jewels and good horses, were as good dead as alive."

A number of Frenchmen were killed in their beds ; others succeeded in resuming their arms, but succumbed to numbers. From the high windows and roofs the women threw on the soldiers who were fleeing, plates and stools. In order that the people of Bruges should recognize each other they cried aloud the three words, " Schild ende vriendt " (" Shield and friend.") Bad pronunciation betrayed the French. Jacques de Châtillon and Pierre Flote succeeded in escaping. This event, which matched the Sicilian Vespers, is known under the name of the Bruges Matins.

In order to avenge those of his subjects who had perished in this ambuscade, Philip the Fair raised an important army, the command of which he confided to Robert d'Artois, the victor of Bonnegarde and of Furnes. " In this company," says the Chronicler, " one could see all the flower of the barons and chivalry of France ranged in splendid battle array." The army of the Flemish communes, in which the Bruges contingents formed the majority, was commanded by Guillaume de Juliers. It was composed entirely of infantry. The opposed armies met on 11th July 1302 in the plain of Groeninghe, under the walls of Courtrai. The Flemish who, for several days, had occupied this land, watered and cut by creeks, had dug in it ditches which they afterwards covered with branches. The cross-bowmen who formed the first line of the French army opened the attack. The Flemish began to retreat so obviously that Robert d'Artois thought the battle won. Wishing to allow the Chivalry to take part in the honour of the day, he gave the order to the infantry to fall back and made the cavalry advance. The Flemish continued to retreat. Then the French Chivalry charged vehemently, when, suddenly, the charge was transformed into a frightful jumble of horses and men, dismounted in the ditches, in which splashed a liquid mud. The ranks behind, carried on by their impetus, pushed those who were in front. Embarrassed by their iron carapaces, the French knights were killed without being able to defend themselves. Almost the entire royal army perished.

"And the Flamens," writes the picturesque author of the ancient Chronicles of Flanders, "the Flemish, who saw their enemies in such peril and danger, pressed on them to such an extent that they were all overturned by so great impetuosity that all were killed or dead. And there could one see all the French noblesse lying in the deep ditches, mouths yawning wide, and the great war-horses feet upwards and the knights below." Only the rearguard, commanded by the Counts of Boulogne and St. Pol, escaped. They took to flight. The beaten army ran terrified along the road to Tournai. "Those who found refuge in the town," writes the Abbé Li Muisis, "were filled with terror, and on the morrow they still trembled so much that it was impossible for them to eat the bread that was offered them."

For the King of France the disaster was irreparable. His power was shaken to its foundations, and his efforts were brought to nothing at the moment that the end seemed certain of attainment.

In the heart of the Vatican the news of the defeat reached the old Pope, Boniface VIII, late at night, and he ordered the procurator of the Count of Flanders at the Court of Rome, the Abbot Michel As Clokettes, to be called. And the Pontiff, who had leaped from his bed, hardly took the time to clothe himself in order to hear from his lips the narrative of the battle.

Philip the Fair lost at Courtrai his most useful assistant and the Pope his most redoubtable adversary: the one-eyed Chancellor of a kingdom of the blind, Pierre Flote, was killed there, bravely fighting sword in hand.

In haste the King of France equipped a new army and advanced with it to Vitry. But he had to beat a retreat. The contingents from his own communes, composed of popular elements, threatened to pass over to the camp of the Flemish.

The embarrassment of the King was increased by his financial distress. In the Middle Ages the State was not organized to be able to meet the sudden calls for money which the necessity of putting rapidly in motion and provisioning great armies summoned to the frontiers entailed. Boniface VIII saw in Courtrai the hand of God and doubted no longer that the moment had come to settle the domination of the Church. On 18th November 1302 was published the Bull *Unam sanctam*, which caused Boniface to be called by the partisans of the supremacy of the Church Boniface the Great. In that splendid style of which he had the secret, the Pope addressed himself to the whole of Christendom. The Church has only one body and one head. It is not a monster with two heads, the Pope and the King of France. Its one head is the Vicar of Christ. There are, it is true, two swords—the spiritual and the temporal; but these two swords are in the hands of the Pope. Those who claim that the temporal sword is not in the hands of the Pope forget that Christ said to Peter when he had struck off the Roman soldier's ear, " Return thy sword to its scabbard." Kings ought then only to make use of the temporal sword for the Church and according to the directions of the Pontiff, which they are bound implicitly to obey " ad nutum sacerdotis."

Boniface went so far as to say that he would rather be an ass or a dog than a Frenchman. He repeated that all the French would be damned because they did not believe in the temporal sovereignty of the Pope. The Archives of England, Belgium, and Germany preserve traces of the activity that the old Pope displayed in this moment to urge on the princes allied against Philip the Fair. He absolved the lords of the Imperial marches from the oaths they had taken to the Crown of France. To strengthen the league formed by the King of England he employed the money which had been sent him for the work of the Holy Land. He said, " I shall quickly make martyrs or apostates of all the French."

Some notes emanating from the English Chancery suggest the profound trouble that the papal policy spread in France; they show how much Philip the Fair and his counsellors dreaded the sentences of excommunication that the Pope was preparing to launch against them. The excommunication would transform into a crusade against France the war which was imminent on the expiry of the truce; the King of England and his allies would draw from it a new strength, the audacity of the Flemish

PHILIP THE FAIR

would increase, the English party would see its forces multiplied tenfold by it; the Languedocians, who in their hearts still preserved the rancours sown by the war with the Albigensians, would find in it a powerful motive to rebel; the leagues of the noblesse of Franche-Comté, whom the Burgundians and the people of Champagne were beginning to join, would by it consolidate their area of action. Already at the very heart of the kingdom did not one see the Archbishop of Tours and his suffragans refusing to pay the war tithe.

The attitude of the Pope thus placed Philip the Fair in a position in which it was impossible to retain his conquests, Aquitaine retaken from the Plantagenets. "Through fear of the said excommunication and interdict," we read in the English Chancery Rolls, "the King of France was compelled to come to terms with the King of England and to restore to him castles and towns, and he did this through fear of the said sentences of excommunication and interdict and of seeing them put into execution by crusade or by aid of the secular arm."

Thus, sick at heart, Philip the Fair was constrained to conclude the Treaty of Paris, 20th May 1303. He restored Aquitaine, for which the King of England once again recognized himself to be a vassal of the French Crown. Moreover, Edward II was affianced to Isabella, daughter of Philip the Fair. From this marriage were to be born Edward III and his pretensions to the Crown of France.

One knows the consequences of the Treaty of Paris without it being necessary to indicate them. A century and a half of wars and sufferings, those frightful times that one includes in the name of the Hundred Years War, hardly sufficed to efface them; but the Papacy which had launched against the Capetian power this terrible blow, suffered from it a counter-blow to which it almost succumbed.

Philip the Fair saw clearly that he could no longer avoid taking the offensive in order to save himself from being conquered. On 12th March 1303, in an assembly of the grandees of the kingdom at the Louvre, Boniface VIII was declared a heretic. The King of France appealed to an immediate Council to depose him. On the following 24th June, in the royal garden, at the centre of the City, the crowd pressed on to the lawns. A procession from the most distant provinces of archbishops and bishops, abbots, priors, a crowd of priests and mendicant friars, and a numberless multitude of the people had been seen arriving. On a platform were the King, his sons, his two brothers, and his Councillors. Near them was standing a clerk. He read the appeal against the "false Pope." It stated that Boniface VIII was a materialist, simoniacal, that he practised sorcery, that he had sworn to destroy the kingdom of France. He was preparing sentences of excommunication against the King and his subjects. The King hoped that all would support the appeal to the future Council. From this point, until the Council met, by the very fact of the appeal, the acts of the Pope became null and the kingdom of France was placed directly under the hand of God. From the crowd a thousand voices replied, "Yes. Yes. We support it." And the notaries, seated in black robes at long tables, drew up the reports.

These scenes were renewed in every locality of any importance throughout France.

But speed was necessary. The thunders of the Church might break out at any moment. Moreover, for the action that the French Court proposed, Italy itself should offer some useful allies: the turbulent nobility of the Roman Campagna whom Boniface's despotism had irritated; the dependants of the Colonna, vanquished but not reduced; the Florentines, against whom Boniface had armed Charles de Valois; the Ghibellines, traditionally hostile to the Holy See; the monks and mendicant orders, who increased rapidly and were contemned by Boniface; the hermits, venerated by the crowd; the devout, who by the mouth of holy people like Jacopone de Todi protested against the literary fantasies of the old Pope. The Colonna refugees in France kept the King correctly informed. Nogaret was then charged to go to Italy to notify the Sovereign Pontiff of the appeal which France lodged against him to the decisions of an immediate Council which the Pope was summoned to convoke without delay. Nogaret took as assistant the Florentine banker, "Monseigneur Mouche"; a legist, Thierri d'Hireçon; and a notary, Jacques de Jasseines.

The Prior of la Chaise, Pierre de Paroi, who had already been in Italy, set out on 15th August to overtake and support the mission of Nogaret. " I was," he says later, " to inform Boniface of the appeals lodged against him. If I could not have secured access to him I was to publish these acts in Rome and have them attached to the doors of the churches in Tuscany, Lombardy, and Campania. At the moment that I received these instructions, one of the great prelates of the Council said to me in the presence of the King :

"'Prior, you know that this Boniface is an evil man, a heretic who piles up scandals. Kill him. I take all the responsibility on myself.'

" But Philip the Fair, putting out his hand, said :

"'No! No! It would displease God. The Prior will do nothing of the sort.'"

Historians think that Nogaret and his companions had been commissioned to seize the Pope at Rome and to bring him back prisoner to Lyons, where he should be tried by the Council. It would have been an extravagant enterprise. The sole purpose of the King and of his councillors was to proclaim as regularly and solemnly as possible the appeal to a future Council against the acts of the Pope, so as to nullify the sentences of excommunication which the Sovereign Pontiff was preparing to launch against Philip the Fair, and which would have the consequences already set forth.

In the task which Nogaret went to carry out he acted with complete sincerity. Only a convinced man could have carried through to the end the duty he had assumed. " I wept," he will say, " over the Church, the King, and my country."

Nogaret and his companions reached Florentine territory, where they lodged in a castle belonging to Monseigneur Mouche. As their arrival became known, and their mission was noised abroad, partisans came to them in a crowd. There were first the Colonna and their dependants : Jacopo Colonna, called Sciarra, whom Boniface VIII had reduced to rowing under the leather whips of pirates ; the children of Giovanni di Ceccano, whose father had been kept for two years chained in the dungeon of a strong château ; and lastly, numerous gentlemen of the Roman Campagna, jealous of the sudden elevation of the Gaetani. And Monseigneur Mouche distributed money with open hands.

Nogaret found a priceless ally in Rinaldo da Lupino, a native of Anagni, like Boniface, and captain of the fortified town of Ferrentino, distant hardly a league from Anagni, where the Sovereign Pontiff lay. Boniface had taken from Rinaldo the Château of Trevi, and, outrageous insult, had broken off the projected marriage between Rinaldo's sister and his nephew, Francesco Gaetani, because he wished to make him a Cardinal. Rinaldo assembled 300 horsemen and 1500 footmen, recruited for the most part in the districts of Anagni, Alatri, Ferrentino, and Subri, of that race of rude countrymen who for two centuries had been producing popes and condottieri.

Nogaret learned that Boniface was going to launch the interdict against the King of France on 8th September, the Feast of the Nativity of Our Lady, from the height of that chair of Anagni from which Frederick I had been excommunicated by Alexander III and Frederick II by Gregory IX.

We have preserved the text of the Bull that the aged Pope had prepared, the Bull *Super Petri solio*. . . . It bore already the date 8th September, and began thus:

" On the seat of Peter, from the elevation of a lofty throne, where the hand of God has placed us, we occupy the place of Him to whom the Father said : ' Thou art my Son, I have begotten Thee ; ask and I shall give Thee the nations for Thy inheritance, and Thy domains shall extend to the ends of the universe. Rule men with a rod of iron, break them like potters' vessels ! . . .' Words which form a warning to kings." In short, the Pope excommunicated the King of France, he absolved his subjects from the oath of fidelity, and the treaties signed in the name of the King of France were declared null.

Anagni is a small town which is set upon an elongated plateau that forms one of the last buttresses of the Hernici. One sees it there to-day still, on the height dominating the plain which is bathed by the warm light of the Roman Campagna. The Cathedral, which preserves some ancient parts, is decorated with a statue of Boniface VIII, overlooking the square which it blesses with a peaceable gesture. The papal palace abutted on the Church : the two buildings communicated by a corridor.

and the fortified houses of the Gaetani pressed all round like a rampart to the dwelling of the Pope. The majority of them still stand.

Nogaret had not a minute to lose. It was essential to prevent the Pope launching the interdict. As to the Pope, he had no idea of imminent peril.

On the morning of 7th September, the vigil of the Feast of Our Lady, a band of Italians, 600 horsemen and 1000 armed ruffians, commanded by Sciarra Colonna, preceded by two standards,—one bearing the fleurs-de-lis, and the other the arms of the Church,—poured into the streets of the little town, hardly yet awake. There were no French among this troop except Nogaret and one or two knights. Thierri d'Hireçon and Jacques de Jasseines had themselves abandoned their companion. The people of Anagni took the part of the assailants. To the cries of " Death to Pope Boniface," and " Long live the King of France," a horde of madmen threw themselves on the papal palace. The Marquis Pietro Gaetani, assisted by his son and some faithful friends, resisted and erected barricades; but their houses were forced, as also the palaces of the few cardinals who remained faithful to the Sovereign Pontiff.

Boniface VIII, terrified, wished to negotiate. What did they want with him?

" That he should abdicate like Celestine; that he should become a monk and shut himself up in the cell of a distant convent! "

The old man of eighty-six years recovered his energy:

" Never."

The papal palace was fortified. They got into it by means of the adjoining church whose doors had been burned down. The clergy in their albs fled like a flock of great white birds. The floor of the church was stained with blood; they threw down there, pierced by a dagger, the Archbishop of Strigovie. Some of the pontifical servants assisted the attackers, who flung themselves into the dwelling of the Pope by the light of the crackling flames. Night was approaching when Boniface heard shaking about him the last doors. Tears fell down his cheeks. He said to two clerics remaining at his side:

" I am betrayed like Jesus Christ. I wish to die as a Pope."

He assumes the cope of St. Peter and puts on his head the tiara of three rows, the *triregnum*, shining with gold and precious stones. With him remained two cardinals, Nicolas Boccasini (who succeeded him under the name of Benedict XI), and Peter of Spain, Bishop of Salerno.

The Pope fixed his eyes on the oaken door, which suddenly, under the pressure of the assailants, flies into splinters. The first to appear is Sciarra Colonna, with bloodshot eyes. He shouted out insults, and uttered violent threats. Behind him was Nogaret, calm and grave. The "venerable professor of laws" saw in all this only a legal process. The planks of the roof fell with a crash; cries were heard and already the disputes over pillage, the noise made by the arms in forcing the coffers of the pontifical treasure. The golden vases, falling on the flagstones, sounded like bells. Standing by the banner of the fleur-de-lis, Nogaret explained to Boniface VIII his purpose. He spoke precisely and distinctly. He explained how "he, Boniface, was accused of heresy, and that not having advanced a defence, he was reputed convicted, in conformity with the laws of the Church; that he summoned him to appear at Lyons, before an œcumenical council, at which he would be deposed, seeing that his guilt was notorious, as a heretic and simoniac."

But the uproar was redoubled. Boniface stared into space with a stupid air; his hands were trembling. Nogaret went on:

"However, as it is necessary that you should be declared guilty by the judgment of the Church, I wish to preserve your life from the violence of your enemies and to present you to the General Council, which I require you to convoke. If you refuse to submit to its judgment, it will function in spite of you, especially as it is a case of heresy. I insist on preventing you also from exciting scandal in the Church, particularly against the King of France. For these reasons I hand you over to the custody of guards for the defence of the faith and the interests of the Church; not to insult you nor for any other reason."

While Nogaret was speaking, Sciarra was boiling with impatience. He thought that the legist was going to speak for ever. The discourse led nowhere. The only thing necessary to do was to put a sword through the Pope's throat and all would be in order.

The old Pontiff repeated, his arms extended in the form of a cross, " Behold my head ! Behold my arms ! "

The plunder of the magnificent papal treasure, of the Gaetani palace and of the houses of the cardinals favourable to Boniface, went on energetically. It was this that the Italians who had followed Nogaret considered the most important feature of the adventure. Nogaret allocated guards to the old Pope, who protected him and shut him up in a room : " an action that saved his life," he will say later. He insisted that only the Pope's own servants should be authorized to prepare his meals. He permitted the cardinals to withdraw to Péronne.

Some surprise has been caused by the inaction of Nogaret on the following day, 7th September. The reason is that he had been involved in the expedition to Anagni in spite of himself, from the necessity in which he found himself of preventing at all costs the publication of the letters of interdict of which he had suddenly learned the imminence. The Colonna and the nobles of Anagni, enemies of the Gaetani, wished to keep Boniface VIII in their hands ; Nogaret would have preferred to remove him to France. But how could he transport a Pope prisoner, across the whole of Italy, in the company of only three men—a banker, a notary, and a cleric ?

The people of Anagni recovered themselves. Rome was moved with lively emotion. Jealousy against the French woke up ; it was thought that if they were allowed to remove the Pope to France, neither he nor his successors would return there : fears sufficiently justified. Four hundred Roman horsemen, led by the Cardinal Matteo of Aqua Sparta, marched upon Anagni. When they arrived, Nogaret had left.

Boniface was brought to Rome. He presented himself at St. Peter's in sumptuous apparel. He ran over in his mind great plans to avenge himself against the King of France. But he had been profoundly injured. He was stifled with rage, his mind was unbalanced. He no longer spoke, looking before him with a fixed and sombre stare. His servants, on entering his room, found him doubled up, his eyes haggard, his teeth

THE MIDDLE AGES

buried in his fists. In this state he died on 11th October 1303, aged eighty-six years.

On 21st October, Nicholas Boccasini, one of the two prelates who had been with the old Pontiff at Anagni on the terrible day of 7th September, was elected pope. He took the name of Benedict XI. Benedict was the baptismal name of Boniface VIII. He was an old man, gentle and timid, who feared to take any action. The great majesty of Philip the Fair overawed him. On 10th February 1304, Nogaret was to return to Béziers, where he rejoined his master. A Bull of 13th May 1304 annulled all the sentences which the Holy See had launched against the King of France or his counsellors. The King was victorious.

Yet Philip the Fair strained his efforts to put an end to the struggle with the Flemish, which threatened to drag on for ever. He put himself in person at the head of his army. The opposed forces met on the 18th August 1304 in the plain of Mons-en-Pévele. The Flemish were on this occasion still commanded by Guillaume de Juliers, elected Archbishop of Cologne. The King disposed of 60,000 men; the Flemish army amounted to about 80,000 men.

In the middle of the action, the French cavalry, suddenly seized with panic, broke. The battle would have been lost but for the coolness of the King, who stood firm against the Flemish. At his side, Anselme de Chevreuse, who held the oriflamme, and Brun de Verneuil, who led the King's horse by the bridle, were killed. The King was himself unhorsed; but reseated in the saddle by two officials of his house, the brothers Jacques and Pierre Gentien, he threw himself on the Flemish; we know that he was of great stature and of a singular physical strength. "He had bones bigger than beams," writes the Templar of Tyr. Then the Flemish, we read in the *Anciennes Chroniques* of Flanders, who thought they had completely won, ran upon him. "The noble King was mounted on a tall war-horse, bearing his full royal arms, and carried a great iron weapon in one hand. He cried '*Montjoye Saint Denis!*' his weapon performed wonders, for those whom he struck full in the body had no resource but the doctor. Indeed, he performed such feats of arms by his valour that, by his own body and own enterprise without the help of any one else, the Flemish might have this day been discomfited. For when the cavalry, who had already fallen back, perceived the King in person, who had advanced and wrought so much with his weapons, they recoiled in a body on the Flemish. And then began once more a violent and cruel battle. But the Flemish, who all this day had been struggling, could bear no more: they were discomfited, and so many of them were killed that the fields were littered with their bodies."

Guillaume de Juliers attempted in his turn to rally his forces, but the Count de Boulogne, by an opportune manœuvre, surrounded him on all sides. Juliers and his faithful men of Bruges were exhausted. The heat of the day had been stifling. "Then the Count Guillaume de Juliers took off his boots and all his people with him, and put the pommels of their swords into their mouths to staunch their thirst and thus waited for death." A French soldier cut off the head of Guillaume de Juliers and carried it stuck on a pike to Philip the Fair, who turned away his eyes from it. The oriflamme was found only on the morrow, torn into two parts. In commemoration of his victory, Philip the Fair caused to be erected an equestrian statue, representing him equipped for battle, in the Church of Notre Dame. It could still be seen there on the eve of the Revolution. As to the Flemish, they were unable to believe in the death of their hero, Guillaume de Juliers. For long years after Mons-en-Pévele, writes the Ghent annalist, it was told in the country and market towns, how in the height of the struggle an invisible hand had removed Guillaume de Juliers and that one day, doubtless near at hand, in the hour of danger, they would see him again, in his shining armour, at the head of the crafts of Bruges, leading them to victory.

The preceding week, the French fleet had won a striking victory over the Flemish fleet, commanded by Gui de Namur in the Bay of Zierickzee; Gui de Namur perished there. Peace could be delayed no longer: it was concluded at Athis-sur-Orge in June 1305. Philip the Fair restored to Robert de Béthune, the heir of Gui de Dampierre, the States he had confiscated from his father, but retaining French-speaking Flanders: Lille, Douai, and Orchies.

THE MIDDLE AGES

We have followed up to this point only a part of the political activity of Philip the Fair. Witness how he united to the French Crown the town of Valenciennes, the County of Bar, the bishoprics of Toul and of Verdun, Viviers, and the whole of Franche-Comté.

The False-Coiner.

Benedict XI was succeeded on 5th June 1305 by a French Pope, the Archbishop of Bordeaux, Bertrand de Got, who took on the pontifical throne the name of Clement V and transferred the seat of the Papacy to France. On all sides Philip the Fair strengthened French influence.

For this vast and complex work, and for the organization of the kingdom, he required financial resources.

In a century and a half the expenses of the monarchy had been tripled, but the sources of the revenues of which the King disposed had remained the same. If the King wished to levy some new contribution what outcries there were! The clergy appeal to the Pope, the nobles form a league, in the towns popular risings break out. In 1306 in Paris the life of the King is even in danger: he is obliged to take refuge in the precincts of the Temple.

The disasters of 1302 in Flanders necessitate new contributions. Philip the Fair adopts the tax proportional to the income. He attempts to show the people that it is in their own interest that he has been inspired to decide upon this form of tax, which was, moreover, softened by the manner in which it was collected.

" Deal amicably," writes the King to his collectors, " with the people of big and small towns; show how in this affair, which touches the interest of all, each is bound to give of his goods according to his power. The King does not wish that his subjects should be exposed to the perils of war; he wishes, on the contrary, to arrange everything so as to cause them the smallest injury. He has taken counsel with wise and prudent men, who have sought to discover the best way for the people, and they have decided that the people should give subsidies to the King for four months, that if the campaign should drag on longer they would pay no more, but the subsidies should be proportionally diminished if the campaign should be

404

shorter." "For each sergeant," continued the King, "only two sous would be paid, although he costs more to the King; and during the whole war neither customs, the fiftieth, nor any other subvention shall be demanded."

The King ended with these words: "Item, if you cannot make a good agreement with the towns taken together, treat with each separately and see how much each should pay; estimate what could be derived from this method and from the other, and see which would yield the greater profit; but the King inclines to that which shall appear best to the people."

At other times the King called to Paris the representatives of the big towns, the prelates, and lords of the realm. An assembly of this sort took place on 1st April 1314 in the garden of the Palace. Some supplies were necessary for the war of Flanders. Enguerran de Marigny, "coadjutor of the realm," stood up beside the King: "Preaching to the people, he explained the complaint of the King." He described the origins of the conflict, the vicissitudes of the war, and the treaty of peace which the Flemish did not wish to observe. "Against these rebels will not the faithful subjects of the King of France consent to assist their lord?" At these words the King rose and approached the edge of the platform in order to receive the engagements of those who were disposed to come to his assistance. The first who responded was Etienne Barbette, burgess of Paris. In the name of the Parisians he said that all would help their King in the measure of their power. The King thanked him for his assurance. And after him, one by one, the delegates from other communes of France spoke in the same sense. And the King thanked them. And then, after this parliament, a subvention was levied . . . for which the said Enguerran fell under the hatred and malediction of the common people."

Enguerran Le Portier de Marigny was the greatest figure of the reign after Pierre Flote. He came of a modest family of Norman origin. In 1298 we find him pantler of Queen Jeanne of Navarre, who was his patron at Court. He became chamberlain of the King. In these functions he displayed his administrative powers. At the end of the reign he could boast that he was the only one who understood the finances of the kingdom.

He was equally well informed as to the resources of the neighbouring peoples and the resources of foreign courts. He writes to Simon of Pisa: "Know, Brother Simon, that I am aware as well as a man of Flanders of the power of the Flemings, of the money they can strike, and that I know as well as you who have been there the agreements which the German nobles make, what they do and what they think."

To these gifts of administration he added oratorical powers already useful to those who wished to acquire influence in France. Geoffroi de Paris calls him "the finest speaker of all in France." He exercised a considerable influence on Philip the Fair during the last years of the reign. "He was key and lock of the kingdom." Foreign sovereigns overwhelmed him with gifts and sought his favour. The Pope offered him a rose of gold. Ministers, Kings, and Pope, says the popular chronicler, were puppets in his hands of which he held the wires:

"He had them all on his line."

In this rapid rise, Marigny appeared not to have maintained necessary moderation. His house at Paris had a golden gable; his luxury overshadowed the King's brothers; in the city court of justice, whose reconstruction he directed, he caused his statue to be erected at the side of that of Philip the Fair. "One sees him when one mounts to the chapel," writes Geoffroi de Paris, "at the right of the King in white head-dress."

Some contemporaries understood the necessity of the contributions which the King levied; but their number was small and the needs were pressing. It was thus that Philip the Fair was brought to the changes in the currency for which he has been so much reproached.

In order to grasp what constituted in the thirteenth and fourteenth centuries the false currency of the Kings, it must be noted that in the Middle Ages there was a double currency—a real money and a nominal money. One reckoned by livres, sous, and deniers, a way of reckoning which passed into England, where the initials have been preserved: £ = pound, livre; s = shilling, sou; d = penny, denier. The golden florin of the middle of the thirteenth century was worth 12 sous 6 deniers, and the groat of Tours was equal in value to a sou. But these ratios were not fixed; they could vary either by the natural

PHILIP THE FAIR

changes of currency or by order of the King. He could ordain, for example, that the groat of Tours should for the future be received for two sous instead of one. The King could also, without altering the nominal value of the Tours groats, reduce their weight and standard, so that in reality their value was the half of what they were previously worth, at the same time maintaining their value in exchange. In this consisted the debased coining of Philip the Fair. In his urgent needs, he declared that the money leaving the coffers should have a value superior to that which it had in reality; or indeed he recoined the money in them, giving an inferior weight and standard. He did not alter the pieces in order to deceive the people, as is generally believed; he warned the public of the diminution in weight which he caused in the Tours groats and the golden florin while imposing on them a forced currency. This is the exact word. Such is our paper-money.

At the time of the great alteration of 1295, necessitated by the war against England, the King expressed himself in this way: " We have been obliged to have a coinage struck which lacks something of the weight and of the alloy that our predecessors put into it." But, adds the King, " I shall accept myself this money in payment of that which is due to me, and later I shall indemnify those who shall have suffered any loss from this cause "; and to this effect he engaged the revenues of his domains.

Finally, as soon as he could, the King invited the holders of " feeble " money to report themselves at his workshops, so that he could cause them to be refunded in " good and ancient money." It was then a form of loan such as the economic condition of the time permitted, and which the King repaid when the state of his finances gave him the means to do so. Notice, for example, a Bull of Benedict XI, the successor of Boniface VIII, which grants to the King (11th May 1305) a year of prebends and two years of the ecclesiastical benefices in France, in order that he should be able to raise his coinage to the standard it possessed under Saint Louis.

Modern times have seen the assignats, forced currency notes, and loans which the organization of great financial concerns permit, resources which were wanting to Philip the Fair.

THE MIDDLE AGES

When in our days the Government issues forty or fifty milliards' worth of paper-money, bank-notes, guaranteed by five or six milliards of gold or silver in the cellars of the Bank of France, it also issues false money—indeed, much more false than that of Philip the Fair, and exposed, like it, to sudden changes and variations in value; but the progress realized since the thirteenth century in monetary circulation, the control of credit and the introduction of a fiduciary money, make the inconveniences no longer as great as in former times.

It is certain that if Philip the Fair had had the disposal of the financial organization which the Knights of the Temple had developed for themselves, he would not have dreamed of debasing the coinage.

The Templars.

This Order, religious and military, founded in 1119 by a knight of Champagne, Hugue de Payns, had rapidly attained an extraordinary prosperity. In 1128 the Council of Troyes, at the suggestion of St. Bernard, gave to the " Poor Soldiers of the Temple " a rule inspired by that of Citeaux. The end of the order was to protect the Holy Land against the attacks of the Infidels. It courageously fulfilled its mission, and at the end of the thirteenth century, those who took in hand the cause of the Temple could say that 20,000 Brothers had died in Palestine with their arms in their hands. But while combating the Infidel and assuring for themselves eternal life, the Poor Soldiers of the Temple fostered their worldly interests. They became the owners of so much property that the Council of the Lateran in 1179 already demanded that they should abandon what they had acquired during the ten preceding years.

They founded "houses" in the West, more particularly in France. On 16th June 1291 the Mohammedans seized St. Jean d'Acre, the last foothold of Christendom in the Holy Land. The Templars returned to their original country. At this moment the order should have been dissolved. It had no longer any *raison d'être*.

The property of the Temple at the end of the thirteenth century was immense.

In 1229 the Emperor Frederick II was obliged to hunt them out of Sicily. The number of knights at the period when Philip the Fair ascended the throne was 15,000 in round numbers. Each of them was a tried soldier. Towards the middle of the thirteenth century, Matthew Paris attributed 9000 castles and manors to them: the number given by the *Chronique de Flandre* is even larger. Each of these manors was the nucleus of a fief, a centre of influence. In the archives of the commanderies of the Temple were preserved by hundreds the titles of the revenues granted to the tenants of the neighbourhood, which involved the obligation of fidelity and of feudal service. The ecclesiastical and lay lords constantly complained to the King that their vassals refused them the service that was due to them on the pretext that they were men of the Temple. Consider the new town of the Temple at Paris, the territory of the Temple near Ypres, and so many others; each of these domains was a veritable feudal lordship, with rights of high, middle, and petty justice, annual fairs, privileges, and franchises and numerous "manants." Among other franchises the Templars claimed that of not being amenable judicially except to the Pope, after the fashion of other religious orders.

Not content to exercise their authority over the territories subject to them, the Templars attempted to acquire new rights, in which they were particularly favoured by the troubles of the war in Aquitaine under Philip the Fair. Their patronage, moreover, was very much sought by the people of the country, who thus armed themselves against the power of the seigniorial bailiffs. Michelet notes that in the seneschal's jurisdiction of Beaucaire alone the order had bought 10,000 pounds' worth of revenues vested in land; and this did not only represent at the epoch a considerable property, but a great territorial power. The Prior of St. Gilles had under him alone fifty-four commanderies. In most of the countries of Europe the Brothers had fortresses; in the kingdom of Valencia they possessed seventeen of them. They had been seen to attack crowned heads—the King of Cyprus and the Prince of Antioch—dethrone a King of Jerusalem, ravage Greece and Thrace.

The origin of their financial power was the immense treasure which they had brought back to the West: 150,000 golden florins, which a skilful financial administration soon increased tenfold. As the Templars had houses in every country, they carried out the financial operations of the international banks of to-day; they were acquainted with bills of exchange, orders payable at sight; they arranged annuities and pensions on paid-up capital, made advances of funds, lent against pledges, managed private deposits, and undertook the levy of taxes for lay and ecclesiastical lords. They lent money to kings.

From the year 1290, Philip the Fair was uneasy on the subject of the power of the Temple. By letters of 29th June he ordered his seneschals and *baillis* to send him the list of the properties acquired by the Brothers of the Temple during the last forty-five years. The same year the Parliament forbade them to extend their patronage over individuals. On 22nd April 1293, Philip the Fair reminded his officials of this decree, ordering them to see to its execution.

The Temple enjoyed insolent prosperity. Richard Cœur de Lion said that he left his avarice to the Cistercians and his pride to the Templars. After the catastrophe in which their power was to collapse, the good chronicler, Geoffroi de Paris, drew this portrait of them: " The Brothers of the Temple, gorged with gold and silver and who commanded such nobility, where are they? What has become of them, those whom no one dare cite in the courts? Always buying and never selling, making themselves feared as much as the King's officers, extending their pride over the world, making themselves richer than the richest: 'So often goes the pitcher to the water that it breaks.'"

They came to the point of braving the King and refusing to pay taxes.

Philip the Fair attempted to divert to the royal authority the power of the Temple. He solicited admission into the Order with a view to becoming the head. He selected the Grand Master as godfather of one of his children. These advances were repulsed: and the destruction of the Temple was decided in his mind.

Imagine what would have become of the power of the King of Bourges in the evil days of the Hundred Years War in the face of an Order counting some thousands of knights, sheltered in some hundreds of fortresses, disposing of infinite resources and

PHILIP THE FAIR

of an immense number of vassals and tenants. We know the history of the Teutonic Order.

The registers of the Trésor des Chartes state that on the 22nd September 1307, in the monastery of Maubisson lès Pontoise, the King gave the seals to Nogaret, and that the matter of the Templars was there directly dealt with. They were arrested throughout France on 13th October. The operation was carried out with so much decision that no resistance could be made. The Templars were prosecuted for heresy.

Already for a long time strange rumours had circulated about the secret practices of the Templars, because they took care that the holding of their chapters and the rules of their Order should remain unknown to the uninitiated. What had they so serious as to require concealment? The Preceptor of Auvergne, one of the dignitaries of the Temple, who was later asked why his Order was always surrounded with such profound secrecy, replied, " Through folly."

The crowd spoke of frightful vices and of idolatry.

Philip the Fair proceeded by way of appeal to the people. In his name Nogaret spoke to the Parisians in the garden of the Palace (13th October 1307). Popular assemblies were summoned throughout France. At Tours the States-General met in immense numbers : the Tiers Etat itself alone counted over 700 delegates (May 1308). The act of accusation against the Templars was read. The people had confidence in the person of the King, who was essentially in their eyes the defender of the Church. With one voice the representatives of the Nobility and of the big towns replied that the Templars deserved death.

On 26th November 1309 the Grand Master, Jacques de Molay, appeared before the judges declaring himself prepared to defend the Temple, although he was only a poor knight, simple and uninstructed. He spoke with force and emotion :

" I know no religious Order whose churches had finer ornaments than the churches of the Temple ; I know no Order in which larger alms were given than in the houses of the Temple, where, three times a week, one gave to all comers ; I know no Order which has shed so much blood in fighting the enemies of the faith."

THE MIDDLE AGES

When it was pointed out to him that all this was nothing without a pure doctrine, he said:

"It is true. It is true. But I believe in only one God in three persons and in the whole Catholic faith; I believe in one God, one faith, one baptism, one Church, and that at the hour when the soul leaves the body we shall see the good and the wicked, and that then each of us will know the truth of that which is at present a matter of debate."

It came to pass that this same Jacques de Molay and many of the dignitaries of the Order recognized as well founded the practices of which the Order of the Temple was accused. Clement V writes that, before him, persons occupying high positions in the Order had admitted freely and without constraint that at the reception of new Brothers they were forced to deny Christ; but more often these admissions were extracted by torture or terror. Ponsard de Gisy declared before the Commissioners: "During the three months which preceded the admissions that I made before the Bishop of Paris, I was placed in a ditch with my arms bound behind my back, and pressed so strongly that all the blood flowed to the nails; I was secured by a cord. If they put me back again into torment, I should say all that they wished. I am prepared to submit to limited punishments, to have my head cut off, to be burned or boiled for the honour of the Order; but I cannot bear long tortures such as those to which I have been subjected for more than two years."

He added that all the admissions made by him were false. It was the Prior of Montfaucon and the monk Guillaume Robert who caused the Templars thus to be put to the question. Thirty-six of his companions had perished at Paris in the tortures. All that they said before the Bishop of Paris against the Order was false.

Another Templar, Bernard Dugue, said that his feet had been roasted until the flesh became detached and the bones from his heels fell off. He held in his hand two bones which the torture had removed from his heels.

The Brothers who appeared before the inquisitors declared that they would defend the Order to the death. Some of them express themselves energetically: "Those who have spoken evil of it have lied with their mouth." A number of them retracted their declarations previously made before the Pope. Those who accuse the Temple of heresy or of evil practices are false Brothers who have left the Order or have been driven from it for their misconduct and wish to avenge themselves.

Brother Jean de Montroyal, in his name and in the name of a great number of his Brothers, read a declaration which alone would have been sufficient to justify the Order, at least in general:

" Our Order is holy; it has been approved by the Roman Church. The Brothers have always lived in the Catholic and Roman faith. They practise fasts and abstinences, confess and communicate publicly at Christmas, Easter, and at Pentecost. They die with the rites of the Church. All the Brothers of our house are bound to say a hundred Paters for the soul of a defunct Brother in the eight days which follow his decease. The High Altar in our churches is consecrated to the Virgin. On Friday we bear a silver-gilt cross before the eyes of all the people in honour of the cross on which our Saviour died. We distribute alms; we give hospitality to travellers. Some Brothers of our Order have become archbishops and bishops. The Kings of France have selected treasurers and almoners from among our Brothers. Item, a number of our Brothers have been prisoners among the Infidels for twenty-five years; neither through fear of death nor by gifts have they been brought to deny Christ; although if the Templars were such as report describes them these prisoners would now be at liberty. The true cross is in the custody of the Templars; if the Templars were what they are said to be the true cross would not suffer itself to be guarded by them. The crown of thorns does not blossom on Good Friday except when it is in the hands of the chaplain of the Temple; and this would not be if the Templars were what they are said to be. St. Euphemia has worked many miracles in one of the houses of the Temple; and this would not have been done if the Templars were what they are said to be. More than 20,000 Brothers have died beyond the seas for the defence of the faith."

Jean de Montroyal ends with these words:

" Item, we have suffered many wounds and hellish imprisonment, and for long periods on bread and water through which many of our Brothers have died; and we should not have suffered so much if our religion were not pure and we were not maintaining the truth, and if it were not to remove evil errors from the world which is without reason on the matter."

The Order of the Temple was innocent. Were there in practice in some houses certain bad customs, imported from the East, a show of renouncing the teaching of Christ imposed as a proof of extreme docility and obedience? It is possible. The heads of the Order were ignorant of it.

On the other hand, the good faith of the accusers is not less evident. Fanatics make bad judges, this has been seen at all times; but the fanatics are convinced. To maintain that Philip the Fair executed so many noble victims with no other motive than the desire to seize the property of the Templars is a suggestion as puerile as that which consists in maintaining that the " patriots " only cut off so many heads in order to seize the goods of the aristocrats and the *émigrés*.

On 12th May 1310, fifty-four Templars who persisted in the determination to defend the Order were burned as relapsed at the edge of the Wood of Vincennes.

The story of this punishment, in the chroniclers of the time, is in the tone of " Père Duchesne," or of the *Revolutions de Paris*, describing a cartload of partisans of the old régime led to the guillotine. On 13th May, Brother Aimeri de Villiers-le-Duc, a Templar for fifty-eight years, appeared in his turn before the Commissioners. " Pale and terrified," he heard the act of accusation read. Brusquely he interrupted: " I have admitted certain articles because of the tortures which Guillaume de Marcilly and Hugue de la Celle, knights of the King, caused me to endure. All that I have said is false. Yesterday I saw fifty-four of my Brothers in wagons, led to the stake, because they did not wish to admit our alleged errors; I thought that I could never resist the terror of the fire. I shall admit all, I feel it; I would declare that I have killed God."

By the Bull *Vox in excelso*, dated 3rd April 1312, Clement V declared the Order of the Temple suppressed. The Templars dispersed : some entered convents ; others married and betook themselves to manual work. On 18th March 1314, were burned alive the Grand Master Jacques de Molay, and Geoffroi de Charnay, the Preceptor of Normandy, in the Ile des Javiaux, also called the Ile aux Juifs, to-day joined to the Ile de la Cité. A rough crowd pressed about the two illustrious victims, and, in the crowd, Geoffroi de Paris, who has left a moving account of the last moments of Molay.

When all was ready, the Grand Master stood " in his shirt." As he had some money with him, he wished to distribute it to the poor, whom he saw at his feet: " That God might have pity on his soul."

> But he found not any soul
> Who wished to hear a word of his;
> They treated him as a dog.

When the executioners bound his hands behind his back he besought them : " Lords, at least let me join my hands a little in order to pray to God."

With a firm voice he proclaimed once more the innocence and purity of the Order ; he asked to be turned towards the Virgin Mary, of whom our Lord was born—that is to say, towards the church of Notre Dame.

> And so sweetly welcomed death
> That each one marvelled at it.

When he had given his last sigh, his companion, the preceptor Geoffroi de Charnay, spoke in his turn :

> Lords, without a doubt
> My master's way I follow,
> You have him as a martyr slain.

The crowd in dispersing discussed the tragedy. Geoffrey of Paris states this and adds philosophically :

> I know not who speaks truth or who the lie,
> May that come of it which ought to be.

What became of the possessions of the Temple ? Philip the Fair decided that they should be handed over to the Hospitallers. Clement V bears witness that the orders given by the King in this matter were executed. The very estate of the Temple in Paris, which, up to the eve of the Revolution,

THE MIDDLE AGES

was the property of the Order of St. John of Jerusalem, bears witness to this up to the threshold of the modern age.

The royal treasury retained certain sums for the expenses of the trial, which were immense. In 1312 the King assembled the Council of Vienne in order that the teaching of the Temple should there be judged.

The great riches and power of the Temple consisted in the hundreds and thousands of contracts of quit-rent (*cens*) and *rente* which all over Christendom attached creditors and tenants to it. These titles were destroyed by the very fact that the Templars were declared to be heretics, every debt to a heretic being reputed null. And perhaps it is in this fact one must seek the reason of the hostility which everywhere manifested itself against the knights, and the facility with which, thanks to the complicity of public opinion, all resistance was stifled.

In these violent conflicts hardly has one been able to catch a glimpse of the legislative work which found its principal expression in the great ordinance of 1303. Philip the Fair so perfected the judicial institutions that we may see in him the founder of the *Parlement*.

End of the Reign.

But here again what obstacles he had to surmount. In 1306 the King was obliged to give way on an essential point in allowing to be re-established the ordeal by battle, even in grave cases—homicide and witchcraft.

The Abbot of St. Denis bears witness that in the last part of his reign the temper of the King was gloomy. He became sad and spoke less and less. To his intimates he confided the anxiety he suffered from the wars, the disturbances and the violences of his reign. Did he recognize the tortures inflicted on the Templars, he who said in setting free the prisoners of the Inquisition, "Prisons exist to retain the guilty, not to torture them."

The death of his wife, Jeanne de Navarre, at Vincennes, 2nd April 1305, in the brilliance of her thirty-two years, had contributed to this sadness. She was a valiant woman who, in spite of her embonpoint and her rosy complexion, when Henri de Bar invaded her county of Champagne, did not hesitate to take horse to lead the troops, who vanquished the

Count de Bar and took him prisoner at Comines. A cultivated woman, who will always preserve the glory of having instigated the old Sire de Joinville to write his immortal life of Saint Louis. The humble monk, Bernard Delicieux, in the course of his campaign for the defence of the people of Languedoc against the Inquisition, calls Jeanne "This other Esther who protects us." Many documents bear witness to the great intimacy which united Philip the Fair and his wife.

She was not then near him to soften the terrible blow he received in learning of the conduct of his daughters-in-law. Isabelle, daughter of Philip the Fair, who had married Edward II, King of England, had given two purses of cloth of gold: one to Marguerite of Burgundy, daughter of the Duke of Burgundy, and wife of Louis le Hutin, son and heir of the King of France; and the other to Blanche, second daughter of Otto IV, Count Palatine of Burgundy, and wife of Charles IV, third son of Philip the Fair. On her return to France she was surprised to find these purses at the belt of two young knights who frequented the Court—Philip and Gauthier d'Aunay. Philip the Fair caused the two brothers d'Aunay to be flayed alive at Pontoise and their corpses dragged through the streets. Some suspicions having also fallen on Jeanne of Burgundy, the wife of Philip the Tall, the King ordered that she should be imprisoned like her two sisters-in-law. Marguerite, wife of Louis le Hutin, was shut up in Château-Gaillard. She admitted her misconduct, and soon perished in the dungeon of the cold prison where she had been thrown.

Jeanne of Burgundy, wife of Philip the Tall, never ceased to protest her innocence. She was taken to the Castle of Dourdan in a four-wheeled car covered with black cloth. She said with sighs, to those who stopped to see her pass: "For God's sake, tell my lord Philip that I die without sin." As a matter of fact, her innocence was recognized, and she returned to her husband.

The third, Blanche of Burgundy, the wife of Charles the Fair, was a child. She was hardly eighteen years of age when she also was shut up in Château-Gaillard. She had no wish to die. She protested that she had done no evil. She had already given Charles the Fair two children, who had died in infancy.

THE MIDDLE AGES

She was questioned several times in the chapel of Château-Gaillard in the presence of her ladies. " The gaiety of her countenance," we read in one of the reports, " showed that at that moment she was without any fear." She allowed herself to be divorced from her husband on the pretext of spiritual affinity. She was then permitted to take the veil in the Abbey of Maubuisson, where her children were buried. There she died in 1325.

On the other hand, Philip the Fair already heard the rumble of the reaction which was to sweep away his work, cause the fall of his chancellor, Pierre de Latilly, and of his chamberlain, Enguerran de Marigny. During the year 1314, in different parts of France, in Brittany, in Normandy, in Picardy, in Champagne, in Burgundy, in Anjou, in Auvergne, in Poitou, in Gascony, and in Languedoc, were formed leagues against the King who " devours his people." " Let the reigning King beware," writes a member of the league, the old Sire de Joinville. " He has escaped great perils. It is only time that he should mend his ways in order that God should not strike him and his cruelly."

The Flemish on their side did not execute the Treaty of Athis. Very weary of this strife, cropping up again incessantly, Philip equipped a new army, to march, once again, towards the Northern frontier.

Did the silent King cast at this moment an anxious glance over the destinies of the kingdom ? Did the prediction of Saint Louis recur to his mind ? His energy is unimpaired; he does not allow his courage to fail. Hiding his projects from his minister selected by himself, Marigny, who, a methodical man concerned with internal affairs, did not like to see the resources of the treasury squandered beyond the frontiers, he engaged in negotiations beyond the Rhine in order to arrange the succession of his brother Charles to the throne of Germany, vacant by the death of Henry VII. He restored to honour the projects of an expedition to the Holy Land, took the Cross with his three sons, an expedition which in his mind ought to assure perpetual peace by concentrating in his hands all the forces of Christendom. To these projects of a Crusade the inveterate servant of the royal magnificence, Nogaret, devoted himself passionately.

PHILIP THE FAIR

But Nogaret dies; then Clement V; and, behold, Philip the Fair is struck down in the strength of his forty-six years. All three rapidly disappear as though obeying the summons of the Templar of Naples, of whom Ferreti de Vicenza speaks.

On 4th November 1314, while hunting in the woods of Pont St. Maxence, the King felt the first attack of the malady to which he was to succumb. He was on horseback and was seized with a fainting fit; his heart ceased to beat. Yet he did not fall from his horse. He was taken by water to Poissy, where he rested ten days. He was able to go on horseback from Poissy to Essonnes; there his illness broke out afresh, and he was carried in a litter as far as Fontainebleau.

On the morning of the 26th, Philip the Fair knew that his end was near. He confessed, communicated, and then went to bed. He put in order the details of his will. From time to time he paused to say, "Fair Lord God, I commend my spirit into Thy hands." Then he received the last sacraments. He whom the others ought to have consoled, writes an eye-witness of his death, consoled them. At the last he calls his eldest son: "Louis," he says to him, "I speak to you before men who love you and are bound to love you; for my part, I love you above all others, but may your life be such that you may deserve to be loved." He tells him how he ought to rule with dignity and moderation, governing by himself, but taking advice from prudent men, in particular of his two uncles, Charles and Louis. "Act so that every one may perceive that you are son of a King, nay more, King of France." And many times, adds the chronicler, he said, "Ponder, Louis, these words: 'What is it to be King of France?'"

Some moments later the King asked that all should retire.

"Secretly, before the confessor alone, he taught his eldest son how he ought to act in touching the sick and the holy words he had been accustomed to use when he touched them. Similarly he told him that it was with great reverence, holiness, and purity that he ought to touch the infirm, clean of conscience as of hands."

Philip the Fair passed away peacefully at Fontainebleau on

THE MIDDLE AGES

29th November 1314, reciting the office of the Holy Spirit. He was forty-six years old.

Philip the Fair has not been understood, and therefore has not received justice. This young Prince was one of the greatest kings and of the noblest characters in history. Speaking of his struggle against the Papacy, the great historians of the sixteenth century will recall that he was surnamed Philip the Catholic, " by the voice of the people and at the request of the clergy."

The generation which succeeded him celebrated with gratitude the prosperity which he gave to France by his far-seeing and active policy. His reign did not appear to the subjects of Philip of Valois the "reign of the devil," but a reign of beauty and of wisdom, worthy of admiration. At the opening of the fourteenth century, commerce, industry, agriculture are in a flourishing state from north to south of France: the cultivation of the vine and of cereals, the raising of cattle, the wool trade are equally prosperous. Agricultural machinery had been brought to perfection. One sees the foundation of joint-stock companies, a marvel for those days. In Provence and in Languedoc one encounters swineherds who possess vineyards; simple drovers have houses in town. And the increase of population becomes more marked with the ease and the active life, to such a point that eminent historians, like Siméon Luce, go so far as to claim that the population of France equalled then, if it did not exceed, the population of France to-day.

SOURCES.—The contemporary chronicles, notably those published in the *Recueil des Historiens des Gaules et de la France*, tomes xx.–xxiii. (1840–76), 4 vols. fol.; *Annales Gaudenses*, 1896; *Chronique Artesienne*, 1898; *Regestum Clementis papæ V*, 1880–90, 7 vols.; Limburg-Stirum, *Codex diplomaticus Flandriæ, 1296–1325*, Bruges, 1878–89, 2 vols.; Thomas Rymer, *Fœdera, conventiones . . . inter reges Angliæ et alios quosvis*, 3rd ed., The Hague, 1739–45, 10 vols. fol.; Michelet, *Procès des Templiers*, Paris, 1841–51, 2 vols.; Buegnot, *Les Olim*, 1839–48, 4 vols.; Edelstan du Meril, *Poésies populaires latines du Moyen Age*, 1847.

HISTORICAL WORKS.—Edgar Boutaric, *La France sous Philippe le Bel*, 1861; Ch. V. Langlois, *Histoire de France*, ed. Lavisse, iii. 1901; P. Dupuy, *Histoire du differand d'entre le Pope Boniface VIII et Philippe le Bel*, 1655; Digard, *Les Registres de Boniface VIII*, 1884–91; Ernest Renan, " Guillaume de Nogaret " in *Histoire Litteraire de la France*, xxviii., 1877, 233–371; Robert Holtzmann, *Wilhelm von Nogaret*, Fribourg-

PHILIP THE FAIR

en-B., 1898 ; P. Funke, *Papst Benedikt XI*, 1891 ; C. Wenck, *Clemens V u. Heinrich VII*, Halle, 1882 ; G. Lizerand, *Clement V et Philippe le Bel*, 1910 ; K. Schottmüller, *Der Untergang des Templer-Ordens*, 1887 ; Ch. V. Langlois, " Le Procès des Templiers," *Revue des Deux Mondes*, 15th January 1891, pp. 382–421 ; L. Delisle, " *Opérations financières des Templiers*," *Memoires de l'Academie des Inscriptions*, xxxiii. (1889) ; Warnkönig-Gheldolf, *Histoire de la Flandre*, 1835–64, 5 vols. ; H. Pirenne, *Histoire de Belgique*, tome i., 3rd ed., 1909.

CHAPTER XVIII

THE END OF FEUDAL FRANCE

Feudalism becomes disorganized. Provincial Leagues. Reaction against the work of the legists. Louis X. Disgrace and punishment of Marigny. Civil troubles in Artois. Rivalry of Robert and Mahaut d'Artois. The provincial charters. Check in the Flanders campaign : "the muddy army." Death of Louis X. Jean I posthumous. Accession of Philip the Tall. Salic Law. Energy of the new King. His death. Accession of Charles the Fair. He dies without an heir. Extinction of the direct line of the Capetians. Who is to succeed to the French Crown ?

THE great King had been able to realize, during his last days, the reaction which would be produced against his work.

The feudal bonds are broken. The vassals of a manor are no longer united to their patron. The feudal lordship is in a state of disintegration. What becomes of the bond of love ? Why, where are the snows of yester year ?

A single baron has become proprietor of several chatellanies. In each he can only reside for part of the year : in several he does not live at all, being replaced by a seneschal who thinks only of the dues to be delivered and makes himself hated.

"The people have not much opinion of the nobles," Philip the Tall will say.

These divisions in the interior of each fief and of each town are complicated by the divisions between the provinces. The Albigensian War has sown profound hatreds. The North has certainly extended over the South its administrative action, its intellectual and artistic influence ; but deep down in the heart the ferments have remained. In the provinces to the south of the Loire, writes towards the end of the fourteenth century the continuator of Girard de Frachet, "those who wished to break away were numerous."

THE END OF FEUDAL FRANCE

Among the Flemish the same thing is happening.

But, behold, the Nobles seek to profit by the embarrassment with which the Crown is overwhelmed by the war in Flanders, which has broken out again. "The moment has come," they think, "to reconquer our rights." The Nobility of Burgundy, of Artois, and of Picardy form a federation directed against the King. At the head of the movement is a lord of Picardy, the Sire de Fiennes. And from Beauvaisis, Vermandois, and Ponthieu support flows in. The Nobles ally themselves to the "commons," that is to say, to the popular class of the towns. The subventions demanded for the war in Flanders provide the pretext for the rebellion.

In order to limit the extent of the movement, Philip the Fair had forbidden, by an edict of the 6th October 1314, the tournaments which gathered together the Nobles of several provinces; but the impulse had been given.

On the 24th November the "alliances" formed in Burgundy, in Champagne, and in Forez joined those of Beauvaisis, Ponthieu, and of Artois. The Nobility of a great part of the kingdom were thus in open revolt.

Our barons no longer wish to allow themselves to be plucked; but above all, they do not intend to allow themselves to be governed by the "paltry folk" of the royal council:

> We are turned upside down
> By villeins and servants;
> Paltry folk who have come
> To the Court and become masters,
> Folk who sew, cut, and snip.

For the rest, if the King did not wish to listen favourably to the grievances of his barons, they are prepared to "enter on a dance against him."

The new King, Louis X, was a young man of twenty-six years. Young and inexperienced, he found himself in the midst of the greatest difficulties. Contrary to what has been too often said, Louis showed himself a resolute follower of the policy of his father; but the "allied" barons, as well as the feudal lords who belonged to the royal Court, the great palatines, believed that the moment had come to get rid of the "little people." The coalition sought a head in the ostentatious Charles of Valois, uncle of Louis X. They obtained the dismissal of the principal ministers of Philip the Fair, of Enguerran de Marigny, of the treasurer, Michel de Bordenai, and of Raoul de Presles, " principal advocate " to the Parliament. The Chancellor, Pierre de Latilly, Bishop of Châlons, had to hand over the seals to Etienne de Mornay, clerk of the chamber to Charles of Valois.

Pierre de Latilly and Raoul de Presles were thrown into prison. The " principal advocate " was accused of witchcraft, and was put to the torture. His strength protected him. Enguerran de Marigny concentrated on himself the unchained passions. Louis X attempted to save him; but in vain. He was accused of peculation. The last campaign in Flanders had ended in the retreat of the royal troops. Marigny, it was said, had been bought by the Flemish. And behold that precisely, at the fair of Ecouis, many flags belonging to him were hung.

> And well it was known to all
> That this honour was done to him
> Because of the treaty he had made. . . .
> *(Geoffroi de Paris.)*

The condemnation of Marigny was pronounced on 30th April 1315. In the midst of a hostile crowd he was taken to Montfaucon. Public opinion, of which Geoffrey of Paris is the echo, is not deceived: Marigny has been condemned

> Only at the request and the instance
> Of all the high barons of France. . . .

Moreover, the people did not delay in going back on their prejudices. Philip the Tall is to render justice to the best servants of his father. He will have the skeleton of Marigny taken down from the gibbet, " where it had a long time hung," and will have it interred in the church of the Monks of Chartreux. He will give £10,000 to his children; and then to Raoul de Presles, Michel de Bordenai, and to Pierre d'Orgemont he will restore their confiscated goods.

But the leagues of Nobles were reconstituted in nearly all the provinces. The Nobles wished to return to the conditions which had ruled their ancestors at the beginning of the thirteenth century, before the time of Philip the Fair and before Saint Louis; the return to the right of private war.

THE END OF FEUDAL FRANCE

The situation was strained to such a point that open hostilities were on the point of breaking out. In Artois the insurgents are about to find a head in the person of Robert, grandson of Robert II, killed at Courtrai, and son of Philip of Artois, who had died in 1298 as the result of a wound received at the battle of Furnes. Robert II had left a daughter, Mahaut, married to Otto III, Count of Burgundy (Franche-Comté), whom the King put in possession of the *Comté-pairie* of Artois in preference to the young Robert.

In a memoir to the King drawn up by the Countess of Artois the situation of the different parties in the town of St. Omer is very clearly shown. At the head of the town is a châtelaine, who out of opposition to the Countess Mahaut, suzerain of the province, takes the part of the " allies." The sheriffs and the patricians, in opposition to the châtelaine, make common cause with Mahaut, and remain faithful to the King. Finally the common people of St. Omer, through hatred of the Patricians, take the part of the châtelaine against the Countess, while the rural population, out of hatred of the country squires, remain faithful to her as well as to the King.

This scheme of parties is infinitely precious to the historian. The same divisions are reproduced in part everywhere. This will be the classing of parties during the first three-quarters of the Hundred Years War.

Under the orders of the lords of Fiennes and of Picquigny, the insurgents invaded the big towns; they there proclaimed the revolution in the public squares at Calais, at Audruicq, Guines, St. Omer, Hesdin, Boulogne, Amiens, Térouanne, and in twenty other places.

There was a similar situation in Burgundy.

And Louis X had engaged in a new campaign in Flanders. Moreover, he resolved to give way by yielding satisfaction to the " allies " as far as possible. He treated separately with the Nobility of each province.

To the Normans he granted, on 19th March 1315, the famous *charte aux Normands*, which was to remain the very constitution of the province, up to the Revolution; but the charters given by him to the other great fiefs will only have an ephemeral life. For this there is a reason: it is not that the charter to the

THE MIDDLE AGES

Normans is better drawn up than the others; but Normandy still lived under a different social constitution from that of the other provinces. We have dealt with this above. Normandy did not know those hierarchies, those aristocratic "superpositions," so complicated in arrangement, produced by spontaneous formation from the feudal aristocracy. It was adaptable to administrative reform.

The charters which Louis X is about to give to the different provinces will not be identical: the charter to the Normans is of pedestrian character; the charter to the people of Languedoc (1st April 1315) swarms with reminiscences of Rome. The charters to the Burgundians and the Picards (April and May 1315) were dictated by an aristocratic caste anxious to recover its ancient privileges; and this character was accentuated in the charter to Champagne (May 1315). The King agreed no longer to exercise justice in the lands of the barons. The escutcheons of the arms of France which individuals fixed to the front of their houses in order to place themselves immediately under the royal authority were removed. But in these same charters, the articles which concern the towns have some opposite tendencies; the royal authority, far from being restricted, is there strengthened.

The inability of the "Alliances" of 1314–15 to establish a representative régime similar to that of the English has been noted. We must not hold the promoters of the movement responsible for this. It was the country which, by its traditions and social formation, was not suited to receive it. After some centuries only, when the traditions and the effects of this formation shall be effaced, will the country be able to accept a representative régime.

In fact, there is no point in talking here (as has been done) of "liberty"; there is no point in inquiring why France was not a free country. France was as free a country as England—freer indeed; but her liberty conformed to her social formation, just as it is true that England had a liberty in conformity with hers. And if one freely grants that the representative régime is not incompatible with the liberty of a people, at least it is not an essential condition of it, any more than the colour

THE END OF FEUDAL FRANCE

of the clothes in which the people in question is wont to dress itself.

Louis X had been forced by the war in Flanders to make these concessions. The autumn rains fell in torrents, drenching the low and marshy lands of the Northern plains. And the army of the King became embogged in the mud without reaching the enemy, whence the name given to this campaign: "the muddy army."

Shortly afterwards Louis X died at Vincennes in the night of 4th–5th June 1316. He was not yet twenty-eight years old. As far as his youth had permitted, he had governed with wisdom. His death was to cause the gravest difficulties.

By his second wife, Clemence of Hungary, Louis X had a son, born posthumously, John I. Born in the night of the 13th–14th November 1316, he died a few days later.

This was the first time since the accession of the Capetians that the throne was without a male heir born of the preceding King.

Three pretenders claimed the throne: Philip the Tall, brother next in age to Louis X; Charles of Valois, his uncle, the brother of Philip the Fair; and lastly, Duke Eude of Burgundy, the brother of Marguerite of Burgundy, first wife of Louis X.

Charles of Valois, an ostentatious and needy prince, accepted money, and Philip the Tall, profiting by the fact that he had exercised the regency, immediately acted as sovereign. He was crowned on 9th January 1317.

Philip the Tall was a tall young man, in his twenty-fourth year, thin, slender, long as a day without bread. He was, the chroniclers insist, bigger than his father, who already, like his grandfather, Saint Louis, exceeded by a head the lords of his Court.

The contemporary miniaturists, who wished to trace his portrait, in order to mark this excessive height, naively make him fold his legs and bow his head, in order to get him to fit into the frame of the picture. But Philip V had not the great breadth of shoulders of his father; he was slender and ungainly.

At the ceremony of the consecration, alone among the great personages of the kingdom, Mahaut of Artois and Charles of

THE MIDDLE AGES

Valois had assisted. Their peers had openly abstained, and some, the old Duchess of Burgundy and the reigning Duke of Burgundy, had put forward lively protestations in order to reserve the rights of Jeanne, a child of five years, the daughter of Louis X and of Marguerite of Burgundy. They demanded that a decision should be given by an assembly of peers. A numerous " parliament " which comprised the nobles and the religious of the Duchy of Burgundy, another at which the nobles of Champagne gathered, pronounced in favour of the little princess. Philip the Tall replied to this by making preparations for war.

He addressed himself to the people of Paris; he made a speech in which he exposed his titles to the crown of France; he visited several large towns. An assembly of nobles and prelates mixed with some burgesses of Paris (February 1317) approved Philip V and decided that " Women did not succeed to the kingdom of France." A second assembly comprised the representatives of some towns of Langue d'oïl: it was also held at Paris (6th March 1317) and approved Philip V, while it demanded at the same time " that the people should be maintained in the manner customary in the time of Saint Louis, and that it should be permitted, in case of disturbances, to repulse force by force." As to the towns of Langue d'oc, Philip V convoked their representatives at Bourges for 27th March 1317. Through these delegates they made a declaration similar to that of the towns of the North.

But the " Allies " did not disarm: they had now a good reason to remain united and to pursue the struggle—the rights to the throne of the little Jeanne, daughter of Louis X.

The Count de Nevers took the field and was beaten. Then a party of the allies consented to some conferences. These were held at Melun (June–July 1317). The allies renounced the claim of Jeanne to the throne of France; they only demanded Champagne and Navarre, the heritage of her grandmother, to which the alleged Salic Law could not be applied. On 27th March the Duke of Burgundy also came to an agreement. He espoused the daughter of Philip V, an alliance which would assure him Artois and Franche-Comté. As to the little Jeanne, in compensation for the crown of France, she received a pension

THE END OF FEUDAL FRANCE

of 15,000 Tours pounds : three millions in actual value. In Maine and in Anjou, the allies were routed by Charles of Valois. Robert of Artois, the nephew of Mahaut, had submitted in November 1316. Nevertheless, the " alliances " dragged on some time still. It was necessary for the Constable Gaucher de Châtillon to march at the head of imposing forces against the Sires de Fiennes and de Picquigny, whose castles were destroyed (1320).

The enterprise of the insurgent barons did not meet with the approbation of the Parisian bourgeoisie, of whom the author of the *Dit des Alliés* forms an echo. He rejoices over their disappointment :

> They have made a storm
> Of March ; but like a white frost
> It will soon have passed away. . . .

It was a March storm which gave warning of an agelong disturbance.

Philip the Tall died at Longchamps in the night of the 2nd–3rd January 1321. He only left daughters. In virtue of the principle he had himself invoked which excluded women from the throne of France, the crown reverted to his younger brother, who became Charles the Fair.

When Charles IV dies at the Château of Vincennes on 1st February 1328, he will leave behind not only no male heir, but not even a brother who can hold the crown. What is to happen ?

Three new claimants were in view :

Philip, Count d'Evreux, husband of Jeanne of Navarre, daughter of Louis X ; the King of England, Edward III, grandson of Philip the Fair by his mother Isabella, wife of Edward II ; finally Philip, Count of Valois, son of Charles of Valois, brother of Philip the Fair. The assembly of the barons, faithful to the alleged Salic Law, gave the crown to Philip of Valois.

SOURCES.—The contemporary chroniclers, published for the most part in tomes xx.–xxiii. of the *Historiens de la France* (D. Bouquet). The documents published in the following works :

HISTORICAL WORKS.—Le Huguer, *Histoire de Philippe le Long*, tome i., " Le Règne," 1897 ; Dufayard, " *La Réaction féodale sous les fils de Philippe le Bel*," *Revue Historique*, 1894 ; Louis Artonne, *Le Mouvement de 1314 et*

THE MIDDLE AGES

les chartes provinciales de 1315, 1912 ; P. Viollet, *Comment les femmes ont été exclues en France de la Couronne*, Paris, 1893 ; Ch. V. Langlois' works quoted.

Conclusion to the History of Feudal France.

Is it not remarkable that the Capetian dynasty should have come to the throne at the epoch when feudal France was being founded, to disappear when feudal France begins to decay ? For more than three centuries the Capetians presided over the destinies of a country which was building up about their throne, with the sole resources of its national genius and of its traditional virtues, a civilization peculiar to itself. In the course of these three centuries the French lived under social forms drawn by them from the bosom of the family in which they were born and where they had grown, and which they developed from generation to generation, until they made of it public institutions extended to the whole nation. And it was also this which gave its beauty to the French civilization and formed its brilliance, originality, power, and popular savour. Who shall celebrate in terms worthy of it the France of the castles and of the cathedrals, of the crusades and tournaments, the France of the religious orders, of chivalry and of the communes, the France of the *chansons de geste*, of the sewing-songs, and of the fables ?

CHAPTER XIX

THE HUNDRED YEARS WAR

Philip of Valois.—His accession. Homage of the King of England. Robert of Artois. Origin and causes of the Hundred Years War. The rupture with Edward III. The Flemish and Van Artevelde. The Brittany Succession. John of Montfort and Charles of Blois. Battle of Creçy (26th August 1346). The fall of Calais (3rd August 1347). Opposition between the popular class (*le commun, minores*) and the Nobility and Patricians (*majores*). Death of Philip of Valois (22nd August 1350). *John the Good.*—He causes the Constable of France, the Count d'Eu, to be put to death. The Battle of the Thirty (27th March 1351). Changes in the currency. Charles the Bad, King of Navarre. Battle of Poitiers (19th September 1356). The captivity of King John. The Great Companies. Bertrand du Guesclin. Etienne Marcel. The Jacquerie (May-June 1358). Assassination of Etienne Marcel (31st July 1358). The Peace of Bretigny (8th May 1360). Return of King John. Death of Charles of Blois. John the Good returns to England, where he dies on 8th April 1364. *Charles the Wise.*—Victory of Cocherel (13th May 1364). Du Guesclin in Spain. Peter the Cruel and Henry of Trastamara. The appeals of Aquitaine rekindle the war. French and English on the sea. The Great Schism. Administration of Charles V. Death of du Guesclin (14th July 1380). Death of Charles V (16th September 1380). *Charles the Well-Beloved.*—Troubles which mark the beginning of his reign. Isabel of Bavaria. The government of the Marmousets. Crusade against the Barbary Pirates. Assassination of Olivier de Clisson. Expedition of Brittany. Madness of the King. Louis of Orleans : antagonism between his policy and that of the House of Burgundy. Richard II, son-in-law of Charles VI, is deposed by Henry of Lancaster ; renewal of the war. Jean sans Peur (the Fearless). He causes Louis of Orleans to be assassinated (23rd November 1407). The Cabochiens. The *Ordinance Cabochienne*. Peace of Bourges between the Duke of Burgundy and the Orleans party (14th July 1412). Accession of Henry V to the English throne (20th March 1413). Battle of Agincourt (25th October 1415). Charles the Dauphin, lieutenant-general of

431

THE MIDDLE AGES

the kingdom (14th June 1417). Armagnacs and Burgundians. Assassination of John the Fearless (10th September 1419). Treaty of Troyes (21st May 1420). Death of Henry V. Henry VI, King of England, proclaimed King of France at St. Denis. *Jeanne d'Arc.*—The King of Bourges. State of France. Defeat of Verneuil (17th August 1424). Mont St. Michel and the Castellany of Vaucouleurs Domrémy. The voices of the Maid. Chinon. Jeanne, *chef de guerre.* The relief of Orleans (8th May 1429). The victory of Patay (18th June). The consecration at Reims (17th July). Charles VII falls back on the Loire. In his company Jeanne comes to Compiègne. She is taken by the Burgundians (23rd May 1430). The trial of Rouen. Death of the heroine (29th May 1431). *Charles the Victorious.*—Reconciliation with the Duke of Burgundy. Treaty of Arras (21st September 1435). Popular risings against the English. Battles of Formigny (15th April 1459), and of Castillon (17th July 1453). The government of Charles VII: the little people of the King's Council.

CHARLES THE FAIR only left a daughter. An assembly of the Grandees of the kingdom hastened to declare women incapable of succeeding to the throne of France, thus setting aside the King of England, Edward III, the grandson, by his mother Isabella, of Philip the Fair, and gave the crown to Philip of Valois, nephew of Philip the Fair.

Philip of Valois.

Philip of Valois was consecrated at Reims on the 29th May 1328.

The death of Charles the Fair extinguished the Capetian line which had furnished so many princes remarkable for their energy, their far-sightedness, and their virtues. In the new dynasty we remark the qualities and the defects of their ancestor, Charles of Valois—showy, brilliant, chivalrous, a friend of the arts and of the elegant life, but having neither a robust good sense, a sense of right, nor pure habits, which were characteristic of the great Capetians. Such, notably, is Philip of Valois.

We have seen how feudal customs, after having brought brilliance and prosperity to the country, had for this very reason ceased to have any *raison d'être.* This was the underlying cause of the Hundred Years War. Historians have formed the habit of judging the feudal epoch from this deplorable war, although it was only that epoch in disorganization.

THE HUNDRED YEARS WAR

To this deep-lying cause are joined accidental causes. We can trace its origin to two treaties, concluded by illustrious and profoundly wise princes who nevertheless were unable to foresee the consequences of the agreement arranged by them. The first is the Treaty of Paris (1259), concluded between Saint Louis and Henry III, King of England, by which the King of France made over again some provinces confiscated from John Lackland, but gave to the feudal homage, which bound the King of England to the King of France, as vassal to suzerain, the force of a written document. Saint Louis had created this situation, intolerable in course of time, of a vassal as powerful as his suzerain and, by the fact of his vassalage, installed in arms in the kingdom of which he was subject. The second treaty is that of Montreuil-sur-Mer, signed in 1299 by Philip the Fair and Edward I, strengthened in 1303 by the second Treaty of Paris. Philip the Fair thought that by it he had settled the question of Aquitaine. He married his sister Marguerite to Edward I, King of England, and his daughter Isabella to Edward II, the eldest son of Edward I. The son who was born of the union of Marguerite and Edward I would assume the crown of Aquitaine, while the son born to Edward II would preserve the crown of England. By the separation of the provinces of the south-west of Franc efrom England, Philip the Fair hoped to put an end to the question of Aquitaine, an incessant source of conflict since the marriage of Eleanor with Henry Plantagenet. Unfortunately, Edward I and Marguerite had no children, and when the three sons of Philip the Fair had themselves died without male issue, Edward III claimed the throne of France on account of his mother. And in this way the treaties of Paris and Montreuil, far from establishing peace between the crowns of France and England, as their framers had thought, were on the contrary the source of the longest and gravest struggle which has stained our annals with blood.

The claims to the crown of France which Edward III was to put forward did not rest, moreover, on any foundation. Even if one admitted the rights of the female line, the rights of Jeanne, daughter of Louis X, married to Philip of Evreux, would take precedence over those of Isabella of France on the death

THE MIDDLE AGES

of Louis X, the unquestioned King, of whom Jeanne was the immediate heir. Philip of Valois made compensation to her by the surrender of Navarre.

But these rights were only a pretext. We have seen how the exercise of English sovereignty over Guienne had become practically impossible. But England in the Middle Ages could not do without Guienne, from which it drew essential commodities, notably wines. The rôle of Guienne *vis-à-vis* the English in the fourteenth century has been compared to that of their colonies to-day.

On the other hand, we have seen the rapid increase of the royal domain in the thirteenth century: the great conquests of Philip Augustus. Philip the Bold added by inheritance Poitou, Auvergne, Toulouse, Rouergue, Albigeois, Agenais, and Comtat. Champagne came to the Crown by the marriage of Philip the Fair. We have just noted the conquests of this last King, and now comes Valois, which is added in its turn by the accession of Philip VI. The royal power had had neither time nor means to assimilate these successive additions; whence numerous differences, the inevitable dissensions between these countries and the old royal domain. And, elsewhere, we have seen the reaction against the reforms of Saint Louis and of Philip the Fair.

This general situation did not escape the notice of the English monarchs. They had made the most skilful efforts to make themselves liked by the people of Guienne. They allowed their subjects in France the greatest liberties and endeavoured to assure their prosperity. It has been said that the English suzerainty over Aquitaine was limited to providing " the witness and the help to its gradual emancipation." There were few English at Bordeaux, few foreign troops. The *jurade* of Bordeaux governed Gascony: and the country experienced, under the distant British sovereignty, a flourishing prosperity.

Moreover, up to the end of the fourteenth century, as Froissart states, Bordeaux, Bayonne, and the frontier towns of Gascony will " nobly " defend the English honour. One will see the towns of Bordelais form a league against the French; they will repel the overtures made by the representative of the King of France: " If the French ruled over us, they would maintain their customs; besides, we prefer to be English, since thus we were born : they keep us unfettered and free " (Froissart). If the French gain a victory over the English, the people of Bordeaux will call it " the bad day." Viollet-le-Duc has noted that during the whole of the fourteenth century the English invasion was not considered, over a good part of the territory of France, as a foreign invasion. And, similarly, M. Bemont has been able to observe that it will be only from the reign of Henry V that the national sentiments of the English against the French will be excited.

The English policy was supported by the Flemish against the King of France and the French Kings acted in Scotland as the English did in Flanders. In 1335 we shall see Philip VI fitting out a fleet. Some French men-at-arms will land, in the spring of the year 1336, on the coast of Scotland.

Philip of Valois had hardly ascended the throne when he sent messengers to Edward III, claiming from him liege homage for the lands which he possessed in France, and, pending the rendering of this homage, the Bishop of Arras and the Sire de Craon were delegated by him in Aquitaine to sequestrate the revenues belonging to the English monarch. And the appeals became more and more frequent. The Sire de Navailles, who called himself a creditor of the King of England, caused lands and castles belonging to his debtor to be seized by the King of France.

In Flanders the social struggles were far from being appeased ; but the Count of Flanders, Louis de Nevers, had passed to the side of the Patricians, with the result that the people of Bruges had arrested him and shut him up in the Grocer's Hall.

At the appeal of his vassal, Philip of Valois marched against them. The Flemish, moreover, and even the popular party, were not united. Once again the people of Ghent separated themselves from those of Bruges. But the men of Bruges believed that they would repeat the day of Courtrai. Armed with their *goedendags*, long iron-covered staves, they entrenched themselves on Mont Cassel, the eminence which dominates the plain of the North. The French army was commanded by the King in person ; the men of Bruges marched under the orders of their burgomaster, no knight having consented to put himself at their head. The engagement took place on 23rd

THE MIDDLE AGES

August 1328. The miracle of Courtrai was not repeated. The men of Bruges were cut to pieces. Almost the entire French army had been destroyed at Courtrai; almost the entire army of Bruges was destroyed at Cassel. Of 16,000 combatants hardly 3000 escaped. The corpses were heaped about that of the burgomaster, Colin Zannekin. The French had lost hardly twenty men.

However, on 3rd June 1329, Edward III decided to come and take the oath of homage to the King of France for his lands of Aquitaine. The ceremony took place in the Cathedral of Amiens. But he paid only simple homage, not liege homage, which made a vassal the man of his suzerain. And as the King of France demanded liege homage, Edward insisted on a delay in order in England to study at leisure the reciprocal obligations of the two Crowns. By letters of 30th March 1331, Edward III in the end declared that he had taken at Amiens, within the hands of the King of France, the oath of liege homage.

He did not, however, hold himself engaged by this. The reciprocal situation of the crowns of France and England was bound to produce a conflict. Here it is rising from a secondary incident.

Robert of Artois, the brother-in-law of Philip VI, had been set aside from the crown of Artois in favour of his aunt, Mahaut. He appealed on the matter to Parliament and, to support his rights, caused some false documents to be drawn up. The trick was discovered. Robert of Artois, who had taken flight, was sentenced in default, his goods confiscated, and himself banished the kingdom. He took refuge in England, where he set himself to excite Edward III against the King of France, encouraging him to claim his rights to the crown of the fleur-de-lis (1332–34). Edward prepared for war, endeavouring to form a coalition against France, as his grandfather had done. Learning of the intentions of the English Prince, Philip of Valois resolved to get in the first blow. He ordered his vassal, the Count of Flanders, to arrest the subjects of the King of England, who were found in his territory. There were many English in Flanders as a result of the active trade between the two countries. The English country districts supplied their wool to the drapery industry of Flanders. Edward retorted by

THE HUNDRED YEARS WAR

stopping the exportation of wool. The looms of the great towns, Bruges, Ypres, and Ghent, ceased to weave (1336). Edward emphasized the bearing of his edict by causing to be sent, in great quantities, sacks of English wool to the manufacturing towns of Brabant. A movement towards emigration among the Flemish artisans was seen taking shape. Very justly the great Flemish cities were much excited by this.

It is the moment when the famous burgess of Ghent, Jacques van Artevelde, comes on the scene. He assumed the rôle of the Bruges leaders, Breidel and Coninc, in the time of Philip the Fair. With an eloquence as great as that of Coninc, he addressed himself, like him, to the artisans of the nation. A decisive assembly was held at la Biloke on 28th December 1337. Artevelde did not intend to break with the King of France, the suzerain of the people of Ghent, but to conclude an economic alliance with England in order to safeguard the industry of the town. The agitation became so strong that Louis de Nevers, the Count of Flanders, found himself forced to relax the reins of government which passed into the hands of the tribune of Ghent.

The decision of the people of Ghent, foreseen by Edward III, had been preceded by letters of defiance sent by the English monarch to the King of France. Philip of Valois had summoned Edward to deliver to him Robert of Artois. The King of England refused. The letters of defiance, dated from Westminster, 19th October 1337, were taken to Paris by the Bishop of Lincoln. The war began in this end of the year 1337; it was only to close in 1453.

It has been rightly pointed out that the men of Ghent who rose at the voice of van Artevelde intended it as much against the great families, the Patricians, the " rich men " of their own town, as against the King of France. In Guienne, the party of the King of England will be very important; but it will be very far from including the whole country. The high Nobles and, in the towns, the Patricians will be for the King of France. In the whole of the first half of the Hundred Years War, up to the end of the fourteenth century, we can be certain that when a town declares for the King of France, that the aristocratic party, the Patricians, supported by its clientele, has got the

THE MIDDLE AGES

upper hand there; when, on the contrary, a locality "turns English," it is a sign that the commonalty, the popular party, has taken in hand the direction of the city. This is an essential characteristic of the prolonged struggle.

And these divisions will go on splitting up, multiplying themselves, breaking into small particles which will spread everywhere: in face of the two great parties opposed to one another, the one leaning on the shield of the fleur-de-lis, the other on the shield of the leopards; the one calling on St. Michael, and the other St. George; the one bearing the white cross, the other the red cross; neighbouring lords, enemies for some personal reason, towns and villages whose territories adjoin, have revived ancient rivalries; even in a family intestine dissensions will find food and force to continue. "The storm of civil war," writes Jean Chartier, "rose everywhere; between the children of the same house, between men of the same rank were committed the outrages of cruel wars; the multiplied wars of the lords became mixed up in these conflicts." Moreover, we see the desolation caused by it. It is no longer only the great battles, the organized expeditions, which afflict the country: it is war divided up indefinitely, multiplied in thousands and thousands of sections with an ill-omened virulence and raging in the smallest out-of-the-way corners.

Jean de Bueil gives a picture of it:

"In going my way, I found myself in a very desolate and deserted country, because there had been war between the inhabitants of the country for a long time, and they were very poor and few in number; for, I may tell you, it seemed rather a place for wild beasts than a habitation for people."

Such was the Hundred Years War.

And so will it be up to the epoch of Jeanne d'Arc. The duration of the war, the excesses of the soldiery, the foreign language spoken by the "Goddam," and their fashions which were not ours, will have then progressively made them foreigners and therefore enemies for the immense majority of the French. And one may say that from this day the English were defeated. Certainly the magnificent impulse given by Jeanne d'Arc will have contributed to this result, but the true cause of it will be that, with time, the national sentiment will

THE HUNDRED YEARS WAR

have formed itself under calamities against the invader. From this moment he will have lost; and he was only able to hold out so long because in every place up till then he had found part of the population ready to support him, namely, the popular faction. From this point of view the rôle played by the Burgundian party, which will be discussed later on, will be most interesting to note: it will make its appearance at the moment when the national sentiment begins to turn against the English. The Burgundian princes are Frenchmen, and they will rally the popular elements when these withdraw from the English, while the Royalist elements will group themselves about the great family of the Armagnacs placed, for more than a century, at the head of the southern Nobility.

The Hundred Years War was a social war; we would dare to say a civil war quite as much as a foreign war, and perhaps in the first part much more a civil war.

The King of England had very carefully prepared to open the campaign. The English monarchy had, in short, remained a monarchy of a military type such as William the Conqueror had established it: the Capetian monarchy, although it had counted great warriors like Henry I, Louis the Fat, and Philip Augustus, had none the less remained a patriarchal monarchy. In England, to meet the expenses of the war, the tax on wool had been doubled. On the English side we are faced with a series of measures in the most modern spirit: the teaching of French to children, a veto on the export of horses, the establishment of a military service in some sort obligatory, the encouragement of games with the bow and the manufacture or improvement of weapons for shooting; and the consequences of these are going to show themselves brilliantly. Whilst in France people were still concerned with chivalrous knighthood and with tournaments, the English princes had learned the importance of infantry in the new war. This infantry, composed of archers and of pikemen, formed two-thirds of their effectives. "The archers," writes Siméon Luce, " were armed with a bow of yew so easy, supple, and portable that one could draw three *saiettes* or barbed arrows in less time than one would take to launch a brick or *vireton* (arrow with a conical end of iron) with a Genoese or French cross-bow. The pikemen were armed with a long knife, or rather, with a lance, like a bayonet lightly bent round, provided at the end with a long staff as a handle. The pikemen attempted to introduce their blades into the joints of the armour. Farewell to the fine military prowess of the noble knights.

The manufacture of the bow had reached a great perfection in England. While the brilliant idea had arisen in France of placing a tax on the cords of bows—oh, French administration, how ancient are thy devices!—the English had encouraged and developed in every way this branch of war industry, and we shall see the King of England so jealous for his country in this superiority in the combats, that the safe-conducts of French prisoners in England will only be issued with a veto on the import across the Channel of bows and arrows. Comines will write still under Louis XI that "the English are the flower of the World's archers."

Lastly, there was the discipline of the English army—a rigorous discipline. It was remarkable, above all, in the cavalry. Albert Malet says very justly that the King of England had in his army a " cavalry," while the King of France had still always only a " chivalry."

The English army did not know those hierarchies in authority, constables, marshals, war leaders, not to mention seigniorial and municipal commands, with which the French army was embarrassed. A lieutenant of the English monarch, clothed with his authority, commanded immediately all his men; while the French army, the image of the society of which it was the expression, continued to be ranged in those ranks of feudal suzerainties which formed the nation. In this once more the two armies reflected the two peoples for whom they fought. May we recall what we have already said on the matter?

Thus we shall see the English gaining surprising victories in view especially of the small number of combatants which they opposed to the French armies. There is not one of the great English victories—Creçy, Poitiers, Agincourt, Verneuil, the Battle of the Herrings—in which the French had not at their disposal a numerical superiority which should have been crushing. The garrisons of places conquered by the English numbered hardly a hundred men : at times only ten or twelve. It is true that at long last this superiority of organization and of command will turn round and come back to the French. From the time when artillery appears, the French will secure in it, in a few years, a mastery of which their adversaries will strive in vain to rob them. Jeanne d'Arc herself will win distinction in it, and the soldiers will admire the expert ingenuity with which she disposed the bombards and culverins.

" In this year 1338," writes the Continuator of Nangis, " the Flemish, particularly the men of Ghent, carried away by the spirit of rebellion, expelled the Count. Gathering a great number of the lower people (*multos minoris populi*), they rose against the great (*contra majores*) and did them great injury ; . . . and they declared that it was not against the kingdom of France that they felt resentment. . . ."

But Edward III pressed them to take up arms against Philip of Valois. Artevelde replied that they could not rebel against their sovereign ; but perhaps a remedy could be found for these scruples. Why should not the King of England bear with his arms the arms of France ? Was he not the legitimate heir of the French Crown ? " And we shall obey you," said Artevelde, " as the King of France."

Edward hesitated ; he hesitated much. Had he not sworn homage to Philip of Valois and confirmed his homage by sealed letters ? At length he decided to follow the counsel of the weaver of Ghent.

The first important battle was a naval engagement, fought on 24th June 1340 off l'Ecluse (Sluis) in Flanders. The French fleet went out to meet the English fleet, which was carrying an army of invasion to France. A reinforcement of Flemish vessels which came up unexpectedly at the crisis of the action turned the balance in favour of the English. The French fleet was in great part destroyed ; its admiral, Nicholas Behuchet, counsellor of the King and *maître des comptes*, was hung at the masthead. This defeat had the gravest consequences for the cause of the French King, who could no longer dream of taking the offensive by carrying his arms into the territory of the enemy.

In the year 1341 a truce was concluded at the instance of

the Sovereign Pontiff. In 1343, in order to meet the needs of the Crown, Philip of Valois established a tax which, under the name of *gabelle*, was to have a long and unhappy course. We know that the law, in virtue of which Philip of Valois reigned in France to the exclusion of women, bore, without any reason for that matter, the name of the Salic Law. In alluding to this tax on salt, Edward III said jestingly that at least his rival justified his title of " Salic " King.

Yet events in Flanders turned against the English. Artevelde had so strongly established his authority that his fellow-citizens began to murmur. Jealousy is the curse of democracies. By his energy, by his valour, by his authority, Artevelde had raised himself above the common herd. The luxury of his house at Ghent, the retinue he affected, his magnificent ways, the brilliant establishment of his daughter, were an offence to the sentiment of equality. We have seen that a town, by the very fact of setting itself up as a commune, became a feudal person. This is an important fact, and sufficient account has not been taken of it.

Bruges united in a brilliant panoply the escutcheons of the towns of which she was suzerain, and after having conquered Bruges, Ghent established over the majority of the towns of Flanders a domination which was to be little different from a feudal suzerainty. In the years 1343-44 some resistance is shown towards the powerful city, at Langemarck, at Ardenbourg, at Oudenarde. On the day of the 17th July 1345, some men of the working class raised a riot about the house of van Artevelde. The weavers, under the pressure of their dean, Gerard Denis, claimed a rendering of accounts. Where does the money go ? Another democratic refrain ! Artevelde demanded a delay of three days, which was refused. The great citizen attempted to fly by way of the stables of his house, where he was killed.

The war between England and France seemed as if it was dying down when it broke out again through the question of the succession in Brittany. John III, surnamed the Good, Duke of Brittany, son of Arthur II, Duke of Brittany, Count of Richemont and of Montfort, died in 1341, without a legitimate heir. His younger brother, the Count Gui de Penthièvre, who had been

THE HUNDRED YEARS WAR

his heir, had died before him, but he left a daughter, Jeanne la Boiteuse (the Lame), married to Charles of Blois, nephew of Philip of Valois. He left also a second brother, son of Arthur II and by a second wife, the Count Jean IV de Montfort. If it had been a case of the throne of France, John de Montfort would have been the heir in virtue of the alleged Salic Law ; but Philip of Valois declared that the Salic Law only applied to the crown of France, and pronounced himself in favour of Jeanne de Penthièvre and of Charles of Blois. Immediately Edward III intervened and supported the claims of Jean de Montfort. We note that in this each of the two sovereigns acted directly contrary to his own principles : because if Philip of Valois shut his ears to the Salic Law when the crown of Brittany was in question, Edward III, who repudiated the whole Salic Law concerning the crown of France, appreciated its excellence at the moment when the question touched the succession of Arthur. In general, Breton Brittany declared for John de Montfort, and French-speaking Brittany for Charles of Blois.

Charles was a strange figure, and he excited the admiration even of his adversaries. He was a replica of Saint Louis, but with still greater piety, more austerity, a more mystical exaltation. In preference even to the gospel he read the *Golden Legend* and delighted himself in these mysterious and trifling stories. He himself resembled a saint of the *Golden Legend* The waves of the sea, it was said, stopped in front of him : the sea went back at the sweetness of his gesture. When he walked with bare feet in the snow, bearing the shrine of St. Yve, flowers sprang up in the prints left by his feet, mingling the carnation of their corollas and their verdant wimples with the whiteness of the winter's carpet. The war went at first in favour of Charles of Blois. Jean de Montfort, taken prisoner, was taken to the Louvre (1341). The conflict might have seemed to be at an end when Montfort escaped and came to kindle once more the ardour of his partisans.

The battle of Creçy was fought on 28th August 1346. The English army was almost a modern army in the bulk of the popular element which it included. There were 10,000 English archers, 6000 Irish infantry, 12,000 Welsh. The army of the

King of France was a throng of jostling dukes and counts and noble bannerets. There was no order, no command: a feudal army which knew no longer the solid cadres, the limited bands which had formed the strength of the first Crusaders. The French army is about to collapse of itself much more than it will succumb to the blows of the enemy. Of the battle of Creçy, the *Chronicle of the First Four Valois* has made this suggestive record:

" King Philip commanded that the Genoese crossbowmen should come to grips with the English; they were soon discomfited and took to flight towards the French, who made an end of them. And then King Philip joined battle with the English, and there was a very hard struggle and wonderful fight. The English archers were in ambush behind the hedges and, by their fire, killed many horses and men. And on this day men were killed by horses; for as the French were thinking to range themselves, their horses were falling dead. What need to prolong the story? By hastiness and disarray were the French discomfited. King Philip performed marvellous feats of arms, but fortune turned against him." The English archers fired their arrows with their white feathers in such numbers that they seemed like snow falling from the sky. We remark that the English made use of three bombards. Is this the most ancient example of the employment of firing bombs in European war?

The effectives of the French army, considerably more than 60,000 men, were double the English contingents. It was at Creçy that was killed in the front ranks the old Count of Luxemburg, the King of Bohemia, John the Blind. The brave knight was indeed blind: but he had demanded that he should be led to the first ranks, in order that there he could still deliver some good blows. The pages consecrated by Froissart to this episode have remained justly celebrated.

On the 2nd September 1346, the English appeared under the walls of Calais, and began this famous siege. The garrison which defended the town was composed, for the most part, of knights of Artois under the orders of a Burgundian, John de Vienne. The siege lasted eleven months. Calais only capitulated on 3rd August 1347. Here the well-known episode

THE HUNDRED YEARS WAR

of the burgesses of Calais falls into place. Six of the principal burgesses of the town—Eustache de St. Pierre, Jean d'Aire, Jean de Fiennes, André d'Ardres, Jacques and Pierre de Wissant—came in their shirts, with ropes about their necks, to put themselves at the disposal of Edward, who wished to put the town to fire and sword. The Queen of England obtained their pardon. The episode has been recounted by Jean le Bel, and popularized by Froissart. Its authenticity has been called in question, since we shall see Eustache de St. Pierre, supporting the English domination, charged with municipal functions by those whom he had fought. But Siméon Luce, after a critical study of the documents, has pronounced in favour of its authenticity. A great number of the inhabitants of Calais, not wishing to become English, left the town in order to remain under the suzerainty of the King of France.

The taking of Calais, after the battle of Creçy, was a matter of high importance for the English. They would have for the future, on the French coast of the Channel, a valuable port of disembarkation. Calais was to remain in English hands until 1558. A month and a half after the battle of Creçy, on 17th October 1346, the Scottish claimant, David Bruce, who had invaded England, beaten at Neville's Cross, fell into the hands of the victors. Everywhere fortune smiled on the enemies of the fleur-de-lis.

We have spoken of the popular sentiments: the hostility which separated the aristocracy and the Patricians on the one side from the common people on the other. The defeat of Creçy went to accentuate this hostility. Note the Remonstrances addressed to the King of France, in the name of the big towns, in the assembly of the States-General meeting at Paris on the 30th November 1347.

The remarkable Continuator of Nangis notes with indignation the pomp, the growing luxury of the rich and of the knights. The misfortunes of the country do not touch them: they care only for feasting, dancing, and dicing, while the common people stoop and weep under the burden. It was at this epoch also, says the Continuator of Nangis, that the people of high rank began to call the workers in the fields " Jacques

Bonhomme" in derision, and the custom spread among the English themselves. The expression, however, was old. In the thirteenth century the authors of the fables call the French peasant "Jacques Bonhomme." "Jacque" designated, moreover, a part of the clothing which the rural worker wore in war: a short shirt stuffed with rough material forming a cushion—the hauberk of the peasants.

The nobles on their side cast the responsibility for the defeat on the commoners. "The King of France," reports Froissart, "said that he wished to make war only with noblemen, and that to draw into the battle the common people was nothing but an encumbrance, because these people in the fray melted like snow in the sun. Hence he would have none of them again, except the crossbowmen."

And to fill up the measure, here comes the Black Death, a bubonic plague, arrived from Asia *via* the port of Genoa. One knows the pages of Boccaccio at the beginning of his *Decameron*: "There was not a day that thousands of them did not fall sick, who, through not being helped or succoured in any way, nearly all died. And there were quite a number who died in the streets, day and night; and others who died in their houses first made their neighbours aware that they were dead by the stench of their decaying corpses." The plague spread in France during 1347. In towns like Avignon four hundred people died daily, and eight hundred in Paris. The people called the scourge the "Great Death." Then there was the famine of 1348. Froissart says that "the third part of the world" died of the double scourge. Jean de Venette (the Continuator of Nangis) goes further, asserting that hardly two out of twenty people escaped. This would confirm the old Burgundian saying:

> In one thousand three hundred and forty-eight,
> At Nuits from a hundred there remained eight.

At first the Jews were held responsible for the calamity. They were supposed to have poisoned the wells. Some thousands of Jews were burnt alive. The monk Jean de Venette does not fail to admire the courage which many of them displayed, especially the women. They threw themselves into the flames which were to consume their husbands, and, lest

THE HUNDRED YEARS WAR

their children should be baptized after their death, they threw them in also. Clement VI intervened. He gave refuge to the Jews in his dominions of Avignon, and shielded them by papal protection. Then came an exaggerated outbreak of mysticism, complicated by nervous crises. The Flagellants tortured themselves with their own hands, swallowing nails and lighted objects. And when the scourge had gone (1349), there came, by way of a reaction of the senses, an afflux of debauchery and luxury, a liberation of brutal appetites.

To this period, however, belong certain acts which are to throw a consoling light on the end of the reign of Philip of Valois, and show that the French monarchy had not fallen so low as appearances might lead us to imagine. Charles IV, the German Emperor, seeks an alliance with Philip VI. It is true that Charles IV was the son of the glorious Jean l'Aveugle (the Blind) who fell in the French ranks at Creçy. The treaty was signed at Metz on the 28th December 1347. And this treaty produced its effects. There will be seen coming from Germany, and especially from the Western marches, contingents of German cavalrymen and knights who will usefully reinforce the troops of the French prince. And then James III, the King of Majorca and suzerain of Montpelier, sells this latter fief to France for 120,000 golden crowns (18th April 1349). More important still was the acquisition of Dauphiné. The district was so named because the reigning house bore a dolphin (*dauphin*) in its arms. The suzerain himself was called the *dauphin*. It was on the 30th March 1349 that the famous agreement was concluded by which Humbert II yielded his magnificent fief to the eldest son of the King of France, on condition that for the future the son of the King should have until his accession the title of "Dauphin." We know in what a touching and charming manner this engagement was kept. Philip VI disbursed to Humbert 120,000 gold florins and besides a life rental of 22,000 pounds of Tours.

These were useful, but heavy, expenses, and came in addition to those incurred by the administration of the kingdom and the war with England. Now we have mentioned the yet rudimentary character of the financial organization. The principal resources of the Crown were still drawn from the revenues of the royal domains. But we can imagine how inadequate these

THE MIDDLE AGES

resources were under the existing conditions. It was necessary to supplement them by contributions levied right and left, in an intermittent, irregular, and unequal manner, and which were even so only obtained by means of concessions to the feudal lordships, to the municipalities, and to individuals, and often to the detriment of the general good. And whatever repugnance the royal government might have for such an expedient it was obliged periodically to have recourse to the debasement of the currency in the way already described. The administration of Philip VI did not fail to give proofs of wisdom. The ordinances relating to the organization of the profession of the notaries, of the power of the *baillis*, of the *Parlements* and the *Chambre des Comptes*, do honour to the end of the reign.

Philip of Valois was far from being a great prince in spite of his courage, which won universal admiration, and his taste for literature and the arts. He loved pomp, fine clothes, splendid feasts, and the brilliance of the life of chivalry, jousts, and tournaments. He liked also beautiful books, artists, and writers, and in this his first wife, Jeanne of Burgundy, had seconded him with very sound taste. Jeanne of Burgundy and Philip of Valois would have liked to keep Petrarch in France.

Philip of Valois died in the Abbey of Coulombs, near Nogent-le-Roi, on the 22nd August 1350.

Jean II, called *le Bon* (the Good or Brave), the son of Philip of Valois and Jeanne of Burgundy, was to bring to the throne the defects and qualities of his father, but in an exaggerated form, so that the faults became very much graver still, and the good qualities, in the circumstances under which they were manifested, became defects. His faults were obstinacy, a passionate nature, and an entire failure to appreciate the things which, in his day, made up modern life. His good points were courage and a very high sense of honour. Hardly was he thirteen years old when his father had given him to wife Bonne of Luxemburg, the daughter of King John of Bohemia. She was three years older than her young husband; but the two formed none the less a very united couple.

Jean le Bon.

One of the first acts of King John caused general stupefaction. On his arrival in Paris he had the Constable of France,

THE HUNDRED YEARS WAR

Raoul de Brienne, Count of Eu and of Guînes, seized and beheaded in the Hôtel de Nesle. One becomes lost in conjecture as to the motives of this execution, which was not preceded by any judicial formality. The office of Constable was given to a lord of whom King John was particularly fond, Charles of Castile, called Charles of Spain, the son of Alfonzo, King of Castile, and grandson of Ferdinand de la Cerda.

The war was going on in Brittany between the partisans of Jean de Montfort and those of Charles de Blois, but the Kings of France and England no longer took part in it. On the 27th March 1351 there took place, "half-way between Josselin and the castle of Ploërmel, in a splendid sloping field, at the spot called the 'Halfway Oak,' beside beautiful green bushes of genets," on the territory of the commune of La Croix-Helléan (Morbihan), the famous "Fight of the Thirty." The encounter rose from the defiance launched against each other by two leaders —the Englishman Bramborough, who commanded Ploërmel, and the Frenchman Beaumanoir, established at Josselin. The initiative came from Beaumanoir, indignant at the bad treatment with which the English overwhelmed the Breton peasants. Each of the two adversaries was to come on the scene as one of a band of thirty men-at-arms. The combat occupied a whole day. In the course of the action Beaumanoir complained of thirst. Geoffroi Dubois cried out to him, "Drink your blood, Beaumanoir!"

> Beaumanoir the Valiant then began to fail,
> Such sorrow and anger possessed him that he was overcome with thirst. . . .

At the end of the day all the combatants were wounded, but the English counted eleven dead, among whom was Bramborough. The survivors yielded themselves as prisoners into the hands of the Bretons, who held them to ransom.

The year 1351 was marked by a recurrence of the debasement of the coinage. We have shown in what these measures consisted. The royal ordinances spoke truly when they said that the alteration of the gold and silver pieces was only a "way of raising taxes, more prompt and easier for those who collected them and less burdensome to those who had to pay them." The King, in fact, did not deny that the money newly issued had not the value which was by necessity attributed to it. The difference constituted the tax deducted beforehand for the needs of the State. But these frequent changes, effected in the value of the medium of exchange, caused much trouble. To remedy it, the traders and the money-changers as well as the public came to take no more account of the nominal value of the gold pounds or the silver sous, but of their weight valued in marks. Through this the authorities were brought to vexatious or violent measures: an oath demanded from the money-changers, traders, and hotel-keepers to respect the ordinances; espionage, perquisitions, confiscations. Up to this time the alterations had been made openly, and, so to speak, honestly. Under the pressure of circumstances the royal government is to proceed to clandestine alterations which will become veritable falsifications. And lest the public should learn of the smaller proportion of gold or silver in the alloy of the new pieces of money, an oath was demanded from the master and employees of the mints that they would reveal nothing. We read in an order of September 1351: "Take care, on your honour, that they (the money-changers) shall not know the power (the standard of the new pieces), under penalty of being declared traitors."

When King John ascended the throne, the silver mark counted against five pounds, five sous; at the end of 1351, it counted as eleven pounds. The intrinsic value of the money in circulation had, then, fallen in a year by 100 per cent. These alterations became more and more frequent, for if the royal power had profited by circulating, with a smaller proportion of gold and silver, the money which it called in, it recast again the "weak" money, with a higher face value, and put it in circulation at a still higher assessment. It put into circulation again sous of Tours or Paris of a better alloy, but demanding two sous of the previous issue for one of the new. And, shortly afterwards, it recommenced the inverse process. During the first ten years of the reign of King John the Tours pound changed in value more than seventy times.

These were certainly vexatious measures, against which modern historians vituperate at their ease. But in the conditions of the time would they have done better ? Is it even certain that they would not have done worse ?

The war had been actively resumed in the South. The lesser nobles, who were suffering from the decrease in the feudal dues, embittered against the great nobles grouped round the powerful lord of Armagnac, had demanded from Edward III effective support, and the English King had sent to Aquitaine his own son, the Prince of Wales, the famous Black Prince, a name he took from the colour of his armour. Edward III was a prince of great intelligence, above all admirable in matters of military administration. The Black Prince proved a skilful strategist, active, quick in his decisions, a clear-sighted leader. He was a young man of twenty-five years, in the strength and beauty of that age at which natures greatly endowed accomplish their most notable achievements. He loved swift horses, finely tempered weapons, works of art. He led a luxurious life, but without relaxing the rigid strength of his character and will. A small number of soldiers sufficed him for the subjection of the land and the pillage of refractory districts. Moreover, on all sides, he found help and support.

However, the finances of the French King were in such a bad state that the pledges of the royal officers were no longer fulfilled. It became necessary to resolve on the summoning of the States-General. It was limited to the country of the *langue d'oïl*, the country of the *langue d'oc* being in the hands of the English. The assembly was held in Paris in the Great Hall of the Palace. The Provost of the Merchants, Etiénne Marcel, was seen there for the first time in his popular rôle. He was the spokesman of the good towns : or, as it would be expressed later, the Third Estate (*le Tiers*). The States realized their duty and showed a sincere devotion to the Crown. They voted subsidies for the war, to be paid by all, beginning with the King and royal family. They proclaimed the right of resistance " by coalition " to the exactions of the royal officials and the pillage of the men-at-arms.

The States met again in March and November 1356. This time the States voted a tax on income, a progressive tax but with a backward progression. Ten pounds of income was liable to 10 per cent. ; a thousand pounds to only 2 per cent. In a later assembly a new imposition was granted to the King by the States, rising to 4 per cent. on incomes lower than a hundred pounds and to 2 per cent. only on incomes higher than this sum.

At first sight this method of " progression " seems revolting. Perhaps it will seem less so if we remember that these impositions were destined for the expenses of the war, and that these already weighed heavily on the feudal aristocracy, who were bound to the service of the army and at that time proportionately to their income.

It has often been asked why the French burgess class and the rural nobility itself did not profit by the weakness and confusion into which the Hundred Years War plunged the royal authority to win public liberties by means of the assembling of the States, to form a national government under the control of representatives elected by themselves, a condition which to some minds seems necessary for liberty. If the representatives delegated to the States did not direct their energies in the sense just indicated, it was because the social and moral conditions of the time rendered impossible the government of the country by an assembly of elected delegates. What militated especially against this kind of " liberty "—in the singular—was precisely the " liberties "—in the plural—which the country enjoyed: on all sides liberties, local franchises, customs individual to each province, to each fief, to each locality, sometimes to a family. We have seen that the population of the region of Bordeaux did not wish to conform to the " usages " of the French. It was the same with the Bretons, the Normans, the Picards, and Burgundians. If a general measure, what we should call a law, had been voted by the majority in an assembly of the States, the good folk in numerous parts of France would have received with blows of pitchforks and picks the officials commissioned to apply them. In England, the Norman Conquest, the levelling of the nation under the rude hand of the reigning sovereigns, the conquerors, the necessity of struggling against these latter, rendered parliamentarism desirable and possible. The very liberties with which France bristled, and the patriarchal and paternal authority which she venerated in her Kings, rendered parliamentarism impossible. And one sees it from these States of 1356. The impositions voted by the representatives of the towns were repulsed with indignation by the very towns whose delegates had caused them to be adopted.

At Arras the great folk (*les gros*), *i.e.* the Patricians, favourable to the fleur-de-lis, declared that they must pay; but the lesser folk (*menus*) were not of this opinion. On the 5th March 1356, seventeen Patricians are killed; on the 7th March the people of Arras kill four more and drive away the remainder. " And thus the said common people remain lords and masters of that town " (*Grandes Chroniques*). But on the 27th April Arnoul d'Audrehem, Marshall of France, appeared at the head of imposing forces; he had twenty heads cut off among those who had proved themselves the most rebellious, and the " Gros " became masters of the city once more.

A new enemy had, however, ranged himself against King John, one who was destined to be for him and for his son, the future Charles V, a source of grave embarrassment. A young Prince of twenty years was living in France, Charles, King of Navarre. He was great-grandson of Philip the Bold, by his father, Count Philip of Evreux (the son of Louis of Evreux, son of Philip the Bold), and great-grandson of Philip the Fair through his mother, the only daughter of Louis le Hutin (Headstrong). This Prince was called Charles the Bad, because of the rather harsh way in which he repressed, in 1350, a rising of the men of Navarre. The throne of Navarre had come to him through his mother, the daughter of Louis le Hutin, for the Salic Law, applied to the crown of France, did not apply to that of Navarre.

The claims of Charles of Navarre to the French throne would have preceded those of Edward III if he had wished to bring them to bear when with the English monarch the succession in the feminine line was claimed; and we shall see that Charles will decide on this course.

The monks of St. Denis draws the portrait of Charles the Bad: " He was little and full of energy, had a penetrating mind, and expressed himself easily with natural eloquence; he was marvellously adroit. Above all, he surpassed all other princes in his affability." In 1352 he had married the Princess Jeanne, daughter of Jean le Bon. History will judge him

THE MIDDLE AGES

severely. With the good qualities of Charles of Navarre there were mingled some shameful faults : a want of character, a lack of straightforwardness, and a certain inclination to lower things.

John the Good was very fond of his cousin, Charles of Spain. We have seen that he had made him Constable after the death of Raoul de Brienne. He gave him, besides, the county of Angoulême. Now, Charles of Navarre and his brothers had some claims to the County of Angoulême : whence arose a rivalry between the two Charles's. It manifested itself one day in violent words. On the 8th January 1354, Charles of Spain was lying, suspecting nothing, in his bed at l'Aigle, in the County of Alençon, when the King of Navarre arrived, followed by the Count of Harcourt and several companions. They pulled the Constable from his bed and killed him miserably.

Two years had passed, and Charles, Duke of Normandy, the eldest son of John the Good, was feasting in his castle of Rouen, to which he had invited the King of Navarre, the Count of Harcourt, the Lord of Granville, and several other boon companions of Charles the Bad, when the door opens silently ; King John and several men-at-arms enter. The King had the Count of Harcourt, the Lord of Granville, a knight, Maubue de Menesmares, and a squire, Colinet Doublet, seized. He had them taken outside the town, to the " Field of the Tournament " (*Champ du Pardon*), and there had their heads cut off and their bodies hanged to a gibbet (4th April 1356). As to the King of Navarre, he was loaded with chains and shut up first in the Château-Gaillard, then in the Châtelet at Paris. By these " cruel judgments " John II avenged the assassination of his Constable.

We read at this date in the *Chronicle of the First Four Valois* : " Edward, King of England, who was very wise in war, saw that it was not to his advantage to fight the French King, and returned to Calais. And then King John sent him a message that he was not acting like a gentleman in not awaiting a battle. Upon this the English King sent word back that he was a gentleman, and there should be no lack of battles." Alas ! Edward III was to keep his word only too well.

THE HUNDRED YEARS WAR

The battle claimed by King John was fought on the 19th September 1356 outside Poitiers. The Black Prince, who had just ravaged Limousin, Saintonge, and Vendée, was returning gorged with booty. He was followed by heavy wagons with rusty iron wheels groaning on their axles. He was aiming at getting back to Bordeaux when a French army, commanded by King John in person, came up with him. The English entrenched themselves on the plateau of Maupertuis, a league from Poitiers. Their position found a natural defence in enclosures of vines and quickset hedges. The numerical superiority of the French army was such that the Prince of Wales considered his fate and that of his men desperate. Through the cardinals, whom the Pope has sent to the adversaries to engineer a peace, the Prince of Wales made a proposal to King John, by which all the French prisoners were to be set at liberty, the latest conquests of the English should be restored, notably Calais and Guînes, and a truce of seven years be made. He demanded only a free opportunity to return to Bordeaux. It would have been the salvation of our country; but King John was boiling over with impatience and anger. In his impetuous ardour he spoke only of falling upon the enemy. However, the Marshall de Clermont pointed out to him that it would be folly to attack the English where they then were. He advised that they should "settle down near them and prevent their receiving new food supplies." Upon which the Marshall d'Audrehem intervened. He was a sort of colossus, with prodigious strength and the blindest courage; which pleased King John:

"Marshall de Claremont," cried Audrehem, "you are upset at the sight of them!"

"To-day you would hardly be brave enough to put the muzzle of your horse against the neck of mine!"

The battle began. From a distance the English archers riddled with darts the French cavalry, who drew back in confusion. King John put the crown on the disorder by telling the knights to alight. One can imagine the fine jumble under the English arrows. The maddened horses rear. And what fine infantry the knights would make hampered by their carapaces of iron! "The clamour and uproar were heard more than three leagues away. And there was great sorrow to see the flower of all nobility and knighthood thus given over to destruction" (*Chronique des quatre premiers Valois*).

In the confusion, King John had at least one gleam of good sense. He ordered his eldest son to retire from the conflict and go back into Poitiers. As for himself, he would not budge from the field of battle. Chandos, the English leader, understood him well, when he gave the advice that the battle should be pressed at the spot where the French King was, for he would let himself be taken alive or cut to pieces rather than fall back. King John, armed with a battle-axe, defended himself like a lion. On his dust-covered brow the blood made little furrows. His second son, known from this day as Philip the Bold (Philippe le Hardi), pressed close to him. And " by force were taken the said King John of France, my lord Philip of France, his son, the Count d'Eu. . . . And a marvellous number of dukes, counts, barons, knights, squires, and good serving-men were killed in the said battle: from which followed irreparable loss."

Siméon Luce has rightly said that Creçy was only a defeat; Poitiers was a disaster. Its first consequence was a recrudescence of anger, hatred, and suspicion among the people against the nobility. Were not the Nobles the cause of the defeat, not only by their inefficiency, as at Creçy, but also by their cowardice? For, in fact, at Poitiers the cavalry had fled. The Continuator of Nangis echoes these sentiments with vehemence:

" From this the affairs of the kingdom went from bad to worse; the republic (*respublica*)—we must not take the word in its literal sense—was falling to ruin, and brigands appeared on all sides. The nobles scorn and detest the villeins; they no longer care for the welfare of the King or of their vassals; they tyrannize over and despoil the peasants in their villages. They have no care for the defence of their country. To trample on those who are subject to them and deprive them of their possessions is their sole preoccupation. From this day the country of France (*patria Franciæ*), which was formerly glorious and honoured throughout the world, happy in her wealth and the benefits of peace, became the laughing-stock of the other nations. Oh, sorrow! she fell into scorn."

The author of the *Plaint of the Battle of Poitiers* expresses himself in still more vivid terms. At Poitiers the Nobles committed treason:

> The great treason which they have long hidden
> Was in that army clearly shown.

And by a counter-movement, it is towards the King who had fought so valiantly with his " little child " (Philip the Bold) that, in a recrudescence of affection and devotion, popular affection turns:

> May God comfort and protect our King
> And his little child who has stayed with him!

Salvation is to be found in the union of the King and brave folk:

> If he (the King) is well advised he will not forget
> To take Jacques Bonhomme in his great company,
> Who will never run away to save his life,

as the knights had done at Poitiers.

In Paris, power passes into the hands of the popular leaders: the illustrious Provost of the Merchants, Etienne Marcel, the Archbishop of Laon, Robert le Coq, and a knight, Jean de Picquigny.

The Nobles are not only incapable and cowardly, say those of the commonalty; they devour the people and rob the King. They insist on payment for the support and wages of the soldiers they take to the army; and they are not afraid, in order to extract larger sums from the public treasury, to falsify their accounts, and to pass off as men-at-arms their servants, valets, and pages:

> When they (the nobles) show themselves to the marshalls to pass muster,
> Their scullions and their pages as soldiers they count,
> Thus there is one for the wages of four which they take. . . .

The people of Paris put themselves in a state of defence. " In this year 1356," writes Jean de Venette, "the Parisians, in fear of their enemies and with no confidence in the nobles, hung chains across the streets and cross-roads; they dug moats round the walls in the western part of the town and around the suburbs in the eastern, where there had been none up to then. They reinforced the fortifications and built bastiles, furnishing the towers with balistas, ammunition, cannons, and engines. They destroyed the houses which inside or out adjoined the ramparts. How many fine dwellings were then destroyed from top to bottom to make room for the moats ! "

And the people of Paris sighed for the return of the King, alone capable, says Jean de Venette, of restoring the country. The scourge of brigandage became a frightful calamity. Some of these brigands were also real soldiers. We have already seen the intimacy of a Richard Cœur de Lion with a Mercadier. The English army, victorious at Poitiers, included a great number of these brigands: mercenaries from Brabant, Flanders, Hainault, and Germany. After the victory and the truce signed for two years at Poitiers, on the 23rd March 1357, the Black Prince left them on French territory.

They took their name from their armour, the brigandine, a corselet composed of scales of iron joined by riveted nails; but other and more reliable historians, such as Siméon Luce, claim that the brigandine received its name from the brigands.

Froissart recounts their doings and achievements. "And every day poor brigands profited in robbing and pillaging towns and castles, and thus won such great possessions that it was a great marvel, and some became so rich, especially those who constituted themselves masters and leaders of other brigands, that there were some who had as much money as 40000 crowns (an enormous sum for the period). To tell the truth, what they did was wonderful: they saw a good town or castle a day or two's journey away; and then they gathered together twenty or thirty brigands, and journeyed day and night by hidden ways until they entered this town or castle which they had seen, exactly at break of day, and set fire to a house. And the people of the town thought that it was a thousand men in armour come to burn the town and so they fled as best they could, and these brigands broke into houses, chests, and coffers, and took as much as they could find and then went their way laden with plunder."

They gave themselves up to frightful excesses. In Bourbonnais they had dug an immense moat where a great fire burned day and night. The brigands called it "Hell." If an unfortunate person could not or would not ransom himself:

"Throw him into Hell!"

"The fear of so terrible a fate," writes Cabaret d'Orreville, "took such a hold on those threatened that all, in order to escape it, consented to give up all their possessions to the brigands."

The English were not alone in employing brigands. Philip of Valois, in order to induce the famous Croquard to enter his service, offered to make him a knight—a fine knight!—and to pay him an annual allowance of £2000 (400,000 francs in our present money). The French King made another bandit named Bacon, clever at surprising fortresses, his usher-at-arms. Some of these brigands, Arnaud de Cervolle, called the Archpriest, and Rodriguez de Villandrando, command armies, treat with sovereigns as one power with another, and play a great part in the defence of the land. Some of these leaders of companies belonged to the highest families, but out of respect for their scutcheon they hid their identity under a nickname. "How we rejoiced," will say one of them named Aimerigot Marchès, "when we were riding at random and met on the countryside a rich abbot or prior, a merchant or a caravan of mules from Montpelier, Narbonne, Limoux, Fougans, or Béziers, from Toulouse or Carcassonne, laden with cloth from Brussels or Moustier-Villiers, or with furs coming from the market at the Lendit (an ancient fair near Paris), or with spices from Bruges, or silks from Damascus or Alexandria. We could take all or ransom it as we liked. Every day we got more money. The peasants of Auvergne and Limousin brought us in our castle corn and flour, bread ready baked, oats and litter for the horses, good wines, oxen, fat lambs, and sheep, chickens, and game. We were stuffed like kings, and when we rode abroad the whole country trembled before us. Everything was ours, going and returning. How we took Carlat, the Bastard of Compans, and myself! and Chaluset, Pierrot le Béarnois, and I! How we took by escalade, just you and I without any help, the fortress of Merquel, which belongs to the Count Dauphin! I held it only five days, and got for it, cash down, five thousand francs. And I renounced another thousand for the love of the Count Dauphin. By my faith, it was a good and fine life."

A bright light was about to shine through this gloom, and it was already shedding its first rays. In July 1357 the Duke of Lancaster raised the siege of Rennes after a fruitless effort lasting nine months. Lancaster had the reputation of being the best warrior of his time, the inspirer of Edward III. This check, which was to make a great stir, and restore confidence to the "white crosses," was due to a Breton gentleman, Bertrand du Guesclin. He was born towards 1320 at the Motte-Broons, some leagues from Dinant, of a noble family. When he distinguished himself at the defence of Rennes he was about thirty-eight years old. Strong, robust, squat, with an ugliness which was to become proverbial, not knowing how to read or write, he is to be, through his courage, wisdom, and good sense, the saviour of his country and the idol of feminine hearts. Bertrand du Guesclin is one of the most complete figures in the perfection of his rôle to be met in all history.

> I think there is none so ugly between Rennes and Dinant,
> Flat-nosed he was and black, uncouth and clownish,

wrote the poet Cuvelier, who consecrated to him a poem in the style of the old epics. He had a flat face and green eyes:

> Fists big and square to carry the sword,
> Legs and thighs for great endurance.

As a partisan of Charles of Blois, he throws himself into Rennes, besieged by Lancaster (3rd March 1357):

> See him come there along that high road
> With a coat of mail black as a pothanger,
> With six squires of his household,
> And carrying at his neck that great axe!
> "By my faith," said the herald who saw the band,
> "He looks just like a brigand catching sight of some merchants." . . .

When the siege of Rennes was over, Du Guesclin was nominated captain of Mont-St.-Michel (13th December 1357), that sublime fortress which was to give an example, in another siege, the finest in all history, of an undaunted resistance of seventy years. At the end of the Hundred Years War, in spite of continual sieges, Mont-St.-Michel will still be French.

THE HUNDRED YEARS WAR

The nomination of Du Guesclin was made at the request of the Abbot of the "Mount." "The glory of Mont-St.-Michel," writes Siméon Luce, "is to have been the sanctuary of national sentiment. For ten years—it is now 1357—during which the struggle with the English lasted, the monks had shown an admirable patriotism. Their abbot, Nicolas le Vitrier, who had been born on the picturesque rock of which the monastery formed the crown, had armed his men and servants, keeping such a strict watch round the rock that the English could never set foot on it. As a reward the Dauphin granted to Nicolas le Vitrier (27th January 1357) that the captain of Mont-St.-Michel should henceforth be only 'the abbot or the nominee of the abbot.'"

In Paris, through the action of Etienne Marcel, the Provost of the Merchants, the democratic element got the upper hand. Marcel, then aged about forty, belonged, however, to one of the richest and best-connected families in the town. He was a woollen-draper, connected with the great woollen-drapers of Flanders. Perhaps the figure of Jacques van Artevelde haunted him. The popular class in Paris was to find in him a guide with broad views, ideas of reform, and by reason of his intellectual power at least, a leader worthy of guiding them.

The provostship of the merchants was a magistracy of the burgesses. All commercial jurisdiction was subject to it: it was the sole bond between the various fiefs whose union had formed the town; it had the policing of the streets. To it belonged the duty of maintaining the fortifications and defence of the place. And through this, later, its prerogatives increased

Let us recall what has been already said. The towns and the places in which the democratic elements were predominant inclined towards the English Crown or, at least, were in opposition to the government of the Valois supported by the aristocracy and the patriciate. But a national sentiment was already beginning to show itself. It was repugnant to the people of Paris and to a man of the quality of Etienne Marcel to seek support in people who were as strangers, even enemies, in France. Thus Marcel and his colleagues, Robert le Coq, Bishop of Laon, and the Vidame of Picquigny, were induced to support the cause of Charles the Bad. He was the Count of Evreux and a French prince. Admitting the transmission of royal rights through women he was the heir of the Capetians. Charles the Bad was held captive in the castle of Arleux-lès-Amiens. At the instigation of Marcel and his friends, a band of men of Amiens seized the castle of Arleux in the night of the 8th–9th November 1357. Restored to liberty, Charles the Bad came to Paris.

Later, when it is no longer possible to support the cause of the King of Navarre, the Parisians pronounce in favour of the Duke of Burgundy. This latter, sprung directly from the French reigning family, will appease any patriotic scruple they may have. Finally, under the evils of invasion, national sentiment will triumph over every other motive in the irresistible movement of which Jeanne d'Arc will be the sublime incarnation, and the people of Paris will come back in its turn to the fleur-de-lis. But up to the death of Jeanne d'Arc the Parisians, and how many other good Frenchmen with them, will follow, and how resolutely, the " Burgundians."

In Paris, Charles the Bad found refuge in the Abbey of St. Germain-des-Prés. He had the people of Paris summoned under the walls of the abbey, in the famous " Clerics' Field " (*Pré-aux-Clercs*), and standing on the wall—*supra muros*—on the 30th November 1357, he " preached " to the crowd " in a loud and clear voice." He described the iniquity of his arrest and his sorrowful imprisonment, " and though he said nothing openly against the King, nor against the Duke (of Normandy, later Charles V), at the same time he said quite enough things dishonourable and shameful to them in covert speech, and such things he spoke for a long time " (*Grandes Chroniques*). The people wept. Finally, under popular pressure, seconded by the widows of Charles the Fair and Philip of Valois, the aunt and sister of the King of Navarre, an apparent reconciliation took place between the latter and the young Charles V (3rd December 1357).

Etienne Marcel seems all powerful in Paris and the surrounding district. He has taken seriously in hand the cares of the administration. He sees to the cleanliness of the streets, and no longer allows pigs to wander freely there. However, the States, after having so loudly blamed the debasement of the coinage, believe themselves authorized to have recourse to this also.

The aim of Etienne Marcel seems to have been to give France an organization similar to that of the Flemish : the administration of the country by urban assemblies, grouped in federation under the direction of Paris—which would play the part held by Ghent in Flanders—under the more or less nominal suzerainty of the King, who would have corresponded to the Suzerain Count in Flanders.

But it was in fact the local liberties of the French which prevented the realization of these plans. M. Coville has seen this clearly. In France the provinces appeared as so many different nations. In Flanders, Ghent could conduct its policy, the policy imagined by Etienne Marcel for Paris, only by means of a veritable dictatorship imposed by force on the other towns of the country. It was with difficulty that Marcel found in some towns, Abbeville, Amiens, Laon, Sens, and Rouen, some good folk ready to assume his caps of red and blue. Even in these few districts, the movement was far from enlisting a decided majority. Elsewhere Marcel's voice found no echo ; it never even reached to the South.

Added to this, Marcel found in Charles V, the eldest son of John the Good, an adversary worthy of him. Charles, in his turn, wanted to harangue the people of Paris. He had them summoned to the market-place. "And when the Bishop of Laon and the Provost of the Merchants knew of this, they thought to prevent it, and said to my lord the Duke (Charles V) that he would be putting himself in great danger by going among so many of the people. But the said lord Duke did not believe them ; and went about terce (10 a.m.) to the said market hall, on horseback, with about five or seven companions. And he said to the great crowd of people who were there, that it was his intention to live and die with them, and that they should not give credence to those who had said and published that he got soldiery to come to pillage and destroy . . . but that he had brought these to help and defend and protect the French people, who had to suffer much, for their enemies were very widespread " (*Grandes Chroniques*).

Charles V had a success equal to that of Charles the Bad.

The common people were flattered to see such great personages coming to speak to them familiarly, and both spoke very well.

When Marcel saw the young prince winning back his authority over the Parisians he resolved to hasten a decision in attacking those whom he considered his chief advisers, the most redoubtable obstacles to his plans, Jean de Conflans, Marshall of Champagne, and Robert of Clermont, Marshall of Normandy. In the morning of the 22nd February he gathered together an armed crowd, about 3000 men, drawn from the class of craftsmen, who flung themselves with furious cries on the dwelling of the King (Palais de Justice) and massacred the two officers in the very apartment of Charles V. The corpse of the Marshall of Champagne rolled at the feet of the horrified Dauphin.

"And (the Dauphin) said to the Provost of the Merchants :

"'Provost, are these my enemies ? Must I beware of them ?'

"'Sire, they are your real well-wishers, for they have only come here for your profit.'

"And then the Provost gave him his red and azure cap, and then the said burgesses dragged the Marshalls, of Clermont and of Champagne, into the courtyard of the Palace, and then departed. And then the governors of the three states (States-General) thought they would enjoy peaceably the government of the kingdom of France" (*Chron. des quatre premiers Valois*).

On the 26th February (1358) Charles the Bad, recalled by Robert le Coq and Etienne Marcel, entered Paris again. On the 14th May the Dauphin Charles informed the Parisians, that after having borne, since the capture of King John, the title of lieutenant of the King, he would henceforth style himself "regent of the kingdom"—a decision which he seems to have taken at the instigation of Etienne Marcel. The Provost hoped, from the moment that the authority of the Dauphin should be entirely substituted for that of the King, to concentrate in his own hands the government of the kingdom, the young regent being at his mercy. He reckoned without his host. Charles V was twenty-one years old. He had a frail appearance, but a strong will, and he was not the man to let himself be the tool of any one. The States-General, which deliberated at Compiègne, pronounced in his favour.

THE HUNDRED YEARS WAR

Having entered on the path of violence Etienne Marcel becomes daily more and more a revolutionary figure. To free himself from his brutal authority the young King left Paris. He went to Meaux and took up his residence in the market of the town, a " very strong place." He had wished to bring the artillery from the Louvre, but the Provost had prevented him.

The Parisians, much moved, tried to get their Prince back again. They charged the King of Navarre with the negotiations. The interview took place on the 2nd May (1358) between Mello and Clermont. " And the said regent (Charles V) said to him (the King of Navarre) that he loved the city of Paris, and he well knew that there were good people within it; but there were some there who had committed great villanies and offences, such as killing his people in his presence, taking his castle of the Louvre and its artillery, and several other offences they had committed against him. And so he had no intention of entering Paris until these things had been redressed " (*Grandes Chroniques*).

The Regent increased still further the fortifications of the market of Meaux, already so considerable. He left there the women of the royal household and departed for Sens. The *Grandes Chroniques*, drawn up, if not by Charles V himself, at least under his inspiration, contain in this connection lines on which we ought to reflect:

The burgesses of Sens, says the Chronicler, received the Dauphin with honour, as they ought to do, as " their rightful lord after the King of France, his father "; at the same time, adds the Chronicler, " there were then few towns, cities, or other places in the *langue d'oïl* which were not roused against the nobles (badly disposed therefore towards the Dauphin) in favour of the people of Paris, who hated them (the nobles)."

The Regent arrived at Sens at the moment that the revolt of the Jacquerie was finishing. The famous rising of the peasants had lasted hardly a month (May to June 1358). The Jacquerie appears to have spread over the country, round Paris and Beauvais, Brie, and a part of Picardy and Champagne.

The bands of armed " Jacques " seized the castles and seigniorial dwellings, which they plundered. " They had made it a custom in the flat (not fortified) towns through which they passed, that the people, men or women, should put tables in the streets, and there the 'Jacques' ate, and then passed on, burning the houses of the gentlemen." They carried flags bearing the fleur-de-lis.

The "Jacques" had come to commit the worst excesses. Etienne Marcel, at first their ally, was horror-stricken by them. And it was the King of Navarre who, at the head of a band of armed knights, crushed the rising in blood. The "Jacques" had chosen as their leader a certain Guillaume Cale or Carle. "He was," says the Chronicler of the first Valois, "a man of knowledge and oratorical powers, of good face and figure." He tried to discipline the rebels and avoid excesses. Charles the Bad took him by treason, in an ambush into which he led him under pretence of concluding an armistice. Then he had him killed in a horrible manner by crowning him with a tripod of red-hot iron. The reaction of the nobles against the peasants was terrible. They could not forgive these rustics for having made them afraid. If we may believe the well-informed author of the *Grandes Chroniques*, in the first three weeks of June they killed more than 20,000 of them. The nobles took advantage to gratify their rancour against the Parisians, who detested them. "And every day the gentlemen burned houses belonging to the inhabitants of Paris, and took and carried off all the furnishings which they found belonging to these inhabitants; and no man travelling through the land dared say he was from Paris."

Marcel had supported the "Jacques" at the beginning of their rising: he saw his popularity impaired by their excesses. He then throws himself into the arms of the King of Navarre. Charles the Bad, on his side, although he was the principal instrument of the repression of the peasants, is to be impelled by the very force of circumstances more and more towards the democratic elements. On the 15th June he makes his entry into Paris, as captain of the town, at the head of English soldiery. The Parisians, says Jean de Venette, welcomed him, for they thought he would defend them against the nobles. But immediately the gentlemen who were attached to him, and particularly in his expedition against the "Jacques," abandoned him. They "left the said King of Navarre, when they saw

THE HUNDRED YEARS WAR

that he had accepted the captaincy of the men of Paris" (*Grandes Chroniques*).

Circumstances prevented the realization of Etienne Marcel's plans. Insensibly and against his will he is to be led from one thing to another, into measures more and more vexatious for a statesman and more and more compromising. He has shown favour to the "Jacques," made an alliance with Charles the Bad, and here he is, in order to resist the Regent's men-at-arms, taking as auxiliaries the bands of brigands known under the name of the "Great Companies." Finally, he turns to the English, some bands of whom Charles the Bad had already introduced into Paris.

Jean de Venette, with his vigour and customary precision, draws a picture of what happened. The nobles, established at Corbeil, were preventing corn and bread coming by water to Paris. They had thrown a bridge across the river between Paris and Corbeil, and passing from one bank to the other did great damage to the people of Paris. The Provost of the Merchants, at the head of an armed troop, went to destroy the bridge. The Regent (Charles V) was living sometimes at Sens, sometimes at Meaux. Another day the nobles, under the orders of the Duke of Normandy (Charles V), came as far as the bridge of Charenton in the desire to fight against the King of Navarre and the Parisians. The King of Navarre, the Captain of the Parisians, went to meet the Duke of Normandy, but instead of fighting him, he made long speeches to his troops and then went back into the town; he was very fond of talking. This rendered him suspect in the eyes of the people of Paris, "for he was noble," says the Chronicler.

The relations between the English soldiers whom Marcel had brought into the town and the Parisians could not fail to be disagreeable. The news spread that the English of St. Denis and St. Cloud were pillaging the country, and the Parisians throwing themselves upon the "Goddams." They killed fifty and shut up a great many more, and some of the most important, in the towers of the Louvre. At which the King of Navarre and Marcel were "very angry."

On the next day, the King of Navarre summoned the Parisians to the Place de Grève, and, from the windows of the

THE MIDDLE AGES

Town Hall, he blamed them for treating the English so badly. Had they not come "to serve the people of Paris"? After which he said, narrates the Chronicler, "fine and gentle words." But the Parisians replied with cries of, "Death to the English!" and that they ought all to be killed. They even forced the King of Navarre and Etienne Marcel to put themselves at their head and march against the English at St. Cloud. They fell there into an ambush and fought confusedly and in retreat, leaving 600 of their men on the ground. Charles the Bad did not dare to enter Paris again. He remained at St. Denis, while Marcel at his return was "severely scolded and blamed" by his subjects. Sixty-seven Englishmen remained shut up in the towers of the Louvre, where the Parisians wanted to kill them. On the 27th July (1358), at the head of an armed troop, Marcel went to deliver them, and, protecting them against the fury of the mob—" and they (the men-at-arms) had their bows at the stretch "—he put them out of Paris by the porte St. Honoré. They went to join their compatriots established at St. Denis. One can see how feelings went. Marcel is fatally drawn to the English; but the contact of the Parisians with the English provokes national sentiment against which the Provost of the Merchants will see his projects break like glass.

The ill-humour of the Parisians was further irritated by the lack of provisions, for the English and the Navarrese, as well as the followers of the Dauphin, stopped them on the way. Feeling his popularity compromised in the capital, abandoned by the provinces where the cause of the Regent was coming more and more into favour, Etienne Marcel was driven to extreme measures. He resolved to let the King of Navarre into the capital, although he knew of the strict alliance concluded shortly before between Charles the Bad and the English. In the night of the 31st July 1358, Marcel was at the *barriere St. Antoine* with some of his party. He held in his hands the great keys of the formidable gate, when he was surprised by the *échevin*, Jean Maillard, who had rallied to the side of the Dauphin. Maillard was accompanied by the knight Pepin des Essarts and several resolute men. With one blow of an axe he split the skull of the Provost of the Merchants. Maillard's companions threw themselves on those of Marcel and killed the majority of them; then they dragged their corpses to the square in front of the church of the Val des Ecoliers. The corpses remained there several days, naked, ignominiously exposed to the gaze of the passers-by. The Parisians would not allow them to be buried, so that the Dauphin, " on his arrival, could see with his own eyes that he was avenged on his enemies."

The peasants furnish touching evidence of the awakening of national sentiment among the people. The people of the villages seized the fortress of Longueil-Ste-Marie (arrondissement of Compiègne) and organized there the resistance to the English companies which were plundering the country. Under the leadership of one of them, Guillaume l'Aloue (Alouette, pretty French name!), they slaughtered the English who fell into their hands. They would not, moreover, admit any gentleman into their ranks. They remained the enemies of the Nobility, at the same time wishing to free the land from the English. L'Aloue was surprised by the " red crosses " and killed, but not without defending himself valiantly in a combat in which he and his peasants killed more than a hundred of the enemy, among them twenty-four knights. L'Aloue left a servant, of herculean stature and strength, the great Ferré. Armed with an enormous woodman's axe, he bore down the English like plaster statues. Jean de Venette devoted to him a page of marvellous vividness and colour, unhappily written in Latin. Following a fight, Ferré, running with perspiration, had drunk some icy-cold water in great mouthfuls. He went to bed shivering with fever. His wife runs to warn him of the approach of the English. The colossus rises, leaning with his back to the wall. He is in his shirt. The attacking party were a dozen in number, armed to the teeth. With his good axe he beats down half of them. The rest flee. But this last effort had weakened him. He took to bed again, never to rise from it. He is a rude and admirable type of the French peasant.

To the miseries of war were added the ravages of bands of brigands, the scourge of the Great Companies. " The sweet sound of the bells," writes Jean de Venette, " was no longer aroused by the praises of God but by enemy invasions. People, seek shelter! A weight of misery lay everywhere, but chiefly on the humble rural class, whose misfortunes the lords increased by extorting their goods. Their cattle was much reduced, but still they had to pay to the lord ten sous for each ox, five sous for each sheep. " In this year 1358," writes Jean de Venette, " numerous unfortified villages transformed their churches into fortresses, surrounding them with deep ditches, arming the towers with machines of war and balistas, and carrying up great stones to resist the brigands; and the precaution proved useful on more than one occasion. Children kept guard in watch-boxes at the top of the tower. If they saw the enemy coming afar off they blew horns or set the bells in motion. The country people ran to take shelter in the church. On the banks of the Loire they were seen taking refuge with their families and beasts, in the islands of the river, or in the boats moored along its course." On the other hand, the peasants tried in many places to destroy the fortresses. We have seen that, in the preceding centuries, these castles with their enclosures had served the workers of the fields as shelter and defence; but they were no longer anything to the workers but centres of offence and oppression. When they could not take it by force, the peasants joined with the inhabitants of the neighbouring town to buy the fortress from the occupants, often from the English, and afterwards destroy it from top to bottom.

The young Regent (Charles V) re-entered Paris on the 2nd August 1358. The aged Charles Toussac and Joceran de Maxon, the chief auxiliaries of Etienne Marcel, had been dragged from the Châtelet into the square, where they had been beheaded, and their bodies then thrown into the river. Executions followed one another until September. On the 12th of that month, Thomas de Ladit, a canon of Paris and Chancellor of the King of Navarre, imprisoned in the Conciergerie of the Palace, was to be transferred to the prisons of the Bishop of Paris. Two men walking one behind the other carried him on horseback on a beam supported on their shoulders. Ladit had irons on his legs. Fearing that he might be delivered from his punishment, some of the Parisian associates threw themselves upon him and, pulling him down, killed him, " and he was stripped naked and remained in this state for a long time on the ground, in the middle of a gutter of rain-water, which ran over his body, and towards vespers (3 p.m.) he was dragged to the river and thrown in " (*Grandes Chroniques*).

Whatever might be the intellectual mediocrity of John the Good, the condition of the kingdom was such that only the return of the King could provide a remedy for the ills endured by the French. Anxious to put an end to these calamities, wishful also of regaining his liberty, King John gave his consent to the Treaty of London (24th March 1359), by which he gave up to Edward III half France and accorded to him for his ransom four million golden crowns, a fabulous sum in those days. At the news of such an agreement there went up in France a cry of stupefaction. The Dauphin summoned the States, which declared such a treaty impossible to execute. The only answer was to make " good war against the English." The Dauphin prepared for it with energy. On the 13th August 1359 he concluded a treaty of friendship with Charles the Bad, who decided, for the sake of great advantages, chiefly in money, to declare himself a " good Frenchman." New forces were set going, of which the English soon felt not only the resistance but the shock. A thing which was truly admirable was that in the then state of the country the Dauphin managed to equip a fleet, and the Parisians contributed two thousand gold pennies to it on condition that some of the boats should be commanded by them and decorated with the arms of their city. Their contingents were commanded by the valiant knight Pepin des Essarts, who had seconded Jean Maillard on the night of the 13th July 1358. The fleet crossed the Straits and reached Winchelsea, where the French landed. They plundered and burned this important seaport, and returned laden with booty. This expedition produced an enormous effect. The King of England was so impressed by it that the preliminaries of a treaty of peace were signed, on the 8th May 1360, at Bretigny-les-Chartres. Edward III was confirmed in the possession of the provinces of which he was suzerain at the beginning of the war, increased by Calais, the counties of Ponthieu, Guînes, Poitou, and Saintonge, Angoumois, Limousin, Périgord, and Agenais ; but he renounced his claims to Boulogne, and also Normandy, Maine, Anjou,

THE MIDDLE AGES

Touraine, and all suzerainty over Brittany and Flanders. King John's ransom, fixed at three million golden crowns, though it was inferior to that which had been agreed upon by the Treaty of London, reached none the less a formidable figure. By the same agreement the King of France repudiated all alliance with the Scotch, as did the English King with regard to the Flemings.

This treaty, which has been considered by the most eminent modern historians as of real advantage to France, was not so regarded by contemporaries. The intelligent author of the *Chronique des quatre premiers Valois* judges it as follows:

"Too lightly was this treaty granted, to the great injury and prejudice of the French realm. For the King of England's army had nothing to eat and no provisions in the open country. For all had retreated into fortresses, castles, and good towns (fortified towns), which were not easy to conquer. Through which the said King of England and his army would have gone away and departed from the kingdom."

On the 14th June 1360, at a fine dinner given by the French King in the Tower of London to his colleague of England, the two princes swore fidelity and friendship with each other. At last, on the 28th July, after a captivity of four years, John landed at Calais. He remained there until the 24th October. Edward III had joined him there. The treaty was sworn on the Gospels by the two Kings. But these fine vows, set off by magnificent feasting, were accompanied by reservations. "The said King of England gave up the name of King of France, and called himself King of England, Lord of Ireland and Aquitaine; but he did not yet give up the said kingdom of France, nor did the King of France renounce the jurisdictions and sovereignties of the lands which he leased to the said King of England, nor to the homage for them." It was, in fact, agreed that the renunciations of these rights which were claimed and these jurisdictions should not become active until after an exchange of documents relating to them which should take place a year later at Bruges, on the 30th November 1361. The "Peace of Bretigny" was really only a truce, accompanied by the setting at liberty of King John on consideration of a ransom.

Petrarch gives a pitiful idea of the state of the kingdom in relating that, to go safely from Calais to Paris, King John

472

found himself obliged to obtain a safe conduct from the bandits commanding the Companies. " A lamentable thing," writes the poet, " and truly shameful ! The King himself, on his return from captivity, found obstacles to his re-entry into the capital. He was forced to treat with the brigands. Posterity will refuse to believe it."

Posterity has had to form the habit of believing in facts much more incredible still.

King John at length crossed the boundary of Paris on the 13th December 1360.

The years which followed the Peace of Bretigny did not, however, bring to the unhappy people the amelioration for which they had hoped. Two scourges tried them cruelly : the plague, which made a new and terrible appearance in 1362, and, more redoubtable still, brigandage. This latter calamity grew worse. Some brigands had at least found employment, or been killed, in war. But now come some years of peace. " The roads were no safer than in the days when the English infested them," says the Continuator of Nangis. These companies of brigands were, moreover, admirably organized. Under the guidance of a proved leader, each of them had at their disposal a complete service, of smiths and farriers, saddlers, tanners, butchers, valets and serving-men, women for pleasure and for good usage, dressmakers, and laundresses ; surgeons for wounds and doctors for health. Arnaud de Cervole, called the Arch-priest, is the King's lieutenant in Nivernais ; he marries the richest heiress in the land and of the highest nobility, the lady of Châteauvilain. He writes to the people of Nimes dating it " the sacred Friday after the holy mystery." He was a frightful bandit, and ended in being vulgarly assassinated by one of his men in a quarrel. These leaders of bands were often of the humblest birth. Robert Knolles had been in his youth a working weaver ; Croquart and the Petit Meschin had been serving-men.

Their luxuriousness witnessed to their character as parvenus : the new rich of the Hundred Years War. They clothed themselves in a sumptuous and showy manner, " wearing caps with ostrich feathers " ; moreover, they were careful to exclude these, by the same title as edged weapons, from the safe conducts which they granted for payment to the baggage of travellers and

THE MIDDLE AGES

merchants. The unfortunate people who cannot live within the walls of a fortified town or a castle with a keep are "tracked down like wild beasts." With what anxiety they travel in the open country. "At the least sign they run madly to hide with wife and children in the spaces of the rocks, in the depths of caves, among the reeds in the marshes or the thickets in the woods."

These bands were gathered in great numbers in the country round Lyons, which they devastated, and whence they threatened the Papacy in Avignon. An expedition was organized against them under the orders of the Count of Tancarville. The leaders of the Companies, English and French, united for plunder; John Hawkwood, Briquet, John Cresway, commanded a mass of mere adventurers of every shape and colour, but brave in battle. The French chivalry suffered another Creçy or Poitiers; in the outskirts of Brignais (Lyonnais) it was defeated, and its leaders killed or captured : the Count of Tancarville, the Count of Joigny, the Count of Sarrebrück, the Count of Furez, Jacques de Bourbon, and his son, Pierre de Bourbon (6th April 1362). For the rest, people hanged these brigands from the highest trees of the forest when they happened to be surprised in small companies.

Moreover, if we believe the Continuator of Nangis, the misery of the times did not bring the nobles to a sense of their duties: "In 1363 were seen only the crushing and oppression of the people . . . not only by the brigands but by the heavy impositions and taxes. What murders in the villages and woods! The people found no defenders. Quite the opposite, the aristocracy seemed pleased at the prevalence of these evils, to which they should have applied a remedy with diligent hands."

In Brittany the war between the two Houses, of Montfort and Blois, went on amid the general lassitude. The death of Charles of Blois, killed at the battle of Auray (1364), by removing one of the claimants, produces a feeling of relief. By the Treaty of Guérande (1365) the French King is to recognize the rights of the House of Montfort. The tenacious and heroic widow of Charles of Blois will be provided with the County of Penthièvre. On the 13th December 1366, Jean de Montfort

THE HUNDRED YEARS WAR

will do homage for the Duchy of Brittany to Charles V, now King.

We touch here on an event which did not at the moment appear of extraordinary importance, but which was to lead to the gravest consequences. In September 1363, King John gave the crown of Burgundy to his fourth son, Philip, called the Bold (*le Hardi*). Philip was twenty-two years old. John remembered the courage of the child at his side in the battle of Poitiers.

The King had inherited the Duchy of Burgundy in 1360 at the death of Philippe de Rouvres, the last prince of the first Capetian dynasty. With Philip the Bold began the second dynasty, whose deeds and history we shall see. According to the words of the Continuator of Nangis (1360) they might have been foreseen.

The English were advancing towards Burgundy after their check before Reims and Châlons. "At this news," says Jean de Venette, "the Burgundians concluded with them the following agreement. They would give the English much money, they would permit them to pass through their provinces, they would furnish them with provisions so long as they should be in France, provided that the English did not inflict any loss upon them." "This at least is what is being said in Paris at the moment I am writing these lines," says the Chronicler; "but I cannot believe it. I cannot believe that this people could have done this in favour of the country's enemies and to the prejudice of the realm. If it were so, and I do not think it is, it would be to their confusion and their eternal shame."

The facts were, unhappily, true. The treaty still exists, dated the 10th March 1360.

One can then imagine what a province would become which was animated by such a sentiment of individualism under the direction of ambitious princes.

However, the clauses of the Treaty of Bretigny were badly carried out or not carried out at all. The populations yielded to the English wished to remain French. The determined resistance of the sea captain, Ringois d'Abbeville, caused him to be shut up in Dover Castle, and as nothing—threats, promises, nor injuries—could induce him to acknowledge himself as an

THE MIDDLE AGES

Englishman, he was "thrown from the cliffs of the Castle of Dover into the sea."

The money for the enormous ransom of King John was only raised with great difficulty. Money became so scarce that pieces of leather, "with a little silver nail," were put into circulation. Comines speaks of them in his memoirs. He saw in his time some of these leather tokens.

In our own days, by means of paper and aluminium and our yellow-boys (*jaunets*) we have recourse to similar means of exchange.

John had left as a hostage in England, his son, the Duke of Anjou, who was to live there until all the clauses of the Treaty of Peace were executed. But the young prince grew weary and ran away. He rigged up a ship and returned to France. "And so that it could not be said that the agreement was broken by him, King John of France crossed the sea to England and went in person to put himself in prison again for his son."

The departure took place on the 6th January 1364. John died in London in the following April.

The poet Cuvelier consecrated to him this funeral oration :

> He crossed straight to London, the good King of France,
> John, the son of Philip of Valois ;
> To England he went back this time
> To keep faith ; for in him was honour,
> Charity and courage, strength, power, and justice ;
> An honourable man he was and loyal, courteous to all.
> The English were very angry at his death.

The poet well defines the qualities of King John. He had the virtues of chivalry. And it was with reason that "the English were very angry at his death." John the Good had none of the qualities necessary to a French King in the circumstances in which he was placed ; his son Charles V will direct public affairs in quite another manner.

Born in the Castle of Vincennes on the 21st January 1337, Charles V ascended the throne at the age of twenty-seven years. He was a young man, gentle and serious, simple and neat in dress, thoughtful and not robust. He was of medium height. He had slender limbs, but broad, straight shoulders. He suffered

Charles the Wise.

from intermittent fevers, headaches, and digestive disturbances. His right hand, slow in movement, could not support a heavy weight. He passed his life between apothecaries and doctors. We are far indeed from those brilliant knights, Philip of Valois and John the Good. Charles loved good books, reflection, study. He sought the company of those who "spoke fine Latin and were argumentative." He himself spoke with a resonant voice, easily and precisely. His eloquence was very simple but charming, and was displayed in the purest style. He meditated at length seated in his "desk" or in his walks in the shades of Vincennes. He would not allow " a man of his Court, however noble and powerful, to wear too short clothes, or shoes with too outrageous a turn upwards, nor women to be sewn up too tightly in their clothes, or to wear too large collars " (Christine de Pisan).

It is said that his grandfather at Creçy, seeing the English afar off, felt his blood boil. From the windows of his Castle of Vincennes, Charles saw rising on the horizon the smoke of the villages to which the English were setting fire.

" It is not with this smoke that they will drive me from the kingdom."

Du Guesclin offered to the young King as a gift for a happy accession the victory of Cocherel (13th May 1364). Neither of the two parties, French or English, desiring that the Treaty of Bretigny should be put into force, war was resumed. Du Guesclin triumphed over the best English leader, the famous Captal de Buch. The consequences were felt immediately: Charles the Bad, whose fidelity remained in the balance, exchanged his Norman domains, which were too near the English, for the distant lordship of Montpelier.

The struggle between Pedro the Cruel and his natural brother, Henry of Trastamara, for the possession of the crown of Castile furnishes a propitious occasion for getting rid, at least in part, of the Great Companies. The Spaniards reproached Pedro the Cruel for his alliance with the Saracen princes and for having married a Jewess. As he was supported by the English, the French pronounced in favour of his rival. Du Guesclin led the undisciplined bands across the Pyrenees. The fortune of war there was varied. As in the French wars,

Du Guesclin distinguished himself in the taking of fortresses. He led his men to the assault of steep walls:

> They have won our walls, so firm;
> Like monkey or cat hideously creeping,
> They have crept upwards. . . .

But at the battle of Navarette (3rd April 1367) the French men-at-arms succumbed once again before the English archers. Du Guesclin was made prisoner. His proud answer to the Prince of Wales, who was surprised at the large sum at which Du Guesclin himself fixed his ransom, has remained famous:

> There is not a woman in France who can spin a thread,
> Who would not rather win my ransom by spinning
> Than not free me from your bonds. . . .

This is all very well; but it is chiefly to the honour of the women of France, and the valiant knight, since it fell to him to fix his own ransom, might have spared them an effort which could only satisfy his own vanity. After this, fortune returned to the French candidate. At the battle of Montiel (14th March 1369) the troops of Pedro the Cruel were crushed by Du Guesclin. The tactics, already quite modern, of the Breton leader, were there shown. Instead of first throwing his army on the enemy, after the traditional manner of chivalry, he takes the precaution of giving advantage to the attack by what our strategists now call "a preparation of artillery."

> At the first meeting, there was discharge of arrows and missiles,
> After this the battle began,
> And they fought hand to hand during its course.

Pedro the Cruel was taken prisoner. A quarrel having broken out between him and his brother Henry, the latter killed him with a blow of a dagger. Henry, King of Castile, gave to Du Guesclin his country of Trastamara raised to a Duchy. Du Guesclin returned to Paris, where he met with a triumphal reception (1370). His biographer shows him entering the capital, with a modest equipage, "in a grey coat and very simply dressed." The Archpriest had been commissioned, for his part, to lead other "companies" across Germany and Hungary, up to the confines of the Greek Empire, to attack the Turks there. For a time, at least, the scourge of brigandage by "companies" seems to have been appeased in France. Jean de Venette describes the happy decay of the brigand hordes :

"Bandits and robbers lost their audacity. Even those who occupied fortified places, abandoned them, either from fear, or after having sold them to the neighbouring towns or to their lawful owners. Along the route of their retreat, it is true, they still robbed; but the product of their thefts melted in their hands like snow in the sun. They sold their horses in the towns. They were seen in a wretched condition, justifying the proverb: Goods evilly come by bring no profit (*bien mal acquis n'est pas profit*). And they died in 'misery.' Glory to God. Amen."

The hostility between the two classes—between those whom contemporaries call the "great" (*gros*) and those whom they call the "small" (*menus*)—remained. It broke out on the least occasion. At Tournai the people were unwilling to pay the salt tax (*gabelle*) or any of the new impositions. If the Patricians had consented to these it was because they made a profit in the collection of the taxes. The "commonalty" had recourse to arms, sounding the alarm-bell in the watch-tower, calling the agricultural workers to the rescue. The Patricians, terror-stricken, fled from the town. The two parties moreover, both implored the intervention of the King of France. Charles V sent as a delegate Edouard de Renty, a Picard knight renowned for his wisdom, who succeeded in putting an end to the quarrel.

We have seen that, in spite of the Treaty of Bretigny, war was not over between the French and the English. It was to be resumed officially in 1369 à propos of the appeals of Aquitaine. A tax of five sous per hearth for five years to the Prince of Wales had been agreed to by the States of Guienne, assembled at Angoulême, on the 18th January 1368. Count Jean d'Armagnac, who had been put, as we have seen, at the head of the nobility of Aquitaine, refused to allow it to be collected on his lands, declaring that he had "a daughter to marry," and as they were trying to force him to pay, he appealed to the Court of France (2nd March 1368). The Sire d'Albret joined him in his appeal on the 8th September 1368, and the brother

THE MIDDLE AGES

of the Count of Périgord on the 13th April 1369. And this appeal resounded not only in the French Court but throughout Aquitaine. Towns and castles emulated one another in uniting their cause with that of Jean d'Armagnac; they opened their gates eagerly to the representatives of Charles V. Towards the middle of 1369 there were in Aquitaine nearly a thousand appellants.

Najac, in Rouergue, had broken with the government of the Black Prince on the 5th January (1369); on the 17th January Jean d'Armagnac defeated a party of English at Puylagarde, in Quercy. Charles V formally declared war against England in April. He added, in the following month : " *Item*, that the said prince put in prison M. Bernard Polot and Monseigneur Jehan de Chaponval, deputed by the King of France to present to the said Prince the letters of the King of France, by which the said prince was appointed a day in a case of appeal before the King or his Court of Parlement in Paris, at the instance of the said Count of Armagnac, and kept them prisoners a very long time and caused them to die, in great contempt of the King and of his Sovereignty."

The movement which had taken form in the South, had its echo in those of the Northern provinces which had passed under the rule of the English ; Abbeville in Ponthieu, Rue in the Somme, and a number of fortresses and districts called themselves the men of the French King. The English said of them, not without spite :

> Truly these villeins have become French again :
> If you had cut them open like a larded pig
> You would have found in their hearts the fleur-de-lis.

" I will go at his summons," the Black Prince had said, in speaking of the citation to the Parlement of Charles V., "but helmet on head and followed by 60,000 men."

Charles V had made his preparations to receive him. He had put good supplies into the fortresses of the kingdom, and had those destroyed which he did not think he could defend victoriously ; finally, he possessed in Bertrand du Guesclin the greatest leader of his day.

Du Guesclin inaugurated a new method of warfare, with surprises and ambushes. The country is left empty before the invader; the people withdraw into the fortresses. The English in the midst of campaign had no means of replenishing their food supplies. The English army will be seen, without fighting, dwindling in a few months to half its numbers. Charles V even prepares to lead a new expedition into England. He goes as far as Honfleur to see the departure of the fleet which he had rapidly equipped. It was put under the command of Philip the Bold. The French fleet reached the English coast, where it burned Portsmouth. But the expedition was not supported by the vessels of the King of Castile, on which they had counted and which could not be got ready in time.

After the Winchelsea expedition and the Portsmouth cruise, an attack of Charles V's fleet on the English port of Rye will bring honour to the French marine. The author of the *Debate of the Heralds-at-Arms* says that King Edward was so upset by it that he fixed his residence at Northampton " because they say it is the town which is at the centre of England."

The English had not at that time the command of the sea so completely as one tends to think. The herald-at-arms of France says to him of England : " The said movement (of the French marine) was partly the cause of your losing Normandy, for your King Edward could not find men to cross the sea, and all were very busy."

The herald-at-arms points out that, in the course of this agelong struggle, the French vessels constantly had the advantage in single combats : " A French vessel on the sea on an equal footing always defeats an English ship." The author attributes this to the advantage on the sea of the crossbow in which the French excelled, over the long bow of which the English were masters. The swaying of the ship is fatal to the archer and prevents his taking aim, while the crossbowman, whatever the movement of the ship, carries the force of his arrow.

It was in the larger conflicts, of fleet against fleet, that the English, by their skill in manœuvre, resumed the advantage.

The strength of Du Guesclin was further increased by his patriotic reconciliation with Olivier de Clisson, who will succeed him as Constable. Brought up in the English methods of warfare, Clisson knew its tricks and windings, and was to have them used against them. Moreover, French artillery was making sensible progress. From the beginning of the reign of Charles V, Girard de Figeac and Bernard de Montfaucon, master armourers, were manufacturing cannons, throwing bullets of stone weighing a hundred pounds. The years 1371–72 were marked by some notable feats of arms, mingled with the efforts of the Pope to re-establish peace. The Sovereign Pontiff was ever thinking of the Holy Land of Jerusalem. His legates intervened, and Charles V consented to " submit himself in all things to the ordinance of the Holy Father "; but the King of England was " wholly recalcitrant." Charles V then said that he would submit to the judgment of the Emperor. To this King Edward was still unwilling to agree. Then the King of France said that " he would put it to the ordinance of four Christian kings." There was a third refusal on the part of the English King. "*Item*, the said legates said to the King of England that he would submit to the judgment of forty persons, knights, and burgesses taken from the realm of England, and as many similarly taken from the kingdom of France, whatever these eighty might say. The King of England refused all this. And so the said legates took their departure."

The Captal de Buch, lieutenant of the English King in Poitou and Saintonge, was defeated and taken prisoner before Soubise (Charente-Inférieure) on the 23rd August 1372 : " And so the English remain very weak in the country." La Rochelle, Angoulême, Saintes, St. Jean d'Angély, open their gates to the French. Poitiers had capitulated on the 3rd August 1372. Du Guesclin had presented himself at the foot of the walls, holding in his hand a branch of flowers :

> A branch in his hand of flowers quite full,
> Before the gate came Bertrand the Knight,
> A branch in his hand with the leaves upon it.
> His page with him but few people.
> He gave his page his helmet to hold.
> " Lords," said Bertrand, " whom here I see,
> May it please you to hear my words,
> Without shooting or aiming or hurling stones.
> I come for the King who has France in his keeping,
> As his Constable. . . ."

THE HUNDRED YEARS WAR

The poet puts some magnificent words into the mouth of the Constable:

> "Hear," says Bertrand, "you cannot hold out;
> For just as one sees the sun shining bright
> Passing through glass all bright and sparkling,
> So shall you see the French pass through your walls."

The Poitevins were no doubt convinced, and lowered their drawbridges. At the taking of St. Sever, Du Guesclin held the garrison to ransom, but had those Frenchmen who had assisted the enemies of the kingdom hanged by their valets and serving-men. At the end of March 1373, Poitou was entirely reconquered. In 1374 there remained to the English in France only a few ports: Calais, Cherbourg, Brest, Bordeaux, and Bayonne. "And so the King of France had such power that his enemies were everywhere most feeble. And in truth not within the memory of man had a King been seen who had accomplished so much."

In 1375 a truce was concluded on the intervention of Gregory XI. The celebrated Black Prince, the Prince of Wales, died on the 8th June 1376. A Frenchman, the Chronicler of the first four Valois, renders him this homage: "This prince was one of the best knights in the world. In his time he was renowned above all." Although he was his enemy, Charles V had his memory celebrated in a solemn service. In September the cunning Gascon leader, the Captal de Buch, who had served the cause of the English with so much skill and valour, died in prison at the Louvre, where he had been maintained in princely captivity. Finally, in 1377 the great English monarch, Edward III, whose strong and active will had supported the war from its beginnings, died in his turn. A child of ten succeeded him with the name of Richard II. Public affairs, already so intricate, were to be further complicated by the Great Schism. Gregory XI, the seventh Avignon Pope, died in 1377. At Rome, a conclave, reduced to sixteen cardinals, elected an Italian, who assumed the tiara under the name of Urban VI; but the next year, on the 2nd August 1378, the majority of the cardinals who had taken part in this election declared that it had been made under the violent compulsion of the people of Rome. A new conclave met at Fondi, in the

THE MIDDLE AGES

kingdom of Naples, and proclaimed Robert of Geneva Pope. He took the name of Clement VII. Christendom was divided between the two Popes. By letters written on the 16th November 1378, Charles V is to notify the cardinals who had remained at Avignon that France recognized as valid only the election of Clement VII. This last, truth to tell, was of his lineage. Even in France there was not a unanimous agreement, as the University of Paris pronounced in favour of Urban VI. The Great Schism is to last until 1415.

There was peace more or less complete on land. It was more difficult to make it respected at sea, where the vessels of the two nations continued to run foul of one another in bloody conflicts. A fairly important naval battle was fought in 1379. The French won and captured a part of the English marine. The policy of Charles V in Brittany, which already tended towards the union of the province with the Crown, joined in a common resistance the partisans of the two rival houses. In March to April 1379 there was formed a league against the King of France, to which rallied Jean de Penthièvre. Du Guesclin himself was on the point of breaking his Constable's sword.

In the towns the struggle over the collection of the taxes still went on between the "Commonalty," the popular party, and the Patricians. Troubles broke out in Puy, Alais, and Clermont-L'Herault; at Montpelier they assumed a sufficiently serious character.

In Flanders the towns went on with their armed struggles against one another. Bruges bore with impatience the domination of Ghent. After some successes the people of Bruges were conquered. The men of Ghent sacked Bruges and extended their authority over the greater part of Flanders.

The year 1380 sees the end of the reign of Charles the Wise. The brigands and highwaymen had found refuge in the mountains of Auvergne. They were masters of Carlat, and threatened Aurillac and St. Flour. Du Guesclin, who marched against them, had stopped before Châteauneuf-Randon (senechausée of Beaucaire), occupied by the King's enemies. He arranged the siege, and the place was at the point of surrender when the great soldier died (14th July 1380). History

THE HUNDRED YEARS WAR

relates that the besieged came to lay the keys of the fortress on his coffin. Shortly afterwards, on the 16th September of the same year, Charles V died at his residence, Beauté-sur-Marne, " at the end of the Wood of Vincennes."

"He was very wise and very moral, and a good judge of honour and estate; and by his great good sense attracted and overcame many of his enemies. He gathered together great treasure. He took pleasure in raising noble buildings."

These lines were written by the Chronicler of the first four Valois. One finds in them nothing to discount and little to add.

Charles V's financial administration is worthy of admiration. We have seen in what condition State affairs were transmitted to him. What efforts he had had to make to re-establish them! He encouraged literature and art and formed a library at the Louvre. He built some magnificent monuments. The "Louvre of Charles V" is known to us, thanks to the marvellous painting of the brothers Malewel. And he left at his death a reserve of seventeen millions.

On his death-bed, however, the excellent Prince regretted having established permanent taxes, thus entering on the road of modern finance and breaking with feudal custom. "Concerning these aids of the kingdom of France," he said to his son in his last moments, "by which the poor people are so heavily burdened, consult your conscience and remove as many as you can; they are things which I have supported, but which grieve me much and are heavy upon me. . . ." He also advised his son to marry a German princess, in order to find in those parts alliance against the English. It must be said that in those days there still reigned in Germany Charles IV of the House of Luxemburg, favourable to the French dynasty, and who had paid a friendly visit to Charles V at the Louvre in 1378.

Charles the Well-Beloved. The revolutionary disturbances, which had begun in the last years of the reign of Charles V, grew worse in the first years of the reign of Charles VI. They also broke out in England as well as in France. There was the insurrection of the *Maillets* (Hammers) in Paris and of the *Harelle* at Rouen. Serious risings accompanied by pillage and bloodshed broke out at Sens, St. Quentin, and Compiègne; but while, in the towns of the North, under the suzerainty of the King of France, the seditious movements against the taxes are the work of the popular party; in Aquitaine, on the contrary, and adjacent provinces, under the English suzerainty, they have for instigators members of the great Nobility and their adherents.

During the minority of Charles VI, the kingdom is governed by his uncles, Louis, Duke of Anjou, and Philip the Bold, Duke of Burgundy, both men of great worth. Louis of Anjou, a skilful diplomat, an elegant speaker, and a splendid nobleman, had won some fine successes in war. He had driven the English from the southern provinces. Philip the Bold is shown to us by Christine de Pisan as "a prince of great knowledge, industry, and will." During the reign of his brother, Charles V, Philip the Bold had inspired his foreign policy. He had inclined him to German alliances in opposition to the English. Under his influence, and, moreover, in conformity with the last wishes of Charles V, the betrothal was concluded of Charles VI with the too famous Isabel of Bavaria, daughter of Duke Stephen of Agrapha, and granddaughter of Bernabo Visconti. In July 1385 the two young fiancés met at Amiens. They were charmed with each other from the first. Charles VI fell violently in love with his wife. On the other hand, Louis of Orleans, the brother of Charles VI, was to marry Valentina Visconti, the daughter of Gian Galeazzo, Duke of Milan. It was stipulated that the rights of Gian Galeazzo over the Duchy of Milan should pass to his daughter. Louis XII, the King of France, the son of Charles of Orleans, and grandson of Louis of Orleans, will one day claim these rights which will prolong the Italian wars with their infinite consequences.

The war with England was resumed in August 1388. A new expedition across the Channel was planned. Charles VI left Paris animated with immense ardour. He said again and again "that he would not return before he had been in England." In November 1388 the young King was declared of age. He was, in fact, twenty years old. Charles VI informed his uncles that he would henceforth rule alone. He wisely again put the administration into the hands of those who had been the good councillors of his father : Bureau de la Rivière, Jean le Mercier, the Constable of Clisson, Le Besgue de Villaine, Jean de Montaigu, men of the burgess class or of the lesser Nobility, whom the great lords, the princes of the blood royal whom they had ousted, called contemptuously the *Marmousets*, from the name of the little stone figures, thick-set and grotesque, sculptured on the walls of buildings.

At twenty, Charles VI was not the Prince worn out by illness and whom we picture, mad and weary, in the arms of the amiable little Odette de Champdivers. He was tall and strong, a fine man, with his fair hair falling in thick curls on his shoulders, and a beard beginning to grow. He loved physical exercises and excelled in them, showed himself of a warlike, bustling, and enterprising temperament; generous to excess, gallant, a patron of the arts: in short, a perfect Valois.

Under the wise administration of the *Marmousets*, the kingdom regained a measure of prosperity. At the entry of Queen Isabel into Paris, on the 22nd April 1389, there was seen a striking display of luxury not only on the part of the lords of the Court, but also among the burgesses : " The houses decorated with cloths of high lustre, silken materials, and precious stuffs ; women and young girls adorned with rich necklaces and long robes embroidered in purple and gold " (Monk of St. Denis).

One must point out this surprising contrast in the Hundred Years War : in the midst of profound wretchedness, of paralysed trade, the devastation of the countryside, of plundering and burning, we suddenly see sumptuous feasts marked by Pantagruelian orgies in which the whole population takes part : dreams of the thousand and one nights. Perhaps the explanation is to be found in the exaggerations of the chroniclers when they are describing both the days of feast and jollity and the scenes of desolation and misery.

A crusade against the Barbary pirates, in 1390, has not been sufficiently noticed. We know that at this time a number of French knights had gone to Hungary to fight the Turks ; here are more of them on the coasts of Africa, where they sail in the company of Genoese and English. Under the command of Louis de Bourbon, the expedition lands in Africa, gains a

THE MIDDLE AGES

brilliant victory over the pirates, forces them to set free their Christian captives, and lays siege to Tunis. A dispute which supervened, not between the French and English, but between the French and the Genoese, prevented the achievement of the results expected.

On the 14th June 1392, there reached the Hôtel St. Paul, where the Royal Court was staying, an astounding piece of news. The Constable of France, Olivier de Clisson, had just been assassinated by Pierre de Craon. The murderer found refuge with the Duke of Brittany. Charles VI put himself at the head of an expedition to avenge his Constable, when, in the plain of Le Mans, on the skirts of the forest, he was seized with an attack of violent madness (5th August 1392).

The Chronicler of the first four Valois has described this famous scene: " When the King of France . . . was about to enter the forest of Le Mans, on the fifth day of August, there came before him a figure with distorted countenance, saying :

" ' King, if you enter the forest to go to Le Mans there will be a misadventure ! '

" Then came a madman with distorted face who seized the King's bridle and said to him :

" ' If you go on you are a dead man ! '

" The King wanted to free himself from the madman, and came to his page to get his sword. And the page was afraid and ran away, and the King after him. And he took the sword and went mad with anger and vexation, having been made desperate, or poisoned, or bewitched, or possessed. For when he had got the sword he ran upon those around him and killed many of them. And no one ever knew what became of the aforesaid messenger or the madman. And the King was only secured with great difficulty; for no one dared to approach him, but he was at length taken by a knight from Caux."

We have spoken of the delicate health of Charles V, the father of Charles VI, and the mental condition of his mother, Jeanne de Bourbon, must be remembered. For a time she lost all sense and memory; and then returned to sanity : a cure which contemporaries attributed to pilgrimages. There lies the origin of Charles VI's madness. It did not affect him

THE HUNDRED YEARS WAR

continuously. His brain sometimes recovered for a time, more or less protracted; then came relapses which, each time, threw him into a more serious condition.

No greater misfortune could have fallen upon France. We have seen that the conditions of the period made the government of the King necessary. There is no use in expatiating on this with vain lamentations. One might regret also that men have not eyes at the back of the head, which would be very convenient, as they could then see behind as well as in front. Let us accept France as she has formed herself through the centuries. Through the fall of the royal authority the country in a fatal manner falls back into anarchy. We have seen the terrible effects of the captivity of King John. The madness of Charles VI is to be for the country another kind of royal captivity and still worse in its effects. Power passes into the hands of the King's uncles, above all, to Philip the Bold, to the exclusion of the younger brother of the King, Louis of Orleans.

This Louis of Orleans is perhaps the most attractive figure of the period. Young, handsome, elegant, he wore with ease the maddest costumes.

He had, through the cares of Charles the Wise, profited by the most splendid education, to which literature and the fine arts had added the brilliance of their fine flowers. He had married Valentina Visconti, the daughter of Galeazzo I, Duke of Milan; but he was no model husband:

"Yes, I have loved," he said, "and I have been loved. Love has done it." Love had a broad back!

He was bold, enterprising, shining in jousts and tournaments; but under this frivolous exterior he hid a wary political sense. Like his father and his uncle, Jean de Berry, he was a great builder. He had the Château of Pierrefonds built and the famous castle of Coucy enlarged.

His domains were very extensive: the Duchy of Orleans, Périgord, the counties of Valois, Beaumont, Dreux, Blois, Dunois, Soissons, Angoulême, and Porcien; the lordship of Coucy, the province of Asti in Italy. But these wealthy and important territories had not the cohesion of those which guaranteed the power of his two uncles, the Dukes of Burgundy and

THE MIDDLE AGES

Berry. Louis, Duke of Anjou, had died on the 20th September 1384. Louis of Orleans endeavoured to unite his lands in one block. He acquired the County of Vertus and the Duchy of Luxemburg. In this way he tended to form between the Marne and the Meuse an important State which would definitely have separated into two slices, at a distance from each other, the possessions of the Grand Duke of the West, as the Duke of Burgundy was called, Artois and Flanders to the North-West, and the Duchy of Burgundy to the South-East, which Philip the Bold, and still more after him his son John the Fearless, will have an ardent ambition to unite. From this comes a first cause of conflict, to which will be added a rivalry for power: the source of the violent hatred which arose between Louis of Orleans and John the Fearless.

Let us read carefully the lines devoted by Christine de Pisan to Louis of Orleans:

"This prince loves gentlemen and men of honour who, from valour, travel and try to increase the honour and the name of France in many lands, helps them with his possessions, honours and supports them. He is to-day the resort and refuge of the chivalry of France, of which he holds a noble and very fine court with gentlemen young, handsome, comely, and well apparelled, all ready to do good deeds: they come to him from all parts by reason of his splendid youth and from hope of his benefits, and he receives them amiably."

To re-establish peace between France and England, Philip of Burgundy succeeded in concluding at Calais, on the 4th November 1396, the marriage of Isabel, the daughter of Charles VI, with Richard II, the English King. The young wife was seven years old. The truce established between the two crowns, which should have ended on the 29th September 1398, had been prolonged on the 9th March 1396 for twenty-eight years. It seemed to be the dawn of a definite peace. France might then have hoped for some years of beneficent and curative repose, when two terrible crimes—one in England, the other in France —came to plunge our unhappy country once more into a period of disturbance, of civil and foreign wars more frightful still than that from which it had emerged.

In 1399 Richard II, King of England, and son-in-law of

THE HUNDRED YEARS WAR

Charles VI, was overthrown by Henry of Lancaster and, in March 1400, was assassinated in the prison in which he had been interned. The Duke of Lancaster ascended the throne of England as Henry IV. The hostility against France, or more accurately the lure of the beautiful towns and countryside of France as plunder for the English soldiery, had been one of the causes of the movement set going against Richard II. Louis of Orleans sent a personal defiance to the new King of England, who had put to death his niece's husband. The war was about to be rekindled.

On the other hand, in Paris, Queen Isabel, who exercised the regency during the mental alienation of her husband, saw the town, and before long the country, divided into two hostile camps. At the Hôtel d'Artois was the Duke of Burgundy with his two sons Jean and Antoine. The Burgundian princes grouped round them many men-at-arms, a great number of them foreigners—Flemings, Brabançons, German cavalrymen. And Christine de Pisan has shown us the Duke of Orleans on his side collecting round him a numerous knighthood. Louis of Orleans held his Court in his house near the gate of St. Antoine. Two enemy camps disputed the government of the kingdom, ready to come to blows; but let us not be deceived: under cover of the Houses of Orleans and Burgundy, it will be the old struggle between the aristocratic and the democratic elements, between the "great" and the "small," which will be pursued. The high aristocracy and the Patricians will support those of Orleans, who are to become the Armagnacs; the popular elements will be Burgundians. And as the English, by the very fact of the war and the cruelties it entailed, will become daily more figured as foreigners and enemies from outside, the Dukes of Burgundy will seem very suitable to give a French physiognomy to those who would have disliked to make common cause with the English.

On the 1st July 1402, Charles VI confirmed to his wife Isabel the authority which he had previously delegated to her, his "absence" making it impossible for him to govern the kingdom. On the 22nd February 1403 was born the young prince who was one day to be Charles VII, and who in memory of his elder brother, the Dauphin, who had died in his ninth year,

THE MIDDLE AGES

was also named Charles. He was the Queen's eleventh child. The father was quite mad.

On the 27th April of the following year Philip the Bold, Duke of Burgundy, died. His son, John the Fearless, was thirty-three years old. He had won this fine name at the battle of Nicopolis against the Turks on the 25th September 1396. "This John," writes Olivier de la Marche, "was very courageous and high spirited, and was a man subtle, doubting, and suspicious, and trusted no one. For this reason he always wore armour under his robe and had his sword girt and made himself redoubted and feared above all others." He was little, with a big head and frog's eyes. He stammered in his speech, was ambitious and greedy, but had a familiar and popular manner. People were surprised, and then flattered, to find a great prince such a good fellow; and this created for him faithful servants.

Queen Isabel of Bavaria, very sensitive to gracefulness and masculine beauty, found him hideous, awkward, silent, and stupid; she could not bear him. She had, on the other hand, the liveliest sympathy for the charming and sprightly Duke of Orleans, her brother-in-law. If we may believe the Monk of St. Denis, Isabel and Louis were seldom away from each other.

"They put all their vanity in wealth, all their pleasure in bodily delight. . . . They so far forgot the rights and duties of royalty that they had become an object of scandal for France and a tale among foreign nations." Charles VI was abandoned by his wife and brother to his lamentable disorder. Pale, dirty, and ragged, he wandered about with vacant eyes, covered with pimples, with his hair, beard, and nails longer than those of a hermit in a forest. A gracious child with a charming laugh and a charming name, Odette de Champdivers, conceived a tender pitifulness towards her King. She took him, washed and cleaned him, cut his nails, cared for him like a sister of charity, but with very tender feelings. She took him on her knees and rocked him, singing to him, like a little child. She was in love with him: an exquisite and poignant idyll.

The hostility between the Houses of Orleans and Burgundy grew more marked. The character of John the Fearless, such as we have seen it, did not make for peace. "The bolts and keys of the gates of Paris were changed, we read in the precious

THE HUNDRED YEARS WAR

Journal of a Burgess of Paris (*Journal d'un bourgeois de Paris*), and my lord of Berry and my lord of Bourbon were made captains of the town of Paris, and there came so great a multitude of men-at-arms to Paris that in the villages around there seemed to be no people left; at the same time the men of the aforesaid Duke of Burgundy took nothing without paying, and gave an account each evening to their hosts, and paid there and then."

On the 23rd November 1407, the Duke of Orleans had gone to the Hôtel Barbette, in Marais, to see Queen Isabel, who was recovering from childbirth. At eight o'clock in the evening he was called. Louis of Orleans set out, followed by six or eight companions, when he was attacked in the rue Vieille-du-Temple by a band of assassins, under the command of a certain Raoul d'Anquetonville, and left dead on the spot.

The cause of the victim was taken up by one of the greatest lords of the Duchy of Aquitaine, Bernard d'Armagnac. His daughter married Charles, the son of Louis of Orleans. His father, Jean d'Armagnac, had had a preponderating rôle in the struggles against the Black Prince in Guienne.

From the reign of Philip the Fair, about the end of the thirteenth century, the Armagnac family appeared in the South at the head of a sort of confederation in which was grouped the Nobility hostile to England. Through the valour of Jean d'Armagnac and of his son Bernard this noble Southern family is to find itself put naturally at the head of the elements favourable to the fleur-de-lis. The Armagnacs will take for their rallying sign the white cross or scarf; the Burgundians will take, in opposition, the red cross of the English, but will make a St. Andrew's Cross of it.

After the assassination of Louis of Orleans, John the Fearless reigned as master in Paris. Popular resentment was bridled. The Armagnacs were set upon "like dogs," says the Bourgeois de Paris. Individual vengeance had a fine field of action. "And whoever was killed henceforward, people said, 'He is an Armagnac!'"

Round the young Charles of Orleans, now the son-in-law of Bernard VII of Armagnac, the great Nobility was grouped: the Dukes of Bourbon and Brittany, the Counts of Clermont and Alençon, the great families of the South, the de l'Isles and the d'Albrets. However, demagogism broke out in Paris. The powerful corporation of the butchers, with their acolytes, the tanners, tripe-dealers, and curriers headed the movement of which the hangman Capeluche and the flayer Simon Caboche, with arms red with blood, were the rude leaders. Caboche gave his name to the Cabochian insurrection.

After scenes of slaughter and pillage, they began to think about reform. The University of Paris, animated by a democratic spirit, lent its light to the movement. From this moment is seen pushing himself to the front, ambitious, active, rough, and devoid of scruple, the cleric who is to become so sadly famous, Pierre Cauchon. In the higher class of burgesses, some minds, moulded on the model of Etienne Marcel, did not fail to make their influence felt. In such circumstances, and favoured by the meeting of the States-General opened on the 30th January 1413, the famous *Ordonnance Cabochienne* was drawn up.

It had been prepared silently, laboriously, by men of study and reflection, among whom were distinguished the Bishop of Tournai and the Abbot of Moutier-St.-Jean, the lord of Offémont, and the *vidame* of Amiens, the King's almoner Jean Courtecuisse, Pierre Cauchon, and Jean de l'Olive, *échevin* of Paris. The butchers and their assistants, the flayers, demanded that it should be published and put into action, following a particularly violent day (24th May 1413), as though to cover with a cloak of wisdom their red saturnalia. The *Ordonnance Cabochienne* was published on the 26th to 27th May 1413. The complaints formulated by the delegates of the various provinces to the States-General in the session of the preceding 3rd February, constituted a preface for it.

The *Ordonnance Cabochienne*, thus named from the circumstances in which it had its origin, although the Cabochiens had taken no part in its compilation—they would not have been able to do it—is a regulation of administration rather than a code of reforms in law and custom. There were measures against dishonest ministers of finance, and in favour of a more rapid process of justice; efforts to produce a less arbitrary central administration, and one which would be simpler and cheaper: the whole was well conceived. It is a pity that these aspirations towards reform should have foundered in the reaction against the Cabochian demagogism which was about to supervene. On the 4th August 1413 the Cabochiens were defeated in Paris itself; those most compromised fled. On the 1st September, Charles of Orleans made a triumphal entry into the great city. The Provost of the Merchants, the *échevins*, the burgesses of Paris in thousands, had donned violet capes in stuff of two shades, bearing a great white cross, with the device embroidered in silver thread: "The right road" (*Le droit chemin*). "And then they began to govern," writes the "Bourgeois de Paris," who belongs to the Burgundian party. "They put in such a state those who had been concerned with the government of the King and the good town of Paris, that some fled to Flanders, others into the Empire or across the sea, no matter where, and they thought themselves lucky when they could escape as vagrants or pages or vendors of harness or in any other way; and none was so bold as to speak against them (the Armagnacs)." In a judicial meeting of the Parlement (*lit de justice*) on the 5th September 1413, the *Ordonnance Cabochienne* will be quashed and nullified, to the great regret of the better minds of whom the Monk of St. Denis forms the sad echo.

On the 14th July 1412, at Bourges, the Duke of Burgundy had been induced to conclude a peace with the confederate princes of the Orleans party. The Peace of Bourges was confirmed at Auxerre on the 22nd August; but the divisions went too deep and were not limited to the heads of the parties. In the very heart of the nation the hostility between the two factions remained active. The hour had not yet sounded when such agreements could be rendered efficacious. We shall see the Duke of Burgundy acting as sovereign over the whole kingdom in the face of the sovereign and his representatives: giving to the French orders which will be carried out, commanding in a number of towns and fortresses. Many Frenchmen hesitated between the parties. We have seen that the Duke of Orleans and his adherents entering Paris in triumph had caused to be embroidered in silver thread on their capes and coats: "The right road." But many Frenchmen questioned whether the right road was indeed in their footsteps. "Fortune worked at random," writes the Bourgeois de Paris, "and there was neither noble nor any other who knew what was best."

The King of England, Henry IV, died on the 20th March 1413. For several years his serious ill-health had prevented his actively directing his government and the French War. The attack will find again its sting under his son Henry V, a young prince of twenty-seven, sharp and harsh, hard and intelligent, with an austere energy, a valour founded in devotion and an ambition devoid of scruples. He dreamed of renewing the exploits of Edward III, whose vast designs he resumed. He had practised war from his earliest youth. He was handsome and very brave, Comines will say, and "had wise and valiant men and very great leaders, such as the Earl of Salisbury (Thomas Montagu) and Talbot."

On the 13th August 1415, Henry V landed on the outskirts of Harfleur. His fleet spread over France 2500 knights, 7000 archers, 120 underminers, and 75 gunners. As a climax of misfortune the German Emperor abandoned the cause of Charles VI, gave to Henry V the title of "King of France," and promised him assistance in the recovery of "his" kingdom. We can understand the ease with which a small number of English are about to conquer extensive territories and establish their domination on solid foundations in considering the division of the kingdom between the two parties, the Armagnacs or partisans of the Court, and the Burgundians, the partisans of John the Fearless. Each side has its banner, its war cry, and its soldiery. To take, as example, the *bailliages* of Rouen, Gisors, and Caux, we see that the orders of the French Court were followed at Neufchâtel-en-Bray, Pont-de-l'Arche, Louviers, Mortemer, Beaussault, Arques, Charlemesnil, Longueville, Fontaines-le-Bourg, Cailly, Bellencombre, Lindebeuf, Préaux, Château-Gaillard, Goulet-les-Vernon, Douville, and Logempré in the valley of the Andelle; while there were ranged under the banners of the opposite party Rouen, Mantes, Vernon, Dieppe, Caudebec, Montivilliers, Fécamp, Bacqueville, Graville, Rouvray, Valmont, and Houdetot. In these last localities the King of England was to find support. These divisions were repeated in the various provinces, and so profoundly

THE HUNDRED YEARS WAR

that sometimes, in the same family, one saw some members wearing the white cross of the French side and the others the red St. Andrew's cross of the "Burgundians."

However, the Armagnacs, under the orders of a great lord of the South, the Constable Charles d'Albret, had advanced to meet the English. The French chivalry has learned nothing since Creçy and Poitiers. The lessons of defeat, the training afforded by Du Guesclin, have been in vain. The encounter took place on the Calais road between Framecourt and Agincourt. The forces of the Constable d'Albret were three times as large as those at the disposal of the English King, who could only draw up 900 lances and 3000 archers. But the French command made their dispositions badly, in land which was ploughed up and muddy. "The King of England won," says Jean de Bueil, "because he kept his men from getting out of breath, and at night saw that they were refreshed; and the French did the opposite. For at night they lay in a field where they were up to their knees in mud, and next day marched across a great stretch of ploughed land to come up to their enemy, and they went so far to seek them that, when it came to fighting, they assembled so few men, and one after another, and out of breath, so that they were defeated (25th October 1415)." It is the story of the Horatii and the Curiatii.

Albret was among the dead, the brave and gentle Charles of Orleans among the prisoners. The son of the victim of John the Fearless is to be taken to England where, contemplating afar off on fine days the azure coast of France, he will compose those poems, delicate and full of emotion, with the graceful rhythm and the fine play of colour which are to place him among the best French poets. As a prisoner of the English, Charles of Orleans will arouse the ingenuous and stirring enthusiasm of Jeanne d'Arc.

The English conducted the war cruelly. Like the horrible Boches in 1914-18 they cut the fruit trees to the ground in order to ruin the country over which they passed. Whole villages were deserted. The good folk encumbered the roads with brambles, thorns, bushes, and knotty trees in fear of being murdered, robbed, set upon, and beaten.

THE MIDDLE AGES

Gerson sketches with a vivid pen the wretched poverty of Jacques Bonhomme.

" Alas ! when a poor man shall have paid his impost, his villein tax, his salt tax, his hearth money, his fourth, the King's spurs, the Queen's belt, the customs, the road tax, the tolls—not much remains to him. Then will come another levy newly created, and sergeants to come and take in pledge his pots and his store. The poor man will have no bread to eat, except by chance some little rye or barley ; his poor wife will be in childbirth, and will have four or six little children round the hearth—or by the oven, if it chance to be warm—asking for bread and crying with the desperation of hunger. The poor mother will have nothing to put into their mouths but a little bread, even if she has this. This should be sufficient misery ; but then will come ruffians who will ransack everything. They will find, perhaps, a hen with four chickens, which the wife was nourishing to sell and pay the remainder of the tax, or a new one just levied—everything will be taken or seized, and who shall pay ? And if the man or woman protest, they will be abused, fined, or maltreated. If they sue for payment they will lose their time, spend double, and get nothing in the end : or sometimes, by chance, a note stating that to such a person so much is owing.

" ' Very well ! ' says the debtor.

" And he goes on owing.

" How could it be worse for a poor fellow ? It could hardly be worse. But still worse is to come—soldiers fighting with each other who are not content to take nothing where there is nothing, but threaten and beat the man and his wife, and set fire to the house unless they pay ransom, and make people pay them in unjust and crooked ways, with money or provisions. I will not speak of the outrages to women. . . . And there are thousands and thousands, and more than ten thousand, in the land in a worse state than I have described."

Is not this an admirable passage—terribly admirable—in its strength, colour, and vividness ?

To Charles d'Albret there succeeded in the office of Constable Bernard VII d'Armagnac, the brother-in-law of the Duke of Orleans. He was a penniless hero, but of an illustrious line, with a head as hard as his iron helmet and with the devil in him.

THE HUNDRED YEARS WAR

With his cadets of Gascony, of the most authentic vintage, he will show the Burgundians some fine doings. Until his death he is to be master of the government.

But he could not prevent the rapid progress of the English who, in a short time, found themselves masters of all Normandy. Thomas Basin points out: "The English had the ways open before them. Everywhere the Armagnacs and the Burgundians were fighting each other, without truce, animated by a burning hate against one another, so that the English had no difficulty in seizing towns and fortresses."

The defeat of Agincourt let loose among the Parisians a reaction against the Armagnacs. The Dauphin, the future Charles VII, nominated on the 14th June 1417 lieutenant-general of the kingdom in the place of his mad father, is obliged to flee. On the 28th May 1418 he reaches Melun at full speed. He was fifteen years old.

The *Bourgeois de Paris*, belonging to the popular party, *i.e.* the Burgundian party, hails the return of his friends. During the night of the 29th May 1418 the gate of St. Germain is opened to the soldiers of John the Fearless. They were grouped in the plain of Grenelle, to the number of six or seven hundred, under the command of the Lord of Bar and the Sire de l'Isle Adam. "The majority of the people," writes the *Bourgeois de Paris*, "were for them. The Armagnacs were hemmed in, the gates of the dwellings broken in, their coffers emptied, their chests broken, their possessions plundered. Very thankful were they who could hide in a cave or cellar or any hiding-place. They were killed 'in great heaps.' They were sometimes killed ruthlessly with great axes and other weapons, . . . and women and children and people who could do them no worse injury cursed them as they passed by, saying:

"'Dogs! traitors! you are in a better state than you deserve. Would that it pleased God to put you all into that state.'

"And you would not have found in Paris a street in which there was not some one killed at every hundred steps. And when they were dead, nothing remained to them but their coats, and they lay, like pigs, in the midst of the mud."

Then there was the horrible massacre of the prisons, the

slaying of the Armagnacs shut up in the Conciergerie. The mob rushed upon it at midnight, " a confusing hour for a man taken by surprise." " They began to cry aloud :

" ' Kill ! Kill these false Armagnacs.'

" They killed, battered, slew, murdered all whom they found." The Constable Bernard d'Armagnac was slaughtered in a horrible manner, his corpse dragged to the Palais de Justice, thrown naked on the marble table in the great hall, where the butchers, expert in the business, flayed a great St. Andrew's Cross on his breast, thus imprinting on his body the red cross of the Burgundians (12th June 1418).

In fighting the Armagnacs the Parisians did not regard themselves as acting in a way hostile to the French Crown. It was the Nobility, they thought, who had laid France open to the English.

" May God curse any who should have pity on those false traitors, the Armagnac-English dogs ! for by them is the kingdom of France, quite spoilt and wasted ; they sold it to the English " (*Bourgeois de Paris*).

The movement spread over the whole of France. To free oneself of an enemy one cried as he passed : " There goes an Armagnac ! " (*Juvenal des Ursins*). Every rich man was labelled " Armagnac."

And the good people of Paris celebrated their bloody triumph with as much devotion as poetry. In the church of St. Eustache, " every one who went in had a crown of red roses (the colour of the blood newly spilt) . . .; but before twelve o'clock the supply of chaplets ran out ; but the church of St. Eustache was quite full of people, and in the church it smelt as pleasant as though it had been washed in rose-water " (*Bourgeois de Paris*).

About the same time, the Great Schism seemed as though it might come to an end through the efforts of the Council of Constance : the two enemy Popes, John XXII and Benedict XIII, were both deposed ; and the unity of the Church momentarily restored by the election of Martin V (November 1417).

Soissons, in imitation of Paris, turned Burgundian. With cries of " Death to the Armagnacs ! " the " common people " fell upon the rich, massacring and plundering. The Armagnacs held the Dauphin; the Burgundians seized the Queen. The entry into Paris of John the Fearless, accompanied by Isabel of Bavaria, was made on the 14th July 1418. The burgesses came to meet them dressed in long blue robes. "And they were received with such honour and joy as never lady or lord had ever been in France. Everywhere they passed, the people cried aloud, 'Noël!' and there were few who did not weep from joy and pity" (*Bourgeois de Paris*).

The Parisians wept with joy—very good; and with pity—better still. Just as the Dauphin, Charles V, had not lost confidence after Poitiers, so was the Dauphin, Charles VII, not discouraged after Agincourt. He reorganized his army, assisted by courageous leaders, notably by the Breton Tanguy du Châtel, the Provost of Paris. Etampes is retaken. The Burgundians besieging Montlhéry quickly decamp. The Parisians could no longer go beyond their ramparts to look after their harvests. We know that Paris was still an agricultural town. "That year (1418) the corn and oats remained uncut all round Paris, for no one dared to go out because of the Armagnacs, who killed all those they could seize who belonged to Paris."

The *Bourgeois de Paris* accuses the noblemen whom the Parisians had chosen as leaders of complicity with the Armagnacs. "And it is the truth that if the common folk had had their way there would not have remained an Armagnac in France. In less than two months they would have been finished off."

In the commission given by the Government to the Admiral Robert de Braquemont, the King's lieutenant in the *bailliages* of Rouen, Gisors, and Caux, appears the care which is taken to put the country into a good state of defence. The castles and fortresses which seem "tenable" are to be "taken and fortified"; the others which are "not tenable" are to be destroyed. In each fortified town, in each castle, is to be put a tried leader. Finally, in some provinces, an agreement is concluded, a veritable treaty of peace directed against the English, between the leaders commanding the places holding to the Dauphin and those commanding the places holding to

THE MIDDLE AGES

the Duke of Burgundy. The public misfortunes lead both sides to begin to consider themselves as natural allies against those who have invaded the country; moreover, a victorious resistance might have been contemplated, when the drama of the Bridge of Montereau came to plunge the country once more into an abyss of dissensions, disorder, and misery.

John the Fearless, after the English had taken possession of Normandy, was affrighted by the conditions which the conquerors sought to impose on him. He wished to be reconciled with the King of France. A meeting was arranged between him and the Dauphin: it took place on the bridge of Montereau-fault-Yonne on the 10th September 1419. Comines has described the scene:

"It had been agreed that the King (the Dauphin) and he (John the Fearless) should come to Montereau-fault-Yonne, and there was made a bridge and a barrier in the middle; but in the middle of the aforesaid barrier there was a little *portillon* which closed the two sides; by which one could go from one side to the other, when both parties were willing.

"Thus the King was on one side of the bridge and the aforesaid Duke John on the other, accompanied by a great number of men-at-arms, and especially the aforesaid Duke. They began to speak together on the bridge, and at the spot where they spoke, there were with the said Duke only three or four persons. Having begun their parley, the Duke was so excited or so annoyed at humiliating himself before the King that he opened from his side, and the other side was opened to him, and he passed with three others. Immediately he was killed."

The affair seems to have been accidental. There was no premeditation. The innocence of Charles VII is established. It was without doubt the officers of the Dauphin's suite who struck John the Fearless, irritated "by some outrageous words" which the latter let fall in the course of the discussion with their master. We know that John the Fearless was hasty and easily carried away, and that he expressed himself awkwardly. But he left a son, Philip the Good, who is to be the "Grand Duke of the West," very noble in character and lofty in his aims and resolutions. Philip the Good will set his heart on avenging his father, and unhappily for our country he will

THE HUNDRED YEARS WAR

succeed only too well. The alliance is cemented between the Burgundians and the English. Queen Isabel and the poor mad King Charles VI are in their power. Thus was brought about the horrible Treaty of Troyes (21st May 1420). Henry V, King of England, was to marry Catherine, the daughter of Charles VI, and would be recognized as heir, to the throne of St. Louis, of his poor father-in-law, Charles VI, who would keep during his deadened life the title of King of France and the revenues of the Crown, but would abandon the reins of government to the English monarch.

The *Bourgeois de Paris*, fundamentally "Burgundian," traces a famous picture of the state of France at that time. Its features are striking. The excellent man sees quite rightly the source of the evils which France is undergoing in the divisions of parties, the responsibility for which he attributes being frankly Burgundian to the Armagnacs and particularly to him who had been their leader, the blunt Constable of France. " . . . The great mass of the people who had had the habit of working and staying safely at home, with their wives and families—merchants, members of merchant companies, churchmen, monks, nuns, people of every condition—have been turned out of their houses like wild beasts, so that people beg who were accustomed to give ; others serve who had formerly their own servants ; some have become thieves and murderers in despair ; good maidens and honest women have come to shame through force or otherwise, having become evil through necessity. How many monks, priests, ladies vowed to religion and other gentle women, have left all by force and yielded body and soul to despair, God knows how. Alas ! so many children born dead for want of help ; so many dying without confession, through tyranny and other causes ; so many dead left unburied in forests and other deserted places ; so many marriages prevented from being solemnized ; so many churches burned, and chapels, hospitals, lazar houses where holy service and works of mercy were performed, and nothing now remains of them but their site ; so many treasures buried of which no good will ever come, and jewels of the churches and relics and other things. In short, I think that no man could enumerate the great, miserable and damnable sins which have been committed since the unfortunate and damnable arrival of Bernard, Count of Armagnac and Constable of France, for, since the names came into France of Burgundian and Armagnac, all the evils which could be enumerated have been committed in the kingdom of France, while the clamour of the innocent blood which has been shed cries to Heaven for vengeance. And I believe in my heart that the aforesaid Count of Armagnac was a devil in the form of a man, for I see none who were for him or use his name, or who wears his badge (the white scarf of the Armagnacs), who keeps the law or the Christian faith; but they conduct themselves towards all over whom they have the mastery like people who have denied their Creator, as can be seen throughout the kingdom of France. For I dare say that the King of England would not have been so bold as to set foot in France, nor would there have been the quarrel of this unhappy name, and all Normandy would still be French, nor would the noble blood of France have been shed, nor the lords of that realm led into exile (as prisoners in England), nor the battle lost and so many good men dead, nor the piteous day of Agincourt have ever been in which the King lost so many of his good and loyal friends, but for the pride of this unhappy name of Armagnac.... Alas! I do not believe that ever since Clovis, France was so desolate and divided as she is to-day, for the Dauphin pays attention to nothing, day and night, him and his, except spoiling the country of his father with fire and blood, and the English on their side do as much harm as the Saracens. But still it is better to be taken by the English than by the Dauphin or his men, who call themselves Armagnacs; and the poor King and Queen stay at Troyes with a poor suite, like fugitives, and driven from their place by their own child, which seems to all good people a great pity to think of."

It is a precious page, and shows by what obliquity of sentiment a good Frenchman can be moved, under the fatal pressure of intestine divisions, to incline his sympathies to the English.

Henry V, King of England, was not to glory for long in his triumph. He died at Vincennes on the 31st August 1422, soon followed to the tomb by poor Charles VI, who died in his house of St. Paul on the 21st October of the same year.

THE HUNDRED YEARS WAR

On his tomb Berry the Herald-at-arms proclaimed the accession of Henry " by the grace of God, King of France and England." The sovereign of this great empire, the son of Henry V and Catherine of France, was hardly eighteen months old.

While at St. Denis, the French King-at-arms was proclaiming the accession of the son of Henry V; at Bourges Charles VII was proclaiming himself King of France: whence the surname " King of Bourges," which was given to him at the beginning of his reign. The young prince was in his twentieth year. It was now the turn of the English to have a minor on the throne. The uncles of Henry VI, the Dukes of Gloucester and Bedford, took the government on themselves in the quality of regents —Gloucester at London and Bedford at Paris.

The Virgin of Battles.

The affairs of the King of Bourges were not, after all, in so bad a state as might appear. The French found again a king, and we know the force of attraction which the royal person exercised over them at this time. Neither the Queen Regent, nor the lieutenant of the King, nor even the Dauphin, could replace him. English chroniclers and historians have recognized this clearly: " Assuredly the death of Charles brought about an important change in France, for a great number of the Nobility, who were previously on the English side, now turned to the Dauphin in a common effort to drive the English from the land."

The Superior of the Carmelites was handed over to justice for having said, on hearing of the proclamation of Henry VI as King of France and England:

" No Englishman was ever King of France or shall be."

In Noyon a poor cobbler went about saying that " the Dauphin (Charles VII) would be master and King, and that, if he came to Noyon, the gates of the town would be opened to him."

At Bourges, Charles VII receives some emissaries from Normandy in "disguising garments": they announce to him that if he were to come to the beautiful land of Normandy he would be well received.

In Normandy the English Government could not manage to extricate itself from a tangled partisan warfare which showed the lively hold national sentiment had taken there in all classes of society. The English dominated the land by their organized forces. They were the masters in the towns; but in the depths of the forests there lurked the indomitable defenders of national independence. At all times of the day and night and everywhere, at the spots where they were least expected, they pounced upon the representatives of the English Government, killed them when they found them in small bands, took from the collectors their money received from the taxes, stopped the messengers, and altogether impeded administration. The peasants were their allies and hid them at need. Brave women brought them provisions in the depths of the woods. When the English managed to catch them they buried these noble patriots alive beneath the gibbets on which were hanged those who had assisted them. They had set dogs to hunt these " outlaws " in their sylvan haunts. They had put a price on the head of the " brigands," as they called the representatives of the cause of France: six pounds per man brought alive to the viscounty. The results of this hunting of men are found in the accounts mingled with those of the hunting of wolves.

All classes and conditions were represented in these bands of partisans: priests who had cast away their frocks to defend their country, traders who had abandoned their counters. Nobles and knights rubbed shoulders with peasants, curriers, shoemakers, and carpenters. It was the first and fruitful example of the drawing together which was to come between the country gentry and the common people. One sees the villagers following in bands their lord who led them in this patriotic brigandage.

Some soldiers were discussing in an inn the means of stamping out this irregular army, when a priest intervened:

" Let the English leave the country and the brigands will soon disappear."

Let us picture to ourselves the state of France at this beginning of the reign of Charles VII: " The rural districts, that is to say, the unfortified lands, the countryside, are turned into the condition of the sea, where each one has just as much command as he has power." The English and Burgundians dominated the great towns; but how many little places, small defended villages, how many castles and strongholds were in the hands of their adversaries. In consequence of the disorder, disorganization, and want of security, of the dilapidation of the bridges and highways, communications had become immensely difficult, slow to the last degree, and extremely rare. Things were going back to the state of stagnation, isolation, and immobility which we described at the beginning of this book. Jean de Bueil gives us a lively picture of it:

"In passing on my way I found myself in a very desolate and deserted district, for there had been for a long time war there between the inhabitants. Nevertheless, there was a certain gathering of common people, as there is often in the open country, and some places inhabited by poor noblemen, that is to say, castles and fortresses of the smaller sort, poorly fortified and old fashioned; among which there were two close to each other and like enough in their poverty; but so opposed were they to each other that they had been a long time at war and enmity for a very small cause. For just as through high and great disputes there come great divisions between rich and powerful men, similarly between the poor there arise brawls and dissensions for little occasions enough: no one wishes to lose his rights.

"Now it was thus that in passing on my way—which I had entered upon without safe conduct to avoid danger from the enemies of the side to which I adhered—I arrived at one of the above-mentioned castles, which was called Luc (Château l'Hermitage, canton de Pontvallain, Sarthe), opposed to the other castle named Verset (one of the little places in Maine occupied by the English). Certainly both of them were badly held and very poorly built. The sentinel's lodge was very exposed and open to the wind, so that he who kept watch was not protected against it. And similarly the gate-keeper was much exposed to the heat and glare of summer and to cold and frost in winter.

"I stayed at the fortress of Luc because it belonged to my party."

Château l'Hermitage is then occupied by Armagnac soldiers whom Jean de Bueil comes to join; Verset is garrisoned by the

English. There is daily war, careful, minute, and punctilious, between the two fortresses.

This was repeated throughout France at least in all the provinces in which the English were installed. "The war," M. Pierre Champion very justly writes, "took on the character of an occupation. It assumed the aspect of a monotonous trench war. Not that they dug out furrows in the earth, but the France of that day was covered with castles and fortresses, which were veritable redoubts, commanding the passage of the rivers, of the ravines, giving the prospects necessary to soldiers for a surprise. Each fortified town had its circle of walls. When the warning was given, the burgesses and the canons themselves mounted guard on the ramparts. Moats full of water were a serious obstacle to any one attempting an attack. A few defenders sufficed for these places, which guarded themselves."

Here, then, are the Armagnacs at Château l'Hermitage and the English at Verset. They spy upon each other, try to surprise each other, and seize each other's provisions and horses. The difficulty of communications which hampered the bringing of fresh supplies, reduced every one to the most precarious and wretched existence.

"I stayed there long enough," says Jean de Bueil, "awaiting the merchants, men or women, who from time to time brought oats to the garrison, but it was not every day. Their horses went fasting most of the time, through which they were weak, sickly, and thin. And some had lost their shoes and had to wait for the farrier, who was not always there. And worse still, they had so few that every time they went on an expedition against their enemies, or for any journey, they took all of them and left none behind, and yet there were not enough; but often they went two on a horse, and the majority went on foot. And to cut the matter short, the greater number, men as well as horses, were either blind or lame, and there was none who did not bear signs of their trade."

If the English got possession of one of these castles occupied by a garrison faithful to Charles VII they treated their enemies with the greatest harshness. The English took the Château d'Orsay. They led its garrison to Paris, "each with a halter round his neck, tightly fastened, coupled with one another like dogs, coming on foot from the said castle to Paris; and there were about fifty of them, not counting the women and young pages."

The aspect of the country is described by Thomas Basin. He has traversed Champagne, Brie, Gâtinais, Beauvais, the country round Chartres, Maine, Perche, Vexin, and Valois. The fields are abandoned, rough, tangled; the trees grow as in virgin forests. Cultivation of the land is found only round fortified towns and castles, over the extent of ground which can be seen by the watchman posted at the top of the towers. When the sentinel discerned at a distance an invasion of brigands or of an enemy, he gave the alarm by the sound of trumpet or bell, and for all to take refuge with beasts and goods within the fortified enclosure. This signal had become so frequent in certain places that on hearing it the oxen and horses ran of their own accord to shelter. "But," says Thomas Basin, "as in these provinces with extensive fields, towns and fortresses are rare—some, too, of the latter had been destroyed in the recent fighting—the land under cultivation round the fortified places was small in comparison with the immensity of the waste ground, encumbered with briars, heath, and wild shrubs." One might imagine oneself at the beginnings of the feudal period.

When a district commanded by a fortified town or powerful castle chanced to be efficaciously defended by the soldiers living there, there was seen, restored again quickly enough, a certain degree of prosperity. Work was organized in security. Jean de Bueil is at Sablé, of which Guillaume de Brezé is captain. Le Jouvencel and his companions "stayed in the town for a time and their fame spread throughout the district. There was talk only of their feats in arms. And they so kept the peace in the town and all the surrounding country that in a short time the population increased and goods became profitable."

On the 26th September 1423, at Graville in Maine, the French, commanded by Jean d'Harcourt, gained a signal success over the English under the command of William Pole; but on the 17th August 1424 they were beaten once more at Verneuil, the bloodiest battle of the war. Once more an army much superior in numbers to that of the enemy was beaten through the mistaken manœuvring of its leaders. The clever strategist Jean de Bueil, who was soon to be in command of the armies as Marshall of France, explains it thus:

"The French put a good number of horsemen in front of them, who were thrown back against them, by which they were discomfited. Foot soldiers should never put cavalry in front of them, for when the horsemen are thrown back, they often charge their own men with their horses' chests and break their ranks; they should be placed on the wings."

The results of the battle of Verneuil was to make the English almost entirely masters of the country north of the Loire. On the seacoast there was always victoriously resisting the admirable Mont-St.-Michel, which a troop of Norman gentlemen defended indefatigably, assisted by the humble burgesses and fishermen who constituted the little town clinging to the sides of the *Mont*; and on the frontiers of the Empire, there resisted another wave, quite inland, the castellany of Vaucouleurs, commanded by a kind of condottiere, pugnacious and energetic, Robert de Baudricourt. From this little corner of the land, faithful to the fleur-de-lis, salvation was to come.

But before recounting the wonderful epic of the Maid of Domrémy, let us mark two facts which show to what an extent the two parties, the Armagnacs and the Burgundians, the aristocratic and the popular parties, continued to divide France.

At the news of the disaster of Verneuil the barons of Auvergne, of Bourbonnais, Guienne, and Languedoc came spontaneously to offer their help to Charles VII with the most numerous show of arms they had been able to muster; but Le Mans fell into the hands of the English (28th May 1428) under the following circumstances: "The common people," writes the *Bourgeois de Paris*, "conceived so great a hatred for the Armagnacs that they allowed the aforesaid leaders (the English) to enter. When they (the English) were within they began to shout, 'The town is won!' . . . And they fought, hand to hand, for a very long time, but in the end the Armagnacs were defeated, for the people had such a great hatred of them for their wickedness that they threw great stones down upon them from the windows, killing them and their horses, and when any of the Armagnacs escaped on a good horse or in any other way he was forthwith killed by the popular party. And so great was their prowess, namely, of the leader named my Lord Talbot and the people of the castle (the English who were in the castle of the town) and the commune, that twelve hundred Armagnacs remained dead on the ground besides those who were beheaded for having consented to the entry of the Armagnacs."

Jeanne the Deliverer was born on the 5th January 1412, at Domrémy, in the castellany of Vaucouleurs, in the marches of Lorraine, within the royal jurisdiction.

Her father, Jacquot d'Arc — pronounced " d'Ai "—was a native of the village of Arc-en-Barrois (arrondissement of Chaumont). Jacquot d'Arc was held in great respect at Domrémy. He was dean (doyen) of the community and commanded the watch. He possessed arable lands, meadows, and woods, enough to form a *gaignage*, that is to say, a domain which necessitated the use of several horses. Jacquot d'Arc and his eldest son, Jacquemin, commanded the fortress of Domrémy, called the " House of the Isle," a defensive position, rough and abrupt, constructed at the point of a kind of peninsula which the Meuse surrounded in its winding course. It was a " refuge " where man and beast found shelter and whose defence in those days of alarms was directed by Jacquot d'Arc and his eldest son. There was collected there an arsenal of weapons and armour, which they shared among the peasants when the alarm went, thus transforming them into a garrison. "What days, and above all what nights, must Jeannette have passed in the open air, her ear strained for the slightest noise, watching for the approach of the English from Montigny and Nogent or the Burgundians from Andelot, Fouvent, Vignory, and St. Dizier " (Siméon Luce).

In June 1425 Jeanne was in her thirteenth year. At midday in her father's garden, which the bells of the neighbouring church filled with their clanging, voices very gentle, very sweet, called her as though coming from the church. There was no one to be seen in the direction from which the sound came. The child was seized with terror. On the following days this call was renewed. The voices were tuneful and tender; they were accompanied by a great light, and a perfume sweeter than that of flowers. The voices were those of the Archangel Michael, the protector of the kingdom of France, and of the two saints, St. Catherine and St. Margaret, whose statues stood in the church of Domrémy, near the altar.

At Domrémy, everybody was Armagnac, that is to say, attached to the royal cause, and it was the same in the neighbouring fortress of Vaucouleurs; while, all round, the Burgundians were in power, and the district was cut up by the English, who occupied many fortresses.

At Vaucouleurs there was in command, faithful to his King, but otherwise without a trace of sentiment, a picturesque person, Robert de Baudricourt. A brave soldier, a bluff leader, skilful in surprises and ambushes, and not less in the tricks of diplomacy and the finesse of a man of affairs. The Duke of Bedford, Regent of France, was preparing an expedition to clear from the country the last wave which had remained hostile to the King of England, at the moment when these luminous voices, gliding through the foliage of a little enclosure of greenery, were murmuring in the ears of a girl of seventeen:

> Jeanne, thou maiden well blessed,
> The God of Heaven sends me to you;
> Fear nothing,
> Be wholly joyful.
> His will and His pleasure
> Is that you go to Orleans,
> Drive away the English,
> And raise the siege.
> Then it will fall to you
> To lead the King to Reims for consecration.
> And to the Lord of Baudricourt,
> Go and bid him lead you
> Immediately by the shortest road,
> That he is your leader,
> And God will guide you always.
> (*Mistère du Siège d'Orléans.*)

Domrémy stood on a road which formed the highway to Italy, the Rhone Valley, Burgundy, and Flanders. The merchants in those days were also the informed newsbringers. The house of Jacques d'Arc was hospitable, and Jeanne heard,

THE HUNDRED YEARS WAR

through the most various accounts, the details of the events which she had so much at heart.

At the beginning of May 1428 Jeanne went to her uncle, Durand Laxart, who lived at Burey-le-Petit, near Vaucouleurs. She succeeded in convincing him of the reality of her mission. Accompanied by her uncle, Laxart, she set out for Vaucouleurs on the 13th May 1428. She arrived there dressed in a frock of red wool, tight to the figure, and falling in straight pleats.

Aged seventeen, Jeanne was pleasing with her lively and attractive air. Her face had a frank and happy expression. She was of medium height, with straight shoulders, black hair, and with big black eyes. She had a robust, slightly rustic appearance. Her strength, her adaptability, and endurance are to be the admiration of the soldiery. All contemporaries agree as to the beauty of her figure and that, a little hard perhaps, of her features.

Jeanne and her uncle, Laxart, had much difficulty in obtaining an audience with Baudricourt. In the end they succeeded, thanks to two young squires, Bertrand de Poulangy and Jean de Metz, who had been charmed by the frank manner and pleasant looks of the young girl. Baudricourt was convinced in his turn. On the 23rd February 1429 a little band left Vaucouleurs to go to Charles VII at Chinon. It included Jeanne d'Arc, Jean de Metz, and Bertrand de Poulangy, four servants, a King's messenger, Colet de Vienne, and an archer named Richard.

The terrible defeat of the 12th February near Rouvray St. Denis, known as the " Battle of the Herrings," seemed to have given the death-blow to the cause of the Valois. The battle had taken its name from the fact that the French had thought they could attack victoriously an English convoy of provisions containing three hundred wagons laden with herrings: the staple food of the people in the Middle Ages, much more so than bread, at least in the towns. Orleans, the last fortress on the Loire, was on the point of succumbing to the attacks of the English.

Jeanne was introduced into the presence of Charles VII, on the 8th March, at nightfall. Nearly three hundred knights filled the great hall of the Castle of Chinon, in which fifty torches shed their glittering light. Some brushwood was crackling under the mantel of the high chimney-piece, still preserved. Jeanne advanced towards the King.

" Most noble Dauphin, I have come on the part of God to help you, you and your kingdom."

Her sweet, clear voice, her rustic beauty in the flower of her eighteenth year, her movements, youthful and free, told in her favour.

" King," said the young girl to him, " be ever humble and gentle towards God and He will help you."

Charles VII was walking next day on the banks of the Loire with his friends, when he stopped, surprised to see with what grace and courage the Maid from Vaucouleurs wielded a lance on a war-horse. The young Duke of Alençon was seized with an enthusiasm for her which never afterwards diminished.

Some provisions had been collected at Blois for the reprovisioning of Orleans. Jeanne declared that she was charged to take them into the town. The King gave her the rank of war leader, *chef de guerre*. This expression has misled the best and most recent historians. It does not mean at all that Jeanne was to be commander-in-chief of the French army. The *chef de guerre* had a fixed rôle in the armies of the fifteenth century. His importance corresponded roughly with that of colonel in the royal armies of the eighteenth century. He was qualified to recruit a band of men-at-arms at will and on his own responsibility, whom he dressed as he liked and to whom he gave a banner of his own designing; it was his company: in the eighteenth century it would have been his regiment. The supreme head of the armies was the King, and in default of him, the King's Lieutenant, and under his orders were the Constable and the Marshalls. Under the direction of these great leaders were the *chefs de guerre*, each of whom represented his company and who were very numerous. Each *chef de guerre* received from him for whom he fought, King, simple lord, or municipality, an agreed sum, which enabled him to equip, feed, and pay his men. Charles of Anjou, the King's Lieutenant, assembled his officers in council (towards 1425) :

" . . . had a great hall prepared in which to hold a council as Lieutenant-General, and he sat on a seat and all the lords and war leaders round him. . . ." He takes their advice and concludes:

"It has seemed good to all the lords, captains, and war leaders here assembled. . . ."

Another passage of *Jouvencel* will show us these war leaders in the midst of their men.

It is on the battlefield at the end of the day. The battle has been fierce: "One is tired, another weighed down by his harness . . . the *chefs de guerre* cannot speak any more from shouting so much. Their men do not hear them, and if they do, they pretend not to. The leaders have not to do with individual men but with the whole company. . . ."

These two passages show us clearly the rôle of the *chefs de guerre*, on the one hand in council, on the other in the heat of action, each ordering, sustaining, rallying, and encouraging the men of his company. Jeanne writes in her letter to Henry VI :

"I am a *chef de guerre*. . . ."

This, then, is quite definitely her rôle in the army. It is a great mistake to attribute to her the command of the whole French army : an error which falsifies the character of her action and prevents us understanding it. Let us add that each of these *chefs de guerre* had in council and the conduct of affairs an importance varying with his personal valour and his reputation. After Orleans and Patay, Jeanne's importance as *chef de guerre* became very great; but officially she never had other functions than those we have just indicated.

At the moment of beginning the story of the Battle of Patay the author of the *Chronique Martiniane* writes : "Those who led the vanguard, the Constable and the Marshall de Boussac, La Hire, Pothon (Xaintrailles), and Anthoine de Chabannes and Jeanne the Maid and other captains . . ." Behold, then, Jeanne d'Arc very exactly placed among the most famous *chefs de guerre* of the time, La Hire, Xantrailles, and Chabannes under the orders of the Constable and a Marshall of France.

The company, of which Jeanne was leader, was of little importance in the beginning, at the moment of the march on Orleans. It included only three lances, which made with the squires and servants fifteen men. Later her company will grow in numbers. In May 1430, when she enters Compiègne, Jeanne will have under her banner three or four hundred men, of whom one hundred will be cavalry, sixty-eight archers and bowmen, and two trumpeters. Her lieutenant was an Italian, Bartolommeo Baretta. There were attached to the company a chaplain and a secretary for accounts and writing. And as one of her most recent historians, M. Jules d'Auriac, well says, " It is pleasant to imagine Jeanne d'Arc, aged eighteen, paying her men, looking after their sustenance, verifying the good condition of their weapons and the solidity of their armour. . . ." Here Jeanne is in her right place. There is none finer nor of which we French, so proud of her, could be prouder.

Jeanne was the virgin of battles, a fighter in her very soul. She had the boldness, the courage, the endurance, and the energy of the warrior. She remained on horseback, in her white armour with its plates of steel, whole days and nights. After a year and a half of incessant riding her beautiful body was deformed by it. She had the bluff manner of the soldier and used language fit for a trooper. The judges at Rouen reproached her with these oaths. She rode marvellously, " riding black and high-mettled horses " (*The Black Book of La Rochelle*).

The " Burgundian " Monstrelet also will say : " She was bold in riding horses, and in leading them to drink, and in performing the feats of soldiers." She hardly liked to be out of the company of the soldiers ; she liked their straightforwardness, their plain dealing, their loyalty. She could not bear lawyers and doctors. " She was simple in everything," one of the witnesses in the process of rehabilitation will say, " except in matters of warfare, in which she was among the most expert." " She was very clever," the Duke of Alençon will say, " in handling a lance, gathering together an army, arranging the order of battles, or disposing the artillery." All the witnesses called on to speak were of accord on this subject. Let us quote what Monstrelet, of the opposing camp, said about it :

" And always Jeanne the Maid was in the front with her standard. And in all the marches there was no greater fame or reputation than there was of her and of no other soldier."

THE HUNDRED YEARS WAR

To which we must add her vanity, one of the charming traits of her character and which does not belittle her, but the contrary. The most acceptable present which could be given to her consisted of fine horses, and beautiful weapons and armour, and then of rich stuffs and precious adornments.

At Domrémy Jeanne wore a dress of red wool. She arrived at Chinon, dressed as a man in dark grey cloth. " She had a black doublet with hose attached, a short frock of dark grey material, her black hair cut straight round, with a black hat on her head." Later she puts on white armour with plates of steel, capes of cloth of gold, red capes, long cloaks of crimson velvet strewn with nettles of the natural colour, the arms of Charles of Orleans, stuffs of purple silk, beaten with gold and silver. When she was not in armour she dressed as a horse soldier with " shoes laced behind the foot, tight-fitting doublet and hose, and a small hat on her head, and wearing magnificent clothes of cloth of gold and silk well trimmed with fur (*Chronique des Cordeliers*).

The Chancellor of France, Regnauld de Chartres, Archbishop of Reims, will reproach her angrily for her vanity and having spent so much money on her toilet. Moreover, will not her beautiful golden cape, which she had thrown over her armour, contribute to her capture under the walls of Compiègne? The Burgundians will seize her by the lappets of her cape to make her fall from her horse.

On the 29th April 1429, Jeanne appeared in sight of Orleans, followed by the royal army. The next day the town was revictualled. On the 4th May the fortress of St. Loup, which the English had built on the banks of the river, was taken at the first attack. The redoubtable girdle of wood and stone, with which seven months of incessant labour had encircled the town, was broken through. The bastille St. Jean le Blanc, full of English, was taken on the 6th May. Amidst the arrows, bricks, and stones which the enemy rained down, Jeanne cried to her men, waving her banner, " In the name of God! be brave! Forward! " It was then the turn of the bastille of the Augustinians and the Fort of the Tourelles.

The English, who had received Jeanne with gross insults, are filled with terror. " I have never heard of such a one,"

THE MIDDLE AGES

cries Suffolk, their leader, "unless it were a devil from hell." The *Tourelles* were taken on the 7th May. Grievously wounded in the shoulder towards the middle of the day, Jeanne had eaten nothing since morning; she had sustained all the effort of the attack in her iron armour, and the evening found her still courageous, active, smiling. From nightfall to dawn the belfries of Orleans filled the air with songs of victory; bonfires were lighted at the cross-roads; streets and lanes repeated in sonorous echo, "Noël! Noël!" while horns and trumpets sounded triumphal marches. And on the next day, the 8th May 1429, the English decamped.

> In the year fourteen hundred and twenty-nine
> The sun again began to shine,

says Christine de Pisan in her fine language.

Such was the panic spread among the "red crosses" that Bedford sent letters to the leaders settled in the French ports to order them to arrest the deserters who flocked there asking for boats to recross the Channel, while in England it was impossible to ship the soldiers destined for the French War.

The towns are taken, one after another, from the English: Jargeau, Meung-sur-Loire, Beaugency.

The battle of Patay takes place on the 18th June (1429). The English, under the most famous captains, Talbot, Fastolf, Ramston, and Scales, were installed behind the hedges and bushes, where they hoped to find a line of defence. The French army was commanded by the Duke of Alençon, the lieutenant of the King. When they asked Jeanne her opinion on the battle to be fought she replied:

"Fall upon the English and strike boldly: they will take flight."

And that was what happened. The illustrious John Talbot was among the prisoners. He was called "England's shield." He bore the title of "Marshall of France." John Fastolf fled. The English made a scapegoat of him, and we know the ridiculous and burlesque silhouette which Shakespeare has traced of him.

After the battle of Patay, Jeanne resumed with increased energy the plan of the march upon Reims, where he who was still called the Dauphin was to be crowned. Historians have

THE HUNDRED YEARS WAR

not all realized the justice of the Maid's views. It was certain that from the day that a unity of sentiment should form round Charles VII, the English would no longer hold in France. One must think of the prestige afforded by the anointing at Reims. The action would rally those who hesitated and rouse the indifferent. Jeanne, with her clear brain, had realized this. The States-General of 1484 will recall it in precise terms: "Before the time that King Charles VII was anointed and crowned, many inconveniences happened in the realm, for the majority of the people before the aforesaid consecration were unwilling to obey him, and the enemy overwhelmed the country, and there was no justice, only pillage and oppression, and as soon as he was crowned he never ceased to prosper and be victorious over his enemies."

The consecration of Charles VII at Reims will strike a mortal blow at the English cause in France. They made their way victoriously to the town across territory still subject to the laws of the enemy. The ceremony took place on the 17th July. The Maid prayed beside the King, near the altar. Beside her a monk held her banner. The crowd filled the nave with cries of "Noël! Noël!" Jeanne threw herself at the feet of the prince, transported with joy. She said to him, embracing his knees, "Noble King, now is the will of God fulfilled, that you should come to Reims to receive your due consecration, showing that you are the true King."

"And a great joy," says a spectator, "came to those who saw her thus, and many wept."

Truth to tell, Jeanne's rôle was now finished. She felt it to be so. She wished to return to her peaceful village and her parents, but she could not make up her mind to it. She loved war too much, the sonorous clamour and the emotions of battles. She could not bring herself to leave her dear soldiers, to give up the broad outlook, the fine feats of the sword. She will be found at the head of the party around Charles VII, which will pronounce in favour of war to the death, without truce or treaty, until the English should be driven out of France; she was followed by the Duke of Alençon, Duke René de Bar, Dunois, and all the *chefs de guerre,* men like La Hire, Chabannes, and Xaintrailles. The opposite party formed of those who

THE MIDDLE AGES

would be called nowadays the "Pacifists," and who wished to negotiate with the Duke of Burgundy or with the English King himself, was headed by the able Chancellor of France, Regnauld de Chartres, Archbishop of Reims, by the King's favourites La Trémoille and Gaucourt, and by the Count of Clermont.

"We will have peace only at the point of the lance," said Jeanne.

"At the point of the pen," said the Chancellor.

Charles VII was inclined by temperament towards the ideas of his Chancellor. These divergences will increase as time goes on. They will cause the check of the attack on Paris (8th September 1429), in which Jeanne did not receive support, and the retreat on the Loire. Charles VII had left Compiègne to go to the central provinces. He had just concluded with the Duke of Burgundy a truce of four months, prolonged soon after. The treaty stipulated that the Burgundians should have the keeping of Paris.

Incapable of conforming to the exigencies of a policy with which a nature like hers, all faith and action, could not harmonize, Jeanne was deeply grieved at being dragged inactive from Gen-sur-Loire to Selles in Berry, then to Bourges, to Montargis, Loches, Jargeau, Issoudun, and finally to the fine castle of Mehun-sur-Yèvre. Certainly the King gave her as much money as she wanted, the thoroughbred horses she loved to ride, the fine dresses, the sumptuous fabrics in which she loved to dress. The King ennobled her, together with her father, her brothers, and all her family; but all this brilliance did not stifle her "voices," which summoned her to new battles. Yielding to her entreaties, at the end of October 1429, Charles VII at last authorized Jeanne d'Arc, *chef de guerre*, to depart with her company, effectively reinforced, to the "conquest" of various fortresses which the Burgundians still possessed in the region of the Loire. She began by going to lay siege to St. Pierre-le-Moutier. Here, again, a characteristic incident takes place.

The assailants were repulsed in a first attack. The faithful D'Aulon, an old squire in the Maid's suite, never ceased to watch over her. He saw her alone on the ramparts. Barely a few soldiers, who were particularly devoted, remained near her. Spurring his horse, D'Aulon joins her and begs her to retire; but Jeanne, raising the visor of her helmet, says:

"I am not alone"—and with her eyes fixed with an inspired look on the crest of the ramparts, of which she felt herself already mistress—"I have still in my company fifty thousand of my people, and I will not depart until I have taken the town. . . ."

Jean d'Aulon looked round in the greatest astonishment.

"Whatever she might tell me," he declared simply, "she had no more than four or five men."

And as D'Aulon insisted, Jeanne's only answer was to make him bring wattles and shelters, faggots and ladders, for the escalade of the ramparts.

"In God's name, to the attack!" cried the young girl; "the town is ours!"

"And the town was taken," concluded the faithful squire, more and more bewildered.

On the 28th March 1430, Jeanne was with the King at Sully-sur-Loire. She was tired of the incessant discussions with him and his councillors, "discontented," says Perceval de Cagny, "with the manner in which he was working for the recovery of the kingdom." She had assembled the men of her company and completed in an unostentatious manner the preparations necessary for her plans. Suddenly, "without taking leave," she slipped away with her troops towards Lagny-sur-Marne, where she knew that "there was good fighting against the English." We touch here on one of the most important moments of her life. Let us picture Jeanne in her relations with the King. There were certainly lively, even violent, disputes between them. "She would not listen to advice, but did everything as she liked," Regnauld de Chartres will say. When she was opposed to the ministers and friends of Charles VII, she said:

"You have been at your council, I have been at mine."

Her council was her voices, the voice of Heaven, the voice of God. It is no detriment to the sublime heroine to say that, at this time of her life, in the councils of Charles VII in which she sat as a *chef de guerre*, she must have been unbearable. How can one discuss things with a young person who speaks all the time in the name of the good God. Regnauld of Chartres, without any doubt, spoke the truth when he claimed that she no longer listened to reason.

And we can understand the feelings of Charles VII after this last escapade. Regardless of the King's orders, of the treaties concluded, and which she would—if she had been acting with the approval of the King—have been openly violating, she returned to the banks of the Seine and the Oise to give, not only to the English but also to the Burgundians, " good buffets and blows." These are her expressions. What monarch would have tolerated such behaviour in a leader under his orders and fighting in his pay and in his name ?

" Let her go and be hanged ! " Charles VII may have said with an impulse of anger, quite justifiable. And Regnauld de Chartres and La Trémoille felt a certain sense of relief : " Ugh ! " At the head of her company Jeanne marched to the relief of Lagny.

Her company was composed of the most curious elements. The Italian Baretta is always its lieutenant, which means that he commands it in the absence of Jeanne d'Arc. There are found in it also some Italians, some Scotchmen, and naturally some French. Some of the most ruthless and grimmest warriors of the period had joined it—highwaymen turned soldiers, the two Potons, namely, Poton de Xaintrailles and Poton the Burgundian, Ambroise de Loré, Jean Foucaut, Jacques de Chabannes, Rigaud de Fontaines, Geoffroi de St. Belin, rough fellows, knowing no other trade, honour or joy, source of profit or means of existence, but ambushes, escalades, and the sword. Some of them, St. Belin, Chabannes, and Xaintrailles, are to figure, after the Peace of Arras, among the captains of the terrible *écorcheurs* (flayers).

The troop turned towards Lagny. On the way they met, followed by his men, a famous Burgundian *chef de guerre*, Franquet d'Arras, a redoubtable veteran, half brigand, half soldier. Jeanne attacked, conquered him and took him prisoner ; and then he had his head cut off. This battle, of the month of March 1430, has not been sufficiently noticed. Here Jeanne commanded her little army efficiently. A *chef de guerre* herself, she commanded her company in this duel with a *chef de*

THE HUNDRED YEARS WAR

guerre of the opposite side, an experienced condottiere, and won a complete victory over him.

The first weeks of May were spent in various skirmishes in the Ile-de-France and Valois. Jeanne was at Crépy when she heard that the army of the Duke of Burgundy had come to lay siege to Compiègne. Philip the Good claimed that this fortress should be delivered to him according to the truce concluded with Charles VII. About midnight she mounted on horseback and, followed by her company—300 or 400 men—rode till dawn. In the morning of the 14th May she entered Compiègne. Now you must know that the municipality of Compiègne had received from Charles VII the order to open the gates of the town to the Duke of Burgundy; but they had obstinately refused. It must be remembered too that Charles VII and his advisers were hoping, following on the truce with the Burgundians, to arrive at a general and definitive agreement. New conferences had been decided upon; but Philip the Good broke off the negotiations, and precisely because Compiègne was not put into his hands. The municipality, supported by a harsh and cruel captain, Guillaume de Flavy, who commanded the fortress, continued to turn a deaf ear to all the injunctions of Charles VII, of the Count of Clermont, and Regnauld de Chartres. And now Jeanne has come to support him in his resistance.

The unfortunate sortie in which the Maid, the victim of her own boldness, was captured by the Burgundians, takes place on the 23rd May 1430. Just as the brave child was always seen in the forefront when the charge was sounded, she wanted to remain last to cover the retreat of her company. It is a Burgundian writer, and one who was on the scene, Monstrelet, who will show us the young *chef de guerre* in the last moments of her admirable military career:

"These French, seeing their enemies increasing in great numbers, retired in front of the town, the Maid always with them at the back, making great efforts to support her men and lead them off without loss." She was the vigilant leader up to the last moment, and even when her life was in peril, thinking only of the most favourable way of retreat for her soldiers. Thus, shouting, fighting, jostling one another, French, English, and Burgundians arrived at the head of the bridge over the town

THE MIDDLE AGES

moat. Guillaume de Flavy, who was in command of Compiègne, saw the fortress threatened by the tide of enemies—more than two thousand men—says Monstrelet. He ordered the drawbridge to be raised. Jeanne was lost.

A human clutch grasps the caparison of her horse, pulls the beast by the bridle, pulls Jeanne herself by the lappets of her cape of gold. She was defending herself with great swordstrokes when a Picard archer, climbing on her horse's croup, seized her round the body and rolled with her on the trampled grass. The prisoner was conducted to the quarters of the Burgundian leader, Jean de Luxemburg. Jean de Luxemburg sold her to the English.

There followed captivity and her trial at Rouen, the eternal shame of those who were consumed with fury against the sublime child. The University of Paris obstinately dishonoured itself in the matter, and it required some centuries to recover from the opprobrium which it brought upon itself. There could be nothing finer than the description of the process of condemnation. It is the highest epic, the most touching drama. Beside the replies of Jeanne to her judges, what are the verses of Homer or the tragedies of Shakespeare? There is nothing in the literature of all time, except one work alone, to compare with these interrogations of a country child morally tortured by prelates and theologians, and that is the Gospels. The same spirit inspires both, the genius of the people—open, candid, intelligent, simple, and honest in face of the Pharisees.

On the 29th May 1431, in the chapel of the old castle of Rouen, Jeanne, the good Maid of Lorraine, was declared by Churchmen to be a relapsed heretic. On the morning of the next day, Wednesday, 30th May, the Dominican Martin Ladvenic came to inform her that she would be burned. At this moment the Maid shuddered with anguish. " My body, clean and whole, which has never been corrupted, will be burned and reduced to ashes. I call God, the great Judge, to witness the wrongs and injuries which are done to me ! "

She asked to be dressed, to go to her execution, in a long chemise. The stake had been erected at Rouen in the old market-place. An inscription was fastened to it bearing these words: "Jeanne who had herself called the Maid, a liar, dangerous, an abuser of the people, sorceress, superstitious, a blasphemer of God, presumptuous, causing injury to the faith of Jesus Christ, a boaster, an idolatress, cruel, dissolute, an invoker of devils, an apostate, schismatic and heretic."

In her long chemise she advanced on the condemned cart, a pointed paper mitre on her head bearing the inscription:

"Heretic, relapsed, apostate, idolatress."

They preached her yet another sermon in the old market-place.

It is impossible to imagine the number of sermons which the Churchmen, who sent her to her doom, preached to this poor child, in her last days. Then the horrible Cauchon—a very appropriate name for this person, but with a fault of spelling (*cochon*, pig)—read the sentence. Some of the English found the ceremony too long drawn out. The prelates were growing weary. The English cried to the Bishop of Beauvais, "Are you going to make us dine here?" Then the Churchmen who had given Jeanne to death drew back. The executioner set fire to the wood. Jeanne asked for a cross. An English soldier made one for her from two bits of wood, which he tied together: Jeanne took it and pressed it against her heart.

The majority of the spectators wept, overcome by the pious courage of the martyr, and the very English burst into sobs. Some of these executioners shuddered with remorse. The flames rose round the Maid, surrounding her with a glory more radiant than that of the saints, and the name of Jesus, which she repeated confidently, still fluttered on her lips at the moment when she left a world too wicked and too stupid for her ideal beauty.

Charles the Victorious.
The capture of Jeanne d'Arc had not brought luck to the Anglo-Burgundians before Compiègne. They had to raise the siege (28th October 1430), abandoning material and artillery, "which was the thing they felt and regretted most." This check, inflicted on the armies of Henry VI and Philip the Good, produced a great sensation from Noyon to Beauvais and from Soissons to Reims. On all sides the Anglo-Burgundians are tracked down and

THE MIDDLE AGES

driven from their haunts. Indeed, from this moment the English cause seems lost in France. The energy and courage of the regent, John of Lancaster, Duke of Bedford, alone prolonged their power.

We come now to the Treaty of Arras, in which the reconciliation of the Houses of France and Burgundy will be sealed. In the matter of this reconciliation so many hands and so many hearts had busied themselves—Jeanne d'Arc, Colette de Corbie, and even the Fathers of the Council of Basle. Jouvenel des Ursins rightly said:

"According to my poor opinion, I think disputes should be more widely condemned as being the cause of the kingdom's ruin."

Olivier de la Marche has noted in touching terms the reasons which determined Philip the Good to appease his resentment at the foot of the French throne:

"And on the part of the good Duke Philip it seems that what made him give in easily was his regard for the salvation of the realm of France, for the noble blood from which he had sprung and which ran in his veins, and for the great benefits which he had received through his predecessors from the royal House. These three things, which are all one, made him forget the offence (the assassination of his father, John the Fearless).

"Secondly, the scanty affinity and liking he had for the English; and thirdly, his honour and virtue, for always throughout his life, however much offended, irritated, or piqued he might be on various occasions, he stretched out a hand efficiently and powerfully to support, maintain, and protect the royal Majesty of France, and lived and died noble and wholly French in blood, heart, and will."

The people of Arras, seeing the friendship so marvellously established between the two princes, Charles VII and Philip the Good, wept for joy at it. Dances and songs were organized spontaneously in the streets; but in England the consternation was so great that it gave rise to disturbances in various directions. Historians say that the illustrious Duke of Bedford died of grief from it (13th September 1435). Everywhere in France the English are outflanked. On the 13th April 1436 the Constable de Richemond entered Paris, and the University of Paris, with a complete change from its attitude in the trial of Jeanne d'Arc, humbly begged Charles VII to return to his good town. In the district of Caux and other places in Normandy the English had had the idea of arming the peasants: these arms were turned against them.

The French, under the sting of resentment, in thinking of all that the English had made them suffer, and for so long, went sometimes beyond bounds in their vengeance: " On the 25th day of September 1441 the men-at-arms led out the prisoners (English) whom they had brought to Paris after the taking of Pontoise to their fortresses, in a very pitiful condition, for they led them forth to the bread of sorrow, coupled two and two with very strong halters, just as dogs are led to the chase, themselves mounted on great horses, which went very swiftly; and the prisoners were without cloaks and bareheaded, each clothed in a wretched rag, all without hose, and the greater number without shoes; in short, everything had been taken from them, even to the breeches; . . . and all who could not pay ransom they led to the Grève, near the Port-au-Foin, and they tied their hands and feet, and there they killed them in sight of all the people. . . ."

Thomas Basin has shown admirably how, after the Treaty of Arras, the divisions between Frenchmen having been appeased, the Englishman became to all the common enemy. " The French and Normans, who were still under the English domination, burned with a more and more bitter hatred against the English. They realized that their suzerainty would mean for them a source of continual misery. They realized that those who had for twenty years afflicted them with constant war, were not seeking the good of the country or the repose of their subjects, but that there burned within them an innate and inveterate hatred of the French nation which they wished to overwhelm with trouble and misery even to its extermination, so that, between French and English, who reciprocally scorned each other, hatred and defiance went on increasing." Thomas Basin says again: " When peace was made between French and Burgundians the French had no longer any one but the English to fight, which ought to assure them an easy victory, if only they could organize their armies."

THE MIDDLE AGES

The two last important battles of the Hundred Years War were those of Formigny (15th April 1450) and of Castillon (17th July 1453). In the first of the two conflicts, the troops of Charles VII were commanded by the Count of Clermont. The English lost the battle, says Jean de Bueil, through a false manœuvre. " When they saw the French in greater numbers than they expected, they decided to take a more advantageous position, and in going, they fell into disorder and so were defeated." At Formigny the French chivalry took its revenge for its former defeats, for it was to the charges of the French cavalry placed on the two wings and put into action at the opportune time that the victory was due. For the first time in a great battle the English were more numerous than the French. The victory of the Count of Clermont made a great stir. Through it the English lost all spirit and heart.

At Castillon (17th July 1453), Jean de Bueil was one of the two leaders of the French army. The other was Jacques de Chabannes, one of the last companions of Jeanne d'Arc. The English were commanded by the illustrious Talbot. As at Formigny they were in greater numbers, twice as many as their adversaries; but since Creçy, Poitiers, and Agincourt the rôles were reversed: the superiority in organization, and above all in the new arm, the artillery, was on the side of the French. At each volley of one of the cannons of M. Girault five or six English were killed. The army of Henry VI suffered a crushing defeat. Old Talbot, the last survivor of the great battles, was among the dead. The few towns of Guienne in which the red crosses still held sway capitulated, Bordeaux on the 17th October (1453). The English had only Calais left in France: the fine port which was not to be reconquered until the sixteenth century by the great Duke of Guise.

In these last and so rapid successes won by the French a large place should be given, as we have just said, to the artillery. The progress made by it was due, chiefly, to the activity of a man of genius, Jean Bureau: "A Parisian," says Thomas Basin, " of plebeian family, small in stature but great in intrepidity and thought. He furnished the fortresses held by the French with an artillery which rendered them impregnable." Besieged in Caen, the English had concentrated there consider-

THE HUNDRED YEARS WAR

able means of defence; but the French put into action a bombardment of such power (for the period) that the besieged were terrified and capitulated at the first volley (1st July 1450). One is reminded of the effects of the Boche 420 in the first days of the late war. At the Siege of Cherbourg the French installed their pieces of artillery on the shore at low tide. They knew how to protect them so that the sea did not damage them when it covered them, and hardly had the tide gone out than the firing began again in the finest manner. The fortress was reduced in less than a month.

The date 1453 is generally considered as ending the Hundred Years War; but it is not until the 3rd November 1492 that the Treaty of Etaples will officially put an end to the great conflict. We have said that this war really began in 1296. The struggle had lasted nearly two centuries.

Charles VII, the little King sickly and stunted, frail and ethereal, timid and reserved, showed himself an admirable organizer. He was small and slender in appearance, with delicate and agreeable features. He dressed with minute care, generally in green. When he put on one of the short tunics which reached only to the thighs, in his tight hose after the fashion of the time, his bandy legs and crooked knees showed plainly. There is much talk of the influence exercised on him in the second part of his reign by Agnes Sorel, Mademoiselle de Beauté, as she was called from the domaine of Beauté-sur-Marne, which Charles VII had given her. As a matter of fact, her beauty was held in high esteem by contemporaries, even if, to our taste, her potato-like nose does not seem very charming. "She was one of the most beautiful women I ever saw," writes Olivier de la Marche, "and did, in her position, much good to the kingdom of France. She put forward to the King's notice young soldiers and noble companions by whom the King was afterwards well served." Her reign was indeed of short duration. She only became the King's friend in 1444, and she died at Jumièges on the 9th February 1450.

A Flemish Chronicler, George Chastellain, will write a fine eulogy of Charles VII: "He, with his kingdom all desolate, vexed and destroyed, like a ship dismantled and demolished on all sides, ruined in its foundations, and in all its beauty and magnificence brought to ruin; without labour, without inhabitants, merchandise or justice, without rule or order, full of thieves and brigands, of poverty and anxiety, violence and exactions, full of tyranny and inhumanity, and with even its royal throne lying low, overthrown, a footstool for men's feet for the English to trample on and plunderers to wipe their feet upon, he, with great labour, restored it to freedom and prosperity."

The end of the Hundred Years War found the old feudality destroyed. It is ruined. The great feudal proprietor has disappeared. The small rural Nobility draws nearer to the peasants: it is to produce those famous country gentlemen who will be one of the elements of the strength, wealth, and prosperity of our country. In the towns the higher burgesses will be recast. They also will draw nearer to the working class and will give birth to the Renaissance. Trade and industry are to receive at the end of the reign of Charles VII an unheard-of impetus. The French flag will float above all others in the ports of the Levant. The great figure of the merchant Jacques Cœur remains as a brilliant witness thereof. The "little people of the King's Council" who replace the great lords and high dignitaries of former days will have greatly contributed to this renewal by the reform of military and financial administration, of judicial organization, and even of the Church itself. A special mention is due to Pierre d'Oriole, who succeeded Jean de Bar on the 4th October 1453 as General of Finance. Pierre d'Oriole will extend his active and beneficent intelligence over the last nine years of the reign of Charles VII and the reign of Louis XI.

Philippe de Comines points out that Charles VII was the first King of France to levy taxes regularly without the grant of the States-General. It is true that the summoning of these latter had become at the same time more and more difficult and illusory. When Charles VII had called together the States-General at Chinon (September 1428) the deputies of Languedoc came only to complain of having been summoned, those of Rouergue came but not to sit, and others did not come at all. "Charles VII," writes Jean de Bueil, "very soon had his artillery set up, and was a man always on his

THE HUNDRED YEARS WAR

guard; and whatever he might have to do, he never laid a great subsidy on the people. He had always an ordinary tax which he collected every year from his subjects, and put in safe keeping, so that he had recourse to it at need without demanding anything else from them. He was well paid in what was due to him, and no one dared to cheat him or make default of payment. He also kept strict justice, and no one dared break his statutes and ordinances, or do wrong to one another." It is thus that good reigns are made.

SOURCES.—*Les Grands traités de la Guerre de Cent ans*, ed. E. Cosneau, 1889; *L'Ordonnance Carbochienne*, ed. Alf. Coville, 1891; Le Père H. Denifle, *La Guerre de Cent ans et la désolation des églises*, 1899; *Continuateurs de G. de Nangis*, ed. H. Geraud, 1848—the part drawn up by J. de Venette in a democratic spirit is extremely remarkable; *Les Grandes Chroniques*, ed. Delachenal, 1910–20, 4 vols.—a work no less remarkable than the preceding and which can be pitted against it, having been drawn up under the inspiration of Charles V; *Journal d'un bourgeois de Paris, 1405–49*, ed. Al. Tueley, 1881—very vivid and interesting; Christine de Pisan, *Le Livre des faits et bonnes mœurs du sage roi Charles V*, various editions; *Chronicles of Froissart et of Jean le Bel*, various editions; *Chronique des quatre premiers Valois*, ed. Siméon Luce, 1862; *Chronique du Mt. St. Michel (1348–1468)*, ed. Siméon Luce, 1879; J. de Bueil, *Le Jouvencel*, ed. Favre and Lecestre, 1887–89, 2 vols.; Cuvelier, *Chron.* (in rhyme) *de Bertrand du Guesclin*, ed. Charrière, 1839; *Chron. d'Antonio Marosini*, ed. Germ. Lefèvre-Pontalis and Leon Dorez, 1899–1902, 3 vols.; *Procès de condamnation et rehabilitation de Jeanne d'Arc*, ed. J. Quicherat, 1861–69, 5 vols.; *Procès de condamnation de Jeanne d'Arc*, ed. Pierre Champion, 1921; *Histoire de Thomas Basin*, ed. Quicherat, 1833–49, 4 vols.

HISTORICAL WORKS.—A. Coville, "Les Premiers Valois et la Guerre de Cent Ans," in the *Histoire de France*, ed. E. Lavisse, iv. 1902; Ch. Petit-Dutaillis, "Charles VII," "Louis XI," *ibid.* iv. 1902; (Maxime Petit), *Histoire de France Illustrée* (Larousse), without date, 4to—we owe a great deal to these three works; J. d'Auriac, *La Veritable Jeanne d'Arc*, 1920; G. du Fresne de Beaucourt, *Histoire de Charles VII*, 1881–91, 6 vols.; Marcellin Boudet, *La Jacquerie des Tuchiens*, 1895; Pierre Champion, *Guillaume de Flavy*, 1906; Pierre Champion, *Charles d'Orleans*, 1911; Cherest. *L'Archiprêtre*, 1879; Alf. Coville, *Recherches sur la-misère en Normandie au temps de Charles VI*, 1886; Alf. Coville, *Les Cabochiens et l'ordonnance de 1413*, 1888; R. Delachenal, *Histoire de Charles V*, 1900, 2 vols.; G. Guigne, *Les tard-Venus en Lyonnais*, 1886; Jarry, *Vie Politique de Louis d'Orleans*, 1886; Germ. Lefèvre-Pontalis, *La guerre de Partisans dans la Haute-Normandie (1424–29)*, Bibliothèque de l'Ecole des Chartes, 1896; Ch. Lénient, *La*

THE MIDDLE AGES

Poesie patriotique en France au Moyen Age, 1891 ; Siméon Luce, *Histoire de la Jacquerie*, 2nd ed., 1895; Siméon Luce, *Histoire de Bertrand du Guesclin et de son époque*, 2nd ed., 1882 ; Siméon Luce, *Jeanne d'Arc à Domrémy*, 1886 ; Moisant, *Le Prince Noir en Aquitaine*, 1894 ; Leon Mirot, *Les Insurrections urbaines au début du règne de Charles VI*, 1905 ; H. Moranville, *Etude sur la vie de Jean le Mercier*, 1888 ; F. T. Perrens, *Etienne Marcel*, 1860 ; G. Picot, *Histoire des Etats Généraux*, 2nd ed., 1888 ; J. Quicherat, *Rodrigue de Villedrando*, 1879 ; Marcel Thibault, *Isabeau de Bavière*, 1903 ; Noël Valois, *Le Conseil du Roi aux XIVe, XVe, et XVIe siècles*, 1888 ; Noël Valois, *La France et le Grand Schisme d'Occident*, 1896–1902, 4 vols.

CHAPTER XX

A MODERN KING: LOUIS XI

Louis XI, Dauphin. His hostility against his father. The League of the Public Weal. Charles the Bold, Duke of Burgundy. The War of the Two Roses in England. Louis XI and the *Liègois*. The Duke de Berry. Nesle and Beauvais. Jeanne Hachette (1472). The ambitions of Charles the Bold. His struggle against the Swiss: Grandson and Morat (2nd March and 22nd June 1476). His death before Nancy (5th January 1477). The heritage of the last Duke of Burgundy. The administrative work of Louis XI. His character. His death at Plessis-lès-Tours (31st August 1483).

LOUIS XI, the son of Charles VII, born at Bourges on the 3rd July 1423, was twenty-eight years old when he succeeded his father (22nd July 1461). At the end of their life, father and son were on the worst possible terms with each other. In his lordship of Dauphiné, which he held as Dauphin of France, Louis had tried to organize a kind of independent state on the model of the Duchy of Burgundy: so much so that his father had sent troops against him. Then Louis had taken refuge with the great Duke of Burgundy, Philip the Good, who welcomed him in princely fashion, and gave him a pension of £30,000. And Charles VII remarked, in speaking of his cousin of Burgundy:

" He receives in his house a fox which will eat all his hens."

At the end of his life Charles VII took food only with the greatest circumspection, persuaded that his son and heir was trying to poison him.

" In my opinion," remarks Comines, " the trouble which he (Louis XI) had in his youth, when he was a fugitive from his father and was under the Duke of Burgundy, where he was for six years (dating from 1456), benefited him very greatly, for he was forced to make himself agreeable to those of whom he had need, and this advantage—which is no small one—adversity taught him."

One of the first acts of the new King was to dismiss the chief ministers and servants of his father, from hatred of the policy of which they had been the inspirers or the instruments. Two of them, Pierre de Brézé and Antoine de Chabannes, were so frightened by his threats that they fled. After this, Louis XI tried to win back the majority of them to co-operate with him, being moved to do them justice and because his policy, whatever there was of it, was the continuation of that of his predecessor. Olivier de la Marche and Thomas Basin have painted the temper of Louis XI, suspicious, changeable. He attached to himself, by means of money, the assistance which seemed desirable, then he suddenly dismissed his most important auxiliaries on a suspicion, an idea, a whim, the motive of which our writers, to tell the truth, have rarely known. Louis XI, that politician wary, cold, and calculating, profoundly meditating for long periods on his plans, was of an impulsive temperament, naturally inclined to sudden, bold, risky decisions. His was a character strange and surprising, made up of contradictions, at the same time avaricious and liberal, dressing himself in so mean a way as to surprise and scandalize his subjects, and spending on birds and dogs for hunting, on building and feasting, excessive sums. This man, reserved, cautious, suspicious, and hypocritical, was extremely lively and fond of gossip. He would hardly let ambassadors and deputies admitted to his presence speak. He spoke at length in a guttural fashion, and without order or apparent logic : but in a language pure and polished, and his discourse did not fail to charm by the sound of his voice, " so sweet that it lulled one like the sirens."

By the Treaty of Arras, which had brought about the reconciliation of the Houses of France and Burgundy, the towns of the Somme had been ceded to Philip the Good. They formed a line of important fortresses : their master dominated the Northern provinces. The treaty had stipulated for the possibility of redeeming them for 400,000 pounds. Louis XI at once set his mind to the recovery of these places : Abbeville, Amiens, Péronne, and St. Quentin. He succeeded by emptying his treasury and levying new taxes (September–October 1463).

A MODERN KING: LOUIS XI

Louis XI followed, with regard to the Count of Charolais, the son of Philip the Good—the prince who was very soon to be the Duke of Burgundy, Charles the Bold—a policy which was not without analogy with that which Philip the Good had followed towards himself when he was Dauphin. He paid him a pension of 36,000 pounds and made him his lieutenant in Normandy; but the pension was not paid regularly, and the redemption of the towns of the Somme caused the breach. The Count of Charolais will be one of the principal authors of the famous League of the Public Weal, an effort of decaying feudalism to seize once more the government of the kingdom from which events were daily removing it farther. "And this war was called *the Public Weal* (*le Bien public*), writes Comines, " because it was begun under colour of saying that it was for the public welfare." It was a struggle for the franchises of the various provinces under the direction of the great seigniorial houses. The Duke of Brittany complained that Louis XI wished to impose on the Breton Parlement the summons to the Parlement of Paris. " The League of the Public Weal," observes Viollet-le-Duc, " marked the last effort of the feudal aristocracy to seize again its ancient power. At this period many lords furnished their castles with new defences suited to artillery. These defensive works chiefly consisted of external works, big thick towers pierced with embrasures to hold cannons, platforms, or bulwarks commanding the outworks."

In reality, this *Public Weal* consisted, as the Duke of Nemours declared cynically enough, in demanding from the King " big pensions for the Nobles," at the head of whom was Louis' own brother, Charles, Duke of Berry; then came the Count of Charolais, the Dukes of Brittany, Lorraine, and Bourbon, the Counts of Armagnac and St. Pol, and the illustrious Bastard of Orleans.

The rival armies met on the 16th July 1465 before Montlhéry. Louis XI commanded in person the "Royalists" (*royaux*); Charles the Bold was at the head of the Confederates.

"The two armies being drawn up in face of each other, several volleys were fired from the cannons, killing some men on both sides. No one wanted to fight any more, and though our band was bigger than that of the King, at the same time his presence (the King's) was a great thing, and the good words he

THE MIDDLE AGES

spoke to the soldiers; and I believe that even if he had been alone all would have fled from him." We owe this picture to the pen of Comines, who was in the ranks of the Confederates. Louis XI, seeing that the action was indecisive, hastened to re-enter Paris so as to make sure of the great town, leaving his young adversary, Charles the Bold, the vain satisfaction of lying on the field of battle.

Comines again points out how much this apparent success, won by a General-in-Chief of thirty-two years, afterwards exercised on his life a malign influence. "My lord of Charolais," writes Comines, "remained on the field, very joyful, judging the glory to be his, which since has cost him very dear; for never since has he taken the opinion of any one, but only his own; and before that day he was very little inclined for war, and liked nothing belonging to it, but after that he changed his mind, for he continued in it until his death."

For the moment the League of the Public Weal ended in the Treaty of Conflans (November 1465). Louis XI restored the towns of the Somme, and one of the members of the League, particularly attached to the Count of Charolais, Louis, Count of St. Pol, was made Constable of France.

Philip the Good, Duke of Burgundy, died at Bruges on the 15th June 1467. He had proved himself an admirable prince, liberal and magnificent, of a large political sense and supreme ability. He did much harm to the French kingdom in his desire to avenge the death of his father, John the Fearless; but he returned to the French cause when he deemed his resentment sufficiently satisfied. It is difficult to picture the pomp and magnificence with which he had made the Court of Dijon resplendent. He died at the age of seventy-one, the wealthiest prince in Europe, not excepting any of the crowned heads, leaving his Duchy in a condition of incomparable prosperity.

The contrast established by Thomas Basin between the lands of the country of France, which the Hundred Years War ruined, with those subject to the Duke of Burgundy, which it spared, is poignant.

"It is unnecessary to point out to the traveller the boundary at which one passes from the Burgundian suzerainty on to

A MODERN KING: LOUIS XI

French territory. Hardly have you set foot in the kingdom before the aspect of the country becomes sordid and rough : uncultivated fields, briars, thorns, and brushwood ; some few field workers, emaciated and bloodless, covered with rags ; in the towns and villages numerous ruins and empty dwellings, and in those which are inhabited, poor and insufficient furniture, a picture of wretchedness, depression, and servitude ; but now behold us under the Burgundian government : everything is flourishing, resplendent, growing ; there are numerous towns and fortresses ; the population is large, the houses are varied and of splendid appearance, full of fine furnishings ; the fields are cultivated, the fences in a good state ; the people are well dressed and smiling."

The Duke of Burgundy required only small contributions from his subjects. He had armies well equipped and trained, but not large. Through his situation between Flanders, Lorraine, Germany, and Italy, through the richness of his soil and the magnificence of his wines, the trade of the country was of the most prosperous. " The Burgundians," writes Comines, " were overwhelmed with riches and in a condition of great repose ; . . . the expenses and clothes of men and women great and superfluous ; the banquets greater and more lavish than in any other place ; the baths and other festivities with women . . ." and this in all classes of society.

Happily for France, England in her turn was to become acquainted with the bloody quarrels from which the kingdom of the fleur-de-lis had suffered so much during the reign of Charles VI and the first part of the reign of Charles VII. In her turn England was divided into two enemy camps—that of the red rose and that of the white, the side of the House of Lancaster and that of the House of York. " And there is no doubt," says Comines, " that if England had been in her former state, that this kingdom of France would have had many fights."

During the War of the Public Weal, Louis XI had fomented a revolt of the people of Liège. The treaty of alliance between the French King and the warlike burgesses was concluded on the 17th June 1465. The prince-bishop of Liège, against whom the town had revolted, was the nephew of Philip the

THE MIDDLE AGES

Good. Since then the war between the Duke of Burgundy and his good town had smouldered with alternating periods of quiet, and violent outbreaks. The men of Liège were beaten in the end. On the 17th November 1467, Charles the Bold entered the town and ordered the destruction of the ramparts.

Louis, however, who relied more on his diplomatic ability than on the uncertain accidents of the war, had demanded an interview with Charles the Bold so as to establish by a common agreement the bases of a definite peace. Charles received the King in his castle of Peronne. The parleys were taking their course when Charles heard that Liège had revolted again, doubtless at the instigation of the French King and by means of his subsidies. He fell into a terrible rage. He had the King in his hands, and Louis XI believed himself lost. It is told that the nearness of the tower in which Herbert de Vermandois had had Charles the Simple killed, made his flesh creep. But this much must in justice be said for him, that after having so imprudently allowed himself to be captured, he showed a brave face and was able to appease his terrible vassal—on the hardest conditions, it is true; the possession of the Somme towns was to be definitely confirmed to Charles the Bold; the Duke of Berry, a close ally of the Duke of Burgundy, was to receive as appanage Champagne and Brie, adjoining the Duchy of Burgundy; finally, Louis XI himself went to Liège to put down there, cheek by jowl with the Duke, the brave burgesses whom he himself had stirred up to revolt (14th October 1468). Louis XI had to be present at the merciless punishment of the town whose citizens welcomed him with cries of " Long live the King ! " (14th October 1468).

Louis XI had committed an imprudence ; Charles the Bold committed another. It is the eternal history of the Caudine Forks. Charles the Bold should either have destroyed the cunning King of France when he was at his mercy or behaved to him like a gentleman. Louis XI returned to Paris, sore, desiring only vengeance. He got the States of Tours to annul the Treaty of Peronne obtained by a trick ; he sent soldiers to occupy the Somme towns, St. Quentin, Amiens, Roye, and Montdidier ; his army beat the Burgundians at Buxy. Charles

A MODERN KING: LOUIS XI

the Bold, "much surprised," formed the second League of the Public Weal. The "surprise" of the Duke of Burgundy was increased by the agreement plotted between Louis XI and his brother Charles de Berry. The King of France had persuaded this latter to accept the remote Guienne in exchange for Champagne and Brie, which had been granted to him; his complicity could no longer be of the same use to Charles the Bold. Then the Duke of Berry dies at Bordeaux on the 24th May 1472. The Duke of Burgundy published a violent manifesto, declaring that Louis XI had poisoned his brother, a calumny which Thomas Basin and Olivier de la Marche echoed.

"On the news of the death of the Duke of Berry," writes Comines, "angrily, the said Duke (of Burgundy) set out and took the road towards Nesle in Vermandois; and he began an ugly and wicked device of war, which he had never used before: it was to have every place to which he came set on fire."

At Nesle the troops of Charles the Bold gave themselves up to frightful excesses. The soldiers cut off the hands of the people. In the church where women and children had taken refuge there was blood higher than one's shins. The next day the town was destroyed. The attack had come (12th June 1472) without warning. The people were living in the security of peace. Charles was immediately punished for it before Beauvais. Terrified at the fate which awaited them, the burgesses made a desperate resistance. The women seconded the men. There were feats of arms in which shone Jeanne Laisné, called Jeanne Hachette, from the little hatchet which she used to fell the Burgundian soldiers at the top of the ramparts (July 1472).

Charles the Bold conceived some outrageous plans. The state of magnificence and prosperity at which his House had arrived and his first military successes, which were exaggerated in his imagination, had turned his head. Olivier de la Marche, who lived in close intimacy with him and never speaks of him except with deference, writes on this subject: "He brewed more enterprises than several men's lives would have been sufficient to fulfil." There was always the plan of uniting his

THE MIDDLE AGES

dominions in Flanders and Artois with those in Burgundy, by the acquisition of Lorraine and Alsace. But his views did not end here. He wanted to form a great kingdom which should stretch from the Mediterranean to the North Sea and which would have made him the most powerful sovereign in Europe. He included in his plans the Rhine lands, Switzerland, Savoy, Dauphiné, and Provence, and on all sides he had begun an actively aggressive policy.

" As for the House of Savoy," writes Comines, " the aforesaid Duke (Charles the Bold) disposed of it as his own." The Duke of Milan was his ally. King René of Sicily (René of Anjou) was willing to put his land of Provence into his hands! From Sigismund, Archduke of Austria, he had obtained, for 50,000 pounds, the Landgraveship of Haute Alsace and the county of Ferrette. Duke Arnold of Gueldre abandoned his States to him. But in the Rhine lands and Switzerland Charles the Bold met with resistance. His ambitions did not end here. He had claims on the throne of England. On the 3rd November 1471, he declared before a notary that his mother, Isabella of Portugal, had declared herself the sole heir of Henry VI, and that she had transmitted her rights to him. His ambitious dreams extended to the Imperial Crown.

The Treaty of Arras had exempted Philip the Good, during his life, from the suzerainty of the French King, but Charles the Bold came under this again with its rights of appeal. The new Duke of Burgundy also planned to free himself from it. He established parliaments at Beaune and at Dôle, a court of appeal at Malines (23rd December 1473). Just as the English King had once thought he could do in Guienne, he forbade his subjects to appeal to the Court of Paris.

With surprising activity Charles the Bold operated on all points at once, with money, diplomacy, and arms. To give himself breathing space he concluded on the 13th September 1475 a nine years' truce with Louis XI, and delivered up to him the Constable of St. Pol, who had committed treason in his favour. Louis had the felonious Constable beheaded (19th December 1475). As to the dreams of Charles the Bold they were dashed to pieces against an obstacle he had scorned. In the two terrible battles of Grandson and Morat (22nd June

A MODERN KING: LOUIS XI

1476) the long Swiss pikes triumphed over the Burgundian bombs and spears.

"His grief at the loss of the first battle of Grandson was so great," writes Comines, "and troubled his spirits so much, that he fell into a serious illness. . . ."

From this time Charles the Bold lost that good sense which is so necessary to statesmen and with which he had never been provided in too great abundance. His fine alliances were broken off. René of Anjou was the first to draw near again to the King of France. "The King of Sicily arranged that his county of Provence should return to the King" (Jean de Roye).

Obstinate, headstrong, tenacious, Charles the Bold was always desirous of uniting by the conquest of the Duchy of Lorraine the two branches of his States, Flanders and Burgundy. The defeat of the Burgundians by the Swiss had brought about the return of René of Lorraine to his capital. On the 22nd October 1477 Charles the Bold came to lay siege to Nancy. With the money secretly provided for him by the French King, the Duke of Lorraine had levied an army of 12,000 Swiss, who marched to the relief of the fortress. It was the depth of winter; the plain lay white under a grey sky. Charles the Bold had for some time put all his confidence in a sort of condottiere, an Italian, Count Niccolo de Campobasso, whom the French chroniclers call Bobache. Charles the Bold advanced boldly against his enemies, although they were two or three times superior in number. The treason of Bobache, who abandoned his protector with his Italian contingent at the beginning of the engagement, completed the defeat. The plans of Charles the Bold foundered in the terrible disaster of Nancy (5th January 1477), amidst the ice and the cold. "On the Tuesday (7th January) following the said battle, a page pointed out plainly the Duke of Burgundy dead and quite naked, and round him 1400 men quite naked, quite far enough away from one another. And the aforesaid Duke of Burgundy had had a blow from the kind of weapon known as a halberd, from the side of the middle of the head above the ear as far as the teeth, a blow of a pike across the thighs, and another in the anus" (Jean de Roye).

THE MIDDLE AGES

The dream of the Grand Dukes of the West, the reconstitution of the ancient kingdom of Austrasia between France and "the Germans," was dead. In the region of the arts at least, by the fusion of the French, Flemish, Rhenish, and Italian elements, the magnificent House of Burgundy, founded by Philip the Bold and destroyed by Charles the Bold, will have left lasting traces.

Speaking of Charles the Bold, Bobache the traitor said correctly enough to the Duke of Brittany, whose relative he pretended to be and who had received him:

" He was cruel and inhuman, and in all his enterprises he had no success and only lost time, men, and lands by his foolish obstinacy." The fate of Charles the Bold no doubt inspired Louis XI with his favourite motto: " When pride rides before, shame and loss follow close."

In virtue of the custom which gave back to the French Crown the appanages which it had granted when the holder died without a male heir, the Duchy of Burgundy fell into the hands of Louis XI, for Charles the Bold left only a daughter, Marie of Burgundy. On the 1st February 1478 the royal army entered Dijon.

Louis XI would have liked indeed to lay hands on the whole heritage of Charles the Bold, for the last Duke of Burgundy owned the Low Countries, Artois, and Franche-Comté; but he came up against the opposition of the English joined with the Flemish. The sinister beginnings of the Hundred Years War were revolved in his mind. Marie of Burgundy was twenty years old. Louis XI at first thought of betrothing her to his son, the Dauphin, who was eight. The plan was not impossible, and flattered the young girl; but Louis XI gave it up. He remembered the way in which he himself, as Dauphin, had behaved towards his father, Charles VII, and fearing that his son might one day behave in the same way towards him, he was unwilling to give him so much power. This moment is one of the most serious in our history. Comines, who had attached himself to Louis XI, speaks of it with due care and attention. Deceiving himself, and without exposing the real motive which decided him, the King declared that he was unwilling to reconstitute so large a State as the old Duchy of

A MODERN KING: LOUIS XI

Burgundy with its dependencies, but on the contrary to divide its different parts among various Powers.

"He was inclined," says Comines, "to undo and destroy this House, and to share its lordships among various people: and he named those to whom he intended to give the counties, such as Namur and Hainault, which are situated near him! With the other great tracts such as Brabant and Holland he wanted to win some German lords, who should be his friends and help him to execute his will. He was pleased to tell me all these things, because, formerly, I had advised him in the other direction, described above (the betrothal of Mary of Burgundy and the Dauphin), and he wanted me to hear his reasons and why he did not follow my advice, and that this plan was more useful for his kingdom, which had suffered much through the greatness of the House of Burgundy and the great lordships which it possessed."

Comines, with his fine political insight, was not convinced; but he made no more objections, impressed by the personality of Louis XI. "At the same time," he said, "the judgment of our good King was so great that neither I nor any other of the company would have been able to see so clearly in these matters as he did himself. For he was without doubt one of the wisest and subtlest of princes. . . ."

However, Comines was right. He was to show it. "In these great matters God disposes the hearts of Kings. . . . If it had been His pleasure that our King should have continued the plan which he had himself advised before the death of the Duke of Burgundy (the marriage of the Dauphin with Marie of Burgundy), the wars which have taken place since, and those which are still going on, would not have been. . . . I say these things at length to show that, in the beginning, when one wishes to embark on so great an undertaking, that one should consult and debate well, in order to choose the better part. I do not mean to blame our King, by saying that he had been wanting in this matter, for, perhaps, others who knew and heard more than I were then of his opinion, however little debate there was, there or elsewhere, on the said subject."

For Louis XI, differing in this from all his predecessors

THE MIDDLE AGES

on the French throne, never acted except as he pleased, without consulting those round him. " The King's horse," said Jacques de Brézé, " carries his whole council."

Troubled by his conscience, Louis XI fell, in this matter, into the greatest political fault that a French King had committed since the divorce of Louis VII from Eleanor of Aquitaine.

On the 18th August 1477, at Ghent, Marie of Burgundy married Maximilian of Austria, son of the German Emperor, and himself future German Emperor, bringing him his rights over Flanders, Brabant, and Hainault. From their union will spring Philip the Fair, Archduke of Austria, who after having married Joanna of Aragon, the daughter of Ferdinand of Castile, will ascend the Spanish throne, after the death of his mother-in-law, and will have a son, Charles V. Two centuries and a half of efforts, the blood of thousands upon thousands of Frenchmen will painfully redeem the mistake committed in 1477 by the ablest and most cunning of our kings. Perhaps even the consequences of this fault still weigh upon us to-day.

The reunion of the Duchy of Burgundy worked without any great difficulty. " On all the roads one met Burgundian lords leading the soldiers of the King "; but if the nobles and the rich burgesses welcomed cordially the banners of the fleur-de-lis it was not the same with the common people, who remained attached to their old Dukes. The old struggle between Burgundians and Armagnacs is continued. As England is out of the game, it is in the House of Austria that the proletariat seeks support. There were some risings. The president of the Burgundian Parlement was murdered, and at Dijon the royal banner thrown down from the tower over which it waved. The great men of the town brought back the people of Dijon to a sense of their duty. " By your good means," writes Louis XI to them, " you have found a way to reduce the town to our obedience." Just the same in Franche-Comté, into which Louis XI had sent forward his troops, the higher burgesses incline towards France, while the artisans wish to resist the King's arms. These facts dominate the policy of Louis XI towards the French towns in which he was generally favourable to the administration of the notables. The roots of this

A MODERN KING: LOUIS XI

policy went back two centuries. But elsewhere also he tried to give to this governing class a wider basis by declaring all possessors of fiefs to be noble. We have already spoken of those invaluable country gentlemen who are to be one of the most active elements in the Renaissance. And in the towns also Louis XI raised to the Nobility a burgess aristocracy which, too, in the Renaissance, will be the inspiration of the fine artistic and commercial expansion.

Tocqueville has pointed out: "Louis XI destroyed all the popular and democratic character of the towns, and kept their government in a small number of families attached to his reform and bound to his power by immense benefits." This policy was a legacy to Louis XI from his predecessors, who had never ceased to support the Patricians in the towns, for it was round the Patricians that were grouped the supporters of the fleur-de-lis.

We have already spoken of the predominance in the councils of Charles VII of "small folk." Those who are to serve as advisers to Louis XI will be of still humbler origin. There was Tristan the Hermit, who had plied the trade of executioner and whom his master made Provost of the Marshalls of France. The Englishman, Robert Neville, however, gave it as his judgment that Tristan was "the most diligent, quick, and subtle mind in the kingdom." Then there was Olivier the Bad, *valet de chambre* and barber to the King. Louis XI ennobled him and changed his name to Olivier le Daim. He was of Flemish origin, from the district near Ghent. Louis XI employed him in diplomatic missions to his native country. He had very great confidence in him. He gave him considerable possessions—the ponds of Meulan, the woods of Sénart; but after the King's death the poor fellow was hanged (24th May 1484). Finally, there was his doctor, Jacques Coitiers, who had a hold on him through the morbid fear the King had of death. All these people, and others of still less importance, were gorged by Louis XI with goods and honours; but they had to give him blind submission. "It was great servitude to be among his suite," says Chastellain.

The financial administration of Louis XI was remarkable, and controlled by men of rare worth, Pierre d'Oriole and

THE MIDDLE AGES

Etienne Chevalier. In this he continued the work of his father. The tax (*taille*), it must be said, was more than doubled ; but the regularity and accuracy of its collection made it lighter ; moreover, the feudal charges which had weighed on the people in previous reigns, were decreased ; and commercial prosperity, partly thanks to the King, took a considerable impetus. Louis XI decreed that the Nobility could devote itself to commerce without depreciation. He was the first King to introduce systematically commercial clauses in the treaties, agreements, or truces which he was called upon to conclude. He entrusted his representatives in foreign countries with commercial missions, and wanted to organize in London, in 1470, an exhibition of the best products of French industry, so " that the inhabitants of the aforesaid kingdom should know that the French merchants were able to provide for them, like the other nations." He favoured the industries connected with art and luxury : lace, tapestries, earthenware. It is to Louis XI that Lyons owes its magnificent silk industry, which was to bring it later such honour and wealth. And we may add that this admirable foundation was imposed on the people of Lyons against their will, through the intelligent persistence of the King.

Louis XI encouraged the beginnings of printing.

He gave a great impulse to agriculture. Waste and untilled ground were divided on his initiative among labourers and lords on condition that they were cultivated.

Louis XI created the postal service in France by letters dated from Lucheux (Somme) (the 19th June 1464). The relays for the horses succeeded each other at distances of four leagues.

Finally, in the military sphere, Louis XI developed further his father's great reforms. His attention was especially directed to the artillery. It has been said that the artillery of Louis XI would have withstood, if the need had arisen, that of all the other Powers of Europe united. Modest and poor in his garments, made of common cloth, black or grey, he had them repaired and new sleeves put in his doublet when they were worn at the elbows. Hiding in his corners, shunning appearing in public and all show, so much so that the streets

A MODERN KING: LOUIS XI

leading off the main streets of the towns through which he passed were barricaded to prevent his slipping away from the receptions organized in his honour; surrounded by nobodies and sometimes by vulgar scoundrels; drinking in taverns, with elbows on the table side by side with common companions, Louis XI showed himself none the less a great prince by the justice of his views in the majority of circumstances, by his liberalities which he knew how to scatter at the opportune moment, and by the power to which he brought the monarchy. Europe considered him the first monarch of his day, and even in Italy, princes and republics called on him to arbitrate in their disputes.

It has been said of Louis XI that he was cruel, and we cannot deny it when we remember the horrible prisons, the " King's little girls " (*Fillettes du roi*), in which he kept shut up those who betrayed him; but the Burgundian Molinet acknowledged that he would have spent without hesitation 10,000 crowns to save the life of a single one of his archers—he was careful of the lives of his men and anxious for their comfort.

Comines has given us a description of the *Fillettes du roi*, the more exact as he was himself kept for a period of eight months in one during the reign of Charles VIII. " It is true that he (Louis XI) had made some rigorous prisons, like iron cages, and others of wood covered with sheets of iron, and within with terrible ironwork, some eight feet wide (two and a half metres) and a foot more than the height of a man. The first who gave him the idea was the Bishop of Verdun (Guillaume de Haraucourt), who was straightway put into the first which was made, and lay there fourteen years. Many since have cursed him, and among them myself, who have had a taste of it (in the castle of Loches) under the present King (Charles VIII) for eight months."

He was religious, and even more devout than religious, frequenting churches and shrines, and submitting his royal person, in profound sincerity, to the most afflicting mummeries. He wore in his black hat of greasy felt little leaden images, pious figures " which, on every occasion when good news reached him, he kissed, falling on his knees, wherever he

THE MIDDLE AGES

happened to be, so suddenly that sometimes he seemed stupid rather than a wise man."

He has been called a tyrant; and in fact he commanded in an imperious way, as we have said, those whom he had chosen as his political instruments, and did not allow them to rest on their oars; but on great occasions he allowed them to oppose him, submitting his will to reason. He had sent for the registration by the Parliament some fiscal edicts involving heavy new impositions. A delegation came to him from the High Court of Justice with the First President at its head:

" Sire, we come to resign our commissions into your hands and to suffer all that it may please you rather than offend against our consciences."

And the King, declaring himself delighted to have such magistrates, put the edicts back in his pocket. In conclusion, Comines, whose chronicle does for Louis XI what that of Joinville does for Saint Louis—each of the two princes found a biographer well adapted to his character—Comines judged the King, his master, as follows:

" In all (the princes of his time) there was some good and some evil, but without having recourse to any flattery, there were in him far more of the qualities appertaining to the office of king and prince than in any other. I have seen them nearly all and know their abilities."

Louis XI spent the last days of his life in the castle of Plessis, which he had had arranged for him near Tours. The fear of death, mingled with the most grotesque terrors, haunted him more and more strangely. He had had " his house of Plessis-lès-Tours closed with great iron bars in the form of gratings, and, at the four corners of the house, four bastions of iron, good, big, and thick. The said gratings were against the wall at the side of the fortress, on the other side of the moat, for it was a flat-bottomed moat; and he had put there several iron pegs, built into the wall, with three or four points, and had them put very close to one another. And he placed ten bowmen within the said ditches, to draw on those who approached before the door was opened, and he saw that they slept in the aforesaid iron bastions."

The gate of the castle of Plessis was opened only at eight

A MODERN KING: LOUIS XI

o'clock in the morning, to shut again at dusk. Only a few people went in, people anxiously chosen by the voluntary prisoner. "The cages in which he had kept others," says Comines once more, "were about eight feet square, and he, who was so great a King, had a very little castle courtyard in which to take his walks." He was particularly suspicious of his son, of his daughter Anne, and of his son-in-law, the Sire of Beaujeu.

He wanted to defer the day of his death. Not only the Pope, but the Grand Turk sent him some relics. The holy ampulla of Reims, "which had never been moved from its place," was brought to him in his room. He brought from Italy the holy hermit Francesco de Paolo.

His last hour sounded on the 31st August 1483.

The work of this King, small in body and morbid in mind, was immense. He had indeed been the man necessary to end the Middle Ages for France and lead her to the new age, in which our country will continue to play a part worthy of its magnificent past : the constant source of modern civilization. In giving back to the Crown Burgundy and Picardy, in giving to it Franche-Comté, Provence, and Roussillon, Louis XI continued splendidly the work of his predecessors, as well as their administrative activity. The Renaissance is announced. Villon, while yet using the language and forms of the Middle Ages, is already a modern poet. In him sings the soul of Verlaine. And now comes printing. The Mohammedans are driven from Spain by Ferdinand the Catholic, but Constantinople falls under the Empire of the Turks. The Portuguese are about to discover the Cape of Good Hope (1486), and Christopher Columbus catches sight of the horizon-blue line of the American coast on the 14th October 1492. A new world shines in a clear dawn ; but its splendours will not efface the fecund beauty of the centuries of Philip Augustus and Saint Louis, to which in all history there is only to compare the century of Sophocles, Phidias, and Pericles.

SOURCES.—*Lettres de Louis XI*, ed. Et. Charavay and J. Vaesen, 1883–1905, 9 vols. ; *Memoires de Comines*, ed. Mlle Dupont, 1840–47, 3 vols. ; *Memoires d'Olivier de la Marche*, ed. Beaune and d'Arbaumont, 1883–88, 4 vols. ; *Journal de J. de Roye*, ed. B. de Mandroit, 1894–96,

THE MIDDLE AGES

2 vols.; *Chronique de Chastellain*, ed. Kervyn de Lettenhove, 1863–68; *Chronique de Molinet*, ed. Buchon, 1827–28, 5 vols.; *Histoire de Thomas Basin*, ed. Quicherat, 1855–59, 4 vols.; Jehan Marcellin, *Journal des Etats généraux de Tours*, ed. A. Bernier, 1835.

HISTORICAL WORKS.—Petit-Dutaillis in the *Histoire de France*, ed. E. Lavisse, iv., 1902; (Maxime Petit), *Histoire de France Illustrée* (Larousse), undated, 4to; P. Champion, *François Villon*, 1913; A. Kleinclauz, *Histoire de Bourgogne*, 1909; Lecoy de la Marche, *Louis XI et la Succession de Provence*, 1888; Michelet, *Louis XI et Charles le Téméraire*, 1857; H. Sée, *Louis XI et les Villes*, 1891; H. Stein, *Charles de France, frère de Louis XI*, 1921; Marcel Thibault, *La Jeunesse de Louis XI, 1423–45*, 1907.

INDEX

ACRE, siege of, 255.
Adèle de Champagne, 246, 247.
Adhémar de Monteil, 109, 110, 114, 119.
Agincourt, battle of, 497.
Agnes Sorrel, 529.
Aimerides, cycle of, 53.
Albert of Austria, 385.
Albigenses, 269.
Alexius, Emperor, 101, 105, 106, 107, 111, 117.
Alods, freeholds, 13.
Amiens, Treaty of, 296.
Antioch, 100, 112, 114, 115, 116, 117, 119.
Aragon Expedition, 319.
Ardres, formation of, 23.
Arles, formation of, 33.
Arnaud, Daniel, troubadour, 195.
Arras, Treaty of, 526, 534, 540.
Arthur of Brittany, claims English throne, 259; is defeated and assassinated, 263.
Association of Peace, peace of God, 161.
Association of Peace, truce of God, 161.
Association of Peace, "Quarantine" of the King, 161.
Auvergne, war in, 136.
Avoues, 365.

Baillis, 284, 358, 359.
Baldwin of Boulogne, 108, 113, 114, 123.
Baldwin of Flanders, 78, 79, 89.
Barbarossa, Emperor of Germany, 252, 253.
Barbary pirates, crusade against, 487.
Beadles, function of, 358.
Beauvais, Bishop of, Philippe de Dreux, 257, 278.
Beauvais, commune of, 152.
Becket, Thomas, 245, 246, 247.
Bernard, St., 243.
Bernard d'Armagnac, 493, 498, 500.
Bertha, wife of Philip I, 90.
Berthe de Bourgoyne, 73.
Bertrade de Montfort, 90, 91, 97.

Bertrand de Bar-sur-Aube, 59, 60.
Bertrand de Born, 170, 195, 196.
Bertrand du Guesclin, 460, 461, 477, 478, 480, 481, 483, 484.
Beyles, 358.
Black Death, 446.
Black Prince, 451, 455, 458, 478, 479, 480, 483.
Blanche of Castile, 262, 289, 290, 291, 292, 298, 303, 315.
Boemund, Prince of Tarento, 108, 114, 115, 116, 117, 118, 123.
Boileau Etienne, Book of Trades, 343, 344, 347.
Boniface VIII, 202; character, 377, 378; elected, 379; conflict with Philip IV, 382, 383; crusades against Aragonese of Sicily and Colonna family, 383, 384; refusal to ratify election of Albert King of Germany, 385; interview with Nogaret, who explains policy of Philip IV, 386, 387; he addresses Bull to Philip IV, 387, 388, 389; he addresses Bull to all Christendom, 394; Council appealed to by King of France to depose him, 395; his palace is attacked by band of Italians and Nogaret, 399; Nogaret informs him that he is accused of heresy, 400; he is brought to Rome, where he dies, 401, 402.
Book of Trades, Etienne Boileau, 343.
Bourges, peace of, 495.
Bouvines, battle of, 279.
Bretigny, peace of, 471, 472, 473, 475, 477, 479.
Bruges, matins, 392.
Butler, office of, 41.

Calais, siege of, 444.
Capet, Hugh, 36; is elected king, 37; proclaimed king, 38; reason of his election, 44; his coronation oath, 45; has his son crowned, 46; his character and death, 47.
Castillon, battle of, 528.
Castles, description of life in, 164, 165, 166.

551

INDEX

Cathari, the, 269.
Chalus-en-Limousin, siege of, 258.
Chamberlain, office of, 39, 41.
Champenois, faction of, 251.
Chancellor Grand, office of, 42.
Chanson de Roland, epic poem, 54, 55 56.
Chanson de Guillaume, epic poem, 54, 57, 58.
Charles IV, the Fair, 429.
Charles V, opposes Etienne Marcel, 463; assumes style of Regent, 464; leaves Paris for Meaux and Sens, 465; re-enters Paris, 470; equips a fleet to make war on England, 471, 472; ascends throne, 476; resumes war with England, 480; conflicts at sea, 481; efforts towards peace, 482; concludes truce, 483; his financial administration and death, 485.
Charles VI, revolutionary disturbance, 485; renews war with England, 486; is seized with madness, 488; delegation of authority to Queen Isabel, 491; is tended by Odette de Champdivers, 492; his death, 504.
Charles VII, his birth, 491; nominated lieutenant-general of kingdom, flees from Paris, 499; reorganises army after Agincourt and retakes Etampes, 501; he meets John the Fearless at Montereau-fault-Yonne, where the latter is killed, 502; proclaimed king at Bourges, 505; receives Jeanne d'Arc, 513; gives her rank of war leader, 514; consecration at Reims, 519; is anxious for peace but opposed by Jeanne, 520, 521, 522; is reconciled with Duke of Burgundy, 526; Treaty of Arras, 526; battles of Formigny and Castillon, 528; his government, 529, 530, 531; fear of his son, 533.
Charles d'Albret, 497
Charles of Blois, 443, 460, 474.
Charles of Navarre, the Bad, claims French throne, 453; assassinates Charles of Spain and is imprisoned by John II, 454; is released and reconciled to Regent Charles V, 462; re-enters Paris, 464; negotiates with Charles V on behalf of people of Paris, 465; crushes the Jacquerie rising, 466; becomes captain of men of Paris, 466, 467, 468; makes treaty of friendship with Charles V, 471; exchanges domain for lordship of Montpelier, 477.
Charles of Orleans, 493, 495, 497.

Charles of Spain constable, 449, 454.
Charles of Valois, 423, 427.
Charpentier, le, 115.
Chateauroux, Treaty of, 253.
Chivalry, institution of, 162.
Cistercians, 69.
Clement V, 404.
Clermont, council of, 101.
Cluny, Order of, influence and work, 69, 70, 94, 95; schools, 199; architecture, 215.
Colleges, foundation of, 210.
Compiègne, siege of, 523, 524, 525.
Conflans, Treaty of, 536.
Constance, wife of Robert the Pious, 74, 75.
Corbeil, Treaty of, 316.
Coucy, 22.
Courtrai, 363, 392, 393.
Crown, the, meaning of term, 39.
Crusades, First, 101.
„ Second, 243.
„ Third, 253.
„ Fourth, 265.
„ Egyptian, 304.
„ of Tunis, 317.

Damietta, capture of, 306.
Dampierre, Guy de, 372, 373, 374, 375, 376.
Dominicans, 69.

Edward the Confessor, 87.
Edward I of England, 364, 365, 371, 372, 373, 375, 433.
Edward III of England, 433, 435, 436, 437, 439, 441, 442, 451, 454, 471, 472, 481, 482, 483.
Eleanor of Aquitaine, 241, 242, 244.
Enguerran Le Portier de Marigny, 405, 406, 418, 424.
Eschevinages, formation of, 340.
Etaples, Treaty of, 529.
Etienne Boileau, book of trades, 343, 344.
Etienne Marcel, 451, 457, 461, 462, 463, 464, 465, 466, 467, 468, 469.
Eude, son of Robert the Strong, 35.
Eustace of Boulogne, 108.

Famines, 75, 76, 100, 103, 115, 117, 446.
Fiefs, 10, 11, 12, 13, 19, 34.
Fight of the Thirty, 449.
Fillettes du roi, 547.
Fortress, castle, 20, 21, 22, 26, 27.
Foulque le Rechin, 90, 91.
Franciscans, 69.
Fulk, Vicar of Neuilly sur Marne, 265.

INDEX

Garlands, Jean de, 344.
Gaudry, Bishop of Laon, 148, 149, 150.
Geoffrey, Count of Anjou, 139, 242, 244.
Gerbert, 37, 65, 66, 74, 199.
Gilles de Rome, Egidio Colonna, 384.
Giraud de Bornelh, troubadour, 195.
Gisors, 245, 246, 258.
Godfrey de Bouillon, 108, 110, 112, 116, 122, 123.
Gothic style of architecture, 219, 220, 221, 222, 223, 226; ornamentation of, 227, 228, 229, 230, 231.
Grandson, battle of, 540.
Graville in Maine, battle of, 509.
Great schism, 483, 484.
Gregory V, Pope, 73.
Gregory VII, 85, 93.
Guèrin Brother, the Hospitaller, 285, 287, 289.
Guilds, formation of, 337.
Guillaume de Julien, 390, 391, 392, 402, 403.
Guillaume de Nogaret, 361, 386, 387, 396, 397, 398, 399–402, 411, 418, 419.

Hanses, formation of, 337.
Harold II of England, 87, 88.
Henry I, conflict with his brothers, 76; war with Normandy and opposition to clergy, 77; marriage and death, 78.
Henry Beauclerc, 89, 90, 129, 133, 138, 139, 148, 171.
Henry Plantagenet, 211; conflict with Louis VII, 244, 245, 246, 247; increase of power in France, 251; trouble with sons, 253; reconciliation with Philip Augustus, 253; preparation for Crusade and death, 254, 255.
Henry III of England, 286, 296, 297.
Henry IV of England, 491, 496.
Henry V of England, 496, 497, 504.
Henry V of Germany, 93, 133, 135.
Hericon, the, 5.
Herrings, battle of, 513.
Honoré, miniaturist, 332.
Hugh du Puiset, 128, 129.
Hugh the Fair, 36.

Ingeburg of Denmark, 260, 261, 263, 264, 265; psalter of, 322.
Innocent III, 264, 286.
Inquisitor-reformers, 363.
Institution of St. Louis, 302.
Isabel of Bavaria, 486, 487, 491, 492, 501.
Isabella of Hainault, 251, 252.

Jacquerie, the, 465, 466.
Jacques van Artevelde, 437, 441, 442.
Jacobins, 361, 362.
Jean II, the Good, 448; has Constable of France seized and beheaded and gives office to Charles of Spain, 448, 449; debases currency, 449, 450; struggle with Charles of Navarre, 453, 454; is taken prisoner in battle of Poitiers, 455, 456; release and return to France, 472, 473; return to England, and death in London, 476.
Jean d'Armagnac, 479, 480.
Jean de Garlande, 344.
Jean de Luxembourg, 524.
Jean de Montfort, 443, 449.
Jean de Montroyal, brother, 413.
Jean Pucelle, miniaturist, 332, 333.
Jeanne of Navarre, 416, 417.
Jeanne d'Arc, hears voices, 511, 512; is taken to Charles VII, 513; receives rank of war leader, 514, 515; her boldness and courage, 516; raises siege of Orleans, 517; battle of Patay, 518; consecration of Charles VII at Reims, 519; lays siege to St. Pierre de Montier, 520; her further exploits, 521, 522, 523; is taken prisoner, tried at Rouen, and executed, 504, 525.
Jeanne Hachette, 539.
John, King of Bohemia, 444.
John Lackland, 254, 259, 263, 278, 279, 283, 284, 285, 286.
John the Fearless, Duke of Burgundy, 492, 493, 495, 499, 501, 502.

Keeps, 16, 17, 21, 26.
Knights, 43, 162, 163, 361.

Laon, 145, 147, 148, 149, 150, 151, 157.
Lateran, council of, 276.
League of the Public Weal, 535, 539.
Legists, 361, 362.
Le Mans, commune of, 147.
Leopold, Duke of Austria, 256.
Liège, revolt of people of, 537.
Lignages, 29.
Lincoln, battle of, 286.
Lorris-en-Gâtinais, charter granted to, 157.
Lothaire, 36, 37.
Louis VI, Le Gros, 126; reduces feudal lords, 127, 128, 129, 130; gains victory over Germany, 133, 134, 135, 136; besieges Montferrand, 136; appoints new Count of Flanders and goes to war with England, 137, 138; failure and

553

INDEX

death, 139, 140; his attitude towards communes, 142, 143.
Louis VII Le Jeune, his accession and marriage with Eleanor of Aquitaine, 241; his struggle against feudatories, 242; takes part in second Crusade, 243; divorces Queen Eleanor, 244; conflict with English Crown, 244, 245; marries Adèle de Champagne, 246; birth of Philip Augustus, 247; character and death, 248.
Louis VIII prepares to claim English throne, 268; lands in England, is defeated at Lincoln and signs treaty renouncing his claim, 286; succeeds his father, invasion of Aquitaine, war against Albigenses and death, 287, 288.
Louis IX, St. Louis, 289, 292, 293; government, 294, 295, 296; war with England, 297; his religious faith and conduct, 298, 299, 300, 301, 302, 303; Egyptian crusade, 304-15; returns to France, makes treaty with King of Aragon, 316; crusade of Tunis and death, 317, 318; kindness to minstrels, 189.
Louis X, 423; campaign in Flanders, 425, 427; gives charters to provinces, 425, 426; death, 427.
Louis XI, hostility to father and friendship with Duke of Burgundy, 533; reverses policy of father, 534; struggle with Charles the Bold, 535, 536, 537, 538, 539, 540, 541, 542, 543; financial administration and rule, 545, 546, 547; piety, 547; fear of death and end, 548, 549.
Louis, Duke of Anjou, 486, 490.
Louis de Nevers, Count of Flanders, 437.
Louis of Orleans, 489, 490, 491, 492, 493.
Luke de la Barre-sur-Ouche, 171.

Magistrat, authority of, 341.
Marie of Burgundy, 542, 543, 544.
Marigny, Enguerran de, 405, 406, 418, 424.
Marle, Thomas de, 150, 151.
Marque, letters of, 368, 369.
Matilda of Flanders, 86, 89, 90.
Meilhan-en-Bazadais, 28.
Mercadier, 256, 257, 258, 259.
Mesnie, 8, 9, 28, 29, 34, 42, 43, 68.
Metz, formation of, 33.
Miniaturists, growth of the art, 321.
„ preparation of colours, 324, 325, 326.

Miniaturists, rules, 323.
„ statutes, 331.
Mirabeau, 263.
Molay, Grand Master Jacques de, 415.
Montreuil-sur-Mer, treaty of, 433.
Montroyat, Jean de, 413.
Mont St. Michel, 460, 461.
Morat, battle of, 540.
Mottes, fortified mounds, 5, 6, 7, 19.

Nancy, battle of, 541.
Nicolas, Miniaturist, 332.
Nogaret, Guillaume de, 361, 386, 387, 396, 397, 398, 399, 400, 401, 402, 411, 418, 419.
Notre Dame, church of, 220, 224, 232.
Noyon, Cathedral of, 219.

Odette de Champdivers, 492.
Ordonnance Cabochienne, 494.
Oriflamme, the, 133, 134.
Ornamentation of churches, 227.
Orleans, relief of, 518.
Otto VI of Brunswick, 278, 281, 282, 283.

Pantler, Grand, office of, 42.
Parages, 29.
Paris, formation of, 277.
„ improvements to, 286, 287.
„ treaty of (1229), 290, 433; (1303), 395, 433.
„ university of, 200, 201, 202, 206, 208, 211, 494, 524.
Paschall II, 94.
Patay, 518.
Pedro the Cruel, 447, 448.
Pelerinage de Charlemagne, 54, 58.
Peter Barthelemy, 118, 119, 120.
Peter the Hermit, 101; preaches Crusade, 102; sets out and crosses Europe, 103, 104, 105; is defeated by Turks, 106, 107; attempts to desert, 115; relieves sufferings of crusaders, 116; returns to Europe and dies, 123.
Peyre, Cardinal, troubadour, 196.
Philip I, accession of, 78; acquirement of Keep of Montlhéry, 83, 84; attitude towards Union of England and Normandy, 89; marriage with Bertrade de Montfort, 90, 91; conflict with Holy See, 91, 92, 96; strengthening power in royal domain, 96; administration of palace, 96, 97; death, 97; mentioned, 124.
Philip Augustus, birth, 247; accession, 250; marriage, 251; struggle with coalition of nobles, 252; reconciliation with Henry II, 253,

554